STRESS MANAGEMENT FOR WELLNESS

SECOND EDITION

by

WALT SCHAFER

Harcourt Brace Jovanovich College Publishers

Fort Worth   Philadelphia   San Diego   New York   Orlando   Austin   San Antonio
Toronto   Montreal   London   Sydney   Tokyo

Publisher:	Ted Buchholz
Acquisitions Editor:	Eve Howard
Developmental Editor:	John Haley
Project Editor:	Steven-Michael Patterson
Production Manager:	Tad Gaither
Art & Design Supervisor:	Vicki McAlindon Horton
Text Designer:	DUO Design Group

Library of Congress Cataloging-in-Publication Data

Schafer, Walter E., 1939–
    Stress management for wellness/Walt Schafer.—2nd ed.
      p. cm.

    Includes bibliographical references and index.
    ISBN (invalid) 0-00-352774-0
    1. Stress management. I. Title.
RA785.S33 1992
155.9'042—dc20

91–7938
CIP

ISBN: 0-03-052774-0

Copyright © 1992, 1987 by Holt, Rinehart and Winston, Inc.

Requests for permission to make copies of any part of the work should be mailed to the Copyrights and Permissions Department, Harcourt Brace Jovanovich, 6277 Sea Harbor Drive, Orlando, Florida 32887.

Address for editorial correspondence: 301 Commerce Street, Suite 3700, Fort Worth, TX 76102

Address for orders: 6277 Sea Harbor Drive, Orlando, FL 32887
              1-800-782-4479, or 1-800-433-0001 (in Florida)

PRINTED IN THE UNITED STATES OF AMERICA

1 2 3 4 016 9 8 7 6 5 4 3 2

Preface

Evidence is mounting that Americans are becoming more healthy: for example, fewer of them smoke, and more of them exercise. Still, a substantial number of Americans continues to experience a high rate of illness-induced absenteeism from school and work, to feel sluggish or depressed, and to see their doctor regularly for one medication or another. And, often, those who are not ill within a medical framework are not truly well either, since they are hardly maximizing their potentials, enjoying daily life, or maintaining high levels of vitality and energy.

Evidence from epidemiological and behavioral medicine studies clearly tells that our wellness is largely a function of our daily habits: sleep, diet, exercise, relationships, how we handle anger, our chronic and acute tension levels, work satisfaction, presence or absence of energizing visions for ourselves and our world. Studies also leave little doubt that how we manage stress vitally influences the degree of illness or wellness we experience.

This book brings together two significant and challenging topics: *wellness* and *stress management*. Both have central relevance, for the ultimate values this book intends to promote are maximization of human potential, good health, and enjoyment of daily life. This volume contains few *I*'s or *me*'s, but it is a very personal book; it is, first and foremost, an expression of my own learning and search for wellness through wise stress management. I have learned from many sources, which I acknowledge later. Most of all, I have integrated information from others' experience and research studies with my own search for a lifestyle of true wellness, a lifestyle with a proper balance of work and play, giving and receiving, mind and body, intensity and recovery.

There is no better time to improve stress management practices than during the college years, although, even if you are beyond that stage, it certainly is never too late. Many of my cardiac rehabilitation students in their 60's and 70's have benefitted from the ideas and techniques presented. My profound hope is that, through this book, you will all be aided in your personal quest for wellness through stress management.

CONTENT AND APPROACH ▼

In terms of content, this book is distinctive in five main ways. First, the approach balances *realism* and *idealism*. We assume that life is and always will be difficult. There is no freedom from challenge, change, or conflict, but you can learn to confront, adapt, and grow by facing your problems. We also assume that personal change comes gradually through effort and patience. There are no magic pills or panaceas for everlasting bliss, yet, for most of us, greater happiness, vitality, and realization of potentials is possible. Idealism, in short, needs to be blended with realism, as in this book.

Second, this book is distinguished by its *integrated, whole-person, lifestyle approach* to stress management. We believe wellness is promoted not by practicing any single stress management method (such as meditation, deep breathing, positive thinking, exercise, managing time better, or assertiveness training), but rather by integrating a number of methods to control stress and tension. It is vital to find the unique combination that works best for you. As noted above, introducing these techniques into your daily life requires time, patience, and gradualism. There are no miracles. Treat yourself as an experiment-of-one, and see what works best for you.

Third, the book weaves together *information* and *application*. The ultimate goal is not abstract learning for its own sake, but rather application of what you learn in the pursuit of higher-level wellness for yourself and others.

Fourth, this book's approach is constructive. Its goal is to assist you in learning to *control* and *channel* stress rather than succumb to it. *Stress* (arousal of mind and body in response to demands placed upon them) is unavoidable, and can, in fact, be highly useful in order to meet performance demands, deadlines, and physical emergencies. This is *positive stress.* On the other hand, *distress* (harmful stress resulting from too much or too little arousal) can do untold harm to your health, career, relationships, and emotional life. It can be very costly to your family, to your employer, and to society.

Fifth, this book places *personal stress within social context.* You are not an island unto yourself, and your experiences with stress are not entirely unique. In many respects, they are shared with others. Furthermore, personal problems do not emerge in isolation—they are the product of larger social forces. This means that understanding the dynamic interplay between self and society is vital in managing stress. Seeking to improve social conditions out of which distress flows becomes just as important as dealing with personal problems, and caring for others as valuable as caring for self. Thus, this book focuses on balancing self-care with social responsibility.

A key assumption here is that wise stress management is a kind of preventive medicine—you will reduce the risk of illness to the degree that you succeed in harnessing stress. This book is designed to assist you in living wisely, thereby enhancing your wellness and preventing illness.

ORGANIZATION OF THIS BOOK ▼

The book is organized into three parts. Part I presents the conceptual and historical groundwork upon which the rest of the book is built. Included are chapters on the nature of stress and wellness; the history of stress theory and research; the nature of the stress response; the relaxation response and human energy; stress-related symptoms and illnesses; and the nature, causes and effects of Type A behavior and its most toxic component, hostility.

Part II presents a range of methods for managing stress, all within a whole-person, lifestyle approach. We focus on coping; self-talk, the health buffers of aerobic exercise, good nutrition, and adequate sleep; relaxation methods, including on-the-spot tension reducers and deep relaxation techniques; managing time, pace, and change; and social support, both giving and receiving.

Part III contains special applications. We deal with coping with stress in college and at work. Attention is then given to the special challenge of thriving under pressure, whatever the setting. The final chapter focuses on balancing self-care and social responsibility, and the epilogue presents a brief review, along with a few personal thoughts from the author about looking ahead.

CHANGES IN THE SECOND EDITION   ▼

Readers familiar with the first edition of *Stress Management for Wellness* will note several key changes here. First, greater emphasis has been placed on wellness than before, not only in the opening chapter but throughout the book. Second, we have added several new chapters: Pioneers and Pathfinders: A History and Theory of Stress (Chapter 2), Type A Behavior and Hostility (Chapter 5), Your Coping Response (Chapter 6), Managing Time, Pace and Change (Chapter 10), Social Support (Chapter 11), Passing the Test of College Stress (Chapter 12), Thriving Under Pressure (Chapter 14), and Balancing Self-Care and Social Responsibility (Chapter 15). These have been added in response to trends in the field, suggestions from readers and reviewers, and the author's judgment.

Third, we have updated scientific references so that support is as current as possible. Many new illustrations and examples are given, with more emphasis on a range of ages and demographic groups.

Fourth, we have placed more emphasis than before on stress in a social context. As noted above, this includes both the roots of stress and approaches to minimizing distress. I increasingly believe in the importance of self-transcendence—getting outside yourself to focus on values and goals dealing with the common good. This is discussed in Chapter 15 along with egoistic altruism (self-fulfillment through contributing to the well-being of others).

What has not changed from the first edition is a balance between learning and application. My hope is that after having read this book, you will not only have a better understanding of stress and wellness, but you will already have begun to take steps to improve your own wellness lifestyle.

ACKNOWLEDGEMENTS   ▼

I am grateful to many people for their contributions to this effort. Some who have influenced and inspired me the most have done so at a distance through their research and writing. Most important among these are the late Hans Selye, Kenneth Pelletier, Kenneth Cooper, Herbert Benson, Meyer Friedman, Ray Rosenman, Robert Eliot, Donald Ardell, Joe Henderson, George Sheehan, Richard Lazarus, Albert Ellis, and Redford Williams.

Ideas in this book have taken shape through my interaction with several groups of people. First, I am grateful to former students in my Human Stress and Occupational Stress classes at California State University at Chico with whom I have shared many of the ideas expressed here. These thousands of students have been invaluable in challenging me to formulate and present my ideas coherently and usefully.

Second, I also wish to acknowledge several thousand community participants with whom I have experienced reciprocal learning at the N.T. Enloe Memorial

Hospital Stress and Health Center, which I founded and, for a number of years, directed. Especially useful has been my interaction with them in my five-month class on modifying Type A behavior, known as Reducing Perfectionism, Irritability and Hurry Sickness. Ranging in age from early 20's to late 70's, these co-learners have sharpened my awareness of the positive and negative features of stress, which techniques seem to be most effective, and what the personal change process is really like.

Third, my interactions with colleagues have been rewarding and instructive. This especially includes fellow instructors of Human Stress at CSU, Chico (Walter Zahnd, Deborah Powers, and Robert Dionne) and my close colleagues and friends Bruce Aikin, Terrence Hoffman, Darrell Stevens, and David Welch. Joyce Norman, a superb CSU, Chico colleague in health psychology and behavioral medicine, provided ideas and shared her personal library as I wrote, for which I am grateful.

In preparation of the book, I have enormously benefitted from feedback, criticism, and suggestions from my several exceptional reviewers:

Ken Briggs	Central Washington University
Linda Davis	Mount Hood Community College
Richard Friedman	State University of New York at Stony Brook
Deena Fuller	Tennessee State University
George Fuller von Bozzay	City College of San Francisco
Frederick Lopez	Michigan State University
Roseann Lyle	Purdue University
Joanne Marrow	California State University at Sacramento
Floyd Whitehead	Fayetteville (N.C.) Technical College

I am grateful to my secretaries in the CSU, Chico Department of Sociology and Social Work, Billie Kanter and Karen Ginno, who have been patient and supportive as I have sought to balance the sometimes difficult demands of writing, teaching, and administering. Dorine Sanders and Christine Schwartz, secretaries at the Enloe Stress and Health Center, have been supportive in a host of ways as we have worked together to bring this material to the community.

The editorial, design, and production staff at Holt, Rinehart and Winston have provided superb support. Special thanks to my editor, John Haley, with whom development and completion of the book has truly been a team effort. He developed a keen sense of what I was trying to accomplish and how I could better bring this about. He did an excellent job at distilling and integrating feedback from the reviewers. Thanks also to Steven-Michael Patterson, Project Editor, for his assistance in managing the final stages of production.

My daughters, Kimberly and Kristin, have witnessed firsthand the evolution of these ideas in my own life and work. Over the years, they have participated in my personal quest for a balanced lifestyle. I am grateful for their support. My special friend, Jasper, whose amazingly effective stress management practices I have carefully watched and learned from, and who has truly been "with me" during the writing, also deserves credit.

Finally, Teresa Kludt, my wife and best friend, has been a source of ideas, caring, energy, and good humor throughout this project. She has not only been patient during my many days at the keyboard, but has also helped me avoid sexist language in my writing. To her I am most grateful of all.

TABLE OF CONTENTS

PART

ONE

Understanding Stress and Wellness

Distress, Stress and Wellness

Chapter 1

CHAPTER 1

I. LESSONS FROM THE SEA PALM

II. WHAT IS STRESS?
A. Brian: A Case Study of Stress
B. Stress and Stressors
  1. Stressor and Distressor
  2. Stress
    a. Pleasant and Unpleasant Stress
    b. Anticipatory, Current and Residual Stress
    c. Stress From Over and Understimulation
    d. Implications for Managing Stress
C. Neustress
D. Distress
  1. Symptoms of Distress
  2. Stress-Related Illnesses
  3. Distress and Disharmony
  4. Costs of Distress
  5. Personal Stress and Public Issues
E. Positive Stress
  1. Ways Positive Stress Can Be Helpful
  2. Personal Growth Through Pushing Your Limits
F. Dispelling Common Myths About Stress

III. STRESS AND WELLNESS
A. What Is Wellness?
  1. Wellness Habits
  2. How Stress Relates To Wellness
B. Six Ways of Relating to Stress
C. What Do Good Stress Managers Do?

IV. ASSUMPTIONS ABOUT STRESS MANAGEMENT

LESSONS FROM THE SEA PALM   ▼

I recently spent several hours on a Pacific Coast cliff wondering at the power of the surf. I was soon taken with a fascinating sight. A particular species of seaweed known as sea palms gave the appearance of miniature palm trees, clinging to the rocks near the surf line. Several parallels between this hardy plant and humans struck me.

Clearly, the sea palm possesses a powerful life force—the drive to survive and grow. Like the sea palm, we too are born with a strong drive to survive and to grow to full potential.

If external conditions such as light, water, or access to food are not right, sea palms and people cannot survive, much less grow to fullness.

For both sea palms and humans, the environment plays an additional role to that of sustenance and support. It is also full of stressors, some major, some minor. A key difference between humans and sea palms is that we possess the ability to modify stressful conditions in the environment—or even to leave it and set up somewhere else.

The sea palm does not avoid its stressors. Rather, it is destined to live where sea conditions are the most challenging— on coastal rocks where waves pound the hardest. Similarly, we find ourselves in difficult circumstances. There are individual differences, of course, in the ability of both sea palms and humans to cope with these stressful conditions. Some thrive, others break or wither.

Like the sea palm, we cannot realize our potential by avoiding challenge. In fact, we need new demands and progressively more challenge. Otherwise, we remain stunted, half-grown, our potentials unrealized rather than fulfilled.

If the sea palm is to survive and grow, it must at once be well-anchored on the rock and resilient. Similarly, we must be well-anchored to our values, our social support networks. We must care for our bodies in order to be strong, yet resilient. We must know how "to bend without breaking."

Unlike the sea palm, you and I can help to determine the extent of fulfillment by the way in which we use two uniquely human qualities: awareness and choice. If we continue to grow in awareness of the self and the world around us, we are more likely to make stress work for us. And if we choose our actions wisely, we increase our chances of becoming winners rather than losers. For example, a loser might react to pressures of final examinations by watching TV and drinking beer every night during final exam week. A winner reacts by planning carefully, studying hard, and finding time to relax and exercise each day during final exams.

Because you have the ability to exercise awareness and choice, you are well ahead of the sea palm. You need not be at the mercy of your surroundings. To a large extent, you can create your own future. When awareness and choice are translated into personal responsibility, stress can be harnessed and directed effectively.

My intention in this book is to assist you in practical, concrete ways to manage effectively your own stress. Along the way, you will learn what stress is, how it affects you, and what we can learn about scientific studies of stress management techniques. You will also learn that managing stress effectively can not only help you avoid its harmful effects. More, it can enhance wellness—and benefit the world around you.

Welcome to the journey.

EXERCISE 1-1. COMPARING SEA PALMS WITH HUMANS ✓

1. How many parallels and differences can you describe between the sea palm and humans in relation to stress?

2. How does each of these parallels and differences apply to you?

WHAT IS STRESS?   ▼

BRIAN: A CASE STUDY OF STRESS

Brian's mounting tension was increasingly apparent to him, his family, and his co-workers. His hands trembled as each day wore on, his stomach churned, his shoulders were tight, his lower back hurt. He felt edgy and anxious and was often depressed for days at a time.

Communication became increasingly difficult, thinking more fuzzy, speech sometimes staccato. He snapped at secretaries, boiled inside as business sales slowed, then blew up at colleagues. Working lunches usually included one or two stiff drinks to dull the tension. His wife and children became targets of irritability and short-temperedness.

Brian knew that tension was inevitable in his work. He even had found in the past that some anxiety was useful before a difficult meeting or speech. Yet chronic tension was getting out of hand. Something had to change and soon. Already his body showed signs of breakdown, his work was inefficient, his business partnership was threatened, his family was becoming progressively alienated. Finally, his drinking was nearly out of control.

Following a series of stress management consultations, Brian was determined to take positive steps.

During the next several months, he began a daily running and deep relaxation program. He improved his diet. He learned new techniques of mental and physical relaxation (on-the-spot tension reducers), which reduced the frequency of destructive stress build-ups. He developed new communication skills for coping with colleagues and for supervising subordinates. He decided to eliminate alcohol consumption completely for at least the next year. Finally, he learned to accept moderate tension as a fact of life and sometimes even as a positive force.

As a result of these steps, Brian's quality of life markedly improved. His energy level rose and he felt better. His productivity increased, and his relationships at work and home improved. A key difference was his moderate reaction to stressful events, compared to his previous over-reactions. These improvements were as apparent to him and others as his distress symptoms had been earlier.

Brian's experiences taught him a great deal. They also illustrate a number of key concepts related to stress. Each of these terms is a building block for a thorough understanding of the stress experience—including its helpful and harmful sides.

STRESS AND STRESSORS

Brian's emotional and physical symptoms clearly suggest too much stress. In order to understand why his body began breaking down, why his emotions became more volatile, why his thinking grew more confused, and why his relationships turned sour, Brian had to learn more about stress. This required understanding several key terms, beginning with stressor.

Stressor and Distressor

A stressor is any demand on mind or body.

A distressor is any demand resulting in harm to mind or body.

Like you and me, Brian finds his life to be a constant process of responding to stimuli, pressures, and changes. Like Brian, you do not live in a vacuum. Rather, you are an "open system," continually exchanging energy, information, and feelings with the environment. You also place demands on yourself. Thus, you are always dealing with stressors—demands on your mind, your body, or both.

Viewed this way, stressors are ever-present. Adaptation is a continuous process. Most of the time, you respond to these demands with ease and familiarity. That is, stressors remain facts of life with no ill effects.

But adjustment can exact a toll in wear and tear on mind or body. Physical upset or emotional turmoil often result. When this happens, stressors become distressors.

One stress expert has written, "The most elementary acquaintance with history, with anthropology, and above all, with literature—be it the Bible, the Greeks, Shakespeare, Dante, or Dostoevsky—reveals the rarity of tranquility in human existence" (Antonovsky, 1979, 87).

EXERCISE 1-2. BELIEFS ABOUT STRESS ✓

Below are 10 common beliefs about stress. With which do you agree or disagree? Write about or discuss your reactions to each one as you begin this book. Later in this chapter you will read more about them.

Belief 1. All stress is bad.
Belief 2. The goal of stress management should be to eliminate stress.
Belief 3. The "good life" should be free of stressors.
Belief 4. The less the stress, the better.
Belief 5. A person can always successfully adapt to difficult circumstances if he or she tries hard enough.
Belief 6. Some people are destined by their heritage to be highly stressed.
Belief 7. Distress has only harmful effects.
Belief 8. Physical exercise drains energy that otherwise might be used to cope with stress.
Belief 9. Meditation is cultish, anti-Christian nonsense.
Belief 10. Stress affects only adults.

This rather gloomy opinion on the possibility of human peace may or may not be valid, depending upon one's point of view and definition of tranquility. We do know that the history of the human species indeed is marked by considerable misery, illness, and struggle. In part, this results from humankind's continual need to adapt—to a changing physical environment, to ever- shifting technology, to neighboring tribes and nations, to the life cycle itself. At a more personal level, human unhappiness results from sharp disagreements in points of view, from blocked- up emotions of hurt and frustration, even from intentional acts of emotional or physical violence. In short, stressors become distressors. Demands no longer are neutral. They result in harmful effects to the individual.

Charlesworth and Nathan (1984) have identified several types of stressors, not exhaustive but informative:

Change stressors	Environmental stressors
Chemical stressors	Family stressors
Commuting stressors	Pain stressors
Decision stressors	Phobic stressors
Disease stressors	Physical stressors
Work stressors	Social stressors

Notice that demands do not cause harmful effects. Rather, harmful effects result from the person's interpretation of those demands. More on this important distinction later.

It is important to note here that awareness of stressors can itself be a deterrent to turning them into distressors. As Hans Selye, a pioneer in the stress field, has said, "It is well established that the mere fact of knowing what hurts you has an inherent curative value" (Selye, 1976, 406). This is illustrated by both animal and human studies showing that the greatest harm results from stressors that are unknown and therefore unpredictable. When stressors are perceived as predictable and manageable, they seem to be less threatening.

EXERCISE 1-3. VARIABILITY OF STRESSORS

Variability of Stressors and Distressors
A useful first step in understanding stressors and distressors is to be aware of some of the key ways they can vary.

1. Origins: Internal vs. external
2. Pleasantness: Pleasant vs. unpleasant
3. Number: Few vs. many
4. Intensity: Micro-stressors vs. macro-stressors
5. Duration: Episodic vs. chronic
6. Familiarity: New vs. familiar

7. How Chosen: Voluntary vs. involuntary
8. Changeability: Easy vs. difficult vs. impossible to change
9. Change agent: Changeable by self vs. by others vs. by both vs. by neither

Recall one or two recent distressors from your own experience. Write or discuss how each of these characteristics of stressors applies.

Stress

Stress is arousal of mind and body in response to demands made upon them.

Definitions are neither right nor wrong. They are useful in varying degrees according to scope and clarity. Definitions can be inclusive or narrow, fuzzy or clear. The above definition of stress has several advantages.

First, the definition makes clear that stress is ever-present, a universal feature of life. Arousal is an inevitable part of living. We constantly think, feel, and act with some degree of arousal. Stress cannot and should not be avoided. Rather, it is to be contained, managed, and directed.

Second, this definition points to the multi-faceted nature of stress. The stress response (arousal) involves virtually every set of organs and tissues in your body. Thoughts and feelings are clearly intertwined with these physiological processes. Brian's anxiety and depression, for example, were not only feelings. They were inseparable emotional-physiological states. Body influences mind, and mind influences body. Behavior often is an outward expression of stress—for example, short-temperedness, fast talking, accidents, and harried movement.

Third, this definition is neutral. Arousal of heart rate, blood pressure, and muscle tension intrinsically are neither helpful nor harmful. Most often, arousal is simply a fact of life, neither particularly helpful nor harmful. It simply is.

But stress can become positive or negative. This feature of our definition is significant because it calls attention to a wide range of experiences with stress, from the positive tension of the Wimbledon tennis tournament finalist to the recurrent colds or flu or the unstable college student who plans time poorly.

PLEASANT AND UNPLEASANT STRESS

Stress may be pleasant or unpleasant. An example of pleasant physical stress might be the excitement of a close football game—even more pleasant if your team wins. The delight of a new intimate relationship is an example of pleasant emotional stress, while the challenge of a debate or a writing assignment may bring pleasant intellectual stress. The surge of energy felt by a basketball player during the last two minutes of the game may be pleasant as well; it is stress, nevertheless. Unpleasant stresses are familiar: headache, depression, the pain of a minor burn, irritation of an abrasive noise, fatigue, anxiety.

All stresses cause some wear and tear. But, as Selye has noted, pleasant stress causes less harm to mind and body than does unpleasant stress, although the internal processes accounting for this difference are not fully understood. Even so, pleasant stresses can build up to turn into physical or emotional upset. Examples are too many consecutive parties, a challenging series of work assignments, or a child playing too hard and too long in the hot sun.

ANTICIPATORY, CURRENT, AND RESIDUAL STRESS

Anticipatory stress is your response to expected stressors. Mind and body prepare in advance for change, crisis, or challenge. Examples of this type of stress are numerous: tension before a test, "butterflies" before a race, apprehension about a parent's response to your breaking a rule, fear of an impending hurricane, dread of forced retirement. Anticipatory stress is useful in moderate amounts because it prepares your body and mind for events that are about to happen. Such stress increases sharpness and motivation. I recently experienced this as I approached Colorado River rapids in the Grand Canyon in an inflatable kayak. You, no doubt, have felt it in preparation for an exam or speech.

George Seifert, head coach of the San Francisco 49ers, knows the value of positive stress. As a recent summer training camp got underway, Seifert was interviewed about the transition between seasons and about positive stress (Dickey, 1990, D3).

> Fishing recharges my batteries. But now, it's time to get away from my "fantasy world" and back to the real one.

> Seifert's "real world" is quite different. During the season, he and his staff are committed to long hours and nights preparing for games, at a level of dedication that few jobs demand.

> During the season, I don't look for a release. It's like I don't even want to think about fishing, let alone do it.

> After I came back from our trip, there were a couple days where my mind was still not quite here. But not now. Really, I get to a point now where I really want to get going again. Even the stress is a motivating factor. You kind of feed on all that. Your whole body seems to come alive, and all your energies are focused.

In short, anticipatory stress can be positive. But it also can interfere with life in the present. This sometimes accompanies chronic overload as a person gives more attention to what *might happen* than to *what is happening*. It also affects people who lack confidence or are seeking an escape from involvement in the present.

Current stress occurs during an experience: the body's extreme alarm during an auto accident, mental alertness in the midst of a debate, the surge of energy in the final 100 meters of a race. Current stress, if harnessed effectively, is vital for optimal performance.

Residual stress occurs after the experience has passed. The body remains in a state of alarm for some time after a near- collision on the highway. Athletes may have difficulty sleeping the night after a victory. Overstimulation, whether pleasant or unpleasant, can have the same effect.

During the spring of 1990, the *San Francisco Chronicle* (Minton, 1990) ran a large story under the banner "The Earthquake Isn't Over Yet: Psychological Scars Still Linger Seven Months After Loma Prieta." This story referred, of course, to the lingering effects of the October 17, 1989 Bay Area earthquake.

A pastor whose church slipped off its foundation regularly feels as if she is listing to the right.

A counselor who lost nothing in particular is terrified of crossing the Bay Bridge, riding in elevators, and entering brick buildings.

A retired schoolteacher who survived nearly every kind of natural disaster without fear now can't shake her earthquake worries.

This is "afterstress." Seven months after the October 17 quake, after much of the rubble has been cleared, the homes and the broken bridge patched and the pancaked freeway demolished, the psychological scars linger.

In a report on the emotional aftereffects of fires, Whiting (1990), the author notes that residual stress often merges into anticipatory stress as victims experience both mourning and fear. Other studies have documented residual distress among police officers involved in shooting accidents, especially within the first three days, but continuing on for about three weeks (Loo, 1986); firefighters exposed to a dangerous chemical, for whom psychological symptoms persisted even after 22 months (Markowitz, 1989); and hurricane victims, for whom symptoms continued for up to an average of 16 months (Krause, 1987). No studies have been reported on the psychological aftereffects of the Chernobyl tragedy, but they must be considerable. Residual distress also has been reported for disaster, rescue, and cleanup workers, rape victims (Rose, 1989), children directly exposed to a sniper attack on an elementary school (Nader, 1989); and, of course, for soldiers ("shellshock" after World War II and "post-traumatic stress disorder" after Viet Nam).

One expert believes that combat even alters the brain. According to Lawrence Kolb, a Veterans Administration psychiatrist, "Excessive and prolonged sensitizing stimulation" may lead to changes in the synapses (Kolb, 1988).

Mardi Horowitz, another expert in the field, estimates that 25 to 30 percent of people who survive car accidents, major burglaries, or other traumas experience symptoms of post-traumatic stress (Butler, 1987).

Entertainer Ben Vereen lost his 16-year-old daughter in a tragic auto accident. He describes his lingering grief: "It devastated me. It still does. You keep hearing the voice that tells you your daughter is dead. I wanted it to stop" (Carter, 1990, 4). Yet he has moved on, painfully but steadily.

"Now when I have a problem and find myself feeling anxious," he added, "a voice inside me says, 'This too will pass.' When I'm going through trauma, the voice says, 'You've suffered greater loss. This is nothing. Get up. Get on.'"

As Carter states, "And so he has. Ben Vereen is back, performing his one-man show across the country, dazzling audiences with his enthusiasm and style and heart" (Carter, 1990, 5).

"God endowed me with a wonderful gift, which I had not awakened to," he said. "My work, my art, what I do. I haven't even begun to fulfill that commitment that God made to me, and I made to Him or Her. I'm really looking forward to the next chapter of my life with great expectations" (Carter, 1990, 5).

As Ben Vereen illustrates, a significant challenge in managing stress is to develop ways of returning the body and mind to normal levels of stress—sooner rather than later—after challenges, crises, and changes. If normalcy is not regained relatively quickly, the individual is likely to experience some type of distress. "After-burn time" must follow intense experiences if a person is to return to normal. Amount of time needed depends on both the event and the person.

STRESS FROM OVER AND UNDERSTIMULATION

Stressors can be few or numerous, with respect to a given time period. Similarly, stress can occur from understimulation or overstimulation with "under" and "over" varying from person to person. Hans Selye developed a chart, known as the "experience continuum" that illustrates stress shading into distress at either high or low extremes of stimulation (Selye, 1974). In slightly modified form, the experience continuum is shown in Figure 1-1.

This chart shows that the amount of stress can increase at either extreme, overstimulation or understimulation. But even in the middle range of stimulation, the experience line does not touch bottom, since the only time one reaches the point of no stress is death. At all other times, some amount of arousal is experienced. This chart also shows that stress can turn into distress under conditions of either overstimulation or understimulation.

Let us examine stress and distress at the two extremes of stimulation. A number of laboratory experiments on "sensory deprivation" shows that most people soon begin to experience disorientation, anxiety, depression, or other discomforts when deprived of light, touch, sound, and smell (Goldberger, 1982). Sometimes these experiments are carried out in a tank of water where the submerged subject breathes through a mask but cannot experience even gravity. One journalist who volunteered for such a study in order to write a story acted confident and pleased immediately after leaving the tank. But toward the end of his interview with the scientist in charge, he said, "I honestly believe if you put a person in there, just kept him and fed him by vein, he would just flat die." He never wrote the story (Tanner, 1976).

FIGURE 1-1. THE EXPERIENCE CONTINUUM

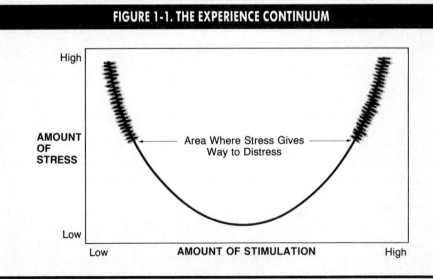

Unfortunately, the elderly too often are plagued with understimulation as a result of withdrawal from previous roles and social supports. Following retirement, there can be reduced opportunity for meaningful and stimulating work. At the same time, senses of hearing and vision sometimes are dulled. Physical abilities diminish (too often as a result of inactivity rather than true aging). Human touch is often totally lacking.

Too little stimulation—"sensory deprivation"—can create serious mental and physical difficulties. A less extreme form of understimulation is boredom. You probably have experienced the heaviness of mind or body, the feeling of depression, or the growing tension that sometimes accompanies too much stillness, too little to do. Prisoners-of-war have been known to break down after only a few days of total isolation.

At the opposite extreme are studies of people on the battlefield, in the workplace, or in school, who simply have too much to do or to absorb in too short a time. The results are familiar—the person may be tense, anxious, fired up, hostile, upset, short-tempered, confused, or unable to sleep. As in understimulation, too much stimulation generates an intricate network of changes in body, mind, and behavior. A vicious cycle starts, in which a series of damaging reactions feed on one another. The chances of high blood pressure and heart attack increase markedly with chronic overload.

IMPLICATIONS FOR MANAGING STRESS

From the above description we can identify a number of targets of stress management.

▼ Anticipate, monitor, and regulate stressors insofar as possible.

▼ Be aware of and control interpretations of stressors.

▼ Practice daily deep relaxation, in order to balance chronic excitation of the stress response with recovery, as well as to keep arousal at a lower level most of the time.

▼ Use mental and physical on-the-spot tension reducers to control arousal when confronted with threatening stressors.

▼ Practice daily exercise, eat well, and get adequate sleep in order to build stress resistance and prevent stress build-up.

▼ Recognize early warning signs of mental and physical distress.

▼ Develop means of mobilizing and controlling stress in performance situations.

▼ Use constructive reactions to distress when it does occur in order to reduce distress, rather than destructive reactions that heighten distress.

NEUSTRESS

As noted at the beginning of the chapter, Brian usually responded neutrally to internal and external demands. His mind and body were aroused but he moved along with little impact from these demands. In short, most of the time, his stress was neutral, neither particularly helpful nor harmful. Morse & Furst (1979) refer to this as neustress.

Neutress is neutral stress—arousal with neither harmful nor helpful effects on mind or body.

DISTRESS

When arousal is too high or too low, distress ensues. The challenge is to identify your own zone of positive stress and to maintain a perspective and lifestyle that will enable you to stay within that zone most of the time.

Distress is too much or too little arousal resulting in harm to mind or body.

An advantage of this definition is that it calls attention to individual meaning and perception. As Lazarus and Folkman (1984) have pointed out, whether a person experiences an event as "harmful" depends on the degree to which a stressor is perceived as exceeding her or his resources to cope with it, and whether personal well-being is threatened. A theme throughout this book is that events are not intrinsically distressing. They become so only when they are interpreted that way—sometimes quite realistically, of course, when they do endanger one's well-being and one is uncertain of his or her ability to handle it.

This definition includes distress from too much or too little arousal. Usually we think of distress only from overload. But as you read above, it can also result from too little stimulation (understimulation, stagnation, boredom). Again, the key is individual interpretation and experience.

Symptoms of Distress

As Brian became more aware of himself, he recognized the following symptoms in himself.

Trembling hands	Depression
Stomach churning	Poor concentration
Tight shoulders	Fuzzy thinking
Sore lower back	Accelerated speech
Edginess	Irritability
Anxiety	Short-temperedness

These distress symptoms served as warning signs—messages that something was wrong and needed to be changed.

Minor distress signals such as trembling hands and tension headaches serve as useful early warning signs when we listen to them and respond constructively. Too often such symptoms remain undetected, become chronic, and turn into full-blown illnesses requiring medical attention. As we shall see in Chapter 4, a variety of health problems can follow.

Stress-Related Illnesses

Below is a partial list of stress-related illnesses among persons referred by physicians to our Enloe Hospital Stress and Health Center for stress management classes or counseling.

Migraine headaches	Non-cardiac chest pain
Tension headaches	Heart attack
Psoriasis	Cancer
Gastritis	Rheumatoid arthritis
Ulcers	Dizzy spells
Colitis	High blood pressure
Lower-back pain	Panic attacks

Experts estimate that between 50 and 80 percent of illness episodes are stress-related (Pelletier, 1977; Charlesworth & Nathan, 1984)). The American Academy of Family Physicians estimates that two-thirds of all appointments with family doctors involve some stress-related problem (Time, June 6, 1983).

Stress contributes to illness in four ways:

▼ By imposing long-term wear and tear on the body and mind, thereby reducing resistance to disease.

▼ By directly precipitating an illness such as heart attack or tension headache.

▼ By aggravating an existing illness such as increased arthritic pain or flare-up of psoriasis.

▼ By being coped with in unhealthy or even illness-generating habits—smoking, alcohol, over-eating, sleep deprivation, for example.

Psychological distress may include severe depression, debilitating anxiety, disorientated thinking, paranoia, or lack of motivation to perform daily routines. Here, too, the line between distress symptoms and full-blown distress illnesses is not distinct. Symptoms tend to shade gradually into more serious disturbed states. Most often, psychological distress symptoms accompany physical illness because of the intricate interplay of mind and body.

Distress and Disharmony

By definition, distress is something to avoid whenever possible. Yet a period of distress can be transformed into a positive experience.

Distress almost always is a sign of some kind of disharmony among different

BOX 1-1. A PERSONAL APPLICATION

Below is a brief "Application Assignment" paper in which a female college student illustrates some of the personal benefits from applying ideas in this book. This paper was written for my course, "Human Stress," in which the first edition of Stress Management for Wellness was used as the main text.

"I have to be honest with you. When I write this, I am absolutely amazed at what I have read and heard in this classroom so far. I had no idea that stress, or actually distress, affected so many people. Throughout my day I find myself watching people and actually noticing signs of stress in their behavior.

"I have taken 'stress tests' in the past and always rank in the lowest category without fail. My first test I took was in 8th grade, and I remember my teacher saying that 'people who scored in the lowest level will be under-achievers.' I never really thought about this until just last week. I would like to think of myself as an achiever. After all, I am sitting in this classroom, and I pay for myself to go to school. I just have always "taken time for myself" in the past. I think that this helps me keep my stress in control, but, at the same point, I feel that I could be doing better.

"I have seen the opposite end of this spectrum far too many times in people that I am close to, not to take it to heart. I see many signs of stress in my father. He works very hard and always has time for his family. About two years ago he had a small stroke. It literally went undetected for two weeks, only because he didn't have time to go to a doctor. With all that I have learned so far through this class it saddens me to say that I really didn't see that much of a change in his behavior or routines.

"I have purchased a copy of your stress management book that I am mailing home tomorrow. I know that they will both read the book. I only hope that they will do something for themselves.

"My mother is generally not a stressful person but is going through a very rough time right now. She [is trying to] quit smoking, lost her brother to cancer and her father to lung failure, all within the last year. She has seen first hand how your behavior has to play a major role in your health. She is beginning to take steps to get her life and my father's life on a healthier track. They both walk a few miles before work, and my mother has stopped smoking. Hopefully, your material will give them just the push they need in the right direction. Thank you so much!"

wants or needs within the person or between the person's inner wants and needs and outside circumstances. Brian learned from his mounting distress. Among other things, he decided it was time to do something about his destructive habits, including heavy drinking. He also determined it was time to take better care of his body through exercise and improved nutrition.

When distressed, then, ask yourself these questions:

1. What is the disharmony within me or between me and my environment?

2. What can I do to resolve this disharmony?

Distress is to be avoided whenever possible. But when unavoidable, it can yield positive benefits by providing the basis for new learning, a change of direction, or resolution of disharmony.

EXERCISE 1-4. SITUATIONS AND SYMPTOMS

On a blank sheet of paper, list these headings at the top of two columns:

SITUATIONS   SYMPTOMS

Under the SITUATIONS column, list common daily situations you would like to handle more effectively so you experience less personal distress.

Under the SYMPTOMS column, list personal symptoms of distress you would like to minimize or avoid in the future.

Costs of Distress

Costs to the individual of prolonged and recurrent distress can include the following.

Physical illness

Lowered energy

Decreased productivity at work or school

Wasted potential

Lack of career advancement

Decreased satisfaction with life, work, and relationships

Low self-esteem

Non-involvement in public issues

Joylessness and meaninglessness

Absence of fun and play

Loss of interest in sex

Unfortunately, the costs of distress do not stop with the individual. They ripple outward, creating negative effects for others. In the family, high personal distress of one member, especially a parent, can contribute to such problems as these.

Tension in the air

A damper on freedom of expression

Open conflict

Psychological put-downs

Physical abuse

Low self-esteem of others in the family

Loss of potential earnings by an ailing family member

Inattentiveness to emotional and physical needs of others

Family breakups

High health-care costs

Costs too are great in the workplace, incurred mainly through the following.

Low productivity	Absenteeism
Worker dissatisfaction	Worker turnover
Conflict with co-workers	High health insurance costs

Matteson and Ivancevich (1987) recently estimated the dollar value of these costs. The probable stress-related expenses to a hypothetical industrial firm employing 1000 people with gross sales of about $40 million per year were estimated at $2,773,000, more than double the three percent profit of $1,200,000 for a given year. The authors point out that if we multiply the estimated $2,773 stress-related cost per employee by 108 million workers (total estimated U.S. work force), we end up with a mind-boggling cost of stress to industry of over $300 billion—a high cost indeed for stress-induced loss of effectiveness and efficiency.

In writing about costs of stress to the society as a whole, the cardiologist Robert Eliot, an expert on stress and heart disease, has stated (Eliot & Breo, 1984, 14):

▼ Painkillers are the leading over-the-counter drugs in this country.

▼ In addition to alcohol, perennially American's most abused drug, the current recreational drug of choice is cocaine, a stimulant that relieves stress by artificially causing the kind of high someone gets right after doing something great in life. Unfortunately, this high only lasts for ten minutes or so, then leaves the user flat.

▼ 13 million Americans are problem drinkers.

▼ One out of every four American adults has high blood pressure, potentially a very serious disease that can be caused or aggravated by stress.

▼ America's number one killer, heart disease, can be caused or aggravated by stress.

▼ According to the American Medical Association, half of this nation's annual $250 billion tab for medical services is due to unhealthy lifestyles.

Time Magazine (1983, 48) states:

> It is a sorry sign of the times that the three bestselling drugs in the country are an ulcer medication (Tagamet), a hypertension drug (Inderal), and a tranquilizer (Valium). Concludes Dr. Joel Elkes, director of the behavioral medicine program at the University of Louisville, "Our mode of life itself, the way we live, is emerging as today's principal cause of illness."

Consider the ten leading causes of death in 1988 in the United States, as shown in Table 1-1. Stress contributes a notable share to all ten through the mediating pathways shown in Figure 1-2.

A recent report concludes that half of all hospital admissions could be prevented by changes in lifestyle habits (Charlesworth & Nathan, 1984). Many of these, such as over- eating, lack of exercise, alcohol abuse, and smoking are maladaptive coping behaviors.

Roglieri (1980), in *Odds on Your Life*, estimates that mismanagement of stress alone probably will contribute to more than one-quarter of all deaths during the next five years in a typical group of white males, aged 40-45.

Costs of distress are not limited to adults. According to a recent news report, "The United States is raising a new generation of adolescents plagued by pregnancies, illegal drug use, suicide and violence, a panel of medical and education leaders said yesterday" (San Francisco Chronicle, 1990). A commission formed by the National Association of State Boards of Education and the American Medical Association concluded that "young people are less healthy and less prepared to take their places

TABLE 1-1. CAUSES OF DEATH, 1988

	PERCENT OF TOTAL
Heart disease	35.4%
Cancer	22.5%
Stroke	6.9%
Accidents	4.5%
Pulmonary disease	3.8%
Pneumonia and influenza	3.6%
Diabetes	1.8%
Suicide	1.4%
Liver disease	1.2%
Other infect. & paras. dis.	1.1%
Other	17.8%
Total	100.0%

SOURCE: (*Statistical Abstract of the U.S.*), 1990. Washington, D.C., Bureau of the Census. Table 115, 79.

FIGURE 1-2. MEDIATING PATHWAYS TO STRESS-RELATED DEATHS

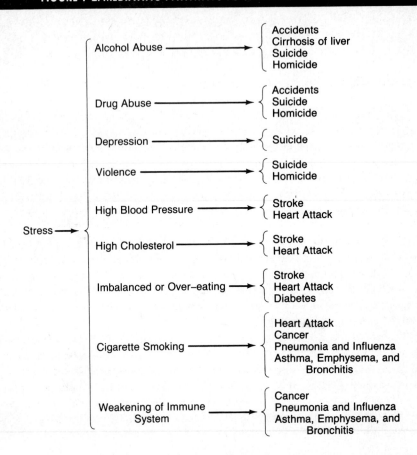

in society than were their parents." Among the statistics that "astonished" commission members were these:

▼ 1 million teenage girls—nearly 1 in 10—become pregnant each year.

▼ 39 percent of high school seniors reported that they had gotten drunk within the two previous weeks.

▼ Alcohol-related accidents are the leading cause of death among teenagers.

▼ The suicide rate for teenagers has doubled since 1968, making it the second-leading cause of death among adolescents. One of 10 teenage boys and nearly 2 of 10 teenage girls have attempted suicide.

▼ Since 1950, teenage arrests have increased 30-fold.

According to a spokesperson for the National Association of State Boards of Education, "We are absolutely convinced that if we don't take action immediately, we're going to find ourselves with a failing economy and social unrest."

In short, excessive distress is extremely costly to individuals, families, employers, schools, and the entire nation. Many experts predict these costs will rise.

Personal Stress and Public Issues

We noted that neither sea palms nor humans live in isolation. John Donne's words still hold: "No man is an island entire of itself." Brian's personal distress did not develop in a vacuum. It resulted from his efforts to adapt to changing circumstances around him, both in his immediate day-to-day environment and in the larger national and international climate. For example, Brian's business had taken a downturn in recent months in response to high interest rates, rising unemployment, and inflation. Periodically, his business faced a cash-flow crisis, a problem that seemed to correlate directly with his physical ailments and flare-ups with employees.

Brian's experience was consistent with research studies showing that a deteriorating economy markedly increases rates of stress-related illness, depression, suicide, child abuse, and alcoholism. During hard times, individuals and families face twin crises. Tension mounts from too little income and job security at the very time when options for day-to-day coping (for example, taking a weekend trip, eating out, beginning a new project around the home, or seeing a counselor) decline because of limited resources.

We all face other chronic pressures from the environment beyond economic ones—from the threat of nuclear war, air pollution, rising crime rates, traffic congestion, daily international tensions, the energy shortage, and urban noise. Like Brian's, each of these strains intrudes into our daily lives in a multitude of small ways. For many, the effect is a build-up of physical, psychological, and social tensions.

Alvin Toffler may well have been correct when he wrote two decades ago in *Future Shock* (1971, 365)

> The assertion that the world has "gone crazy," the graffiti slogan that "reality is a crutch," the interest in hallucinogenic drugs, the enthusiasm for astrology and the occult...the attacks on science, the snowballing belief that reason has failed man, reflect the everyday experience of masses of ordinary people who find they can no longer cope rationally with change.

Faced with these challenges, some people collapse, get sick, abuse others, or become seriously demoralized and resort to alcohol or drugs to numb their pain and depression. Others press onward in pursuit of their own private goals.

Still, others not only pursue their own goals but transcend themselves to do all possible to improve social conditions. They practice *constructive maladjustment*. That is, they are appropriately indignant about social conditions they find unacceptable and they are motivated to seek to improve these conditions. In other words, they link their personal problems with public issues—and they get involved.

Effective stress management, then, includes not only self-care in pursuit of personal wellness. It also includes social awareness and social responsibility in pursuit of the common good.

We have focused attention here on the dark side of stress. Let us now turn to the brighter side, with a discussion of positive stress.

POSITIVE STRESS

Brian's experience illustrates the curious duality of stress. On one hand, moderate, occasional elevations of anxiety helped prepare him for meetings, difficult conferences, and complex business negotiations. On the other, excessive chronic arousal seriously threatened his health, productivity, satisfaction, and relationships. Let us examine more closely the brighter side of stress.

Positive stress is helpful arousal—arousal that promotes health, energy, satisfaction, and peak performance.

Ways Positive Stress Can Be Helpful
Positive stress can be helpful in a number of specific ways. for example:

▼ Positive stress helps us to respond quickly and forcefully in physical emergencies, such as averting an auto collision, avoiding a dropped brick, lifting a heavy object off a child, fighting a fire, or administering cardiopulmonary resuscitation to a heart attack victim.

▼ Positive stress is useful in performing well under pressure, such as in the U.S. Tennis Open, the Law School Admission Test, a job interview, or a speech to the Rotary Club.

▼ Positive stress helps to prepare for deadlines—a term paper, 5:00 check-out time, or the income tax filing date.

▼ Positive stress helps realize potential over a period of years in athletics, academics, and career.

▼ Positive stress adds zest and variety to daily life.

▼ Positive stress helps you push your limits.

Personal Growth Through Pushing Your Limits
In Chapter 3, you will read about "zones of positive stress." You will see that we each have an optimal zone of arousal for peak performance and peak living.

Personal growth comes through sometimes pushing your limits beyond what is immediately comfortable. If you stayed in your zone of positive stress constantly, you would begin to stagnate. You will grow through sometimes deliberately pushing yourself in pursuit of a meaningful goal, to reach a higher level of performance than before, or to cope with an emergency. Marathon running, mountain climbing, studying very hard for a final examination, working very long hours on a project at work, missing sleep while caring for a loved one—all are examples of dedicated, meaningful efforts requiring you to push your mental or physical limits.

If distance runners never entered physical distress, they would never approach

BOX 1-2. PUSHING HER LIMITS

Below is a paper written by a college student in her 40's who had returned to school after many years. This was an Application Assignment in my Human Stress class.

"'Personal growth through pushing your limits' is something I have been doing both physically and mentally during the last six years. This has been the most difficult effort I have ever made, but the most rewarding experience, which I wouldn't trade for anything in the world.

"I am now a completely different person than I was, and it took pushing through a 'brick wall' of many phobias, severe lack of self-esteem and self-confidence, Type E behavior (see Chapter 8) which was a cover-up for my insecurities, and a life- threatening disease. I came from being a 'doormat,' terrified of everything and everybody, to a self-confident, healthy, well- balanced individual.

"In 1984, I discovered for the first time that I had some choices in my health status, started listening to my body to discover what it was telling me, and took one step at a time to make changes. As I pushed to get well, I discovered there were more steps I could take in my emotional status as well. I see the last several years as climbing a ladder, as I struggled to climb out of my pit and discover life on the outside of my 'prison.' Every step I took was terrifying, because it was new to me, but my survival depended on climbing out.

"Gradually, I discovered I survived each step! The steps got slightly easier, and I saw it as the beginning of an adventure! Now, the adventure keeps me going, and I see the obstacles as 'rocks to climb on for a better view' instead of 'boulders to crush me.' There is no stopping now, as I see life as an incredible opportunity to discover ever new ideas. The more I learn, the less I know, because each open door opens to many more open doors!

"My life up to 1984 was extremely distressful, and for several years I had felt like my stress response was stuck on 'ON.' My body was continually in a state of panic. I finally depleted my energy reserve and had to rebuild my system. Now, I am distressed only occasionally, because I look for the positiveness of my situations. I no longer am terrified of being well, because I have dealt with both my internal and external barriers to wellness and have discovered it feels wonderful! The hard work of pushing to literally hundreds of unknowns has brought a life that I had never imagined. My car license plate reminds me that—I DUN IT."

physiological potential. Similarly, if you are never willing to work very, very hard in pursuit of a goal, you will remain half-developed. You may never know the trade-off of temporary emotional or physical pain for the joy of accomplishment and approaching potential.

This principle applies to many spheres of life—and to one's total growth as a person, as illustrated by the story in Box 1-2.

Clearly, then, you do not want to avoid stress altogether. Without it, life would be stagnating and unsatisfying. Positive stress, sometimes called *eustress*, is vital. In fact, positive stress is an important part of wellness, a topic to which we now turn.

EXERCISE 1-5. PERSONAL ILLUSTRATIONS OF POSITIVE STRESS

1. Think back over the past week or two. In what specific situations has stress been HELPFUL?
2. Now think ahead. In what upcoming events might stress play a positive, constructive role for you?

DISPELLING COMMON MYTHS ABOUT STRESS

Earlier in the chapter (Exercise 1-2), you read and reacted to several common beliefs about stress. As you may have concluded by now, all 10 beliefs might better be described as myths.

These and many other false beliefs about stress exist in the minds of people who know they have too much distress and are searching for what to do about it. If these beliefs remain simply beliefs, little concern need exist. However, too often they are translated into action—action that is destructive at worst and ineffective at best in handling stress. Therefore, it is important to dispel these common myths.

1.   **All Stress is bad.** Stress can be helpful as well as harmful. Positive stress can provide zest and enjoyment, as well as attentiveness and energy for meeting deadlines, entering new situations, coping with emergencies, achieving maximum performance, and meeting new challenges. In moderate amounts, stress is useful. Even in large doses, it is often appropriate and vital.

2.   **The goal of stress management should be to eliminate stress.** Stress cannot and should not be eliminated. As Hans Selye, father of this field, has stated, only the dead are free of stress. Arousal is part of life. The goal of stress management should be control stress so it turns into harmful distress as infrequently and as briefly as possible.

3.   **The "good life" should be free of stressors.** Stressors, demands on mind or body, are an ever-present part of existence, just like stress. It is vital, insofar as possible, to control stressors and your interpretations of them so they are not overburdening in intensity or number. But fulfillment of human potential, in fact life itself, depends on exposure to appropriate kinds of stressors.

4.   **The less the stress, the better.** Not necessarily. The more the arousal the better when facing challenges or emergencies, up to a certain point. Stress mobilizes for action, shapes interpretations of events, and heightens attention. The less distress, the better, since, by definition, distress is harmful.

5.   **A person can always successfully adapt to difficult circumstances if he or she tries hard enough.** This belief is false on two counts. First, each person has limits of adaptability. If physical, social, or psychological pressures exceed your upper stress limit for an extended period, wear and tear will lead to eventual breakdown. This state of resistance gives way to the stage of exhaustion. Second,

"trying harder" is not always the answer to distress. The opposite may be true, in that activity needs to be alternated with rest and recovery.

6. **Some people are destined by their heritage to be highly stressed.** It is true that, to some degree, genetic and social background can affect resistance and vulnerability to pressure. But environmental and biological inheritance sets only very broad limits, except in cases of severe mental or physical handicap. Whatever the background, most people can take constructive steps, which can dramatically increase ability to handle and reduce stress.

7. **Distress has only harmful effects.** By definition, mental and physical distress are harmful to self and others. Yet even intense distress can have positive side effects—new learning about self or others, a new beginning, or a renewed relationship with someone, for example.

8. **Physical exercise drains energy that otherwise might be used to cope with stress.** Moderate, progressive physical exercise increases energy through the body's marvelous adaptive process. The claim, "I don't have enough energy to exercise, I need it to meet the demands of my life," is a hollow excuse without foundation in the reality of exercise physiology. The only exception is when a very hard workout might leave one temporarily too tired to cope well.

9. **Meditation is cultish, anti-Christian nonsense.** Some forms of meditation indeed are associated with gurus and cults. But meditation itself is a highly effective method of controlling stress by means of quieting the body (releasing the relaxation response) with a repeated mental focus, such as a silent sound, word, or thought. Research clearly shows that deep relaxation through meditation is effective in preventing and reducing stress-related illnesses. It is important to assess meditation as a method separately from any persons or organizations that might promote it.

10. **Stress affects only adults.** Stress is part of everyone's life, young or old. Children, adolescents, and youth experience the same responses as adults and run the same risks of distress illnesses. Therefore, the guidelines and techniques presented in this book apply equally to persons of all ages.

EXERCISE 1-6. PERSONALIZING AND REWRITING MYTHS

1. To what extent has each of these myths been part of your own thinking?
2. For each myth, formulate a sentence that encapsulates the truth.

STRESS AND WELLNESS   ▼

Most attention by those who conduct research and write about stress focuses on the darker side of stress. For example, what circumstances and life experiences contribute to stress illnesses? How can distress be prevented or treated? What are the harmful effects of stress on self or others? Indeed, parts of this book will address issues such as these. Yet there is another framework within which to view stress—the wellness framework.

WHAT IS WELLNESS?

Americans typically have grown up with the widespread cultural belief that if they are not ill, they must be well. This perspective is reinforced by our medical system. If I go to a typical doctor with a physical complaint and nothing is diagnosed through usual medical tests, I probably will be sent on my way with the message, "I can't find anything wrong with you. You are well. Be on your way and don't worry."

While it may be true I am not *sick*, this does not necessarily mean I am *well*. For wellness means to *live at one's highest possible level as a whole person*. Included in optimal well-being is:

Absence of illness

Low illness risk

Maximum energy for daily living

Enjoyment of daily life

Continuous development of one's abilities

Participating in supportive, satisfying relationships

Commitment to the common good.

Wellness, then, is maximizing one's potentials while enjoying the process and maintaining optimal health along the way. A wellness lifestyle is a way of living that enhances the whole person. As Don Ardell (1982) states, high-level wellness contrasts with low-level worseness.

If the U.S. Army had not already co-opted the phrase, one might say that wellness is being all you can be—as a whole person.

Wellness Habits
Wellness is attained through positive habits in the following areas:

Environmental
Intellectual
Emotional
Spiritual
Physical
Social
Time

Environmental Wellness Habits include awareness of the precarious state of the global environment and of the effects of one's daily habits on the physical environment; maintaining a way of life that minimizes harm to the environment; and being involved in socially responsible activities to protect the environment.

Intellectual Wellness Habits include the abilities to engage in clear thinking and recall, with minimal interference from emotional baggage; to think independently and critically; and to possess basic skills of reasoning. Also included is the broadest and deepest possible knowledge of cultural heritage.

Emotional Wellness Habits include awareness of one's emotions at any given time; the ability to maintain a relatively even emotional state with moderate emotional responses to the flow of life events; the ability to maintain relative control over emotional states; and the ability to experience a preponderance of positive over negative emotional states.

Spiritual Wellness Habits include concern with issues of meaning, value, and purpose; if not clarity or certainty in these respects, at least attentiveness to their importance and a continuing quest for clarity.

Physical Wellness Habits include sound nutritional practices; regular exercise, including aerobic exercise several times a week; consistent and adequate sleep; nonabuse of alcohol, drugs, and tobacco; use of seat belts and cycle helmets and practice of other safe traffic practices.

Social Wellness Habits include sharing intimacy, friendships, and group memberships; practicing empathy and active listening; caring for others; and being open to others' caring.

Time Wellness Habits include maintaining a pace of life that is within one's comfort zone most of the time; maintaining relative control over one's time; minimizing chronic hurry and hassle, on one hand, and boredom and stagnation, on the other; balancing activity and rest, work and play, solitude and relationships.

How Stress Relates to Wellness

Stress relates to wellness in two ways. On one hand, constructive, adaptive stress habits will enhance wellness, including peak performance under pressure. On the other, living a wellness lifestyle will help prevent distress.

The point of managing stress effectively, then, is not only to *avoid* harmful distress—emotional upset, headaches, or heart attacks. Managing stress is for the higher purpose of *promoting* well-being and fulfillment. Others in turn will benefit.

Wellness and "normal health," are not synonymous. To be "well" includes more than simply being "normal or "nonsick." To illustrate the point, it is useful to examine in Table 1-2 contrasts provided by Harold Elrick (1980) between standards of "normal" and "optimal" health. Our concept of wellness is the same as Elrick's notion of optimal health.

Several of these values can be debated in view of recent medical research. Nevertheless, these contrasts effectively illustrate the difference between normal health

TABLE 1-2. NORMAL AND OPTIMAL HEALTH STANDARDS

STANDARD	NORMAL	OPTIMAL
1. Diet	Calories,* Fat,* Salt,* Cholesterol,* Sugar,* Protein,** Fiber,** Calcium**	Optimal amount nutrients
2. Exercise	0—Occasional	Daily
3. Smoking	Common	None
4. Alcohol	Common	0—Occasional
5. Blood Pressure	100/70—150/95	90/60—120/80
6. Pulse	60—100	35—65
7. Body fat (Male)	12—25%	5—10%
8. Cholesterol	150—300	125—135
9. Triglycerides	30—200	30—100
10. Uric Acid	2.8—8	2.5—6.5
11. Magnesium	20—40	40—80

* Excessive
** Deficient
Source: Elrick (1980).

and wellness. To be well is to have the best possible test values, not just minimally acceptable ones.

A key element of wellness is possessing maximum energy for daily living. In many of my workshops and classes, I ask how many people feel tired most of the time. Consistently, 80 to 90 percent raise their hands. "General fatigue and heaviness" has been reported in studies of college professors (McKenna, 1980) and city managers (Schafer and Gard, 1988) to be the most common symptoms of distress.

This need not be so. Part of a wellness lifestyle—and part of managing stress effectively—is maintaining daily practices and attitudes that promote and sustain one's energy level. Being truly well—that is, more than just nonsick—is to have energy available when needed.

Figure 1-3 illustrates the role of perceived energy in protecting against distress and in contributing to a sense of general well-being, measured with a question on happiness.

In a before-after questionnaire given to more than 1171 participants in my community class at the Enloe Hospital Stress and Health Center called, "Reducing Perfectionism, Irritability, and Hurry Sickness," respondents were asked to indicate on a 10- point scale their "sense of vitality or energy level these days." They also

FIGURE 1-3. DISTRESS SYMPTOMS AND HAPPINESS BY PERCEIVED ENERGY

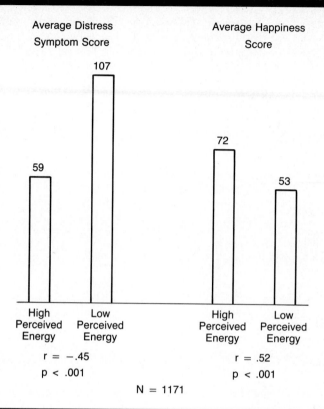

were asked to complete a 50-item checklist of mental, physical and behavioral distress symptoms during the past two weeks. In addition, they were asked to indicate on a ten-point scale "how happy are you these days, all things considered." Figures reported here are from the "before" questionnaires. Responses are mulitplied by ten to create whole numbers.

Figure 1-3 clearly shows that the higher the perceived energy, the lower the distress symptoms. Causal direction probably runs both ways: high energy protects against distress, while high distress saps energy. The key point is that the higher the energy, the lower the distress.

On a more positive note, Figure 1-3 reveals that the higher the perceived energy, the higher the happiness. Again, energy is a vital part of wellness.

Being truly well includes the ability to sustain high energy for long days, long weeks, long semesters—and a long lifetime.

Managing stress effectively, then, can not only assist in avoiding the perils of distress. It can enhance wellness.

Six Ways of Relating to Stress

People vary in how they relate to stress. Recognizing that no one is ever totally one or the other, we can distinguish among the following types of people and their approaches to stress. Consider how each "stress style" relates to wellness as well.

STRESS-SEEKING OR STRESS-AVOIDING?

Stress seekers thrive on challenge, risk, and sensation.

Stress avoiders thrive on security and familiarity, avoiding challenge, sensation, and risk.

DISTRESS-SEEKING OR DISTRESS-AVOIDING?

Distress-seekers thrive on misery, illness, crisis, and martyrdom. Often addicted to this pattern since childhood.

Distress-avoiders thrive on health, contentment, and involvement. They do all they can to avoid and reduce distress.

DISTRESS-PROVOKING OR DISTRESS-REDUCING?

Distress-provokers thrive intentionally or unintentionally on creating misery, disharmony, illness, or upset for others.

Distress-reducers thrive on doing all possible to promote health, happiness, and growth in those whose lives they touch.

These patterns of thought and action often are set in motion during childhood through the *life script,* one's blueprint for living developed through early internalized messages from significant others and early decisions in response to these messages. The pattern is perpetuated through a powerful internal drive of habit known as the repetition compulsion.

EXERCISE 1-7. PERSONAL APPLICATION OF SIX STRESS STYLES

1. To what degree does each of the labels in the section "Six Ways of Relating to Stress" apply to you? How would you rank yourself on each of the six, using these categories?

Applies QUITE A BIT to me

Applies SOMEWHAT to me

Applies VERY LITTLE to me

2. If needed, what steps might you take during the next six months to create a more positive profile?

BOX 1-3. 12 STEPS TO WELLNESS

Donald Ardell, who several years ago authored a pioneering book (Ardell, 1977) that helped launch the wellness movement, believes that "wellness is too important to be presented grimly." Accordingly, he has presented "12 steps to wellness." He cautions, "Like AA's steps, these are SOMEWHAT redundant, preachy and oriented to what a screw-up you've been. But, for lots of people, AA's steps worked, so who knows? Maybe these will work, too.

THE 12 STEPS TO WELLNESS

STEP 1: Acknowledge that you are a wimp in the face of worseness. By admitting your obsessive, chemical and spiritual abdication of responsibility to the siren song of abusive self-ruination and slovenly destructive near-term gratification of an inappropriate nature, you take the FIRST STEP to liberation by wellness. Namely, you conclude that you are a pox on the Earth, a slime-bag of a human being, but that you need not and will not stay that way.

STEP 2: Decide that you need to GAIN POSITIVE support and LOSE NEGATIVE support in getting started. Ask for the former from wellness seekers and dump your low level worseness "friends". Plant yourself in a healthful garden environment while weeding your social garden.

STEP 3: Choose yourself as guru or sovereign master for the course of your life. Make a commitment to independence and self-sufficiency tied to friendships, professional guidance, and a belief in a benevolent spirit or force that wants you to live joyfully and well.

STEP 4: Conduct a searching inventory of where you are. Assess liabilities and strengths, with an emphasis on the latter. Look at extremes of past self-abuse. For instance, consider old patterns of blaming, denial, worry, anger, self-pity, and dead-end relationships and grim associations that reinforce worseness. Make a conscious decision that these kinds of patterns are no longer acceptable.

STEP 5: Write out, analyze, and discuss your old profile. By disclosing who you used to be as well as what you are becoming with special wellness-oriented friends and colleagues, you put the past in the past, where it belongs.

STEP 6: Create a personal plan for wellness. Since the lack of wellness planning got you into a worseness frump in the first place, a written wellness plan is a sure way to lock-in that lifetime slow-fix to self-actualization.

STEP 7: Pursue realistic, worthy goals in a systematic way. Consider what you want from life and why that seems important.

STEP 8: Identify very special people crucial for your wellness quest—and include them in your support network. Avoid isolation; wellness is challenging under any circumstances. Only die-hards could sustain wellness on uninhabited land.

STEP 9: Explain your commitment to a wellness lifestyle to anyone who was a willing or other participant in your worseness past. Make amends, if necessary, in order to secure a tranquil spirit—and eliminate your guilt. Take a few disclosure chances.

STEP 10: Reassess along the way. A wellness lifestyle is never finished as long as life remains; adjustments, variations, and fine-tuning are always appropriate— if you think so.

STEP 11: Add a dash of imagery, meditation, or any other form of self-dialogue, if doing so helps you find inner peace. There are many ways and diverse paths to deepening your spiritual reservoir and finding balance and serenity.

STEP 12: Reach out and assist others. Becoming involved, sharing insights about personal rewards and satisfactions are services to those who need support. The joy of living is potentially too great to keep to yourself. Offer to share it—without being a bore or a bothersome proselytizer.

SOURCE: Ardell (1990, 3). Donald Ardell is publisher of the *Ardell Wellness Report.* Copies can be obtained by writing to *Ardell Wellness Report.* 9901 Lake Georgia Drive, Orlando, FL. 32817. First copy free with SASE.

WHAT DO GOOD STRESS MANAGERS DO?

As you approach the challenge of examining stress in your own life and how you might manage it better, consider what research findings tell us about effective stress managers—those who not only survive adversity but even thrive on it.

INTERNAL CONTROL
Good copers believe they can influence events and their responses to events. In the words of some experts, they have a strong sense of personal efficacy. They don't feel helpless when faced with adversity. Rather they turn difficulty into challenge.

SOCIAL SUPPORT
Effective stress managers know the importance of social support. Family, friends, church, and neighborhood can lend stability, guidance, and caring. And strength flows from giving as well as receiving.

ANCHORS
Good copers know that other personal anchors besides social support are vital. Included are personal beliefs and values, satisfying daily routines, enduring and meaningful objects, favorite places in nature.

PHYSICAL CARE
Effective stress managers take care of their bodies, no matter what. When times get tense, poor copers don't bother to exercise—too little time, too many pressures. By contrast, successful copers practice sound health and fitness habits during both bad

and good times. They eat well, exercise daily, and take twenty minutes a day for deep relaxation.

INVOLVEMENT

Good copers get involved. Helpless alienation breeds depression and disease. Active participation in community and political affairs adds to a sense of control and belonging. Not only do individuals benefit, but so does the community. Effective stress managers do their best to make a difference.

INTERPRETATION OF EVENTS

Those who handle stress well see the world in a generally positive way. They don't see events through rose-colored glasses, but they do try to see the good even in adversity and even in "bad" people. Most of all, they perceive themselves as competent and in control. They see difficult times as challenges to be mastered, rather than as threats.

REACTIONS TO DISTRESS

Finally, they respond to distress in ways that are adaptive and constructive, thereby reducing temporary tension or upset. They usually avoid maladaptive reactions that would escalate stress and tension.

EXERCISE 1-8. SELF-ASSESSMENT OF COPING SKILLS

How do you measure up on each of the qualities of good stress managers?

> Applies QUITE A BIT to me
> Applies SOMEWHAT to me
> Applies VERY LITTLE to me

ASSUMPTIONS ABOUT STRESS MANAGEMENT ▼

The whole-person, lifestyle approach to stress management presented in the following chapters is based on several guiding assumptions.

1. **Personal Responsibility.** Effective management of stress can be accomplished only by you. Your doctor, counselor, spouse, or minister cannot do it for you. They can help. You will need them as partners from time to time. But self-care rather than dependence on others is a keystone in the chapters that follow. The opposite of personal responsibility is helplessness, a bedfellow of distress.

2. **Holism.** There is no single magical way of controlling stress and minimizing distress. Regular running or swimming can help. So can improved diet, regular

meditation, slowing down, expressing feelings, taking vacations, and a number of other activities. The approach presented in Part II involves the whole person and total lifestyle.

3. Gradualism. No one should adopt too many new stress management methods at once. If you try too hard or expect change too soon, you will be frustrated and overloaded. You must be patient. Introduce one or two new stress management methods at a time so you can concentrate and carry through. Change comes gradually, not overnight. Wholeness is a long-term ideal, gradualism the short-run way to get there.

4. Balance. As you search for the pace of life and daily habits that are best for managing your stress, you stand to gain from striving for balance between all of the following.

> Self-interest and the well-being of others
> Work and play
> Intensity and ease
> Thought and action
> Risk and safety
> Change and stability
> Stimulation and quiet

Only you can determine the balance that is right for you in each of these respects—and what is right for you can change over time. You must be continually alert to internal cues that tell you what balance your body and mind need for health and growth.

5. Rhythm. Stress and distress come and go in stages and rhythms, some of which are quite predictable. Perhaps the greatest contribution of Gail Sheehy's best-selling book, *Passages,* has been the message to millions of readers that many adult crises are predictable, that many people experience the same crisis, and that these crises will pass (Sheehy, 1976). The same holds for the pre-adult years and for the later years.

Knowing that distress ebbs and flows can be reassuring. Your inner drive toward health and growth can take you from the deepest valleys to new peaks of authenticity and self-expression.

An important ingredient of wise stress management is conscious control of the rhythms of stress and distress. In daily life there inevitably are stressful periods of intensity and effort. If you are to manage stress wisely, you must deliberately return your stress level to normal relatively quickly, so you can handle the next stressful event of the day. The same is true for weeks and seasons: extended periods of deliberately induced calm, relaxation, and recovery.

6. Awareness. This book has emphasized the key role of understanding stress and distress—what they are, what causes them, how they can play useful and harmful roles in your life, how you can handle them. Continually increasing your understanding of both can be useful in two ways. First, awareness can be directly useful. If, for example, you are aware that a particular mental or physical state is stress-related (and that you are not "going crazy"), your worry about it almost always will subside. Similarly, anticipating a crisis and that it might produce illness or upset can lessen the tension. In short, understanding in itself can aid in handling stress.

Second, enhancing awareness can play an indirectly useful role, by leading to coping responses that are constructive rather than irrelevant or destructive. Knowing through experience, for example, that two long nights of sleep are vital for reducing accumulated tensions can aid you in coping with depression or intense anxiety. Conversely, the awareness that simply working harder may not help can encourage you to slow down or take a vacation. Awareness of stress often comes with *hindsight*—after-the-fact awareness. Next comes *mid-sight*—for example, awareness during a destructive coping response. Finally comes *foresight*—awareness before getting into severe distress or before a harmful coping response starts.

7. Action. Awareness by itself is only half the picture. The other half is paying attention to what you *do* as you seek to manage stress. How you spend your time, the actions you take, what you do in relation to others and your daily tasks—ultimately these will determine how well you manage stress. Both understanding and action are necessary, but neither is sufficient alone. Action guided by informed understanding—that is the necessary and sufficient combination required for handling stress well.

8. Experiment-of-One. People are different and the same approach will not work for everyone. Scientists can tell us what sometimes works to improve health or reduce tension for different kinds of people. But in the final analysis, you are unique. You have your own particular needs, you live your life in your own way, and your social setting is not exactly like anyone else's. You need to test out what fits your own body, personality, and way of living. Through experimentation, you will discover your own methods for controlling stress and preventing distress. This means that you must adopt the perspective of a scientist toward yourself—testing, observing, drawing conclusions, repeating what works, discontinuing what doesn't, searching for new stress methods when needed. The artful application of wisdom gained in this manner is an exciting and continuing challenge.

9. Lifelong Process. Managing stress is not something you do once, and then forget. Rather, in my life as in yours, managing stress is an ongoing, never-ending, sometimes joyful and sometimes frustrating challenge. This underscores the vital importance of deeply internalizing the principles in this book, making them part of your everyday approach to time, your body, other people, and daily activities.

You need not be helpless. Your fate is not sealed at birth or by the circumstances of your life. You can take affirmative steps to build personal protection against the mounting forces creating distress for millions. You can learn from those who handle life's pressures without illness or unnecessary strain.

Notice that good stress managers don't rely on one single technique or approach.

They weave together a blend of stress management methods. This is a *whole person, lifestyle approach*—the theme of this book.

In Chapter 2, we will present a brief history and summary of theories related to stress and wellness.

EXERCISE 1-9. QUALITY OF LIFE ASSESSMENT

Before reading further, you are invited to answer the following questions, then complete Exercise 1-10.

1. Circle the number below which best describes how much *in control of your own life* you feel these days.

1	2	3	4	5	6	7	8	9	10

Not at all   Moderately   Completely
in control   in control   in control

2. Circle the number below that best describes your *emotional tension* these days.

1	2	3	4	5	6	7	8	9	10

No emotional   Moderate   A great deal
tension at all   emotional   of emotional
                              tension   tension

3. Circle the number below that best describes your feeling of *depression* these days.

1	2	3	4	5	6	7	8	9	10

No depression   Moderate   A great deal
at all   depression   of depression

4. Circle the number below that best describes how *satisfied* you are with *life as a whole* these days.

1	2	3	4	5	6	7	8	9	10

Not at all   Moderately   Completely
satisfied   satisfied   satisfied

5. Circle the number below that best describes how *satisfied* you are with your *health* these days.

1	2	3	4	5	6	7	8	9	10

Not at all   Moderately   Completely
satisfied   satisfied   satisfied

6. Circle the number below that best describes how *satisfied* you are with your *job* these days.

1	2	3	4	5	6	7	8	9	10

Not at all   Moderately   Completely
satisfied   satisfied   satisfied

7. Circle the number below that best describes how *satisfied* you are with your *home life* these days.

1	2	3	4	5	6	7	8	9	10

Not at all   Moderately   Completely
satisfied   satisfied   satisfied

8. Circle the number below that best describes how *optimistic* you are about your *health* during the next five years.

1	2	3	4	5	6	7	8	9	10

Not at all   Moderately   Completely
optimistic   optimistic   optimistic

9. Circle the number below that best describes how *optimistic* you are about your *life as a whole* during the next five years.

1	2	3	4	5	6	7	8	9	10

Not at all   Moderately   Completely
optimistic   optimistic   optimistic

10. Circle the number below that best described how *happy* you are these days, all things considered.

1	2	3	4	5	6	7	8	9	10

Not at all   Moderately   Completely
happy   happy   happy

11. Circle the number below that best describes how much *fun and playfulness* you are having these days.

1	2	3	4	5	6	7	8	9	10

None at   Moderate   A great
all   amount   deal

12. Circle the number below that best describes your *self-esteem* or *self-liking* these days.

1	2	3	4	5	6	7	8	9	10

Very low   Moderate   Very high
self-esteem   self-esteem   self-esteem

13. Circle the number below that best describes your *sense of vitality* or *energy level* these days.

1	2	3	4	5	6	7	8	9	10

Very low energy level				Moderate energy level				Very high energy level

---

EXERCISE 1-10. LEARNING FROM YOUR QUALITY OF LIFE QUESTIONS

1. For comparisons, see Chapter 5 for before-and-after average scores among middle-aged participants in a six-month class designed to reduce Type A behavior.

2. How satisfied are you with the picture you see of yourself through these scores?

3. Which scores would you especially like to improve? Why?

4. What would it take, within yourself or within your life circumstances, or both, to improve your scores?

REFERENCES   ▼

Antonovsky, A. (1979). *Health, Stress and Coping.* San Francisco: Jossey-Bass Publishers.

Ardell, D.B. (1977). *High Level Wellness: An Alternative To Doctors, Drugs and Disease.* Emmaus, PA.: Rodale Press. Also see revised edition (1986). Berkeley: Ten Speed Press.

Ardell, D.B. (1982). *14 Days To A Healthy Lifestyle.* Whatever Publishing, Inc.

Ardell, D.B. (1990). 12 Steps to a Wellness Lifestyle. *Ardell Wellness Report,* No. 22, 3.

Associated Press (1990). Experts Say New Generation in Trouble Already. *San Francisco Chronicle,* June 9, A1.

Butler, K. (1987). Survivors of Sudden Tragedies Face Rage, Tears. *San Francisco Chronicle,* November 11, B3.

Carter, C. (1990). What a Father Learned From Grief. *Parade Magazine,* July 29, 4-5.

Charlesworth, E.A. & Nathan, R.G. (1984). *Stress Management: A Comprehensive Guide To Wellness.* New York: Atheneum.

Dickey, G. (1990). Seifert Wants 49ers Hooked on "Three-peat." *San Francisco Chronicle.* July 20, D3.

Eliot R. S. and Breo, D.L. (1984). *Is It Worth Dying For?* New York: Bantam Books.

Elrick, H. (1980). A New Definition of Health. *Journal of the National Medical Association,* 72, 695-699.

Goldberger, L. (1982). Sensory Deprivation and Overload. In L. Goldberger & S. Breznitz (Eds.), *Handbook on Stress: Theoretical and Clinical Aspects.* New York: Free Press.

Krause. N. (1987). Exploring the Impact of a Natural Disaster on the Health and Psychological Well-being of Older Adults. *Journal of Human Stress, 13,* 61-69.

Kolb, L. (1988). Combat Trauma May Alter Brain. *Brain/Mind Bulletin,* 13, 2.

Lazarus, R.S. & Folkman, S. (1984). *Stress, Appraisal and Coping.* New York: Springer Publishing Company.

Loo, R. (1986). Post-Shooting Stress Reactions Among Police Officers. *Journal of Human Stress,* 12, 27.

Markowitz, J.S. (1989). Long-term Psychological Distress Among Chemically Exposed Firefighters. *Behavioral Medicine,* 15, 75- 83.

Matteson, M.T. & Ivancevich, J.M. (1987). *Controlling Work Stress.* San Francisco: Jossey-Bass Publishers.

McKenna, J.K. (1980). *Occupational Stress and The University Professor.* (Unpublished Masters Thesis, California State University, Chico).

Minto, T. (1990). The Earthquake Isn't Over Yet: Psychological Scars Still Linger Seven Months After Loma Prieta. *San Francisco Chronicle,* May 25, B3.

Morse, D.R. & Furst, M.L. (1979). *Stress For Success: A Holistic Approach to Stress and Its Management.* New York: Van Nostrand Reinhold Company.

Nader, K. (1989). Stress persists after sniper's attack on school. *Family Practice News,* 19, 33.

Pelletier, K.R. (1977). *Mind as Healer, Mind as Slayer.* New York: Dell.

Roglieri, J.L. (1980). *Odds On Your Life.* New York: Seaview.

Rose, D.S. (1989). Post-traumatic Stress Disorder Said to Affect Most Rape Victims. *Family Practice News,* 19, 52.

Schafer, W. & Gard. B. (1988). Stress and California's City Managers. *Western City,* 64, 13-15.

Selye, H. (1974). *Stress Without Distress.* Philadelphia: Lippincott.

Selye, H. (1976). *The Stress of Life,* Rev. Ed. New York: McGraw-Hill Book Company.

Sheehy, G. (1976). *Passages: Predictable Crises of Adult Life.* New York: Dutton.

Tanner, O. (1976). *Stress.* New York: Time-Life.

Time. (1983). Stress: Can We Cope? June 6, 48-53.

Toffler, A. (1971). *Future Shock.* New York: Bantam Books.

Whiting, S. (1990). Waiting for the Fire: Survivors Live in Fear of the Next One. *San Francisco Chronicle,* August 1, B3.

Pioneers and Pathfinders:
A History of
Theories of Stress

Chapter 2

CHAPTER 2

I. INTRODUCTION

II. EARLY ORIGINS OF THE STRESS CONCEPT
A. The Yerkes-Dodson Law
B. Walter Cannon: Fight-or-Flight
C. Hans Selye: The General Adaptation Syndrome

III. RECENT THEORIES
A. Holmes and Rahe: Stress as Result of Clustering of Life Events
B. Maddi and Kobasa: Hardiness and Stress Resistance
C. Antonovsky: Sense of Coherence and Generalized Resistance Resources
   1. Sense of Coherence
   2. General Resistance Resources
D. Friedman and Rosenman: Stress as Result of Type A Behavior
E. Seligman: Stress and Learned Helplessness
F. Social Factors and Stress
G. Cognitive Interpretation of Stressors
H. Contributions from War Research
I. Lazarus and Folkman: Stress—A Dynamic, Transactional Coping Process

IV. A WHOLE-PERSON, LIFESTYLE MODEL OF STRESS MANAGEMENT

INTRODUCTION   ▼

Popular magazines are filled these days with self-help tips for how to achieve better health, happiness, love, appearance, and much more. Our approach is distinguished from most of these how-to articles by being soundly grounded in scientific research and theory.

This chapter's review of highlights of scientific research and theory—past and current—is intended to enhance your understanding of how we got to this point in our understanding of human stress—its nature, causes, effects, control, and prevention. This review also will provide useful guidance in formulating an integrated, coherent stress management approach.

Of course, time and space will allow only a brief discussion of key ideas. You might want to consult other sources for more detail. We will refer back to these theories and lines of research throughout the book.

EARLY ORIGINS OF THE STRESS CONCEPT   ▼

Like many other ideas in the behavioral sciences, the concept of stress had its origins in the physical sciences (Hinkle, 1977). Dating back at least to the last century, "load" referred to an external force on, say, metal or wood. "Stress" was the ratio of resulting internal forces to the area over which the force acted. The term "strain" was applied to disruption or distortion of the material being acted upon, such as a building beam or a floor.

In the 19th century, first applications of stress to human experience began to occur in the medical literature. For example, the mind-body pioneer Sir William Osler made this comment about Jewish businessmen:

> Living an intense life, absorbed in his work, devoted to his pleasures, passionately devoted to his home, the nervous energy of the Jew is taxed to the uttermost, and his system is subjected to that stress and strain which seems to be a basic factor in so many cases of angina pectoris (Hinkle, 1977, 30).

As Lazarus and Folkman (1984) have noted, this description is an old version of the modern concept of Type A behavior. Note that it makes direct connections between mind and body, and between lifestyle and health.

A specific early link between hostility and heart disease also was suggested by the story of a famous 18th century English medical professor named Sir John Harvey, who made a sad prediction when he said, "My life is in the hands of any fool who chooses to annoy and tease me" (Williams, 1989, 18). He apparently recognized the link between his anginal chest pain (shortage of oxygen to the heart) and his run-ins with colleagues.

One evening in 1793, his prediction came true. After a heated argument with other doctors at a hospital board meeting, Dr. Harvey stormed out, groaned, and fell dead.

While Harvey was not credited posthumously with applying the term stress to his experience, he clearly understood the connection between tension and the well-being of his body, in this case his heart. What he apparently failed to recognize, or at least to apply in his life, was the fact that it was not those "fools" around him who caused his upset, but rather his own self-talk—that is, his interpretation or appraisal about those individuals.

THE YERKES-DODSON LAW

Another important early contribution was the *Yerkes-Dodson Law*, first formulated in 1908 (Yerkes & Dodson, 1908). Still useful, this model generates important insights about the association between arousal and performance. As shown in Figure 2-1, this law postulates that, up to a point, arousal increases performance. After an optimum arousal peak, however, performance goes down as arousal continues to rise. At very high levels of arousal, performance may be no better than if the person were not aroused at all.

> As Mike mentally prepared during the last week for his moment in the state rollerskating championships, he recalled his ups and downs during that season. He had done very well several times, mediocre twice, and was definitely "off" at three meets. He had tried a number of different mental and physical techniques to prepare himself, sometimes entering the rink emotionally too high—pent-up, anxious, on edge—at others with a feeling of listlessness and lack of concentration. In looking back, it became clear to him that those meets in which he performed at his peak were instances where his stress level was in the middle, neither too high nor too low. He realized after further thought that the same had been true of his test performances at college, speeches he had given, even job interviews. He was struck by the vital importance of optimum stress in peak performances.

The Yerkes-Dodson law also can be illustrated by performance in a basketball tournament game, a final examination in college, or a speech before the corporate board of directors. The lesson is the same: people usually perform best when mental and physical arousal are moderate, rather than extreme, in either direction.

This model also suggests the notion of zones of positive or optimal stress, zones which vary from one individual to the next, but within which performance and good health are at their peak.

A personal challenge is to determine one's optimum arousal level. Another is to learn techniques, including one's lifestyle itself, for creating and maintaining that optimum stress level.

A challenge facing managers, supervisors, teachers, and coaches is to learn techniques for creating the right stress level for those they influence—and to learn how to recognize it when present.

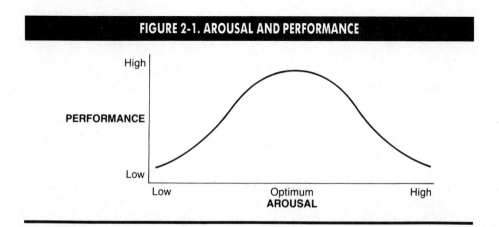

FIGURE 2-1. AROUSAL AND PERFORMANCE

EXERCISE 2-1. PERSONAL APPLICATION OF STRESS-PERFORMANCE CURVE

1. Can you recall a performance situation in which your arousal level was either too high or too low, thus adversely affecting your performance? Exactly how did you feel? What happened?

2. During the near future, observe your own mental and physical arousal level during demanding performance situations (e.g., speech, interview, athletic contest, musical or acting performance). Be aware of your arousal level and its effect on your performance? Was it too high? Too low? Optimal?

3. Try applying some of the techniques presented throughout Part II for regulating your arousal level in such situations.

WALTER CANNON: FIGHT-OR-FLIGHT

Walter Cannon (1932), a Harvard medical professor who was an early mind-body pioneer, made the first real application of the stress concept to human experience. He considered stress to be a disturbance of homeostasis (balance or staying power) under conditions of lack of oxygen, cold, heat, low blood sugar, and the like. He especially emphasized the role of the sympathetic nervous system during periods of disturbance. Cannon also provided rather detailed accounts of how the body responds during such emotional upsets as rage.

Perhaps Cannon's greatest contribution was to identify the *fight-or-flight response,* the body's mobilization to face external threat. Cannon noted a cluster of inter-related physiological changes that prepare one to stand ground and fight or to escape the danger through flight. He described, for example, an increase in respiration and heart rate, tightening of muscles, increase in blood pressure, dilation of pupils, and more. In Chapter 3, we examine the stress response in some detail.

HANS SELYE: THE GENERAL ADAPTATION SYNDROME

Building on Cannon's work, Hans Selye, a young medical student at McGill University, began more detailed investigations of the body's response to changes in external conditions (Selye, 1950, 1951-56, 1974, 1976). Selye pointed out that the initial focus of his work was on "the syndrome of just being sick." "In my second year of training I was struck by how patients suffering from the most diverse diseases exhibited strikingly similar signs and symptoms, such as loss of weight and appetite, diminished muscular strength, and absence of ambition (Selye, 1982, 9)."

His curiosity about the "sick syndrome" led him to detailed study of the stress response in laboratory rats. In the course of this research, Selye discovered a curious thing: whatever "noxious agents" (stressors) he introduced into the bodies of rats, the response always seemed the same.

Three types of changes were produced: (1) the cortex, or outer layer, of the adrenal glands became enlarged and hyperactive; (2) the thymus, spleen, lymph nodes, and all other lymphatic structures shrank; and (3) deep, bleeding ulcers appeared in the stomach and upper intestines. Being closely interdependent, these changes formed a definite syndrome (Selye, 1982, 9).

Selye coined this syndrome the *general adaptation syndrome* (GAS). In response to a local infection or bruise, the body undergoes a series of specific adaptations at the site. These Selye called the "local stress response." But he noted that the body goes through a general, systemic response as well. This general response is what Selye meant by the stress response. Although subsequent stress research has shown the GAS to be overly simplistic when applied to the complexities of human stress, this was an important early contribution to the field.

Selye's well-known definition of stress, based on his research, is "the non-specific response of the body to any demand made upon it" (Selye, 1974). This definition is very similar to the one introduced in Chapter 1. The only differences are that the definition used throughout this book includes mental as well as physical reactions and introduces the somewhat more descriptive term "arousal." By including mental arousal, we focus on a much wider range of human experience under the category of stress.

Selye also noted that sometimes stress is experienced as positive, "eustress" (Selye, 1974). An example is the thrill of a job promotion. Even though the person is required to adjust, the experience is pleasant. Other times stress is negative, "distress", as in a job demotion. Of course, whether an event is experienced as eustress or distress depends, not on the event itself, but on the individual's appraisal or interpretation of the event. Job promotions or demotions can be interpreted in directly opposite ways by two different persons.

Another fascinating, though controversial, idea set forth by Selye was that we possess two types of adaptive energy: superficial and deep (Selye, 1974). *Superficial adaptive energy* is not depletable. In fact, it can be increased through good health and fitness practices. *Deep adaptive energy* is like an inherited fortune, held in reserve for times of intense stress. Selye suggested that our deep adaptive energies may be limited and finite, like oil reserves in the earth. In times of distress, we use up small amounts of this reserve. "Chemical scars" remain. As the reserve is depleted, we wear down. This is aging. Total depletion brings death.

EXERCISE 2-2. EVALUATING THE IDEA OF SUPERFICIAL AND DEEP ADAPTATIVE ENERGY

1. How accurate do you believe Selye's notions of superficial and deep adaptive energy to be? Why?

2. To what extent do you believe energy depleted from major life events can be renewed? How, if at all?

3. To what extent do you believe energy depleted from the hassles of daily life can be renewed? How, if at all, can superficial adaptive energy be renewed?

Wise management of our lives, especially pace of life, means using adaptive energies sparingly and for the right purposes. As Selye (1974, 40) states, "We can squander our adaptability recklessly, 'burning the candle at both ends,' or we can learn to make this valuable resource last long, by using it wisely and sparingly, only for things that are worthwhile and cause least distress." Proper pacing is vital in daily life, just as in running a marathon. So is choosing activities and goals that are meaningful—worth using up some of our deep adaptive energy.

Important as Selye's contributions were over the period of more than 40 years of his research and writing, critics have pointed out important limitations in his model of human stress. For example, he tended to ignore individual differences in response to stressors. Since his work was almost entirely based on animal research, he could not adequately take account of the influences of mental appraisal, emotions, coping style, or social factors in his accounts of stress. As noted above, the General Adaptation Syndrome now seems too simplistic when applied to human experience.

Mason (1975) maintains that the nonspecificity of the stress response is an artifact of the animal laboratory and that emotions associated with that response play a vital role in influencing the body's reaction. Thus, he maintains that the stress response is most likely a specific rather than general response.

Nevertheless, this field owes Selye a great debt for his pioneering and detailed accounts of physiological changes elicited by the stress response. His work set the stage for further research and theory about the nature of stress and its influences on health and disease. Let us now examine some of the most important recent theories of stress which followed Selye's lead. In each case, we will identify key implications for understanding human stress and key leads for stress management strategies.

RECENT THEORIES   ▼

HOLMES AND RAHE: STRESS AS RESULT OF CLUSTERING OF LIFE EVENTS

During the 1960s, a group of researchers led by Richard Rahe and Thomas Holmes noticed that illness seemed to increase during times of rapid personal change. However, no systematic evidence had ever been gathered to test their hunch against reality. Therefore, they set out on a program of research about the link between life change and illness.

Their initial studies focused on two questions (Holmes & Rahe, 1967; Rahe, 1974). First, how do people rank life-change experiences in degree of stressfulness? Second, is there an association between the clustering of life changes and frequency of illness? Through a series of steps we need not review in detail here, Holmes and Rahe developed a rank ordering of 43 events, weighted in terms of average stressfulness among several thousand respondents. An important insight from this research was that not only do "big events," such as death of spouse, loss of job or retirement, lead to stress, but so do seemingly minor events such as change in number of family get-togethers.

Known as "The Social Readjustment Rating Scale" (see Chapter 10), the resulting measure provided the needed tool to tackle the second question about the effect of life change on risk of illness. Literally hundreds of studies using this and similar scales have documented that the greater the clustering of life events within six months or a year's time, the greater the chances of illness, both major and minor. While negative life events are especially stressful, researchers have found that even positive events can increase chances of getting sick, since all life changes require mental and physical adjustment. The more choice and control over events, the less harmful the effects.

More recently, research by Lazarus and colleagues (DeLongis, et al., 1982; Lazarus, 1984) has extended the view that minor adjustments can exact mental and physical damage. In fact, it may be that these "daily hassles" have more negative impact on well-being than major life events. Lazarus notes that the two usually are linked. That is, a major life event, such as a divorce, sets in motion a series of new and challenging daily adjustments. The divorcee may need to learn how to handle family finances, plumbing problems, shopping, child care, yard work, and more. Thus, major events may have their harmful effects through daily hassles (Dohren-wend, 1986). In Chapter 12, you will read that daily hassles can impact students as well.

EXERCISE 2-3. Change and Illness in Your Life

1. Looking back over your life during the past year, identify changes you have experienced. Which were major and which were minor—as you experienced them? Which have been pleasant, which unpleasant? Which were initiated by you, which could you not control?
2. Were you ill during or after any of these changes?
3. Do you believe change and illness might be related in your own experience? Why or why not?
4. Do you have any ideas about the mental or physical pathways through which change might have influenced illness?

In Chapter 10, we will describe this line of research in more detail. It is important to note here, however, that despite recent criticisms of life events studies, the work of Holmes, Rahe and others provided important early insights into the impact of life experiences on the body and mind.

MADDI AND KOBASA: HARDINESS AND STRESS RESISTANCE

A key criticism of life events research has been its assumption that the individual is a passive recipient of whatever events life happens to send his or her way. Another is the implicit assumption that change, indeed stress itself, is bad and should be avoided.

These assumptions troubled a group of researchers led by Salvadore Maddi and his student, Suzanne Kobasa, at the University of Chicago. They decided to pose the reverse question. Given that people sometimes go through periods of turmoil and change, whether by choice or not, who stays well? What are the characteristics and habits of those who seem to be stress-resistant?

Maddi and Kobasa initiated a research program of their own, resulting in findings with important implications for both research and prevention (Kobasa & Maddi, 1977; Kobasa, 1979; Kobasa, Maddi & Courington, 1981; Kobasa & Hiller, 1982;

Kobasa, Maddi & Kahn, 1982; Maddi & Kobasa, 1984). They found that stress-resistant individuals possess a cluster of attitudes and beliefs which Maddi and Kobasa termed hardiness.

Hardy individuals manifest three C's: *Challenge, Commitment and Control.* They thrive on adversity and pressure, turning these experiences from potential threats into challenges and opportunities. They are highly involved and committed in what-ever they set out to do. And they have a strong belief that they will be able to influence events in their lives and control their responses to events. In Chapter 7 you will read more about these components and how to strengthen them in your own life.

This line of work by Maddi and Kobasa has been an important addition to our understanding of susceptibility-vulnerability to distress and disease in a fast-paced, rapidly changing world. It underscores the idea that environmental pressure and stress are not just matters of stimulus-response. Rather, personal perspective and interpretation can make a real difference. Some writers refer to this as "self-talk." Others see hardiness as one of several potential "stress-resistance resources." This research also suggests that stress involves a give-and-take between person and environment and is a dynamic process through time.

EXERCISE 2-4. PERSONAL ASSESSMENT OF THREE C'S OF HARDINESS

1. Can you identify anyone you know who exemplifies high hardiness? How does this individual display a sense of challenge, a sense of commitment, and personal control?

2. How would you rank yourself on each of the three C's, using the following categories:
Applies QUITE A BIT to me
Applies SOMEWHAT to me
Applies VERY LITTLE to me

ANTONOVSKY: SENSE OF COHERENCE AND GENERALIZED RESISTANCE RESOURCES

Sense of Coherence
An Israeli sociologist, Aaron Antonovsky, has proposed a theory of stress susceptibility and resistance based on the concept, "sense of coherence" (Antonovsky, 1979, 1987).

The sense of coherence is a global orientation that expresses the extent to which one has a pervasive, enduring though dynamic feeling of confidence that (1) the stimuli deriving from one's internal and external environments in the course of living are structured, predictable, and explicable; (2) the resources are available to one to meet the demands posed by these stimuli; and (3) these demands are challenges, worthy of investment and engagement (Antonovsky, 1987, 19).

Antonovsky contends that sense of coherence is vital for distress since it ". . . is a generalized, long-lasting way of seeing the world and one's life in it." More, it is

". . . a crucial element in the basic personality structure of an individual and in the ambience of a subculture, culture, or historical period" (Antonovsky, 1979, 124). In other words, the greater the presence of sense of coherence, the more stress- resistant will be a person, a group, or a society.

Sense of coherence is both cognitive and affective in nature. It provides a sense of stability, yet the term "dynamic" in the definition means it can tolerate minor fluctuations of life experiences and minor emotional ups and downs.

Central to this idea is a sense of relative control over events, to the extent that they are controllable, and acceptance when they are not.

Antonovsky does not believe one needs to believe everything will turn out rosy to be well and happy. Quite to the contrary.

> A sense of coherence is not at all equivalent to feeling that everything in life is handed to one on a silver platter or that one has the Midas touch. Quite the contrary may even be true. Life may well be seen as full of complexities, conflicts, and complications—which one understands. Goal achievement may be seen as contingent on immense investment of effort. Moreover, one may be fully aware that life involves failure and frustration. The important thing is that one has a sense of confidence, of faith, that, by and large, things will work out well. Not that things will have a Hollywood happy ending. This is why the proviso "as can reasonably be expected" is added. A strong sense of coherence includes a solid capacity to judge reality (Antonovosky, 1979, 126).

Generalized Resistance Resources

Linked to his concept of sense of coherence is Antonovsky's concept of "generalized resistance resources," or GRRs (Antonovsky, 1979). He maintains that sense of coherence is likely to develop to the extent that GRRs are present in our lives. He points out that, "A pathogenic orientation . . . particularly within the framework of the traditional medical model of the single bullet, immunological or therapeutic, pressures one to focus on specific resistance resources relevant to a particular disease" (Antonovsky, 1979, 99). He defines GRRs, on the other hand, as "any characteristic of the person, the group, or the environment that can facilitate effective tension management" (Antonovsky, 1979, 99).

Several categories of GRRs are the focus of his attention:

▼ Physical and biochemical GRRs (immunological strength, neurological adapt-ability)

▼ Cognitive and emotional GRRs (knowledge, intelligence, identity)

▼ Valuative-attitudinal GRRs (cognitive appraisal habits, flexibility, farsighted-ness)

▼ Interpersonal-Relational GRRs (social supports, social commitment)

▼ Macrocultural (beliefs, rituals, norms, values embedded in larger culture)

In short, Antonovsky's position is that stress and stress- induced illnesses develop to the degree that generalized resistance resources are lacking, resulting in turn in a weak sense of coherence. Conversely, health in part is a product of GRRs and sense of coherence.

Following Antonovsky's lead, it is important to attend to resources within and around us that can contribute to stress resistance, as well as to our generalized view about events now and in the future—that is, our sense of coherence, which can vitally affect how we interpret specific events.

FRIEDMAN AND ROSENMAN: STRESS AS RESULT OF TYPE A BEHAVIOR

Another influential line of research emerged in the 1960s from quite another source: the medical specialty of cardiology. During the 1950s, two cardiologists, Meyer Friedman and Ray Rosenman, had already been engaged in studying risk factors contributing to coronary heart disease. They found that so-called conventional risk factors, such as elevated cholesterol, high blood pressure, and cigaret smoking explained many heart attacks, but by no means all of them. They began to wonder if something about emotions, behavior, or personality might have heretofore-unrecognized harmful effects on coronary arteries and the heart.

After numerous impediments to securing federal funds to study this possibility—most medical researchers were extremely skeptical then that psychological factors could possibly have anything to do with heart disease—Friedman and Rosenman began a series of carefully designed studies. They first identified a syndrome they called Type A, marked by chronic time urgency, drive to accomplish, perfectionism, and easily aroused hostility and anger (Friedman and Rosenman, 1974).

A key early study of more than 3500 subjects found that Type As were about twice as likely as Type Bs (subjects without Type A qualities) to develop coronary artery disease and suffer heart attacks over an eight and one-half year period (Friedman & Rosenman, 1974; Rosenman, et al., 1975). A later study by the same team in San Francisco found that the risk of a second heart attack dropped by about half among patients who completed a program for reducing Type A behavior (Freidman & Ulmer, 1984; Friedman, et al., 1986).

As we will see in Chapter 5, considerable criticism has been leveled at the theory of Type A behavior, partly because of recent non-confirming research findings. Part of the problem may lie in the too-broad scope of what is measured by the interviews and questionnaires used in the Type A studies.

During the 1980s and continuing into the 1990s, scientific investigators have been zeroing in on specific components of the Type A pattern in an effort to discover if specific parts might be more toxic than others. As we shall see, they are finding that one specific culprit—hostility—seems to be the sole toxic element contributing to increased risk of heart attacks. Even standing alone, in the absence of any of the other Type A qualities, hostility appears to contribute to coronary heart disease and to premature death from all causes.

Again, despite the problems and limitations, Type A theory and research during the past quarter century have extended our understanding of stress and health. One of its merits has been to demonstrate that lifestyle—the pace at which we live and how we experience daily events—can influence the body. Another has been to show implicitly that stress does not occur in isolation, but rather is tied into social relationships. Hostility and anger occur in relation to others.

Thus, in seeking to understand and manage stress we are led to attend to how we relate to others in a fluid process of give and take as well as how we respond mentally and physically to static events. Stress is part of a dynamic, interpersonal process of coping with the environment.

SELIGMAN: STRESS AND LEARNED HELPLESSNESS

We noted in Chapter 1 that distress develops when the individual perceives demands from the environment as exceeding his or her coping resources. Seligman (1975, 1979) has developed a theory of learned helplessness that helps understand how some individuals get to the point of feeling overwhelmed by environmental demands. We all experience trying unsuccessfully to make an event happen: calling someone for a date and being turned down, applying for a job and never getting that call for an interview, trying to get an idea across to a professor who never seems to get the point of what you are saying. Most people go on with only minor disappointment.

Sometimes, these uncontrollable events become chronic occurrences. Research shows that both animals in the laboratory and humans in society can develop learned helplessness in response. In other words, people sometimes learn to become helpless when faced with repeated uncontrollable events.

In one experiment with students, for example, Hirito and Seligman (1975)

BOX 2-1. LEARNING AND UNLEARNING HELPLESSNESS

Below is an example of how learned helplessness can be taught to children by parents. This was written by a woman who had returned to college in her 40s and sought to understand family influences on her development.

"For myself, I found I would be crtiticized by my mother whether I did something correctly and nicely or if I did something unpleasant. Criticism would come my way even in the presence of strangers who were paying me compliments. My mother would have to negate any positive input that would come my way. This kind of ongoing, negative environment left me with a psychology of 'why bother trying.' If I did anything well it would not be appreciated anyway.

"I recall one incident, while listening to a barrage of criticism, I said to my mother, 'Well, Mom, there must be something I do well, I couldn't be doing everything wrong.' She answered, quite seriously, 'I'm sorry, S-----, but there is nothing you do right, nothing.'

"Intellectually, I did not accept this, but emotionally I was crushed. I am certain that a little more of me gave up hope of ever being loved by mother. It did not, however, stop me from trying. . . .

"It has been a long, painful struggle for me to learn that I could indeed set myself a goal and then go about reaching that goal. Each time I was able to reach a goal I had set for myself, I gained a little more confidence in my ability to set and reach a new goal. This learning is still occurring in my life, and I seem to take two steps ahead and one step back."

SOURCE: Berger, (1990).

assigned subjects to one of three groups. Group one was exposed to loud noise that could be terminated by pushing a button. Group two received loud noise but had no control over its termination. Group three received no noise. In the second session, all three groups were exposed to loud noise that, unknown to them, could easily be stopped by pushing the button. The "controllable" and "no noise" group quickly discovered how to stop the noise and did so. By contrast, the "uncontrollable noise" group failed to discover how to stop the noise and, instead, passively endured it. They had "learned," quite incorrectly, that the noise was uncontrollable.

Seligman and his colleagues (Maier and Seligman, 1976) concluded from this and many other studies that learned helplessness takes on three dimensions: motivational, cognitive, and emotional. The result is earlier entry into the "stage of exhaustion," described by Selye in the general adaptation syndrome. According to Seligman, learned helplessness heightens chances of depression.

This theory of learned helplessness has generated a great deal of interest. Yet it has been criticized on a number of grounds, including its failure to take account of individual differences as well as the duration of helplessness (Taylor, 1986). Thus, Seligman and colleagues reformulated the model to take greater account of individual explanations of negative events (Abramson, Garber and Seligman, 1980).

According to this revised model, three dimensions of cognitive interpretation become important for explaining and predicting the depth, pervasiveness and duration of helplessness. First is *internality-externality*. When the individual experiences negative events (for example, not getting a job she very much wanted), does she attribute the cause internally ("If only I had tried harder") or externally ("I did my best; they must have wanted different skills than mine")?

The second dimension is *stability*. Stable attributions assume it will always be this way ("I'll never get a job that amounts to anything"). Unstable attributions see this event as a minor and short-lived glitch in personal growth and success ("I know I will get a good job; it will just take patience and perseverance").

Third is *globality*: the extent to which the interpretation is limited to one sphere of life ("I have lots of other things going on in my life right now") or many spheres ("This is one more part of my life where things don't go my way").

A host of studies by Seligman and others show that interpretations that are internal, stable and global lead to losses in motivation, cognition and emotional well-being. The result is greater frequency, depth, and duration of depression.

Taylor (1986, 157) gives an example of how the learned helplessness model might fit the situation of coping with a romantic relationship in which one person is continually disappointed. Here is how someone who tends toward internal, stable, and global interpretations might react.

> Every time you think a problem is solved, it arises again or a new one takes its place. Eventually, you will lose interest in the relationship, think about it less, and make few efforts to keep it afloat. With repeated unsuccessful efforts, you may conclude that internal, stable, global factors are responsible. Consequently, you may give up trying in the expectation that future relationships will be as disappointing as those in the past. Jaded lovers who flee from all but the most casual romantic encounter fit this pattern well.

Individuals vary, of course, in their tendency to attribute the cause of negative events to internal, stable, and global factors. When they do, they are likely not only to experience greater depression, but to cope with ongoing events in ways that become self-fulfilling—and therefore dissatisfying and distressful.

This model also helps explain why uncontrollable events are more distressing than controllable ones. When events are interpreted as uncontrollable and unmodifiable, the person is more likely to conclude that no personal effort can possibly make any difference anyway. Thus, one's perceived inner sources to cope soon are overwhelmed by perceived demands of the environment. Subjective feelings of distress follow—and so do physical and behavioral consequences (Taylor, 1986).

On the other hand, presenting opportunities for beneficial, controllable events is likely to enhance chances of "learned optimism" (Seligman, 1991). Since helplessness and attributional style are learned, it stands to reason that educational and therapeutic programs can succeed in teaching learned optimism and attributional styles that are based on external, unstable, and nonglobal interpretations.

The learned helplessness theory, then, sheds further light on the complex interplay of individual and environment in the emergence of distress and the person's response in coping with it. It is clear that both personal and situational factors must be acknowledged.

SOCIAL FACTORS AND STRESS

Early writing by several sociologists focused attention on other aspects of the relationship between the individual and the social environment. For example, Durkheim (1893) wrote extensively about alienation. By alienation (or anomie) he meant a condition in which individuals experience the lack or loss of clear, socially agreed upon guidelines (social norms) to guide their behavior. Later on, other sociologists elaborated the concept of alienation to include powerlessness, meaninglessness, normlessness, isolation, and self-estrangement (Seeman, 1959, 1971). Alienation of these various types has come to be seen as aspects of stress—aspects that have special relevance in modern times.

C. Wright Mills carried on this tradition in the 1950s by asserting that "personal problems" need to be seen as "public issues" (Mills, 1956). He maintained and carried on qualitative sociological analyses to support his position, that personal experiences are patterned. That is, rates of personal difficulties are structured according to individuals' location in social structures; for example, whether people are excluded from access to power in the society. Thus, social structures directly influence personal experience. He maintained, then, that individuals need to try to change social systems, not just their adjustment to those systems, in order to improve their lives. He maintained this can best be done through political action.

Contemporary sociologists have tended to use the term strain, rather than stress, and have applied it to social, rather than personal disturbances. For example, analyses of riots, panics, and rates of crime, mental illness, homicide, and suicide refer to social rather than personal problems. Yet the line between psychology and sociology blurs when attention is given to:

natural disasters	the impact of the depression on individuals and families
work strikes	
examination stress	the effects of nighttime work
rates of high blood pressure among various groups	the impact of organizational climate or administrative style on an employee's health
the effects of poverty	
	the effects of divorce

In most studies on these topics, emphasis is put on the dynamic interplay between individual and environment as a process through time.

Individual differences often are noted, based on the influences of coping style and psychological appraisal. Yet the person is not seen in isolation, but rather as vitally connected with—and influenced by—outside influences.

More recently, studies by Lynch (1977), Berkman & Syme (1979), House (1981) and others have continued to document the role of social support in stress, illness, and mortality. The greater the social connectedness, the better off is the individual.

COGNITIVE INTERPRETATION OF STRESSORS

Since the 1950s, a great deal of attention has been devoted to the role of thinking in the stress experience.

In an excellent book on the topic, Lazarus and Folkman raise the question, why is a concept of appraisal necessary? They point out that even though circumstances may heighten chances of distress, they do not alone explain it (Lazarus and Folkman, 1984, 22).

> Although certain environmental demands and pressures produce stress in substantial numbers of people, individual and group differences in the degree and kind of reaction are always evident. People and groups differ in their sensitivity and vulnerability to certain types of events, as well as in their interpretations and reactions.
>
> Under comparable conditions, for example, one person responds with anger, another with depression, yet another with anxiety or guilt; and still others feel challenged rather than threatened. Likewise, one individual uses denial to cope with terminal illness, whereas another anxiously ruminates about the problem or is depressed. One individual handles an insult by ignoring it and another grows angry and plans revenge. Even in the most devastating of circumstances, such as the Nazi concentration camps, people differed as to how threatened, disorganized, and distressed they were. Their patterns of coping differed as well (Benner, Roskies, and Lazarus, 1980). In order to understand variations among individuals under comparable conditions, we must take into account the cognitive processes that intervene between the encounter and the reaction, and the factors that affect the nature of this mediation. If we do not consider these processes, we will be unable to understand human variation under comparable external conditions.

Beck (1976), Burns (1980), Berne (1964, 1972), Ellis (1962, 1975), Lazarus (1966; Lazarus & Folkman, 1984), Helmstetter (1986, 1987), and others have generated theory and research emphasizing that it is not outside circumstances alone that produce stress, but rather a combination of circumstances and the individual's self-talk about them. This view, of course, is consistent with the "hardiness" and "sense of coherence" theories reviewed above.

Study after study has shown that two different individuals—indeed the same person at different points in time—can interpret the same event quite differently. Consequences for emotion, physical state, and behavior will vary accordingly.

Hamilton (1982, 118) has presented a useful review of this area of stress research, including a clear illustration of the impact of self-talk on anxiety.

> Let us now consider the nature of the data by which conditions, events, etc., are identified as stressors. Why do we respond with anxiety if we think that we are being followed while walking through a dark and empty park? Clearly, we *interpret,* rightly and wrongly, the situation as being favorable to a mugging. We impose a *meaning* on a stimulus field on the basis of what we mean—as a result of learning—by being alone in the dark and being followed. The meaning is established vocally, subvocally, or without vocalization by retrieving the implications of "walking behind," "dark," "lonely," and "mugging." These lexical units form a so-called semantic network. Should it transpire that the stranger following is the park keeper, the whole interpretation and its lexicon is revised. The identification of this official person changes the semantic network and, therefore, the conceptual structure of the previous anxiety response to one of support and relief.

Research in the psychological laboratory and in the field has reinforced the assumption that interpretation or appraisal influences people's responses to external events. This line of research underscores again the fact that the person is not a passive object being acted upon by outside events. Rather, stress is a result of an interplay between circumstances, events, appraisal, and response.

You may recall that one criticism of Selye's definition of stress as the nonspecific response of the body to demands made upon it and his theory of the general adaptation syndrome was that it did not take account of individual differences, nor cognitive factors. As Mason (1975) has noted, understanding stress can be enhanced by understanding the body's response to *pathogens.* As Taylor (1986, 114) has noted:

> Pathogens such as viruses and bacteria act on an organism to produce disease. However, not all organisms exposed to pathogens develop disease; some resist and remain disease free. So individual differences show up in susceptibility to infectious illnesses. Mason suggested that stress can be viewed in the same way. Stress may have the potential to cause disease, but individual factors must also be taken into account. The tuberculosis bacterium does not inevitably cause the disease in those exposed to it. Some people exposed to the bacterium will develop tuberculosis, but some will not. The same can be applied to stress. Some people exposed to stress will succumb to its pathogenic effects, but others will not.

Interpretation of events is one key factor influencing susceptibility to distress and disease, given adversity in the environment.

EXERCISE 2-5. PERSONAL APPLICATIONS OF COGNITIVE MODEL

1. Identify a recent event about which you became more upset or uptight than you wish.
2. What emotional and physical reactions occurred?
3. What did you say to yourself—what was your self-talk—just before and during your reaction?
4. To what extent was your reaction a result of your self-talk, rather than the event itself?
5. Looking back, how might you have interpreted this event in a more realistic or positive way?

CONTRIBUTIONS FROM WAR RESEARCH

World War II, the Korean War, and the Viet Nam War all resulted in landmark studies on stress. For example, Grinker and Spiegel (1945) published a classic study of "shell shock," a condition of immobilization or panic under fire. New studies during the Korean War focused on the role of stress hormones in the stress response, as well as on performance under pressure. Studies during the Viet Nam era also focused on combat stress and its aftermath, now called the Post-Traumatic Stress Disorder (Blank, 1982). Military studies during these conflicts also paid attention to manipulation of the minds of prisoners of war, the impact of bombing on civilians, and concentration camp survival. Again, these studies were important contributions not only to the subjects at hand, but to building a body of knowledge about the human stress experience. Most focused in one way or another on the intricate and fascinating interplay among body-mind-behavior-environment.

LAZARUS AND FOLKMAN: STRESS—A DYNAMIC, TRANSACTIONAL COPING PROCESS

Lazarus & Folkman maintain that stress is most accurately seen as ". . . a particular relationship between the person and the environment that is appraised by the person as taxing or exceeding his or her resources and endangering his or her well-being" (1984, 19). From their perspective, stress can best be understood from "a transactional, process, appraisal- and coping-centered approach."

Lazarus and Folkman maintain there are several advantages of viewing stress from a dynamic, active point of view. First, the original use of this term in the physical sciences implied an inactive or passive object that is strained or harmed by the environment. The dynamic view, however, sees the human body as actively responding back, engaging in continuous effort to adapt and restore homeostasis. In other words, adaptation is active, not passive, and continuous, not static.

Second, biological stress as a process of defense offers a useful analogy to the process of psychological "coping," in which the person struggles to achieve psychological balance.

Third, stress as a dynamic process brings to the fore the importance of aspects of human stress that would be ignored by a static and passive view of stress. Included, for example, are such factors as the resources available for coping, such as physical fitness, social support, and money; the costs of stress, such as illness and disturbed relationships; and the benefits of effective coping including energy, joy of accomplishment, and peak performance.

Fourth, focus on stress as a dynamic state turns attention to the ongoing relationship between the individual and the environment, including continuous feedback and interplay.

Fifth, attention is directed, not only to the influence of major life events, but to how individuals experience common daily hassles. As noted above, Lazarus and colleagues have devoted a good deal of attention to the study of minor hassles of daily life. Their studies suggest that the experience of many small events as negative hassles has more influence on mental health than do major life changes (DeLongis, et al., 1982).

A sixth implication, not mentioned by Lazarus and Folkman, is that attention is directed to intervening with the environment as a method of managing stress. As noted in Chapter 1, in fact, being socially responsible sometimes requires involvement in social issues. To be content with simply adapting to unjust or unfair social conditions is to misuse the notion of stress management.

As Lazarus and Folkman (1984, 6) point out, "Since the 1960s there has been growing recognition that while stress is an inevitable aspect of the human condition, it is coping that makes the big difference in adaptational outcome." The experience of stress is influenced not only by internal appraisals and physical responses but by the cultural and subcultural context, since it is these contexts out of which specific stressors emerge and which influence the accessibility and form of coping.

Thus, we are led to be aware of the individual's cognitive, emotional, physical, and behavioral interplay with the environment in the ongoing, dynamic effort to resolve difficulties and maintain mental and physical health. In this way, we are led to a multi-focused, complementary set of steps to harnessing stress—an approach we refer to as a *whole-person, lifestyle model of stress management.*

A WHOLE-PERSON, LIFESTYLE MODEL OF STRESS MANAGEMENT ▼

Many other theories of stress have been proposed, and a number of other lines of research have been carried on. Our purpose here is not to present an exhaustive survey of these writings. Rather, our effort has been to draw on key ideas from the human stress literature to bring guidance to our search for effective strategies and techniques of stress management.

A whole-person, lifestyle model of stress can be synthesized from the above theories of stress. This framework is very useful for approaching stress management, its main advantage being its emphasis on the complex nature of stress. In turn, you see that any wise approach to stress management must be multi-targeted. Let us briefly examine this framework, part by part.

1.   **Social and Physical Context.** Stressors do not impinge upon the person in a vacuum. Rather, as we saw in the above discussion about social factors and stress, specific stressors are part of a larger environment. Nor does the individual respond in isolation. For example, a manager's oppressive behavior toward

employees is best seen as a part of the context of the larger organization. Similarly, the specific stressors confronting each employee and the way he or she responds are imbedded within and influenced by his or her surroundings, including the physical setting, the organizational climate, the work group, the family, the community, and the society. It is sometimes vital, then, to focus stress management efforts on this surrounding context, rather than simply on the specific stressor or on the sole individual affected by it. Chapters 13 (Managing Job Stress), and 15 (Balancing Self-Care and Social Responsibility) will focus on the social context of stress as a key target of stress management.

2. **Stressors.** Very early in the history of stress theory and research, Selye distinguished between stimulus (stressor) and response (stress). In Chapter 1, we identified a number of types of stressors and ways they can vary. A vital target for stress management is to monitor and manage stressors insofar as possible. This may mean avoiding, changing, or accepting them—all forms of coping. We saw that an important implication of the transactional, process-oriented model of stress proposed by Lazarus and Folkman is that attention is given to the continuous interplay between self and others. We will examine detailed suggestions for managing stressors, including communication techniques' throughout Parts II and III.

3. **Health Buffers.** You are not destined by biological or social background to react to stress in a given way, as noted in Chapter 1 in our discussions of myths about stress. By developing effective health buffers, you can add physical and mental resistance against distress, as we saw in the review of theories of generalized resistance resources. In Chapter 8, we will focus on several health buffers: aerobic exercise, good nutrition, and sleep.

4. **Interpretation of Stressors.** Another vital link intervening between stressors and your mental, physical, and behavioral reactions to them is your interpretations of those stressors. For example, a change in job location or assignment can be perceived as a threat or an opportunity for growth. Interpretations of stressors can be controlled, a position taken by several of the theorists we reviewed above. Chapter 7 will focus on a number of specific and practical methods for managing your interpretations.

5. **Emotional and Physical Stress Response.** Selye and others since have described in considerable detail how the brain and body process interpretations of stressors through either the conscious or unconscious appraisal pathways. Learning to regulate and control these responses immediately prior to, during, or after arousal is another important target of stress managment, and it will be addressed in Chapter 9. Special attention is given to controlling the physical part of the stress response.

6. **Coping.** We noted above that Lazarus and Folkman call attention to stress as a dynamic process through time in which the person perceives, interprets, reacts internally with thoughts and feelings, responds behaviorally, is responded to, and becomes aware of and reacts to his or her own earlier responses—including one's own response of distress. Unfortunately, a sizable

proportion of stress problems results not from the original stress, but from ineffective or maladaptive steps for dealing with distress. We will discuss in Chapter 6 steps for responding to temporary distress adaptively, decreasing the distress level, or maladaptively, making it worse. This is what we call "reactions to distress."

In the next chapter, we will examine in more detail the physiology of the stress response and the relaxation response. This discussion will shed further light on what is needed for an effective whole-person, lifestyle approach to stress management.

REFERENCES ▼

Abrahamson, L.Y., Garber, J. & Seligman, M.E.P. (1980). Learned Helplessness in Humans: An Attributional Analysis. In J. Garber & M.E.P. Seligman (Eds.), *Human Helplessness: Theory and Applications.* New York: Academic Press.

Antonovsky, A. (1979). *Health, Stress and Coping: New Perspectives on Mental and Physical Well-Being.* San Francisco: Jossey-Bass Publishers.

Antonovsky, A. (1987). *Unraveling the Mystery of Health: How People Manage Stress and Stay Well.* San Francisco: Jossey-Bass Publishers.

Beck, A.T. (1976). *Cognitive Therapy, and The Emotional Disorders.* New York: International Universities Press.

Benner, P., Roskies, E., & Lazarus, R.S. (1980). Stress and Coping Under Extreme Conditions. In J.E. Dimsdale (Ed), *Survivors, Victims and Perpetrators: Essays on the Nazi Holocaust.* Washington, D.C.: Hemisphere.

Berger. S. (1990). A Self-Portrait. (Unpublished paper, California State University, Chico).

Berkman, L.F. & Syme, S.L. (1979). Social Networks, Host Resistance and Mortality: A Nine-year Follow-up Study of Alameda County Residents. *American Journal of Epidemiology,* 109, 186-204.

Berne, E. (1964). *Games People Play.* New York: Grove Press.

Berne, E. (1972). *What Do You Say After You Say Hello?* New York: Grove Press.

Blank, A.S., Jr. (1982). Stresses of War: The Example of Viet Nam. In L. Goldberger & S. Breznetz (Eds.), *Handbook of Stress: Theoretical and Clinical Aspects.* New York: Free Press.

Burns, D.D. (1980). *Feeling Good.* New York: William Morrow.

Cannon, W.B. (1932). *The Wisdom of The Body.* New York: Norton.

Delongis, A., Coyne, J.C., Dakof, G., Folkman, S., & Lazarus, R.S. (1982). Relationship of Daily Hassles, Uplifts, and Major Life Events to Health Status. *Health Psychology,* I, 119-136.

Dohrenwend, B.P. (1986). Note on a Program of Research on Alternative Social Psychological Models of Relationships Between Life Stress and Psychopathology. In M.H. Appley & R. Trumbull, *Dynamics of Stress: Physiological, Psychological and Social Perspectives.* New York: Plenum Press.

Durkheim, E. (1893). *The Division of Labor in Society.* (Trans. George Simpson, 1966). Glencoe, Ill.: Free Press.

Ellis, A. (1962). *Reason and Emotion in Psychotherapy*. New York: Lyle Stuart.

Ellis, A. (1975). *How To Live With a "Neurotic" at Home and At Work*. New York: Crowne.

Friedman, M. & Rosenman, R.H. (1974). *Type A Behavior and Your Heart*. New York: Knopf.

Freidman, M. & Ulmer, D. (1984). *Treating Type A Behavior and Your Heart*. New York: Knopf.

Friedman, M., Thoresen, C. E., Gill, J.J., Ulmer, D., Powell, L.H., Price, V. A., Brown, B., Thompson, L., Rabin, D.D., Greall, W.S., Bourg,. E., Levy, R., & Dixon, T. (1986). Alteration of Type A Behavior and Its Effect on Cardiac Recurrences in Post Myocardial Infarction Patients: Summary Results of the Recurrent Coronary Prevention Project. *American Heart Journal*, 112, 653-665.

Grinker, R.R., & Spiegel, J.P. (1945). *Men Under Stress*. New York: McGraw-Hill.

Hamilton, V. (1982). Cognition and Stress: An Information Processing Model. In L Goldberger &. S. Breznetz, *Handbook of Stress: Theoretical and Clinical Aspects*. New York: Free Press.

Helmstetter, S. (1986). *What To Say When You Talk To Yourself*. New York: Pocket Books.

Helmstetter, S. (1987). *The Self-Talk Solution*. New York: Pocket Books.

Hinkle, L.E., Jr. (1977). The Concept of "Stress" in the Biological and Social Sciences. In Z.J. Lipowski, D.R. Lipsitt, & P.C. Whybrow (Eds.), *Psychosomatic Medicine: Current Trends and Clinical Implications*. New York: Oxford University Press.

Hiroto, D.S. & Seligman, M.E.P. (1975). Generality of Learned Helplessness in Man. *Journal of Personality and Social Psychology*, 31, 311-327.

Holmes T.H. & Rahe, R.H. (1967). The Social Readjustment Rating Scale. *Journal of Psychosomatic Research*, 11, 213-218.

House, J.S. (1981). *Work Stress and Social Support*. Reading, MA.: Addison-Wesley.

Kobasa, S.C. (1979). Stressful Life Events, Personality and Health: An Inquiry into Hardiness. *Journal of Personality and Social Psychology*, 37, 1-11.

Kobasa, S.C. & Hiller, R.R. (1982). Executive Work Perceptions and the Quality of Working Life. *Journal of Occupational Medicine*, 24, 25-29.

Kobasa, S.C., Maddi. S.R., & Courington, S. (1981). Personality and Constitution as Mediators in the Stress-illness Relationship. *Journal of Health and Social Behavior*, 22, 368- 378.

Kobasa, S.C., Maddi, S.R., & Kahn, S. (1982) Hardiness and Health: A Prospective Study. *Journal of Personality and Social Psychology*, 42, 168-177.

Lazarus, R.S. (1966). *Psychological Stress and The Coping Process*. New York: McGraw-Hill.

Lazarus, R.S. (1984). Puzzles in the Study of Daily Hassles. *Journal of Behavioral Medicine*, 7, 375-389.

Lazarus, R.S. & Folkman, S. (1984). *Stress, Appraisal and Coping*. New York: Springer Publishing Company.

Lynch, J.J. (1977). *The Broken Heart: The Medical Consequences of Loneliness*. New York: Basic Books.

Maddi, S.R. and Kobasa S.C. (1984). *The Hardy Executive: Health Under Stress.* Homewood, Ill.: Dow Jones-Irwin.

Maier, S.F. & Seligman, M.E.P. (1976). Learned Helplessness: Theory and Evidence. *Journal of Experimental Psychology: General,* 195, 3-46.

Mason, J.W. (1975). A Historical View of the Stress Field. *Journal of Human Stress,* 1, 22-36.

Mills, C.W. (1956). *The Power Elite.* New York: Oxford University Press.

Rahe, R.H. (1974). The Pathways Between Subjects' Recent Life Changes and Their Near-future Illness Reports: Representative Results and Methodological Issues. In B.S. Dohrenwend and B.P. Dohrenwend, *Stressful Life Events: Their Nature and Effects.* New York: John Wiley & Sons, 73-86.

Rosenman, R.H., Brand, R.J., Jenkins, C.D., Friedman, M., Straus, R., & Wurm, M. (1975). Coronary Heart Disease in the Western Collaborative Group Study: Final Follow-up of 8½ Years. *American Journal of Cardiology,* 233, 872-877.

Seeman, M. (1959). On the Meaning of Alienation. *American Sociological Review,* 24, 783-791.

Seeman, M. (1971). The Urban Alienations: Some Dubious Theses from Marx to Marcuse. *Journal of Personality and Social Psychology,* 19, 135-143.

Seligman, M.E.P. (1975). *Helplessness: On Depression, Development and Death.* San Francisco: W.H. Freeman.

Seligman, M.E.P. (1979). *Helplessness.* San Francisco: W.H. Freeman.

Seligman, M.E.P. (1991). *Learned Optimism: The Skills To Overcome Life's Obstacles.* New York: Random House.

Selye, H. (1950). *The Physiology and Pathology of Exposure To Stress.* Montreal: Acta.

Selye, H. (1951-1956). *Annual Report of Stress.* Montreal: Acta.

Selye, H. (1974). *Stress Without Distress.* Philadelphia: Lippincott.

Selye, H. (1976). *The Stress of Life* (Rev. Ed.). New York: McGraw-Hill.

Selye, H. (1982). History and Present Status of the Stress Concept. In L. Goldberger & S. Breznetz (Eds.), *Handbook of Stress: Theoretical and Clinical Aspects.* New York: Free Press.

Taylor, S.E. (1986). *Health Psychology.* New York: Random House.

Williams, R. (1989). *The Trusting Heart: Great News About Type A Behavior.* New York: Times Books.

Yerkes, R.M. & Dodson, J.D. (1908). The Relation of Strength of Stimulus to Rapidity of Habit-Formation. *Journal of Comparative Neurology and Psychology,* 18, 459-482.

The Dynamics of Stress, Relaxation and Energy

Chapter 3

CHAPTER 3

I. INTRODUCTION

II. THE INTERPLAY OF MIND, BODY, AND BEHAVIOR

III. THE STRESS RESPONSE
A. Physiology of the Stress Response
   1. Interpretation of Stressors
   2. Interpretation and the Brain
   3. The Sympathetic Nervous System
   4. The Endocrine System
   5. Readiness for Physical Action
B. Behavior, Thoughts, and Feelings in the Stress Response
C. Stress and Immunity
D. Stress and Adaptation
   1. The General Adaptation Syndrome
   2. How Humans Adapt to Stress

IV. THE RELAXATION RESPONSE AND HOMEOSTASIS
A. The Relaxation Response
B. Physiology of Deep Relaxation

V. ENERGY: A COMPONENT OF WELLNESS
A. Energy, Stress, and Relaxation
B. The Nature of Human Energy
   1. Defining Energy
   2. Beliefs About Energy
   3. Two Dimensions of Energy
   4. Types of Energy People
   5. Sources of Energy
   6. Energy Qualities
   7. Blocked Energy
   8. Energy Rhythms
   9. Energy in Relationships
C. Correlates of Energy: Research Evidence
D. Changing Energy Levels

INTRODUCTION   ▼

> During a five-mile run in the foothills where I live, my easy rhythm was severely interrupted by the sudden, silent approach of a full-grown, teeth-baring Doberman Pinscher. Some months earlier the same dog had bitten my 16-year-old daughter, so I saw him as a genuine threat. Already my heart had been beating at 130-140 beats per minute during the run. Suddenly it sped up, probably to 160-170 beats per minute. My breathing accelerated. My muscles tensed, my eyes dilated and opened wide. I could feel adrenaline pouring into my limbs.
>
> My attention focused immediately on coping with this threat. I had two alternatives: fight or flee. Experience had taught me that fighting, or at least pretending readiness to fight, would prove most effective. I yelled at the dog, reached for stones on the road, and threw two or three at the ground in front of him. The dog turned tail and vanished, but it took my body several minutes to "come down" from intense arousal to its previous normal condition associated with running at an easy eight-minute per mile pace.

In certain respects, this experience was unique. I had never met this particular dog at this particular time of day or in this particular place. Yet the reactions in my body and mind were not at all unique. What I experienced was the stress response, a distinctive mental-neurological-muscular-hormonal reaction that I had known many times before. So has everyone. And so have animals other than humans.

My encounter with the dog was a genuine physical threat, eliciting an appropriate, useful response from my body. Arousal helped me cope. Most stressors, however, are social and psychological, rather than physical. Hence, such physical arousal usually is quite useless. As we shall see, in fact, the stress response can be hazardous to well-being when chronic and unreleased.

My stress response was *episodic* and intense, that is, *a maxi fight-or-flight response*. Normally, intense episodic arousal does no harm, and in fact, can prove helpful. But the pressures of daily living too often result in a chronic stress response at too high a level. In short, *chronic* daily hassles often produce a continuous, erosive *mini fight-or-flight response*. Its damage is cumulative and often imperceptible, like a low-grade fever.

In this chapter, you will learn more about the *stress response* and how it affects you. You also will read about its opposite, the *relaxation response*. Finally, we will discuss *energy*, another vital dimension of human experience with relevance to stress and wellness. Focusing on these topics will provide an important base of understanding upon which to build attitudes and practices for managing stress and maximizing wellness.

THE INTERPLAY OF MIND, BODY, AND BEHAVIOR   ▼

A fundamental assumption in our whole-person, lifestyle approach to stress is that mind, body, and behavior are closely intertwined. In fact, they are inseparable. Cause-effect arrows depicting these linkages run both ways, as illustrated in Figure 3-1. These interconnections occur in response to major events as well as to minor daily hassles.

Physical wear and tear (body) often results from chronic mental strain (mind) associated with coping with (behavior) a difficult marriage, an unsatisfying job, or overload at school. Distress often results as mind, body, and behavior affect each other in an accelerating cycle of stress build-up.

A fascinating illustration of mind-body-behavior interplay is blood pressure during conversation. Recent studies by James Lynch and his associates at the University of Maryland clearly show that each time a person talks (an action), his or her blood pressure goes up (physical arousal), most likely in response to thoughts and feelings (in the mind) associated with the act of communicating. When the person stops talking, blood pressure declines (Lynch, 1985).

This nearly universal pattern is illustrated in Figure 3-2 by the average blood pressure readings of six nurses before, during, and after talking.

Lynch has found that whether the spoken content is negative or positive, blood pressure arousal results. However, the more emotionally intense the content, the greater the arousal.

The likely mediating role of thoughts and emotions is further illustrated by Figure 3-3, which shows that reading alone elevates blood pressure somewhat, but not as much as reading in someone else's presence. It also shows that reading in the presence of a "high status" person (an experimenter dressed up as a physician) raised blood pressure more than did reading in the presence of an "equal status" experimenter (a graduate student dressed casually in blue jeans, sport shirt, and tennis shoes).

This strongly suggests that interpretation (thoughts) affected emotions ("performance anxiety" with the physician), which in turn affected blood pressure through changes in the heart and blood vessels (body).

FIGURE 3-1. MIND-BODY-BEHAVIOR

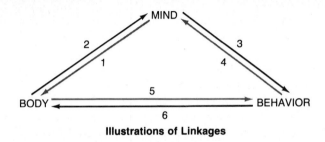

Illustrations of Linkages

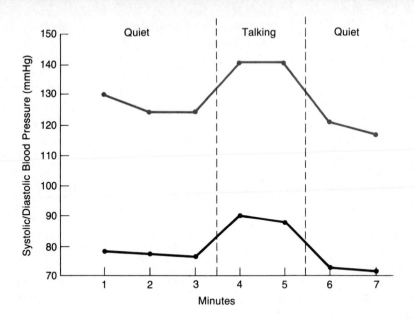

FIGURE 3-2. BLOOD PRESSURE AND TALKING

SOURCE: Lynch (1985, 123).

Here is another fascinating illustration of mind-body interaction. Phillips & King (1988; Phillips, 1990) have found in several samples that people seem able to postpone their own deaths until after a meaningful date or event, such as their own birthday, Passover, and, among elderly Chinese women, the Harvest Moon Festival.

For many years, studies of "placebo power" also have consistently shown that the mind can influence the body. As reported by Norman Cousins, one Harvard medical researcher concluded the following after reviewing results of 15 studies involving 1082 subjects:

> He discovered that across the broad spectrum of these tests, 35 percent of the patients consistently experienced "satisfactory relief" when placebos were used instead of regular medication for a wide range of medical problems, including severe postoperative wound pain, seasickness, headaches, coughs, and anxiety. Other biological processes and disorders affected by placebos, as reported by medical researchers, include rheumatoid and degenerative arthritis, blood-cell count, respiratory rates, vasomotor function, peptic ulcers, hay fever, hypertension, and spontaneous remission of warts (Cousins, 1979, 58).

Another important mind-body-behavior link is that exercise (behavior) improves mental clarity and emotional stability (mind), as well as energy level and cardiovascular capacity (body). More will be presented about exercise and stress in Chapter 8.

FIGURE 3-3. BLOOD PRESSURE RISE IN PRESENCE OF PERSON OF HIGH AND EQUAL STATUS

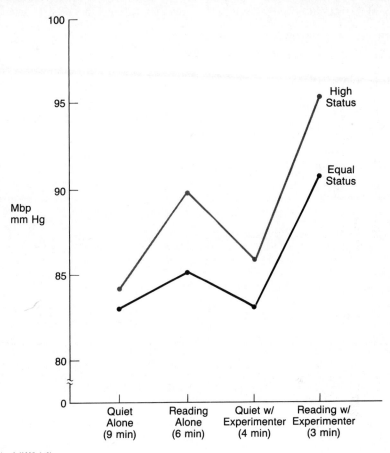

SOURCE: Lynch (1985, 149).

A recent study found a direct link between anxiety and heart rate experienced among U.S. Border Patrol officers participating in a simulated field shooting test. The author reports:

> Pulse rates were well within normal limits at baseline; they began to show an elevation during the control and the briefing intervals and demonstrated a dramatic rise—to nearly 150/minute—during the judgment shoot. Pulse rates began to return to normal during the debriefing session and reached normal levels once again at the second baseline period (Rahe, 1988, 121).

Later in this chapter you will read that mind, body, and behavior also interrelate during the relaxation response, the opposite of the stress response. Because of these interlinkages, you will come to understand why an integrated, whole-person, lifestyle approach to stress management is so important.

The key point here is that mind-body-behavior are intimately intertwined. We will now examine how this happens in relation to the experience of stress.

THE STRESS RESPONSE
PHYSIOLOGY OF THE STRESS RESPONSE

This section describes the physiology of the stress response and its integration with thoughts, feelings, and behavior. As shown in Figure 3-4, the proper place to begin in understanding the stress response is with the stress trigger, or stressor. We noted in Chapter 1 that stressors may be intense (word of death of a relative) or mild (a child's dirty shoes on the living room carpet); pleasant (a daughter's high school graduation ceremony) or unpleasant (an unexpected medical bill).

An important target in managing stress is to manage stressors. This might mean, for example, changing one's pace of life by slowing down or simplifying, avoiding certain individuals or situations, changing the lighting in the workplace, or requesting that a roommate be more respectful of your study time.

Whatever the stressor, it elicits a physical and mental response, once it is perceived.

Interpretation of Stressors

The stressor-stress response link is not a direct stimulus- response connection. Intervening between the two is a distinctive, higher-level mental process: perception/ interpretation/appraisal of the stressor.

Humans are not unique in this respect. My dog sometimes pauses before responding to determine whether an approaching person is friend or foe. His behavior and physical response will vary markedly depending upon his assessment of the situation. Similarly, the nature and strength of a person's internal reactions are affected by whether a stressor is perceived at all, and, if so, how it is interpreted. As Shakespeare stated, "There is nothing either good or bad, but thinking makes it so."

Interpretation refers to the process of becoming aware of and appraising stimuli.

When perception is aroused, the stress response is set in motion. For example, the simple act of listening usually elicits an increased tone on a biofeedback monitor known as the galvanic skin response, which measures electrical conduction on the skin. As you read earlier in this chapter, a recent study reported that blood pressure usually rises while a person is talking and falls immediately afterward.

These are two simple illustrations of the fact that almost any perception of a stimulus elicits the stress response. In relation to stress, the important questions are how intense, prolonged, and frequent the response is and what effects it has on the body. The important question for stress management is how this response can be managed. This book provides guidelines and techniques for managing the stress response.

Sometimes, arousal occurs through the *unconscious interpretation pathway*. For example, chronic arousal in response to chronic loud or low-grade noise, fluorescent

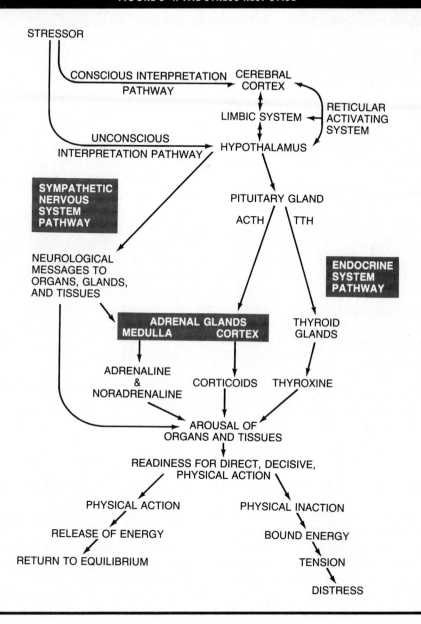

FIGURE 3-4. THE STRESS RESPONSE

lights, or the "bad vibrations" of certain individuals may occur below the level of conscious awareness and interpretation. Here the stress trigger may enter directly into the sub-cortex, one of the two major divisions of the brain.

The second and more familiar pathway is the *conscious interpretation pathway*, which involves conscious perception, assessment, and interpretation. This is an important distinction, because it calls attention to the existence of stress at a moderate or high chronic level, even in the absence of conscious arousal. Bringing these stressors into awareness can be a vital step to adapting constructively.

Interpretation and the Brain

When conscious appraisal occurs, the *cerebral cortex* becomes aware of, assesses, and interprets the stress trigger (Asterita, 1985). The cerebral cortex is far more developed in humans than in other animals, and it allows for more thoughtful reactions to stress triggers.

> The addition of the vast number of cortical cells (in humans) allowed the development and storage of analytical skills, verbal communications, writing ability, empathy, fine motor control, additional emotion, memory, learning and rational thought, as well as more sophisticated problem-solving and survival abilities (Girdano & Everly, 1986, 23).

For better or worse, an individual's reality can be determined by his/her interpretations. Behavior can be weighted against possible outcomes. Symbolism, goals, motivation, and anticipation become part of the functioning human being.

Human beings also are gifted with a more highly developed *limbic system* or midbrain, which is part of the of the sub-cortex. This further removes us from a simple stimulus-response relationship to the world around us. Among other things, the limbic system attaches feelings to pieces of information in the cerebral cortex. These feelings may include fear, anxiety, anger, joy, or pleasure. Thus a continual interplay takes place between awareness and feeling as the cerebral cortex and limbic system exchange messages.

The *reticular activating system* (RAS) is a two-way pathway of nerve cells or neurons extending from the spinal cord up through the lower brain centers and mid-brain to the cerebral cortex. Its main function is to transmit messages and impulses among different parts of the brain. These messages may be specific or general. For example, the perception of an unusual sound is transmitted via the RAS to various lower- and mid-brain points, and this results in general attentiveness arousal. Even before the cortex appraises the situation, the limbic system may produce a feeling of fear, and the hypothalamus, which regulates various body processes, may send messages to the body to prepare for action. This may include tensing muscles and increasing blood flow to the limbs.

An important feature of the RAS is that when it is turned on too frequently at too high a level, it will stay aroused. It essentially says, "If you're going to ask me to turn on like this so often, I'll simply stay turned on continuously." Continuous arousal throughout the body can contribute to such stress-induced ailments as hypertension and insomnia.

A key link in the stress response is the *hypothalamus*, which is a virtual dynamo of potency even though only the size of a pea. When a stress trigger enters the brain through either the conscious or unconscious appraisal pathway, the hypothalamus is stimulated. Despite its small size, it is the control center regulating both the stress response and its opposite, the relaxation response.

As shown in Figure 3-4, the hypothalamus activates the body through two avenues, the sympathetic nervous system and the endocrine system.

The Sympathetic Nervous System

When Blanca Hernandez decides it is time to check the mail, she activates the voluntary nervous system, which controls striate, voluntary muscles throughout the body, controlling posture and movement. Along the way, she quickly dodges a falling digger pine cone, which can be quite lethal with its weight and dagger-like points. Here she activates her *autonomic nervous system,* which is often referred to as the involuntary system because it controls such internal processes as the circulatory, reproductive, and digestive systems.

This name reflects the past belief in the involuntary nature of the autonomic system. However, biofeedback monitoring has taught us that such internal activities as heart rate, blood pressure, brain waves, and temperature can be controlled through volition. As Kenneth Pelletier (1977, 54) has stated, "This discovery is one of the most profound discoveries of contemporary medicine, with far-reaching implications for the future of holistic, preventive health care."

Most of the time, however, the autonomic nervous system does operate outside our conscious control. It is divided into two interconnected branches, the *sympathetic nervous system,* which arouses the body, and the *parasympathetic nervous system,* which quiets the body. These sometimes are referred to as the emergency branch and the calming branch.

When a stressor stimulates the brain, the sympathetic nervous system sends neurological messages to glands, organs, and tissues to arouse, to prepare for action. Our bodies cannot know what the stressor is and whether a physical reaction indeed is called for. It simply does what it is told by the sympathetic nervous system: prepare to react, to defend by fighting or fleeing. One important target of this activation is the *adrenal medulla.*

The adrenal glands are located just above the kidneys and are divided into two distinct parts—the adrenal medulla (inner part) and the *adrenal cortex* (larger, outer part). The medulla is stimulated during stress by the sympathetic nervous system. When this happens, the medulla secretes into the bloodstream two main hormones, *adrenaline,* or *epinephrine,* and *noradrenaline,* or *norepinephrine,* which together comprise the *catecholamines.*

Adrenaline acts upon the liver, which sends more glucose into the blood stream, assuring a quick source of energy. Adrenaline also increases carbohydrate metabolism, dilates arteries and capillaries throughout the body, accelerates pumping by the heart, elevates body temperature, increases the amount of blood sent out by the heart (stroke volume), and speeds up respiration. At the same time, noradrenaline works with adrenaline in circulating free fatty acids, while also raising blood pressure and constricting certain blood vessels in the body.

The Endocrine System

Simultaneously, a part of the *endocrine* or *hormone system* is turned on to work in tandem with the sympathetic nervous system. When the cortex detects a threat, it sends a message through the RAS to the hypothalamus. A tiny organ at the base of the brain, the hypothalamus controls the body's response to threat.

One of the ways it does so is by activating the sympathetic nervous system, which we have just described. The second is by sending a chemical message through a small network of blood vessels to the *pituitary gland,* which is located nearby. The pituitary in turn sends two chemicals into the bloodstream. One, *thyrotropic hormone* (TTH) is designed to activate the *thyroid gland* when it reaches that destination. The thyroid, in turn secretes *thyroxine* into the bloodstream. Thyroxine increases the rate at which the body consumes fuel. During the stress response, thyroxine

---

BOX 3-1. STRESS AND SURGICAL COMPLICATIONS

The stress response can affect the mind and body in unexpected ways. One is risk of surgical complications.

Physicians are aware that some surgical patients recover quickly and completely, while others suffer complications. Recent evidence suggests a key factor influencing chances of complications is stress of the patient (Linn, Linn and Klimas, 1988).

Researchers at the Miami Veterans Administration Medical Center studied 24 men, average age 59, undergoing elective hernia repair. A control group with the same average age and medical history also was followed.

Stress was measured in two ways. One was a questionnaire about recent stressful events. The second was a physical measure: reactivity of blood pressure to putting one's hand in cold water (known as the cold pressor test).

Those patients who had a high response to the cold pressor test ("hot reactors") experienced more complications after surgery than did "cold reactors." Although these complications were relatively minor, they did result in a longer average hospital stay and in more medication.

Those patients who had both high life-event stress and high reactivity used three times more medication after surgery than any other group.

The researchers also cited other studies suggesting that immune function and risk of postoperative infection also are affected by stress. And one Ohio State study suggests that perhaps reduction of stress can enhance immune function. Relaxation training three times a week for a month improved immune function among nursing home residents compared with a control group who received only social contact or no intervention.

The authors of the VA study suggest it might be worthwhile for surgeons to do all they can to allay patients' pre-surgical anxiety and fears, even in routine surgery such as hernia repair. This view is certainly consistent with the American College of Surgeons, who some years ago recognized that the emotional state of the patient was an important consideration when they concluded that an optimistic octogenarian was a better surgical risk than a pessimistic younger patient.

speeds up metabolism in tissues and cells. Thyroxine also seems to make the body more sensitive and responsive to adrenaline.

The pituitary gland at the same time secretes *adrenocorticotropic hormone* (ACTH), which stimulates the outer part of the adrenal gland, the adrenal cortex. It is interesting to note that the greater the production of TTH and ACTH, the less the production of sex hormones. This probably accounts for the loss of interest in sex during stressful periods.

The adrenal cortex, in turn, secretes another important hormone, *gluco-corticoids*, which stimulate the liver to produce more blood sugar. More fats and proteins also are released into the blood for more energy. Release of too much protein for energy can reduce protein normally available for construction of white blood cells and other antibodies, thereby weakening the body's immune system over the long run. Release of too much fat, in turn, can promote atherosclerosis, build-up of plaque in arteries of the brain and heart. This may be one reason Type A behavior can increase risk of heart attacks, as we shall see in Chapter 4.

Mineral corticoids, primarily aldosterone, are the other products of the adrenal cortex. This hormone, in turn, helps to dissipate heat and water generated by increased metabolism, as well as to retain water and raise blood pressure and blood salinity through retention of sodium (salt). It also is a vital link in the body's mobilization of the immune response to fight infection.

Readiness for Physical Action

Through the sympathetic nervous system and endocrine system, the body is prepared for direct, decisive, physical action. Key observable or measurable signs of this preparedness include the following.

Pupils dilate

Throat tightens

Neck, upper back and shoulders tighten

Breathing quickens and becomes shallow

Heart pumps faster

Muscles and legs become taut, especially in front

Skin cools

Brain waves become shorter

Blood pressure rises

Blood shifts from abdomen to limbs

More glucose enters the bloodstream

More white blood cells enter the bloodstream

Metabolism speeds up

Cholesterol remains in bloodstream longer

Arteries and capillaries constrict

As Pelletier notes (1977), many of these internal changes have entered our common language.

Trembling with fear	A lump in my throat
Cold feet	Clammy hands
Chills ran up and down my spine	A knot in my stomach
A racing heart	Butterflies inside

Part of effective stress management is learning to monitor and recognize these and other warning signs of distress, especially when they become chronic.

Through these intricate pathways, then, the body is prepared for direct, decisive, physical action. In an extremely threatening situation, this is the maxi fight-or-flight response. In smaller ways, these changes occur constantly, resulting in chronic excitation of the mini stress response.

When physical action occurs, this readiness—this pent-up energy—is released. At one time in human history, such physical activity was constant, not necessarily at the moment of arousal, but certainly through the day as people worked, moved about, and played. In the past, too, more stress triggers were physical threats, in which a physical stress response was appropriate.

However, three important changes have occurred. First, the faster pace of life in this century has increased the number of stressors we face. Second, most stressors today are psychological and social, rather than physical. Third, we have become more sedentary, resulting in less release of energy build-up. Hence, an increase occurs in the *need* for physical action to release energy and tension at the very time physical action no longer is included as a natural part of most of our daily lives. Thus, we find the build-up of *bound energy* and the rise of mental and physical tension. Stress-related disturbances and diseases often result.

On the other hand, the stress response can be very useful, aiding us in responding to emergencies, in reaching higher levels of performance, in meeting deadlines, and more. Without the stress response, positive stress would be unavailable.

BEHAVIOR, THOUGHTS AND FEELINGS IN THE STRESS RESPONSE

At the beginning of this chapter, we emphasized that body, mind, and behavior are all interconnected. Yet thus far we have said little about behavior. What part does it play? As we have defined stress, behavior is not part of the stress response itself. Yet it is closely related in four ways:

▼ Mental and physical arousal often are expressed in behavior.

▼ Behavior such as exercise and self-disclosure, for example, can help protect against out-of-control stress responses.

▼ Behavior is used to cope or interact with stress triggers.

▼ Behavior is used to react to distress, either constructively or destructively.

Thoughts and feelings also are related to the stress response because emotional and intellectual stress are closely interrelated with physical stress. The interplay of these forms of stress will be discussed in more detail later. Here it is sufficient to recognize that thoughts and feelings may either trigger or reflect physical stress. However, thoughts and feelings do not exist apart from physical stress. This is important because altering the physical basis of stress through relaxation or exercise can alter troubling thoughts and feelings.

STRESS AND IMMUNITY

The immune system is the body's surveillance system, guarding against allergens, infection, cancer, viruses and bacteria. This protection occurs through two immuno-logic reactions. The first, *humoral immunity,* is mediated by B lymphocytes. When stimulated by antigens, B lymphocytes differentiate into several cells that produce antibodies which in turn flow through the bloodstream to the needed site. The second reaction is *cell immunity,* a slower-acting process. When T lymphocytes receive the message from the thymus gland that a threatening invader is present, they secrete chemicals that in turn kill unwanted cells and aid in phagocytosis, a process through which invading cells are ingested.

A number of other cells and elements of the blood stream, which we need not explain here, also are involved in the immune response, including monocytes, natural killer cells, mast cells, polymorphonuclear leukocytes, macrophages, and inter-feron (Jemmott and Locke, 1984; Borysenko and Borysenko, 1983; Taylor, 1986; Borysenko, 1987; Kiecolt-Glaser and Glaser, 1988; Pelletier & Herzing, 1988).

Immunocompetence refers to the body's ability to defend successfully against a microbial invader. Taylor (1986, 197) has noted that immunocompetence occurs through a number of complementary processes.

> Measures of immunological functioning are manifold and include the ability of lymphocytes to kill invading cells (lymphocyte cytotoxicity), the ability of lymphocytes to reproduce when stimulated artificially by a chemical (mitogen), the ability of the lymphocytes to produce antibodies, the ratio of suppressor and helper T cells, the ability of the white cells to ingest foreign particles (phagocytotic activity), and others.

A considerable and growing body of research shows that stress can suppress the immune response, thereby increasing chances of immune-related illness (Rogers, Dubey, and Reich, 1979; Jemmott and Locke, 1984; Borysenko and Borysenko, 1983; Dantzer and Kelley, 1989; Leclere and Werhy, 1989; Kiecolt-Glaser and Glaser, 1988; Pelletier and Herzing, 1988.) Animal research conclusively demonstrates that experimentally manipulated stressors can reduce immunological functioning and in-crease susceptibility to disorders that are influenced by the immune system. Animal studies have shown, for example, that lymphocytes are suppressed by exposure to loud noise (Monjan and Collector, 1977), infant-mother separation (Laudenslager, Reite, and Harbeck, 1982), separation from peers (Reite, Harbeck, and Hoffman, 1981), and electric shock (Keller, et al., 1981).

Studies of human populations under stress also are revealing. Infectious diseases have been shown to increase among children when their families are exposed to stressful events (Hinkle, 1974). Stressful events among adults have been linked to immune-related disorders such as the common cold, trench mouth, herpes recurrences, and mononucleosis (Jemmott and Locke, 1984). Levy (1989) found an association between stressful life events and natural killer (NK) cells. The lower the NK count, the more the sick days and the greater the illness. Apollo and Skylab astronauts have been shown to have immunological deficiencies following splashdown (Leach and Rambaut, 1974; Kimzey, 1975). Both men and women in unhappy marriages have been shown to have weakened immune systems (Kiecolt-Glaser & Glaser, 1988).

Naturally occurring severe stressors also have been shown to depress immune strength. These include loss of spouse (Bartrop, et al., 1977; Schleifer et al., 1979) and student examinations (Jemmott and Locke, 1984). In a recent study by Norman (1989), for example, undergraduate students' IgA levels (an indicator of immune response in the saliva) were measured one month before a regularly scheduled examination week. They were retested during the exam week. Sure enough, the IgA count was lower during exam time than one month before. And the higher the test-related anxiety, the lower the IgA. Perhaps this explains why so many students "catch" colds and flu during exam time.

Emotions also have been linked with immunocompetence. For example, depression has been shown to suppress lymphocyte and T cell activity (Kronfol, et al., 1983; Schleifer, et al., 1989; Nerozzi, et al., 1989; Targum, et al., 1989).

On the other hand, laughter induced by a humorous video has been shown to result in proliferation of lymphocytes and natural killer cell activity (Berk, 1989). Epinephrine levels decreased even before the videotapes were shown, suggesting that even the anticipation of a good time can help reduce stress level and enhance immunocompetence. Berk states, "The effect of anticipation of the event becomes as real for the individual as the event itself." He points out that nervous or uncomfortable laughter that does not necessarily reflect good feelings may not have the same effect.

How does stress depress immunocompetence? This question is still under investigation. There is strong suspicion among experts that the catecholamines (epinephrine and norepinephrine) and corticosteroids that are stimulated during the stress response may have anti-inflammatory and immunosuppressive effects. Stress might also suppress endorphins.

Although mediating pathways are not entirely clear at this point, evidence mounts that stress can sometimes suppress the immune system, heightening chances of stress-induced physical disorders. Psychoneuroimmunology is a new hybrid, interdisciplinary field of scientific study of these complex mind-body linkages (For reviews of research in this field, see, for example, Borysenko and Borysenko, 1983; and Pelletier and Herzing, 1988.)

STRESS AND ADAPTATION

The General Adaptation Syndrome

As noted in Chapter 2, Hans Selye many years ago identified a universal pattern of physical stress known as the *general adaptation syndrome* which helps us understand how the body handles stress over time and how physical stress sometimes gives way to distress. The GAS also is useful in explaining the role of adaptation in managing stress effectively.

Selye maintains we go through three phases as we seek to handle stress, whatever the specific stressor and location in the body: alarm reaction, sustained resistance, and exhaustion.

These phases, shown in Figure 3-5, can be seen most easily in the body's reaction to physical trauma, such as fire, cold, or an accident. But Selye suggested that the same sequence is likely as you react to personal and social situations in daily life, such as a verbal attack, prolonged isolation, or chronic overload.

During the alarm reaction, the body is immediately prepared for direct, decisive physical action (the fight-or-flight response), largely through instantaneous activation of the sympathetic nervous system, sometimes before the person is even aware of the stressor. Large amounts of glucose and oxygen are supplied to organs most active in warding off danger, such as the heart, the brain, and the skeletal muscles. The curving line in Figure 3-5 falls below normal stress level because the body often is temporarily set back as it fights to restore internal balance.

As the body mobilizes additional resources, largely through arousal of the stress hormones, the stage of resistance ensues. The body and mind cope with the difficulty in a sustained way, usually quite effectively. If the stressor is too intense for too long, however, the body's adaptive reserves begin to become depleted, at which time the stage of exhaustion begins. At this stage, wear and tear is progressive. Stress becomes distress, and illness is likely. The type of illness will be determined by particular weaknesses in the individual's organ systems.

FIGURE 3-5. THE GENERAL ADAPTATION SYNDROME

The General Adaptation Syndrome

NORMAL LEVEL OF RESISTANCE		
ALARM REACTION	STAGE OF RESISTANCE	STAGE OF EXHAUSTION

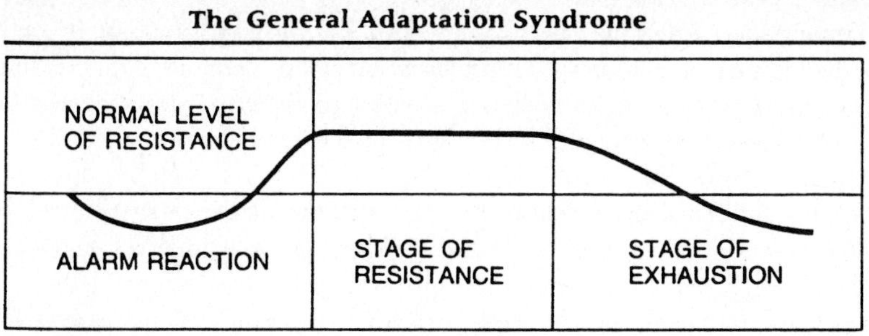

SOURCE: Selye (1974, 27).

As noted, Selye demonstrated with laboratory rats that this sequence of adaptation occurs irrespective of the specific stressor, such as electric shock, cold, forced muscular work, drugs, or injections. He suggested the same is true of humans. This discovery and Selye's resulting general adaptation syndrome have important implications for understanding how humans adapt to stress.

How Humans Adapt to Stress

A remarkable feature of human beings is the ability to adapt—both to changing external circumstances and to internal stress levels. As you move from one place to another, change jobs, meet and lose friends, confront challenges in the classroom or on the athletic field, you may experience intense stress. Sometimes you wonder if you will make it. Yet you do. And you will again—because you adapt to stressors and to stress. You get used to new situations.

Some years ago, selected inmates from Oregon State Prison participated in Project Newgate, a college education program. They attended classes inside the prison until a few months before parole or discharge. Their last several months as prisoners were spent at a halfway house at the University of Oregon campus.

From the prison to the campus, the increase in stimulation level was enormous. Sometimes inmates found themselves overwhelmed by sounds, sights, choices, competition, dates, and the availability of alcohol and drugs. A few inmate-students were so overwhelmed that they broke down, broke a rule, or simply asked to be returned to the "joint." Yet most adapted. Their zone of positive stress shifted upward. They learned to live with the higher stimulation of campus life. Their stress levels went down.

In track and field, swimming, and other sports, coaches deliberately control their athletes' adaptation to stress. The usual training program calls for practicing at a certain speed and distance for a designated period of time. During the first few days at a certain level of output, performance goes down while fatigue increases. After a few days, the athlete adapts to the new level of effort. The workouts, initially so demanding, become relatively easy within two or three weeks. In a systematic fashion, still more speed and distance are added until limits are reached. In this incremental manner the athlete progresses to the point where maximum possible performance is attained.

Performance limits may be set by mental barriers, by effort, or by breakdown in muscles, joints, or tendons. The athlete must adapt carefully to increasing levels of stress, while remaining just below the point of distress—that fine edge beyond which one goes into injury, physical fatigue, or mental exhaustion.

You also have this capability to adapt, to adjust to different stresses as you take on new challenges. Adapting to stress is important to achieve higher levels of self-fulfillment in the various facets of your life. What you need is *stress without distress* (Selye, 1974).

An important word of caution is needed, however. We sometimes delude ourselves into believing we are adapting within our zone of positive stress. We become comfortable with a highly demanding job, fast pace of life, or troubled marriage, for example. We assume we are adjusting within our own tolerance limits and that our health will not be adversely affected. Often, however, this apparent adjustment is not successful adaptation at all. Rather, we continue quite unaware for a lengthy period in Selye's stage of resistance without returning to our optimum stress level.

In time, our bodies give way in one form or another, depending on the individual. It may be chronic colds, hypertension, a skin disorder, migraines, or even a sudden heart attack. All reflect wear and tear as we enter the stage of physical exhaustion.

Selye maintains that our deep adaptive reserves are limited and can be used up. Disharmony exacts a toll in the long run. Premature aging is the ultimate result.

In brief, adaptation to stress does not mean simply becoming comfortable with a stressor or set of stressors. True adaptation means adjustment of your spirit and your body to those circumstances within the limits of your unique zone of positive stress. What is comfortable may not be healthy over the long run.

THE RELAXATION RESPONSE AND HOMEOSTASIS   ▼

Just as the body possesses capabilities to arouse, it can recover and relax. The mind plays an equally important part in the relaxation response as in the stress response.

THE RELAXATION RESPONSE

THE RELAXATION RESPONSE IS QUIETING OF MIND AND BODY

The human organism, like other animals, possesses a strong and persistent drive toward equilibrium or homeostasis. As Herbert Benson states in *The Relaxation Response* (1975, 18):

> If the fight-or-flight response resides within animals and humans, is there an innate physiologic response that is dramatically different? The answer is yes. Each of us possesses a natural and innate protective mechanism against "overstress," which allows us to turn off harmful bodily effects, to counter the effects of the fight-or-flight response. This response against "overstress" brings on bodily changes that decrease heart rate, lower metabolism, decrease the rate of breathing, and bring the body back into what is probably a healthier balance. That is the relaxation response.

The relaxation response is a natural process. Each time we are aroused, the body tends to restore itself to a more natural, lower level. This occurs through the parasympathetic nervous system, which counters the sympathetic nervous system, and through quieting of the endocrine system. Problems arise when the stress response is triggered too frequently or continuously without adequate recovery or when people do not know how to relax. Stress build-up results.

At the same time that physical exercise is needed to release bound energy and to prevent its accumulation, deliberate steps are needed to induce the relaxation response each day through mental and physical relaxation practices such as meditation or self-hypnosis.

PHYSIOLOGY OF DEEP RELAXATION

Research shows that during deep relaxation, physical and mental responses are the opposite of the fight-or-flight response.

Slower breathing

Lower oxygen use rate

Slower heart rate

Less blood per heart beat

Relaxed muscles and skin

Decreased blood lactate

Slowing down of brain waves

Greater harmony among brain waves

Quieting of key hormonal glands

This gives the body time to restore itself, to recuperate from the stresses of daily life. As shown in Figure 3-6, metabolism during deep relaxation is slower, even after a minute or two, than during the deepest sleep after five or six hours.

After daily relaxation, your energy level increases. You feel rested, and you are able to recover more quickly from unexpected threats or alarms.

In short, activity needs to be alternated with rest, arousal with relaxation, excitation with quiet. Research shows that 15-20 minutes set aside once or twice

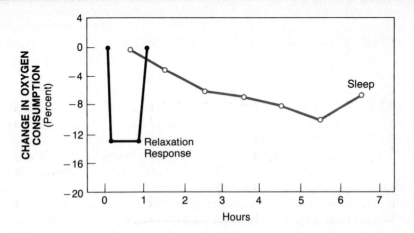

FIGURE 3-6. METABOLISM DURING SLEEP AND THE RELAXATION RESPONSE

SOURCE: Benson (1975), 65.

each day for deep relaxation, which takes body processes into a deeper quiet than the normal equilibrium level of daily living, can prove effective for both coping with distress already present and for preventing stress build-up from occurring in the first place. Later chapters will present a number of techniques for releasing the relaxation response. For an initial experience, see Exercise 3-1.

EXERCISE 3-1. BREATHING AWAY TENSION

1. Sit or lie in a comfortable position with hands open and legs uncrossed.

2. Be aware of the weight of your entire body on the floor, bed, couch, or chair. Your muscles need not help support your body at all.

3. Softly close your eyes.

4. Focus attention on your nostrils and "see" the air entering each side. Follow its path down into your lungs, "watch" it swirling around, and "observe" it moving back up and out.

5. As it leaves, tell yourself it is carrying away tension, pain, and disease if present.

6. Continue for 1–5 minutes.

It is important here to note that popular notions of relaxation may be quite inaccurate. A non-work activity may be pleasant but not necessarily relaxing in the sense that physical and mental quieting occur. In fact the exact opposite may ensue. The familiar coffee break may elevate the stress response through the stimulating effect of caffeine. A round of golf may arouse competitive urges, rather than quiet the hypothalamus, the pituitary gland, the adrenal cortex, and the sympathetic nervous system. The same may happen with a do-it-yourself home project. The activity may be beneficial by being a diversion, but may not be relaxing. Certainly it does not produce deep relaxation, so vital to counteracting chronic arousal of the stress response. In short, diversion and recreation may not be true relaxation.

ENERGY: A COMPONENT OF WELLNESS   ▼

Jose is an energetic college student who thrives under pressure, gets a great deal done in a day's time, and seldom seems tired or discouraged. He works out nearly every day, gets six to eight hours of sleep most nights, and catnaps when needed.

Josephina pays her own way through a western university where she carries a 3.4 grade point average. She is active in several campus organizations, yet somehow finds time for her friendships, play, and her aerobics class. She seldom feels run down or fatigued. In fact, she surprises most of her friends with her apparently boundless supply of energy.

Jennie is a community college student who feels tired most of the time. She sleeps restlessly, eats sporadically, and is either cranky or depressed most of the time. She seldom exercises—there never seems to be enough time.

> *Jonathan is a likable college sophomore who moves through his days more like a turtle than a race horse. He is quite content with his pace and he seems to know his limits. He sleeps nine to ten hours most nights. Jonathan turns down many opportunities to party with his friends, preferring instead to spend time alone reading or working on computer graphics.*

These cases illustrate the considerable variety among us in energy levels. They also point to the importance of energy in health, productivity, and emotional well-being.

Energy, in fact, is a central component of wellness. With it, you can reach your highest possible levels of performance, maintain satisfying relationships, provide the basis for emotional stability, think clearly, and ensure good health. Without it, you will underachieve, become irritable, burn out, break down, and more. In short, energy is vital.

Unfortunately, many among us are chronically tired, with too little energy to meet zestfully the demands of daily living. When I ask participants in my classes and workshops how many are tired more often than they would like, about 80 percent raise their hands. My physician friend, a family practitioner, tells me fatigue by far is the most common presenting symptom among his patients. He and his colleagues note this in their medical charts with *TATT—Tired All The Time.*

Studies of college professors (McKenna, 1980) and city managers (Schafer and Gard, 1988) both found "general fatigue and heaviness" to be the most commonly cited symptom on a 50-item Distress Symptom Scale (this scale is presented in Chapter 4). The "chronic fatigue syndrome" has become a major medical problem in this country, baffling scientific experts (Cowley, 1990).

ENERGY, STRESS AND RELAXATION

Energy relates to the stress response and the relaxation response in a host of ways, positively and negatively. The stress response greatly increases energy in emergencies, of course, through the fight-or-flight processes described earlier in the chapter. Yet chronic stress can deplete energy, as Selye described in the exhaustion stage of the general adaptation syndrome. The result often is physical illness or emotional disorders.

As Kuntzleman (1981, 9) notes, this can be avoided.

> Stress need not rob you of energy. The key to stress and energy is how you handle it—whether you can manage stress or allow it to manage you. And that's why trying to avoid stress just doesn't work. You can run away from it all, build a log cabin in the wilderness, and sit by the fire the rest of your life and still be plagued by stress—if you are a worrier, uncomfortable with change, and angry at the world. It's all a matter of learning how to cope with stress and understanding your place in the world.

The relaxation response helps restore energy. When elicited regularly, the relaxation response can provide stress resistance in the face of challenge, change and crisis. Yet if the relaxation response is your state of being most of the time, stagnation results.

Energy can be a vital element in stress resistance. This is consistent with the theory of generalized resistance resources by Antonovsky (1979, 1987), which we reviewed in Chapter 2. Implied in his formulation is that personal energy is a key ingredient in one's ability to cope effectively with potentially distressful life events.

Energy also is implicit in the theory of stress by Lazarus and Folkman (1984). In their transactional, process, contextual, meaning-centered model of stress and coping, Lazarus and Folkman define stress as ". . . a particular relationship between the person and the environment that is appraised by the person as taxing or exceeding his or her resources and endangering his or her well-being" (Lazarus & Folkman, 1984, 19). They maintain that appraisal of events influences behavioral, emotional, and physical responses to events. They emphasize the ongoing, interactional process of coping through time in their effort to understand why some individuals are more effective than others in staying healthy under pressure. Among ". . . the resources upon which people draw in order to cope with the myriad demands of living is health and energy." They point out that "A person who is frail, sick, tired, or otherwise debilitated has less energy to expend on coping than a healthy, robust person" (Lazarus and Folkman, 1984, 159). As with Antonovsky's theory, in other words, the greater the energy, the greater the resources for dealing effectively with the stressors of daily life.

Let us examine more closely the nature of energy, its various dimensions, some of the factors that influence it, and some of its effects.

THE NATURE OF HUMAN ENERGY

Defining Energy

In physics, "energy" is defined as "the capacity for doing work and overcoming resistance" (Webster's New World Dictionary, 1980, 463). Energy in humans too can be viewed as potential for action. Thus, one has high energy to the degree one has high physical and emotional reserves available when needed.

While human energy can be measured physiologically, it is most useful here to conceive of it subjectively. Thus, we will follow the definition of energy set forth by Flora Davis in her informative book about energy, *Personal Peak Performance: Making The Most of Your Natural Energy* (Davis, 1980, xxvii):

"Energy is your own perception at any given moment of your potential for action. It's your sense of what you could do if you chose to."

Stated differently, perceived energy is a subjective feeling that one has the internal resources to respond to demands when needed. Davis (1980, xxx) uses the term *"body truth"* to describe your awareness of energy. A "body truth" is a personal, internal experience. High energy is the relative presence of such internal resources. Low energy is their relative absence.

Beliefs About Energy

Davis points out that Americans have mixed feelings about energy (Davis, 1980, xxxi).

> Because we live in a highly competitive society that is very accomplishment-oriented, we value and envy people who seem to have unusual vitality. On the one hand, we sometimes denigrate them as well, insisting that if they're constantly on the go, it's because they're driven by their own private demons. "I'm not high-energy at all," one woman replied indignantly when I asked to interview her. "I'm not the nervous type." I never said she was.

Our cultural beliefs about work and achievement usually lead us to place greater value on high than low energy. Most Americans equate energy with accomplishment. As one interviewee told Davis (1980, xxxi), "Energy is what it takes to do work." It apparently never occurred to her it also takes energy to play. And we sometimes forget that low energy is intrinsically no better or worse than high energy—unless it is the result of emotional impairment, irresponsibility, selfishness, or poor health habits.

Another common belief is that energy belongs more in the masculine than the feminine realm, especially energy related to accomplishment. At least traditionally, men are supposed to possess drive and vitality, while women are supposed to be more passive and subdued. Of course, neither gender is supposed to have a monopoly on sexual energy.

Two Dimensions of Energy

Energy has two key dimensions: endurance and intensity. *Endurance* refers to your ability to sustain a moderate or high level of energy over a given period. A high energy person is someone who stays "up" without wearing down throughout the day, as energetic at 9:00 PM as at 9:00 AM. You are high energy if you are as fresh Friday noon as you were Monday noon; as fresh in May as you were in September if you are a teacher or student; as active, alert and productive at age 72 as at age 32. Endurance over the lifetime is illustrated, for example, by Paul Reese, a 73-year-old retired school administrator from Sacramento (Reese, 1990) who recently became the oldest person to run from coast to coast (3182 miles in 122 days) and by 70-year-old Bert LeFevre, who in 1990 traveled 700 miles through the Far West—by mule (Gray, 1990). Thus, endurance refers to maintaining energy throughout the day, week, season, and lifetime.

Intensity is the second dimension of energy. A high energy person is fully present, fully engaged and attentive at whatever she is doing. Energy can be too intense, of course, as in people who are "hyper." What is best is to be involved and able to concentrate when needed. The low energy person is detached, too tired to concentrate or put out to his fullest.

Types of Energy People

As Davis (1980) has noted, there are several types of energy people:

▼ **Strollers** are low-energy types who move relatively slowly. They thrive under relatively low levels of stimulation and enjoy a slow pace of life.

▼ **Joggers** move at a moderate, steady pace with a moderate and even energy level. They know their limits, are often quite productive and know how to take care of themselves.

▼ **Sprinters** go very hard for brief periods, then need to come down for recuperation. Like Carl Lewis in the 100 meter dash, they can sustain their full-tilt pace for only a short while.

▼ **Long-distance athletes** are like joggers in that they are steady over the long haul, but they differ in that their energy is sustained at an unusually high level for a long period.

EXERCISE 3-2. ASSESSING YOUR ENERGY TYPE

1. Which energy type best describes you?
Stroller
Jogger
Sprinter
Long-Distance Athlete
2. How satisfied are with your own energy type?
3. In your opinion, what hereditary and environmental factors have influenced your own energy type?
4. How satisfied are you with your energy type? Why?
5. What will you do, if needed, to increase the intensity or endurance of your energy?

Sources of Energy

Anyone who has visited a hospital nursery knows that infants vary in energy levels in their first hours, surely the result of *hereditary* influences. Yet, there is a considerable effect later on of *social learning*. Early examples set by parents and peers, the nature of rewards and punishments, the community, region, culture and subculture in which one lives—all play a role in determining one's energy level. Finally, *personal choice* plays a part. Whether you choose to live at a fast or slow pace; whether or not you take care of yourself by maintaining good habits of sleep, nutrition and exercise—these too influence your energy level.

Energy Qualities

Energy can be *natural* or *nervous*. Natural energy is energy that flows easily with little effort or struggle. Nervous energy comes from fear, low self-esteem, anger, or anxiety. It is marked by struggle. This distinction corresponds with Maslow's terms "deficiency motivation" and "self-actualization motivation" (Maslow, 1962).

Energy can be *satisfying* or *unsatisfying* to the person in question. Of course, this is a matter of degree and is entirely subjective.

Energy can be distinguished by whether it is *helpful* or *harmful,* according to its effects on others.

Finally, energy can be *wasted* or *directed.* Having high energy does not necessarily mean you are productive or useful. A great many people endure lives of futility and frustration because they drift, flail, or sputter.

To live a wellness lifestyle, then, is to live so your energy is as *natural, satisfying, helpful,* and *directed* as possible. Stress can interfere with this ideal. Managing stress effectively—through wise balance of the stress response and the relaxation response—can promote it.

Blocked Energy

You no doubt have experienced writer's block at some time in your life. You have been afraid to take a risk in this way or others. In short, you have blocked your energy.

Energy can be blocked for several reasons: perfectionism, fear of failure, fear of success, fear of disapproval, self-doubt, unexpressed anger or frustration from the past, either immediate (yesterday) or long-term (childhood).

Maximizing your energy, then, includes clearing away these blockages so that energy is available when needed. Sometimes therapy or other professional assistance is needed. Learning self-talk techniques, such as those in Chapter 7 also can help.

EXERCISE 3-3. ASSESSING YOUR ENERGY QUALITIES

1. Please circle the number below that best describes how *natural* or *nervous* your energy tends to be these days.

1	2	3	4	5	6	7	8	9	10

Very Nervous   A Mix of Both   Very Natural

2. Please circle the number below that best describes how *satisfying* your energy is these days.

1	2	3	4	5	6	7	8	9	10

Very Unsatisfying   A Mix of Both   Very Satisfying

3. Please circle the number below that best describes how *helpful* or *harmful* your energy is these days.

1	2	3	4	5	6	7	8	9	10

Very Harmful   A Mix of Both   Very Helpful

4. Please circle the number below that best describes how *wasted* or *directed* energy level is these days.

1	2	3	4	5	6	7	8	9	10

Very Wasted   A Mix of both   Very Directed

5. How satisfied are you with the results of this self-appraisal?

6. What will you do during coming days and weeks to improve your energy profile, if needed?

Energy Rhythms

People differ in the stability and variability of their energy throughout the day. Some are relatively even in physical and mental energy, others experience definite highs and lows. Some are morning people, others night people, others are in between. A catnap, a deep relaxation break, or physical exercise can be very effective for countering down times throughout the day. One study found a 10 minute walk to be more effective than a "candy bar break" for restoring energy and reducing anxiety (Thayer, 1986).

Energy in Relationships

As Davis (1980) notes, couples sometimes vary in energy levels, creating potential for conflict. Consider the following case (Davis, 1980, 371).

> "My husband has much more energy than I do," Amy said. "That's something that became uncomfortably obvious to me when we were on our honeymoon years ago. I was exhausted from all the wedding preparations, and I just wanted to lie on the beach and rest, but Arthur was all set to swim and play tennis, go do snorkeling and scuba diving; in the evenings he wanted to go dancing until all hours. I trailed around after him, but it was hard. In fact, I thought we were so mismatched that I was ready to leave him."

Amy and Arthur are still together 12 years later, partly because it was Arthur's energy to which Amy was attracted. Yet, the potential for conflict and disagreement is apparent.

Davis points out that energy gaps can be good or bad, depending on the meaning to those involved. Certainly energy is one personal quality to be considered in selecting a partner. When serious differences do exist, several solutions are available: compromise by both, one person moving toward the other's energy level, vice versa, or learning to live with the difference.

CORRELATES OF ENERGY: RESEARCH EVIDENCE

As noted above, human energy can be conceptualized and measured as purely a physiological phenomenon. Or it can be treated as a subjective experience. As a behavioral scientist, my approach is the latter: to think of energy as one's own "body truth." Thus, measuring energy is to measure "perceived energy."

For the past nine years, I have taught a 10-session community class at the Enloe Hospital Stress and Health Center called, "Reducing Perfectionism, Irritability, and Hurry Sickness." Participants complete pre and post questionnaires and receive feedback about their progress on a number of aspects of stress and health over the 20 weeks of the course. Results of these comparisons are presented in Chapter 5.

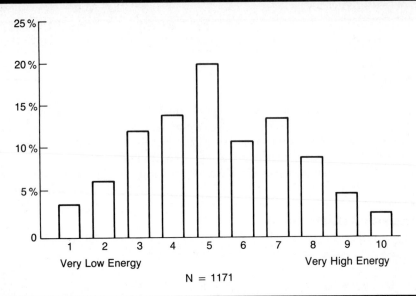

Of interest here is the statistical association of perceived energy with other factors. You may recall that in Exercise 1-9 we presented a number of "quality of life questions." Among them was an item about energy: "Please circle the number below that best describes your *sense of vitality or energy level* these days." Response options ranged over a 10-point scale, from Very Low Energy Level (1) to Very High Energy Level (10).

Figure 3-7 shows the distribution of responses across these 10 response categories.

Table 3-1 presents the association between perceived energy and a number of other factors. The table reveals that those scoring high in perceived energy were significantly more likely to score:

Lower in distress symptoms

Lower in Type A behavior

Higher in internal control

Lower in depression

Lower in emotional tension

Higher in life satisfaction

Higher in health satisfaction

Higher in home satisfaction

TABLE 3-1. ASSOCIATION BETWEEN PERCEIVED ENERGY AND OTHER VARIABLES

	MEAN SCORES	
VARIABLE	HIGH PERCEIVED ENERGY GROUP	LOW PERCEIVED ENERGY GROUP
Distress Symptom Scale	59	107
Framingham Type A Scale	26	29
Internal Control	66	50
Depression	36	55
Emotional Tension	55	95
Life Satisfaction	67	50
Health Satisfaction	66	44
Home Satisfaction	70	58
Job Satisfaction	68	53
Health Optimism	78	62
Life Optimism	78	63
Happiness	72	53
Fun and playfulness	59	38
Self-esteem	71	49
Anxious reactivity	22	25
Irritability	49	54
Wellness Behavior	2.70	2.28
Time-Related Stress	103	136

N = 1171. All Associations are significant at P <.001
Items from Internal Control through Self-esteem are based on a 10-point scale multiplied by 10 to produce whole numbers.

Higher in job satisfaction

Higher in health optimism

Higher in life optimism

Higher in happiness

Higher in self-esteem

Lower in anxious reactivity

Lower in irritability

Higher in wellness behavior

Lower in time-related stress

Clearly, perceived energy is part of a "syndrome" of wellness. Since this is a cross-sectional or single-point-in-time survey, we don't know what causes what. For example, we can speculate that high perceived energy causes greater happiness—or the other way around. What is clear is that doing all we can to increase energy reserves and energy accessibility is likely to improve wellness in our lives.

EXERCISE 3-4. INTERPRETING TABLE 3-1.

The statistical associations in Table 3-1 are based on cross-sectional, rather than longitudinal or experimental-design data. Therefore, we can only speculate as to whether perceived energy is cause or effect in each case.

1.   For each relationship (the association between distress symptoms and perceived energy) create two hypotheses: one with perceived energy as cause, the other with perceived energy as effect. An example: self-esteem contributes to high energy.

2.   Provide a one or two sentence rationale for each hypothesis.

3.   How do the findings in Table 3-1 relate to your personal experience? To your observations of others?

ENERGY FOR WHAT?

You may have lots of energy, but for what purpose? What values direct your energy? What is the role of spirituality— that is, matters of value, meaning and purpose— in the direction of your energy (Chapman, 1986, 1987)?

We noted in Chapter 1 that personal well-being needs to be balanced with concern with the common good. Hopefully, this book will stimulate you toward self-care, not merely as an end in itself but in order to provide more energy for contributing to the well-being of others.

CHANGING ENERGY LEVELS

It is entirely up to you, of course, whether you need to change your energy level at all. The key question is, what does your present energy level do for you and others? Is it constructive in terms of your stress and wellness? How does it affect others?

For some, reducing energy level may be needed, especially when it is now more nervous than natural, if you are setting the stage for later burnout or breakdown by imposing undue wear and tear on your body, or if others are negatively affected by your present pace.

For others, increasing energy may be desirable. This probably is the most common perceived need. Low energy in a potentially high-energy person often results from chronic overload, chronic and unexpressed emotional tension, depression, poor sleep habits, inadequate nutrition, or lack of exercise (Chopra, 1985). Following guidelines and techniques from this book can help overcome these barriers to full energy.

For still others, changing energy habits might mean smoothing out erratic energy rhythms or increasing accessibility to energy reserves by removing energy blockages.

Whatever your specific energy need, awareness of your own "body truth" is a starting point. Acceptance of your own potential for modifying energy level is next. And action follows.

In this chapter, we have explained the stress response, the relaxation response, and the need for proper balance between them. You also read about energy, a central element in wellness. In Chapter 4, we will examine some of the ways stress turns into distress, with special attention to stress-related illnesses.

REFERENCES ▼

Antonovsky, A. (1979). *Health, Stress and Coping: New Perspectives on Mental and Physical Well-being.* San Francisco: Jossey-Bass Publishers.

Antonovsky, A. (1987). *Unraveling The Mystery of Health: How People Manage Stress and Stay Well.* San Francisco: Jossey-Bass Publishers.

Asteria, M.F. (1985). *The Physiology of Stress.* New York: Human Sciences Press.

Bartrop, R.W., Lockhurst, E. Lazarus, L, Kiloh, L.G., & Penny, R. (1977). Depresssed Lymphocyte Function After Bereavement. *Lancet,* 1, 834-836.

Benson, H. (1975). *The Relaxation Response.* New York: William Morrow.

Berk, L. (1989). Laughter and Immunity. *Advances,* 6, 5.

Borysenko, J. (1987). *Minding The Body, Mending The Mind.* New York: Bantam Books.

Borysenko, J, & Borysenko, M. (1983). On Psychoneuroimmunology: How the Mind Influences Health and Disease . . . and How to Make the Influence Beneficial. *Executive Health,* 19, 1-7.

Chapman, L.S. (1986). Spiritual Health: A Component Missing from Health Promotion. *American Journal of Health Promotion,* 1, 38-41.

Chapman, L.S. (1987). Developing a Useful Perspective on Spiritual Health: Well-being, Spiritual Potential and the Search for Meaning. *American Journal of Health Promotion,* 1, 31-39.

Chopra, D. (1985). *Creating Health: The Psychophysiological Connection.* New York: Vantage Press.

Cousins, N. (1979). *Anatomy of an Illness.* New York: W.W. Norton.

Cowley, G. (1990). Chronic Fatigue Syndrome: A Modern Medical Mystery. *Newsweek.* November 12.

Dantzer, R. & Kelley, K.W. (1989). Stress and Immunity: An Integrated View of Relationships Between the Brain and the Immune System. *Life Sciences,* 44, 1995-2008.

Davis, F. (1980). *Personal Peak Performance: Making The Most of Your Natural Energy.* New York: McGraw-Hill.

Girdano, D.A. & Everly, G.S., Jr. (1986). *Controlling Stress and Tension: A Holistic Approach.* (2nd. Ed.). Englewood Cliffs: Prentice-Hall.

Gray, E. (1990). LeFevre Trek: Paradise to Idaho on Horseback. *Chico Enterprise-Record,* August 25, 1B.

Hinkle, L.E., Jr. (1974). The Effects of Exposure to Culture Change, Social Change and Changes in Interpersonal Relationships to Health. In B.S. Dohrenwend & B.P. Dohrenwend (Eds.), *Stressful Life Events: Their Nature and Effects.* New York: John Wiley and Sons.

Jemmott, J.B. III, & Locke, S.E. (1984). Psychological Factors, Immunologic Mediation, and Human Susceptibility to Infectious Diseases: How Much Do We Know? *Psychological Bulletin, 95,* 78-108.

Keller, S.R., Weiss, J.M., Schleifer, S.J., Miller, N.E., & Stein, M. (1981). Suppression of Immunity by Stress: Effect of a Graded Series of Stressors on Lymphocyte Stimulation in the Rat. *Science, 213,* 1397-1400.

Kiecolt-Glaser, J.K. & Glaser, R. (1988). Psychological Influences on Immunity. *American Psychologist, 43,* 892-898.

Kimzey, S.L. (1975). The Effects of Extended Spaceflight on Hemotologic and Immunologic Systems. *Journal of the American Medical Women's Association, 30,* 218-232.

Kronfol, Z., Silva, J., Greden, J., Dembinski, S., Gardner, R., & Carroll, B. (1983). Impaired Lymphocyte Function in Depressive Illness. *Life Sciences, 33,* 241-247.

Kuntzleman, C.T. (1981). *Maximum Personal Energy: Unleash Your Energy Potential and Enjoy Life.* Emmaus, PA.: Rodale Press.

Laudenslager, M.L., Reite, M., & Harbeck, R.J. (1982). Suppressed Immune Response in Infant Monkeys Associated with Maternal Separation. *Behavior and Neural Biology, 36,* 568-570.

Lazarus, R.S. & Folkman, S. (1984). *Stress, Appraisal and Coping.* New York: Springer Publishing Company.

Leach, C.S. & Rambault, P.C. (1974). Biochemical Responses of the Skylab Crewmen. *Proceedings of the Skylab Life Sciences Symposium, 2,* 427-454.

Leclere, J. & Weryha, G. (1989). Stress and Auto-immune Endocrine Diseases. *Hormone Research, 31,* 90-93.

Levy, S.M. (1989). Age, Stress, and Immunity. *Advances, 6,* 7.

Linn, B.S., Linn, M.W. & Klimas, N.G. (1988). Effects of Stress on Surgical Outcome. *Psychosomatic Medicine, 50,* 230-244.

Lynch, J.J. (1985). *The Language of the Heart.* New York: McGraw-Hill.

Maslow, A. (1962). *Toward A Psychology of Being.* New York: Van Nostrand.

McKenna, J.K. (1980). *Occupational Stress and The University Professor.* Unpublished Masters Thesis, California State University, Chico.

Monjan, A. & Collector, M.I. (1977). Stress-induced Modulation of the Immune Response. *Science, 196,* 307-308.

Nerozzi, D., Santoni, A., Bersani, G., Magnini, A. Bressan, A., Pasini, A., Antonozzi, I., & Frajese, G. (1989). Reduced Natural Killer Cell Activity in Major Depression: Neuroendocrine Implications. *Psychoneuroendocrinology, 14,* 295-301.

Norman, J. (1989). Stress and the Immune System. Paper presented at Annual Meetings of Pacific Division of American Association for the Advancement of Science. Chico, Ca. June.

Pelletier, K.R. (1977). *Mind as Healer, Mind as Slayer.* New York: Dell.

Pelletier, K.R. & Herzing, D.L. (1988). Psychoneuroimmunology: Toward a Mindbody Model. *Advances, 5,* 27-56.

Phillips, D.P. & King, E.W. (1988). Death Takes a Holiday: Mortality Surrounding Major Social Occasions. *Lancet*, 2:8613, 728-732.

Phillips, D.P. (1990). Postponement of Death Until Symbolically Meaningful Occasions. *Journal of the American Medical Association*, 263, 1947-1951.

Rahe, R.H. (1988). Acute vs. Chronic Psychological Reactions to Combat. *Military Medicine*, 153, 365-372.

Reese, P. (1990). Reese Runs the U.S. *RunCal*, No. 41, 8.

Reite, M., Harbeck, R., & Hoffman, A. (1981). Altered Cellular Immune Response Following Peer Separation. *Life Sciences*, 29, 1133-1136.

Rogers, M.P., Dubey, D., & Reich, P. (1979). The Influence of the Psyche and the Brain on Immunity and Disease Susceptibility: A Critical Review. *Psychosomatic Research*, 7, 520-526.

Schafer, W. & Gard, B. (1988). Stress and California's City Managers. *Western City*, 64, 13-15.

Schleiffer, S.J., Keller, S.E., McKegney, F.P., & Stein, M. (1979). The Influence of Stress and other Psychosocial Factors on Human Immunity. Paper presented at the American Psychosomatic Society Annual Meetings, Dallas, March.

Schleiffer, S.J., Keller, S.E., Bond, R.N., Cohen, J., & Stein, M. (1989). Major Depressive Disorder and Immunity: Role of Age, Sex, Severity and Hospitalization. *Archives of General Psychiatry*, 46, 81-87.

Selye, H. (1974). *Stress Without Distress*. Philadelphia: Lippincott.

Targum, S.D., Marshall, L.E., Fischman, P., & Martin, D. (1989). Lymphocyte Subpopulations in Depressed Elderly Women. *Biological Psychiatry*, 26, 581-589.

Taylor, S.E. (1986). *Health Psychology*. New York: Random House.

Thayer, R. (1986). Energy, Tiredness and Tension Effects of a Sugar Snack Versus Exercise. *Journal of Personality and Social Psychology*, 52, 199-225.

Stress-Related Symptoms and Disorders

Chapter 4

CHAPTER 4

I. INTRODUCTION

II. ZONES OF POSITIVE STRESS
    A. Variability in Zones of Positive Stress
    B. Eight Common Stress Difficulties
    C. Getting to Know Your Zone of Positive Stress

III. MONITORING DISTRESS SYMPTOMS
    A. Caution: Over-Concern with Symptoms
    B. Emotional Distress Symptoms
        1. Anxiety
        2. Depression
        3. Anger
        4. Fear
        5. Sadness
        6. Frustration
        7. Mislabeling Emotional Difficulties
    C. Cognitive Distress Symptoms
    D. Behavioral Distress Symptoms
        1. Direct Symptoms
        2. Indirect Symptoms
    E. Physical Distress Symptoms

IV. STRESS-RELATED ILLNESSES
    A. High Blood Pressure
        1. Causes of Hypertension
        2. Labile Hypertension
    B. Coronary Artery Disease
        1. Development of Coronary Artery Disease
        2. Risk Factors for Coronary Disease
    C. Migraine and Tension Headaches
        1. Behavior, Emotions, and Migraines
        2. Treatment and Prevention
        3. Tension Headaches
    D. Ulcers
    E. Rheumatoid Arthritis
    F. Cancer
        1. The Role of Stress in Cancer
        2. Emotional Factors in Cancer
    G. Insomnia
        1. Occasional Insomnia
        2. Chronic Insomnia
    H. Sudden Death

INTRODUCTION   ▼

In previous chapters, we saw that stress in moderate amounts can be pleasant, stimulating, and even helpful for meeting challenges and emergencies. Positive stress can help you to reach your potentials. But distress from either overstress or understress must be avoided whenever possible. Otherwise, wellness is impeded, health can be impaired, quality of life suffers.

Occasional distress is unavoidable. For example, two or more people can relate through time only imperfectly. The physical environment is largely uncontrollable. Financial problems are bound to arise for most people. Illness and death of loved ones is inevitable. But the less distress the better.

In this chapter, we will point out some of the ways moderate stress turns to harmful distress, resulting in stress-induced illnesses and in various forms of mental distress. At the outset, it will be useful to examine the concept of "zone of positive stress."

ZONES OF POSITIVE STRESS   ▼

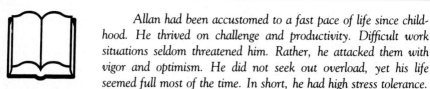

Allan had been accustomed to a fast pace of life since childhood. He thrived on challenge and productivity. Difficult work situations seldom threatened him. Rather, he attacked them with vigor and optimism. He did not seek out overload, yet his life seemed full most of the time. In short, he had high stress tolerance. He seldom missed work because of illness. He was productive and quite satisfied with his work and family life.

Fred was awed by Allan's seemingly endless ability to tolerate challenge without showing signs of wear and tear. Fred by nature was more slow-going and required more time per work task. He tended to become flustered and ineffective when work piled up. He deliberately let others take on difficult confrontations with clients because he disliked the tension. Fred had considerably lower stress tolerance than Allan, and became emotionally and intellectually overloaded at a point where Allan thrived.

Each of us possesses a distinctive zone of positive stress. A vital part of managing stress is to learn the range and limits of that zone. We must learn to recognize warning signs near its edges and to live within that zone most of the time.

Zone of positive stress: the tolerance range of stress within which the person is healthy, productive, and satisfied.

VARIABILITY IN ZONES OF POSITIVE STRESS

We can visualize the zone of positive stress better by studying Figure 4-1. The scale on the left represents an objective range of stress tolerance, which might be measured

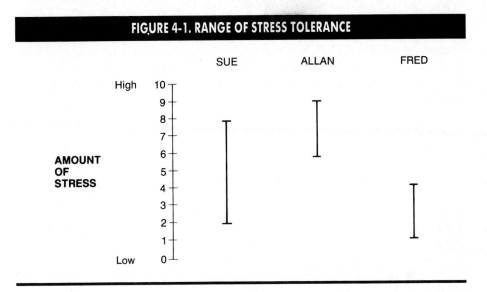

FIGURE 4-1. RANGE OF STRESS TOLERANCE

by physical indicators such as blood pressure, heart rate, muscle tension, or brain waves, or by indicators of emotional anxiety.

Three illustrative cases are shown in Figure 4-1. Sue, with a zone of positive stress from eight to two, is the most adaptable of the three, because she is comfortable, productive, and healthy at either a fast or slow pace, with high or low arousal. Her well-being is more independent from her environment than the other two in that she thrives within a wider range of stimulation and personal stress.

Allan's zone is narrower at a relatively high level. He is what Selye (1974) calls a "racehorse," a person with intrinsically high energy. He is bored and even experiences a bit of distress at point four or five on the scale, which is Sue's mid-range. Allan generates a high activity level at home and work to keep his stress level high when his outside environment does not do it for him. He is a "sensation seeker" (Ogylvie, 1973; Zuckerman, 1979), and perhaps even what one psychologist calls a Type T—a thrill seeker (Farley, 1986; Leo, 1990).

Fred is what Selye (1974) would call a "turtle," a low energy person with a narrow zone near the lower end of the scale. As noted above, he quite wisely avoids challenge and unfamiliar situations. He is somewhat of a plodder, yet he is dependable and effective in his work.

A common source of job stress is a misfit between the demands of the job and the zone of positive stress of the worker. A key challenge for managers and supervisors is to achieve an optimal job-personality fit among employees. Another is to fit employees together with relatively compatible tolerance zones whenever possible.

Another common problem is incompatible zones of positive stress between marriage partners. Let us hope that Allan's twin sister Eileen, who also is a racehorse, does not fall in love with and marry Fred, the turtle. Such a marriage would be destined for difficulty from the start because of the quite different paces of life.

Zones of positive stress are determined and shaped by a variety of influences: physical energy levels, background, personality, choice, and demands of the home, work, or school situation.

Everyone's zone is changeable to some degree, of course. The decision to leave a life of relative leisure in order to return to law school brings with it a choice to raise the upper limit of one's zone. Entering a demanding new job also may require living with a higher stress level than before. Similarly, getting married or having a baby results in the need for greater tolerance than before. Each person has limits of adaptability. A great deal of ill health and unhappiness results from efforts to push one's limits too far—at either the upper or lower end of the scale.

Mental and physical distress can result from either too little or too much stress. Each person, then, possesses three zones—zone of positive stress, zone of overload distress, and zone of underload distress. Symptoms of the two types of distress may be similar or different (emotional anxiety, insomnia, or irritability, for example).

Thus far, we have used one dimension (zero to ten) to describe the zone of positive stress. In order to enhance the usefulness of this model for understanding common stress difficulties, we will add a horizontal dimension.

A relatively distress-free day is presented in Figure 4-2. Note that stress level fluctuates throughout the day. In reality, of course, blood pressure, brain waves, and other physiological processes vary throughout the day in much finer degrees than shown here. Larger swings, however, are shown. This individual stayed within the zone of positive stress most of the time, exceeding the upper limit only briefly. This is a desirable stress pattern.

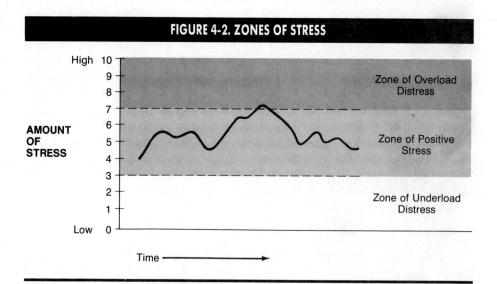

FIGURE 4-2. ZONES OF STRESS

EIGHT COMMON STRESS DIFFICULTIES

Figure 4-3 shows the same tolerance limits (between three and seven) that appeared in Figure 4-2. Here, however, are eight common stress difficulties. Each illustrates actual cases I have seen in the Enloe Hospital Stress and Health Center. No individual, in reality, would experience all eight in the same day—or even the same year. For graphic simplicity, I have drawn together a composite of separate persons and time periods into a single chart. Baseline stress level refers to hour-after-hour tension level when the individual is neither pressed nor experiencing deep relaxation. The following stress difficulties are illustrated in this figure.

1.   Baseline stress level too low. Following retirement by her and her husband, Mildred was perpetually bored, with no personal goals, little social contact, and little meaning in her life. She had difficulty sleeping at night, yet was listless, devoid of energy and irritable during the day.

2.   Baseline stress level too high. José, an ambitious college junior, felt over-whelmed much of the time. He constantly was aware of the need to excel, to serve on various campus committees, and to show his best side to classmates and friends. He not only studied hard most nights, he also spent several hours each week helping friends with study problems, as well as attending a variety of organizational meetings. He had a robust dating life, and he was a do-it-yourselfer at his apartment, frequently offering to fix his roommates' cars and appliances. He had been a perfectionist since childhood, driven ever upward toward some illusory standard with little satisfaction along the way. José suffered from gastritis, insomnia, and frequent colds.

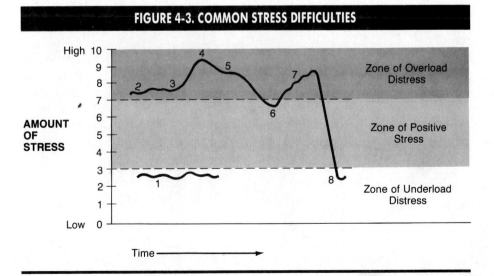

FIGURE 4-3. COMMON STRESS DIFFICULTIES

3.   Hair-trigger stress reaction. John, an insurance agent whose baseline stress level was too high, had virtually no tolerance for the noise or flippancy of his 11-year-old son. In earlier years, they often had joked and played together. Now, however, the slightest disturbance or demand on John after work produced an outburst of put-downs and discounts toward the boy. John often was defensive with his wife, co-workers, and friends.

4.   Peak arousal too high. Sharon, a 38-year-old mother of four teenagers, decided last year to return to college after a 19-year lay-off. Understandably, her baseline stress level was too high much of the time, and she, too, was often over-reactive to high demands or deviations. In addition, she sometimes experienced debilitating test anxiety. She knew some anxiety helped her to prepare, but lately this arousal had gotten out of hand, resulting in serious mental blocks during tests. She also sometimes had angry outbursts at home, far out of proportion to the situation. Both the test anxiety and the displays of anger were instances where peak arousal was too high.

5.   Recovery too slow. Julie, a teacher and mother of three, had been quite involved during recent months with the marriage break-up of her best friends, who lived nearby. She became the primary listener for both the man and the woman, which often put her in a considerable bind, since she had to be careful what she said to whom. This involvement began to interfere with her own family life, especially as her concentration and attentiveness diminished at home. She found it difficult to put her friends' problems out of her mind as she tried to find possible solutions to suggest. Her sleep was frequently disturbed. In short, her recovery from emotions and complex events was too slow.

6.   Recovery not low enough. Alberta, a 58-year-old bank manager, was hardly able to tolerate the thought that four years stood between her and retirement. The volume of her work was not only overwhelming, it had become meaningless. During a series of stress consultations, she became aware that she had no effective means of releasing tensions, of bringing her mental and physical stress level down to a more tolerable level in the evenings. Not only was her baseline stress level too high and her recovery too slow, but her recovery was not low enough. Although she had not exercised since her teens, she began a moderate program of walking and jogging after work, which served to get her out of the office earlier and to help her release built-up physical tension from the day, thereby bringing her emotional tension down to a reasonable level for the evening.

7.   Stress build-up. Willie was a pleasant, kind, responsive, overweight elementary teacher of 41, who not only kept his family of seven in bread, butter, and shoes on a meager salary but gave a great deal of time to the activities of his children. He car-pooled to scouting events, went camping often, built a swimming pool and deck for his family, and went to church regularly. He also was a superb cook, especially for large banquets. Not surprisingly, he was asked often, usually as a volunteer, to cook for school and church events. He was a responsible and helpful teacher who took his job seriously. Thus, he was an easy target to organize special events or to take on difficult committee assignments. After several years of this, Willie became aware of a severe stress build-up. His easy-going manner became more tense, he snapped at others more often, he felt joyless, he put on weight, and he had recurrent bouts with psoriasis, an uncomfortable and potentially dangerous skin disorder.

8.   Recovery too low. George was a 23-year-old university student who decided to return to school after working for three years as a gas station attendant. He studied hard to compensate for his limited abilities and his three-year absence from book learning. At mid-term and final exam time, he would cram very hard, often long into the night, then resume studying in the morning. He would be emotionally up during these periods, but then would take a depressive nose-dive after exams were over. It sometimes took three to four weeks for him to recover his usual emotional level. In short, he experienced too low a recovery period. He was not seriously manic-depressive, but his pattern resembled manic-depression in its basic form.

These eight common stress difficulties can occur in combination or independently. When baseline stress level is too high, several other difficulties tend to follow: hair-trigger stress reaction, too high peak stress, too low recovery, recovery not low enough and too slow, and stress build-up. These illustrations underscore the fact that effective stress management does not rest on a single, simple solution, but on an integrated lifestyle approach involving control of time, release of physical tension, relaxation skills, altered relationships, and more. These stress difficulties manifest themselves physically, emotionally, intellectually, and in behavior.

GETTING TO KNOW YOUR ZONE OF POSITIVE STRESS

You may recall that each person possesses his or her own zone of positive stress—the tolerance range of stress in which the person is healthy, productive, and satisfied. You may also recall this can be translated into a numerical scale ranging, for example, from 0 to 100. In order to get to know your zone of positive stress, you are invited to complete the following exercise.

EXERCISE 4-1. ASSESSING YOUR ZONE OF POSITIVE STRESS

1.   With one or more persons you know well, compare and contrast your zones of positive stress on a scale of 0-100 (see below). What signs of stress indicate your upper and lower limits? The limits of others with whom you compare yourself?

2.   How has your zone of positive stress changed over time?

3.   How well does your zone of positive stress match up with the demands of your environment?

4.   How does your ideal zone of positive stress differ, if any, from present reality?

Positive Stress Zones

Very High Stress   100____

                           90____

                           80____

                           70____

                           60____

                           50____

                           40____

                           30____

                           20____

                           10____

Very Low Stress   0____

You read in the above discussion of eight common stress difficulties that problems arise from too much or too little arousal, which can be easily understood and applied to yourself within the framework of "zone of positive stress." In order to know your stress pattern more completely, and as an additional basis for targeting your stress management efforts, you might want to complete the following exercise.

EXERCISE 4-2. MONITORING STRESS DIFFICULTIES

1. Please indicate by checking the appropriate blank how often you have experienced each of the following stress difficulties during the past three months.

	Occurred Almost Constantly	Occurred Several Times	Occurred Once or Twice	Did Not Occur
Too High Baseline Stress Level	____	____	____	____
Too Low Baseline Stress Level	____	____	____	____
Hair-Trigger Stress Reaction	____	____	____	____
Too High Peak Arousal	____	____	____	____

	Occurred Almost Constantly	Occurred Several Times	Occurred Once or Twice	Did Not Occur
Too Slow Recovery	_____	_____	_____	_____
Recovery Not Low Enough	_____	_____	_____	_____
Stress Build-Up	_____	_____	_____	_____
Recovery Too Low	_____	_____	_____	_____

2. Write a brief description of what symptoms you experienced during those times you experienced a stress difficulty almost constantly or several times.
3. Now go back and underline stress difficulties that you have encountered during the past week.
4. What have you learned?
5. Specifically, what do you need to do to prevent this (these) from recurring so often in the future? When will you start?
6. What do you need to do now to remedy the item(s) you underlined for this week? Do it.

EXERCISE 4-3. OTHERS' PERCEPTIONS OF YOUR STRESS DIFFICULTIES

Now ask someone close to you to give you scores on the same eight stress difficulty items.

1. Were his or her ratings of you similar to or different from your own?
2. What can you learn from this?
3. Discuss.

It is important to remember that distress makes itself known first through minor symptoms. It is important to be aware of these signals in mind, body, and behavior—and then to respond constructively to them—before they turn into major stress-induced illness. Stated differently, recognizing distress signals at an early stage is a vital first step in preventing moderate, useful stress from turning into harmful, destructive distress. Having reviewed and personally assessed a number of common stress difficulties, we will discuss four main types of distress symptoms: emotional, cognitive, physical, and behavioral. But first, a word of caution.

MONITORING DISTRESS SYMPTOMS   ▼

CAUTION: OVER-CONCERN WITH SYMPTOMS

Carried to the extreme, the following information about stress symptoms could readily be misunderstood and misused. I do not advocate narcissism, "blissing out," disengaging from people or activities, or hypochondriasis. Rather, I advocate continued awareness of what you are experiencing inwardly as you focus your energies and activities outward. Learning to self-monitor and regulate your life accordingly is intended to help you stay healthy, satisfied, and productive, while engaged with the world around you.

This point is reinforced negatively by the fact that "neurotic" individuals, as well as many drug-oriented youth, are often are so preoccupied with themselves that they find it extremely difficult to see beyond their own eyelashes, much less engage constructively with people or issues around them. For many who begin our stress health management programs this is true. Certainly, I do not want to reinforce such inward fixation. Chapter 15 discusses the need to balance self-care with social responsibility.

As noted in Chapter 1, research shows that "good copers" are highly committed to and involved in activities in the world around them. They engage life rather than hang back on the fringes of it. This is the opposite of alienation and narcissistic preoccupation with subjective symptoms and signs of stress.

What I suggest, then, is an inward-outward balance with appropriate concern about self in order to promote the self-in-action. The following discussion is intended to sharpen your perception of stress signals and to help you understand how to use them as a basis for continually regulating your daily activities and personal care. In this way, hopefully, you will be better able to realize your potentials while contributing to the world around you.

EMOTIONAL DISTRESS SYMPTOMS

Soldiers react to the extreme stressors of battle in a variety of ways. Some are relatively calm and confident. Most react at some time with emotional distress of one type or another. Similar reactions occur among refugees and among victims of natural disasters. Toffler (1971, 348) has pointed out that different types of people show striking parallels in their reactions to overstimulation.

> First, we find the same evidence of confusion, disorientation, or distortion of reality. Second, there are the same signs of fatigue, anxiety, tenseness or extreme irritability. Third, in all cases there appears to be a point of no return—a point at which apathy and emotional withdrawal set in. In short, the available evidence suggests that over-stimulation may lead to bizarre and anti-adaptive behavior.

The stressors facing soldiers, refugees, and victims of disaster are much more intense than those generally faced in daily life. Yet each time you move, change jobs, go away to college, or in some other way drastically alter your daily patterns of living, you run the risk of becoming emotionally upset—depressed, angry, fearful. When you live so fast that you experience the chronic overload of micro-stressors, mild emotional stress ("nervousness" or "tension") may give way to severe depression, anxiety, or disorientation. Similar results may accompany a chaotic life with little routine. Emotional and physical distress often feed on one another, as illustrated by the following all-too-common tragedy.

Mrs. Loren was a 76-year-old grandmother who had lived alone since her husband of 52 years died. She had been a faithful, devoted wife who looked after husband, children, home and garden with great care and pride throughout her life. She had never been sickly, although her general condition had weakened somewhat in recent years. After her husband's death she took a serious nose-dive, emotionally and physically. She seemed lost, lonely, and unable to find meaning. Last month she died of a lethal stroke.

Traumatic as the death of a long-time spouse may be, most surviving mates do not experience such a severe downturn in health and spirit. This suggests that there must be more effective ways of adapting to such crises. Yet the fact remains that the death rate is very high for surviving spouses during the year after a mate's death.

Let us examine more closely six of the most common distress emotions: anxiety, depression, anger, fear, sadness, and frustration.

Anxiety

Anxiety in moderate amounts is a normal part of living. In sports, optimal performance is achieved when pre-contest anxiety is in the middle range, neither too high nor too low. The same is true of occupational or academic performance.

Anxiety can become a stress problem in two ways. One is when arousal before or during a critical event is debilitating or otherwise interferes with performance. Earlier we referred to this stress difficulty as too high peak arousal. Difficulty in speaking before a group, disoriented thinking because of panic during a test, profuse sweating during an uncomfortable conversation, the intense fear before a job interview—all are examples of out-of-control situational anxiety. Some experts believe that panic attacks in such situations have unknown chemical or other biological origins, rather than cognitive or emotional causes, and that in these cases medical treatment is needed (Rifkin, 1990).

The second type of anxiety problem is chronic anxiety, sometimes referred to as anxiety neurosis. As Mason notes, "A person suffering from anxiety neurosis may exhibit certain physical symptoms: palpitations, chest pain, cold and sweaty extremities, band-like pressure around the head, constriction of the throat, fatigue, lack of appetite, vomiting, and diarrhea" (Mason, 1980, 140). Thus, anxiety is not just an emotional state, it is intellectual, physical, and behavioral as well.

BOX 4-1. SYMPTOMS OF GENERALIZED ANXIETY DISORDER

KEY FEATURE: Unrealistic or excessive anxiety and worry (apprehensive expectations) about two or more life circumstances.

MOTOR TENSION
Trembling, twitching, or feeling shaky
Muscle tension, aches, or soreness
Restlessness
Easily fatigued

AUTONOMIC HYPERACTIVITY
Shortness of breath or smothering sensations
Palpitations or tachycardia
Sweating or cold, clammy hands
Dry mouth
Dizziness or lightheadedness
Nausea, diarrhea, or other abdominal distress
Flushes or chills
Frequent urination
Trouble swallowing or lump in throat

VIGILANCE AND SCANNING
Feeling "keyed up" or on edge
Exaggerated startle response
Difficulty concentrating or mind going blank due to anxiety
Trouble falling asleep or staying asleep
Irritability

SOURCE: American Psychiatric Association, (1987, 252).

Depression

Depression, the second primary stress emotion, also is multi-faceted, as reflected in the following list of symptoms.

Emotional: a dull, tired, empty, sad, numb feeling with little or no pleasure from ordinarily enjoyable activities and people

Behavioral: irritability, excessive complaining about small annoyances or minor problems, impaired memory, inability to concentrate, difficulty making decisions, loss of sexual desires, inability to get going in the morning, slowed down reaction time, crying or screaming, excessive guilt feelings

Physical: loss of appetite, weight loss, constipation, insomnia or restless sleep, impotence, headache, dizziness, indigestion, and abnormal heart rate (Cohen, 1977, 13)

Specific combinations of symptoms vary from one person to the next. All sufferers tend to have the following in common: reduced energy level, withdrawal from interactions with others, gloomy and dark affect, self-criticism, and a sense of helplessness (Klein & Wender, 1988).

Like anxiety, depression is a common and expected reaction to events that temporarily seem overwhelming or negative in other ways (Goode, 1990). Short-run bouts are little to be concerned about. But depression which lasts for weeks or months is cause for concern and may require positive, aggressive steps. Major depression affects 2.5 million men and about 5 million women at any one time in the United States (Tollefson, 1990).

Sometimes depression has chemical origins (Dalack & Roose, 1990). Other times it is a temporary result of a traumatic loss, such as the death of a spouse. Other times depression results from accumulated fatigue, and in still other instances, it can accompany a profound sense of disharmony with work and marriage.

While medications may help in the short-run, lifestyle modification may be called for. As we shall see, running has been shown to be very effective in reducing depression, partly by helping to overcome the helplessness so often inherent in depression.

Anger

Anger, the third distress emotion, may be apparent as mild irritation, hostility, or intense aggressiveness. Often, anger results from blaming others. As Parrino states,

> The angered individual is intent on placing blame and leveling punishment for some misgiving. The angry self-dialogue often includes statements such as, "You should not have done that to me." "It is your fault, and you should be punished." "If it weren't for you, I wouldn't be in this situation." "I'll get you for that."

Anger brings with it physical arousal much like anxiety. When unexpressed and unresolved, it can lead to clear damage in tissues and organs. A study by University of Michigan researchers reported that blood pressure was highest among people who resolved anger by repressing it, next highest among those who explode with it, and lowest among those who discuss it (Harburg, et al., 1973). Other alternatives, perhaps even more effective, are discussing your anger, daily aerobic exercise, and deep relaxation. These practices are likely to reduce anger as an emotional and physical state through dissolving or releasing it.

The challenge still remains, of course, to look behind the immediate anger at the patterns of interpretation that produce anger in the first place. When we discuss anger in more detail in Chapter 5, you will note three key questions about managing anger:

▼ How can I prevent anger in the first place?

▼ How can I catch it in progress?

▼ How can I handle it constructively, once present?

Fear

Fear, the fourth distress emotion, involves a mild to severe feeling of apprehension about some perceived threat. Fear may be residual (consequence of something that already has happened), current (an immediate physical threat), or anticipatory (something believed likely to happen).

Fear is based on conscious or unconscious appraisal of a threat. This appraisal may or may not be based on reality. Someone once said that the letters in the word "fear" stand for "faulty evaluation of actual reality," which often is true, especially among phobic, paranoid, or other persons lacking in confidence. Fear can elicit a very powerful and immediate stress response.

Sadness

Sadness, the fifth primary distress emotion, is the dreary, dark feeling associated with a real, imagined, or anticipated loss. This loss may be a thing, achievement, expectation, illusion, limb, or whatever. The result is a gap in internal reality. Physical consequences can include, for example, insomnia, chest pain, upset stomach, fatigue, or loss of appetite. Behavior may become withdrawn. Thought processes may become fuzzy and characterized by loss of concentration.

Frustration

Frustration, the sixth primary distress emotion, is the sense of irritation, anger, or outrage at being blocked from something you want to have, experience, or do. It is familiar to everyone, since part of living with others is to compromise, giving up bits and pieces of what you would like for yourself.

The key issue is your reactivity to frustration. Very disturbed or deranged persons are hyper-reactive, often become violent when they do not get what they want. Handling frustration calmly is a continuing challenge, especially when you are blocked from something you very much want. High internal reactivity without expression is perhaps the most dangerous of all to health, because it can result in chronic excitation of the stress response. Essential (unexplained) hypertension often is the result of this pattern.

Mislabeling Emotional Difficulties

"Mental illness" is a term often applied to stress-related emotional difficulties. Application of this label, however, sometimes leads to feelings of hopelessness and helplessness. The "mentally ill" often are stigmatized by neighbors and friends. Emotional strains sometimes are better understood and handled if they are seen for what they are— acute stress, too much stress for too long, or a harmful reaction to stress—rather than as "mental illness."

"Nervous breakdown" is another term often mistakenly applied to stress-related emotional and behavioral difficulties. A "nervous breakdown" has nothing to do with a breakdown of nerves or the nervous system. Usually it refers to a feeling of helplessness, loss of control, or confusion in a temporary crisis. People who feel they are about to break down or lose control may need the help of family, clergy, or mental health specialists in getting through a crisis. But their sense of helplessness usually passes as the stressful circumstances are overcome.

People differ, of course, with respect to the point at which mild emotional stress gives way to harmful distress.

Let us look now at a sampling of emotional distress symptoms. Recognizing the following emotional symptoms requires no great skill or insight. Understanding them as messages about stress does require greater attentiveness and awareness. Do they reflect positive, temporary arousal associated with an intense but positively challenging situation? Or do they reflect more troublesome, ongoing distress? What can you learn from the following list of symptoms?

Depressed feelings—blue, down, helpless, gloomy

Emotional ups and downs

Strong urge to cry

Strong urge to "run away from it all"

Strong urge to hurt someone

Feelings of being emotionally unstable

Feelings of joylessness

Feelings of anxiety

Feelings of being "fed up"

Feelings of sadness

Fear of the future

Fear of others' disapproval

Fear of failing

Fear that others are "out to get me"

Difficulty falling asleep

Difficulty sleeping through the night

Decreased interest in sex

More impatience than usual

Struggling to get up to "face another day"

Feeling that things are out of control

Feelings of hopelessness

These signals may be temporary and even positive, reflecting, for example, a temporary "high" from a thrilling challenge. Or they may be messages from your mind and body that arousal has been too high (or too low) for too long. Distress may be present or on the way. Positive steps to regulate inputs or your responses to them may be called for.

Cognitive Distress Symptoms

Stressful situations sometimes produce a lack of concentration, poor memory, fuzzy or illogical thinking, or confusion. Students who have not paced themselves properly often find their heads "jammed up" in the middle of final exam week—they are unable to think clearly or remember very well. Young people who feel caught between pressures from their parents and those from their friends, or between the tugs and pulls of divorced parents, often find they cannot concentrate in class, complete assignments on time, or perform well on tests. These are examples of intellectual distress from overload—too many stressors in too short a time.

Toffler (1971) has pointed out that overload can lead to three forms of intellectual distress. First, too much stimulation at the point of sensory intake can distort and twist perceptions of reality. Second, overload can lead to disturbances in the processing of information—how you remember, reason, or solve problems. Third, overstimulation can cause the decision-making function to become irrational, blocked, out of control. In an accelerating society with many of us leading faster and faster lives, these three types of intellectual distress seem to be on the rise.

At the other extreme, assembly-line workers often become bored, dull, and intellectually stifled after many years on the job. This also happens to isolated retirees, to housewives, and to students who find school unchallenging. Such people also are victims of intellectual distress—from understimulation rather than from overload.

Which of these symptoms of cognitive distress have you experienced lately?

Fuzzy, foggy thinking

Forgetfulness

Mental block

Difficulty organizing thoughts

Inability to concentrate

Bizarre, disjointed thoughts

Inward preoccupation interfering with listening

Nightmares

Disturbed thinking is closely intertwined with emotions, especially with emotions of fear, anxiety, depression, and anger. Disturbed thinking also may be associated with a distressed body. Observing your thought processes sometimes can cue you about other distress warning signals that otherwise might not be noticed.

For many people, signs of distress are more apparent behaviorally than emotionally or cognitively. Let us examine behavioral distress.

BEHAVIORAL DISTRESS SYMPTOMS

Direct Symptoms
Following are direct behavioral symptoms. They usually are direct reflections of internal tension.

Irritability

Compulsive, spur of the moment actions

Talking faster than usual

Easily startled

Stuttering or stumbling in speech

Grinding teeth

Difficulty sitting still

Verbal attack on someone

Difficulty staying with one activity very long

Significant interpersonal conflict

Short-tempered

Withdrawn

Crying spells

Lashing out at something or someone

Indirect Symptoms

Following are indirect symptoms. These are indirect in that they reflect increased use of specific actions to release the physical and mental pain of distress. In other words, if these increase in frequency, they may reflect an increased level of distress to which they are a response.

Increased smoking

Increased alcohol consumption

Increased use of prescribed medications to reduce tension

Use of sleep as an escape

Use of TV as an escape

Increased use of over-the-counter aids for sleeping or relaxing

Use of illegal drugs

Increased consumption of coffee or colas

Seeing medical doctor for tension-related health problem

Irrational spending sprees

PHYSICAL DISTRESS SYMPTOMS   ▼

How you move and hold your body conveys a great deal about your internal tension.

Toe jiggling and foot tapping often reflect impatience and irritability.

Tight, hunched shoulders, which can become chronically sore, can signal anxiety, fear, or embarrassment.

Tightly folded arms may signal disapproval, anger, apprehension, or the desire to be left alone.

Tightly crossed or coiled legs can convey several messages—wanting to be left alone, anxiety, fearful anticipation.

Sagging, sloping shoulders and back can reflect fatigue, temporary or cumulative; feeling burdened (or simply not knowing how to stand straight).

Nail biting often conveys worry, tension, anxiety—and low self-esteem.

A jutting jaw often shows apprehension and tension.

Clinched fists or taut fingers reflect anxiety, usually of a current or anticipatory kind.

Furrows and frowns in the forehead are another sign of worry, fatigue, or depression.

These are illustrations of a more extensive list of physical stress signals, which also includes the following. The specific meaning and importance of these signals can best be determined by the person experiencing them. All have been described to me by participants in my stress management workshops, groups, and classes in recent years.

Dryness of mouth or throat

General fatigue or heaviness

Trembling or nervous twitch

Pounding of heart

Diarrhea

Constipation

Frequent need to urinate

Upset stomach

Neck pain

Back pain

Dizzy spells

Decreased interest in sex

Loss of appetite

Increase of appetite

Chest pain

Heart palpitations

Tension throughout the body

Sometimes these occur in clusters, at other times singly. In many instances, they are only minor irritants, but sometimes they interfere with behavior and performance.

A fascinating form of physical distress is "network nerves," a phenomenon experienced by people who appear on TV talk shows. Network nerves can include "panic, stomach distress, flushed skin, tightness of the larynx, poor circulation, fast pulse, even vomiting." Psychologists sometimes help performers overcome their intense fear of on-camera blundering by suggesting pleasant, relaxing images they can call forth before their appearance.

Minor physical distress symptoms, when cumulative, do not remain minor. They often turn into full-blown stress illnesses. Whether or not this progression occurs is tied to effectiveness of the dynamic, interactive coping process, which we discussed in our review of Lazarus and Folkman's theory in Chapter 2. Part of this process is whether one responds to early warning signs with constructive or destructive responses.

Exercises 4-4 through 4-10 provide a range of opportunities to assess and monitor your own distress symptoms.

EXERCISE 4-4. DISTRESS SYMPTOM SCALE

You are invited to complete the following inventory of your current distress signals, which includes many of the above items. While some of these items may reflect positive stress (for example, talking faster than usual or difficulty falling asleep), the scale as a whole is intended to measure distress. It correlates highly with a number of other stress-related scales, suggesting that it is a valid measure of distress symptoms. The most important thing for you is that it will give you a fairly vivid picture of what you are experiencing in mind, body, and behavior. When you are finished, add your score, using the numbers given at the top of the scale.

Please indicate which of these occurred during the past two weeks. Use numbers as follows:

___**0**___ Did not occur
___**1**___ Occurred once or twice
___**5**___ Occurred several times
___**10**__ Occurred almost constantly

_____ Irritability

_____ Depressed feelings

_____ Dryness of mouth or throat from tension

_____ Impulsive, spur-of-the-moment actions

_____ Emotional ups-and-downs

_____ Strong urge to cry

_____ Strong urge to "run away from it all"

_____ Strong urge to hurt someone

_____ Fuzzy, foggy thinking

_____ Talking faster than usual

_____ General fatigue or heaviness

_____ Feelings of being "overwhelmed by it all"

_____ Feelings of being emotionally unstable

_____ Feelings of joylessness

_____ Feelings of anxiety

_____ Emotional tension

_____ Easily startled

_____ Hostility

_____ Trembling or nervous twitch

_____ Stuttering or stumbling in speech

_____ Inability to concentrate

_____ Difficulty organizing thoughts

_____ Difficulty sleeping through the night

_____ More impatience than usual

_____ Grinding teeth

_____ Difficulty sitting still

_____ Nightmares

_____ Diarrhea

_____ Verbal attack on someone

_____ Mental block

_____ Frequent need to urinate

_____ Upset stomach

_____ Headache

_____ Neck pain

_____ Pain in back

_____ Loss of appetite

_____ Decreased interest in sex

_____ Increased appetite

_____ Forgetful

_____ Chest pain

_____ Significant interpersonal conflict

_____ Struggling to get up to "face another day"

_____ Feeling things are "out of control"

_____ Feelings of hopelessness

_____ Difficulty staying with one activity very long

_____ Short-tempered

_____ Withdrawn

_____ Difficulty falling asleep

_____ Slow recovery from a stressful event

_____ Pounding of heart from tension

EXERCISE 4-5. QUESTIONS ABOUT YOUR DISTRESS SYMPTOM SCORE

1. Add your score.
2. In which of these three categories does your score fall?

High Distress Symptoms   50 or higher
Medium Distress Symptoms   20–49
Low Distress Symptoms   0–19

3. Is your score higher than you would like?
4. What do you see that is new or surprising?
5. Underline the two or three items most troublesome to you during periods of overload.
6. Underline the two or three items most troublesome to you during periods of underload.
7. What can you learn about your zone of positive stress from the items you have underlined?
8. How do you suppose your mate, a close friend, or a working partner would rate you on the scale? Ask him or her.

EXERCISE 4-6. COMPARING YOUR DISTRESS SYMPTOM SCORE

Compare your score with the scores of the following groups who have recently taken the same self-assessment.

TABLE 4-1. GROUP SCORES ON DISTRESS SYMPTOM SCALE

GROUP	NUMBER OF RESPONDENTS	MEDIAN SCORE	PERCENTAGE WITH SCORES HIGHER THAN 100
Participants in weight loss clinic	26	36	15%
Employees of county housing authority	15	74	33%
Mothers of nursery school children	70	52	16%
Dental support staff	71	35	8%
Dentists	41	19	5%
Special education teachers	54	50	17%
Elementary school teachers	15	40	20%
Physicians	24	37	0%
College students (First week of classes)	63	53	8%
College students (Final exam week)	79	54	32%
Small town newspaper editors	48	41	8%
Certified Public Accountants (non-tax season)	52	34	5%
Certified Public Accountants (tax season)	52	45	19%
Realtors	29	22	7%
Pharmacists	40	27.5	10%
Members of secretarial organization	78	40	11%
College custodians	54	20	4%
College dept. secretaries	26	9	8%

EXERCISE 4-7. MONITORING DISTRESS SIGNALS

Without becoming overly preoccupied, use this list of 50 distress signals as a guide to more closely monitoring messages from your mind, body, and behavior during the next two days. What can you learn? What stressors seem to lead to specific types of distress?

EXERCISE 4-8. DISTRESS SIGNALS AND DISHARMONY

When stress signals are not related to a perceived or actual positive stress, they probably indicate unwanted and potentially harmful distress, either current or anticipated. As pointed out in Chapter 1, distress is a signal of disharmony somewhere in your life. Distress is, after all, internal disharmony—an equilibrium gone wrong, an imbalance between mind and body, or a conflict among different parts of yourself. If your score on the Distress Symptom Scale is higher than you think it ought to be, you are invited to complete the following exercise.

1. Given what you have learned thus far from this book, what is your best guess as to the disequilibrium or imbalance within your body? Between your mind and body? With what simple words would you describe this disequilibrium?

2. What is there about your life right now that is contributing to your high distress symptom score? In other words, where is the disharmony? Here are a few possibilities.

I am not getting something I want or need very much—love, affection, approval, food, money, recognition, or advancement, for example.

Two feelings about someone or something are in conflict, doing battle. Examples might be: the desire to live together conflicts with wanting time alone; desire for more money conflicts with wanting to stay in my present job; I like certain things about him or her, but others I can't stand.

Uncertainty about the future—job change, marriage, divorce, school, move.

Something I am doing that I hate myself for—like smoking, overeating, being inaccessible to others, overspending, or abusing my body in other ways.

Conflict with someone else—boss, mate, friend, co-worker, neighbor.

Disharmony between job requirements and my personality.

Conflict between my need for slower pace and demands of my current situation.

Others?

EXERCISE 4-9. BODY SYMPTOMS: TRACKDOWN ON DEEPER MEANINGS

We learn time and time again that illness, pain, and accident are manifestations of deeper needs that are going unmet. Perhaps this trackdown method will help you to get in touch with some of these needs.[1]

Symptom	Trackdown	Regina's Example	Your Example
tension headache	1. It feels like:	a knife over my right eye	_____
	2. It happens when:	I've been pushing myself hard for several days	_____
	3. It prevents:	reading, feeling excited about life	_____
	4. It encourages:	more sleep, less work, admitting my weaknesses	_____
	5. It provides the reward:	attention and help from Jere	_____
	6. It may indicate the deeper need for:	Jere's acceptance of me	_____
	7. A more direct way to meet this need might be:	expressing this to him; scheduling more special time with him	_____

SOURCE: Ryan & Travis (1981, 14).

EXERCISE 4-10. MONITORING YOUR HEART RATE

A simple, fascinating, highly accessible means of monitoring what is happening inside your body is to take your pulse rate. Use your wrist or the carotid artery in your neck. Right now, count the number of beats for 15 seconds, multiply times four. This is your pulse rate per minute.

1. Take it for four days as follows, recording it each time.
   Days One and Two
   _____ Before getting out of bed
   _____ At 10:00 A.M.
   _____ After running up at least two flights of stairs
   _____ At 3:00 P.M.
   _____ At 7:00 P.M.
   _____ Before getting into bed.
   Days Three and Four
   _____ Just before getting out of bed
   _____ Just before exercising

_____ Immediately before dinner
_____ Immediately after deep relaxation
_____ During a stressful situation (no one will notice)
_____ Thirty minutes after a stressful situation

2. What did you learn? Discuss your findings with a friend.

Let us now examine a number of stress-related illnesses—the all-too-frequent result of escalation of once-minor distress symptoms.

STRESS-RELATED ILLNESSES ▼

The term "psychosomatic illness" is popularly misused to refer to an illness which has no organic origin, but is "all in your head." To be sure, disease states often are imagined rather than real, as any practicing physician can attest. This may be why placebo pills are effective about one-third of the time.

Psychosomatic illness properly refers to sickness in which the mind plays a causative part. Illnesses usually do not have one single origin, but rather result from the convergence of a number of factors: deficient nutrition, fatigue, exposure to germs, weakened immunity, and more. Through emotional and cognitive distress, the mind sometimes contributes to illness in four ways:

▼ Long-term wear and tear from excessive stress makes the body more susceptible to breakdown, such as peptic ulcers, colitis, cancer, migraines, or high blood pressure.

▼ An acute episode of intense emotional stress can directly precipitate a physical ailment, heart attack, tension headache, or muscle spasm in the back.

▼ High stress, chronic or acute, can aggravate an existing illness, such as angina, diabetes, arthritis, or hypertension.

▼ Stress can alter health habits such as alcohol consumption, exercise, sleep, or adherence to prescribed medications, thereby raising chances of illness.

Box 4-2 describes one expert's summary of hypotheses about pathways between stress and pathology of organs and tissues.

As we noted in Chapter 1, experts on stress and health estimate that between 50 and 80 percent of all illnesses are stress-related in one of these ways. This is not to say that all such illnesses are unreal or imagined. But stress helped to induce or aggravate them in one of these ways. More effective management of stress may be among the most effective means of reducing the soaring costs of health care (or, more accurately, illness care) in this country.

BOX 4-2. HYPOTHESES ABOUT STRESS AND ILLNESS

Below are hypotheses about how the experience of stress sometimes leads to pathology of tissues and organs (Zegans, 1982).

1. The acute body response itself may cause damage, particularly if an already compromised organ is involved.

2. The acute response may cause transient insult to a tissue, but repeated occurrence of the stress may cause permanent tissue damage.

3. The acute physiological reaction can become chronic if it becomes conditioned to a benign stimulus resembling the stressor. Such a benign stimulus may be a more regular part of the individual's environment and provoke an unnecessary coping response.

4. A coping strategy may be used successfully, but the physiological component is not terminated when the challenge is mastered. A *reverberating circuit* is established, which puts unusual strain on the body.

5. A minor stress provocation releases an inappropriately severe physiological response. Modulation is lacking that grades the body's reaction according to the nature of the threat. When all stresses are responded to as major assaults, abnormal physiological reactions are possible.

6. A physiological response appropriate and adequate to cope with a given threat may result in damage to some other aspect of the body through inhibiting a benign but vital body process or stimulating an irritating one.

7. Coping strategies can misfire when the behavioral component is inhibited but the physiological aspect is expressed (fight behavior inhibited but not its physiological component). The physiological aspects of a blocked action can be continuously repeated, since no appropriate cutoff signal is received.

SOURCE: This summary of Zegan's work appears in Genest and Genest (1987, 98).

In *The Doctor's Guide to Living With Stress*, Graham-Bonnalie (1972) listed the following illnesses as sometimes induced or aggravated by excessive stress.

Acne	Asthma
Alcoholism	Cancer
Allergies	Colitis
Anorexia nervosa	Constipation
Appendicitis	Dermatitis and eczema

Diabetes	Hypertension
Diarrhea	Impotence
Enuresis	Insomnia
Eye condition	Obesity
Fatigue	Peptic ulcers
Frigidity	Psoriasis
Gout	Rheumatic fever
Headache and migraine	Rheumatoid arthritis
Heart conditions	

Let us examine several prevalent stress-related illnesses in more detail.

HIGH BLOOD PRESSURE ▼

Hypertension, or high blood pressure, is among the most lethal, widespread, and baffling ailments of our time (Weinberger, 1990). One in five Americans suffers from it, with the incidence among blacks exceeding that among whites by 50 to 100 percent (Galton, 1973; Pelletier, 1977, 1979). High blood pressure alone accounts for thousands of deaths per year, but if its indirect mortal impact through long-range effects on strokes, heart attacks, and kidney ailments are taken into account, it is a contributing factor in millions of deaths. The absence of subjectively detectable symptoms makes hypertension especially insidious and dangerous.

Hypertension is excessive pressure against the walls of blood vessels throughout the body. It is the direct result of constriction of the size of those blood vessels through chronic contraction of small muscles in the blood vessel walls.

Blood pressure is measured with two numbers, *systolic* and *diastolic*. Systolic blood pressure, the numerator and larger number, refers to millimeters of mercury raised on a scale at the moment of contraction of the heart. Diastolic blood pressure, the denominator and smaller number, refers to the millimeters of mercury raised on a scale at the moment between beats, when the ventricles (pumps) of the heart are refilling with blood and less pressure is exerted against blood vessel walls.

Blood pressure tends to rise with age. Most medical authorities, however, agree that in younger and middle-aged people, repeated readings above 140/90 warrant careful monitoring. Repeated readings higher than 150/95 often are treated with medications.

CAUSES OF HYPERTENSION

While glandular and other disorders contribute to hypertension in some cases, most cases are considered to be "essential hypertension"—of unexplained origin. A medical textbook states that ". . . a specific cause for the increase in peripheral resistance which is responsible for the elevated arterial pressure cannot be defined in approximately 90 percent of patients with hypertension disease" (Isselbacher, 1981, 86).

We do know that high salt consumption contributes to high blood pressure, at least among the genetically predisposed. So can lack of exercise, overweight, and certain glandular disorders.

Herbert Benson and other experts (Benson, 1975; Benson, Kotch, & Crassweller, 1978) contend that a substantial proportion of essential hypertension may result from prolonged, unreleased chronic excitation of the stress response. Conditions of modern life expose us to greater risks of hypertension. Benson (1975, 45) begins by quoting Ostfeld and Shekelle (1967):

"There has been an appreciable increase in uncertainty of human relations as man has gone from the relatively primitive and more rural to the urban and industrial. Contemporary man, in much of the world, is faced every day with people and with situations about which there is uncertainty of outcome, wherein appropriate behavior is not prescribed and validated by tradition, where the possibility of bodily or psychological harm exists, where running or fighting is inappropriate, and where mental vigilance is called for." The elevation of blood pressure will depend upon the extent to which the individual is exposed to accelerated environmental change uncertainty, and on his innate and acquired abilities to adapt.

Numerous studies lend credibility to this position that hypertension, at least in part, results from social stressors (Mustacchi, 1990). For example, hypertension is a major problem for black Americans, a fact which may be due less to genetic disposition than to the greater life stresses of blacks. A study of blacks residing in middle-class neighborhoods showed that they had a rate of hypertension only about one-half that of blacks residing in ghetto environments, for whom crime, unstable neighborhoods, pollution, and over-crowding are likely to create much more daily tension (Harburg, et al., 1970).

Another study shows that air traffic controllers have a rate of hypertension about five times greater than comparable work groups, probably because of the intensely demanding pressures in the air traffic towers (Greenberg and Velletutti, 1980). Cottington (1986) found that men with high job stress who suppress their anger are more likely to experience hypertension than those who do not suppress their anger. At the same time, other studies show that both exercise and meditation are sometimes effective in reducing blood pressure (Benson, 1975, 1984; Thomas, et al., 1981; Johnsgård, 1989).

Labile Hypertension

Recently, medical researchers have given attention to a pattern called labile (unstable) high blood pressure. Some persons appear to have resting blood pressure in the normal range, yet their blood pressure shoots up to very high levels when they are emotionally aroused (Pickering, and Gerin, 1990; Manuck, Kasprowisz, and Muldoon, 1990; Fredrikson and Matthews, 1990).

One form of this pattern is "white coat hypertension"—high blood pressure seems to appear only in the presence of a nurse but never at home. Curiously, Eliot (1989) reports that about 17 percent of family physicians also manifest labile hypertension. Another pattern is the "hot reactor"—blood pressure soaring in response to emotional upset, especially from anger (Eliot & Breo, 1984).

Since studies suggest that the chances of eventual chronic hypertension are greater later in life among such "hot reactors," it is vital for young people with this pattern to learn ways to control it.

In the previous chapter, we cited Lynch's research showing that blood pressure tends to rise each time a person talks. He also found that hypertensives usually have greater elevations during talking than normotensives (Lynch, 1985). Lynch raises the fascinating question of whether the chronic elevation of blood pressure might be the result of years of minor hot reactions during millions of communications over many years. Learning early to keep one's body as calm as possible during conversation might be especially vital, then, among persons disposed by family history toward hypertension.

In short, hypertension is a severe health hazard resulting in part from the stresses of late twentieth-century existence, especially for certain population groups. In the long run, understanding and minimizing stress may be a more potent means of containing this epidemic than even the most effective medications. Meanwhile, treatment programs using exercise, diet modifications, and relaxation training have been shown to be effective in many cases in treating this dangerous disorder.

CORONARY ARTERY DISEASE ▼

The coronary arteries wrap around the heart to furnish the heart muscle with newly oxygenated blood. If these arteries are partially blocked, insufficient blood supply reaches the heart. When the continuous flow of blood through the arteries is cut off, death to heart tissue results. This is a heart attack.

Development of Coronary Artery Disease

Beginning early in life (Wissler, 1990) and continuing into adulthood, the inner lining of some individuals' coronary arteries develops tiny streaks of fat and cholesterol. Research continues into precisely how this occurs biochemically and why people differ in the number and severity of such lesions. What is known is that in some persons, especially in Western nations, this process continues on for some years until larger deposits develop. These partial blockages are called *atherosclerosis*.

The deposits (*coronary plaques*) not only increase in size, but they sometimes develop tiny breaks and tears. Fortunately, the body is equipped to repair these minor internal injuries, just as it can repair a minor external trauma. Through a complex series of messages from the brain, blood clots and scar tissues emerge. New cells develop and the tiny wound is repaired. But as this happens, the size of the passageway through the coronary artery is narrowed slightly. The scar tissue continues to build up on new lesions along the coronary arteries or on old scar tissue.

Scars continue both in number and size, partly because of continued clotting and partly because fat-like substances get stuck in tiny openings in the scar tissue. After a time, the scar tissue contains many of these fatty substances.

The most dangerous of these is *cholesterol*, a wax-like chemical that is vital for building cells through the body, for constructing hormones, and for other purposes. When too much cholesterol travels in the bloodstream, it tends to attach itself to the walls of the arteries. This is especially true if the bloodstream has a high percentage of *low density lipoproteins* (LDL), which "deliver" the cholesterol throughout the body, and a low percentage of *high density lipoproteins* (HDL), which "discard" cholesterol to the liver. LDL's, then, are the "bad guys" in the cholesterol family, HDL's the "good guys."

More lesions, more clotting and scarring, more closure, less blood flow, more lesions—on the cycle goes. Finally, a blood clot may break away, blocking the line at a narrowed spot. Or arteries narrowed from high blood pressure may completely close off blood flow, the rhythmic pumping of the heart may go awry (*arrhythmia*) and stop altogether. The part of the heart deprived of blood soon dies and nearby cells are severely weakened. The heart can no longer pump blood to the lungs or throughout the body. If enough heart muscle dies from lack of oxygen, the result is death.

The term *coronary artery disease* refers to the partial closing of one or more coronary arteries. A *heart attack* or *myocardial infarction* occurs when a coronary blockage causes a complete cessation of blood to an area of the heart. The result is death of heart tissue.

You read in Chapter 1 that coronary heart disease is by far the leading cause of death in this country. Over half of all deaths of middle-aged men are caused by coronary disease (Green & Shellenberger, 1991). One in four of the people who die from heart disease are under age 65 (American Heart Association, 1985). On the positive side, the rate of heart attacks and death from heart disease has dropped steadily for the past 25 years.

Risk Factors for Coronary Disease

The emergence of heart attacks as a major cause of death in this century has stimulated scientists to devote substantial time and energy to studying causes. While much remains to be learned, a number of fairly definite "risk factors" have been identified (Kannel, 1990). These include:

▼ Family history

▼ Cigaret smoking

▼ Elevated blood pressure

▼ Elevated cholesterol

▼ A high ratio of total cholesterol to HDL

▼ Low aerobic fitness

▼ Obesity

▼ Diabetes

▼ Coronary-prone behavior

Note that all these risk factors except for family history are related to lifestyle and choice. Even diabetes is influenced, of course, by diet, exercise—and sometimes emotions. Fortunately, risk factors can be changed—even in entire communities, as recently reported by Farquhar and colleagues (Farquhar, et al., 1990). Evidence has even been reported that the combination of exercise, low-fat diet, social support, and meditation can reverse coronary plaque buildup (Ornish, 1990).

In Chapter 9, we will describe in some detail the significant role of coronary-prone behavior in coronary artery disease and heart attacks. You will read that recent studies strongly suggest that the most dangerous part of coronary-prone behavior is hostility and frequently aroused anger.

MIGRAINE AND TENSION HEADACHES ▼

Behavior, Emotions, and Migraines

Migraine headache is a painful condition associated with alternating constriction and dilation of cerebral arteries that supply blood to the brain (Blanchard and Andrasik, 1985; Kunkel, 1990). During the first stage (prodrome), arteries constrict. Subjective signs of the prodrome include dizziness, flushness, visual static, and a familiar sense of uneasiness. Little or no pain may be felt at this stage. The second stage is the intense, usually one-sided pain associated with dilation of the arteries. Migraines can be devastating, often leading to nausea and to complete temporary incapacitation. Women suffer from them more often than men.

A curious feature of migraines is that they do not usually occur simultaneously with intense stress, but afterwards. Sundays and vacations are notorious migraine days, as if internal permission finally can be given to let down.

Migraines resemble heart attacks in that both are vascular problems. In many respects, the migraine sufferer also resembles the coronary-prone individual. Both tend to have perfectionist tendencies, for example. But whereas coronary-prone individuals are more likely to be aggressive, controlling, and hostile as they struggle to control their environment, the so-called migraine personality is more likely to be characterized by self-sacrifice, compliance, and inability to delegate.

Research on migraine patients many years ago by Harold Wolff (1950), still considered definitive by many experts, suggests that the typical migraine sufferer is at bottom insecure. As McQuade and Aikman (1974, 41) have stated:

> What he really wants is to be loved, but he will settle for being admired, or simply approved of—anything to still his gnawing sense of worthlessness. It is for this reason that he drives himself so hard, selflessly taking on thankless chores, burdening himself with ever-increasing responsibilities, conscious, rigid, somewhat fanatical. It is not surprising, then, that when leisure finally does catch up with him, he cracks.

The talking-vascular system linkage discovered has relevance for migraines, as noted by Lynch (1985, 209).

> As I have already noted, the abnormalities of the circulatory system in the hypertensive patient and the disordered vascular responsiveness of the typical migraine patient can both be viewed as hidden

or internal blushing. That is, just as the ordinary blush denotes an alteration in blood flow—triggered by human interaction—to a particular vascular bed, so too the circulatory changes observed in migraine and hypertensive patients also are triggered by human dialogue

Another consistent behavior pattern often preceding onset of the migraine is withdrawing emotional energy from another person. Emotion is blocked from flowing outward. Anger and resentment are contained—turned inward where they boil and fester. At this point, the patient often will report a cold, clammy feeling in feet and hands, sometimes contributing to sleep-onset insomnia.

A recent study at the Johns Hopkins School of Medicine asked 324 people, half of whom had frequent migraines, to complete a questionnaire (Brandt, et al., 1990). The migraine group was 2.5 times more likely to be anxious, depressed, or tense than the control group. Of course, it could be that the migraines caused the emotional distress, rather than the other way around. Yet, most experts agree that emotional distress probably does help cause migraines.

Migraines occur most often between the ages of 16 and 35 and tend to decline by age 50.

Treatment and Prevention

Experts continue to search for medical and behavioral methods of preventing and treating migraines. Several types of medications sometimes are prescribed, with mixed results.

Through meditation, autogenic relaxation, or biofeedback, the individual often can learn to arrest progression of the migraine at the point of the prodrome by learning to divert blood to the extremities and away from the head area. One stress specialist reports that "85 percent of migraine patients I work with respond positively to stress reduction practices." He also reports (Mason, 1980, 118):

> The people who do not get better usually are not practicing consistently because for their own reasons, they are not quite ready to give up their migraines and discover a headache-free existence. I strongly recommend that migraine sufferers study the secondary gains they get from migraines and evaluate their lives to determine what needs are not being met appropriately.

Tension Headaches

Tension headaches differ from migraines in that pain comes from tense muscles rather than from constricting and dilating of blood vessels (Kunkel, 1990b). As Holroyd, Appel, and Andrasik (1983) point out, however, it is not always easy to distinguish between the two types of headaches.

Tension headaches tend to appear in late afternoon and evenings for many persons, corresponding to their general fatigue level. One study found tensions tend to be more associated with minor hassles of daily life than with major life events (Howarth, 1965).

Tension headaches are part of a more general category of body discomforts from partially constricted or tense muscles. As a result of aroused emotions, muscles around the head tighten and don't let go (Gannon et al., 1987). For others the target muscles for tension are in the neck and shoulder areas or the lower back.

A recent study found a significant correlation between frequency of headaches and depression (Chung & Kraybill, 1990). In fact, three of four persons with headaches recurring almost every day had a significantly elevated level of depression. The authors, writing in a medical journal, concluded, "Headache is an important marker for depression in the primary care setting. It can be inferred from this study that the clinician may need to focus more on treating the entity of depression than on treating just the symptom of headache." Of course, the causal direction could also be reversed: perhaps depression is a response to chronic headaches, rather than the other way around. In any event, this study suggests they tend to be associated.

In all these cases, relaxation techniques usually can help. For example, I frequently have students in my classes tell me they come to class with a headache but that it disappears during or after a deep relaxation exercise. Regular exercise, consistent sleep, healthy nutrition, and daily deep relaxation can help prevent tension headaches in the first place. So can use of self-talk methods to prevent emotional volatility and worry.

BOX 4-3. HEADACHE FACTS

Here are a few facts about headaches, based on a national Harris Poll of 1254 adults.

Headaches are America's number one pain problem.

Three of four adults suffered at least one headache during the past year.

Eighty-five percent of those aged 18-24 reported one or more headaches during the past year, compared with only 50 percent among those over age 65.

Working mothers suffer headaches more frequently than homemakers.

In addition to incalculable individual discomfort from heachaches, the report concludes that, "These numbers reflect a massive social cost to the quality of life of Americans and a massive loss of production to the economy . . . This lost time cost the American economy an estimated $55 million."

SOURCE: National Headache Foundation (1985).

ULCERS   ▼

Among the most common and clearly understood stress-related maladies are gastric and duodenal ulcers (Weinstock & Clouse, 1987; Young, et al., 1987; Sanowski,

1990a). Peptic ulcers result from excessive gastric secretion in the stomach. Ultimately a lesion or open sore develops, causing pain and, sometimes, bleeding. Recent evidence by Phillips (1990) strongly suggests that a bacterium is the dominant cause of peptic ulcers, although stress most likely plays a part, sometimes as an independent cause, other times in aggravating bacterium-caused peptic ulcers.

Duodenal ulcers, which are similar to peptic ulcers, except that lesions occur in the small intestine just beyond the stomach, usually take longer to heal because of the constant flow of food and gastric juices through that area. Experts believe that stress plays a greater role in the development and exacerbation of duodenal than peptic ulcer disease (Whitehead and Schuster, 1985).

Clear evidence points to greater elevation of digestive acids from elevation of the stress response (Tennant, 1988; Weiner, 1977; Feist and Brannon, 1988; Folkenberg, 1989). This was observed directly for a number of years by Stewart Wolf in a patient who was forced to live with an opening in his stomach because of an unusual injury to his esophagus (Wolf, 1965). Wolf found that whenever his patient became more emotional, greater amounts of stomach acids were secreted.

Selye, who began his research on ulcers in rats more than 45 years ago, has summarized the link between stress ulcers as follows (Selye, 1976, 259):

> The gastro-intestinal tract is particularly sensitive to general stress. Loss of appetite is one of the first symptoms in the great "syndrome of just being sick," and this may be accompanied by vomiting, diarrhea, or constipation. Signs of irritation and upset of the digestive organs may occur in any type of emotional stress. This is well known, not only in soldiers who experience it during the tense excitation of battle, but even to students who pace the floor before my door awaiting their turn in oral examinations.

Ulcer-prone people usually are driven "go-getters" who strive very hard in pursuit of ever-receding career goals. Underlying hostility often is present but seldom is expressed. An even stronger unconscious urge to be accepted and loved similarly is expressed. Men with ulcers have a high incidence of unhappy marriage. Curiously, one study found that wives with rheumatoid arthritis often have husbands with peptic ulcers. Such women tend to possess strong drives to achieve public recognition and esteem, something the traditional husband cannot accept or understand. The husband is driven by his own success need, yet also craves emotional support, something the wife does not offer because of her resentment. "So the wife's bones and the husband's digestive tract ache to a common beat" (Tanner, 1976, 49).

Other studies on both animals and humans suggest that controllability of stressors influences chances of ulcers. Feist and Brannon (1988, 129) point out:

> Ulcers are most likely when the animal anticipates painful stimuli, but is helpless to do anything to avoid it, when it is not warned prior to pain and, thus, has not time to prepare, or when it must make decisions and remain constantly vigilant. If these findings can be generalized to the human situation, then it would appear that jobs with strongly distasteful elements that cannot be avoided, those with

unexpected nuisances and exasperations, and those which require tough decisions with little real control, are the ones most likely to lead to the development of ulcers.

Smith and others (Smith, et al., 1978) indeed found that lower- and middle-level jobs, where employees are harassed by the public, by supervisors, or by subordinates, were found to have ulcers more often than upper-level managers.

Physical exercise, controlling pace of life, containing the drive to prove oneself, deep relaxation, and support from a warm accepting partner—all are likely to help reduce emotional pressures toward ulcers. Conventional medical treatment may also be needed (Rogers, 1990; Sanowski, 1990b).

RHEUMATOID ARTHRITIS   ▼

Rheumatoid arthritis usually starts during young adulthood or middle age, continues into old age, and affects women three times more often than men (Pelletier, 1977). This illness manifests itself through swelling and soreness in joints throughout the body. Stress often appears to play a part in the course of this illness and perhaps in its inception.

Like ulcerative colitis and, perhaps, cancer, rheumatoid arthritis is a disease of the immune system. Specifically, it is an autoimmune illness in which antibodies become directed against the body's own cells, thereby inflicting tissue damage. Usually the immune system has little difficulty distinguishing self and non-self. For reasons not entirely understood, this discriminating ability breaks down in rheumatoid arthritic patients, resulting in chronic joint inflammation, usually in shoulders, elbows, hips, wrists, fingers, knees, ankles, and feet. Ultimately, cells of the synovial joint multiply at an abnormally faster rate, contributing to the swelling and, finally, filling up the joint space itself and eroding the cartilage and bone ends. Scar tissue may form, resulting in deformation and pain.

Rheumatoid arthritis, like other illnesses, has varied causes. For example, heredity seems sometimes to play a part through a blood protein called the "rheumatoid factor," which is found in about half of rheumatoid arthritics. The factor increases susceptibility, but does not always cause rheumatoid arthritis.

Research has not yet produced definitive conclusions as to why rheumatoid arthritis develops when it does in specific people. However, certain personality traits have been associated in many cases. According to Mason (1980, 128):

> The following are typical: shy, inhibited, masochistic, self-sacrificing, anxious, depressed, resentful, and repressed anger. People who possess these characteristics along with the rheumatoid factor are the most likely to be candidates for this disease; people who have a healthy psychological balance and risk factor rarely suffer from this disease.

My experience working with a handful of rheumatoid arthritic patients is consistent with references by a number of writers to a common pattern: emotional tension significantly worsens the symptoms.

> *A 48-year-old woman had developed rheumatoid arthritis soon after marrying at age 18 while pregnant. The swelling and pain had plagued her off and on ever since. Three years prior to her entering our hospital-based 12-week stress control program, her husband had left her after a bitter series of feuds in which she felt discounted and unloved. For several months after the split, she was almost totally bed-ridden with pain and swelling. Gradually, she made her way back to independence and strength, though she was still very vulnerable and emotionally unstable. During and after our work together, she enrolled in a community college, began to swim daily, and practiced deep relaxation. Her symptoms subsided in harmony with the increase in her physical fitness, confidence, and optimistic outlook toward the future.*

This case is consistent with studies showing that emotional distress, especially depression and anxiety, are sometimes tied to the exacerbation of this illness (Backus & Dudley, 1977; Crawford, 1981; Taylor, 1986; Weiner, 1977).

A study by Flor and Turk (1988) found that the belief systems and interpretation patterns had considerable bearing on pain and disability among a sample of rhuematoid arthritis patients.

Like other stress-induced or stress-aggravated illnesses, rheumatoid arthritis often can be contained, if not diminished, through an integrated program of stress management.

CANCER ▼

A hazard in discussing stress and cancer is that readers with cancer will conclude that they induced their own illness in a direct cause-effect fashion. Cancer is not that simple. No one knows for sure why cancer appears when and where it does. A number of factors can contribute: diet, carcinogens in the environment, viruses, the immune system, and others. While stress and personality probably do not cause cancer in a straightforward way, they may well play a part. Therefore, it is important to understand how they sometimes interrelate.

Everyone's body conducts its own continuous surveillance for outside invaders and internal imperfections, including cell mutations. Cell mutations, unpredictable changes in hereditary material, usually are recognized immediately and the deviant cell is quickly destroyed before it can multiply and turn into a wayward, uncontrolled tumor. But in rare instances, the mutant cells escape destruction, gradually multiply, and become a runaway tumor, sometimes consuming normal tissue and organs as they grow. If not stopped, the tumor can cause death as it impedes normal functioning of key body parts. In other instances, cancer can metastasize, a part breaking away to take up residence and multiply at another location in the body. This process of growth and metastasis can occur within a few weeks or over many years. Tragically, many cancers are not diagnosed and treated with radiation, chemotherapy, or surgery until too late.

The Role of Stress in Cancer

Stress sometimes contributes to cancer by weakening the body's immune system. McQuade and Aikman (1974, 76) have stated:

> Stress helps to cause cancer because it depresses the immune system, the body's only real means of defending itself against malignant cells. It does this through the action of the adrenal cortex hormones, which partly affect t-lymphocytes. Searching out foreign antigens in the body is one of the tasks of the t-lymphocytes, and significantly they measure at low levels in the tissues of most cancer patients.

Other studies have shown the number of t-cells to be lower in mice that have been exposed to stressful experiences (Riley, 1975). Though subject to criticism (Fox, 1978; Feist & Brannon, 1988), other studies have found an association between cancer and previous clustering of multiple life changes (Graham, et al., 1971; Horne & Picard, 1979). A study by Shaffer and others (1987) found a 16-times-greater incidence of cancer over a 30-year period among 972 physicians who had been tested as "loners," likely to suppress emotion when in medical school.

Emotional Factors in Cancer

What kinds of emotional patterns or experiences have been linked with increased risk of cancer? There are no simple answers since mind-body interplay here is quite complex and varied. Several studies, however, are suggestive. In a well-known study of 455 cancer patients, LeShan (1966, 482) found four common elements:

1. A childhood marked by loneliness, guilt and self-condemnation, usually because of painful, troubled relations with parents and siblings. Often this is accentuated by specific events, such as divorce, death of parent or sibling.

2. During late adolescence or early adulthood, the individual perceived a chance to come out of this deep loneliness by developing a "safe" relationship—usually with a spouse, child, or career. Feelings of isolation and loneliness greatly diminished, though never completely disappeared. A great deal of emotional investment was poured into this new linkage, which lasted anywhere from one to over forty years.

3. Then the safe world collapsed—retirement, death of spouse, children leaving home, divorce. On the surface, the person "adjusted," going about daily business as usual. But underneath, despair and hopelessness had returned. "Nothing gave them real satisfaction. It seemed to them as though the thing they had expected and feared all their lives—utter isolation and rejection—was now their eternal doom . . ."

4. Helplessness and hopelessness followed. Meaning and zest went out of life. Energy declined. The fantasy from childhood that something was basically wrong with them returned. At some time between six and eighteen months later, the cancer appeared.

This scenario does not lead inevitably to cancer. Rather, LeShans's work suggests an increased risk, given such a sequence of events.

A study of experimental mice by Vernon Riley (1975) of the Fred Hutchinson Research Center in Seattle also is suggestive. Laboratory mice born to mothers with a known mammary tumor virus were exposed to a variety of environmental stressors, including isolation and severe crowding. Mice demonstrated that mammary tumor occurrences in these already vulnerable offspring increased up to 90 percent under stress, but remained at seven percent in a protected stress-free environment. A generalization from experimental mice to humans cannot be made without extreme caution, yet this study is consistent with the position that stress may play a part in cancer. In *Getting Well Again,* Simonton, Simonton and Creighton (1978) cite other important studies.

Schmale and Iker (1966) noted a tendency among their female cancer patients to have given up, to have fallen into a sense of hopeless frustration in dealing with an unresolvable conflict. Their study revealed that this conflict often seemed to occur about six months before diagnosis of cancer.

Schmale and Iker then studied a sample of women who were presently cancer-free, but were determined to be a high biological risk for cancer of the cervix. After obtaining these women's scores on a psychological measure of "helplessness-prone personality," they predicted which ones would develop cancer. They were accurate 74 percent of the time. The authors did not claim that this proves that the feelings of helplessness causes cancer. Rather, they suggested that a helpless orientation may have been a contributing factor, along with others.

In another study, this one lasting 15 years, W. A. Greene (1966) investigated the previous personal and social experiences of patients who contracted leukemia and lymphoma. He found an unusually frequent incidence after a death or threat of death of a mother or, for men, a "mother figure" such as a wife. For men, other significant losses or threatened losses included job termination and career termination through retirement. For women, major losses included menopause or change of residence.

The linkage between stress and cancer is complex and not entirely understood. Controversy and disagreement remain (Cooper, 1984a; Cooper, 1984b; Blaney, 1985; Levy, 1985). It is safe to assert that there is considerable likelihood that stresses of certain types can, in some instances, increase chances of cancer. On the positive side, evidence was recently presented that group therapy can prolong survival time for breast cancer patients (Spiegel, 1990).

INSOMNIA ▼

Among self-observable signs of stress, Selye lists "insomnia, which is usually a consequence of being keyed-up." He also notes, "Muscular activity or mental work which leads to a definite solution prepares you for rest and sleep, but intellectual efforts which set up self-maintaining tensions keep you awake" (Selye, 1976, 175).

Difficulty sleeping takes two forms: inability to fall asleep (onset insomnia) and inability to sleep through the night. Onset insomnia usually results from being keyed-up or excessively aroused throughout the day and especially during the evening. The mind fails to quiet itself, and the body stays aroused. Even though physical fatigue may be very great, continuing excitation of the stress response makes quieting of brain waves into the delta zone, which is needed for sleep, difficult or impossible.

Either type of insomnia can result from excessive residual or anticipatory stress—inability to leave events, thoughts, and feelings from the previous day or mental preoccupation with events anticipated for the next day. In either case, the challenge is to control the mind, which in turn can exert control over bodily tension.

Occasional Insomnia

It is important to accept occasional insomnia without too much concern. A "high" from an intimate encounter, worry over something left unsaid or undone the previous day, excitement or worry about a challenge the next day—all will result in occasional sleeplessness, even for the healthy, well-balanced person. Missing part or even all of a night's sleep will have little effect on one's performance. As a collegiate middle-distance runner, one of my best-ever times came after not sleeping at all the previous night.

Some people find it useful to get up during a sleepless night to read, write, study, think, or work on some other project. This is one way to turn a potential problem—lack of sleep—into an opportunity. I view such nights as "gifts of time."

Chronic Insomnia

Quite a different matter is chronic insomnia, which can contribute to wear and tear and to stress build-up over days and weeks. Unfortunately, loss of sleep, worry, and tension often reinforce each other in a frustrating cycle, as shown in Figure 4-4.

Sometimes, this problem has purely physical origins (Moore, Clay, and Williams, 1990). When physical causes are not involved, the key questions with chronic insomnia are: Where is the disharmony creating chronic off-balance, tension, arousal? What needs to be done to resolve it? Meanwhile a number of steps can be taken to

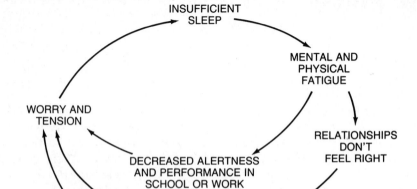

FIGURE 4-4. SLEEP AND STRESS

INSUFFICIENT SLEEP

MENTAL AND PHYSICAL FATIGUE

RELATIONSHIPS DON'T FEEL RIGHT

WORRY AND TENSION

DECREASED ALERTNESS AND PERFORMANCE IN SCHOOL OR WORK

STRESSOR

facilitate sleep: regular daily exercise, daily deep relaxation, deliberate steps to taper off activity during the evening, avoiding caffeine late in the day, and practice of specific techniques of relaxation just before and after going to bed. Such techniques are discussed in more detail in Chapter 8.

SUDDEN DEATH   ▼

Robert Eliot, who has written extensively on the role of stress in high blood pressure and heart disease, made a startling discovery during his service as a cardiovascular consultant to the U.S. space program in 1967: "Young aerospace workers, some as young as twenty-nine, were dropping dead of heart attacks at an alarming rate" (Eliot & Breo, 1984, 15). Though showing no unusual coronary risk factor patterns, these employees did experience dangerous levels of emotional stress.

> What I found instead were anxiety and depression and a universal, pervasive feeling of hopelessness and helplessness. Cape Canaveral families led the nation in drinking, drug-taking, divorce, and sudden heart attacks. The space workers were a whole population suffering from the acute stress of knowing that at any moment they could lose their work income, status, and identity as skilled professionals.
>
> At the lab, I analyzed autopsies of workers who had dropped dead without warning. What I found suggested that adrenaline and other stress chemicals had spewed into their bodies with such strength that they had literally ruptured the muscle fibers of their hearts. It appeared that the brain had the power to trigger heart-stopping emotional reactions to distress.

Stress not only contributes to illness, it can contribute to sudden death. George Engel (1971) has investigated the circumstances surrounding the unexplained sudden deaths of a large number of persons who died unexpectedly. Most were healthy at the time of their demise. Engel (1977, 118) discovered four categories of stressful life events that precipitated sudden death.

> The most common (135 deaths) was an exceptionally traumatic disruption of a close human relationship or the anniversary of the loss of a loved one. The second category (103 deaths) involved situations of danger, struggle, or attack. Loss of status, self-esteem, or valued possessions, as well as disappointment, failure, defeat, or humiliation, accounted for the third group of deaths (21 in all). And the fourth category (16 deaths) consisted of people who died suddenly at moments of triumph, public recognition, reunion, or "happy ending." Fifty-seven deaths in the first category were immediately preceded by the collapse or death—often abrupt—of a loved one. Some survivors were reported to have cried out that they could not go on without the deceased. Many were in the midst of some frantic activity—attempting to revive the loved, get help, or rush the person to the hospital—when they, too, collapsed and died.
>
> One common denominator emerges from the medical literature and the 275 press reports on sudden death. For the most part, the victims are confronted with events which are impossible to ignore, either because of their abrupt, unexpected, or dramatic quality or because of their intensity, irreversibility, or persistence. The individual experiences or is threatened with overwhelming excitation.
>
> Implicit, also is the idea that he no longer has, or no longer believes that he has, mastery or control over the situation or himself, or fears that he may lose what control he has.

Engel suggests these sudden deaths often can be explained by "derangement of cardiac rhythm" in response either to overwhelming discharge of catecholamines or to breakdown from rapid shifts between excitatory and withdrawal responses. Homeostatic balance within the organism is lost.

Engel (1971, 774) cites several specific cases:

> A dramatic example is the death of the 27-year-old army captain who had commanded the ceremonial troops at the funeral of President Kennedy. He died 10 days after the President of a "cardiac irregularity and acute congestion," according to the newspaper report of the medical findings.

> A 39-year-old pair of twins who had been inseparable died within a week of each other; no cause of death was mentioned.

> A 64-year-old woman who was said never to have recovered from the death of her son in an auto accident 14 years earlier died 4 days after her husband was murdered in a holdup.

While such incidents are rare, they illustrate the intricate mind-body connection and the extremes to which this linkage can go awry.

BOX 4-4

A CONTEMPORARY FABLE UPSTREAM/DOWNSTREAM

Here is a story about prevention versus treatment, wellness versus medicine.

"It was many years ago that villagers in Downstream recall spotting the first body in the river. Some old timers remember how spartan were the facilities and procedures for managing that sort of thing. Sometimes, they say, it would take hours to pull 10 people from the river, and even then only a few would survive.

"Though the number of victims in the river has increased greatly in recent years, the good folks of Downstream have responded admirably to the challenge. Their rescue system is clearly second to none: most people discovered in the swirling waters are reached within 20 minutes— many in less than 10. Only a small number drown each day before help arrives—a big improvement from the way it used to be.

"Talk to the people of Downstream and they'll speak with pride about the new hospital by the edge of the waters, the flotilla of rescue boats ready for service at a moment's notice, the comprehensive health plans for coordinating all the manpower involved, and the large number of highly trained and dedicated swimmers always ready to risk their lives to save victims from the raging currents. Sure it costs a lot but, say the Downstreamers, what else can decent people do except to provide whatever is necessary when human lives are at stake.

"Ah, a few people in Downsteam have raised the question now and again, but most folks show little interest in what's happening Upstream. It seems there's so much to do to help those in the river that nobody's got time to check how all those bodies are getting there in the first place. That's the way things are, sometimes."

SOURCE: Ardell (1979, 189). Donald Ardell publishes the *Ardell Wellness Report*. A free sample copy can be obtained by sending a SASE to *Ardell Wellness Report*, 9901 Lake George Drive, Orlando, FL 32817.

We have reviewed how stress can contribute to hypertension, coronary heart disease, migraines, rheumatoid arthritis, cancer, insomnia, and sudden death. All result from some direct or indirect difficulty with the stress response—a part of human experience so useful, yet potentially so harmful. Other illnesses shown to be linked with stress, as either a contributing cause or an aggravating influence, include back pain, certain dental disorders, asthma, allergies, irritable bowel syndrome, ulcerative colitis, panic attacks, premenstrual syndrome, and hyperthyroidism, premature births, and even certain eye disorders.

In Chapter 5 we will focus in more detail on Type A and hostility, factors shown in recent years to be significant contributors to stress-related disorders, especially heart disease.

REFERENCES ▼

American Heart Association. (1985). *Heart Facts.* Dallas.

American Psychiatric Association. (1987). *DMS-III R.* Washington, D.C.

Ardell, D.B. (1979). *High Level Wellness: An Alternative to Doctors, Drugs, and Disease.* New York: Bantam Books. Also see revised edition: (1986) Berkeley: Ten Speed Press.

Backus, F. I., & Dudley, D.L. (1977). Obsvervations of Psychosocial Factors and their Relationship to Organic Disease. In Z. J. Lipowski, D.R. Lipsitt, & P.C. Whybrow (Eds.), *Psychosomatic Medicine: Current Trends and Clinical Applications.* New York: Oxford University Press.

Benson, H. (1975). *The Relaxation Response.* New York: William Morrow.

Benson, H. (1984). *Beyond the Relaxation Response.* New York: Times Books.

Benson, H., Cotch, J.B., & Crasswell, K.D. (1978). Stress and Hypertension: Interrelations and Management. *Cardiovascular Clinics, 9,* 113-124.

Blanchard, E.B., & Andrasik, F. (1985). *Management of Chronic Headaches: A Psychological Approach.* New York: Pergamon Press.

Blaney, P.H. (1985). Psychological Considerations in Cancer. In N. Schneiderman & J.T. Tapp (Eds.), *Behavioral Medicine: The Biopsychosocial Approach,* 533-563.

Brandt, J., Celentano, D., Stewart, W., Linet, M. & Folstern, M.F. (1990). Personality and Emotional Disorder in a Community Sample of Migraine Headache Sufferers. *American Journal of Psychiatry, 147,* 303-308.

Chung, M.K., & Kraybill, D.E. (1990). Headache: A Marker of Depression. *The Journal of Family Practice, 31,* 360-364.

Cohen, J. (1977). Depression: The Sickness of the 70's. *San Francisco Chronicle,* April, 13.

Cottington, E.M. (1986). Job Stress and Suppressed Anger Lead to Hypertension. *Family Practice News, 16,* 43.

Cooper, C.L. (Ed). (1984a). *Psychosocial Stress and Cancer.* Chichester, England: Wiley.

Cooper, C.L. (1984b). The Social-Psychological Precursor to Cancer. *Journal of Human Stress, 10,* 4-11.

Crawford, J.S. (1981). The Role of Rehabilitative Medicine. In D.A.Gordon (Ed.), *Rheumatoid Arthritis.* New York: Medical Examination Publishing.

Dalack, G.W. & Roose, S.P. (1990). Perspectives on the Relationship Between Cardiovascular Disease and Affective Disorder. *The Journal of Clinical Psychiatry, 51 Supplement, 4-9.*

Eliot, R.S., & Breo, D.L. (1984). *Is It Worth Dying For?* New York: Bantam Books.

Eliot, R.S. (1989). Labile HT Is Found in About 17% of FPs; Prevalence Appears to Vary by Specialty. *Family Practice News, 19, 3)*

Engel, G.L. (1971). Sudden and Rapid Death During Psychological Stress. *Annaas of Internal Medicine, 74, 771-782.*

Engel, G.L. (1977) Emotional Stress and Sudden Death. *Psychology Today, 11, 115-121.*

Farley, F. (1986). The Big T in Personality. *Psychology Today, 20, 44-52.*

Farquhar, J.W., Fortmann, S.P., Flora, J.A., Taylor, C.B., Haskell, W.L. Williams, P.T., Maccoby, N, & Wood, P.D. (1990). Effects of Communitywide Education on Cardiovascular Disease Risk Factors: The Stanford Five-city Project. *Journal of The American Medical Association, 264, 359-365.*

Feist, J. & Brannon L. (1988). *Health Psychology: An Introduction to Behavior and Health.* Belmont, CA.: Worth Publishing Company.

Flor, H., & Turk, D.C. (1988). Chronic Back Pain and Rheumatoid Arthritis: Predicting Pain and Disability from Cognitive Variables. *Journal of Behaviorial Medicine, 11, 251-266.*

Fredrikson, M. & Matthews, K.A. (1990). Cardiovascular Responses to Behavioral Stress and Hypertension: A Meta-analytic Review. *Annals of Behavioral Medicine, 12, 30-39.*

Folkenberg, J. (1989). Ulcers and Stress: The Missing Link? *Psychology Today, 23, 24-25.*

Fox, B.H. (1978). Premorbid Psychosocial Factors as Related to Cancer Incidence. *Journal of Behavioral Medicine, 1, 45-133.*

Galton, L. (1973). *The Silent Disease.* New York: Signet.

Gannon, L.R., Haynes, S.N., Cuevas, J., & Chavez, R. (1987). Psychophysiological Correlates of Induced Headaches. *Journal of Behavioral Medicine, 10, 411-423.*

Genest, M. & Genest, S. (1987). *Psychology and Health.* Champaign, IL: Research Press.

Goode, E. (1990). Beating Depression. *U.S. News & World Report,* March 5, 48-56.

Graham, S. Snell, L.M., Graham, J.B., & Ford, L. (1971). Social Trauma in the Epidemiology of Cancer of the Cervix. *Journal of Chronic Diseases, 24, 711-725.*

Graham-Bonnalie, F.E. (1972). *The Doctor's Guide to Living With Stress.* New York: Drake, 102.

Green, J., & R. Shellenberger. (1991). *The Dynamics of Health and Wellness: A Biopsychosocial Approach.* Fort Worth: Holt, Rinehart and Winston.

Greenberg. S.F., & Valletutti, P.J. (1980). *Stress and The Helping Professions.* Baltimore: Brooks.

Greene, W.A. (1966). The Psychosocial Setting of the Development of Leukemia and Lymphoma. *Annals of the New York Academy of Sciences, 125, 794-801.*

Harburg, E., Schull, W.J., & Erfurt, J.C. (1970). A Family Set Method for Estimating

Heredity and Stress: A Pilot Study of Blood Pressure Among Negroes in High and Low Stress Areas. *Journal of Chronic Diseases, 23,* 69-81.

Harburg, E., Erfurt, J., & Chape, C. (1973). Socioecological Stress Areas and Black-white Blood Pressure: Detroit. *Journal of Chronic Diseases, 26,* 595-611.

Holroyd, K.A., Appel, M.A., & Andrasik, F. (1983). A Cognitive-behavioral Approach to Psychophysiological Disorders. In D. Meichenbaum & M.E. Jaremko (Eds.), *Stress Reduction and Prevention.* New York: Plenum Press.

Horne, R.L., & Picard, R.S. (1979). Psychosocial Risk Factors for Lung Cancer. *Psychosomatic Medicine, 41,* 503-514.

Howarth, E. (1965). Headache, Personality, and Stress. *British Journal of Psychiatry, 111,* 1193-1197.

Isselbacher, K. (1981). *Principles of Internal Medicine.* New York: McGraw.

Johnsgård, K. (1989). *The Exercise Prescription for Depression and Anxiety.* New York: Plenum.

Kannel, W.B. (1990). CHD Risk Factors: A Framingham Study Update. *Hospital Practice, 25,* 119-130.

Klein, D.F., & Wender, P.H. *Do You Have A Depressive Illness?* New York: New American Library.

Kunkel, R.S. (1990a). Office Management of Benign Headache Syndromes: I. Migraine Headache. *Modern Medicine, 58,* 50-58.

Kunkel, R.S. (1990b). Office Management of Benign Headache Syndromes: III. Tension-type Headache. *Modern Medicine, 58,* 62-74.

Leo, J. (1990). Looking for a Life of Thrills. *Time Magazine, 125,* 92-93.

LeShan, L. (1966). An Emotional Life-history Pattern Associated with Neoplastic Disease. *Annals of the New York Academy of Sciences, 125,* 780-793.

Levy, S.M. (1985). *Behavior and Cancer.* San Francisco: Jossey-Bass Publishers.

Lynch, J.J. (1985). *The Language of The Heart.* New York: McGraw-Hill.

Mason, J.L. (1980). *Guide To Stress Reduction.* Culver City, CA: Peace.

Manuck, S.B., Kasprowisz, & Muldoon, M.F. (1990). Behaviorally-evoked Cardiovascular Reactivity and Hypertension: Conceptual Issues and Potential Associations. *Annals of Behavioral Medicine, 12,* 17-29.

McQuade, W., & Aikman, A. (1974). *Stress.* New York: Bantam Books.

Moore, C., Clay, H., & Williams, R.L. (1990). Sleep Disorders: Practical Management. *Hospital Medicine, 26,* 96-104.

Mustacchi, P. (1990). Stress and Hypertension. *Western Journal of Medicine, 153,* 180-185.

National Headache Foundation. (1985). *Newsletter,* No. 55, 1.

Ogylvie, B.S. (1973). The Stimulus Addicts. *The Physician and Sports Medicine, 1,* 61-65.

Ornish, D. (1990). *Dr. Dean Ornish's Program for Reversing Heart Disease.* New York: Random House.

Ostefeld, A.M., & Shekelle, R.B. (1967). Psychological Variables and Blood Pressure. In J. Stamler, R. Stamler, and T.N. Pullman (Eds.), *The Epidemiology of Hypertension.* New York: Grune and Stratton, 321-331.

Pelletier, K.R. (1973). *Holistic Medicine: From Stress To Optimum Health.* New York: Delacourte Press.

Pelletier, K.R. (1977). *Mind As Healer, Mind As Slayer*. New York: Dell.

Pickering, T.G., & Gernin.,W. (1990). Cardiovascular Reactivity in the Laboratory and the Role of Behavioral Factors in Hypertension: A Critical Review. *Annals of Behavioral Medicine, 12*, 3-16.

Phillips, P. (1990). Bacterium-ulcer Link Clinched. *World Medical News, 31*, 17.

Riley, V. (1975). Mouse Mammary Tumors: Alterations of Incidence as Apparent Function of Stress. *Science, 189*, 465-467.

Rifkin, A. (1990). Solving Panic Disorder Problems. *Postgraduate Medicine, 88*, 133-138.

Rogers, A.I. (1990). Medical Treatment and Prevention of Peptic Ulcers. *Postgraduate Medicine, 88*, 57-60.

Ryan, R.S., & Travis, J.W. (1981). *Wellness Workbook*. Berkeley: Ten Speed Press.

Sanowski, R.A. (1990a). Peptic Ulcer Disease: Update on its Etiology and Diagnosis. *Modern Medicine, 58*, 46-47.

Sanowski, R.A. (1990b). The Changing Spectrum of Therapy for Active Peptic Ulcer Disease. *Modern Medicine, 58*, 50-51.

Schmale, A.H., &. Iker. H. (1966). The Psychological Setting of Uterine Cervical Cancer. *Annals of the New York Academy of Sciences, 125*, 807-813.

Selye, H. (1974). *Stress Without Distress*. Philadelphia: Lippincott.

Selye, H. (1976). *The Stress of Life*. (Rev.Ed.). New York: McGraw-Hill.

Shaffer, J.W., Graves, P.L., Swank, R.T., & Pearson, T.A. (1987). *Journal of Behavioral Medicine, 10*, 441-448.

Simonton, O.C., Matthews-Simonton, S., & Creighton, J.L. (1978). *Getting Well Again*. New York: Bantam Books.

Smith, M., Colligan, M., Horning, R.W., & Harrel, J. (1978). *Occupational Comparison of Stress-Related Disease Incidence*. Cincinnati: Cincinnati National Institute for Occupational Safety and Helth.

Spiegel, D. (1990). Group Therapy Said to Prolong Breast Cancer Survival. *Family Practice News, 20*, 9.

Tanner, O. (1976). *Stress*. New York: Time-Life Books.

Tennant, C. (1988). Psychosocial Causes of Duodenal Ulcer. *Australian and New Zealand Journal of Psychiatry, 22*, 195-201.

Thomas, G.S., Lee, P.R., Franks, P., & Paffenbarger, R.S., Jr. (1981). *Exercise and Health: The Evidence and The Implications*. Cambridge, MA.: Oelgeschlager, Gunn & Hain, Publishers.

Toffler, A. (1971). *Future Shock*. New York: Bantam Books.

Tollefson, G.D. (1990). Recognition and Treatment of Major Depression. *American Family Physician, 42* Supplement, 59S-69S.

Young, L.D., Richter, J.E., Bradley, L.A., & Anderson, K.O. (1987). Disorders of the Upper Gastrointestinal System: An Overview. *Annals of Behavioral Medicine, 9*, 7-12.

Weinberger, M.H. (1990). Advances in Hypertension in the 1980s. *Practical Cardiology, 16*, 58-65.

Weiner, H.M. (1977). *The Psychobiology of Human Illness*. New York: Elsevier.

Weinstock L.B., & Clouse, R.E. (1987). A Focused Overview of Gastrointestinal Physiology. *Annals of Behavioral Medicine, 9*, 3-6.

Whitehead, W.E., & Schuster, M.M. (1985). *Gastrointestinal Disorders: Behavioral and Physiological Basis for Treatment.* New York: Academic Press.

Wissler, R.W. (1990). Autopsy Findings in Large Study Confirm that CHD Starts Early. *Family Practice News, 20,* 7.

Wolf, S. (1965) *The Stomach.* New York: Oxford.

Wolff, H.G. (1950). Life Stress and Cardiovascular Disorders. *Circulation, I,* 187-203.

Zegans, L.S. (1982). Stress and the Development of Somatic Disorders. In L. Goldberger & S. Breznitz (Eds.), *Handbook of Stress: Theoretical and Clinical Aspects.* New York: Free Press, 134-152.

Zuckerman, M. (1979) *Sensation Seeking: Beyond The Optimal Level of Arousal.* Hillsdale, NJ: Lawrence Erlbaum Associates.

Type A Behavior and Hostility: Causes, Effects, and Alternatives

Chapter 5

CHAPTER 5

I. EARLY STUDY OF EMOTIONS AND THE HEART

II. WHAT IS TYPE A BEHAVIOR?
A. Insecurity of Status
B. Sense of Time Urgency
C. Hyperaggressiveness
D. Free-Floating Hostility
E. The Drive to Self-Destruction
F. Other Type A Qualities
G. Type A Behavior and the Social Environment
H. Gender and Type A Behavior

III. TYPE B BEHAVIOR
A. Absence of Time Urgency
B. Absence of Free-Floating Hostility
C. A Sense of Self-Esteem
D. Type B's as Leaders

IV. DIAGNOSING TYPE A BEHAVIOR

V. ROOTS OF TYPE A BEHAVIOR
A. Social-Cultural Roots
   1. Value on Material Gain
   2. Infatuation with Speed
   3. Competitiveness
   4. People as Numbers
   5. Secularization
   6. "Atrophy" of the Body and the Right Brain
B. Socialization of Type A Behavior
   1. Through the Family
      a. Instruction
      b. Social Modeling
      c. Reward and Punishment
   2. Through the School
   3. Through Television

VI. EFFECTS OF TYPE A BEHAVIOR
A. Quality of Life
B. Heart Disease and Other Causes of Death

VII. HOSTILITY: THE HARMFUL COMPONENT OF TYPE A BEHAVIOR
A. Toxic and Benign Elements of Hostility

Every now and then, a concept from the behavioral sciences so captures the public's attention that it enters into mass consciousness and becomes part of our common parlance. *Type A behavior* is one such term. As noted in Chapter 2, Type A behavior has been one of the most intensely studied topics in the stress field.

For this reason, and because so many readers of this book no doubt display at least some Type A qualities, the topic warrants a chapter by itself. This chapter has three goals: to deepen your understanding of Type A behavior, to clear up several popular misconceptions (including the mistaken notion that Type A behavior is all bad), and to provide guidelines and techniques for preventing and managing Type A behavior, especially its most harmful component: hostility.

We will describe the historical antecedents of this concept, what Type A behavior is, how it is reinforced by American culture and socialization, its measurement, its effects on health and well-being, and how and why it has these effects. We then will discuss the one component of Type A behavior, hostility, that is most toxic. Finally, we will explore various approaches for preventing and managing Type A behavior, especially hostility.

EARLY STUDY OF EMOTIONS AND THE HEART ▼

The idea that emotions affect the heart is hardly new. Redford Williams notes that, "Over the centuries, two Roman emperors, a Catholic pope, and a king of Spain have been reported to have died suddenly while in the throes of acute emotional distress" (Williams, 1989, 18). We noted in Chapter 2 that as early as the 17th century some physicians spoke of the link between emotions and heart problems. For example, William Harvey, one of the founders of modern physiology and medicine, wrote in 1628 that, "Every affection of the mind that is attended with either pain or pleasure, hope or fear, is the cause of an agitation whose influence extends to the heart" (Williams, 1989, 19). In 1868 a German doctor, T. von Deusch, described the person prone to heart attacks as often speaking in a loud voice and working through the night (von Deusch, 1868).

While a professor of medicine at Oxford University, Sir William Osler contributed some of the most significant early ideas about mind-body connections (Osler, 1892). As Williams points out, Osler specifically wrote important insights about the role of emotions in heart disease. Osler described the typical heart patient as ". . . not the delicate, neurotic person . . . but the robust, the vigorous in mind and body, the keen and ambitious man, the indicator of whose engine is always at 'full speed ahead'" (cited in Williams, 1989, 19). Osler saw coronary heart disease as caused by ". . . the high pressure at which men live and the habit of working the machine to its maximum capacity" (Williams, 1989, 19).

More recently, Menninger and Menninger (1936) wrote about heart patients' frequent tendency toward an aggressive personality. Dunbar (1943), another pioneer of psychosomatic (mind-body) medicine, went a step further, believing heart patients possessed a coronary-prone personality. Dunbar's sample was based on nonstructured interviews with only 22 patients, more than half of whom shared a common cultural heritage, since they were Jewish (Storement, 1951; Weiss, et al., 1957). Since these observations were based on patients already diagnosed with heart disease, nothing was proven. Still needed were studies of the development of coronary disease in individuals who exhibited some or all of these emotional tendencies but who at the outset of the study were free of the disease (Roskies, 1987).

BOX 5-1. EMOTIONS AND THE HEART IN EVERYDAY LANGUAGE

A few years ago, a friend and fellow Chicoan, Ruth Hornaday, began to experience symptoms of heart valve disease. Open heart surgery eventually corrected the problem, but along the way she inquired deeply into the interplay of emotions and the heart, a subject that interested her for both personal and professional reasons, as a heart patient and a psychotherapist.

In the course of her studies, she was struck by the multitude of linkages in our common language between emotions and the heart. Here is the list she constructed from various sources and passed along to me one day during a morning walk at our Enloe Hospital Cardiac Rehabilitation Program.

Heartaches & sorrows	Down hearted
Heartaches & suffering	Faint hearted
Heartburn	Heavy hearted
Soft hearted	Hard hearted
Hardened his (her) heart	Big hearted
Light hearted	Bleeding heart
Weak hearted	False hearted
Chicken hearted	Broken hearted
Understanding heart (responds)	Aching heart

Lonely heart	Tender hearted
Stingy hearted	Black hearted
Cracked heart	Heartsick & weary
Sick at heart	Heart like a stone
Heart of stone	Disheartened
Heart pounding like a (trip) hammer	Heart fluttering
Bent heartstrings	Plucked the strings of my heart
Pain in my heart	Played on heart strings
Take heart	On the strings of my heart
Lose heart	Pure in heart (See God)
Corner of my heart	Change of heart
Pain in my heart	Bottom of my heart
Warmed my heart	Learned by heart
Warmed the cockles of my heart	Eat "hearty"—"hearty" appetite
Eat your heart out	Right to the heart of. . . .
The heart of the matter	Heart association
Heart fund	Touched my heart
"A merry heart doeth good like a medicine" (Bible)	Like a knife in my heart (betrayal)
Cut to the heart (neg feeling of hurt)	Heart if closed off
Open hearted & open heart surgery	
Cross my heart & hope to die	

In the 1950s, Friedman and Rosenman led a team of medical scientists investigating the role of cholesterol and other risk factors in the development of coronary artery disease. After finding that as much as half of all heart attacks could not be explained by "conventional risk factors" (for example, family history, cigaret smoking, high blood pressure, elevated cholesterol), they began to suspect that emotions or personality should be studied.

Not only were they influenced by the early hunches of Harvey, von Deusch, Osler, the Menningers and others, they were influenced by a couple of leads of their own. One was the casual observation by an upholstering company that the front edges of the waiting room seats in Friedman and Rosenman's clinic seemed to be unusually worn down. The workmen wondered what kind of patients came here—

people who would be so impatient and on edge that they would wear down the front edge of the seats (Friedman and Ulmer, 1984).

The other lead came from what Friedman has described as the "first bona fide research effort in this field," a study of 40 volunteer public accountants (Friedman and Ulmer, 1984, 6).

> The blood cholesterol of these accountants and also the speed at which their blood clotted in January, 1957 was completely normal and remained so when they were studied biweekly for the remainder of January and through February and March. During these same months the accountants did not alter either their eating or exercise habits. During the first two weeks of April, however, as the tax-filing deadline approached and our subjects were desperately striving to finish their clients' tax forms and get them signed and in the mail, their average blood cholesterol level rose abruptly and their blood began clotting at a dangerously accelerated rate. In May and June, with no further deadlines to face, the blood cholesterol and clotting times of these men returned to normal levels. For the first time in medical history, a clear-cut demonstration of the power of the mind alone to alter man's blood cholesterol and clotting time had been achieved.

When this finding was reported at the annual scientific meetings of the American Heart Association, it met with dead silence (Friedman, Rosenman & Carroll, 1958). Scientific experts in the audience were highly skeptical that anything other than diet could affect cholesterol level in the bloodstream.

When Friedman and Rosenman applied for government agency funding to conduct a broader study of the effect of "emotional stress" on coronary heart disease, they were twice turned down. After inquiring what had gone wrong, they were advised informally to avoid the term "emotion" in their grant application in order not to offend psychiatrists who reviewed the applications—and who apparently believed that cardiologists could not possibly be equipped to study emotional matters. Said a government employee, "I believe you fellows are describing a behavior pattern, something you've actually witnessed. Why don't you just label it Type A behavior pattern?" (Friedman and Ulmer, 1984, 6). They did, they were funded—and a new term entered the American lexicon.

Before summarizing the results of this research, it is important to describe the nature of Type A behavior.

WHAT IS TYPE A BEHAVIOR? ▼

In their informative book, *Treating Type A Behavior and Your Heart*, Friedman and Ulmer (1984, 31) provide the following definition of Type A behavior.

> Type A behavior is above all a continuous struggle, an unremitting attempt to accomplish or achieve more and more things or participate in more and more events in less and less time, frequently in the face of opposition—real or imagined—from other persons. The Type A personality is dominated by covert insecurity of status or hyperaggressiveness, or both.

The various components of Type A behavior and their relationships to "pathophysiological processes" are described in Figure 5-1 (Friedman and Ulmer, 1984, 70). Let us examine several of these key components.

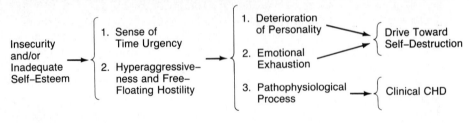

FIGURE 5-1. THE NATURE OF TYPE A BEHAVIOR AND ITS OUTCOMES

Source: Friedman & Ulmer (1984, 70).

INSECURITY OF STATUS

Why do Type A persons engage in their incessant, never-ending struggle? The key reason is that they typically suffer from a hidden lack of self-esteem which in turn results in "insecurity of status." Thus, they feel compelled to compare themselves with others. They usually come out looking deficient in their own eyes. A fascinating by-product of this perceived deficiency is greater tendency to self-referencing in conversation (Fontana, et al., 1990), part of an on-going struggle to protect or enhance self-esteem.

Self-esteem is a product of the gap between self-expectations and personal achievement. Type A's usually hold such unrealistically high expectations of themselves and are so self-critical that they feel chronically driven to do more and get more—with never a let-up.

SENSE OF TIME URGENCY (HURRY SICKNESS)

Type A behavior is a common antecedent to perpetual overload, as noted in more detail in Chapter 10. Out of her or his insecurity and low self-esteem comes the Type A's struggle with time. Most often this means, very simply, taking on more obligations or commitments than time available—and then taking on still more.

The person swirling in this maelstrom feels driven, yet overwhelmed. The only way out seems to be to accelerate, to speed-up. Friedman and Ulmer (1984, 37) point out:

> To keep up with his overload of projects, the Type A is forced to accelerate the rate at which he thinks, plans, and executes almost all his daily functions. Thus he increases not only his own rate of speech, but also forces others to speak more quickly to him; attempts to read and write faster; to walk and eat faster; to drive his car as fast and as cleverly as he can without actually violating traffic regulations (or getting caught at it). Even his minor activities will be accelerated. For example, the male Type A may seek to shave faster by discarding soap, brush, and blade for the most efficient electric razor he can find. One Type A physician friend of ours has already bought ten different electric

razors, in a search for the one that shaves fastest. And we know of three Type A's who use two electric razors, so that they can save time by shaving both sides of the face simultaneously!

One notable aspect of time urgency is "polyphasic thinking and behavior"—thinking and doing more than one thing at a time. Not satisfied with accomplishing enough every minute of the day, the Type A person, consciously or not, tries to get still more done by doing (or thinking about) more than one thing at a time.

Commonly this takes the form of thinking about something else while "listening" during a conversation. While on the phone, he or she might read the paper, write a check, prepare dinner, or check the mail. He might read the paper and eat breakfast—while shaving. Or read the morning paper while driving to work.

HYPERAGGRESSIVENESS

To possess a high achievement-orientation means to strive for high goals. Hyperaggressiveness goes beyond that to include a desire to dominate, with little regard for the feelings or rights of others (Friedman and Ulmer, 1984). As author Jess Lair once stated, "Before I had my heart attack, I didn't have any friends. When I played poker, I played to win from the bastards" (Friedman and Ulmer, 1984, 33).

This pattern often develops very early, sometimes manifesting itself in the play and social habits of small children. Low self-esteem and status insecurity usually accompany this characteristic even at an early age.

As Type A's become frustrated in their incessant struggles, their self-esteem is further damaged—and they struggle even more, typically causing still more aggressiveness.

FREE-FLOATING HOSTILITY

"Free-floating hostility is a permanently indwelling anger that shows itself with ever-greater frequency in response to increasingly trivial happenings" (Friedman and Ulmer, 1984, 34). The person with this pattern is perpetually agitated. In their earlier book, Friedman and Rosenman referred to this tendency as AIAI (Anger, Irritation, Aggravation, Impatience).

The Type A person generally sees the darker side of other people, displaying suspiciousness and distrust. Free-floating hostility is always present and ready to be triggered by whatever the Type A person judges to be wrong. This may be almost anything in the environment—too-loud stereos, slow store clerks, laughter of children, the neighbor who has not mowed his grass for three weeks, a co-worker who displays idiosyncratic habits, government regulations, welfare mothers who should be working, police who aren't tough enough in enforcing traffic laws, the idiot-driver in the next freeway lane, and more.

Friedman and Ulmer (1984, 34) report:

One of our Type A patients, for example, having stopped for a red light, lit a cigarette just as the signal turned green. The female motorist behind him honked several times. Reacting, he slowly got out of his car, sneeringly smiled at her and then sauntered to the front of his car, opened the engine hood, and pretended to look for some mechanical breakdown. "I think the bitch got the message," he later remarked to a friend.

THE DRIVE TO SELF-DESTRUCTION

Less obvious, especially to the Type A person himself or herself, is the drive toward self-destruction. This was not apparent to Friedman and Rosenman when they wrote *Type A Behavior and Your Heart* in 1974. Subsequently, it has become more clear.

To illustrate this point, Friedman and Ulmer (1984, 41) quote Henry Kissinger's comment about Richard Nixon: "It was hard to avoid the impression that Nixon, who thrived on crisis, also craved disasters." A close friend told Peter Sellers' son after Sellers's death, "Your father was always searching for a bloody heart attack as if it were a letter he knew had been posted and hadn't arrived" (Friedman and Ulmer, 1984, 41).

Type A's usually feel the crush of their pressured lifestyle and know they cannot sustain it indefinitely. Thus, they unconsciously pursue some avenue of escape, some way out. Friedman and Ulmer (1984, 41) quote these heart attack patients as they lay in their respective intensive care units.

"I'm glad it finally came. I just couldn't seem to find any other way to get out from under all the junky stuff loading me down."

"It may seem strange to you, but I knew I was going to get this attack and I sort of looked forward to it."

"I wouldn't ever admit this, not even to my wife, but I knew this was coming and so I wanted to get it over with, one way or the other. And frankly, I didn't care a damn which way it came out just as long as I didn't have to have someone wheeling me around the rest of my life."

OTHER TYPE A QUALITIES

The components above are the core elements of Type A behavior. Others include:

▼ A tendency to use numbers a great deal when thinking and talking.

▼ Failure to use imagery, metaphors, and similes.

▼ Love of competition.

▼ Intense concentration and alertness.

TYPE A BEHAVIOR AND THE SOCIAL ENVIRONMENT

It is important to note that Type A behavior can remain latent or can become overtly manifest, depending upon the social situation. If a person with Type A tendencies lives and works in a culture, subculture, or work setting that is relatively easy-going with a preponderance of Type B people, the Type A person may never display many of his Type A qualities. The same person in a rapid-paced, frenetic setting is much more likely to show her or his Type A personality.

This fact is consistent, of course, with the transactional, coping theory of stress of Lazarus and Folkman (1984) noted in Chapter 2, since from the point of view of this theory, stress is the result of the interplay between situation and self.

Before reading about Type B behavior, you are invited to read Box 5-2, which presents a hypothetical scenario of Mr. A and Mr. B. This example helps to convey the contrast between the two patterns. Then turn to Exercise 5-1 to compare these scenarios with your own experience.

GENDER AND TYPE A BEHAVIOR

It is important to realize that Type A behavior characterizes women as well as men in our society (Lawler, et al., 1990; Thoreson & Low, 1990). To be sure, most of the Type A qualities we have described seem to fit more readily into a male perspective and style of life. Yet, as Friedman and Ulmer (1984) have noted, there has been a dramatic rise in Type A behavior among women since the 1970s, as more women have entered workplaces dominated by Type A men and a Type A climate of work. More recently, Bedeian, Mossholder, and Touliatos (1990) found that males and females respond differently to similar work-related challenges. For example, hours worked and role conflict tend to be associated with Type A behavior among men but not women. Greenglass (1990) found that university faculty women tended to be much more Type A than Type B and that the greater the Type A behavior, the greater the conflict of their work roles with family roles, mostly because Type A women worked longer hours.

Research investigators have found a four times higher incidence of coronary heart disease among Type A employed women than Type B employed women (Haynes, 1984). Yet for reasons not well understood, women are more likely to develop angina pectoris (chest pain from inadequate flow of blood through the coronary arteries to the heart muscle) as their first sign of blocked arteries than men, for whom myocardial infarction (heart attack) is usually the first sign. Perhaps women simply recognize and acknowledge the early warning sign of anginal chest pain earlier than do men.

BOX 5-2

ONE DAY IN THE LIFE OF MR. A AND MR. B

Potential Stressors	Mr. A: (Stressed, ineffective responses)	Mr. B: (Relaxed, effective responses)
1. 7:00 A.M. Alarm clock did not go off. Overslept.	**Action** Rushed through shaving, dressing. Left without any breakfast.	**Action** Called colleague to say he would be 30 minutes late. Got ready for work and breakfasted as usual.

Potential Stressors	Mr. A: (Stressed, ineffective responses)	Mr. B: (Relaxed, effective responses)
	Thoughts I can't be late. This is going to foul up my whole day.	**Thoughts** This is not a big problem. I can manage to make up the 30 minutes later on.
	Results Left home in a hurried state.	**Results** Left home in a relaxed state.
2. 8:00 A.M. Traffic jam caused by slow driver in fast lane.	**Action** Honked horn, gripped steering wheel hard; tried to pass and later tried to speed.	**Action** Waited for traffic jam to end. Relaxed and listened to the radio while waiting; later drove at his normal rate.
	Thoughts Why can't that jerk move into the slow lane? This infuriates me.	**Thoughts** I'm not going to let this upset me because there is nothing I can do about it.
	Results Blood pressure and pulse rate rose. Arrived at work hurried and harried.	**Results** Remained calm and relaxed. Arrived at work fresh and alert.
3. 10:00 A.M. Angry associate blew up over a staffing problem.	**Action** Was officially polite but nonverbal behavior signaled impatience and anger.	**Action** Relaxed while listening attentively and mentally rehearsed how to handle this encounter. Remained calm in demeanor.
	Thoughts This guy is a prima donna. I can't tolerate outbursts like these; I'll never get my work done.	**Thoughts** Beneath all his anger he does have a point. I can take care of this problem now before it gets more serious.
	Results Associate stormed out unsatisfied. Mr. A.	**Results** Associate's temper was calmed. He thanked Mr.

Potential Stressors	Mr. A: (Stressed, ineffective responses)	Mr. B: (Relaxed, effective responses)
	was too aggravated to take care of important business on his agenda.	B. for hearing him out. Mr. B. was glad that he was able to take care of the problem.
4. 12:00 noon. Behind.	**Action** Ate lunch in office while working. Could not find needed materials in files. Made telephone calls but parties were out.	**Action** Went for a 20-minute walk in park. Ate lunch in park.
	Thoughts I'll never get out from under all this work. I'm going to plow through this if I have to work through dinner.	**Thoughts** A break in routine refreshes me. I work better when I allow myself intervals to relax.
	Results Made mistakes in work because of exasperation.	**Results** Returned refreshed. Proceeded with work rapidly and with fresh insight.
5. 11:00 P.M. Bedtime	**Action** Couldn't get to sleep. Had insomnia for two hours.	**Action** Fell asleep rapidly.
	Thoughts Why don't I accomplish more? I am a disappointment to myself and my family.	**Thoughts** This has been a good day. I'm glad I was able to head off several potential problems.
	Results Awoke exhausted and depressed.	**Results** Awoke refreshed and happy.

SOURCE: Farquhar (1978, 64).

After reading Box 5-2, consider these questions:

1. To what extent can you identify with the experiences of Mr. A and Mr. B?

2. What specific similarities do you see between characteristics of Mr. A and Mr. B, on one hand, and yourself, on the other?

3. From this comparison, what do you see about yourself that you would like to change? Be specific.

TYPE B BEHAVIOR ▼

We noted at the beginning of the chapter that the image of the Type A individual has become very well-known throughout this society as the term "Type A" has taken hold in our language: a person who is hurried, hassled, driven, irritable, quick-tempered. Much less attention has been given either by scholars or by popular writers to the Type B person. The image we do often hear about is that Type B's lack ambition and are rather dull.

Friedman and Ulmer (1984, 71) point out that this image of the Type B individual is quite inaccurate.

> It is important to us that no one get the idea that all Type B's lead sane but dull lives, or that their main excitement in life comes from changing the brand of cereal they eat at breakfast, the route they drive to work, or the television programs they view in the evening. Actually ... many Type B's live magnificent lives, lives in which their capacity to appreciate beauty, affection, and creative novelty offers them the chance to experience a myriad of wonderful events—the first flowering of a cattleya orchid they have been nurturing, their grandchild stutter-mumbling his first sentence, the shy smile of thanks of an old lady on the street, granted because they took the time to notice her existence by smiling at her. Some Type A men *talk* with more spice and zing, but Type B's often *do* far more satisfying things.

Type B behavior is the absence of any of the qualities we have described. Friedman prefers to label as Type A anyone who displays even one of the Type A qualities, even though such a person would be a mild Type A (Friedman and Ulmer, 1984). The more of these qualities a person possesses, the more Type A she or he is. Thus, Type A ranges from very mild to very severe. Let us examine Type B behavior.

ABSENCE OF TIME URGENCY

Friedman and Ulmer (1974) point out that Type B's are distinguished by being on "gracious terms with time." That is, they seldom experience time urgency. They are responsible and diligent in relation to time, but they seem able to move through their day without the Type A's "overtones of frenzy and rage."

One Type B quoted Jonathan Swift in explaining his attitude toward time: "Whoever is out of patience is out of possession of his soul." Type B's take "the long view" toward their activities, being more concerned with the calendar than the minute and second hands of their watch. Type B's feel sufficiently secure not to feel compelled to approach every task from the point of view of a deadline.

Type B's find it easier to delegate, since they are more likely to accept others', including subordinates', divergent ways of doing things. By contrast, Type A's usually delegate with reluctance, trepidation and impatience, sure that tasks will not be completed to their high standard.

Friedman and Ulmer (1984, 74) note the contrast between Lyndon Johnson, a flaming Type A with constant impatience, a monumental temper, and a critical attitude toward most around him, and Harry Truman. Truman no doubt would have agreed with Thoreau's statement that, "Nothing can be more useful to a man than a determination not to be hurried." His cousin remarked that, "There was no sense of frantic urgency, no burning need to hurry; Harry was always a deliberate man."

Type B's usually take time for contemplation. They value each moment and are less compulsively preoccupied with the future than Type A's. They take time to appreciate themselves, as well as those they care about. Type A's seldom "have time."

ABSENCE OF FREE-FLOATING HOSTILITY

Unlike Type A's, Type B's need not control everyone and everything in their environments. Because of their greater personal security, they find it reasonable to tolerate diversity in the thinking and actions of those around them. Consequently, Type B's are frustrated much less often by the flow of daily events.

Friedman and Ulmer (1984, 76) tell this humorous story about the contrast between Type A's and Type B's in toleration.

> In recent years, we have run into a curious illustration of the way Type A men, in marked contrast to Type B's, are likely to take the silliest things seriously. More than half of them seem to be prepared to argue heatedly about the manner in which a toilet paper roll is placed in its receptacle: so that the paper unrolls over the top, or comes out underneath. It may be hard to believe, but we have witnessed grown men very nearly come to blows over this issue. The medieval churchmen who fought over how many angels can dance on the head of a pin must have been Type A's.

> The blunders of other drivers make a Type B more cautious. A Type A becomes irritated, angered, and even outraged. Because Type B's are able to overlook small mistakes by others, their family life is marked by less tension and displays of AIAI.

Perhaps most importantly, Type B's are more able to practice empathy—to put themselves in the shoes of the other, to see events through her or his eyes. They seldom sermonize to their spouses or children and seldom find it necessary to resort to corporal punishment. They find it much easier than Type A's to express affection.

Why the relative absence of hostility in Type B's? Again, the answer is their higher self-esteem and sense of personal security.

A SENSE OF SELF-ESTEEM

Friedman and Ulmer maintain that the most important difference between Type A's and Type B's is that Type B's possess adequate, rather than deficient, self-esteem. Type B's, having received a greater abundance of unconditional love and afffection, grow up believing they are worthwhile human beings—irrespective of their achievements. Consequently, they find no need to develop the burning drive to win approval through unending achievements.

This does not mean Type B's are unmotivated to succeed or that they don't work hard. But Type B's are more likely to feel at peace with themselves whether or not they are accomplishing something. And their self-expectations are ". . . in healthy balance with their perceived capabilities" (Friedman and Ulmer, 1984, 78).

A man well over 90 years of age told a friend of his secret to a long and happy life: "My mother told me to always do the best I could and be satisfied with the result. I've tried to do just that" (Freidman and Ulmer, 1984, 78).

As Type B's give and receive love and affection from those close to them, their self-esteem is further enhanced.

TYPE B'S AS LEADERS

It is a myth that one must be Type A to succeed in America. Type A's who make it to the top generally do so despite many of their Type A qualities, not because of them. Are aggravation, impatience, anger, or irritability assets in any profession? Doubtful.

Friedman and Ulmer present the following data to make the case that many

TABLE 5-1. THE PRESENCE OF TYPE A AND TYPE B BEHAVIOR IN 106 NATIONAL LEADERS

TYPE OF LEADERS	TOTAL NUMBER	TYPE A BEHAVIOR	TYPE B BEHAVIOR
1) University Presidents	11	6 (55%)	5 (45%)
2) Bank Presidents	5	3 (60%)	2 (40%)
3) Corporation Chairmen	30	21 (70%)	9 (30%)
4) Generals, Admirals	11	6 (55%)	5 (45%)
5) Archbishops, Bishops, Rabbis	4	2 (50%)	2 (50%)
6) Journalists, Publishers	22	16 (73%)	6 (27%)
7) Nobel Laureates	11	6 (55%)	5 (45%)
8) Congressmen, Senators	7	3 (43%)	4 (57%)
9) Federal Judges	5	2 (40%)	3 (60%)
Total:	106	65 (62%)	41 (39%)

SOURCE: Friedman and Ulmer (1984, 81).

Type B's make it to the top of their professions. They note that the overall percentage of Type A's among these leaders (62 percent) is less than the estimated percentage of Type A's in the general urban male population (75 percent).

DIAGNOSING TYPE A BEHAVIOR   ▼

How do you know the degree to which you are Type A? (Note that the question is posed as a matter of degree rather than either–or.) Two main techniques have been developed for measuring this pattern. First, Friedman and Rosenman have developed a structured, videotaped interview that is designed to elicit the verbal and body language signs of Type A behavior. The judges who study these videotapes base their assessments on the criteria listed in the following exercise.

Check those criteria you think apply to you. The more you check, the greater the possibility that you exhibit a Type A pattern. Ask someone who knows you to do the same.

EXERCISE 5-2. MANIFESTATIONS OF TYPE A BEHAVIOR

Identifying and Assessing Hyperaggressiveness and Free-Floating Hostility

Psychomotor Signs

_____ a. Facial hostility which usually reveals itself in the set of the jaw and mouth muscles and the belligerence of the eyes. On occasion, something approaching a chronic sneer is evident.

_____ b. A tic-like grimace in which the corners of the mouth are twitched back, partially exposing the teeth. When this grimace is observed, it invariably indicates the presence of severe free-floating hostility.

_____ c. A hostile, jarring laugh.

_____ d. Fist-clenching during ordinary conversation.

_____ e. Unpleasant, frequently irritating, grating speech.

_____ f. Frequent use of Anglo-Saxon obscenities.*

_____ g. Teeth-grinding.

_____ h. A tic-like tendency to open the eyes widely, exposing the whites around the pupil.*

Biographical Manifestations

_____ a. Eagerness to undertake all activities in a spirit of competition.

_____ b. Intense compulsion to win at all costs, even when playing in minor contests or with pre-teen-age children.

_____ c. Inclination to dominate in social as well as in business situations.

_____ d. Easily aroused irritability, particularly in regard to the actions of other persons which do not conform to his sense of propriety or correctness.

_____ e. Fixed and angrily defended opinions on various sociological, economic, and political matters.

_____ f. Failure to be elated or joyful at the success of others.

Diagnosis and Assessment of a Sense of Time Urgency

Psychomotor Signs (Voice and Body)

_____ a. Facial tension and, often, a tense body posture.

_____ b. Rapid blinking (over 30 times per minute).*

_____ c. Rapid speech, with characteristic elision or telescoping of the terminal words of sentences.

_____ d. Hurrying or interruption of the speech of others.

_____ e. Sucking in one's breath during speech while continuing to speak.*

_____ f. Rapid, vigorous finger-tapping or jiggling of knees.

_____ g. Browning of skin of eyelids and of skin immediately below the eyelids. This tan pigmentation is due to a chronic excess discharge of a pigment-inducing hormone (melanocyte-stimulating hormone, MSH) by the pituitary gland. Unlike the tan coming after exposure to excess sunlight, this type of periorbital pigmentation never seems to disappear. Although it is by no means common to all persons exhibiting Type A behavior, its presence in Caucasians invariably indicates severe Type A behavior and usually a relatively high level of serum cholesterol.

_____ h. Lip-clicking while speaking.* (If you compress your lips closely, bring the tip of your tongue to the back of your upper incisors and then open your mouth quickly, you will make this sound.)

_____ i. Expiratory sighing.* This brief sigh or muffled grunt occurs during breathing out. It is usually preceded by a slight lifting of the shoulders.

_____ j. Head-nodding while speaking.* Normal persons often nod affirmatively while someone is speaking to them, to show their agreement with what is being said. Type A nodding occurs in the speaker while he himself is speaking.

_____ k. Rapid body movements. The Type A tends to move and act rapidly.

_____ l. Excessive perspiration on forehead and upper lip.*

Biographical Manifestations

_____ a. Self-awareness of impatience.

_____ b. Pace of activities so rapid as to attract frequent advice from others to slow down.

_____ c. Difficulty in sitting and doing nothing.

_____ d. Intense dislike of waiting in line.

_____ e. Fast walking, fast eating, and unwillingness to dawdle at table after meals.

_____ f. Habitual substitution of numbers for metaphors and nouns, even in casual conversations.

_____ g. Polyphasic thought and actions. As already noted, the Type A has a strong tendency to attempt to think of or do more than one thing at a time.

Most Type A's also exhibit at least six of the above listed 12 psychomotor signs indicative of the presence of a sense of time urgency: rapid speech with elision of the terminal words of sentences, hurrying or interrupting the speech of others, rapid finger-tapping or jiggling knees, lip-clicking, head-nodding when speaking, and rapid body movements. Most Type A persons will admit having all of the biographical manifestations associated with a sense of time urgency. On the other hand, fewer than two percent of Type A's exhibit profuse facial sweating.

*Newly discovered indicator
SOURCE: Friedman & Ulmer (1984, 57–60).

The second way Type A behavior is measured is through questionnaires. Friedman and his associates maintain that questionnaires are a less effective measure than interviews. Nevertheless, it may increase your self-awareness to complete the Pace of Life Index below.

EXERCISE 5-3. PACE OF LIFE INDEX

Indicate how often each of the following applies to you in daily life. After you have checked the appropriate column, total your score using the number that appears above each column.

	3 Always or Usually	2 Sometimes	1 Seldom or Never
1. Do you find yourself rushing your speech?	_____	_____	_____
2. Do you hurry other people's speech by interrupting them with "umha, umhm" or by completing their sentences for them?	_____	_____	_____
3. Do you hate to wait in line?	_____	_____	_____
4. Do you seem to be short of time to get everything done?	_____	_____	_____
5. Do you detest wasting time?	_____	_____	_____
6. Do you eat fast?	_____	_____	_____
7. Do you drive over the speed limit?	_____	_____	_____
8. Do you try to do more than one thing at a time?	_____	_____	_____

	3 **Always or Usually**	2 **Sometimes**	1 **Seldom or Never**
9. Do you become impatient if others do something too slowly?	_____	_____	_____
10. Do you seem to have little time to relax and enjoy the time of day?	_____	_____	_____
11. Do you find yourself over-committed?	_____	_____	_____
12. Do you jiggle your knees or tap your fingers?	_____	_____	_____
13. Do you think about other things during conversations?	_____	_____	_____
14. Do you walk fast?	_____	_____	_____
15. Do you hate dawdling after a meal?	_____	_____	_____
16. Do you become irritable if kept waiting?	_____	_____	_____
17. Do you detest losing in sports and games?	_____	_____	_____
18. Do you find yourself with clinched fists or tight neck or jaw muscles?	_____	_____	_____
19. Does your concentration sometimes wander while you think about what's coming up later?	_____	_____	_____
20. Are you a competitive person?	_____	_____	_____

Total Score _____

EXERCISE 5-4. QUESTIONS ABOUT THE PACE OF LIFE INDEX

Here are categories for assessing your score.

45–60 High Type A behavior
35–44 Medium Type A behavior
20–34 Low Type A behavior

1.   Is your score higher than you wish?

2.   During the next two days, focus on reducing Type A behavior by modifying two or three specific things on which you scored "always or usually."

3.   Ask your mate or a friend to rate you on this scale. Then ask for his or her suggestion for how you might slow down, if needed.

ROOTS OF TYPE A BEHAVIOR   ▼

Consideration of the causes of Type A behavior brings attention to two inter-related questions. First, what is there about modern Western society that seems to breed such a high—and probably increasing— rate of Type A behavior? Second, what happens in the early lives of specific persons that causes Type A behavior to develop? In short, we need to focus on social- cultural antecedents and socialization patterns.

SOCIAL-CULTURAL ROOTS

Friedman and Rosenman (1974) suggest that in the past, even in prehistoric times, there probably were some individuals who were engaged in a chronic struggle to achieve more "numbers" and who were hostile toward their families and others in their clan or tribe. Yet they probably were the exception. Why has Type A behavior grown to such a point that, in America and most other Western countries, perhaps three of four persons in most urban areas display this pattern? What is there about contemporary urban-industrial, Western society that causes this phenomenon?

Friedman and Rosenman (1974; Rosenman, 1986; Rosenman, 1990) correctly point out that emergence of Type A behavior probably is the combined result of personality and social environment. They point to several environmental factors in American society.

Value on Material Gain

First, early New England Puritanism gave way to "an unbridled drive to acquire more and more of the world's material benefits." As early as 1835, Alex de Tocqueville was struck by Americans' acquisitiveness.

This quest for things sometimes takes the form of pursuing money for its own sake, as though merely possessing it had intrinsic meaning. Writing in *Fortune* magazine, Myron Magnet (1987, 26) recently called attention to the glorification of "the money society" during the 1980s. (See Box 5-3 for excerpts)

BOX 5-3. THE MONEY SOCIETY

"Money, money, money is the incantation of today. Bewitched by an epidemic of money enchantment, Americans in the Eighties wriggle in a St. Vitus's dance of materialism unseen since the Gilded Age or the Roaring Twenties. Under the blazing sun of money, all other values shine palely. And the . . . decade acclaims but one breed of hero: He's the honcho with the condo and the limo and the Miro and lots and lots of dough.

"The evidence is everywhere you turn. Open the scarlet covers of the Saks Fifth Avenue Christmas catalogue, for starters, and look at what Santa offers today's young family, from Dad's $1,650 ostrich-skin briefcase and Mom's $39,500 fur coat to Junior's $4,000 15-mph miniature Mercedes, driven by a 5-year-old Donald Trump look-alike in pleated evening shirt, studs, and red suspenders. Take a stroll along Manhattan's Madison Avenue and gape at the Arabian Nights' bazaar of shop windows, where money translates life's commonest objects into rarities, rich and strange. Behold embroidery-encrusted sheets fine enough for the princess and the pea, or ladies' shoes as fanciful and elaborate as any that artisans painstakingly toiled over when Marie Antoinette graced the throne, or sumptuous lace underwear that makes the inconspicuous consumption and adds the charm of wealth to the ordinariness of seduction. Visit Bijan, the temple of excess on Rodeo Drive and Fifth Avenue, and pick up five matched crocodile suitcases for $75,000—yes, thousand—perhaps to be filled with business shirts at $550 and $650 apiece.

". . . An overwhelming 93% of recently surveyed teenage girls deemed shopping their favorite pastime, way ahead of sixth-rated dating. Back in 1967, around 40% of U.S. college freshmen told pollsters that it was important to them to be very well off financially, as against around 80% who listed developing a meaningful philosophy of life as an important objective. But by 1986 the numbers had reversed, with almost 80% aspiring plutocrats as against 40% philosophers.

". . . Today, we obsessively talk about money almost nonstop: how much they paid for their house, their boat, their painting; how big the deal was; how much this one makes—and that one and that one.

". . . Says historian Maury Klein, 'Money tends to be more or less important in an age, depending on the degree of turbulence and social change that is taking place.' Like the rapidly urbanizing and industrializing era of the robber barons, Klein says, ours is an 'age where traditional self-identities are under great attack and great strain just from the pace of change. In that situation, money becomes a way of defining who you are by what you have.' That way of defining a self is rampant in the money society.

"Now we live in a world where all values are relative, equal, and, therefore, without authority, truly matters of mere style. Says Dee Hock, former chief of the Visa bank-card operation, 'It's not that people value money more but that they value everything else so much less—not that they are more greedy but that they have no other values to keep greed in check.' Or as University of Pennsylvania sociologist E. Digby Baltsezz puts it, 'When there are no values, money counts'"

SOURCE: Magnet (1987, 26-31).

EXERCISE 5-5. THE MONEY SOCIETY AND YOU

After reading about "the money society" in Box 5-3, consider the following questions.

1. Do you agree or disagree with the writer's basic premise that the United States is "the money society"? Why?

2. To what degree and in what ways are you influenced by "the money society"?

3.   If you are a college student, which is more important from your education, a clear philosophy of life, or wealth? Why?

4.   What values compete with money in your own life? Explain.

5.   How, if at all, can "the money society" lead to specific components of Type A behavior?

Infatuation with Speed

Friedman and Rosenman point to a second social-cultural factor contributing to a high rate of Type A behavior in America: our collective infatuation with speed. As Friedman and Rosenman (1974, 194) note, we seem to have accelerated our minds and behavior as our machines have sped up, sometimes at considerable cost.

> Your great-grandfather, for example, trotting along in his horse-drawn buggy at a leisurely pace, might very well have stopped to chat with a passing neighbor for ten minutes or so. Encased in your car, you will be fortunate even to glimpse your neighbor as you each hurtle by. That both of you might stop and pass the times of day is wholly unthinkable. It is as if your automobiles might resent the interruption. If that sounds silly, think about it. Isn't there truth in the idea that the faster a machine is made to operate, the faster the operator feels he must think and act?

Urbanization and industrialization have encouraged and reinforced this acceleration in the pace of daily life. Specialization increases as we hire out many things we need to have or need to get done. This is done in part, of course, because we cannot possibly have the expertise to manufacture our own automobiles, washers, and refrigerators. But in part, specialization is driven by a desire to save time. As Friedman and Rosenman (1974, 195) state, "We take turns selling each other our services, always hoping that the exchange will somehow save us a bit of time."

Yet in the process we each get tied into interdependent relationships in which we deal with others whom we know are time-conscious. Thus, we try to do things a bit faster, both to save time for ourselves and to satisfy those we know to be dependent upon us. All this is reinforced, of course, by the quest for money we discussed above. The frequent result of these influences of material acquisitiveness and quest for speed often is Type A behavior.

Competitiveness

Competitiveness, deeply embedded in our culture, heightens chances of Type A behavior (Rosenman, 1990). This is an open society—relatively speaking. We believe in an open contest in the race for wealth, power and prestige. The reality, of course, is that not all have an equal chance. Some are given a head start, others are handicapped at the starting line—by race, sex, social class, even community or region of residence. Still, we must all compete and, as Friedman and Rosenman (1974, 195) state, "It is performance, not pedigree, that achieves high economic status."

However, many people over-respond, taking competition so seriously that it becomes a way of life, infusing all aspects of life—work, driving, leisure activities, conversation. This "excess of competitive spirit" (Friedman and Rosenman, 1974,

195) usually goes hand in hand with time urgency and further heightens chances of Type A behavior. Van Egeren (1990) refers to this as the "success trap." Partly as a result, Type A's tend to have a stronger need for control and less interest in cooperating with others on tasks (Clark & Miller, 1990).

People As Numbers

Our society's bureaucratization and computerization add to the trend toward quantification—turning people into numbers and encouraging a view of life based on numbers. We are standardized and stripped of individuality by all levels of government, the bank, the insurance company, the mortgage company, the phone and utilities, and more. This trend only encourages the Type A tendency toward a world view based on categories and numbers.

Secularization

Secularization adds to this world view and loss of sense of individuality. Friedman and Rosenman (1974) maintain that the decline of the church, of belief in the sacred, of faith in a force or being larger than self—all add to susceptibility to materialism, empty competitiveness, and linking self-esteem to achievement. These losses also have helped contribute to declines of intimacy and social connectedness, individual competitiveness, and acceleration in the struggle to acquire and achieve. Some replace faith and social anchorage with a never-ending struggle to make it in society. Frustration, irritability and hyperaggressiveness—elements of Type A behavior— sometimes result.

"Atrophy" of the Body and the Right Brain

Friedman and Rosenman speculate that our reliance on rationality and machines have led to "atrophy" of both the body and non-rational parts of the brain. Because we are relatively inactive in the course of daily living, tensions mount as arousal turns into bound energy. At the same time, the part of the brain (the right hemisphere) having to do with music, poetry, appreciation of beauty, and other aspects of aesthetic living becomes relatively inactive. For some, Type A behavior emerges as a result.

These, then, are several ways Type A behavior is produced in relatively high rates by this society. Yet not everyone becomes Type A. According to Freidman and Rosenman (1974), perhaps a third become clearly Type B. This means there are differences in socialization, personality development and individual choice.

Let us now examine some of the socialization influences likely to produce the Type A pattern. In a sense, these intervene between the cultural-social roots reviewed above and the individual. Stated differently, these socialization influences may help explain how Type A-related factors in the larger environment get into the individual.

SOCIALIZATION OF TYPE A BEHAVIOR

Disagreement exists among experts as to the likely contribution of genetic inheritance to Type A behavior. Both animal and human studies suggest there might be inborn differences between individuals in such attributes as hyperreactivity, hyperaggressiveness, and hostility (Matthews and Krantz, 1976; Krantz and Durel, 1983; Rose,

Grim, and Miller, 1984; Williams, 1989; Swan, Carmelli, and Rosenman, 1990). Yet most specialists agree that environment and social learning probably play a far greater part in the emergence of Type A behavior (Freidman and Rosenman, 1974; Glass, 1977; Price, 1982; Friedman and Ulmer, 1984; Williams, 1989).

We will never know precisely how much environment and heredity cause Type A behavior. As long as environment plays some part—and it no doubt is the more important of the two—then Type A behavior can be prevented and changed. It becomes important, then, to understand both its cultural-social roots and how it is taught to children (Blaney, 1990).

Through the Family

Price (1984) maintains children are socialized into the Type A pattern through the family in three main ways.

INSTRUCTION. Children who continually are told to "hurry up," "try harder," "never waste time," "do it perfectly or don't do it at all," or "always strive to be number one" soon learn the lesson that the way to please parents is to unremittingly strive for achievement and perfection. The child internalizes these messages very early and accordingly begins to form habits of thinking and feeling with an appropriate orientation (Elkind, 1981).

SOCIAL MODELING. Even the most subtle actions of parents are copied by children. As noted earlier, one characteristic of Type A behavior is hypervigilance—being constantly on the alert for something threatening to happen. As Price (1982, 52), says:

> Being hypervigilant implies the need to be in a state of constant readiness prepared for something to happen. One way a child learns hypervigilance is by observing his parents in a chronic state of anticipation of threat from their external environment. A child whose parents are always on the alert for hidden challenges across the dimensions of situation and time would be expected to grow up thinking such behavior was completely appropriate, even necessary. Similarly, parents who are engaged in a chronic struggle against time and other persons may teach their children by example to be Type A. Parents who are hard-driving, set excessively high performance standards for themselves, rejoice when their achievements are recognized by others, and reproach themselves when they fail to meet their self-imposed standards are likely to produce children who exhibit these characteristics.

Price also points out that children are most likely themselves to take on the behavior patterns of their parents if they value the consequences they see their parents derive from that behavior. Examples of perceived benefits from Type A behavior include recognition, wealth, prestige, and self-esteem.

REWARD AND PUNISHMENT. Children learn habits of thinking, feeling and behavior from repeated patterns of reward and punishment as well. Children are born helpless and physically dependent. During her early years, the child also becomes emotionally dependent. If the environment is seen by the child as threatening—for example, if parents are unresponsive, unloving, or highly unpredictable—she may develop a response pattern of suspiciousness, dread, and anticipation of threat (Price,

1982). If this social style continues, she is likely at some point to become hostile and angry—precursors to Type A behavior.

This pattern of development receives support from research from Waldron et al. (1980) who found that Type A men were more likely than Type B men to report that they had fathers who were more severe, punished physically more often, and produced feelings of resentment from such punishment. Type A women, too, recall being punished physically more often than Type B women. Such child-rearing experiences also are more likely to result in diminished self-esteem, further reinforcing a need to prove oneself through performance and further raising the likelihood of anger and hostility.

Perhaps equally powerful is the experience of parents giving approval for performance and perfection while giving disapproval for moderation or "underperformance" (as perceived by the parent). In such environments, children learn that their parents' love is contingent on achievement. They conclude they must continually strive for peak performance and for behavior that is beyond reproach.

Several studies have reported that adolescents who have high achievement needs come from homes where parents have set high goals and frequently reward them for achievement behavior (Crandall, Preston, and Rabsen, 1960; Smith, 1969). Mothers have been found to habitually escalate the performance standards of their Type A sons more often than mothers of Type B sons (Matthews and Krantz, 1976). Such child-rearing practices emphasize outcome over process.

EXERCISE 5-6. RAISING THE PERFECT TYPE A CHILD

If you wanted to raise the perfect Type A boy or girl from birth, how would you go about it? What messages would you repeatedly send? How? How would you use rewards and punishments? What example would you set?

Through the School

Price (1982) points out that the school also is a major transmitter of Type A beliefs and behavior. Schools not only emphasize competitiveness and achievement as part of the "covert curriculum," they also promote time urgency through reinforcement of timed tasks, rapid learning and test performance, and chronic overload (Cohen, Matthews, and Waldron, 1978). Self-esteem comes to be contingent on performance. One learns the implicit message that self-worth is gained through comparison with others.

In conducting stress management workshops, I usually have participants complete the 50-item Distress Symptom Scale (See Exercise 4-4). The highest average scores I have seen during the past decade have been among "gifted" junior and senior high school students. Their tension and obvious sense of internal pressure no doubt reflect the socialization patterns we have discussed in both the school and the family. Type A behavior often results.

Through Television

American eighth-graders watch an average of 21.7 hours of television each week (Superintendent of Documents, 1990). The average 18-year-old has spent more time watching TV than any other single activity other than sleep. Evidence exists that a good part of the programming and commercials emphasize the very qualities that comprise Type A behavior. For example, Gerbner (1972) found some years ago that characters most often portrayed on television are assertive, aggressive, and violent. DeFleur (1964) found leading characters to be most often clever, aggressive, temperamental, and hardened. As Price notes (1982, 54), ". . . it is almost always the relentlessly hard-driving policeman, detective, or doctor who obtains the greatest and most coveted rewards of recognition, power, and material gain."

Price (1982) also points out that children's cartoons and even *Sesame Street* are exceedingly fast-paced and may promote chronic time urgency. Television commercials place high value on Type A behavior: for example, a young executive barking commands to his secretary while talking simultaneously on two phones—following which he gets into his luxury car and drives off into the sunset. The message is clear: if you engage in this type of hurried, polyphasic, aggressive, frantic activity, you too can succeed in the only ways that really count—prestige and wealth.

It is clear, then, that every day we observe on television the idea that self-worth is tied to things and achievement, that a fast-paced life is inherently good, and that being hard-driving—perhaps even a bit nasty—is the way to go. For many, especially those whose families, schools, and friends emphasize the same things, Type A behavior gradually emerges.

EXERCISE 5-7. INFLUENCES TOWARD TYPE A BEHAVIOR IN YOUR CHILDHOOD

After reading the above section on socialization of Type A behavior and thinking back on your own childhood, you are invited to answer the following questions.

1. What specific family influences toward Type A behavior can you recall?
2. School influences?
3. Media influences?
4. To what extent and in what specific ways were you—and are you still—affected by these influences?

EFFECTS OF TYPE A BEHAVIOR

Type A behavior inherently is neither good nor bad. Rather, it is to be judged by its consequences. Like most things in life, it has mixed effects, some positive, some negative.

Most research on the effects of Type A behavior has focused on coronary artery disease, heart attacks and cardiac-related mortality. Later we will examine this research literature. Before doing so, however, let us examine the effects on quality of life.

QUALITY OF LIFE

While there may be positive benefits of some elements of Type A behavior (for example, being hard-driving helps one get ahead and complete tasks—including those that may be socially beneficial), my research indicates that, on balance, its effects are more negative than positive.

Participants in my 10-session community class, Reducing Perfectionism, Irritability and Hurry Sickness, complete before and after the class the Personal Stress Assessment, a questionnaire measuring various aspects of stress, health, and quality of life. Included is the Pace of Life Index, a 20-item measure of Type A behavior.

When we compare several of these quality of life measures among those who are Type A and Type B (top and bottom quartiles on the Pace of Life Index), we find that Type A's come out significantly less positively on every single variable. When compared with Type B's, Type A's display the following:

More distress symptoms	Less happiness
Less internal control	Less fun and playfulness
More depression	Lower self-esteem
More emotional tension	Less energy and vitality
Less life satisfaction	More anxious reactivity
Less health satisfaction	More irritability and anger
Less job satisfaction	More time-related stress
Less home satisfaction	

These findings are consistent with personal reports from many of my students from both community and campus classes. They often report that life seems like a constant struggle. They feel perpetually overwhelmed, pressed, frustrated, and unhappy. Relationships usually are rocky and a source of added frustration. One study also found a higher incidence of upper respiratory infections among Type A students compared with Type B's (Stout and Bloom, 1982). Another found a higher incidence of migraine headaches (Woods, et al., 1984). The same researcher, as well as others, have found a wide range of more frequent symptoms and illnesses among Type A's (Woods and Burns, 1984; Offutt and Lacroix, 1988; Suls and Sanders, 1988).

In a recent study of Type A behavior among runners, 572 members of six Northern California running clubs completed the Pace of Life Index (Schafer and McKenna, 1985). They also provided other information about their health patterns, including stress and running injuries. The results were striking and significant: the higher the Type A behavior, the greater the distress symptoms, the higher the perceived stress level during the past three months, the more the running injuries, the greater the number of running days missed or reduced because of injury, the greater the number of health-care appointments because of running injuries, the more the days of work missed because of illness, and the greater the number of health-care appointments for illness other than injuries. Runners are likely to be protected to some degree from ill effects of Type A behavior, although this has not been proven by research studies. Even so, the greater the Type A behavior, the more adverse the effects on stress and health.

In the same study, we were interested in the emotional results of being injured. Most devoted runners know it is never easy to adjust to sedentary living when they cannot run because of injury. Having one's pursuit of performance goals interrupted makes it even more frustrating. But how do Type A's and Type B's respond differently? One might suspect that Type A's would find it especially difficult.

All runners find it very difficult to interrupt their running when injured. But significantly, Type A runners react with even more emotional upset. Our survey asked, "When you have been forced to stop or reduce your running because of injury, how have you been affected in each of the following ways—more, less, or no change?" Responses of Type A's and Type B's are shown in Table 5-2.

Whatever the impact of Type A behavior on illness and injury, it is clear that it tends to erode quality of life. This is reflected in questionnaire responses by participants in my class offered through the Enloe Hospital Stress and Health Center for modifying Type A behavior.

Recent studies by Bryant and Yarnold (1990) reported that Type A college

TABLE 5-2. TYPE A AND TYPE B RESPONSES TO RUNNING INJURIES

PERCENT REPORTING	TYPE A	TYPE B
More tense	76	62
More irritable	76	58
More anxious	71	53
More depressed	70	57
Less energetic	63	55
Less restful sleep	45	42
Less satisfied at work or school	40	37
More physical stress symptoms	38	31
More family conflicts	34	19
Less sociable	31	21
More withdrawn	28	18
Less productive at work or school	26	20

SOURCE: Schafer and McKenna (1985, 251).

students report more positive scores of subjective well-being and emotional state. These findings, discrepant with mine, might result from different measures or samples. Alternatively, they might suggest that Type A's begin with more emotional vigor and positiveness early in adulthood, but that this subjective "advantage" disappears over the years, since my sample's average age was early forties.

To be sure, there may be positive elements of Type A behavior, as suggested earlier—drive, ambition, dedication, high personal standards. Unfortunately, these potential positive ingredients often are accompanied with the negative and harmful elements of hostility, chronic time urgency, struggle, hyperaggressiveness, and irritability.

BOX 5-4

EXERCISE: A BUFFER AGAINST TYPE A BEHAVIOR?

The following table, based on a survey of 129 college students, suggests that if you are Type A (or Type B), distress symptom scores are lower by exercising five or more times per week than three or fewer times per week. Notice that distress symptom scores are highest for Type A's who exercise infrequently and lowest for Type B's who exercise frequently.

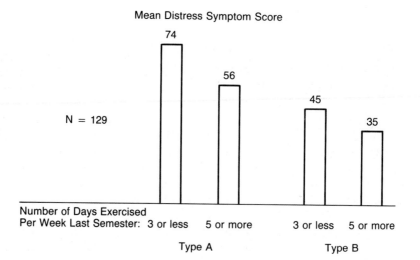

Mean Distress Symptom Score

N = 129

Number of Days Exercised
Per Week Last Semester: 3 or less   5 or more   3 or less   5 or more

Type A   Type B

MEASURES

Exercise: "On the average last semester, how many days per week did you exercise for at least 20 minutes?"

Distress symptoms: Distress Symptom Scale (See Chapter 4).

Type A Behavior: Pace of Life Index (See page 157).

HEART DISEASE AND OTHER CAUSES OF DEATH

We noted earlier that physicians as long ago as the 17th century suspected that emotions affected the heart. It was not until the 1960s that the first scientific investigators, Friedman and Rosenman, began systematically to examine the effect of Type A behavior on coronary artery disease and heart attacks.

Coronary artery disease (CAD), the number one cause of death in this country, is the progressive buildup of plaque on the inside of the coronary arteries which supply blood to the heart muscle. Medical scientists have long known that a number of risk factors increase chances of CAD:

Family history (especially heart attacks before age 50)

High blood pressure

High cholesterol in the blood

Cigaret smoking

Overweight

Physical unfitness

Diabetes

Being male (pre-age 50)

Friedman and Rosenman concluded after several years of research that in combination these risk factors account for less than half of all heart attacks in this country. We noted earlier in the chapter that they suspected back in the 1950s that emotions or personality might help explain much of the remaining incidence of heart attack.

In the early 1960s Friedman and Rosenman created a longitudinal, prospective research design to study the impact of Type A behavior among previously heart-healthy subjects. The results of this Western Collaborative Group Study made headlines everywhere (Friedman and Rosenman, 1971). Over the 8½ years of the study, Type A subjects were twice as likely to suffer from coronary disease, to have heart attacks, and to die from heart attacks than Type B's. This effect held up even after Type A and Type B subjects were equated on such potential confounding factors as smoking, elevated blood cholesterol, and high blood pressure.

This and other early studies prompted two panels of scientific experts to conclude that Type A behavior indeed is a risk factor for heart disease, that it exerts an effect independent of other risk factors, and that it is equal in impact to high blood pressure, elevated cholesterol, and cigaret smoking (Review Panel, 1981).

Subsequent studies documented that not only could Type A behavior predict to coronary artery disease and heart attacks, but also to degree of coronary disease (for example, number of blocked arteries and percentage of blockage in given coronary arteries) (Blumenthal, et al., 1978; Frank, et al., 1978; and Zyzanski, et al., 1976).

Experts continue to speculate as to why Type A bevhaior has these harmful cardiovascular effects. Possible mediating pathways include increased insulin and adrenaline secretion of Type A's, their greater blood pressure volatility, the tendency of Type A's to secrete more cholesterol and platelets when under pressure, and their greater difficulty in removing cholesterol from the bloodstream (Friedman and Rosenman, 1974; Friedman and Ulmer, 1984; Abbott and Sutherland, 1990; Rosenman, 1990).

As noted at the beginning of the chapter, Type A behavior entered into the common language of most Americans as a result of these studies and the publicity that ensued. Wives and friends hastened to warn Type A's to slow down and simmer down—mostly to slow down. Wisely so, since the costs appeared to be high, both for quality and length of life.

Yet the full scientific story had not yet been written about Type A behavior. For by the mid-1980s a series of new studies, most notably the Aspirin Myocardial Infarction Study (Shekelle, et al., 1985) and the Multiple Risk Factor Intervention Trial, MRFIT (Case, et al., 1985), reported no association at all between Type A behavior and coronary artery disease, heart attacks, or heart attack-induced deaths. (For a review of these and other negative studies, see Matthews and Haynes, 1986; Haynes and Matthews, 1988; Rosenman, 1990). To some extent, these negative findings might have resulted from measurement problems (Haynes and Matthews, 1988; Rosenman, 1990).

Yet, as Williams (1989) has noted, euphoria turned to uncertainty among behavioral medicine and cardiology researchers in this field. As Joel Dimsdale stated in a 1988 *New England Journal of Medicine* editorial (Dimsdale, 1988, 110):

> It is important to acknowledge that something is going on in terms of the relation between personality and heart disease. However, the nature of that influence is far more complex than is conveyed by the simple assertion that Type A behavior is a risk factor for coronary heart disease.

Then clarity and renewed optimism began to return. For scientists now turned to a new question. Might there be one or more components of Type A behavior that are harmful to the heart, even if the syndrome as a whole might not be? After a series of studies in which the negative effects of the various Type A elements were separated out, attention focused on one key component: *hostility.*

HOSTILITY: THE HARMFUL COMPONENT OF TYPE A BEHAVIOR   ▼

Regrouping 50 questions from the Minnesota Multiphasic Personality Inventory (MMPI), Cook and Medley previously had developed a hostility scale (Cook and Medley, 1954). Using this scale as their measure of hostility, a series of investigators found a definite association between hostility, on one hand, and coronary artery disease, heart attacks, and all-cause mortality, on the other. Here is a sampling of those studies (Smith and Pope, 1990; Swan, Carmelli and Rosenman, 1990):

▼ Williams and colleagues (1980) found that the higher the hostility score among 424 Duke heart patients, the greater the likelihood of having one or more blocked coronary arteries.

▼ Shekelle and colleagues (1983) reported higher mortality from heart disease, cancer, and all causes among 1877 middle-aged men (employees of Western Electric) who had scored high on the Cook-Medley measure 20 years before.

▼ University of North Carolina researchers found a seven-times-higher mortality rate by age 50 from all causes among a group of physicians who had scored high on the MMPI hostility scale 25 years before, when compared with those who had scored low on that same scale (Barefoot, Dahlstrom, and Williams, 1983).

▼ Using a new 27-item combination of hostility items from the Cook-Medley scale, Barefoot and others (1988) found that over a 20 year period the death rate (all causes) was four times higher among high than low hostility individuals among 118 lawyers.

▼ Williams and Siegler (1990) found that college students who scored high on a hostility scale in the 1960s were significantly more likely 20 years later to have elevated total cholesterol and lowered levels of HDL, the good kind of cholesterol.

TOXIC AND BENIGN ELEMENTS OF HOSTILITY　　▼

Just as Type A behavior has toxic and benign components, so apparently does hostility. Kenneth Dodge, a Vanderbilt psychologist who specializes in the study of aggressive children, recently grouped the Cook and Medley hostility items from the MMPI into six categories. Redford Williams (1989, 67) summarizes these categories as follows:

Cynicism: a generally negative view of humankind, depicting others as unworthy, deceptive, and selfish; reflects beliefs regarding the behaviors of others or toward the world in general, with the target of this behavior unspecified.

Hostile Attributions: a tendency to perceive others as intentionally trying to harm one; suspicion, paranoia, and fear of threat to self.

Hostile Affect: the experience of negative emotions in association with social relationships; admissions of anger, impatience, and loathing, when dealing with others; does not imply overt actions on the basis of the emotions.

Aggressive Responding: a tendency to use anger and aggression as a response to problems, or to endorse these behaviors as reasonable and justified; overt interpersonal behavior is indicated or implied.

Social Avoidance: admission that one avoids others; does not have the flavor of interpersonal confrontation contained in the other groups above.

Other: a miscellaneous category for items that do not fit any of the other groups' definitions.

The study of lawyers cited above (Barefoot, et al., 1988) found that combining three of these six (Cynicism, Hostile Affect, and Aggressive Responding) predicted increased mortality more accurately than did the previously used 50-item hostility scale. As Williams states, this revised 27-item scale measures ". . . a cynical and untrusting view of humankind, the frequent experience of negative emotions when dealing with others, and the frequent expression of overt anger and aggression when faced with frustration or problems" (Williams, 1989, 69).

This triad, then, seems to be not only dysfunctional but dangerous to your health: a cynical attitude, frequently aroused anger feelings, and a tendency to display anger overtly (Smith and Pope, 1990). See Exercise 5-8 for Redford Williams' three-question index of these toxic elements of hostility.

EXERCISE 5-8. THREE-QUESTION INDEX OF HOSTILITY

1. When family members or even persons I don't know do things (or fail to do things) that hold me up or prevent me from doing something I wish to do, I begin to think that they are selfish, mean, inconsiderate, and the like:

NEVER   SOMETIMES   OFTEN   ALWAYS

2. When strangers, friends, or members of my family do things that seem incompetent, messy, selfish, or inconsiderate, I quickly experience feelings of frustration, anger, irritation, and even rage; at the same time I become aware of these feelings, I notice unpleasant bodily sensations, like trouble getting enough breath, my heart pounding rapidly in my chest, my palms sweating, and the like:

NEVER   SOMETIMES   OFTEN   ALWAYS

3. When I have the thoughts, feelings, and bodily sensations just described, I am very likely to express my feelings in some way—whether by words, gestures, tone of voice, or facial expressions—to the other person or persons whom I see as responsible for my unpleasant thoughts and feelings:

NEVER   SOMETIMES   OFTEN   ALWAYS

SOURCE: Williams (1989, 174).

PHYSIOLOGICAL LINKAGES BETWEEN HOSTILITY AND HEART DISEASE   ▼

Proof that hostility helps cause coronary artery disease rests on research findings showing that hostility precedes CAD in time and on identification of physiological pathways between the two. Research on these physiological linkages is as yet in an early stage. Yet Williams maintains enough is known to identify tentatively two inter-related processes (Williams, 1989).

First, hostile individuals (like Type A persons more generally) have been found to be physiologically more reactive to challenge than nonhostile persons. Stated differently, they are more likely to display heightened "emergency branch" (that is, sympathetic nervous system and endocrine) reactions under pressure, as in a timed mathematics quiz in a laboratory. This physiological volatility may damage coronary arteries directly through the impact of adrenaline and nor-adrenaline on the inner walls of the arteries. And, indirectly, it may do harm through repeated episodes of blood pressure and cholesterol elevation. Still further, the greater emotional and cognitive vigilance of hostile persons tends to be associated with heightened testosterone secretions. We know that testosterone tends to decrease high density lipoproteins, the good kind that carries cholesterol away from deposits on arteries to the liver for discharge. This may also help explain why hostility does damage to the coronary arteries.

Second, hostile individuals have been found by Suarez, McRae, and Williams (1988) to display a weaker "braking" action of their parasympathetic nervous system—that is, their calming branch. Thus, they not only over-react in their bodies, they also stay aroused for a longer time.

These combined effects of heightened arousal in the emergency branch of the autonomic system and a weaker braking effect of the calming branch may help explain not only the harmful effects of hostility on the coronary arteries and the heart, but on the body more generally.

NATURE AND NURTURE IN THE DEVELOPMENT OF HOSTILITY   ▼

You have read that the most dangerous component of Type A behavior for the development of coronary artery disease is hostility. Williams (1989) points out that propensity toward hostility probably develops as a combined result of heredity, especially the tendency toward hyper-reactivity, and environment. After detailed analysis, Carmelli, Swan, and Rosenman (1990) recently suggested that about one quarter of hostility is inherited, the rest the result of environment.

In an argument consistent with the interactional, dynamic, coping perspective toward stress (Lazarus and Folkman, 1984), to which we have referred a number of times, Williams notes that a parent who tends to hyper-react physically, emotionally, and behaviorally to common daily events is more likely to engender unfriendly responses from others, including his or her own children, than a parent who reacts more evenly and moderately. This occurs in very subtle ways through facial expression, body language, and tone of voice.

When this type of interaction occurs thousands of times over the course of the child's early life, he is likely to see the world as an unfriendly, hostile, even dangerous place. Then if the child in turn has inherited a tendency toward quick and strong physical and emotional responses (accompanied with relatively few endorphins that would make interactions more pleasant), he is likely to behave in ways that turn the world into what he has expected, since others around the child feel the same apprehension, distrustfulness, and hostility that the child picked up from the parent.

For example, he squirms and cries a lot when held; he wears facial expressions of disgust, tension, apprehension, or anger; he is not very outgoing. In turn, adults are likely to be less kind and to withdraw from the child, confirming his assessment that the world is an unfriendly, unpredictable, hostile place, justifying again his social distancing behavior, his hostility, and even his overt anger. The cycle mounts.

While nature (heredity) no doubt plays a role in development of hostility, then, social learning plays an even greater part, probably in interaction with biological tendencies. Since hostility is learned, it probably can be prevented and even unlearned.

CAN TYPE A BEHAVIOR BE CHANGED?   ▼

It is one thing to recognize Type A behavior in self and others. But can it be changed? A number of studies strongly suggest that indeed it can. Here is evidence to consider.

The most important research on reducing Type A behavior has been conducted by Friedman and associates, who studied over one thousand post-heart attack patients in California. (Friedman, et al., 1984; Friedman, et. al., 1986). These investigators were interested in two questions. First, can Type A behavior be changed? Second, if it can be changed, will doing so reduce the risk of a second heart attack? Nearly 80 percent of an experimental group who completed monthly behavior-change groups over a three-and-one-half-year period did show measurable reductions in Type A behavior. And those in the behavior-change groups reduced their incidence of repeat heart attacks by one-half, compared with two control groups. Friedman and associates note that this is a more significant reduction in the occurrence of repeat attacks than any medication ever studied and is even greater than bypass surgery.

But does reducing Type A behavior depend on having experienced such a life-threatening event as a heart attack? Can it be changed among those who have not been face-to-face with death? A more recent study, again by Friedman and colleagues, strongly suggests that reducing Type A behavior can be accomplished among adult men who have not suffered a myocardial infarction (Gill, et al., 1985). This time, the investigators sought the cooperation of the U.S. Army War College. Half of a group of healthy, middle-aged career officers who volunteered for the study were assigned to a control group and received no special attention or instruction. The other half participated in classes over a nine-month period aimed at reducing Type A behavior. Again, a significantly higher percentage of those in the experimental group decreased their Type A patterns. Of interest is that their colleagues reported no adverse effects on the subjects' work performances—allaying the apprehension that to reduce Type A qualities would endanger one's chances of a successful career.

The third study is one I have been conducting for several years at the Enloe Hospital Stress and Health Center. Several hundred community residents have taken my class aimed at reducing Type A behavior. Called Reducing Perfectionism and Hurry Sickness, this class meets in groups of 10–15 persons (61 percent have been females; average age is 42) every other week for ten sessions. Individual relaxation training sessions are optional. A blend of behavior and attitude change methods is used to reduce Type A behavior. These include heightened awareness of Type A behavior and of the physiology of stress in general, brief and deep relaxation techniques, time management methods, steps for redefining situations so they become less irritating, methods of handling anger more effectively, and more.

At the outset and again at the end of the class, participants complete a questionnaire containing a series of stress-related scales. Unfortunately, we have no control group, so findings must be viewed with caution.

As shown in Table 5-3, several positive findings have emerged among persons who have completed the class and filled out both pre- and post-measures. First, Type A behavior did appear to change, using three measures: the Pace of Life Index, the Framingham Type A Scale (a well-known ten-item measure), and the Pace of Life Rating Scale, which is completed before and after by someone who knows the participant.

Second, stress level seemed to decline markedly, based on responses to the Distress Symptom Scale described in Chapter 4. Third, health habits seemed to improve, based on responses to the Wellness Behavior Test. Fourth, participants

TABLE 5-3. AVERAGE BEFORE-AFTER SCORES FOR PARTICIPANTS IN A FIVE-MONTH CLASS ON REDUCING TYPE A BEHAVIOR

MEASURE	BEFORE	AFTER	DIRECTION OF CHANGE*
Pace of Life Index	42	34	+
Pace of Life Rating Scale (Completed by another)	40	34	+
Framingham Type A Scale	28	22	+
Distress Symptom Scale	93	35	+
Irritability Quotient	52	41	+
Internal Control**	56	71	+
Emotional Tension	71	49	+
Depression	47	33	+
Life Satisfaction	56	69	+
Health Satisfaction	53	67	+
Job Satisfaction	59	68	+
Home Satisfaction	62	73	+
Health Optimism	68	75	+
Life Optimism	68	76	+
Happiness	60	73	+
Fun and Playfulness	46	62	+
Self-Esteem	58	74	+
Vitality and Energy	53	67	+
Anxious Reactivity	24	20	+
Wellness Behavior Test	2.50	2.86	+
Time Stress Questionnaire	128	86	+

* All differences are significant at <.001 except for Time Stress Questionnaire, which is significant at .01.
** Internal control through vitality and energy are from the Quality of Life Index (Chapter 1). All of these scores are given after being multiplied times 10.
N = 429

seemed to become less easily irritated and angered, based on responses to a 25-item Irritability Quotient. Fifth, quality of life seemed to improve in a number of other respects among most participants—for example, a sense of being in control of things; depression; emotional tension; happiness; satisfaction with job, home, and life in general; self-esteem; vitality and energy; fun and playfulness. Sixth, participants seemed to experience less stress associated with time, based on responses to the Time Stress Questionnaire, described in Chapter 10.

In short, Type A behavior does appear to be amenable to change. It is not locked into our thinking, feeling, and acting forever. Reducing it does appear to improve the quality of life. Perhaps it can also improve the length of life. For a complete review of studies on alteration of Type A behavior, see Roskies (1990).

Box 5-5 contains Redford Williams' suggestions for developing a more "trusting heart"—one with less hostility and more love.

BOX 5-5

12 STEPS TO A TRUSTING HEART

1. MONITOR YOUR CYNICAL THOUGHTS
2. CONFESSION IS GOOD FOR THE SOUL
3. STOP THOSE THOUGHTS
4. REASON WITH YOURSELF
5. PUT YOURSELF IN THE OTHER PERSON'S SHOES
6. LEARN TO LAUGH AT YOURSELF
7. LEARN TO RELAX
8. PRACTICE TRUST
9. LEARN TO LISTEN
10. LEARN TO BE ASSERTIVE
11. PRETEND TODAY IS YOUR LAST
12. PRACTICE FORGIVING

SOURCE: Williams (1989, Chap. 11).

MANAGING ANGER ▼

Anger is a familiar state that includes emotions, thoughts, physical arousal, and sometimes actions (Hauck, 1974; Ellis, 1977; Tavris, 1982; Doty, 1985). In Chapter 3, you read about "bound energy" resulting from arousal for physical action that remains unexpressed. Bound energy can evolve into tension, illness, emotional distress, and disorganized thinking.

DISTINGUISHING BETWEEN POSITIVE AND NEGATIVE ANGER

It is vital at the outset to understand the distinction between positive anger and negative anger. It is my position that negative anger is a harmful and nearly always avoidable part of human experience. Positive anger on the other hand, is a constructive, positive experience. Let us examine the difference between the two.

Negative anger involves the following steps.

1. I want something. "You must act like I think you should."

2. I am not getting it. "You are not meeting my expectations."

3. This frustrates me. "I'm boiling at what you just did."

4. This is intolerable. "I can't stand it."

5. You are to blame for my frustration. "You make me SO mad."

6. Therefore, you deserve to be punished. "I'll teach you not to do this to me again."

Positive anger, by contrast, begins the same but ends up at quite a different point.

1. I want something. "I sure like peace and quiet in my neighborhood."

2. I am not getting it. "Those neighbors' dogs bark and bark."

3. This frustrates me. "I sure have a terrible time getting to sleep with those dogs barking."

4. This is unacceptable. "This cannot go on."

5. I am motivated to do something to improve this situation. "I am going to call the neighbors and tell them something must be done to quiet down their dogs at night."

6. I will take constructive action to remedy the source of my frustration. "Hello, I need to talk with you about your dogs."

Notice that negative anger leads to hostility, aggressive impulses—and distress within oneself. Positive anger leads to motivation to alter the situation in a positive way based on assertiveness.

This, of course, is how conditions of living improve. People become indignant and take action. The world around us becomes a better place—not just a source of frustration and upset.

Positive anger, then, is constructive and desirable from time to time. Negative anger is harmful, avoidable—and the source of a good deal of evil, if by evil we mean harm by humans toward each other.

A step toward understanding how to handle anger effectively is to recognize that it is often a secondary emotion, a cover-up for a prior, even stronger feeling that, for one reason or another, we keep hidden. It can cover up each of the following:

Frustration

Fear

Self-doubt

Feeling rejected and lonely

Defensiveness

Guilt

Hurt

Negative anger usually arises in response to a perceived threat, frustration, or injustice. Perhaps the most difficult of all to allow into consciousness is anger from having been exposed, shown to be wrong, questioned, doubted. These are threats to personal worth. The greater the threat, the greater the potential anger. A key to dealing with negative anger as a cover-up emotion is to find out what the underlying emotion is, what is causing that feeling, and what can be done about it.

A number of constructive suggestions can be offered for dealing with anger in ways that minimize its unnecessary occurrence as a harmful experience, acknowledge its existence, and allow for expression in harmless yet fruitful ways.

THREE QUESTIONS IN MANAGING ANGER ▼

When most people think of managing anger, their first question usually is, "Should I express it or hold it in?" Important as it is, this question needs to be set in a broader context of anger management.

Three key questions need to be addressed. You will note that our answers draw upon suggestions and guidelines from previous chapters.

1. **How can I prevent negative anger?**
   A. Enter each day with an attitude of patience, tolerance and good humor
   B. Use these self-talk statements:
      Is this truly worth getting upset about?
      I remain calm with difficult people.
      I value diversity in others' opinions and behavior.
      I am okay no matter what.
   C. Maintain good health buffers
      Exercise
      Nutrition
      Sleep
   D. Practice active listening (See Chapter 11)
   E. Express feelings honestly and promptly
   F. When needed, avoid distress-provokers

2. **How can I catch negative anger in progress?**
   A. Use the Six-Second Quieting Response (See Chapter 9)

    B. Use Instant Replay or P and Q Method for managing situational self-talk (See Chapter 7)
       Catch (Recognize) my negative self-talk
       Challenge it
       Change it
       or
       Pause and Question
    C. Use thought-stopping and thought-switching (See Chapter 9)
    D. Change actions from upset to reasonable
    E. If appropriate, leave scene momentarily

3. **How can I handle negative anger constructively, once present?**
    A. Reduce destructive responses
       Anger in—repress
       Anger out—explode
       Poison darts
       Dumping on innocent bystanders
    B. Use constructive options
       Discuss with person at whom you are angry
       Discuss with someone else
       Dissolve it through self-talk
       Release it through exercise
       Channel anger energy into constructive activity
       Take constructive action to remedy situation—turn negative anger into positive anger
       Express anger in harmless ways

OTHER ANGER TIPS   ▼

1. When anger is present, ask: What am I really feeling? Am I truly frustrated at being wronged, blocked, or misunderstood? Or is anger a cover-up for another feeling hidden beneath? If so, what is that other emotion, and how can I deal with it directly and constructively?

2. Waste no time in dealing with anger within the limits of what is appropriate. The longer it boils away, the greater the potential for physical harm and boil-over later on.

3. Ask: Is my anger partly the result of being overloaded? As pointed out earlier, anger often will partly or totally subside when this awareness is brought to the surface.

4. Get to the root of your anger. What can be changed in self, others, or the larger situation to reduce this anger and the chances that it will happen again?

5. In expressing anger to the target person use "I" rather than "you" openers. "I am angry because dinner is late," rather than, "You are late again with dinner."

"I am upset at your failure to do your household chores this week," rather than, "You failed again to fulfill your responsibilities."

"I feel really discouraged by your forgetting my birthday," rather than, "Well, you blew it again this year."

"You" messages set the stage for a defensive response from the listener. "I" messages lay the groundwork for understanding dialogue and continuation of the conversation. This is a simple formula, but it can work wonders for the person who is angered, as well as for the person who is the target of anger.

6.   Avoid collecting anger credits for your "slush fund" of bad feelings, tense body tissue, and righteous indignation. Far better that you deal with them one at a time, piece-by-piece, immediately or soon after they arise. Otherwise, your bubble will explode or will eat away at your insides.

7.   Express anger with forethought and good taste. Be rational about it. Does it really make good sense to explode at your 86-year-old father because of how he treated you when you were ten? Again, the key ethical questions are: What will the consequences be for others? And for myself? Is it moral to clear out my angry emotions in such a way that someone else clearly is hurt? Is there an alternative for reducing my anger while not inflicting harm on others? Obviously there is.

8.   Avoid displaying anger at those closest to you who may be quite undeserving. A particularly common pattern is to transfer anger from job to family. Why? There are several reasons.

They are available

They are safe to dump on (that is, relatively safe)

They won't hurt us (not in the way a boss or customer can)

Their personalities might be receptive to this

They will still love us

They won't reject us

They might understand us (if their emotional temperature is not too high)

Far better to handle anger at its source—at work—or at least to talk it out at home and then leave it, rather than to drip it out at home through poisonous darts or to create volcanic explosions.

9.   Use techniques of giving negative feedback and assertiveness, both discussed in Chapter 11, for expressing anger constructively, and for getting what you want, but not at someone else's expense.

10.   Be available to your co-workers, spouse, children, and friends to talk out their anger, using the techniques of active listening described in Chapter 11. Help enlighten them about some of these principles for handling anger in the future.

11.   Pick the appropriate time and place to express anger.

You may choose to complete the next exercises on a sheet of paper, in a diary, or in a notebook.

EXERCISE 5-9. MONITORING YOUR ANGER

1.   List several family situations in which you get angry.
I get angry at home when:
2.   List and discuss several work situations in which you get angry.
I get angry at work when:
3.   List several things about what you do or feel that makes you angry.
I get angry at myself when:
4.   List several other situations in which your anger is aroused.
I get angry when:

EXERCISE 5-10. ANGRY ANSWERS

You are invited to answer the following questions from the *Wellness Workbook*. Again, use a separate sheet.

1.   Messages I heard about expressing anger:
2.   These things/events/people stimulate anger in me:
3.   The last time I felt anger was:
4.   Is it OK for me to feel angry?
5.   I express it:
6.   Unhealthy ways I express anger:
7.   Healthy ways I express anger:
8.   What I've learned about myself from these questions:
9.   Share with a friend.

Note: From Regina S. Ryan and John W. Travis, *Wellness Workbook,* Berkeley, Calif.: Ten Speed Press, 1981, p. 1320.

EXERCISE 5-11. MONITORING ANGER TRIGGERS AND REACTIONS

For the next week or two, monitor situations in which your anger is aroused. Write them in your stress diary. Use the following questions as guides for your observation.

Do any of them involve blaming others for your behavior or feelings? Might you have been less upset with greater patience, humor, or tolerance?
Was your baseline stress level too high to begin with?
Exactly what did you feel emotionally and physically? At the moment? One hour later? Four hours later?
How did you handle your anger? Was this a constructive or destructive response to your anger?
Looking back, what might you have done differently in handling the anger?

OTHER TIPS FOR MANAGING TYPE A BEHAVIOR   ▼

Many of the guidelines and suggestions in Chapter 10 for managing time, pace, and change also apply to managing the time urgency part of Type A behavior. Self-talk methods related to self-esteem also apply here (See Chapter 7). So do relaxation methods, both on-the-spot tension reducers and deep relaxation techniques (See Chapter 9). Exercise also can help (See Chapter 8). Below are several additional suggestions from Friedman and Rosenman's important book, *Type A Behavior and Your Heart* (1974, Chapter 15).

1.   **Review your successes.** You will find that your successes are not caused by Type A behavior but occur in spite of it. Impatience, hostility and hyperaggressiveness do not contribute to success, but detract from it. Friedman and Rosenman note that they never met anyone who failed because they failed to do a job too slowly or too well. But they have met many who failed because they rushed too fast.

2.   **Believe in your ability to change.** Type A behavior is learned. Therefore, it can be changed.

3.   **Enter into a thorough self-appraisal.** This often is difficult for the entrenched Type A, who typically is set in her or his ways and thoroughly believes in the virtuousness of present commitments and patterns of conduct. Become aware, especially, of patterns of negative self-talk that produce insecurity, time urgency or hostility. Box 5-6 contains Friedman and Rosenman's suggestions for such a self-appraisal.

BOX 5-6

FRIEDMAN AND ROSENMAN'S GUIDELINES FOR A THOROUGH SELF-APPRAISAL

1.   In a meaningful self-appraisal, you must first attempt to determine just how intelligent, how percipient, and how creative you have been in your job.

2.   You must examine your sense of humor to determine how it has served you. Is it chiefly a repository for jokes and anecdotes? Or does it function—as it should—to help you perceive your own occasionally ludicrous aspects?

3.   You must assess your capacity for flexibility, for change of pace, and for rapid adaptability to change.

4.   You must look at your leadership qualities and determine their worth.

5.   You must examine all the activities that now absorb your intellectual, emotional, and spiritual interests. How many of these activities have to do

with your concern with art, literature, music, drama, philosophy, history, science, and the wonders of the natural world that envelop you?

6.   You must seek out and assess the intensity of your free-floating hostilities. As you do so, don't allow either rationalization or sophistry to blind you to their possible presence.

7.   You must try to estimate the ease with which you can receive and give loyalty and affection.

8.   You must attempt to determine the amount of sheer courage you possess. And if in this assay you detect some very large yellow splotches of frank fear in your personality, don't overlook them. Treasure them, just as you will treasure the steel-gray masses of frank courage you are likely to find there, too.

9.   You must dare to examine critically your ethical and moral principles. How honest have I been in my life, how often and under what circumstances have I cheated, lied, and borne false witness against my neighbor? are questions you must not fail to present to yourself. And painful as it may be in the beginning, stubbornly persist in providing yourself with true answers.

10.   Finally, you must not be afraid to ask, and to persist in asking yourself over and over, until you have answered the question: *What apart from the eternal clutter of my everyday living should be the essence of my life?*

SOURCE: Friedman & Rosenman (1974, 218).

4.   Retrieve your total personality. Reactivate your right brain—the part that relates to literature, art, music, appreciation of beauty in the environment. These are the sorts of interests that tend to bore hard-driving, impatient Type A's. Take time to take in the beauty around you each hour of the day. Surround yourself with symbols of beauty and tranquility.

5.   Make gestures toward myth, ritual and tradition. Friedman and Rosenman (1974, 225) note that:

Perhaps our Western Society will prove to have acted in a supremely wise fashion when it began to replace them (myth, ritual and tradition) with mechanization, automation, and total bureaucratic social security. Except for one thing: this is the first time in the experience of man on earth that a large group of individuals is attempting to live in so absolute a spiritual void.

Find routines with family and friends that you repeat regularly. Place high value on long-term friendships. Nurture and cultivate them. Find means of "centering," looking inward for guidance if that is your spiritual bent. Or pray to whatever higher power gives you strength.

Certain components of Type A behavior clearly have advantages: strong drive, achievement-orientation, attention to detail. Similarly, elements of Type B are desirable: patience, empathy, ability to listen, calm under pressure, flowing more easily with time.

In their stimulating and helpful book, *The C Zone: Peak Performance Under Pressure*, Kriegel and Kriegel (1984) propose a third option that combines the best elements of Type A and Type B, plus other qualities, into a model of attitude and behavior for thriving under pressure. In Chapter 14, we will examine the Type C option in detail, along with its potential uses in your own life. Meanwhile, let us turn to Part II, which focuses on methods of preventing and coping with distress. In Chapter 6 we discuss the concept of coping and its various applications.

REFERENCES   ▼

Abbott, J., & Sutherland, C. (1990). Cognitive, cardiovascular and haematological responses of Type A and Type B individuals prior to and following examinations. *Journal of Social Behavior and Personality,* 5 (Special Issue), 343-368.

Barefoot, J.C., Dahlstrom, W.G., & Williams, R.B. (1983). Hostility, CHD Incidence, and Total Mortality: A 25-year follow-up study of 255 physicians. *Psychosomatic Medicine,* 45, 59-63.

Barefoot, J.C., Dodge, K.A., Peterson, B.L., Dahlstrom, W.G., & Williams, R.B. (1988). Predicting mortality from scores on the Cook-Medley Scale: A follow-up study for 118 lawyers. *Psychosomatic Medicine,* 51, 46-57.

Bedeian, A.G., Mossholder, I., & Touliatos, J. (1990). Type A status and selected work experiences among male and female accountants. *Journal of Social Behavior and Personality,* 5 (Special Issue), 291-305.

Blaney, N.T. (1990). Type A, effort to excel, and attentional style in children: The validity of the MYTH. *Journal of Social Behavior and Personality,* 5 (Special Issue), 159-182.

Blumental, J.A., Williams, R.S., King, Y., Schanberg, S.M., & Thompson, L. Type A behavior pattern and coronary atherosclerosis. *Circulation,* 58, 634-639.

Bryant, F.B., & Yarnold, P.R. (1990). The impact of Type A behavior on subjective life quality: Bad for the heart, good for the soul? *Journal of Social Behavior and Personality,* 5 (Special Issue), 369-404.

Carmelli, D., Swan, G.E., & Rosenman, R.H. (1990). The heritability of the Cook and Medley hostility scale revisited. *Journal of Social Behavior and Personality,* 5 (Special Issue), 107-116.

Case, R.B., Heller, S.S., Case, N.B., & Moss, A.J. (1985). Type A behavior and survival after acute myocardial infarction. *The New England Journal of Medicine,* 312, 634-639.

Clark, L.K., & Miller, S.M. (1990). Self-reliance and desire for control in the Type A behavior pattern. *Journal of Social Behavior and Personality,* 5 (Special Issue), 405-418.

Cohen, J.B., Matthews, K.A., & Waldron, I. (1978). Section summary: Coronary-prone behavior: Developmental and cultural considerations. In Dembroski, T.M.,

Weiss, S.M., Shields, S.G., Haynes, G., & Feinleib, M. (Eds.), *Coronary-Prone Behavior.* New York: Springer-Verlag, 184-190.

Cook, W., & Medley, D. (1954). Proposed hostility and pharasaic-virtue scales for the MMPI. *Journal of Applied Psychology,* 38, 414-418.

Crandall, V.S., Presosn, A., & Rabsen, A. Maternal reactions and the development of independence and achievement behavior in young children. *Child Development,* 31, 243-251.

DeFleur, M. (1964). Occupational roles as portrayed on television. *Public Opinion Quarterly,* 69, 57-74.

Dimsdale, J.E. (1988). A perspective on Type A behavior and coronary disease. (Editorial). *The New England Journal of Medicine,* 318, 110-112.

Doty, B. (1985). *Break The Anger Trap.* Redding, CA: The Bookery Publishing Co.

Dunbar, H.F. (1943). *Psychosomatic Diagnosis.* New York: Paul B. Hoeber, Inc.

Elkind, D. (1981). *The Hurried Child: Growing Up Too Fast.* Reading, MA: Addison-Wesley.

Ellis, A. (1977). *How To Live With and Without Anger.* New York: Reader's Digest Press.

Farquhar, J.W. (1978). *The American Way of Life Can Be Hazardous To Your Health.* Stanford, CA: Stanford Alumni Association.

Fontana, A.F., Rosenber, R.L., Burg, M.M., Kerns, R.D., & Colonese, K.L. (1990). Type A behavior and self-referencing: Interactive risk factors? *Journal of Social Behavior and Personality,* 5 (Special Issue), 215-232.

Frank, K.A., Heller, S.S., Kornfield, D.S., Sporn, A.A., & Weiss, M.B. (1978). Type A behavior pattern and coronary angiographic findings. *Journal of The American Medical Association,* 240, 761-763.

Friedman, M., & Rosenman, R.H. (1971). Type A behavior pattern: Its association with coronary heart disease. *Annals of Clinical Research,* 3, 300-312.

Friedman, M, & Rosenman, R.H. (1974). *Type A Behavior and Your Heart.* New York: Fawcett.

Friedman, M., Rosenman, R.H., & Carroll, V. (1958). Changes in the serum cholesterol and blood clotting time in men subjected to cyclic variation of occupational stress. *Circulation,* 17, 852-861.

Friedman, M., & Ulmer, D. (1984). *Treating Type A Behavior and Your Heart.* New York: Knopf.

Friedman, M., Thoreson, C.E., Gill, J.J., Powell, L., Ulmer, D., Thompson, L., Price, V.A., Rabin, D.D., Breall, W.S., Dixon, T., Levey, R.A., & Bourg, E. (1984). Alteration of Type A behavior and reduction in cardiac recurrences in post-myocardial infarction patients. *American Heart Journal,* 108, 237-248.

Friedman, M., Thoreson, C.E., Gill, J.J., Ulmer, D., Powell, L.H., Price, V.A., Brown, B., Thompson, L., Rabin, D.D., Breall, W.S., Bourg, E., Levy, R., & Dixon, T. (1986). Alteration of Type A behavior and its effect on cardiac recurrences in post-myocardial infarction patients: Summary results of the recurrent coronary prevention project. *American Heart Journal,* 112, 653-665.

Gerbner, G. Violence in television drama: Trends and symbolic functions. In Comstock, G., & Rubinstein, E. (Eds.), *Television and Social Behavior. Vol. 1: Media Content and Control.* Washington, D.C.: U.S. Government Printing Office, 28,178.

Gill, J.J, Price, V.A., Friedman, M., Thoreson, C.E., Powell, L.H., Ulmer, D., Brown, B., & Drews. (1985). Reduction in Type A behavior in healthy middle-aged American military officers. *American Heart Journal*, 180, 503-514.

Glass, D. (1977). *Behavior Patterns, Stress, and Coronary Disease*. Hillsdale, NJ: Erlbaum.

Greenglass. E.R. (1990). Type A behavior, career aspirations, and role conflict in professional women. *Journal of Social Behavior and Personality*, 5, (Special Issue), 307-322.

Hauck, P. A. (1974). *Overcoming Frustration and Anger*. Philadelphia: The Westminster Press.

Haynes, S.G. (1984). Type A behavior, employment status, and coronary heart disease in women. *Behavioral Medicine Update*, 6, 11-15.

Haynes, S.G., & Matthews, K.A. (1988). Review and methodological critique of recent studies of Type A behavior and cardiovascular disease. *Annals of Behavioral Medicine*, 10, 47-59.

Krantz, D.S., & Durel, L.A. (1983). Psychobiological substrates of the Type A behavior pattern. *Health Psychology*, 2, 393-411.

Lawler, K.A., Schmied, L.A., Armstead, C.A., & Lacy, J.E. (1990). Type A behavior, desire for control, and cardiovascular reactivity in young adult women. *Journal of Social Behavior and Personality*, 5 (Special Issue), 135-158.

Lazarus, R.S., & Folkman, S. (1984). *Stress, Appraisal, and Coping*. New York: Springer Publishing Company.

Magnet, M. (1987). The money society. *Fortune*, July 6, 26-31.

Menninger, K.A., & Menninger, W.C. (1936). Psychoanalytic observations in cardiac disorders. *American Heart Journal*, 11, 10.

Matthews, K.A., & Haynes, S.G. (1985). Type A behavior pattern and coronary risk: Update and critical evaluation. *American Journal of Epidemiology*, 123, 23-96.

Matthews, K.A., & Krantz, D.S. (1976). Resemblences of twins and their parents in pattern A behavior. *Psychosomatic Medicine*, 38, 140-144.

Offutt, C., & Lacroix, J.M. (1988). Type A behavior pattern and symptom reports: A prospective investigation. *Journal of Behavioral Medicine*, 11, 227-237.

Osler, W. (1892). *Lectures on Angina Pectoris and Allied States*. New York: Appleton.

Price, V.A. (1982). *Type A Behavior Pattern: A Model for Research and Practice*. New York: Academic Press.

Review Panel on Coronary-Prone Behavior and Coronary Heart Disease. (1981). Coronary-prone behavior and coronary heart disease: A critical review. *Circulation*, 63, 1199-1215.

Rose, R.J., Grim, C.E., & Miller, J.Z. (1984). Familial influences on cardiovascular stress reactivity: Studies of normotensive twins. *Behavioral Medicine Update*, 6, 21-24.

Rosenman, R.H. (1986). Current and past history of Type A behavior pattern. In Schmidt, T.H., Dembroski, T.M., & Blumchen, G. (Eds.), *Biological and Pscyhological Factors in Cardiovascular Disease*. Heidelberg: Springer-Verlag, 15-40.

Rosenman, R.H. (1990). Type A behavior pattern: A personal overview. *Journal of Social Behavior and Personality*, 5 (Special Issue), 1-24.

Roskies, E. (1987). *Stress Management for the Healthy Type A.: Theory and Practice.* New York: The Guilford Press.

Roskies, E. (1990). Type A intervention: Where do we go from here? *Journal of Social Behavior and Personality,* 5 (Special Issue), 419-438.

Suarez, E.S., McRae, A., & Williams, R.B. (1988). High scores on the Cook and Medley Hostility (Ho) scale predict increased cardiovascular responses to harassment. Paper presented at the annual meeting of the American Psychosomatic Society, Toronto, March.

Schafer, W.E., & McKenna, J. F. (1985). Type A behavior, stress, injuries, and illness among adult runners. *Stress Medicine,* 1, 245-254.

Shekelle, R.B., Gale, M., Ostfeld, A.M., & Paul. O. (1983). Hostility, risk of coronary disease, and mortality. *Psychosomatic Medicine,* 45, 219-228.

Shekelle, R.B., Hulley, S., Neaton, J., Billings, J., Borhani, N., Gerace, T., Jacobs, D., Lasser, N., Mittlemark, M., & Stamler, J. (1985). The MRFIT behavioral pattern study: II. Type A behavior pattern and incidence of coronary heart disease. *American Journal of Epidemiology,* 122, 559-570.

Smith, C.P. (1969). The origin and expression of achievement-related motives in children. In Smith, C.P. (Ed.). *Achievement-Related Motives in Children.* New York: Russell Sage Foundation.

Smith, T.W., & Pope, M.K. (1990). Cynical hostility as a health risk: Current status and future directions. *Journal of Social Behavior and Personality,* 5 (Special Issue), 77-88.

Storement, C.T. (1951). Personality and heart disease. *Psychosomatic Medicine,* 13, 304-313.

Stout, C.W., & Bloom, L.J. (1982). Type A behavior and upper respiratory infections. *Journal of Human Stress,* 8, 4-7.

Suls, J., & Sanders. G.S. (1988). Type A behavior as a general risk factor for physical disorder. *Journal of Behavioral Medicine,* 11, 201-226.

Swan, G.E., Carmelli, & Rosenman, R.H. (1990). Cook and Medley hostility and the Type A behavior pattern: Psychological correlates of two coronary-prone behaviors. *Journal of Social Behavior and Personality,* 5 (Special Issue), 89-106.

Superintendent of Documents. (1990). *A Profile of the American Eighth-Grader.* Washington, D.C.: U.S. Government Printing Office.

Tavris, C. (1982). *Anger: The Misunderstood Emotion.* New York: Simon and Schuster.

Thoreson, C.E., & Low, K.G. (1990). Women and the Type A pattern: Review and commentary. *Journal of Social Behavior and Personality,* 5 (Special Issue), 117-133.

Van Egeren, L.F. (1990). A "success trap" theory of Type A behavior: Historical background. *Journal of Social Behavior and Personality,* 5 (Special Issue), 45-58.

von Deusch, T. (1868). *Lehrbuch der Herzkrankbeiten.* Leipzig: Verlag von Wilhelm Engelman.

Waldron, I., Zazinski, S., Shekelle, R.B., Jenkins, C.D., & Tannenbaum, S. (1980). The coronary-prone behavior pattern in employed men and women. *Journal of Human Stress,* 3, 2-18.

Weiss, E., Dlin, B., Rollin, H.R., Fischer, H.K., & Bepler, C.R. (1957). Emotional factors in coronary occlusion. *Archives of Internal Medicine,* 99, 628-641.

Williams, R. (1989). *The Trusting Heart: Great News About Type A Behavior.* New York: Times Books.

Williams, R.B., Haney, T.L., Lee, K.L., Kong, Y., Blumenthal, J., & Whalen, R. (1980). Type A behavior, hostility, and coronary atherosclerosis. *Psychosomatic Medicine, 42,* 539-549.

Williams, R.B., & Siegler, I. (1990). Hostility tied to heart trouble. Paper presented at annual scientific meetings of American Heart Association, Dallas, November.

Woods, P.J., Morgan, B.T., Day, B.W., Jefferson, T., & Harris, C. (1984). Findings on a relationship between Type A behavior and headaches. *Journal of Behavioral Medicine, 7,* 277-286.

Woods, P.J., & Burns, J. (1984). Type A behavior and illness in general. *Journal of Behavioral Medicine, 7,* 411-415.

Zyzanski, S.J., Jenkins, C.D., Ryan, T.J., Flessas, A., & Everist, M. (1976). Psychological correlates of coronary angiographic findings. *Archives of Internal Medicine, 136,* 1234-1237.

P A R T

T W O

Methods of Managing Stress

Your Coping Response

Chapter 6

CHAPTER 6

I. INTRODUCTION

II. UNDERSTANDING THE COPING PROCESS
A. What Is Coping?
B. Stages of Coping
C. Coping Resources
D. Constraints against Using Coping Resources
E. Deliberate vs. Scripted Coping Responses
F. Adaptive vs. Maladaptive Coping

III. COPING OPTIONS
A. Emotion Focus vs. Problem-Solving Focus
B. Five Coping Strategies
C. Transformational vs. Regressive Coping
D. Schafer Coping Model
   1. Option 1: Alter The Stressor
   2. Option 2: Adapt to The Stressor
     a. Manage Self-Talk
     b. Control Physical Stress Response
     c. Manage Actions
     d. Maintain Health Buffers
     e. Utilize Available Coping Resources
     f. Avoid Maladaptive Responses to Distress
   3. Option 3: Avoid the Stressor

IV. EXTINGUISHING MALADAPTIVE REACTIONS TO DISTRESS
A. Alcohol Abuse
B. Smoking
C. Drugs
D. Overeating
E. Escapism
F. Spending Sprees
G. Physical and Verbal Abuse
H. Blaming Others
I. Overworking
J. Denial
K. Magnification
L. Martyrdom
M. Lethal Effects of Maladaptive Responses to Distress

V. STRENGTHENING ADAPTIVE REACTIONS TO DISTRESS
A. Medications
B. Solitude

C. Music
D. Play
E. Prayer
F. Intimacy
G. Massage
H. Professional Assistance
I. Hobbies
J. Humor
K. Exercise
L. Deep Relaxation

INTRODUCTION ▼

After a long and distinguished career as a family therapist and writer, Virginia Satir died of cancer in 1989. In her obituary in the *Los Angeles Times* (1989, 24), she was quoted as saying:

> Life is not the way it's supposed to be. It's the way it is. The way you cope with it is what makes the difference. I think if I have one message, one thing before I die that most of the world would know, it would be that the event does not determine how to respond to the event. That is a purely personal matter. The way in which we respond will direct and influence the event more than the event itself.

Satir was correct. Life is tough. The world in which we live is imperfect. The Garden of Eden went out some time back in Genesis. The very facts of social and personal change inevitably produce pressures, strains and challenges. So does the life cycle as we move through phases and transitions. Economic uncertainties and international tensions will continue.

This chapter is about how we cope with ever-present stressors—and with our own temporary distress as we deal with them. We will explore the coping process, coping styles, and coping options.

   Maria came to the University from a working class family fully supported by her mother. Her father, an alcoholic, had left when Maria was two and had not been heard from in years. She, her three brothers, and one sister were proud of their home and their strong support for each other. As a college junior, she worked 20 hours a week waiting tables. She delegated her time carefully and still managed to nurture several close friendships. She drank an occasional beer, but no more. She did not do drugs. During final exams, she was confident she would do well, having kept up with her studies all semester. She seemed to thrive under this kind of pressure. Clearly, she coped actively and constructively.

Sally's coping style contrasted sharply. Attending the same university, she came from a home where life was relatively easy and predictable. Her parents, both prominent professionals in a small valley town, had provided all the money and support Sally needed to be among the "in" crowd in high school, and later, in her college sorority. Yet Sally felt overwhelmed with college most of the time. She had a habit of procrastinating her term papers and preparation for exams. Several sorority sisters resented her "mopiness" and her tendency to come off as helpless, put upon, and passive. She drank heavily on weekends and sometimes even during the week. The next morning, she always felt terrible—hungover and guilty. But the pattern continued. She caught the flu twice last semester and felt TATT—Tired All The Time. Sally's coping style clearly was maladaptive.

Both coeds faced multiple stressors. Both responded in patterned ways. They engaged in a continuous process of coping, each reflecting her own coping style.

UNDERSTANDING THE COPING PROCESS   ▼

What Is Coping?
Lazarus and Folkman (1984, 141) define coping as:

". . . constantly changing cognitive and behavioral efforts to manage specific external and/or internal demands that are appraised as taxing or exceeding the resources of the person."

In other words, your coping response is what you think and do as you deal with demands. Notice that this definition calls attention to a process through time. It is also specific to the circumstance. Thus, your coping response is constantly shifting and changing as you react and adapt to the situation or persons with which you are dealing. Coping is not what you should, would, or could do, it is what you, in fact, do as you react to particular conditions—and to your own responses to the event. Thus, coping is an *ongoing, dynamic, interactional process*. Your repeated pattern of coping becomes your *coping style*. Sally's and Maria's coping styles constrasted clearly.

Stages of Coping
According to Lazarus and Folkman (1984), you go through three stages as you cope with a difficult situation (such as three exams, two papers, a speech, and an important date—all within two days). First, you engage in *primary appraisal* of the stressor (or cluster of stressors, as in this example). Here, you decide, given your knowledge of yourself and the situation, whether you are potentially threatened or are in jeopardy. In other words, is this worth being concerned about? If the situation is judged to be irrelevant or trivial, the coping process ends. If the circumstance is meaningful

and potentially threatening, the stress-coping process continues. In the example just cited, most students would regard this circumstance as meaningful and potentially threatening.

Next, you engage in *secondary appraisal*—you assess your resources for dealing with the stressor. As Holroyd and Lazarus note (1982, 23), this assessment is influenced by "previous experiences in similar situations, generalized beliefs about the self and the environment, and the availability of personal (for example, physical strength or problem-solving skills) and environmental (for example, social support or money) resources." Following our example, you would ask, "Given that I want to succeed in school, given my past experiences and my knowledge of myself, and given my options right now, what will I do to get through this?" Important to this secondary appraisal is an assessment of how much control you have over the situation. The less the perceived control, the more threatening the situation will be and the greater the probability of mental and physical distress.

The third phase is *coping.* You take whatever actions seem appropriate. This response might involve action or merely a cognitive adjustment—redefining the situation through self-talk. Whether your coping response is helpful and constructive is, of course, another matter (Frese, 1986; Krohne, 1986; Laux, 1986).

Coping Resources

Lazarus and Folkman (1984, 159) note that a wide variety of personal and environmental resources are potentially available as you appraise your coping options. Included are these examples, all of which are discussed in more detail later in the book:

- ▼ Exercise

- ▼ Situational self-talk skills

- ▼ Positive Beliefs
  Sense of Coherence
  Sense of Challenge, Commitment, Control (Hardiness)
  Optimism

- ▼ Problem-solving Skills

- ▼ Communication Skills

- ▼ Social Support

- ▼ Material Resources

- ▼ Community Services

Constraints Against Using Coping Resources

Of course, there are internal and environmental constraints against using these resources. These include guilt, unexpressed anger, hostility, fear, lack of confidence, perceived social prohibitions, unwillingness to seek or accept assistance from others, social norms emphasizing self-sufficiency, poverty, absence of health care or counseling services, lack of available child care programs.

Deliberate vs. Scripted Coping Responses

Are your reactions to stressful events, including your own temporary distress, deliberate or scripted? If you react with little awareness or deliberate choice, your coping behavior probably is scripted. Many people cope in the same ways as their parents without realizing it. Others handle stressful events much like they did as children. Others respond with thoughtfulness and intention.

Unless you become aware of your coping style, you may be seriously limited by your *life script*—a blueprint for thinking, feeling, and acting that usually emerges from adolescence as a result of repeated early messages and early decisions (James & Jongeward, 1971; Steiner, 1974). As an actor follows a stage script, people most often spend their lives blindly living out their own life script. Included in the script are directives related to:

How to be masculine or feminine

How to get love and attention

How to feel good about yourself

How to feel about others

How to spend time

Whether and how to succeed or fail

How to cope with stressful events

Maturity and independence includes freedom from one's life script, especially if it keeps one bound to old, destructive, maladaptive patterns.

Adaptive vs. Maladaptive Coping

Coping can be *adaptive*, helping the individual deal effectively with stressful events and minimizing distress. Or it can be *maladaptive*, resulting in unnecessary distress for self or others. Positive coping outcomes depend on having a range of options available and on accurate linking of options with situation. Let us now explore a range of coping options.

Adaptive coping options, especially when part of a broader positive coping style (cluster of coping habits), contribute to wellness—good health, productivity, life satisfaction, personal growth. Maladaptive coping options, and especially a negative coping style, erode wellness.

COPING OPTIONS   ▼

There are literally hundreds of options available to the individual as one copes with specific stressful events and circumstances. It is useful to examine coping categories several experts have identified.

EMOTION FOCUS VS. PROBLEM-SOLVING FOCUS

Several writers (Pearlin and Schooler, 1978; Folkman, Schaefer, and Lazarus, 1979; Leventhal and Nerenz, 1983) have identified two broad options:

Emotional regulation, in which the focus is dealing with your own fear, anger, or guilt as you react to the situation.

Problem-solving efforts. Here the focus is attempting to deal constructively with the stressor or circumstance itself. In the example of a crunch of exams, papers, a speech, and a date, this option would include deciding how to organize time and energy during the next two days.

Both of these options can be adaptive or maladaptive, of course. Table 6-1 shows the possibilities.

TABLE 6-1. TARGET AND OUTCOME OF COPING		
OUTCOME OF COPING	**TARGET OF COPING**	
	STRESSOR	**SELF**
Adaptive	Put communication problem on agenda for next meeting.	Share frustrations with friend.
Maladaptive	Blow up at boss.	Drink away frustrations.

FIVE COPING STRATEGIES

Cohen and Lazarus (1979) propose five optional strategies in confronting a stressful event. Let's take the example of airport noise (Taylor, 1986, 202).

Information-seeking. What is the noise level at different neighborhood locations throughout the day?

Direct action. Circulate petitions among neighbors.

Inhibition of action. Controlling the urge to shoot down the next noisy airplane.

Intrapsychic efforts. Using self-talk to tolerate the noise.

Turning to others. Sharing frustrations with neighbors, working together to circulate petitions and confront officials.

TRANSFORMATIONAL VS. REGRESSIVE COPING

Maddi and Kobasa (1984) maintain that hardiness is likely to lead to *transformational* coping—taking constructive action to change the stressor. This coping option emerges from a sense of internal control, a sense of challenge, and a sense of commitment. Fundamentally, it is based on optimism. This was Maria's approach.

Regressive coping is thinking pessimistically and avoiding the stressor. This was Sally's way.

SCHAFER COPING MODEL

Having explored various coping approaches, let us now examine a range of options when dealing with stressful situations and your reactions to them, keeping in mind that this is a complex, dynamic, interactional process.

Assuming an event is perceived to be important and sufficiently taxing of your resources to need a response, what are your adaptive options? Consider the following. Each of these steps is discussed in detail in later chapters.

Option 1. Alter the Stressor
Is the stressor controllable, changeable or influenceable? Can I take action by myself? Is group action possible and desirable? What are likely gains and costs—for myself and others? This action might include the following:

▼ Seeking to change a specific situation

▼ Changing a physical stressor

▼ Pacing myself and my stressors better

▼ Spacing my life changes better

▼ Increasing challenges in my life (if the problem is boredom)

▼ Organizing time better

▼ Asking someone to alter her behavior

Option 2. Adapt to the Stressor
Is it best to accept the stressor, finding ways to prevent or lower my distress? These might include:

1. **Manage Self-Talk**

   Alter my irrational beliefs
   Control my situational self-talk
   Take it less seriously
   Turn the "threat" into an opportunity
   See this person or event as temporarily bearable
   Be okay no matter what

2. **Control Physical Stress Response**

   Breathing methods
   Muscle relaxation methods
   Mental methods

3. **Manage Actions**

   Use effective listening
   Be assertive
   Be self-disclosing
   Use an appropriate communication style
   Take action that will get all involved what we want

4. **Maintain Health Buffers**

   Exercise
   Nutrition
   Sleep

5. **Utilize Available Coping Resources**

   Social support
   Money
   Community or campus services
   My beliefs or faith

6. **Avoid Maladaptive Reactions to Distress**

   Alcohol or drug abuse
   Smoking
   Overeating
   Dumping on or abusing others
   Escapism
   Spending sprees
   Blaming others

Option 3. Avoid the Stressor

Is it best for me to avoid or withdraw from this stressor? What would be the gains and costs? Have all other options been exhausted?

EXTINGUISHING MALADAPTIVE REACTIONS TO DISTRESS   ▼

Part of the coping is reacting to one's own temporary distress. Handling distress maladaptively means trying to reduce it in ways that make it worse for self or others. Many times what seems constructive in the short run (getting high on drugs or buzzed on alcohol) turns out to be destructive in the long run.

A great proportion of stress problems seen by physicians, therapists, and stress consultants are not from reactions to original stressors, but are outcomes of coping behavior that makes things worse rather than better.

Just as one must identify and change destructive ways of coping with stressors, so must we recognize our maladaptive reactions to our own distress. Let us now examine some of these maladaptive reactions to distress, what effects they have, and how they can be reduced or extinguished. In each case, the key to stopping is substituting constructive alternatives.

ALCOHOL ABUSE

According to the American Psychiatric Association's official manual on psychiatric disorders (1987), two alcohol disorders exist. The first is *alcohol abuse,* distinguished by repeated use of alcohol in physically hazardous situations or continued use in the face of knowledge that doing so worsens a personal problem. The second, more serious disorder is *alcohol dependence.* Here, all the symptoms of alcohol abuse occur, plus inability to control the drinking. *Tolerance* often occurs at this stage—increasing amounts of alcohol are needed to achieve the desired effect. *Withdrawal* usually is present, in which shakiness, malaise or behavioral disturbance accompany stopping or reducing consumption.

Per capita alcohol consumption has increased during the past two decades, rising 33 percent since 1964 (Prokop, et al., 1991). According to the National Center for Health Statistics (1989), about eight percent of the adult American population drinks heavily—one ounce or more per day of pure alcohol. The rate of heavy drinking is nearly five times greater for males than females. Approximately one-tenth of the U.S. population consumes about half of the alcoholic beverages sold in this country.

Alcohol consumption is higher among younger age groups, especially males, than often thought. For example, national surveys of the young in 1985 revealed that 34 percent of males and 28 percent of females between ages 12 and 17 had used alcohol during the past month. Fully 78 percent of males and 64 percent of females between 18 and 25 reported use during the past month (National Center for Health Statistics, 1989).

A 1989 Gallup Poll found that among those who drink, 35 percent answered "yes" when asked, "Do you sometimes drink more than you should?" This response was given by 42 percent of the males who drink, compared with 26 percent of female drinkers. The age group with the highest percent responding "yes" was 18-29 years (Gallup Organization, 1990).

Costs of alcohol abuse are extremely high in this country: premature death from liver disease, fatal auto accidents associated with drunk driving, lost productivity and absenteeism, spousal and child abuse, crime, incarceration, medical treatment, and more. Combined costs from these and other consequences of alcohol abuse are estimated to total more than $100 billion each year (Green & Shellenberger, 1991).

A commonly accepted guideline is slight or moderate consumption (no more than a single drink daily) for healthy people without central nervous system, liver, cardiovascular, or gastrointestinal disorders. Any more than this should never be used as a means of coping with tension, upset, or distress.

A key problem, of course, is that in many subcultures heavy use of alcohol is supported as acceptable coping behavior—social norms that receive strong support from alcohol advertisements. Closely related is the social norm equating "a good time" or "partying" with heavy drinking. A persistent danger is that many individuals, especially those with a family history of alcoholism, probably inherit a genetic predisposition to become addicted to alcohol. What begins as "good times" in youth too often transforms in later years into severe alcoholism.

Box 6-1 contains a personal assessment questionnaire on problem drinking, which you are invited to complete and contemplate.

BOX 6-1. ARE YOU A PROBLEM DRINKER?

Section One: Yes   No

1. Do you occasionally drink heavily after a disappontment, a quarrel, or when the boss gives you a hard time?
2. When you have trouble or feel under pressure, do you always drink more heavily than usual?
3. Have you noticed that you are able to handle more liquor than you did when you were first drinking?
4. Did you ever wake up on the morning after and discover that you could not remember part of the evening before, even though your friends tell you that you did not pass out?
5. When drinking with other people, do you try to have a few extra drinks when others will not know about it?
6. Are there certain occasions when you feel uncomfortable if alcohol is not available?
7. Have you recently noticed that when you begin drinking you are in more of a hurry to get the first drink than you used to be?
8. Do you sometimes feel guilty about your drinking?

Section Two:

9. Are you secretly irritated when your family or friends discuss your drinking?
10. Have you recently noticed an increase in the frequency of your memory blackouts?
11. Do you often wish to continue drinking after your friends say that they have had enough?
12. Do you usually have a reason for the occasions when you drink heavily?
13. When you are sober, do you often regret things you have done or said while drinking?
14. Have you tried switching brands or following different plans for controlling your drinking?
15. Have you often failed to keep the promises you have made to yourself about controlling or cutting down on your drinking?
16. Have you ever tried to control your drinking by making a change in jobs or moving to a new location?
17. Do you try to avoid family or close friends while you are drinking?
18. Are you having an increasing number of financial and work problems?
19. Do more people seem to be treating you unfairly without good reason?
20. Do you eat very little or irregularly when you are drinking?
21. Do you sometimes have the shakes in the morning and find that it helps to have a little drink?

Section Three:

22. Have you recently noticed that you cannot drink as much as you once did?
23. Do you sometimes stay drunk for several days at a time?
24. Do you sometimes feel very depressed and wonder whether life is worth living?
25. Sometimes after periods of drinking, do you see or hear things that aren't there?
26. Do you get terribly frightened after you have been drinking heavily?

If you answered "yes" to two or more questions in any of these three sections, the National Council on Alcoholism urges you to re-evaluate your drinking behavior. Each section focuses on a more advanced stage of problem drinking.

Section One: Early stage—drinking is a regular part of your life.

Section Two: Middle stage—you are having trouble controlling when, where, and how much to drink.

Section Three: Advanced stage—you can no longer control your desire to drink.

SOURCE: National Council on Alcoholism

SMOKING

The bottom line is that smoking will increase chances of dying prematurely from heart attack, lung cancer, emphysema or bronchitis, pneumonia, or stroke. Roglieri (1980, 81) estimates the increased odds of death from each of these causes increased as follows, compared with nonsmokers.

The idea that smoking reduces stress is a cruel illusion. Smoking decreases energy level for coping with daily hassles. By coating the lungs with tar and nicotine, surrounding red cells with carbon monoxide, by making it more difficult for them to transport oxygen, and by accelerating heart rate, smoking means less ability to take in, circulate, and use oxygen—hence a greater struggle to do the same as a nonsmoker can do more easily, other things equal.

	1-1½ PACKS PER DAY	2 PACKS OR MORE PER DAY
Heart Attack	80 percent	220 percent
Lung Cancer	480 percent	500 percent
Bronchitis/Emphysema	70 percent	210 percent
Pneumonia	300 percent	300 percent
Stroke	50 percent	50 percent

SOURCE: Roglieri (1980, 81)

BOX 6-2. HEALTH BENEFITS OF SMOKING CESSATION

Here are major conclusions of a recent report from the Surgeon General on stopping smoking.

1. Smoking cessation has major and immediate health benefits for persons of all ages and provides benefits for persons with and without smoking-related disease.

2. Former smokers live longer than continuing smokers.

3. Smoking cessation decreases the risk for lung and other cancers, heart attack, stroke, and chronic lung disease.

4. Women who stop smoking before pregnancy or during the first 3 to 4 months of pregnancy reduce their risk for having a low-birth-weight infant to that of women who never smoked.

5. The health benefits of smoking cessation substantially exceed any risks from the average 5-lb. weight gain or any adverse psychological effects that may follow quitting.

SOURCE: Surgeon General (1990).

Smokers may feel a lessening of tension from drawing that first smoke after a 20- or 40-minute break from smoking. But ironically, this is a slight reduction of tension caused by a mini–withdrawal crisis from going 20 to 40 minutes without a cigaret. The cigaret relieves tension caused by the very addiction to smoking. Smoking not only shortens life, decreases coping ability through less energy, and creates tension, it also decreases life chances and causes immediate discomfort for those who must inhale used smoke. It is expensive, and a poor example for children. Smoking is a maladaptive response of the worst kind to distress.

The American Cancer Society, The American Lung Association, The Seventh Day Adventist Church, and other groups now conduct very effective smoking cessation programs. Recent evidence suggests that stopping cold-turkey may be the most effective way. Social support from others helps make the struggle easier.

Drugs

Prescribed medications sometimes are temporarily useful and appropriate in reducing stress, as we will explain later in this chapter. Unfortunately, the "pill for every ill" approach is widely embedded in the popular mind and in medical practice.

Three groups of psycho-active substances are widely used to relieve tension.

Depressants—tranquilizers, barbiturates, and alcohol, for example

Stimulants—caffeine and amphetamines, for example

Distortants—LSD, mescaline, and marijuana, for example

In the short-run, all these may relieve distress by one means or another. However, in the long-run, they lose their effectiveness because of increased tolerance to the drug, because the stress triggers remain the same, because the person's ability to cope with the stressors remains undeveloped, or some combination of these reasons. The diminished capacity to cope through drug-induced numbness or psychological distortion may increase tension later. Psychological or physical dependency becomes worse and tension increases in the long-run. Yet illegal drug use continues to mount. So does reliance by patients on prescribed stress-related medications. Valium alone is consumed to the tune of 3.2 billion pills per year in the U.S.—a 25 million dollar business in itself. Except for short-run, special situations, medications are a non-productive, ineffective substitute for long-term relief of distress. Alternatives suggested in .this book are far better.

Here is a sound principle to follow: don't take anything to feel better emotionally, except after careful consideration with your physician.

BOX 6-3. A NATION OF DRUG-USERS

" 'Americans represent only 2 percent of the world population, but consume 60 percent of the world's illicit drugs,' says Dr. Arnold Washton, an expert on addiction.

" 'If that is not an indictment of our culture, I don't know what is.'

"Washton is co-author of a new study that provides some clues to a question rarely touched in the debate over the war on drugs: Why do Americans use more drugs than anyone else?

"Experts say U.S. per-capita consumption of illicit drugs is the world's highest. In addition, millions abuse prescription drugs from tranquilizers to sleeping pills. Alcohol and tobacco, usually excluded from the drug debate, account for 450,000 deaths a year.

" 'We are not only talking about cocaine or crack,' Washton said.

" 'We are now seeing high school kids who are getting high from typewriter correction fluid. We are becoming a nation of compulsive drug users, a chemical people.'

"The reason is rooted in a society driven by obsessions with perfection, performance, possessions, money, and power, according to the study, titled *Willpower's Not Enough.*

"At the same time, the support traditionally provided by the extended family or community is breaking down.

"In this environment, the study says, people are vulnerable to the temptation of 'mood changers.'

"Addictions in the United States go beyond drugs, according to Washton. No other country has as many compulsive overeaters (estimated at 40 million to 60 million) or gamblers (12 million).

" 'It is a form of collective insanity to believe that if all illicit drugs were somehow removed from this country, we would become a society of noncompulsive, life-embracing people,' said Washton, director of the Washton Institute on Addictions in New York and founder of the first national cocaine hot line.

"The fact that so many other types of compulsive behavior are springing up testifies to the fallacy of that belief."

SOURCE: Debussman (1990).

OVEREATING

Curiously, calorie consumption per person in the U.S. has decreased since 1900, yet the percentage of the population that is at least 20 percent overweight has increased dramatically. This has been caused largely by decreasing physical activity throughout the population, as we have suburbanized, industrialized, mechanized, and "automobilized." An increased percentage of fat in our diets has contributed to a lesser extent. So, too, no doubt, has been the tendency to eat in response to stress—especially when food is high in sugar or fat.

Eating to "relieve" tension often is learned in childhood. Mother feeds child at any sign of distress. As a consequence, the child may never learn to distinguish between hunger and emotions such as fear, anxiety, and anger. Any state of arousal is experienced as hunger. In other cases, the child learns by parental example that a quick way to deal with tension is to stuff it, hide it, not let it out, by overeating.

I have found that about half of those I ask in workshops about appetite during stress report an increase, the other half a decrease. For many, it depends on the type of stress: overeating (often through hurried stuffing) during anger, irritation, or rush, but losing appetite during worry or apprehension, or vice versa.

Overeating is a maladaptive response to distress for several reasons.

▼ It often evokes guilt.

▼ It leaves the stress emotion not faced directly.

▼ It ignores the distress-producing situation.

▼ It adds weight. More weight means less energy. More weight often erodes self-liking.

Finding suitable substitutes for eating binges or chronic overeating in response to stress is vital. Regular aerobic exercise is perhaps the best alternative of all, because it will reduce inches and pounds at the same time that it helps relieve physical and emotional tension.

ESCAPISM

In coping with original stressors, escapism through T.V., flight, drugs, books, or fantasy can be highly destructive. The stress response is likely to remain elevated, the distress emotion denied, the stress triggers unchanged. While temporary, intelligently used withdrawal may be constructive, escapism as a habit is potentially dangerous, both for self and others.

SPENDING SPREES

Often part of a manic-type response to tension, this can be devastating in its consequences. Like escapism, it is actually a form of evasion of true stress emotions and the original situation.

BOX 6-4. DRUGS AND THE GOSPEL OF MATERIALISM

The following letter appeared recently in the *Chico Enterprise-Record*. The author, Albert Mitchell (1989), clearly believes the solution to the U.S drug problem must go deeper than Red Ribbon Day or "Just Saying No." **What do you think?**

Dear Editor—

Who is kidding who? This nation has a drug abuse problem for the simple reason that American society has been, for the most part, spiritually dead for years. There is an emptiness that millions seek to assuage by indulging in booze, pills, crack, uppers, downers, heroin, whatever.

The most gigantic communications juggernaut the world has ever seen—television, radio, motion pictures, the press, billboards—are at work incessantly preaching the gospel of materialism to the corporate consumer cattle we have become.

Never has a nation been so ravaged by venality, by greed. Anyone with sufficient money can have a go at raping society if it is thought a buck can be made doing so. In the process we have created vast fear, vast suspicion, vast loneliness, vast emptiness of spirit.

"Just say no," we say to the kids, or 'Let's all wear a red ribbon to show we're against all that stuff.' This simplistic prattle goes on while other Americans go about coughing up over two hundred billion dollars a year to pay off drug suppliers around the world. Why do they do so? Because there is a spiritual vacuum.

We have created a society that is lawless, greedy, self-indulgent, with a devil-take-the-hindmost attitude toward the weak, the poor, the elderly. The fault lies not with Colombia, or the poppy fields of Peru or Thailand. The fault lies with a society whose great god is money. A society where greed tramples on whatever lies in its path.

We reap the whirlwind, and it is of our own making. Until we do something about re-ordering our rapacious society there will be drugs, drugs, and more drugs.

Albert Mitchell

PHYSICAL AND VERBAL ABUSE

Too often, personal distress does not remain personal. Rather it is transferred to others in the form of physical and verbal abuse. Tragically, we seem to take out our frustrations on those closest to us—especially our spouses, lovers, and children. Recent studies show a surprisingly high percentage of college students are involved in abusive love relationships. Most murders are inflicted on friends or family members. Wife beating and child abuse are among the most destructive of all reactions to our own distress.

BLAMING OTHERS

By blaming others, one can escape responsibility both for being distressed and for doing anything about it.

OVERWORKING

Another form of deflection is overworking. Digging in harder sometimes is a way to reduce distress. Often, however, it is a temporary palliative, ultimately multiplying problems for health, frame of mind, and family.

DENIAL

The subculture of masculinity is especially prone to teach boys and men: "keep moving," "if you don't think about it, it will go away," "be tough," "boys don't cry," and above all "maintain an image of strength." Temporary denial may be useful for seeing a difficult event or period through, but not when it is extended for very long. The result for both men and women who use this response to stress for extended periods is internal wear and tear until relationships and performances are seriously affected, emotional disturbances become extreme, or the body breaks.

MAGNIFICATION

"Making a mountain out of a molehill" can directly add to a stress build-up already started by other stressors. In essence, the stress response itself becomes a new stressor. This is a very common maladaptive reaction to stress that needs to be extinguished. One approach is to ask: What is the worst possible outcome of this situation? Usually, you will find you could live even with that outcome.

MARTYRDOM

Unfortunately, many people are habituated to distress—so addicted that they go out of their way to find it. This happens not out of deliberate choice, but because misery and pain are so familiar, the person seems to need his or her daily dose. The repetition compulsion overpowers the drive toward growth.

Self-created distress is perpetuated by rackets or games (Berne, 1964). *Rackets* are what people do inside their heads to keep themselves miserable—angry, anxious, or afraid. *Games* refers to interpersonal exchanges people use to make themselves or others feel bad. A "kick-me" game-player handles distress by encouraging others to make him feel useless or incompetent. A "stupid" player blunders again and again in order to be constantly reminded by others how inept or dependent he is.

Strange as it may seem, many people who have a history of distress go to great lengths to cope with their distress by creating more of it—thereby playing out their life script as a loser. This often is the tragic story of the alcoholic, the heroin addict, the habitual criminal, the psychotic. Changing this pattern requires enormous courage, awareness, and support. Most of all, it requires overcoming the immense inertia of the repetition compulsion.

Except when very stressful circumstances cannot be changed or when temporary distress is self-chosen for a good reason (like preparing for a concert performance), the approach of simply living with distress is unacceptable to people who seek good health and self-development. There usually is a better way.

LETHAL EFFECTS OF MALADAPTIVE RESPONSES TO DISTRESS

These, then, are illustrative maladaptive responses to distress. Focusing on death, the ultimate distressful side-effect of maladaptive coping responses, Roglieri (1980) estimates that through the effects of overeating, depression (which he takes to be a type of coping rather than a distress symptom), smoking, heavy drinking, and high blood pressure, about five or six of every 1,000 white males aged 40–45 will die an early death directly as a result of "mismanagement of stress." This does not include, of course, the contribution of the original stress itself to various causes of death, such as heart attacks or cancer. Roglieri argues that you are responding inappropriately to your distress if:

1. You light up a cigaret whenever challenged by a person, event, or situation.

2. You take a drink in response to, or in anticipation of, a stressful event.

3. You put your heart into your driving by speeding or driving aggressively.

4. You use food to calm yourself down.

5. You feel your heart beating rapidly, or your heart pounding when frustrated (indicating high blood pressure).

6. You use sleeping pills or tranquilizers frequently.

7. You become depressed (loss of appetite, loss of sleep, loss of libido).

Roglieri (1980, 202) concludes, "Because prolonged dependence on these inappropriate mechanisms for dealing with stress leads to a lifestyle that increases your risk of premature death and disability, these habits have been referred to as 'slow motion suicide.'" Short of that, these and other maladaptive responses to distress lessen the *quality* of life for others, if not oneself.

EXERCISE 6-1. MONITORING YOUR REACTIONS TO DISTRESS

During the past six months, how often have you used each of the following methods of trying to reduce your physical and emotional tension—Never, Rarely, Sometimes, or Often?

_____ 1. Drink alcoholic beverages

_____ 2. Smoke

_____ 3. Take a tranquilizer, sleeping pill, or other prescribed medication

_____ 4. Take aspirin.

_____ 5. Take an over-the-counter relaxant

_____ 6. Drink coffee, cola, or tea

_____ 7. Eat

_____ 8. Yell, hurt, or otherwise take it out on someone else

_____ 9. Forget about it and keep going

_____ 10. Use T.V., books, or something else to "escape" for awhile

_____ 11. Take a leisurely walk

_____ 12. Grin and bear it

_____ 13. Redefine the situation more positively in your mind

_____ 14. Change your approach to the person or stressor

_____ 15. Exercise

_____ 16. Do deep relaxation

_____ 17. Do a breathing or muscle relaxation technique

_____ 18. Talk it over with somebody

_____ 19. Pray

_____ 20. Use humor

_____ 21. Take a day off or a vacation

_____ 22. Other _____

_____ 23. Other _____

EXERCISE 6-2. REACTIONS TO DISTRESS DURING NEXT WEEK

During the next week, watch yourself and others close to you.

1. Observe which of the above reactions to distress are used by you or others.
2. With what effects?
3. What constructive alternatives might have been used?

STRENGTHENING ADAPTIVE REACTIONS TO DISTRESS ▼

MEDICATIONS

Most stress experts believe medications are over-prescribed and over-used. Yet there are four conditions when they may be called for.

1.   **To reduce intense pain.** Certainly medications are called for in cases of terminal cancer, post-surgery, or accident trauma, intense headaches, and other intensely painful stress-induced pain.

2.   **When a temporary crisis interferes with ability to carry on with daily life.** A prescribed relaxant may help you to continue to function until the circumstances are resolved by lowering your anxiety level, raising your mood in times of depression, or helping you sleep.

3.   **Chronic long-term disturbances.** Included, for example, are schizophrenia, hypertension, and manic depression.

4.   **When life is threatened by elevated stress.** For example, if a heart patient has anxiety-induced arrhythmias that could cause cardiac arrest, tranquilizers certainly may be called for.

After reviewing available literature on sleeping patterns, The National Academy of Medicine Institute of Sciences concluded that rarely, if ever, should sleeping pills be prescribed for longer than two to four weeks (Roglieri, 1980). Similarly, other medications usually should be viewed as temporary treatment while attempts are made to find long-term coping and lifestyle buffer methods.

SOLITUDE

When was the last time you were away by yourself, truly alone, for 24 hours? Forty-eight hours? A week? Ever? We are in almost constant contact with others—and need to be for emotional and practical reasons. Yet we also can benefit from being alone from time to time, perhaps routinely each year for a few days, perhaps occasionally to remove ourselves from stressful situations. As I write this, I am in a mountain cabin, truly alone, and I have been for many days. The experience is exhilarating—the opportunity to focus, rest, renew my spirit, appreciate the environment, experience simplicity. For more on solitude in modern life, read Anne Morrow Lindberg's *Gifts From the Sea* (Lindberg, 1978). This is a beautiful, inspiring personal statement about the beauty of solitude.

MUSIC

Music can have a variety of effects: arousal, warmth, sexuality, playfulness. Music can create a sense of structure about you, it can rekindle nostalgia, it can create moods and memories. It can stir you to action, add to your fear, make you angry or mournful, kindle religious sentiments, lower tensions, slow you down. Clearly, music can do many things, mentally and physically. People differ widely in musical tastes, and each person varies from time to time. Thoughtfully chosen music can indeed be restful, relaxing, and renewing. Find which kind works for you for specific occasions. Try to disregard what your particular social group thinks you should like. Listen to your body and spirit.

PLAY

George Sheehan, the runner-doctor-author, has stated that man is animal, child, scholar, and saint (Sheehan, 1978). Perhaps it would be more accurate to say man is *potentially* all of these. Too often, an imbalance is reached where man the animal and man the child are lost in the quest for money and status. Play is part of a good balance. Whether through active games, dance, running, frisbee, cards, pranks, parties, or practical jokes, play can be enormously valuable in dealing with periods of distress—and in reducing chances of its occurrence in the first place.

Reflect on your answer to question 11 in the Quality of Life Questions in Chapter 1. (How much fun and playfulness are you having?) How much time are you taking for your playful self? What would you most like to do during the next two weeks to lift your morale and provide a fun diversion? If you have fallen prey to the trap of all work–no play, see what specific steps you can take to bring a better balance back into your life.

During periods of overload, trauma, or depression, play seems far away. Yet it can be created, rediscovered. One of the gifts children give to adults is to stimulate us to play every now and then. Try it.

PRAYER

For centuries, prayer has been used to cope with tension. Prayer perhaps can be effective. Repetition of a verse as a focus of meditation can be relaxing. In fact, the relaxation response can be produced just as during secular methods of meditation. The time away to pray can lower activity level and anxiety. Prayer can increase hope and optimism. It can bring practical solutions. It can help tune in to one's "inner voice," which can be a source of enlightenment and direction. All these benefits can occur whatever one assumes about divine intervention—which may be the most important benefit of all.

Certainly, the belief in divine guidance and solace helps create a positive self-fulfilling prophecy. Unfortunately, the religious pathway sometimes leads to dependency and escape from personal responsibility for managing stress. Yet managing stress wisely through awareness of self-direction is entirely consistent with religious belief and practice. After all, God helps those who help themselves.

INTIMACY

Unfortunately, marriage or courtship can be terribly destructive, adding to, rather than lessening, distress during difficult periods. Yet there is perhaps no more powerful antidote to weariness, tension, upset, or depression than the authentic touching of two human spirits at the level of true intimacy. Something magical can happen that words fail to convey. Spirits rekindle, barriers come down, true emotion emerges from its submerged place, reassurance is given, distress lessens.

MASSAGE

Massage can be beneficial in response to tension in a number of ways, as Jane Madders (1979, 2) explains:

> Massage helps muscles relax. Physiological massage stimulates the flow of blood and improves the muscle tone. It assists in a clearing away of waste products, reduces muscle tension, and its assorted pain. It does far more than this, however. During massage, there is a subtle calming down of the whole body, a reduction of anxiety, a feeling of trust develops enabling the receiver to feel rather than to think. It offers recuperative rest from the turbulence of stress.

Learning to offer massage to one's partner is a true gift. Receiving massage is to receive a noble gift of love.

Massage for infants can promote bonding, as well as relieve tension in the child. Our Enloe Hospital Stress and Health Center now conducts training programs for new parents in how to massage infants carefully and effectively. Vimala Schneider, author of *Infant Massage* (1982), trained our instructor, Audrey Downes, in the same methods she is teaching other parents and instructors across the country. For further information about infant massage, including training programs for parents and instructors, write to: Audrey Downes, R.N., Infant Massage Programs, Stress and Health Center, Fifth Avenue and the Esplanade, N.T. Enloe Memorial Hospital, Chico, CA 95926.

A number of different massage techniques for adults are available from professionals in most medium-sized and larger cities: chiropractic, acupressure, Rolfing, reflexology, Touch for Health, and more. Taking a class or receiving individual treatments can be most useful, both for immediate stress-reduction and to learn techniques for use at home.

PROFESSIONAL ASSISTANCE

This book is based on the principle of personal responsibility for one's health and stress control. In the past, far too much reliance has been placed on one or another professional: the doctor, the chiropractor, the minister, the psychologist, the marriage counselor, the social worker. The techniques presented throughout this book can be learned and used at home, using your good judgment and willpower. Certain circumstances can be identified, however, when professional assistance definitely is called for.

▼ To learn more about specific stress control methods, such as aerobic exercise, meditation, massage, time management, and active listening

▼ To express frustrations, worries, plans, and the like to an objective trained listener

▼ To jointly problem-solve on a specific problem

▼ To trace under careful guidance the present or past roots of a specific emotional or practical problem in order to leave or solve it

▼ To receive a massage or other physical treatment

▼ To receive inspiration to do something on your own

▼ To receive group support for lifestyle change

HOBBIES

Favorite recreational activities, such as gardening, woodworking, golf, backpacking, fishing, hunting, rock collecting, birdwatching, watching professional basketball on TV—all can help prevent or reduce distress in several ways.

Diversion—getting away from the stressor

Solitude

Companionship

Enhancement of self-worth

Play

Appreciation of the minor nature of your
immediate problem within the larger picture

HYDROTHERAPY

An approach to relaxation many find very effective is as primitive as imaginable: warm water. Whether in the form of a hot bath, a hot shower, or the more contemporary form of a hot tub or flotation tank, this can be a most effective relaxation method, especially at the end of a hard day of work. While formal resarch on the stress-reduction benefits of this approach are limited at best, anecdotal reports are endless, including from this writer.

HUMOR

The ability to infuse humor into everyday life is invaluable for health and happiness. Research evidence supports what folk wisdom has long held: chuckling at situations and self is healthy (Dixon, 1980; Brody, 1983; Martin and Lefcourt, 1983; Long, 1987; Nezu, Nezu & Blissett, 1988). Humor at the expense of others is something else altogether, of course (Blumenfeld and Alpern, 1986). But mirthful laughter, funniness, joking in a playful spirit can enhance mental and physical well-being— and sometimes can even heal (Cousins, 1981; Orstein and Sobel, 1989; Wellingham-Jones, 1989; Graham, 1990). Studies suggest that humor may promote health partly through bolstering the immune system (Dillon, Minchoff and Baker, 1985; Berk, 1989).

EXERCISE

In Chapter 8 you will read extensive evidence that exercise is a highly effective coping step—perhaps the most effective of any presented in this book. Consistent daily or near-daily aerobic exercise can serve as prevention of distress, a type of health buffer. When you are going through a difficult period—interpersonal conflict, adjustment to a new circumstance like a job or new college, depression, time pressure, even overload—exercise can help release physical tension, lift you out of an emotional sink, provide time to plan solutions, and more. By itself, of course, exercise will not solve problems. But it can certainly help bring forth the strength and creativity to approach those problems with zest and vitality (Johnsgard, 1989).

DEEP RELAXATION

Meditation, yoga, self-hypnosis and other methods for eliciting the relaxation response have been used for centuries to cope with the stressors of daily living. Like exercise, deep relaxation is best utilized as an everyday, routine part of living. As such, it becomes a natural part of one's repertoire of coping tools. Deep relaxation restores energy, yields creative solutions to problems, and creates mental and physical calm for facing difficult episodes. Deep relaxation is discussed in more detail in Chapter 9.

HEALTHY PLEASURES

David Sobel, physician and co-author of two well-known books on stress and health, *The Healing Brain* (Ornstein and Sobel, 1986) and *Healthy Pleasures* (Ornstein and Sobel, 1989), recently was featured in an article about how stress experts handle theirs (Castleman, 1990).

In addition to his usual work as Regional Director for Patient Education and Health Promotion for Northern California Kaiser-Permanente (a large Health Maintenance Organization), and his laborious writing work, Sobel had faced a very challenging series of events in his personal life during the 18 months prior to the interview about how he handles his own stress.

Among other things, he had had to contend with the unexpected death of a family member, and he and his family had had several rooms added to their San Jose home. During the renovation, they had had to move out for two months, then return after the work was completed.

Said Sobel, "It's been quite a time. Very stressful. But that's life."

How does Sobel cope? Here is what he told the interviewer (Castleman, 1990, 38, 39):

> Frankly, I don't worry much about managing my stress. I don't use any specific techniques. I'm not opposed to formal stress-management programs or exercises; some people need them. But I'm not involved in any. I simply try to fill my life with activities I personally find pleasurable, things that help rejuvenate me.

Beyond health, family and friends, and having your basic needs met, it's not the big things in life that make the difference. It's the little pleasures you create for yourself: playing with your kids, phone calls to old friends, a hug, a compliment, gardening, having pets, gazing into an aquarium.

Whenever I get upset about something in my little corner of the world, I spin my globe. San Jose is a tiny dot. California is a little sliver. It's a big world out there, and each of us is just a microscopic part of it.

I agree with Sobel. Cultivating healthy pleasures can be a very effective approach to coping with the stressors of everyday life, large and small. For me, this includes, for example:

▼ A cleansing conversation with my wife about our work that day

▼ The beauty of my daily run, usually along rural trails

▼ The quiet morning and evening routine of feeding our farm animals

▼ Cleaning up llama dung on a sunny Sunday afternoon while listening to "Prairie Home Companion" on my Walkman

▼ Enjoying my dog lying quietly at my side for hours on end as I write

▼ Long-distance telephone conversations with my grown daughters

▼ Strolling in our pasture with my wife, cat, and dog on a sunny weekend morning

▼ Inserting my earplugs, going to my recliner chair, and sinking into deep relaxation in the midst of a busy afternoon at the office

▼ Reading the newspaper before a sparkling, warm fireplace on a nippy winter evening

▼ Taking a hot tub under the stars at the end of the day

▼ Kayaking down a Class I, II, or III river in Northern California with my wife and friends.

For me, these healthy pleasures are more than means of coping. They have become personal anchors, offering stability in the midst of a hectic, fast-paced, rapidly changing world. I look to my healthy pleasures for quiet stability.

In this chapter, we have discussed the concept of coping— what you think and do as you deal with the large and small demands of daily living, including how you respond to your own temporary distress. Chapter 7 focuses on a very important part of coping, namely your interpretations of stressful events. We call this self-talk.

REFERENCES ▼

American Psychiatric Association, (1987). *Diagnostic and Statistical Manual of Mental Disorders*, III-R. Washington, D.C.

Berk, L. (1989). Laughter and immunity. *Advances, 6,* 5.

Berne, E. (1964). *Games People Play.* New York: Grove Press.

Blumenfeld, E., & Alpern, L. (1986). *The Smile Connection.* Englewood Cliffs, NJ: Prentice-Hall, Inc.

Brody, R. (1983). Anatomy of a laugh. *American Health,* 43-47.

Castleman, M. (1990). How the stress experts deal with theirs. *Medical Self-Care,* No. 57, 35-40, 74.

Cohen, F., & Lazarus, R.S. (1979). Coping with the stresses of illness. In Stone, G.C., Cohen, F., & Adler, N.E. (Eds.), *Health Psychology: A Handbook.* San Francisco: Jossey-Bass Publishers.

Cousins, N. (1981). *Anatomy of An Illness As Perceived By The Patient: Reflections on Healing and Regeneration.* New York: Bantam.

Debussman, B. (1989). A nation of drug users. *San Francisco Chronicle,* November 25, C1.

Dillon, K.M., Minchoff, B., & Baker, KH. (1985). Positive emotional states and enhancement of the immune system. *International Journal of Psychiatry in Medicine,* 15, 13-17.

Dixon, N.F. (1980). Humor: A cognitive alternative to stress? In Sarason, I.G., & Spielberger, C.D., (Eds.), *In Stress and Anxiety* (Vol. 7). Washington, D.C.: Hemisphere.

Folkman, S., Schaefer, C., & Lazarus, R.S. (1979). Cognitive processes as mediators of stress and coping. In Hamilton, V., & Warburton, D.M. (Eds.), *Human Stress and Cognition: An Information Processsing Approach.* London: Wiley.

Frese, M. (1986). Coping as a moderator and mediator between stress at work and psychosomatic complaints. In Appley, M.H. & Trumbull, R. (Eds.). *Dynamics of Stress: Physiological, Psychological, and Social Perspectives.* New York: Plenum Press, 183-206.

Gallup Organization. (1990). A measure of worry. *Boston Globe,* April 16, 24.

Graham, B. (1990). The healing power of humor. *Mind/Body/Health Digest,* 4, 1-2.

Green, J., & Shellenberger, R. (1991). *The Dynamics of Health and Wellness: A Biopsocial Approach.* Fort Worth: Holt, Rinehart and Winston.

Holroyd, K.A., & Lazarus, R.S. (1982). Stress, coping, and somatic adaptation. In Goldberger, L., & Breznetz, S. (Eds.), *Handbook of Stress: Theoretical and Clinical Aspects.* New York: Free Press, 21-35.

James, M., & Jongeward, D. (1971). *Born to Win.* Reading, MA.: Addison-Wesley.

Johnsgård, K. (1989). *The Exercise Prescription To Depression and Anxiety.* New York: Plenum Press.

Krohne, H.W. (1986). Coping with stress: Dispositions, strategies, and the problem of measurement. In Appley, M.H., & Trumbull, R., (Eds.), *Dynamics of Stress: Physiological, Psychological, and Social Perspectives.* New York: Plenum Press, 207-228.

Laux, L. (1986). A self-presentational view of coping with stress. In Appley, M.H., & Trumbull, R., (Eds.), *Dynamics of Stress: Physiological, Psychological, and Social Perspectives.* New York: Plenum Press, 233-254.

Lazarus, R.S., & Folkman, S. (1984). *Stress, Appraisal and Coping.* New York: Springer Publishing Company.

Levanthal, H., & Nerenz, D.R. (1983). A model for stress research with some implications for the control of stress disorders. In Meichenbaum, D. & Jaremko, M. (Eds.), *Stress Prevention and Management: A Cognitive Behavioral Approach.* New York: Plenum.

Linderg, A.M. (1978). *Gifts From The Sea.* Westminster: Random.

Long, P. (1987). Laugh and be well? *Psychology Today,* 21, 28-29.

Los Angeles Times. (1989). Obituaries, September 12, 24.

Madders, J. (1979). *Stress and Relaxation.* New York: Arco.

Maddi, S.R., & Kobasa, S.C. (1984). *The Hardy Executive: Health Under Stress.* Homewood, Ill.: Dow-Jones Irwin.

Martin, R.A., & Lefcourt, H.M. (1983). Sense of humor as a moderator of the relation between stressors and moods. *Journal of Personality and Social Psychology,* 45, 1313-1324.

Mitchell, A. Drugs and the gospel of materialism. *Chico Enterprise-Record,* September 9, 1989, 4B.

National Center for Health Statistics. (1989). *Health, United States, 1988.* DHHS Publication No. PHS 89-1232. Washington, D.C.: U.S. Government Printing Office.

Nezu, A.M., Nezu, C.M., & Blissett, S.E. (1988). Sense of humor as a moderator of the relation between stressful events and psychological distress: A prospective analysis. *Journal of Personality and Social Psychology,* 54, 520-525.

Ornstein, R., & Sobel, D. (1986). *The Healing Brain.* New York: Touchstone.

Ornstein, R., & Sobel, D. (1989). *Healthy Pleasures.* Reading, MA.; Addison-Wesley.

Pearlin, L.I., & Schooler, C. (1978). The structure of coping. *Journal of Health and Social Behavior,* 19, 2-21.

Prokop, C.K., Bradley, L.A., Burish, T.G., Anderson, K.O., & Fox, J.E. (1991). *Health Psychology: Clinical Methods and Research.* New York: MacMillan.

Roglieri, J.L. (1980). *Odds On Your Life.* New York: Seaview.

Schneider, V. (1982). *Infant Massage.* New York: Bantam.

Sheehan, G. (1978). *Running and Being.* New York: Simon.

Steiner, C. (1974). *Scripts People Live.* New York: Grove Press.

Surgeon General. (1990). *The Health Benefits of Smoking Cessation: A Report of the Surgeon General.* Washington, D.C.: U.S. Government Printing Office.

Taylor, S.E. (1986). *Health Psychology.* New York: Random House.

Wellingham-Jones, P. (1989). *Successful Women.* Tehama, CA: PWL Publishing.

Self-Talk:
It's All in How
You See It

Chapter 7

INTRODUCTION ▼

Jason faced three midterms, two term papers, an oral report, and an accounting club meeting during the next three days. He determined the only way to get through this period successfully was to dig in, take it as a challenge, focus his energy, and organize his time very carefully. Jonathan faced a very similar circumstance. He reacted quite differently: he felt overwhelmed and depressed,

saw this as one more instance of how unfair his professors were, and procrastinated by watching TV for hours and allowing himself to be distracted by his roommates.

Terri was a court clerk who was caught in the middle between a court administrator who gave her one set of orders and a judge who tried to pull her in other directions. She found this role conflict unpleasant, but she nevertheless found satisfaction in her work and did her best to clarify for her two role partners the bind she was in, so they would better agree on their expectations of her. Laurie was another court clerk in much the same situation. Her response, however, was to feel angry most of the time, and to fantasize about not having to work at all. Her work performance was below par.

You are in a crowded elevator taking you to the sixth floor. As the elevator stops at floor three, you are jabbed from behind, then pushed as others get out. You feel slightly irritated. The same thing happens at floor four. You feel your aggravation rise as you tell yourself, "What the——does that person think he's doing? Can't he see I can't move because it's so crowded in here? Why doesn't he just relax?" As a bit of a hot reactor, you turn around—only to discover that the person is blind and that what jabbed you was his cane. Immediately, your thoughts change: "This person is blind. Now I understand why he couldn't see what was going on. No big deal. But how chagrined I feel for getting so upset."

SELF-TALK AND STRESS   ▼

UNDERSTANDING SELF-TALK

These stories illustrate two simple points:

1. Your interpretation of stressors, not stressors themselves, cause distress.

2. You can control your interpretation of stressors.

You will recall from Chapter 2 that soon after it began, stress theory departed from the simplistic notion that human stress is a direct response to external stimuli. We noted that cognitive theory emphasizes the role of individual interpretation. So do other theories we reviewed: stress is a result of a transactional, meaning-centered coping process, hardiness theory, and sense of coherence theory.

This view is not new, illustrated by the following quotations:

Epictetus: "People are disturbed, not by events, but by their view of those events."

Shakespeare: "There is nothing either good or bad but thinking makes it so."

Donne: "The mind is its own place and it can make hell of heaven or heaven of hell."

Twain: "I have had a great many troubles in my life, and most never happened."

The assumption expressed in these statements—that how we think matters most—has profound implications. Most of all, it gives power back to the person to shape her own experience. It is no longer those stupid, irresponsible, threatening, or inconsiderate people who cause upset. Rather, it is your self-talk about them—your interpretations and beliefs.

You talk to yourself 100 percent of the waking time. You constantly process thoughts—about what to do next, what you just did, what you feel at the moment, what others think of you, what your senses tell you, how to deal with an upcoming event, and on and on. Some refer to this as "stream of consciousness."

In *The Bonfire of the Vanities* (1987), author Tom Wolfe does a superb job of describing Sherman's stream of consciousness. For example, Sherman, who considered himself to be a Master of the Universe (he sold institutional bonds on Wall Street and paid monthly bills of $1.2 million to maintain his style of life), told his wife he was taking their dog, Marshall, for a walk outside their Park Avenue apartment. His real intention, of course, was to get out of the house to call his lover. His wife says, "Did you know it was raining?"

> Still not looking up [Sherman responds]: "Yes, I know." Finally he managed to snap the leash on the animal's collar. "You're certainly being nice to Marshall all of a sudden." *Wait a minute.* Was this irony? Did she suspect something? He looked up.

> But the smile on her face was obviously genuine, altogether pleasant . . . a lovely smile, in fact . . . *Still a very good-looking woman, my wife* . . . with her fine features, her big clear blue eyes, her rich brown hair . . . *But she's forty years old!* No getting around it . . . Today *good-looking* . . . Tomorrow they'll be talking about what a *handsome* woman she is . . . Not her fault . . . *But not mine either!* (Wolfe, 1987, 11)

Self-talk, the term I prefer to apply to this kind of internal dialogue, is an ever-present part of life. The question is, how much is it under your control and how much does it take on a life of its own, pushed along by the **repetition compulsion**—the force of habit. You can learn to manage your self-talk.

EXERCISE 7-1. IDENTIFYING PERSONAL USES OF SELF-TALK MANAGEMENT

Self-talk can be used for a variety of personal issues and problems. Below is a partial list.

Preventing worry
Exercising
Listening
Assuming responsibility
Being self-directed
Building hardiness
Increasing self-esteem
Reducing self-criticism
Preventing anger and irritability

Giving constructive feedback
Avoiding procrastination
Organizing time
Reducing chronic hurry and hassle
Reducing chronic overload
Being criticized or attacked.
Meeting a challenge
Eating right
Making transitions
Stopping smoking
Acting with authority
Balancing work/family or community/family
Maintaining good posture
Staying calm under pressure
Pulling out of depression
Enjoying the present
Coping with unexpected emergencies
Reducing shyness
Reducing fear of disapproval
Avoiding working too hard
Avoiding overindulging
Increasing control over emotions
Avoiding taking work home (mentally)
Reducing perfectionism
Turning "musts" into "preferences"
Reducing "shoulding" toward self or others
Giving yourself credit
Building confidence

Check those items on the list to which you believe self-talk might be usefully applied. Then underline the three you want to begin to work on first.

Self-talk not only occupies your mind and your time. Self-talk influences emotions, mental pictures, physical states, and behavior. In short, you are a product of what you think.

Of particular relevance for human stress is that self-talk is self-fulfilling. If you believe others are untrustworthy and selfish, that probably is what you will get. If you assume you are capable and up to the task at hand, you probably will be relatively anxiety-free and will succeed. If you blame yourself when events don't go your way, if you think it is always this way, and it's this way in most parts of your life, you probably will be easily depressed.

Most of all, *self-talk can be self-regulated,* although it is not easy. Changing self-talk habits often takes hard work and lots of patience.

The place of self-talk or interpretation in stress can be expressed in a simple chart.

$$Stressor \longrightarrow Interpretation \longrightarrow Stress$$

If Epictetus, Shakespeare and Donne are correct, then blaming, feeling victimized, pointing the finger—all become wholly inappropriate. For the nature of your response to potentially stressful events is determined by your own thinking and not by the events themselves.

You might find yourself thinking, "But sometimes events in fact are awful and terrible. To think otherwise would be Pollyannish." I agree that events often are unpleasant and unwanted. Sometimes even terrible. Yet most often events are terrible only because they are seen that way. Still, it is important to elaborate a bit about the role of interpretation in stress.

STRESSFUL EVENTS, SELF-TALK, AND STRESS

My reading, personal experience, and work with thousands of people experiencing unwanted distress have led me to the following conclusions about the part interpretation plays in stress and distress.

1.   Stressors are distressors only when they are interpreted as threatening.

Stressors may be interpreted as a threat to any one of several parts of your existence.

To life and safety: "I could get shot by this guy robbing me."

To basic needs: "Getting laid off my job will eliminate income for me and my family."

To self-worth: "Her bad grades mean I am a failure as a parent."

To image or reputation: "My co-workers in this meeting will think I am incompetent if I don't give an intelligent answer to this question."

To acceptance or approval: "If I don't do things just right tonight, he will never ask me out again."

To satisfaction and enjoyment: "I will be miserable for two weeks if I blow this project."

To pain limit: "This is more than I can bear."

2.   Sometimes it is rational and realistic to interpret stressors as threatening and therefore to be temporarily distressed.

For example:

Fear and physical tension at hearing about an earth slide up the hill from your house

Grief and pain at word of death of a loved one

Concern, disappointment, and temporary insomnia at word of an unwanted job transfer

Anger and readiness for action at an attack by a neighbor's dog on your child

3. Stressors often are unnecessarily and unrealistically interpreted as threatening, thereby causing unnecessary distress.

This is especially true of perceived threats to self-worth, image, acceptance, and satisfaction. As we shall see, alternative interpretations are possible.

4. Stressors are unnecessarily interpreted as threatening when you:

Perceive yourself as helpless to control your reactions to stressful situations.

"I can't do anything about my test anxiety."

"I can't control my temper when she makes me angry."

"My depression is out of my control."

"I can't help feeling like a wall flower."

"I can't cope."

"I'm totally overwhelmed."

"I will have a nervous breakdown if this happens."

Perceive yourself as helpless to influence events or people in the surrounding environment.

"There is nothing I can do about that neighbor kid's blaring stereo."

"Vandalism is out of control in this neighborhood."

"My boss is oppressive and insensitive, but I am just a little guy here and can't do anything about it."

"There is no way the poor quality of teaching in this school can be changed."

Perceive the environment as unrealistically dangerous.

"I know those teachers are out to get me, pure and simple."

"Those bright graduate students will make me look bad for sure."

"All whites (or blacks) are a threat to me."

5. Unnecessarily interpreting a specific stressor as threatening results from unreasonable beliefs.

A number of common unreasonable beliefs are held by specific participants in my stress control program.

"I must maintain an image of strength and invulnerability."

"I must be sure to act so others will like me."

"I must always please others."

"If I don't say yes to this, I will never have the opportunity again."

"Anything new is dangerous."

"I must appear feminine at all times—to both men and women."

"I must appear masculine at all times—to both men and women."

"If I relax, disaster will strike."

"If I relax, I will fall behind."

"Spending time on exercise, relaxation, or fun is wasteful."

"If I am really me, I will get hurt."

"Taking one hour a day for me would be selfish."

"If I don't do it, nobody else can or will."

"I must always say 'yes' when asked to help."

"My actions are the main cause of others' emotions."

"Most people are out to get me."

6.   Faulty interpretations resulting in unnecessary distress can be prevented or altered in two ways.

Controlling self-talk as it occurs in the immediate situation

Altering unreasonable beliefs out of which negative self-talk arises

---

EXERCISE 7-2. FAULTY INTERPRETATIONS DURING PAST WEEK

Looking back over the past month, identify circumstances in which you:

1.   Felt unnecessarily helpless to control your emotional or behavioral reactions to a stressor.

2.   Felt unnecessarily helpless to influence people or events around you.

3.   Unnecessarily interpreted the surrounding environment as dangerous.

4.   In retrospect, how might you have thought and acted more realistically or positively to create less upset for yourself?

EXERCISE 7-3. MONITORING THREATENING INTERPRETATIONS

During the next three days, identify each instance when you feel emotional or physical distress. You may want to use a diary for this.

1.   To what do you interpret the stressor to be a threat in each instance?

2.   Is your interpretation realistic or faulty?

3.   What alternative interpretations might you have used in each case?

COMMON STYLES OF NEGATIVE SELF-TALK

Self-talk is an ever-present part of life. You continually appraise or assess stressors as to their nature and likely effects on your experience. In short, you think about them. We noted above that the content of this thinking affects the emotional, physical, and behavioral responses that follow.

Life is challenging, hard, sometimes downright difficult. Yet people's thinking often makes events worse than they truly need be. Several common styles of negative self-talk can be identified through which individuals sometimes make themselves miserable—or miserable to be around.

1. **Negativizing.** Filtering out positive aspects of a situation, while focusing only on negatives.

Example of distorted self-talk:	This job is nothing but one headache after another.
Example of rational self-talk:	This job has many negative things about it, but then it has some positive ones, too. Like most things, it is a mixture of good and bad.

2. **Awfulizing.** Turning a difficult or unsatisfactory situation into something awful, terrible, and intolerable.

Example of distorted self-talk:	Drivers in this town are the worst this side of the Rockies. I can't stand it.
Example of rational self-talk:	Many drivers around here make bad judgments and sometimes even bad mistakes. However, like me they are Fallible Human Beings (FHB's) who sometimes make mistakes—a circumstance hardly worth getting very upset about.

3. **Catastrophizing.** Expecting that the worst almost certainly will happen.

Example of distorted self-talk:	I absolutely know that if my husband goes through with his plan to fly to New York, his plane will crash.
Example of rational self-talk:	I wish my husband didn't have to fly to New York, but the chances of anything happening to him are so remote it is hardly worth worrying about.

4. **Overgeneralizing.** Generalizing from a single event or piece of information to all or most such things.

Example of distorted self-talk:	(After a salesman's failure to sell a product to a prospective client.) This again shows that I am totally inept in relating to people.
Example of rational self-talk:	What can I learn from this situation to continue to improve my effectiveness as a salesman?

5. **Minimizing.** Diminishing the value or importance of something to less than it actually is.

Example of distorted self-talk:	(Self-deprecating professor after having his article accepted for publication by a professional journal.) It was accepted, but it certainly is not the quality of writing I expected to be turning out at this point in my career.

Example of rational self-talk: The article may not be the greatest contribution I will ever make, but it is something I can be satisfied with for now.

6. **Blaming.** Attributing responsibility for events, especially negative ones, to someone else, even when such responsibility rightfully belongs to self.

Example of distorted self-talk: If only my mother had been more loving, then I could have been happy.

Example of rational self-talk: It would have been nice if my mother had loved me more. However, I am now responsible for my own happiness or unhappiness.

7. **Perfectionism.** Impossibly demanding standards toward self, others, or both in many situations.

Example of distorted self-talk: Other drivers should obey all traffic laws and always should drive according to the standards of common courtesy I believe in.

Example of rational self-talk: It would be desirable if other drivers obeyed all traffic laws and followed standards of common courtesy. However, many don't and won't—a fact of life hardly worth getting very upset about.

8. **Musterbation.** The demand that events must turn out as I want them to—otherwise, it inevitably will be very upsetting to me.

Example of distorted self-talk: I must have constant approval and acceptance if life is to be worthwhile and if I am to be happy.

Example of rational self-talk: It would be nice to be approved and accepted most of the time. However, my happiness does not depend upon it.

9. **Personalizing.** Believing that others' behavior or feelings are entirely caused by self.

Example of distorted self-talk: I know he is depressed because of what I implied in my remarks yesterday.

Example of rational self-talk: I will handle situations like yesterday better in the future. However, his depression may or may not be related to what I said. In any case, if he chooses to be depressed, that is his problem, not mine.

10. **Judging Human Worth.** Evaluating total worth of self or others on the basis of traits or behavior.

Example of distorted self-talk:	I really muffed that situation yesterday. How terrible of me. This proves again what a Rotten Person (RP) I am.
Example of rational self-talk:	I didn't handle that situation yesterday very well. What can I learn from it so I can do better next time?

11. Control Fallacy. The belief that happiness depends on cajoling or coercing others to do what I think they should.

Example of distorted self-talk:	There is no way I can enjoy my work unless I can get my employees to work as hard and effectively as I believe they should.
Example of rational self-talk:	I will continue to strive to upgrade the work of my employees. Meanwhile, I refuse to let my job satisfaction depend on them.

12. Polarized Thinking. Things are black and white, right or wrong, good or bad. There is no middle ground.

Example of distorted self-talk:	Either I do perfectly on this test or I am a failure.
Example of rational self-talk:	I will do my best on this test—and then be satisfied with my performance this time around.

13. Being Right. I am continually on trial to prove that my opinions and actions are correct. Being wrong is unthinkable. Therefore, I must go to any length to demonstrate my rightness.

Example of distorted self-talk:	I must be certain they *know* I know what I am talking about.
Example of rational self-talk:	I have no need here to prove myself, because my self-worth does not depend on what others think of me.

14. Fallacy of Fairness. Feeling resentful because the world does not conform to my sense of what is fair.

Example of distorted self-talk:	It is just not fair that those questions were on that exam. I have every reason to be upset.
Example of rational self-talk:	I don't agree that those questions were on the exam. However, they were—something I cannot change and need not get upset about.

15. Shoulding. Constant imposition of *shoulds* and *should haves* on self, others, or both.

Example of distorted self-talk:	I should have said that differently. I should never behave like that.
Example of rational self-talk:	I would like to have handled that situation more effectively. Next time I will do it differently.

16. **Magnifying.** Making more of an event than it actually is.

Example of distorted self-talk:	This low grade is the worst thing that ever happened to me. It's horrible. What a Rotten Person I am!
Example of rational self-talk:	How unfortunate I didn't do well on this test. I genuinely blew it. Yet it's not the end of the world. Next time I certainly will study harder.

EXERCISE 7-4. IDENTIFYING YOUR STYLES OF NEGATIVE SELF-TALK

1. Re-read the list of common styles of negative self-talk. Circle the number of those you recognize as present in yourself more often that you would like.
2. Underline the ones you would most like to change.

TURNING SELF-TALK INTO A POSITIVE FORCE ▼

The 16 common styles of negative self-talk manifest themselves in two forms: situational self-talk and long-term beliefs. Therefore, transforming negative self-talk habits into positive or realistic self-talk habits can be accomplished by two categories of self-talk methods: methods for managing situational self-talk and methods for managing one's perspective—that is, one's cluster of beliefs that endure though time.

MANAGING SITUATIONAL SELF-TALK

> John tended to react defensively each time his wife even hinted that he had done something wrong. He knew she usually did not intend to hurt his feelings, question his competence or offend him. Yet he seemed to react automatically, with little apparent ability to control his flare-ups. He wanted very much to change this negative habit.

John learned in his stress class that either of two techniques can be very effective in managing his situational interpretation whenever this repetitive episode with his wife arises.

Tool #1: The P and Q Method

As John finds himself reacting defensively in the above situation, he now quickly turns to the P (Pause) and Q (Question) Method. He tells himself to take a deep breath, hesitate before going further, and ask of himself:

▼ What is my self-talk here?

▼ How am I upsetting myself?

▼ Is this truly worth getting upset about?

▼ How can I interpret this situation so I will respond with reasonable feelings and actions?

John soon discovered what he usually tells himself when his wife questions something he has just done: "I can't stand to be criticized. Being criticized is awful, intolerable, and I can't let her get away with this. That would diminish my worth and stature. I must and will defend myself here at all costs. If she wins, I lose." As he began to question his self-talk, it gradually began to change.

John sometimes uses another method to manage his situational self-talk.

Tool #2: Instant Replay

This method sometimes works for John's defensiveness (Bedford, 1981). An alternative to the P and Q Method, it too can work for you when you find yourself reacting to a stressor in an undesirable fashion (depression, anxiety, irritability, anger). Instant replay involves using 3 C's:

▼ Catch (recognize) my negative self-talk

▼ Challenge it

▼ Change it. Substitute realistic or positive self-talk.

Below are questions to ask in challenging negative self-talk:

FACTUAL OR DISTORTED?

1. Is this self-talk based on *fact*—that is, on objective reality?

2. What *evidence* is there that this self-talk is *true*?

3. Is this self-talk a *distortion* of reality? If so, what type of distortion am I creating?

MODERATE OR EXTREME?

1. Is my self-talk part of an unnecessarily *hot reaction*?

2. Can I get along just as well with a *cooler* reaction?

3.   Is this self-talk an unnecessarily demanding *should* on myself and others?

4.   Am I thinking in a *rigid* or *extreme way?*

HELPFUL OR HARMFUL?

1.   Is this self-talk helpful or harmful to me? For others?

2.   How does this self-talk affect:
My *emotional stability* or *upset?* Others' emotional stability or upset?
My *physical state* and *health?* Others' physical state and health?
My *relationships* with others?
My *behavior?* Will this self-talk lead to helpful or harmful behavior for me and others?

Below are a number of realistic self-talk statements that can be helpful in reacting to potentially stressful situations— at the moment they occur.

This too shall pass, and my life will be better.

I am a worthy person.

I am doing the best I can, given my history and awareness.

Like everyone else, I am an FHB (Fallible Human Being).

What is, is.

Look how far I have progressed, and I am still moving forward.

There are no failures, only different degrees of success.

I will be true to myself.

I will feel okay—guilt-free—about being temporarily upset.

I know I am not helpless. I can and will take necessary actions to pull through this difficult event.

I will remain engaged and involved rather than pulling back and retreating from this difficult set of circumstances.

This is an opportunity rather than a threat—to learn something new, to change direction, or to try a new approach.

One step at a time.

I can remain calm with this difficult person.

I know I will be okay no matter what happens.

He or she is responsible for his or her reaction to me.

This unpleasant situation will soon be over.

This unpleasant situation is merely unpleasant—hardly horrible.

I can bear anything for awhile.

In the long run, does this really matter?

Is this truly worth getting upset about?

I really don't need to prove myself in this situation.

Don't over-react. React appropriately.

Don't sweat the small stuff. It's all small stuff (Almost).

EXERCISE 7-5. YOUR FAVORITE STYLES OF NEGATIVE SITUATIONAL SELF-TALK AND REALISTIC ALTERNATIVES

1.   Divide a sheet of paper in half. Over the left-hand column, write *Style of Negative Self-talk.* Over the right-hand column, write *Realistic Self-talk Alternative.*

2.   In the left-hand column, write in the four styles of negative self-talk you underlined above.

3.   In the right-hand column, write in positive alternatives from above that will help eliminate each negative style.

4.   Write the one positive self-talk statement you would most like to learn and use on an index card. Review and apply your card many times each day.

EXERCISE 7-6. USING THE SITUATIONAL SELF-TALK METHODS

1.   During the next several days, deliberately use either of the two situational self-talk methods—P and Q Method or Instant Replay—when you find yourself becoming upset.

2.   Discuss with someone close to you what you experienced. Alternatively, write about your experiences in a personal journal.

BOX 7-1. EXAMPLE OF RE-EXAMINING SELF-TALK

Below is the report from one of my students about how she recently applied Exercise 7-5.

1. The activating event that spurred the stressor was a very personal situation that occurred between my mother and myself. My family is not one for touching each other to show affection. But my mother and I have grown increasingly closer day by day. When it was time for me to leave for Chico after spending Christmas with her, I felt an urge to hug her—showing my love for her. Anyway, we both stood in the driveway, hesitant of what should come next. So we said our goodbyes verbally, and I drove off.

2. The negative self-talk with which I upset myself was negativizing, awfulizing, and blaming her to not show me affection when I was younger. To prove to her that I do not need her warmth and do not need to take a risk would be a couple more negative self-talks.

3. Here are the unwanted consequences I created for myself: the awaiting of another chance to show affection toward her, blaming her, blaming myself. I created our barrier to continue. I also made myself feel less of a loving creature of earth.

4. The realistic self-talk statements that would have led to more positive results are: be true to myself, engage rather than pull back from the situation, take this as an opportunity rather than a threat, believe that I will be okay no matter what happens. I feel the most important self-talk is to be true to myself because this turns out to be true to others.

5. The desirable consequences I would like to create in similar future situations are to be true and recognize that benefits outweigh the negative consequences. I will gain more self-confidence, friends, and happiness.

Managing Stress-Related Beliefs

Whenever you respond to specific situational stressors, your self-talk is influenced by your long-term perspective—that is, by your ongoing beliefs. A belief is an enduring assumption that you carry along from day to day, week to week, year to year. Perspective refers to a cluster of beliefs.

Behind every specific instance of negative self-talk are one or more unreasonable beliefs. Albert Ellis, founder of Rational-Emotive Therapy, refers to these as irrational beliefs (Ellis, 1957, 1962, 1969, 1973; Ellis & Harper, 1975).

A belief is irrational or unreasonable if it is:

Distorted rather than Factual

Extreme rather than Moderate

Harmful rather than Helpful.

As Rathus states, "We carry them (irrational beliefs) with us; they are our personal doorways to distress. They can give rise to problems in themselves, and, when problems assault us from other sources, these beliefs can magnify their effect" (Rathus, 1990, 438). It becomes vital as a first step, then, to be aware of your beliefs that influence situational interpretations. It also is important to find means of changing them when needed.

Tool #1: Rewriting Old Beliefs
Below are 20 common unreasonable or irrational beliefs that often lead to negative situational self-talk. Read them, then turn to Exercise 7-7.

Irrational Beliefs

1.   Other people and outside events upset me.

2.   I am thin-skinned by genetic nature—I was born that way.

3.   I cannot control my thoughts and feelings.

4.   I cannot change. I am too old, too set in my ways, beyond hope.

5.   It is imperative that I be accepted by others, especially by those who are important to me.

6.   Most people are bad and wicked and cannot be trusted.

7.   If things do not go my way, it will be awful, terrible or catastrophic.

8.   The only way to improve my stress is to shape up others around me who do such dumb things.

9.   It is easier to avoid responsibilities and difficulties than to face them.

10.   My early childhood experiences determine my emotions and behavior, and there is little I can do about it.

11.   I deserve to be upset or depressed over my shortcomings.

12.   I am fully justified in being aggravated over others' shortcomings, deficiencies and blunders.

13.   I should be thoroughly competent, adequate, and achieving in all respects.

14.   The world should always be fair, justice should always triumph, and I am fully justified in feeling angry when these do not occur.

15.   I feel like I should do perfectly in nearly anything I attempt.

16.   There usually is one solution to a problem. It is pretty intolerable when this solution is not found or followed.

17.   I have a clear idea how other people should be and what they should do most of the time.

18.   Others should treat me kindly and considerately at all times.

19.   I have a right to expect a relatively pain-free and trouble-free life.

20.   When people around me are upset, it is usually because of something I have said or done.

EXERCISE 7-7. REWRITING IRRATIONAL BELIEFS

1.   Circle the irrational beliefs you recognize as more present in yourself than you would like.
2.   List those you would like to change in a separate list, leaving several lines between each one.

3.   Below each one, write a more rational or reasonable version, keeping in mind the three criteria of rational beliefs: factual, moderate, helpful.

4.   After rewriting each one, ask: What concrete differences would it make in my life to act upon these new reasonable beliefs?

Tool #2: Disputation

Ellis and colleagues (Grieger and Boyd, 1980; Whalen, DiGiuseppe, and Wessler, 1980) have developed a simple and effective technique for challenging and changing irrational beliefs. This technique, called "disputation," includes several steps.

1.   What symptoms of distress do I want to reduce or eliminate?

2.   What stressor is associated with my distress?

3.   What specific interpretation intervenes between the stressor and my distress symptoms?

4.   What is the unreasonable belief causing me unnecessary distress that I want to change? Here is an illustration in the life of Carla Bunin, a young university professor.

> *Carla frequently "freezes" and stumbles when talking in a department faculty meeting. She perceives the situation as threatening because she believes the impression she leaves on colleagues will influence their votes for or against her tenure next year. Her fear of looking bad creates the very blundering she so much wants to avoid. The unreasonable belief she wants to change is: "If I don't say the proper intelligent things in the proper intelligent manner, they will think I am not a worthy professor and will vote against me next year."*

5.   What evidence is there that this belief is true?
Carla: "None really. Tenure votes are influenced much more by publication records and teaching evaluations than on impressions left in faculty meetings."

6.   What evidence is there that this belief is false?
Carla: "I have never known or heard of anyone who failed to be granted tenure because of what he or she said or did not say in a faculty meeting. Besides, no one has ever given any sign that they think less of me because of what I say or don't say in these meetings."

7.   What alternative reasonable beliefs can you substitute for this unreasonable one?
Carla: "It makes no difference whether any colleagues approve or agree with what I say in faculty meetings. If I just relax, be myself, and do the important parts of my job well, I will probably get tenure; even if I don't, I will survive."

This process of disputation can be applied alone or with someone else, such as a spouse, close friends, or a counselor, who can assist you to re-think your unreasonable beliefs and try to change them.

EXERCISE 7-8. PERSONAL APPLICATION OF DISPUTATION

Apply the disputation steps described above to a recent stressful event in your life. You can do this as a writing or discussion exercise.

1. Distress symptoms?
2. Stressor?
3. My interpretation of the stressor?
4. Unreasonable belief influencing my interpretation?
5. Evidence this belief is true?
6. Evidence this belief is false?
7. Alternative beliefs?

Tool #3: From Vicious Cycle to Vital Cycle

The key role of beliefs in human experience is illustrated in Figure 7-1, which shows how beliefs can set in motion a self-fulfilling prophecy.

FIGURE 7-1. VICIOUS CYCLE OR VITAL CYCLE?

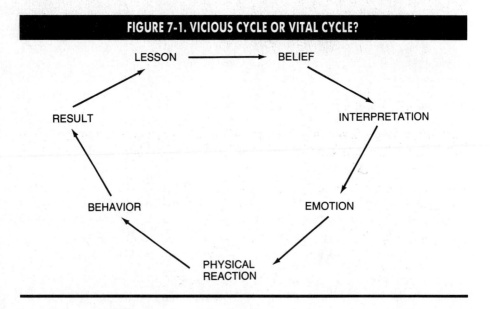

Consider the following examples of how a negative belief can set in motion a vicious cycle.

BELIEF: I never come through in the clutch.

INTERPRETATION (of challenging exam): This is the one exam I know I will fail. EMOTION: Fear, test anxiety.

PHYSICAL REACTION: Headache, fatigue, upset stomach.

BEHAVIOR: Procrastinates during three days before test. Unable to concentrate, lets mind wander during test.

RESULT: Does poorly on test.

LESSON: See, I never come through in the clutch. This proves again that I'm a loser.

Suppose the same individual had begun with a contrasting assumption. "I am reasonably intelligent. I come through when I need to." The interpretation is likely to be, "This test will be difficult, but I will take it on as a challenge." Emotions are likely to include appropriate anxiety that helps mobilize her for study. She may be a bit tense, which does no harm in moderate amounts. She prepares with confidence, although it takes a good deal of time and effort. She stays focused, directed, and confident during the test, convinced she will do reasonably well. The result? A reasonably good grade. The lesson? "See, this proves again that I thrive under pressure."

EXERCISE 7-9. CREATING VICIOUS AND VITAL CYCLE SCENARIOS

Create hypothetical vicious and vital cycle scenarios, beginning with the following beliefs.

1a. I am at my best when challenged.
1b. I am at my worst when challenged.
2a. Nobody ever likes me.
2b. I am a reasonably likable person.
3a. Most people are out to take advantage of me.
3b. Most people are motivated primarily by good will.
4a. Outside events upset me.
4b. I upset myself through my interpretation of events.
5a. I cannot change.
5b. I can change, although it sometimes takes lots of hard work and patience.

Tool #4: Reprogramming

Old, irrational beliefs will continue to provide the basis for situational interpretations—and for harmful distress—unless they are changed. As we have seen, doing so is not easy, although a number of methods are available for attempting this challenge.

Perhaps the most powerful tool I have used and taught is what I call simply, **Reprogramming.** Let us again consider the case of John, who reacts more defensively to his wife's suggestions than he wants. Underlying his situational interpretations were several assumptions or beliefs. For example:

"It is vitally important that others accept me—and my actions— at all times."

"To be criticized is to be diminished."

"For others to criticize me is awful and intolerable."

"My worth as a human being depends on defending myself against any and all criticism."

Clearly, if John is to learn to respond more constructively, he needs to reprogram his thinking, including these enduring assumptions. Here is a simple self-talk statement that can counter the negative beliefs noted above:

"I respond to criticism with humor."

To be effective, new self-talk needs to meet several criteria. It must be:

Personal—Not general or abstract

Positive—To increase potency of the statement

Present-tense—As though you already are doing it

Practical—Achievable, do-able

Brief—So it can be remembered and used

Note that the alternative belief about responding to criticism with humor meets these criteria. So do the following:

"I thrive on challenge."

"I am calm and confident."

"I have quiet self-assurance."

"I draw strength from my inner peace."

Three steps are followed in reprogramming self-talk, whether it be situational self-talk or long-term beliefs:

Step 1. Deliberate use of new self-talk.

Step 2. Repetition and familiarity.

Step 3. New self-talk becomes natural.

Two principles need to be kept in mind in reprogramming self-talk.

Old self-talk habits will always resist change due to the repetition compulsion.

Strength of new self-talk depends upon the amount of repetition.

An effective tool for the process of reprogramming is to write the desired new self-talk statement on a 3 X 5 card, carry it with you or put in a conspicuous place, and review it many times each day. Soon the new statement will become so familiar it will seem to be a natural part of your thinking. Continue for two or three weeks for each statement. You will soon find your self-talk reprogrammed in those areas of your life you want to improve.

EXERCISE 7-10. REPROGRAMMING YOUR SELF-TALK

1. Identify a specific repetitive situation in which you respond emotionally or behaviorally in unwanted ways.
2. Identify the negative self-talk you use to upset yourself.
3. Create a new self-talk alternative for reprogramming your thinking (or draw one from a list in this book). Be sure the new statement meets the five criteria—personal, positive, present-tense, practical, brief.
4. Write this statement on a 3 X 5 card. Carry this card with you or put it in a conspicuous place where you will see it many times each day. Repeat it over and over—perhaps 30 times per day. After two or three weeks, you will find the new statement a natural part of your thinking, influencing your emotions and behavior quite differently than the old self-talk.

APPLICATIONS OF REPROGRAMMING   ▼

The method just described for reprogramming situational self-talk and beliefs can be applied to a number of specific problem areas. Examples from throughout this book include:

Improving exercise habits (Chapter 8).

Avoiding procrastination (Chapter 10).

Reducing chronic hurry and hassle (Chapter 10).

Reducing anger and hostility (Chapter 5).

Turning anxiety into a positive force in performance situations like tests (Chapters 12 and 14).

Building confidence (Chapter 14).

Increasing social responsibility (Chapter 15).

Next you will read about how you can apply reprogramming to perfectionism, worry, hardiness, and self-esteem.

PERFECTIONISM

Perfectionism refers to impossibly demanding expectations toward others (external perfectionism), self (internal perfectionism), or both.

Life is never easy and seldom enjoyable for a perfectionist (Grieger and Boyd, 1980; Burns, 1980a; Burns, 1980b; McKay, Davis and Fanning, 1981; Pacht, 1984). There is nothing wrong, of course, with high standards. Genuine pleasure comes from healthy pursuit of excellence. As a University of Pennsylvania psychologist states, "Without concern for quality, life would seem shallow and true accomplishment would be rare" (Burns, 1980b, 34).

Types of Perfectionists

External perfectionists constantly find fault with others who seldom seem to match their standards of conduct. They believe they know what is right and how things should be done. There almost always is a gap between their standards and others' behavior. Consequently, they are plagued by frustration and hostility.

Internal perfectionists put unrelenting and excessively demanding expectations on themselves. Burns (1980b, 34) makes an important distinction between those who seek personal improvement through striving for realistic standards and true perfectionists.

> The perfectionists I am talking about are those whose standards are high beyond reach or reason, people who strain compulsively and unremittingly toward impossible goals, and who measure their own worth entirely in terms of productivity and accomplishment. For these people, the drive to excel can only be self-defeating.

> Evidence is mounting that the price this kind of perfectionist pays for the habit includes not only decreased productivity, but also impaired health, poor self-control, troubled personal relationships, and low self-esteem. The perfectionist also appears to be vulnerable to a number of potentially serious mood disorders, including depression, performance anxiety, test anxiety, social anxiety, writer's block and obsessive-compulsive illness.

Characteristics of Perfectionists

Perfectionists suffer under their burden of unrealistic pressures because of several beliefs, including the following.

"I must be perfect in anything I attempt."

"I should not make mistakes. Neither should others."

"I try so hard to do the right thing that I deserve exemptions from life's pains and frustrations."

"There is always a right way that things should be done."

"If I do something wrong, I have totally blown it."

"When others don't do what they should, they are rotten human beings."

"I must be perfect or I am a failure."

Perfectionists usually engage in all-or-nothing thinking, seeing things as all black or all white (Butler, 1981). For a student perfectionist, a "B" is a catastrophe.

The perfectionist fears mistakes and tends to overreact to them. He is also perpetually at odds with others around him who "in their shades of grayness" seldom meet his standards. The perfectionist overgeneralizes, fearing that a single negative performance will start a downward drive toward inevitable failure. "I never do anything right." Self-punishment, rather than self-reward prevails with predictably depressing effects.

Perfectionists are beset and preoccupied with "shoulds" in relation to both self and others. They harangue themselves with some of these "shoulds" (McKay, David and Fanning, 1981, 24):

I should be the epitome of generosity, consideration, dignity, courage, unselfishness.

I should be the perfect lover, friend, parent, teacher, student, spouse.

I should be able to endure any hardship with equanimity.

I should be able to find a quick solution to every problem.

I should never feel hurt. I should always be happy and serene.

I should always be spontaneous and at the same time I should always control my feelings.

I should never feel certain emotions, such as anger or jealousy.

I should love my children equally.

I should never make mistakes.

My emotions should be constant—once I feel love I should always feel love.

I should be totally self-reliant.

I should assert myself and, at the same time, I should never hurt anybody else.

I should never get tired or sick.

I should always be at peak efficiency.

One study found that perfectionistic insurance salespersons sold less insurance than those not so perfectionistic (Burns, 1980b). This illustrates that perfectionism can block productivity and creativity.

Perfectionists fear self-disclosure because of their fear of appearing foolish or inadequate. They are greatly concerned with maintaining an outward image of doing everything "right." Not surprisingly, perfectionists usually are lonely and isolated. Because of their vulnerability to rejection and disapproval, they tend to react defensively to harmless—and even helpful—criticism. They keep their distance, missing out on the warmth that would provide the very assurance and comfort they so badly want and need.

In summary, perfectionists exhibit the following tendencies.

1.   Plagued by "shoulds" and "should-haves."

2.   Self-critical, self-punishing, rather than self-rewarding (internal perfectionists).

3. Hyper-critical of others (external perfectionists).

4. Over-generalize from single events.

5. Use all-or-nothing thinking.

6. Guarded and protective of image.

7. Plagued by frustration, guilt, or both.

8. Hostile (especially external perfectionists).

9. Less productive, less creative.

10. Unhappy

EXERCISE 7-11. ASSESSING YOUR OWN PERFECTIONISM

Do you sometimes:

		YES	NO
1.	take life too seriously?	—	—
2.	feel intense, uptight, and defensive?	—	—
3.	hate to admit when you are wrong?	—	—
4.	feel overwhelmed with responsibilities?	—	—
5.	worry about making a mistake?	—	—
6.	fail to organize your affairs effectively?	—	—
7.	get impatient with people?	—	—
8.	believe that people should follow the rules?	—	—
9.	feel anxious when things get out of order?	—	—
10.	think you are nobody unless successful?	—	—
11.	get impatient when things get out of order?	—	—
12.	easily find fault with others?	—	—
13.	go from one extreme to another?	—	—
14.	refuse to accept limitations?	—	—
15.	feel aggravated by your lover's physical imperfections?	—	—
16.	have trouble making decisions?	—	—
17.	feel upset because you are wasting your potential?	—	—
18.	think you are better than most other people?	—	—
19.	feel an urgent need to stay in control?	—	—
20.	worry about giving the wrong impression?	—	—

There is no standard norm for this scale. But the more questions you answered "yes," the greater your perfectionism.

Source: (Knaus & Hendricks, 1986, 108)

EXERCISE 7-12. PERFECTIONISM AND ACHIEVEMENT.

One might ask, is not internal perfectionism vital for personal, academic and professional success? Doesn't setting exceedingly high standards motivate one to strive higher? It is my position that perfectionism is counterproductive, rather than helpful for success. Consider the following contrasting philosophies of achievement.

Perfectionism Philosophy of Achievement	Wellness Philosophy of Achievement
1. I *must* do it perfectly.	**1.** I will strive to do my best.
2. If I do not do it perfectly, I deserve to *punish* myself.	**2.** I will accept what I have done—for now.
3. Since I *did not* do it perfectly, I certainly *must* do it perfectly next time.	**3.** I will learn from that effort to seek to improve next time.

1. What do you think are the results of each philosophy?
2. Which philosophy most closely fits your current outlook?
3. Which philosophy will you strive toward in the future?

Self-Talk for Reprogramming Perfectionism

Below are a number of self-talk statements for reprogramming your perfectionistic thinking. You will note that some of these can be used for reprogramming situational self-talk, others for long-term beliefs.

▼ I stop myself whenever I engage in all-or-nothing thinking. ("If I don't get an A, I will be a total failure.")

▼ I stop myself whenever I over-generalize from a single negative event. ("I'm always screwing up like this. I never seem to learn.")

▼ I am a fallible human being (FHB), doing my best most of the time.

▼ Others are FHB's. It is unfair for me to expect them to be perfect—or to think and act like I think they should.

▼ I am becoming less critical and more accepting of others.

▼ I reward myself for what I do rather than punishing myself for what I do not do.

▼ I set realistic goals and standards for myself.

▼ I sometimes am satisfied with just getting the job done, even if it is not perfect.

▼ I am conscious of how far I have come, rather than dwelling on how far I have to go.

▼ I laugh at my own imperfections—and at my perfectionism.

▼ I strive to do my best. I accept what I have done. I learn from my mistakes.

EXERCISE 7-13. REPROGRAMMING YOUR PERFECTIONISTIC THINKING.

1.   Find which of the self-talk statements for reprogramming perfectionism would be most useful for changing your own perfectionistic tendencies. Create your own if needed.

2.   Write this statement on a 3 x 5 card, review, and apply it for the next two or three weeks.

EXERCISE 7-14. OTHER HINTS FOR TEMPERING PERFECTIONISM

In addition to reprogramming, here are other suggestions for tempering perfectionism:

1.   Eliminate "should" from your vocabulary. For "I should," substitute, "I choose to;" "I will;" "I choose not to;" "I need not." For "I should have," substitute, "Next time I will."

2.   List the things from which you get satisfaction—despite doing them imperfectly at times.

3.   List the advantages of and disadvantages of being perfect. See whether perfectionism is worth it.

Knaus and Hendricks (1986) offer a number of useful suggestions for reducing and preventing perfectionism. Included is to establish sensible standards. How do you know if a standard is sensible? Knaus and Hendricks (1986, 122) suggest it is probably sensible if you can answer yes to these questions:

▼ Is your standard realizable and does it allow you to challenge yourself, take risks, and feel good about trying?

▼ Is your standard pliable? You can't expect that you will perform as well fatigued as alert.

▼ Can you modify your standard to accommodate slowly changing circumstances?

▼ Does your standard allow you to improve the quality of your life and feel pleased with yourself?

▼ Does your standard incorporate the concept of progressive improvement and human limitations and fallibility?

Knaus and Hendricks suggest you apply these five guidelines to a perfectionistic standard like, "I must be great or I'm nothing."

WORRY

Characteristics of Worriers

In *Not To Worry*, Mary and Robert Goulding (1989, 13) describe worriers in this way:

> Worriers are really nice people. They are the kind of people who pay their taxes, vote in all elections, and put their garbage into secured garbage cans that dogs cannot pry open. They don't carry knives. They try hard to do what is right. Their children are clean and, if they too are worriers, tend to be polite and well-mannered.
>
> Worriers are creative. They can take any small stimulus and weave it into an elaborate fiction. One bounced check can grow into an entire bankruptcy scenario, and one poor report card can become a fantasized failure of epic proportions.
>
> Worriers are more intelligent than average, which can be seen by their quick ability to move from the concrete to the abstract and back, within seconds.
>
> Worriers are sufferers. When people worry, they leave the here-and-now in order to create unpleasant, imaginary stories. During a wonderful meal at a fancy restaurant, they imagine a burglar breaking into their home and stealing everything. During the peaceful moments of the late afternoon before the children have returned from play, they write imaginary horror stories of child abduction. During sex, they think about contraceptive failure.
>
> Worriers are caring people. They will tell you, "If I didn't love you so much, I wouldn't worry about you."
>
> In fact, worriers are exactly the sort of people everyone wants for neighbors, as long as they don't corner you to talk about their worries. The worst fault worriers have is that they tend to be boring. Listening to their worries is about as fascinating as listening to a recital of bowel problems.

Goulding and Goulding point out a number of messages parents give to their children as ways of teaching them to worry. (Goulding & Goulding, 1989, 29)

"What if . . ."

"You never know when lightning will strike!"

"Someday you won't be so lucky!"

"Watch out!"

"Be careful!"

"Troubles come in threes!"

"When you're a mother, you'll know what it is to worry!"

"If you feel so good, something bad is sure to happen!"

"A person can't help worrying about . . ."

"The time to worry is when everything seems to be going right."

"I worry myself sick about you kids."

"This job is one big worry."

"Troubles come when you're not looking."

"It's crazy not to worry about . . ."

"You kids be quiet. Your father is worried about something."

"If you don't worry, you must not care."

"It's the things you don't worry about that happen."

"Just when you think everything is going well, all hell breaks loose."

"If you expect the worst, you'll never be disappointed."

Goulding and Goulding note that families weave their own "worry myths" of beliefs out of such self-talk as those above. These myths include the following (Goulding and Goulding, 1989, 30).

- ▼ Worrying keeps your worries from coming true.
- ▼ Other people make you worry.
- ▼ Events make you worry.
- ▼ If you care, you worry.
- ▼ If you love, you worry.
- ▼ If you are sensitive, you worry.
- ▼ If you are intelligent, you worry.
- ▼ If you are human, you worry.

Self-Talk for Reprogramming Worry

Concern is appropriate, of course. Worry is over-concern. Worry can be situational self-talk, it can be a theme of long-term beliefs, or both. In either case, what is needed is reprogramming, using the 3 X 5 card technique or other methods.

Here are illustrative antidotes to worry.

I am free of worry.

I concern myself only with those things I can do something about.

I control my own thinking.

I can stop worrying.

I am in tune with the positive.

I am confident, calm and self-assured.

I think in a clear, decisive way.

I know things will work out okay.

Worrying won't help at all.

I think thoughts that create health and well-being for myself and others.

I am an optimistic person.

I focus only on those things truly worth being concerned about.

I am in full control of those events that are controllable.

HARDINESS: A STRESS RESISTANCE RESOURCE

Hardiness and Stressful Life Events

You have read that self-talk takes two forms: immediate interpretations and long-term perspective. You also read in Chapter 2 that during the last decade, a fascinating line of theory and research has underscored the value of *hardiness* as a stress resistance resource that combines both types of self-talk.

Maddi and Kobasa (1984) developed several reservations about the clustering of life events research and conclusions based on it. First, they noted that even though findings consistently were reported showing a correlation between life event scores and illness, the correlations usually were not very strong (Kobasa, 1979). Second, they questioned the recommendations that emerged from the early studies on life events—that change ought to be avoided or at least minimized. "Popular accounts of the research often advise people simply to avoid stressful life events if they want to stay healthy" (Maddi and Kobasa, 1984, 22). They question whether such advice is realistic or even desirable. Third, they observed that these studies tend to ignore individual differences in perceptions of stressful events and responses to them. "By these omissions, stress researchers appear to be saying that individuals' perceptions and coping responses do not matter. We are all poor victims of our environments and the changes they impose on us; when stressful life events mount, we are all at risk" (Maddi and Kobasa, 1984, 23).

In response to these concerns, Maddi and Kobasa initiated a different type of study on clustering of life events: who stays well and why, given lots of personal change? During the next several years, they and others identified a pattern they called hardiness that clearly set apart those who succeeded in surviving change without illness. Many of their subjects, in fact, seemed to thrive under conditions of rapid and clustered change.

Characteristics of Hardiness

Hardiness is a personality style showing a liking of challenge, a strong sense of commitment, and a strong sense of control.

Thus, hardiness has come to be known by its three C's:

Challenge
Commitment
Control

People high in hardiness display several qualities. They:

> Work hard because they enjoy it, rather
>   than because they feel compelled or driven.
>
> React optimistically and take positive action.
>
> Experience events as stressful, but also as:
>   Interesting
>   Important
>   Influenceable
>   Of potential value for personal growth

By contrast, those low in hardiness see stressful events as:

> Terrible.
> Outside their influence.
> Disruptive to their security.

Let us examine more carefully each of the three C's. People high in Challenge:

> Consider it natural for things to change.
> Anticipate change as a useful stimulus for creativity.
> Thrive under conditions of challenge, difficulty, and adversity.
> Turn change and difficulty into opportunity and challenge.
> Rise to the occasion.

People high in Commitment:

> Find it easy to be contented in whatever they are doing.
> Do what they love and love what they do.
> Rarely are at a loss for things to do.
> Make a maximum effort.
> Do so zestfully.

People high in Control:

> Believe they can influence events and their reactions to events.
> Reflect on how to turn difficult situations into opportunities.
> Have a strong sense of initiative.
> Are slow to give up on a challenge.

Selected Research Evidence on Effects of Hardiness

Studies by Kobasa, Maddi, and Kahn (1982), as well as many others, clearly show that hardiness offers protection against distress and illness in the face of clustered change. Table 7-1, for example, shows that among 259 executives, having a high life events score increased severity of illness with or without hardiness. But the presence

TABLE 7-1. AVERAGE SEVERITY OF ILLNESS FOR GROUPS DEFINED BY HARDINESS AND STRESSFUL EVENTS SCORES

		Hardiness	
		High	Low
Stressful Events	High	514	1061
	Low	415	529

Source: Kobasa, Maddi, and Kahn (1982)

of hardiness resulted in lower illness severity risk among both those with low stressful events scores (415 vs. 529) and high stressful events scores (513 vs. 1061). The impact of hardiness was greatest among those with high stressful events scores.

In Chapter 14, you will read other data showing that hardiness characterizes those who thrive under pressure. The key point here is that hardiness is a valuable antidote to distress from too much change in too short a time. And hardiness has other benefits as well, something you will also read more about in Chapter 14.

EXERCISE 7-15. SELF-ASSESSMENT OF HARDINESS

1. How do you measure up on the three C's of hardiness? Rate yourself on Challenge, Commitment, and Control using these categories:

Applies QUITE A BIT to me

Applies SOMEWHAT to me

Applies VERY LITTLE to me

2. Give an example of situations in which you have experienced each of these during recent circumstances of clustered change.

EXERCISE 7-16. SELF-TALK FOR HARDINESS

Below are several self-talk statements—affirmations—for building hardiness. After reading them over, select the one you would most like to memorize and imprint in your mind. Write it on a 3 X 5 card, carry the card with you, and read it many times each day. Continue for two or three weeks. By the end of that time, this statement will be part of your natural thinking. You will have strengthened your own hardiness.

I THRIVE ON CHALLENGE.
THIS IS AN OPPORTUNITY, NOT A THREAT.
I COME THROUGH WHEN I NEED TO.
I CAN DO ALMOST ANYTHING I SET MY MIND TO.
I AM A SPECIAL PERSON.
I HAVE CONFIDENCE.
I LIKE WHO I AM—AND I AM GETTING BETTER ALL THE TIME.
I MAKE THINGS HAPPEN.
I HAVE MORE TALENTS AND SKILLS THAN EVEN I HAVE YET DISCOVERED.
I HAVE LOTS OF ENERGY AND VITALITY.
I AM POSITIVE. I AM CONFIDENT.
I THRIVE UNDER PRESSURE.
I AM HIGHLY COMMITTED TO. . . .

SELF-ESTEEM

Nature and Origins of Self-Esteem

Self-esteem is appreciation of your own worth and importance. Out of self-esteem flow caring for self, caring for others, and translation of this caring into action (California Task Force, 1990).

Self-esteem begins in childhood, of course, as a result of early messages and early decisions in relation to significant others. High self-esteem is reinforced and sustained by self-talk that is supportive and loving. Low self-esteem is perpetuated by negative, self-deprecating self-talk. Self-esteem rests on self-appraisal. Dimensions and standards for such self-appraisal vary, of course, by individual.

Another way of thinking of self-esteem is to see it as the result of the size of the gap between one's self-standards and perceived "performance" relative to that standard.

Low Self-Esteem and High Distress: Research Evidence

At the core of much distress is low self-esteem—that is, low self-acceptance or self-liking. Figure 7-2 shows that among participants in my Enloe Stress and Health Center class on Reducing Perfectionism, Irritability, and Hurry Sickness, there is a significant correlation between self-esteem and distress symptoms: the higher the self-esteem, the lower the distress symptoms.

Self-Talk for Strengthening Self-Esteem

It helps to have had unconditionally loving parents and to have been surrounded by siblings, extended family, peer groups, and community that continually gave reassuring, loving messages. It also helps to have had lots of success experiences growing up.

But given that many of us did not enjoy these early beginnings, how can self-esteem be raised? The most direct way is to learn to reprogram your thinking about

FIGURE 7-2. SELF-ESTEEM AND DISTRESS SYMPTOMS

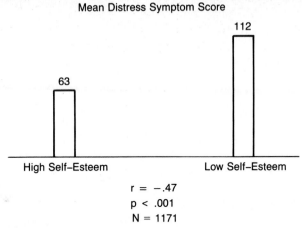

Mean Distress Symptom Score

High Self–Esteem: 63
Low Self–Esteem: 112

$r = -.47$
$p < .001$
$N = 1171$

See Exercise 1-10 for questions measuring self-esteem.
See Exercise 4-4 for Distress Symptom Scale.

yourself. Some of the same self-talk messages and exercises we noted for hardiness apply here as well.

Butler (1981, 72) has proposed a five-step process for improving self-esteem:

1. What am I telling myself?

2. Is my self-talk helping?

3. What Driver, Stopper, or Confuser is maintaining my inner speech?

4. What permission and self-affirmation will I give myself?

5. What action will I take based on my new supportive position?

Exercise 7-17 presents Butler's steps for helping "uncover" your inner speech.

EXERCISE 7-17. STEPS FOR DISCOVERING NEGATIVE SELF-TALK ABOUT SELF

1. Think of a recent compliment. What was your verbal response to it?

2. What criticism have you faced? What was your internal and external reply?

3. List a project or activity that you have begun or considered beginning. What did you tell yourself as you started or failed to start it?

4. What beliefs about yourself have you shared in intimate conversation with another? Were these beliefs negative or positive?

5.   Think of a situation (time, place, surroundings) where you tend to feel negative about yourself. What do you typically say to yourself while in this situation?

6.   Consider a time when you generally feel positive about yourself.

7.   Do you have any common physical symptom? What is your symptom telling you?

8.   Do you find yourself engaging in 'wistful thinking?' Do you often procrastinate? If so, from what negative self-talk are you escaping?

SOURCE: Butler (1981, 79)

Helmstetter (1986, 169) has proposed a number of self-talk statements for building self-esteem. Though somewhat lengthy in some cases, these can be very useful when following the three steps for reprogramming described earlier in the chapter.

▼ "I really am very special. I like who I am and I feel good about my self.

▼ Although I always work to improve myself, and I get better every day, I like who I am today. And tomorrow, when I'm even better, I'll like myself THEN, too.

▼ It's true that there really is no one else like me in the entire world. There never was another me before, and there will never be another me again.

▼ I am unique—from the top of my head to the bottom of my feet. In some ways, I may look and act and sound like some others—but I am not them. I am me.

▼ I wanted to be somebody—and now I know I am. I would rather be me than anyone else in the world.

▼ I like how I feel, and I like how I think, and I like how I do things. I approve of me, and I approve of who I am.

▼ I have many beautiful qualities about me. I have talents and skills and abilities. I have talents that I don't even know about yet. And I am discovering new talents inside myself all the time.

▼ I am positive. I am confident. I radiate good things. If you look closely, you can even see a glow around me.

▼ I am full of life. I like life, and I'm glad to be alive. I am a very special person, living at a very special time.

▼ I am intelligent. My mind is quick and alert and clever and fun. I think good thoughts, and my mind makes things work right for me.

▼ I have a lot of energy and enthusiasm and vitality."

As you will read in more detail in Chapter 15, giving to others is among the most effective means of enhancing your own self-esteem. So is becoming physically

---

BOX 7-2. SELF-TALK AND SELF-WORTH

Here are several inter-related points about self-talk and self-worth. Do you agree or disagree? How does each apply to you?

1. I create my own inner reality.

2. I deserve to create feelings of self-worth—because I am a unique human being.

3. My self-worth can be (even if it isn't now) positive, steady, and independent of social position, accomplishments, others' opinions, and my own fallibilities.

4. Because my own self-worth can exist unconditionally, it need be neither proven nor protected.

5. Self-created distress associated with perfectionism, hurry sickness, anger, and anxiety often results from unnecessary struggles to prove or protect my self-worth.

6. I accept responsibility for my own inner reality.

---

fit, as you will read in Chapter 8. Self-talk messages to yourself about yourself, like those above, become easier and more authentic.

You have read that thoughts affect feelings, mental images, physical states, and behavior. Specifically, thoughts can create distress or they can result in constructive coping when faced with challenging, difficult events. Most importantly, you have the power within to control your own thinking.

Managing self-talk needs to focus on situational self-talk, at the moment you encounter stressors, as well as on long-term stress-related beliefs out of which immediate interpretations emerge. We have reviewed a number of specific methods for managing self-talk, and we have shown how reprogramming your thinking can be applied to reducing perfectionism and worry and to building hardiness and self-esteem.

The next chapter focuses on health buffers—exercise, nutrition, and sleep—that can complement the self-talk approach to stress management by helping to build stress resistance through your lifestyle habits. Thus, health buffers are best seen as preventive steps in managing stress.

REFERENCES ▼

Bedford, S. (1981). *Stress and Tiger Juice.* Chico, CA.: Scott Publications.

Burns, D.D. (1980a). *Feeling Good: The New Mood Therapy.* New York: Signet.

Burns, D.D. (1980b). The perfectionist's script for self-defeat. *Psychology Today,* 14, 34-38.

Butler. P.E. (1981). *Talking to Yourself: Learning the Language of Self-Support.* New York: Harper & Row.

California Task Force to Promote Self-Esteem and Personal and Social Responsibility, (1990). *Toward a State of Esteem.* Sacramento: California State Department of Education.

Ellis, A. (1957). *How To Live With A "Neurotic."* New York: Crown Publishers.

Ellis, A. (1962). *Reason and Emotion in Psychotherapy.* New York: Lyle Stuart.

Ellis, A. (1969). A congitive approach to behavior therapy. *International Journal of Psychiatry,* 8, 896-900.

Ellis, A. (1973). *Humanistic Psychotherapy: The Rational-Emotive Approach.* New York: McGraw-Hill Paperbacks.

Ellis, A., & Harper, R.A. (1975). *A New Guide to Rational Living.* Hollywood: Wilshire Book Co.

Grieger, R., & Boyd, J. (1980). *Rational-Emotive Therapy: A Skills-Based Approach.* New York: Van Nostrand Reinhold Company.

Helmstetter, S. (1986). *The Self-Talk Solution.* New York: Pocket Books.

Knaus, W.J., & Hendricks, C. (1986). *The Illusion Trap: How To Achieve A Happier Life.* New York: World Almanac Publications.

Kobasa, S.C. (1979). Stressful life events, personality and health: An inquiry into hardiness. *Journal of Personality and Social Psychology,* 1-11, 37.

Kobasa, S.C., Maddi, S.R., & Kahn, S. (1982). Hardiness and Health: A prospective study. *Journal of Personality and Social Psychology,* 42, 168-177.

Kriegel, R. & Kriegel, M. (1984). *The C Zone: Peak Performance Under Pressure.* New York: Anchor Press/Doubleday.

Maddi, S.R., & Kobasa, C.S. (1984). *The Hardy Executive: Health Under Stress.* Homewood, IL.: Dow Jones-Irwin.

McKay, M., Davis, M., & Fanning, P. (1981). *Thoughts & Feelings: The Art of Cognitive Stress Intervention.* Oakland: New Harbinger Publications.

Pacht, A.R. (1984). Reflections on perfectionism. *American Psychologist,* 39, 386-390.

Rathus, S. A. (1991). *Psychology.* 4th Ed. Fort Worth: Holt, Rinehart and Winston.

Whalen, S.R., DiGiuseppe, R., & Wessler, R.L. (1980). *A Practitioner's Guide to Rational-Emotive Therapy.* New York: Oxford University Press.

Wolfe, T. (1987). *The Bonfire of the Vanities.* New York: Farrar, Straus and Giroux.

Health Buffers: Exercise, Nutrition, Sleep

Chapter 8

CHAPTER 8

I. INTRODUCTION

II. AEROBIC EXERCISE
A. The Need for Physical Activity
B. Exercise and Emotions: A Sampling of Scientific Evidence
C. What is Aerobic Exercise?
D. How Much Aerobic Exercise is Needed?
E. Physiological Changes with Aerobic Training
F. How Aerobic Exercise Can Help Control Stress?
   1. Psychological and Physiological Pathways
   2. Exercise, Stress, and "Toughness"
G. Running—My Way
   1. Benefits of Running
   2. Cautions About Running
H. Are Other Physical Activities Beneficial?
 I. Tips for Getting Started—And Sticking With It

III. NUTRITION
A. Linkages between Nutrition and Stress
B. America's Nutritional Habits
   1. The Surgeon General's Report
   2. The National Cancer Institute
C. Nutritional Guidelines for Building Stress Resistance
D. Controlling Dietary Habits
   1. Reduce Fat in Your Diet
   2. Cholesterol and Stress
      a. Understanding Cholesterol
      b. Lowering Cholesterol
   3. Vitamins and Other Supplements
   4. Eating Disorders
   5. Is Nibbling Healthy?
   6. Yo-Yo Dieting

IV. SLEEP
A. Stages of Sleep
B. How Much Sleep Do You Need?
C. Insomnia and Sleep Deprivation
   1. Consequences of Sleep Deprivation
   2. Tips for Preventing and Coping With Insomnia

INTRODUCTION ▼

A central theme of this book is that events do not cause distress. How the individual assesses and responds determines whether an event is neutral (neustress), positive (eustress), or negative (distress).

You read in Chapter 2 about several theories of stress that emphasize factors intervening between stressors and stress. Cognitive theories emphasize perspective, self-talk, or interpretation, the focus of Chapter 7. Lazarus and others emphasize the individual's coping response in dealing with major events and especially with daily hassles (Lazarus and Folkman, 1984).

Of particular relevance here is the notion of "general resistance resources," (GRR's) which we noted in our review of sense of coherence theory (Antonovsky, 1979, 1987). GRR's help build stress resistance. They enable the individual to build up a protective reserve so that when tough times come along, the person is ready to cope effectively.

In this chapter, you will read about three resistance resources—called here "health buffers"—that can help build protection against distress: aerobic exercise, good nutrition, and adequate sleep.

AEROBIC EXERCISE ▼

THE NEED FOR PHYSICAL ACTIVITY

Two health-related trends have marked the twentieth century.

Acceleration in pace of life. This takes two forms: more personal changes in shorter periods of time and a faster daily tempo, topics to be discussed in Chapter 10.
Sedentary living. At the turn of the century, most of our grandparents were physically active. They depended more on their bodies than on machines to move from place to place, to work, to maintain their households, to play. Experts estimate that in 1860 one-third of the American economy was human-powered. Today that figure is less than one percent.

How do these two historical trends affect stress and health? Increasing personal adjustments are required, year by year and day by day. Tension mounts, physically and mentally. Without sufficient release through physical activity, this tension turns into bound energy, pulling and tearing inside our bodies.

Stress-induced illnesses result. You read in Chapter 3 that these include migraine and tension headaches, ulcers, back pain, high blood pressure, and atherosclerosis. These ailments can have other causes as well, of course. Emotional distress abounds, evidenced by irritability, joylessness, depression, chronic anxiety, insomnia. Overweight reaches epidemic proportions. Destructive coping behavior is rampant—alcohol and drug abuse, smoking, violence, escapism, attraction to cults, and overeating. The United States leads the world in many forms of addictive behavior.

Social and technological change has deluded us into the false belief that inactivity is a normal way to live. But the fact is that exercising—if not during work then during play—restores your body to its true optimum condition. Those who take time to exercise live as the body was intended—actively. Exercise prevents and reduces bound energy, thereby preventing and reducing distress. Even modest amounts of physical activity add to well-being—and to life expectancy (Paffenbarger, et al., 1986; Blair, 1989).

You may not be able to control the pace of life and the rate of change around you. But you can control your readiness to cope with the stresses of modern life by becoming—and staying—physically active.

In one of his early influential books on exercise, Kenneth Cooper (1977, 11), uses the following conversation with a patient to underscore the central importance of cardiovascular fitness for health and vitality.

> Doc, I don't need much endurance. I work at a desk all day, and I watch television at night. I don't exert myself any more than I have to, and I have no requirements for exerting myself. Who needs large reserves? Who needs endurance?
>
> You do. Everyone does. Surely, you know the usual symptoms caused by inactivity as well as I do. Yawning at your desk, that drowsy feeling all day, falling asleep after a heavy meal, fatigue from even mild exertions like climbing stairs, running for a bus, mowing the lawn, or shoveling snow. You can become a social cripple, "too tired" to play with the kids, "too tired" to go out to dinner with your wife, "too tired" to do anything except sit at your desk or watch television, and maybe you're even getting tired of doing that. And the final clincher, "I guess I'm getting old." You're getting old all right, and a lot sooner than you should.

For most who read this book, employment affords little chance for physical exercise. For full-time homemakers, housework requires lots of movement but little real exercise of any benefit for stress control or health. The answer is to set aside 30 to 60 minutes each day to exercise.

Not surprisingly, most people turn to other options when emotionally troubled. These include alcohol, food, cigarets, prescription medicines, street drugs. These may provide temporary relief, of course, but are hardly long-term solutions. Regular exercise is a far better approach that utilizes the body's natural resources and restores you to being fully human.

EXERCISE AND EMOTIONS: A SAMPLING OF SCIENTIFIC EVIDENCE

As Johnsgård points out (1990), it has long been folk wisdom that exercise has a positive effect on mood. When children drive their parents to distraction from being cooped up too long, parents know enough to send them outside to play in order to "work off some steam." When friends or family are mired in the blues, we do all we can to "get them up and moving."

Such folk wisdom has received countless support in recent years from scientific studies. Here is a sampling.

▼ Dr. John Griest and associates at the University of Wisconsin conducted a pilot study comparing the effects of running therapy with two kinds of conventional individual psychotherapy (Griest, et al., 1978) Subjects were depressed students who came to the University Counseling Center for help. At the end of the treatment, all three groups showed similar reductions in depression. Running reduced depression more rapidly than the other types of treatment and had more lasting effects after several months of followup.

▼ Griest and colleagues (Griest, et al., 1979) next expanded their studies by taking in referrals from private psychiatrists in the local community. An 80 percent recovery rate was reported—and most of those few who did not show quick recovery never did begin to run. This success rate is much higher than for most studies of anti-depressant medications.

▼ A recent study conducted by *Runner's World Magazine* (1989) found that 82 percent of the nearly 700 respondents to a random survey of magazine readers reported that running had enhanced their energy level, 73 percent said it had helped their life control, and 69 percent said running had increased their optimism. Most reported that running exceeded their initial hopes in increasing mental fitness and relieving stress. Other perceived gains included improved diet, weight loss, and fewer colds.

▼ Aerobic exercise was shown in a study conducted through the Veterans Administration Medical Center in Salt Lake City to improve cognitive function in formerly sedentary elderly patients (Dustman, 1989). Specifically, after a four-month exercise program, participants improved in mental flexibility, reaction, and memory—mental skills likely to make coping with the stressors of living during the later years more constructive and effective.

▼ Fifty-five college students who reported a high number of recent negative life events participated in an experiment comparing physical exercise, relaxation training, and no treatment. While all reported improved health over the 11-week period of the study, the exercise group showed a greater drop in depressive symptoms (Roth & Holmes, 1987).

▼ McCann and Holmes (1984) conducted a similar study among 47 female undergraduate students who had been found through a psychological test to be mildly depressed. Like the Roth study, those assigned to an exercise group showed a greater decline in depression than either a relaxation or no-treatment group.

▼ A telephone survey of 401 Illinois residents found a positive association between amount of exercise and psychological well-being, especially among low and middle income groups (Hayes and Ross, 1986).

▼ Dr. Wesley Sime of the University of Nebraska Stress Physiology Laboratory found that among 15 moderately depressed men and women ranging in age from 26 to 53, depression scores were significantly lower after 10 weeks, six months, and 21 months in an exercise program (Sime, 1987). Interestingly, Sime found that durability of positive change was dependent upon continuation of exercise.

▼ A study at the University of London found that among 75 sedentary adults, those assigned to a moderate aerobic exercise group showed improvements in tension and anxiety, while no changes occurred in the high intensity or no activity groups (Moses, 1989). The authors suggest that the high intensity group, perhaps, experienced too much demand for this brief 10 week period.

▼ A great deal of research has been conducted on the influence of exercise on self-esteem. For example, Brown (1986) found a positive effect on self-concept of a 12-week program of exercise for both young and mature women. One reviewer points out that ". . . self-esteem is more likely to be elevated when exercise is introduced to special populations" (Johnsgård, 1989, 200).

▼ Brown (1987) has been testing students for many years through his mental health courses at the University of Virginia. Studies of over 5000 men and women show that regular exercise is inversely associated with hostility.

▼ Berger and Owen (1983) found that exercise has an immediate or acute effect in reducing hostility among both conditioned and unconditioned swimmers.

▼ Morgan and Costill studied male world-class marathoners and college runners compared with normative college samples. They reported that runners' scores were much lower than college students in general on depression, fatigue, confusion, and tension, but significantly higher in vigor (Ungerleider, et al., 1989).

▼ A larger study of 348 non-elite male and female marathoners compared their Profile of Mood scores to those of 856 college students. Marathoners were significantly less tense, less fatigued, less depressed, less confused, and more vigorous than the male and female college students. No difference was found on the anger scale (Ungerleider, et al., 1989).

▼ Another study of 464 non-elite female runners found that their moderate running program was at least as beneficial than the marathoners' heavier training regimen (Ungerleider, et al, 1989).

▼ Many studies have demonstrated that adolescents, like adults, are vulnerable to stress life events. A recent study of 220 adolescent girls showed that among non-exercisers, clustering of stressful life events had notable debilitating effects on emotional and physical health of non-exercisers, but that these negative effects were significantly less among girls who exercised frequently (Brown & Lawton, 1986).

▼ Finally, I have conducted a series of studies on exercise and stress among my undergraduate students. In Figure 8-1 are findings from one survey of 129 students in which students were asked a number of "quality of life" questions (See Quality of Life Questions, Chapter 1). They also were asked how many times on the average they exercised the previous semester for at least 20 minutes. The average was the same for both males and females: 3.4 times per week. All but 12 reported averaging at least once per week.

The results showed no significant differences in any of the quality of life measures between not exercising and exercising 0-3 times per week. But when those who

FIGURE 8-1. STRESS AND QUALITY OF LIFE BY FREQUENCY OF EXERCISE

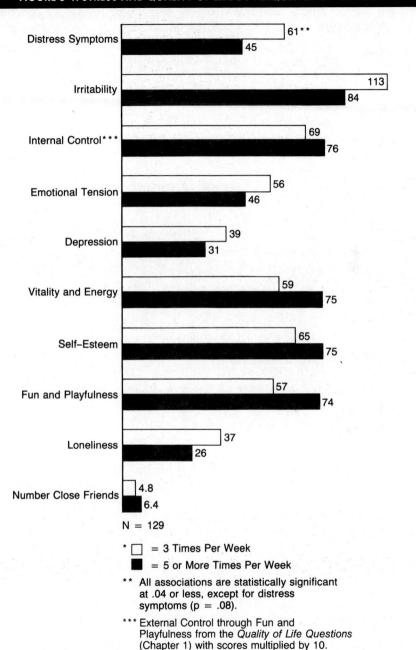

N = 129

* ☐ = 3 Times Per Week
  ■ = 5 or More Times Per Week

** All associations are statistically significant at .04 or less, except for distress symptoms (p = .08).

*** External Control through Fun and Playfulness from the *Quality of Life Questions* (Chapter 1) with scores multiplied by 10.

exercised 0-3 times per week were compared to those who exercised five or more times per week, the pattern became clear: the greater the frequency of exercise, the better the quality of life, whatever the measure. More frequent exercisers reported fewer distress symptoms, less irritability, more internal control, less emotional tension and depression, more vitality and energy, higher self-esteem, more fun and playfulness, less loneliness, and more close friends.

Of course, since this was a cross-sectional, one-time survey, we don't know which causes which. That is, more frequent exercise might be the effect rather than the cause of higher quality of life. At a minimum, we can conclude that the data support the hypothesis that exercise helps control stress and adds to a positive quality of life among this sample of college students.

This is a mere sampling of studies showing positive effects of exercise on emotions. Countless anecdotes also could be cited. To illustrate, note the following from a letter to Johnsgård (1989, 203):

> ". . . I started running and gave up smoking at age 33 when I began to take over responsibility for my health. I began walking and jogging around a golf course near my home long before the running craze hit us. I noticed that after I exercised, I always felt so much better. It left me with a warm afterglow. I was a very aggressive lacrosse player (even a dirty player), but I found that running left me calm and relaxed without any desire to hurt or even dominate. I just love gentle running. . . ."

WHAT IS AEROBIC EXERCISE?

Any form of exercise is better than none. A recent study shows, for example, that even minimal physical activity increases life expectancy (Blair, et al, 1989). But the most effective type of exercise in terms of stress control is *aerobic*. Aerobic means literally, "activity with air."

Other forms of exercise are *anaerobic* exercise (activity without air), such as all-out sprinting or swimming underwater while holding breath; strengthening exercises, such as weight-lifting and isometrics; and stretching, such as yoga and warm-ups before running. Still other forms of physical activity combine these various ways within the context of recreation or games such as golf, softball, volleyball, or ping-pong.

Aerobic exercise is any form of activity in which heart rate is elevated substantially above resting level in response to sustained movement by large muscle groups. Examples of aerobic exercise include the following:

Running

Brisk walking

Swimming

Bicycling

Stationary bicycling

Cross-country skiing

Mini-trampolining

Aerobic dancing

Rope skipping

Stair climbing

How Much Aerobic Exercise Is Needed?

For minimum cardiovascular fitness, the following criteria need to be met, according to the American College of Sports Medicine (1990). You can recall these by remembering the acronym, F.I.T.

Frequency—At least three times per week.
Intensity—Heart rate between 60 and 90 percent of maximum for entire exercise session. To estimate these percentages, subtract your age from 220, then multiply that figure by times .60 and .90.
Time—At least 20 minutes per session.

My experience with stress management clients and students leads me to recommend the following aerobic exercise guidelines for purposes of **effective stress control and high-level wellness**—beyond minimal cardiovascular fitness. This recommendation is consistent with findings reported here in Figure 8-1.

Frequency—Five to seven days per week.
Intensity—Heart rate between 60 and 90 percent of estimated maximum.
Time—At least 30-40 minutes per session.

Physiological Changes with Aerobic Training

Three main changes will occur, all of which improve your overall energy level through more efficient use of oxygen. This is called the "aerobic training effect" (Clarke, 1975).

1. **Improvements in oxygen intake (respiration)**
   Strengthening of diaphragm muscle
   Greater lung flexibility and capacity

2. **Improvements in oxygen circulation**
   More output per heart beat
   Slower heart rate at given exertion level
   More blood volume
   More red corpuscles
   Less blood stickiness
   Expansion in size of blood vessels and capillaries
   Opening of new capillary networks

3. **Improvements in oxygen use (metabolism)**
   More efficient extraction of oxygen from blood
   More efficient burning of oxygen within muscle cells
   More efficient discharge of carbon dioxide

HOW AEROBIC EXERCISE CAN HELP TO CONTROL STRESS

Psychological and Physiological Pathways

Research continues on the mental and physiological pathways through which aerobic exercise helps control tension, anxiety, depression, and other stress symptoms. Here is a summary of what is currently known or considered by experts as likely in terms as explanations for the exercise-stress control linkages.

Psychological pathways related to tension control are likely to include the following.

▼ Release of pent-up emotions

▼ Creative problem-solving during the exercise session—resulting in more constructive coping the rest of the day

▼ Enhanced self-liking, self-acceptance, self-esteem

▼ Heightened internal control

▼ Feeling of well-being and calm—"afterglow" from exercise

▼ Mood stabilization

▼ "Time away" benefit (not unique to exercise, of course)

▼ Decrease of negative thinking and rumination

Physiological pathways through which exercise is thought to improve stress control involve a number of factors.

▼ Release of muscle tension

▼ Burning off of stress-induced adrenaline, which leaves the bloodstream and is consumed in the muscles

▼ Post-exercise reduction of adrenaline production

▼ Post-exercise quieting of the sympathetic nervous system (the part of the system that produces tension)

▼ Production of beta-endorphins, the body's own morphine pain-killer and source of pleasure

▼ Lower baseline tension level

▼ Faster recovery time from acute stress

▼ Body becomes familiar with and habituated to physiological arousal

Exercise, "Toughness," and Stress

In an important article on exercise and mental and physical health, Richard Dienstbier (1989) recently focused on positive and negative views of arousal. Based on studies of both animals and humans, he suggests that physiological arousal can have a positive role in coping and health. However, one needs to distinguish between two types of arousal—arousal through the sympathetic nervous system (SNS)-adrenal medulla pathway versus arousal through the adrenal-cortical pathway. Dienstbier (1989, 88) points out that the ideal for "an emotionally stable and competent individual" is a pattern in which:

> . . . . SNS-adrenal-medullary and adrenal-cortical base rates for the fit individual are low, but in a challenge/threat situation, SNS-adrenal-medullary arousal onset is fast and strong, whereas cortisol remains relatively low; arousal decline is fast with stressor off-set; and across repeated episodes, arousal levels for both kinds of peripheral arousal decline more quickly than in less fit controls (this is particularly apparent with cortisol). If stress is continuous, the fit individual will sustain SNS-adrenal-medullary arousal longer, and both catecholamine depletion and large pituitary-adrenal-cortical responses will be delayed. These parameters add to the characterization of a toughened individual.

In sum, emotionally healthy persons have a low ongoing (baseline) arousal level. However, when faced with challenging or difficult situations, they experience a sharp and fast upswing of adrenal-related arousal. However, they return to baseline much more quickly than less emotionally fit individuals.

Dienstbier refers to this pattern of response as "toughness." And, most important for our discussion here, he concludes that the most effective way to enhance such toughness is through aerobic exercise (Dienstbier, 1989, 96).

> . . . the . . . obvious avenue toward toughening is a program of aerobic exercise. In contrast to the high level of mental challenge available (to many) in technologically advanced environments, advanced civilization (like the living conditions for lab animals) has led to dramatic underuse of human physical abilities. Even modest physical training programs should, therefore, have an impact on toughening. Research reviewed earlier affirmed that exercise training builds toughness that is relevant to either physical or mental challenge/threat situations.
>
> The physiological benefits demonstrated from exercise programs include all of those linked with toughening; for example, lower arousal base rates, including heart rate and blood pressure, quicker return to arousal base rate after stress, improved glucose utilization, and more circulating monocytes (active in resisting bacterial infection). Physiological benefits not emphasized by this system are also achieved: for example, relative increases in high density lipoprotein ("good cholesterol") with lower serum triglyceride levels.

Potential direct psychological benefits from a successful exercise program include feelings of mastery or "effectance" and of improved body image (exercise usually results in lowered weight "set points" for both humans and nonhumans).

"Exercise is also useful in relieving physiological arousal after acute stress. An episode of exercise reduces muscle tension, lowers SNS arousal indicators to stressful stimuli induced even hours later (a situation in which arousal-supported coping is clearly not adaptive; lowers free fatty acids in blood, and lowers self-reports of anxiety and tension.

In short, a vital step in harnessing stress, preventing illness, and reaching higher levels of potential is to restore exercise into daily life. Doing so meets a basic need of the healthy human body—to be physically active.

RUNNING—MY WAY

My particular aerobic exercise is running, although I do bike at times and lift weights at a modest level. I have run for 38 years. Someone asked if I am addicted. "Perhaps," I said. "Let's wait and see."

Benefits of Running

While other types of aerobic exercise can be equally beneficial and enjoyable, I do want to share a few thoughts about running as an approach to stress control.

Judy Marshall, a woman in her mid-thirties, wrote to me in a letter:

I had such a lovely run yesterday. I left home at 5:30 A.M. trying to race the sunrise to the top of my ridge two and one-half miles away (up). I run on a winding dirt road until the last two hundred feet or so. Then it is straight to the top. Just as I rounded the last bend and could see the top, the sun broke over the hills and across the valley. The sky was a brilliant red-orange and pink with rays of sunlight streaking up through high rain clouds. Standing in the middle of the road on the horizon were a doe and buck (his horns were in full velvet) staring at me. The deer silhouetted against the sky was incredible. At that point, even though I was running uphill, I lost all conscious feeling of my running. The sight before me and movement of my body simultaneously became one glorious experience. I ran another three miles on top of the ridges with the cool early morning air and the sun bathing me. It then suddenly began to softly rain large summer rain drops. Wow! I was home by 6:30. I had already experienced so much and my day was just beginning! Stress? What stress?

Running can be immensely rewarding and surprisingly easy. People often associate running with pain and competition. Many athletes stop exercising after high school or college because of their memories of painful training or pressure from coaches to win. And fans who watch them never begin for the same reasons.

Recently millions of Americans have discovered an entirely new way to run—for health, friendship, and the beauty of the body-in-motion. Some compete in low-key races, but competition is less important than the process of running. This type of running can be started at any age, regardless of ability. It can become a regular part of everyday life. And it can be continued into old age.

Running for the purposes of enjoyment and good health has several features. First, it is done as regularly as eating or sleeping. You do not feel guilty about taking time to eat or read the newspaper. Nor do runners feel guilty about taking 20 to 60 minutes each day or two to run. Rain or shine, good mood or bad, they run.

Second, running involves a minimum of strain or pain. Runners usually run at a pace at which they can carry on a reasonable conversation. They are willing to push into the "pain zone" once in a while, but not every day. For they know they can achieve substantial benefits by running fairly easily—and can enjoy it at that pace.

Third, runners can run alone or with others. They do not require the presence of others to get their regular run, but they often do "run socially." Sometimes, in fact, deep friendships develop "on the run."

Fourth, running is a long-term proposition. Continuing to exercise in this way over many years is more important than achieving short-range goals. Running, therefore, is approached with patience. Comments from runners interviewed by Glasser (1976, 108, 109, 113) for his book on positive addictions include the following.

> When I am settled into my run I concentrate on running as much as possible but the mind wanders to thoughts of most anything. The state of mind is one of almost total complacency and privacy. Although you are in sight of people, cars, buses, school kids, dogs, etc., I feel a very privateness when I run. People may yell at me or a kid may bug me for a few hundred yards, but due to the nature of running (it is hard and physically demanding) you are pretty much left to yourself and no one can invade your runners' world because they physically are not able. If another runner enters or intrudes it is fine because he is running for the same reasons and for a lot of the same feelings.

> Running is extremely personal to each runner. Its importance shapes the lives of many people who enjoy running long distances. I can really never see myself quitting unless an accident should occur. It has been an integral part of my life for a number of years, and I am quite happy with myself and my life and I wouldn't trade places with anyone.

> I can describe two states of mind when I have settled into my run. Sometimes both will occur when I am settled into a run. Strangely enough these minds seem to be a function of the weather. Nice crisp days yeah, hot humid days, too. Novelty of the course, physical features of the course include whether the course is beautiful, easy to run, etc. The first mind state that I would describe is that of a rational cognitive nature and coincides with runs that are generally unsatisfactory in some way. The weather is hot, the dogs are harassing me, the course is becoming boring because I have been on it many times. The second mind state is (and here I believe he describes the PA state quite clearly) not cognitive or rational, instead it is ego-transcending. I simply perceive as I run. I react instinctively to obstacles which suddenly appear. I float. I run like a deer. I feel good. I feel high. I don't think at all. My awareness is only the present. Even that cannot be called awareness. Brain chatter is gone. This mind set normally coincides with running along a cross-country course in autumn on a crisp day but definitely appears other times of the year as well.

Cautions about Running

A word of caution is needed when discussing running. Running carries its risks, the main one being injury to joints or muscles. A high percentage of habitual runners, especially those who diligently train for and participate in competitive road races, periodically experience injuries of sufficient seriousness to require complete rest for days, weeks, or months. Because of anatomical anomalies, some individuals are especially injury-prone. The most common injuries are to knees.

Many runners believe the sense of accomplishment from pushing their limits justifies this risk of injury. At the same time, it is wise to be cautious if your primary goal is to run for many years. Effective exercise need be quite moderate over the long run.

If you suffer from chronic back pain or have chronic joint problems, running may not be for you. Walking can produce many of the same benefits as running, especially for older adults, while greatly reducing injury risk.

BOX 8-1. RUNNING: HER PERSONAL ANCHORAGE

A female student—a mother in her thirties who had returned to college—recently submitted this brief "Application Assignment" in my Human Stress class.

"Personal anchorages are referred to in this class as things, places, activities, people, and beliefs that hold us together, even when things around us may be dynamically changing.

"Before taking this class, I had not realized the importance of running as a personal anchorage. What I now recognize is that the benefit of running is more than for health and fitness. It is always there for me, supporting, challenging, and encouraging me whether the chips are up or down.

"Running is something I can do alone, with friends, on vacation, in most any weather, to meet new people, to let off steam, to start my day, to compete for time, to collect thoughts, and so on. Running is always there for me. It keeps me disciplined, builds self-esteem, and maintains vitality and energy.

"One of the favorite things about running is the social support attained. I have run with a group of people for over four years. If we were not all runners looking for early morning partners, our paths may not have ever crossed. As it is, stong friendships have formed. We help one another when the waters are troubled and celebrate when achievements are made. Much of our socializing is preceded by exercise. In fact, we have our own personal half-marathon once a year, followed by brunch and a swim. We also enjoy training for such events as the Bidwell Classic Half-Marathon and Whiskeytown Relays.

"Running is also something I share with my husband. Since we both have hectic schedules, we most always can share an hour of the day running together. As a result, much discussion and problem-solving can be accomplished. Furthermore, running keeps our marriage stable, moods and tempers are mellowed, and we enjoy a harmonious relationship—at least most of the time!

"Running can also be productive. Running alone is an especially good time to collect and organize thoughts for upcoming tests, assignments, speeches, etc. In fact, much of the context of this paper was mentally organized while I was running!

"Running has become second nature to me. No matter where I am or what the pressures are, running most always starts my day."

ARE OTHER PHYSICAL ACTIVITIES BENEFICIAL?

Quality and, perhaps, even length of life can benefit from such activities as walking several blocks to work, climbing stairs rather than taking the elevator, doing yoga and other stretching exercises, and working vigorously on the job.

Other physical activities, such as gardening, fishing, hunting, softball, and golf clearly can have diversionary and recreational value. All these activities certainly can be beneficial in controlling tension and rejuvenating one's spirit. But aerobic exercise is the most beneficial of all for maintaining high-level wellness and managing stress. As noted earlier, this is simply returning the body to its normal state of existence.

Brisk walking is an especially attractive and beneficial form of life-long aerobic exercise. More Americans walk than do any other fitness activity. As Rippe and associates have noted in the *Journal of the American Medical Association* (Rippe, et al., 1988), there are a variety of positive mental and physical benefits from walking. Lamb (1981) has listed some of the key ones as follows:

▼ Walk to stay lean.

▼ Walk to clean out your arteries.

▼ Walk to lower your blood pressure.

▼ Walk to control your blood sugar.

▼ Walk to condition your heart.

▼ Walk to stimulate your bone marrow.

▼ Walk to improve other physical functions (for example, strengthen leg muscles, improve bowel function, strengthen bone).

TIPS FOR GETTING STARTED—AND STICKING WITH IT

Here are 11 tips for getting started and sticking with an exercise program, whatever your personal preference.

1.   **FIND THE TYPE OF EXERCISE YOU LIKE.** You will stay with it if it's fun. Be sure to include at least 20 minutes (preferably 30 or more) of some form of aerobic exercise at least three times a week (preferably five or more).

2.   **MAKE A FOUR-MONTH COMMITMENT.** Decide, come hell or high water, you will stick with it.

3.   **MAKE A WEEKLY PLAN.** Before going to bed on Sunday night, for example, write down when you will work out the next week.

4.   **PRACTICE MODERATION, GRADUALISM AND PATIENCE.** Your fitness buildup need not be painful. Start walking, rather than running, for instance. Add a few steps of running each week. This type of gradual buildup minimizes discouragement, fatigue, and injury.

5.   **IF HELPFUL, EXERCISE WITH A FRIEND OR GROUP.** Knowing someone is waiting at 7:00 AM can make the difference. Companionship adds to the enjoyment. Of course, some prefer to experience this solitude time. That's okay, too.

6.   **IF HELPFUL, SET GOALS.** Look forward to completing a three-mile fun-run six months from now. Swim one mile by spring. Bicycle to the bridge 25 miles away within a month.

7.   **INTRODUCE VARIETY.** This may mean changing the course where you walk, run, or bike. Or it may mean alternating types of exercise, within a given week or by season.

8.   **DO IT EVEN WHEN YOU DON'T FEEL LIKE IT.** The fatigue you feel at the end of the workday is more mental than physical. The moment you begin to dance, run, swim or bike, you'll forget you ever felt tired.

9.   **IF YOU MISS A SESSION OR TWO, DON'T QUIT ALTOGETHER.** Be tolerant of your own imperfections. View a missed session or two as a mere wrinkle on your way to a lifetime of fitness.

10.   **BE AWARE OF NEGATIVE SELF-TALK ABOUT EXERCISE.** Use thought-stopping. Change it to positive thinking.

11.   **START.**

EXERCISE 8-1. PERSONAL EXERCISE PLANNING

1.   Do you now meet the minimal criteria of aerobic excercise described above (frequency, intensity, time)?
2.   If not, what are the barriers now interfering, (time, habit, weather, cost, child-care)?
3.   Which aerobic activity do you choose?
4.   Where will you do it?
5.   What time of week and day?
6.   With whom?
7.   What equipment and supplies will you need?
8.   What barriers do you expect to interfere with starting? With continuing?
9.   What specific steps will you take to overcome these barriers?
10.   How long a commitment are you making, rain or shine, no matter what?
11.   When will you start?

EXERCISE 8-2. SELF-TALK FOR EXERCISE

Non-exercisers use a variety of negative self-talk statements to continue their sedentary ways. If this is so for you, use the 3 x 5 card technique for reprogramming. Here are several optional self-talk statements. Pick one to begin with.

▼ I love being in good shape.

▼ I take care of myself and keep myself fit.

▼ Regular exercise gives me energy, mental clarity, and emotional stability.

▼ My daily exercise is my daily mini-vacation.

▼ I like the positive effects that exercising creates in my life.

▼ I am proud of how I look, feel, think, and live. Exercise helps me continue to become better and better.

▼ I can MAKE TIME to exercise.

▼ Exercising is my long-term commitment. Missing a day or two is no reason to stop altogether.

▼ Some of the busiest and most important people in this country make time to exercise. So can I.

▼ I love my body. Taking good care of it is very important to me.

▼ Getting fit takes time. I am patient.

NUTRITION   ▼

A second vital health buffer is good nutrition. Just as regular aerobic exercise helps build stress resistance, so will sound nutrition practices.

The linkages between nutrition and stress are complex and numerous. Before setting forth practical nutritional guidelines for helping build stress resistance, let us examine some of the fascinating ways nutrition relates to stress, positively and negatively. This is a mere sampling.

LINKAGES BETWEEN NUTRITION AND STRESS

The most basic place to start is that sufficient calories are needed to provide energy for coping with the stresses of life. The TATT feeling (Tired All The Time) so often reported by students, housewives, laborers, and executives alike sometimes is the result of skipping meals, going on crash diets, or simply undereating in the press of daily life. The amount of calories needed varies by body size and activity.

More common among Americans is overconsumption of calories, which relates to stress in several ways. When caloric intake exceeds energy outgo, the obvious result is overweight. Overweight increases chances of cancer, diabetes, and heart disease, which in turn are obvious sources of stress. Overweight is damaging to self-esteem, especially in our appearance-conscious culture. This problem is intensified when the overweight individual repeatedly tries without success to shed pounds. Excess weight decreases energy available for daily living and coping.

Irregular and inconsistent eating habits are a leading nutritional problem for many in modern life. Students allow the press of midterms to interfere with the regularity of meals. So do harried salespersons, fulltime mothers, busy executives, the urban poor struggling to make ends meet and coping with the dangers and tensions of daily life—and too often with barely enough money to make ends meet.

Too much or too little of specific food substances also relate to stress. Perhaps the most damaging is excess fat in most of our diets. The widely accepted ideal is less than 25 to 30 percent of all calories in the form of fat is ideal. Most Americans exceed this amount. This is one factor contributing to the high rates of death from cardiovascular diseases and cancer in this country, which is noted in Chapter 1. Especially damaging is our too-high proportion of saturated fats. Since fat concentrates calories more than do carbohydrates or protein, high fat consumption increases chances of obesity.

Excess cholesterol also heightens risk of heart disease, which in turn leads to untold fear, anxiety, disability, and grief. Later in this section, we will review ideal figures for fat, cholesterol and other foods.

High amounts of refined sugar—sugar put back into foods such as soft drinks, ice cream, candy bars, and cakes—can also be a stress-related problem for several reasons. Refined sugar is "empty calories" in the sense that it brings with it no vitamins or minerals. It quickly adds up to caloric excess. And it can result in mood swings. Glucose in the blood stream quickly rises with ingestion of high sugar foods. Glucose just as quickly elicits secretion of insulin, which quickly brings energy and emotions down. So the sugar addict alternates between blood sugar-related ups and downs.

Inadequate vitamins and minerals can contribute to loss of energy, irritability, insomnia, and anxiety. Vitamin B is used in construction of adrenaline. While B-complex vitamins (thiamine, riboflavin, niacin, pantothenic acid, and pyrodoxine hydrochloride) can be consumed in unusually large amounts, there is growing agreement that a well-balanced diet can provide daily needs, even during times of high stress. More on this later.

High salt consumption, especially in salt-sensitive individuals, increases chances of high blood pressure. And the higher the blood pressure, the more reactive blood pressure will be during stressful episodes. Stated differently, hypertensives are more likely to have sharp increases of blood pressure when challenged by stressors.

There is some evidence that stress interferes with absorption of calcium in the intestine. At the same time, it can increase excretion of calcium, potassium, zinc, copper, and magnesium. This becomes especially significant in women who are disposed to osteoporosis, a condition of weak and brittle bones.

Excess alcohol consumption is another obvious stress-nutrition link. Excess alcohol intake brings with it many risks: high caloric intake, damage to the liver and the brain, danger in driving, addiction, emotional dependence, and impaired judgment. There is little evidence that modest consumption—a drink a day or so—does harm. The problem is some individuals seem genetically disposed toward easy addiction. And many resort to alcohol overuse, either chronically or episodically, as a way to "numb out" or to blindly conform to group pressure during stressful times.

Sympathomimetic agents—especially caffeine—simulate the stress response through activation of the sympathetic nervous system. Not only do they increase baseline arousal level, they also increase reactivity. These agents include coffee, cola, tea, chocolate, and, perhaps especially in some children, food coloring and preservatives. Tea also contains other sympathomimetic agents: theobromine and theophylline, which are thought to stimulate increases in metabolism and alertness. Like other foods, moderation is the key. More than the equivalent of two or three cups of coffee per day can increase risk of high blood pressure, heighten reactivity to stressful events, and contribute to insomnia.

This, then, is a sampling of nutrition-stress linkages. Next, we examine generally sound nutritional principles. A key assumption here is that wise nutritional principles and practices in general are sound guidelines for stress control as well. Later we will make several recommendations specifically related to stress.

A number of national bodies have issued nutritional reports in recent years. Most display a high degree of agreement. As an example, we will briefly examine recent reports from the U.S. Surgeon General and the National Cancer Institute.

AMERICA'S NUTRITIONAL HABITS

The Surgeon General's Report
Former U.S. Surgeon General C. Everett Koop will best be remembered for his reports and statements on smoking. But he also issued a significant report on diet and health in America (Surgeon General, 1989). This 712-page study was the first ever issued by a U.S. Surgeon General and reflects the growing concern in health circles that dietary flaws represent a real threat to the health of Americans. Several basic and urgent recommendations comprised the core of this report:

▼ Reduce fats, especially saturated fats such as butter and untrimmed red meat.

▼ Reduce cholesterol consumption.

▼ Increase consumption of fish, poultry, lean meats, and low-fat dairy products.

▼ Reduce total calorie intake; balance caloric intake with energy expenditure.

▼ Increase consumption of foods containing complex carbohydrates and fiber such as whole grains, cereals, leafy vegetables, dried beans and peas, and fruit.

▼ Choose foods low in sodium, and minimize addition of table salt.

▼ Consume no more than two alcoholic drinks per day and none during pregnancy.

Other recommendations included caution when purchasing products labeled "natural" or "organic." Koop noted that Americans spend far too much on unproven vitamin and mineral supplements and on fad diets.

Curiously, he said, this country suffers from twin problems: On one hand, malnourishment among the poor, especially children; and, on the other, widespread overeating and obesity.

The recommendations in this report from the U.S. Surgeon General are congruent with those from the American Heart Association, the American Cancer Society, and most other leading groups and experts. Says Dr. Richard J. Havel, Director of the Cardiovascular Research Institute at the University of California at San Francisco and Chairman of the National Research Council's Food and Nutrition Board, "There is now a broad consensus among people in all fields related to nutrition. There just is not a lot of conflict among the experts" (Petit, 1989).

How are Americans doing relative to these guidelines? Not very well, although some improvements are showing, according to Koop and others. When issuing his report, Koop noted that most of the leading causes of death in this country are diseases of "dietary excess and imbalance." Of the 2.1 million Americans who died during 1987, he said, 1.5 million were killed by diseases associated with poor diet. According to Dr. J. Michael McGinnis, Koop's Deputy Assistant Secretary in charge of health promotion, "Five of the ten leading causes of death in the United States— coronary heart disease, certain types of cancer, stroke, diabetes mellitus and athero-sclerosis—are diseases in which diet plays a part" (Perlman, 1988).

The National Cancer Institute Report

The National Cancer Institute recently issued a report on daily eating habits of Americans as part of a long-term study of diet and health (Associated Press, 1988). In interviews with more than 11,000 people, researchers found, for example:

▼ On a typical day, 40 percent of Americans do not eat any fruit and 20 percent consume no vegetables.

▼ More than 80 percent of those surveyed ate no high-fiber cereals or whole-grain breads. Overall, daily fiber intake averaged less than half the recommended amount.

▼ More than four of 10 reported eating at least one serving each day of lunch meat or bacon—foods high in salt and fat and usually cured with nitrates.

Stated Gladys Block, a National Cancer Institute scientist and co-author of the report, "We really need to change the way we eat. I really believe that could make a difference in the amount of cancer we have." A more recent survey of eating habits of Californians found similar eating patterns and came to similar conclusions (Lowman, 1990).

The director of another recent national nutrition study by the National Research Council concludes that Americans need to cut protein consumption by 10 percent, overall fat by 20 percent, and saturated fat and salt by 25 percent. At the same time, they need to increase complex carbohydrates by 20 percent (Petit, 1989).

NUTRITIONAL GUIDELINES FOR BUILDING STRESS RESISTANCE

Based on what we know about nutrition and health in general and about nutrition and stress in particular, three simple guidelines need to be followed to ensure that

---

BOX 8-1. THE STRESS DIET

BREAKFAST
½ grapefruit
1 slice whole wheat toast
8 oz. skim milk

LUNCH
4 oz lean broiled chicken breast
1 cup zucchini—steamed
1 Oreo cookie
Herb tea

MID-AFTERNOON SNACK
Rest of the package of Oreos
1 quart Rocky Road ice cream
1 jar hot fudge

DINNER
2 loaves garlic bread
Large pepperoni and mushroom pizza
Large pitcher of beer
3 Milky Way candy bars
Entire frozen cheesecake eaten directly from the freezer

Source: Unknown.

---

we eat in ways that will ensure good health and maximum stress-resistance. After presenting these, we will discuss a number of related tips and suggestions.

1. Eat a balanced, consistent diet with sufficient but not excessive calories, vitamins, and minerals.

2. Minimize the following in response to stress:
Undereating
Overeating
Excess alcohol—no more than one or two drinks per day
"Sugar hits"
Excess caffeine—no more than the equivalent of a cup or two of coffee
per day

3. Follow these simple principles:
Low salt—less than 6 grams per day
Low fat, especially saturated fat—less than 30 percent of calories through
fat; less than 10 percent through saturated fat

Low cholesterol—less than 300 milligrams per day
Low refined sugars
High complex carbohydrates—50 percent or more of total calories

High fiber—20 to 30 grams per day

Plenty of water—6 to 8 glasses per day

EXERCISE 8-3. FOOD SCRIPTING

Your "food script" is part of your broader life script—a blueprint for living developed through early messages and early decisions. This exercise is intended to increase your awareness of your own food script.

Recall some childhood experience that involved food and eating. What messages did you receive about food and eating from family and friends? Examples might be:

"If you love me, you will eat everything I put on the table."
"Good times always have food connected with them."
"Follow my example and eat in response to stress."

What problems, if any, did these messages cause you? What steps can you take to update them?

CONTROLLING DIETARY HABITS

Reduce Fat in Your Diet

Evidence continues to mount that high-fat dietary habits heighten risk for coronary artery disease, cancer and other illnesses. A recent study suggests that among teenagers the main source of saturated fat—the bad kind—is dairy products (Associated Press, 1989a). The Florida Department of Citrus and the Mazola Fat and Cholesterol Tip Service recently provided the following guidelines for reducing fat in your diet (Associated Press, 1989b):

▼ Eat more fish, chicken, and turkey, or non-meat alternatives such as legumes or tofu.

▼ Make sandwiches with lean meats or skinless poultry rather than with high-fat hamburgers, bologna, or yellow cheeses.

▼ Select beef cuts that are trimmed of excess fat, with little marbling.

▼ Remove skin from poultry before cooking.

▼ Select low-fat dairy products.

▼ Use yogurt instead of sour cream, ice milk or sherbet rather than ice cream, skim milk cheeses rather than regular cheeses.

▼ Use margarine instead of butter.

▼ Use only a small amount of oil in salad dressings and in frying or sauteing.

▼ Eat more fruits, legumes, vegetables, oats, and oat bran.

▼ When making selections from the salad bar, avoid high-fat items such as bacon bits, olives, and creamy dressings.

▼ For a light dessert or snack, serve fresh fruits. Choose sorbet or nonfat frozen yogurt instead of creamy ice cream.

▼ Read labels carefully. Limit foods high in saturated fats such as palm and coconut oils, lard, and animal shortenings.

Cholesterol and Stress

UNDERSTANDING CHOLESTEROL AND STRESS. Cholesterol has a bad reputation, of course, since it is the substance which helps clog coronary arteries, as you read in Chapter 5. But cholesterol has a positive side as well. In fact it is a vital element for the human body, used for construction of adrenaline, for repair of cell walls, and other important functions. It is a waxy type of fat that originates from two sources: food intake (about 10 percent) and the liver (about 90 percent).

Cholesterol does not travel by itself but attaches to small protein substances called lipoproteins. These come in three forms: very low density lipoprotein (VHDL), low density lipoprotein (LDL), and high density (HDL) (Brand, 1988). HDL is known as the "good guy" of the cholesterol family, because it is the type of lipoprotein that picks up cholesterol already deposited on the inside of coronary arteries and takes it away to the liver for discharge. The higher the HDL, the better.

LDL is the "bad guy" of cholesterols, in that it is the type of lipoprotein that carries cholesterol from the liver and intestines out to the body and deposits some of it along walls of the coronary arteries (Gotto, 1988).

Cholesterol in the bloodstream is influenced by a number of factors, one of which, though not widely recognized, is emotional stress. For example, studies show that cholesterol is elevated among students during exams, among night shift workers, during unemployment, during flight training, during periods of high anxiety, and during tax season among public accountants (Friedman and Rosenman, 1959; van Doornen & Orlebeke, 1982).

LOWERING CHOLESTEROL. On the positive side, studies show that cholesterol can be controlled or reduced by regular practice of deep relaxation and aerobic exercise, as well as by reduction of saturated fat and cholesterol in the diet. One might speculate that other stress management methods such as modification of self-talk habits might have similar effects.

It is commonly assumed that cholesterol in the bloodstream is influenced by diet mainly through cholesterol consumed in foods we eat. However, serum cholesterol also is influenced by fat in the diet. Specifically, the higher the proportion of fat intake that is saturated—mostly from animal sources such as meat and dairy products—the higher the cholesterol in your bloodstream. That, in fact, is the main reason it is so important to minimize dietary fat.

Fortunately, one recent study found that an occasional high-fat meal does not elevate cholesterol in your bloodstream if your routine dietary habit is low-fat (Denke, 1988). Stated Margo Denke in her presentation to the American Heart Association:

> As a doctor, I can't recommend high-fat meals, but these findings suggest that it is the overall consumption of saturated fat over time, rather than occasional high-fat meals, that have the most effect on the lipid profile. It means that when your best friend gets married and they put out a big buffet dinner . . . or when you have a board room lunch meeting and the sandwiches are brought in . . . you don't have to worry too much if you stick to the good diet most of the time.

Another study suggests that if a person follows a low-fat, high-fiber diet, then even an egg a day does not raise cholesterol levels in the blood. In the group studied, the major reduction in cholesterol occurred after the participants had changed to a low-fat diet (Edington, 1987).

Vitamins and Other Supplements

One expert estimates that 40 to 60 percent of Americans use dietary supplements, such as vitamin pills, calcium powder, and high fiber compounds or capsules (Petit, 1989). Yet, their value for health or stress control (prevention or reduction) is highly questionable. Says Dr. Arno Motulsky, a University of Washington professor of medicine and director of a nutrition and health study by the National Research Council, "Although supplements make some people think they feel better, the evidence that this helps prevent chronic disease is nonexistent. Having no evidence of scientific benefits, we don't recommend it" (Meyeroff, 1990).

Similarly, a coalition of health and consumer groups led by the American Dietetic Association has charged that the nation's $2.6 billion-a-year vitamin supplement industry markets products most adults and children do not need to maintain good health and that can cause toxic reactions if overused (*Eugene Register-Guard*, 1987). The report asserts that "there are no demonstrated benefits" in the use of vitamin supplements by otherwise healthy men, women and children. The American Medical Council on Scientific Affairs issued a report at nearly the same time reaching the same conclusion: ". . . healthy adults, 18 years of age and older, receiving adequate diets should have no need for supplementary vitamins" (*Eugene Register-Guard*, 1987).

Exceptions to this general rule may be smokers who, perhaps, need vitamin C supplementation, endurance athletes who sometimes need additional zinc and other trace minerals (although a wholesome diet usually is sufficient even for them), women who take in too little calcium in their diets to prevent osteoporosis, women who need iron supplementation, pregnant women, and other special groups, including the very elderly.

Supplementation may also be needed, of course, for individuals who do not eat a balanced, consistent diet with plenty of vegetables and fruits. In general, however, eating a balanced diet rich in fruits and vegetables will yield sufficient vitamins and minerals to meet daily needs.

What about the association between vitamin B and stress? Vitamin supplements, especially in the B group, are commonly advertised as helpful in combating stress.

Some companies mention physical stress, others refer to mental stress as well. Still others do not distinguish between the two, relying instead on "stress" to sell their products.

One leading company until recently based its promotion of a "stress vitamin" on a 1952 report of the National Academy of Sciences. Close examination of this report, however, shows that it recommends vitamin supplements only for people suffering from severe physical trauma, such as major surgery, major fractures, and serious burns. Even in the case of physical stress, the report stated that ". . . in minor illnesses or injury where the expected duration of the disease is less than 10 days and when the patient is essentially ambulatory and is eating his diet . . . a good diet will supply the recommended dietary allowances of all nutrients" (Schafer, 1987). Nutrition experts agree that, with rare exception, recovery from or prevention of physical stress associated with illness or injury seldom requires vitamin supplements, since needs seldom exceed recommended daily allowances.

What about emotional stress? No evidence exists that emotional stress increases our need for vitamin supplementation—or that vitamin supplements will prevent such stress. Again, a normal dietary regimen will provide all vitamins needed by most people. The chief of nutritional science at Lederle Laboratories, manufacturers of Stresstabs, acknowledged this fact in an interview in *Consumer Reports* magazine when he stated that ". . . people who eat a balanced diet do not need stress vitamins— or for that matter, any vitamin supplement at all" (Schafer, 1987).

In New York state, one vitamin manufacturer was successfully prosecuted in 1986 for advertising that "stress resulting from work situations, physical activity, smoking, and complications of everyday life can increase your need for certain vitamins."

In short, don't be misled by advertisements for "stress vitamins." Except in rare cases, you don't need them.

EXERCISE 8-4. FOOD DIARY

Keep a food diary for the next three days. What can you learn about good and bad foods you eat? About how eating and drinking relate to stressful events in your life? What can you do differently to improve your diet for better buffering against distress? For more effective reactions to distress?

Eating Disorders

The message women constantly get from mass media in this country is, "You are not quite right like you are. You had better do something about your . . . weight, eyes, hips, feet, skin, hair, scent, breast size, etc., etc." One result is hyperconcern with appearance, especially weight.

Since weight is associated with health risks and with aerobic fitness, there is good reason to try to minimize weight gain. Among many young people, especially women, this concern becomes an obsession, often resulting in the eating disorders of anorexia nervosa and bulimia nervosa. These disorders most often are the direct result of intense stress, and they in turn add immeasurably to human distress.

Anorexia nervosa remains a disorder mainly affecting young women, with onset usually between ages 12 and 25 (Giannini, Newman & Gold, 1990). It includes refusal to maintain minimal normal body weight over time, intense fear of weight gain or looking fat, and distorts body image (like feeling "fat" even when emaciated, believing that one area of the body is "too fat" even when obviously underweight).

Anorexia afflicts between two and five percent of young women, with women of upper-middle socioeconomic status over-represented. It carries a mortality rate of about five percent during the first two years, but when untreated can carry a mortality risk of 20 percent.

According to one source, "A perfectionistic lifestyle, punctuated by one or more performance-related stresses, predisposes to anorexia nervosa" (Giannini, Newman & Gold, 1990, 1170).

Bulimia nervosa, which has a prevalence of about five percent among adolescent females and less than one percent among adolescent males, most often takes the form of binge eating, accompanied by voluntary vomiting, use of laxatives, or use of diuretics to prevent weight gain. Vigorous exercise and distorted body image usually go along. According to the same source, those afflicted disproportionately come from families with a history of emotional instability and obesity.

A study in the mid-1980s found young girls dieting at an alarming rate, perhaps an indication of more eating disorders still ahead and certainly underscoring the obsessive concern about weight and appearance in our society (Associated Press, 1986). University of California, San Francisco researchers surveyed 500 girls in grades 4-12 at San Francisco parochial schools about their attitudes and behavior related to body weight. Consider these findings.

▼ Thirty-one percent of the nine-year-olds said they were worried they were or would become fat.

▼ Almost half of the nine-year-olds and almost 80 percent of the 10-and 11-year-olds reported dieting to lose weight.

▼ The number of girls who reported binge eating increased steadily with age, and all of the 18-year-olds reported current episodes of vomiting, using laxatives, fasting, or taking diet pills.

▼ Although 58 percent of the sample said they considered themselves overweight, their actual height and weight showed that in reality only 17 percent were, an indication of the extent of distortion of body image among young females.

According to the study director, Laurel Mellin, "While eating disorders in adolescents have been studied before, the prevalence of these patterns in children had not been investigated. The results, which are both surprising and alarming, underscore the need for preventive education in the very early school years, possibly even pre-school."

Unfortunately, available data suggest a rise in eating disorders. The most common and difficult barrier to treatment is denial of the extent of the problem, with resulting resistance to change. Often a multi-disciplinary focus is needed, including physician, counselor, dietitian, and support group. Willingness to change is vital to success. Learning to manage tension, anxiety, boredom, or depression can help.

Is Nibbling Healthy?

A common debate among those struggling to lose weight is whether it's best to skip a meal a day, to eat three modest-sized meals, or to nibble all day long. This same issue is equally important, of course, to anyone who eats—which does, after all, include most of us.

Most dietitians agree on two key principles. First, skipping meals does more harm than good, for several reasons.

▼ Resting metabolism slows down when the digestive system is inactive for long periods. Therefore, fewer calories are burned.

▼ When a meal is skipped (and even more if two are missed), the body believes it is entering a period of prolonged deprivation. In response, it is more likely to convert calories to fat to be stored for later survival.

▼ Skipping meals leads to low energy, which can negatively affect productivity, relationships, and emotional well-being.

Second, eating small meals combined with several snacks is better than eating three big meals a day. Again, there are several reasons.

▼ For one thing, energy level is likely to be higher and more stable. This in turn will improve productivity, relationships, and emotional stability.

▼ A higher proportion of calories you eat is likely to be burned rather than stored, resulting in better weight control.

▼ You will never feel very hungry nor very full.

▼ An unexpected benefit recently found by medical researchers is that both total cholesterol and low density lipoprotein cholesterol (the bad kind) are lower than if the same foods and the same amount of calories are consumed in three meals per day (Jenkins, et al., 1989).

For someone trying to lose weight, here is a suggested plan for taking in 1500 daily calories through three meals and three snacks (*Running & Fitnews*, 1990).

Breakfast	300 calories
Snack	200 calories
Lunch	300 calories
Snack	200 calories
Dinner	400 calories
Snack	100 calories

The authors suggest designing menus of this type for about a week at a time.

Yo-Yo Dieting

There is no question that obesity increases risk of distress, illness, and a shortened life span. Yet, recent evidence suggests that cyclical or "yo-yo" dieting can sometimes do more harm than good.

Steen, Opplinger and Brownell (1988) point out that weight cycling has the following effects:

▼ Increases preferences for fatty foods

▼ Lowers metabolism rate, making subsequent dieting even more difficult

▼ Increases risk of cardiovascular disease

In a recent presentation to the American Dietetic Association, Brownell stated, "There is evidence that the more dieting one does, the harder it is to lose weight. This seems to be due to the body's adaptation to weight loss by lowering its energy requirements" (Higgins, 1988).

For example, Brownell's study of high school wrestlers found that some were cyclical dieters, others "noncyclers." (Brownell, 1988). The investigators discovered that the weight cyclers had a significantly lower resting metabolic rate and lower resting energy expenditure than did noncyclers.

Preliminary results from a Swedish epidemiological study suggest that ". . . a history of weight fluctuation is associated with a risk of heart disease" (Higgins, 1988).

The implication appears to be that while obesity has its costs, continually losing and regaining weight has even more. Most experts agree regular moderate exercise is the key to losing weight and keeping it off. Without exercise, the probabilities are very high that within a few months lost weight will return.

BOX 8-2. MORMON LIFESTYLE AND LIFE EXPECTANCY

A recent study by a UCLA epidemiologist credits the positive lifestyle habits of Mormons with their unusually low mortality rate and their high life expectancy (Enstrom, 1989).

Enstrom studied the health habits and death rates of about 5000 Mormon men who had risen to the highest lay rank of their church, as well as similar data on their wives. Here are highlights of his findings:

Middle-aged Mormon men who adhered to three key positive health habits— never smoking, getting regular exercise, and consistently sleeping seven to eight hours per night—had only 34 percent of the mortality rate from cancer and only 14 percent of the mortality rate from cardiovascular disease of middled-aged white U.S. males. The overall rate of these Mormon men was only 22 percent of the overall rate of middle-aged U.S. males.

Middle-aged Mormon wives adhering to all three habits had mortality rates, compared with middle-aged white women, of 55 percent (cancer-related death), 34 percent (cardiovascular-related death), and 47 percent (overall rate).

Enstrom points out that positive characteristics of the Mormon lifestyle other than the three noted above might also contribute to their longer life expectancy (85 for a 25-year-old Mormon male, compared with 74 for a comparable white non-Mormon): avoidance of caffeine, alcohol, and drugs; a low-fat, well-balanced diet; higher than average education; and a strong family life.

Concludes Enstrom, "If people want to minimize their mortality rate and maximize their longevity, this (maintaining positive lifestyle habits) is certainly one way of doing it. I'm not a Mormon, and I don't recommend that people have to become Mormons to do this" (Scott, 1989).

SLEEP   ▼

STAGES OF SLEEP

The third health buffer that helps protect against distress is adequate sleep. Sleep is vital for rejuvenating the body and mind. Sleep deficiency, either in amount or quality, makes one more vulnerable to irritability, anxiety, depression, disturbed thinking, and physical disorders.

Sleep is an altered state of consciousness in which brain waves go through five stages: four stages of non-rapid-eye movement (NREM) and one stage of rapid-eye-movement sleep (REM). As you close your eyes and sink into deep quiet, your brain emits *alpha waves*, low amplitude waves of about eight to 13 cycles per second (Rathus, 1990). This is the same brain wave zone that can be learned through biofeedback and meditation. Entering Stage 1 sleep results in further slowing of the brain, into the zone of *theta waves* with a frequency of about six to eight cycles per second. The transition from alpha to theta waves may be accompanied by a *hypnogogic state*, in which you experience dreamlike images. Yet this is the lightest stage of sleep.

After a half hour or so of Stage 1 sleep, you experience a rather steep dive into Stages 2, 3, and 4. Here your brain emits *delta waves*, from about one-half to seven cycles per second. Stage 4, reached after less than an hour, is the deepest sleep from which it is most difficult to be awakened. After perhaps half an hour in the depths of Stage 4, you begin a relatively rapid climb back upward through the stages into the stage of REM. During REM sleep you experience relatively rapid, low-amplitude brain waves similar to those of Stage 1. During REM sleep most intense dreaming occurs.

HOW MUCH SLEEP DO YOU NEED?

Most adults function best when getting about eight hours of sleep, but there are individual differences. On one hand, Albert Einstein typically slept 11 hours a night and Calvin Coolidge slept 12 (Carlinsky, 1990). By contrast, short sleepers include Margaret Thatcher, Leonard Bernstein, Bryant Gumbel, David Stockman, Cloris Leachman, Jerry Falwell, and John Barrymore. Robert Maxwell, the British publishing baron, sleeps (grudgingly) only about four hours a night and is still going strong at nearly 70.

A Cornell University sleep researcher, James Maas, estimates that more than 100 million Americans—nearly every other adult and teenager—work and play with insufficient sleep (Kates, 1990). He suggests that our on-the-go lifestyle is turning the nation into "walking zombies." Berman and colleagues, medical sleep researchers, point out that, "Excessive daytime sleepiness and inappropriate sleep may constitute the most under-rated health-risk factor in America today" (Berman, Nino-Murcia & Roehrs, 1990). *Time Magazine* (Toufexis, 1990, 79) recently noted in an article called "Drowsy America" that ". . . millions of Americans are chronically sleep deprived, trying to get by on six hours or even less. In many households, cheating on sleep has become an unconscious and pernicious habit."

Studies show that high school seniors average 6.1 hours per night—but need about 10 hours to function effectively. Close to one-third fall asleep in class at least once each week (Kates, 1990).

INSOMNIA AND SLEEP DEPRIVATION

Insomnia can be caused by anything from calcium deficiency to breathing difficulties. According to one report, 90 percent of the time insomnia is caused by stress (*Chico Enterprise-Record*, 1985). It is estimated that one-third of all Americans have difficulty falling asleep on any given night, while half have an occasional episode of disturbed sleep. About one in five have prolonged bouts of insomnia. Twice as many women as men are affected.

Consequences of Sleep Deprivation

Consequences of sleep disturbance and deprivation can be quite minor if short-term and temporary—for example, increased irritability, sensitivity to criticism, difficulty concentrating, memory problems, the blues, increased physical and emotional tension. Most agree there is little harm caused by a short night or two.

Prolonged sleep deprivation can evoke more serious results. Sometimes these difficulties are associated with night or shift work. The Three Mile Island disaster happened at 4:00 AM, Chernobyl at 2:00 AM, the Bhotal accident at midnight, and the Exxon Valdez disaster at about midnight. Flight crew sleep deprivation and disturbed sleep rhythm may have played a part in several major commercial airline disasters in recent years, according to chronobiologists William Holley and William Price (Perrin, 1987).

As we noted in Chapter 4, chronic sleep problems themselves can become major stressors as the individual worries and frets about not getting enough sleep. Beyond that, emotional volatility is likely to increase, thought processes become less effective, performance suffers, and health is impaired. *Time* correctly points out (Toufexis, 1990, 80):

Perhaps the most insidious consequence of skimping on sleep is the irritability that increasingly pervades society. Weariness corrodes civility and erases humor, traits that ease the myriad of daily frustrations, from standing in supermarket lines to refereeing the kids' squabbles. Without sufficient sleep, tempers flare faster and hotter at the slightest offense.

Most of us know the time we are most susceptible to colds and flu—when we are "run down" from too many short nights of sleep. William Dement, director of Stanford University's sleep center states that "Most Americans no longer know what it feels like to be fully alert" (Toufexis, 1990, 79). The only country with greater sleep deprivation may be Japan.

Tips for Preventing and Coping with Insomnia

While medications can sometimes work, experts agree it is far more desirable to try lifestyle approaches first. Here are a number of suggestions made by sleep experts:

1. **Establish a regular sleep routine.** Although this sometimes is difficult because of the changing demands of school, job, community meetings, and family, it is important to seek to go to bed at a regular time. It is also useful to follow established habits during the 15-30 minutes before falling to sleep—reading a novel or a newsmagazine, watching the news, watering the plants, massage.

2. **Use relaxation methods.** In Chapter 9, you will read about several techniques that sometimes work in sleep inducement: progressive relaxation (tense and relax muscles), autogenic relaxation (inducing warmth and heaviness in muscles), meditation, imagery, producing alpha waves through biofeedback-learning.

3. **Exercise regularly.** There is some evidence that those who exercise regularly experience a deeper, more restful sleep. It makes sense that daily release of emotional and physical tension will decrease chances of going to bed in a pent-up state. Intense exercise shortly before bedtime, however, can leave the body in a state of residual arousal, making it harder to get to sleep.

4. **Minimize noise.** Using earplugs often can do wonders when outside noise cannot be avoided.

5. **Practice sleep-congruent nutritional habits.** For example, avoid alcohol before going to bed. While a drink may help you fall asleep faster, alcohol disturbs sleep later in the night. A light snack, including milk, sometimes can help. Avoid a heavy meal just before bedtime, since that will stimulate the body. Avoid caffeine for several hours before sleep.

6. **Stop smoking.** Nicotine too is a stimulant. Further, withdrawal symptoms occur during the night, often disturbing sleep.

7. **Get up if you can't sleep.** New York clinical psychologist Roy Shapiro advises insomniacs to get out of bed for 15-60 minutes and occupy their minds with thoughts other than sleeping. He states, "The worst thing a person can do is to stay in bed. All you accomplish is to brood even more about your problems

and count the time you are not sleeping. Reading and watching TV are activities that will absorb the mind without stimulating it too much. Then, when you're sleepy, go back to bed. If another 15 minutes pass by, and you can't get to sleep, get out of bed again" (Levine, 1990).

8.   Maintain realistic self-talk about sleep. As noted above, sleep deprivation itself can become a major stressor. Believing your day will certainly be ruined unless you get to sleep only makes things worse. Rathus (1990, 179) has identified a number of beliefs that increase bedtime tension and realistic alternatives.

Exaggerated Belief	Alternative Belief
If I don't get to sleep, I'll feel wrecked tomorrow.	Not necessarily. If I'm tired, I can go to bed early tomorrow night.
It's unhealthy for me not to get more sleep.	Not necessarily. Some more people do very well on only a few hours of sleep.
I'll wreck my sleeping schedule for the whole week if I don't get to sleep very soon.	Not at all. If I'm tired, I'll just go to bed a bit earlier. I'll get up about the same time with no problem.
If I don't get to sleep, I won't be able to concentrate on that big test/conference tomorrow.	Possibly, but my fears may be exaggerated. I may as well relax or get up and do something enjoyable for a while.

In short, adequate sleep is important for good health and prevention of distress. Like regular exercise and sound nutritional practices, management of your sleep habits is important to a whole-person, lifestyle approach to stress management.

In the next chapter, we will examine meditation, biofeedback and other relaxation methods.

REFERENCES   ▼

American College of Sports Medicine. (1990). *The Recommended Quantity and Quality of Exercise for Developing and Maintaining Cardiorespiratory and Muscular Fitness in Healthy Adults.*

Antonovsky, A. (1979). *Health, Stress and Coping: New Perspectives on Mental and Physical Well-Being.* San Francisco: Jossey-Bass Publishers.

Antonovsky, A. (1987). *Unraveling The Mystery of Health: How People Manage Stress and Stay Well.* San Francisco: Jossey-Bass Publishers.

Associated Press. (1986). Study shows alarming rate of young girls dieting. *Chico Enterprise-Record*, October 30, 3A.

Associated Press. (1988). Cancer group finds Americans eat all wrong. *San Francisco Chronicle*, March 14, A1.

Associated Press. (1989a). Milk biggest source of bad fat in kids. *Chico Enterprise-Record*, February 19, 8D.

Associated Press. (1989b). Easy, painless changes that can cut fat from your diet. *Chico Enterprise-Record,* September 5, 8B.

Berger, B.G., & Owen, D.R. (1983). Mood alteration with swimming—Swimmers really do "feel better." *Psychosomatic Medicine,* 45, 425-433.

Berman, T.E., Nino-Murcia, G., & Roehrs, T. (1990). Sleep disorders: Take them seriously. *Patient Care,* June 15, 85-104.

Blair, S. N., Kohl, H.W. III, Paffenbarger, R.S., Jr., Clark, D.G., Cooper, K.H., & Gibbons, L.W. (1989). Physical fitness and all-cause mortality: A prospective study of healthy men and women. *Journal of the American Medical Association,* 262, 95-2401.

Brand D. (1988). Searching for life's Elixir. *Time,* December 12, 62-66.

Brown, J.D., & Lawton, M. (1986). Stress and well-being in adolescence: The moderating role of physical exercise. *Journal of Human Stress,* 12, 125-131.

Brown, R.D. (1986). *Effects of a Strength Training Program on Strength, Body Composition, and Self-Concept of Females.* Unpublished Doctoral Dissertation. Brigham Young University.

Brown, R.S. (1987). Exercise as an adjunct to the treatment of mental disorders. In Morgan, W.P. & Goldson, S.E. (Eds.), *Exercise and Mental Health.* Washington, D.C.: Hemisphere, 131- 137.

Carlinksy, D. (1990). Not everyone needs eight-hour slumber. *San Francisco Chronicle,* March 14, B1.

Chico Enterprise-Record. (1985). Insomnia: If it's stress-related, fighting can only make it worse, October 27, C4.

Clarke, D.H. (1975). *Exercise Physiology.* Englewood Cliffs, N.J.: Prentice-Hall, Inc.

Cooper, K. H. (1977). *The Aerobics Way.* New York: Evans.

Denke, M.A. (1988). Occasional high-fat meal may not cancel effect of prudent diet. *Family Practice News,* 18, 5.

Dienstbier, R.A. (1989). Arousal and physiological toughness: Implications for mental and physical health. *Psychological Review,* 96, 84-100.

Dustman, R.E. (1989). Aerobics fitness helps cognitive function in aged. *Family Practice News,* 19, 37.

Edington, J. (1987). Egg may not need to be resticted in low-fat diet. *Family Practice News,* 17, 6.

Enstrom, J.E. (1989) Health practices and cancer mortality among active California Mormons. *Journal of the National Cancer,* 6, 1807-1814.

Eugene Register-Guard. (1987). Vitamin overuse alleged, April 9, 3A.

Friedman, M., Rosenman, R.H., (1959). Association of specific overt behavior pattern with blood and cardiovascular findings. *Journal of the American Medical Association,* 169, 1286-1296.

Giannini, A.J., Newman, M., & Gold, M. (1990). Anorexia and bulimia. *American Family Physician,* 41, 1169-1176.

Glasser, W. (1976). *Positive Addiction.* New York: Harper.

Gotto, A.M., Jr. (1988). Lipoprotein metabolism and the etiology of hyperlipidemia. *Hospital Practice: Symposium Supplement,* 23, 4-13.

Griest, J.H., Klein, M.H., Eischens, R.R., & Faris, J.T. (1978). Running out of depression. *The Physician and Sportsmedicine,* 6, 49-56.

Griest, J.H., Klein, M.H., Eischens, R.R., Faris, J.T., Gurman, A.S., & Morgan, J.P. (1979). Running as a treatment for depression. *Comprehensive Psychiatry*, 20, 41-54.

Hays, D., & Ross, C.E. (1986). Body and mind: The effect of exercise, overweight, and physical health on psychological well-being. *Journal of Health and Social Behavior*, 27, 387-400.

Higgins, L.C. (1988). Cyclical dieting poses dangers. *Medical World News*, November 14, 25-26.

Jenkins, D.A. J., Theiss, M.S., Vuksan, V., Brighenti, F., Cumnae, S.C., Rao, V., Kenkins, A.L., Buckly, G., Patten, R., Singer, W., Corey, R., & Josse, R.G. (1989). Nibbling versus gorging: Metabolic advantages of increased meal frequency. *New England Journal of Medicine*, 321, 929-934.

Johnsgård, K. W. (1989). *The Exercise Prescription for Depression and Anxiety*. New York: Plenum Press.

Kates, W. (1990). America is not getting enough sleep. *San Francisco Chronicle*, March 30, B3.

Lamb, L. E. (1981). Walking to health. *The Health Letter*, XVIII, 1-2.

Lazarus, R.S., & Folkman, S. (1984). *Stress, Appraisal and Coping*. New York: Springer Publishing Company.

Levine, D. (1990). Relief from insomnia via lifestyle favored. *Medical Tribune*, 31, 2.

Lowman, M. (1990). Californians have a ways to go toward a well-balanced diet. *Chico Enterprise-Record*, C1.

McCann, I.L., & Holmes, D.S. (1984). The influence of aerobic exercise on depression. *Journal of Personality and Social Psychology*, 46, 1142-1147.

Meyeroff, W.J. (1990). Vitamin use debated. *Medical Tribune*, 31, 4.

Moses, J. (1989). Light exercise may yield more mental benefit. *Family Practice News*, 19, 51.

Paffenbarger, R.S., Jr., Hyde, R.T., Wing, A.L., & Hsieh, C. (1986). Physical Activity, all-cause mortality, and longevity of college alumni. *New England Journal of Medicine*, 314, 605-613.

Perlman, D. (1988). Koop says bad diet kills 1 million a year in U.S. *San Francisco Chronicle*, July 28, A5.

Perrin, F. (1987). Is weariness in cockpit contributing to crashes? *Medical Tribune*, 27, 7-9.

Petit, C. (1989). A new report tells Americans how to eat. *San Francisco Chronicle*, March 2, A4.

Rathus, S.A. (1990). *Psychology*. Fourth Edition. Fort Worth: Holt, Rinehart and Winston.

Rippe, J.M., Ward, A., Porcari, J.P., & Freedman, P.S. (1988). Walking for health and fitness. *Journal of The American Medical Association*, 259, 2720-2723.

Roth, D.L., & Holmes, D.S. (1987). Influence of aerobic exercise training and relaxation training on physical and psychological health following stressful life events. *Psychosomatic Medicine*, 49, 355-365.

Runner's World. (1989). Up with people, May, 49.

Running and Fitnews. (1990). It's better to nibble than to gorge. April, 2.

Schafer, W. (1987). On stress vitamins. *Stress and Health Report*, 5, 1

Scott, J. (1989). Mormon ways shown to be healthy. *Sacramento Bee*, December 6, A5.

Sime, W.E. (1987) Exercise in the prevention and treatment of depression. In Morgan, W.P., & Goldston, S.E. (Eds.), *Exercise and Mental Health*. Washington, D.C.: Hemisphere, 145-152.

Steen, S.N., Oppliger, R.A., & Brownell, K.D. (1988). Metabolic effects of repeated weight loss and regain in adolescent wrestlers. *Journal of The American Medical Association*, 260, 47-50.

Surgeon General. (1989). *The Surgeon General's Report on Nutrition and Health*. Washington, D.C.: U.S. Government Printing Office.

Toufexis, A. (1990). Drowsy America. *Time Magazine*, December 17, 78-85.

Ungerleider, S., Porter, K., Golding, J., & Foster, J. (1989). Mental advantages for masters. *Running Times*, No. 156, 18-20.

van Doornen, L.J.P., & Orlebeke, K.F. (1982). Stress, personality and serum-cholesterol level. *Journal of Human Stress*, 24-29.

Quieting the Mind
and Body: Relaxation Methods

Chapter 9

CHAPTER 9

INTRODUCTION   ▼

> The first time Joe gave a class presentation during his first
> semester in college, he trembled beforehand, sweated, stumbled
> several times over simple words and phrases, and developed a
> temporary mental block in the middle of his speech. Afterwards,
> he felt extremely depressed, resolving never to get up before a
> group again.
>   Six weeks later, after working with a stress counselor, it was his turn to give
> another speech. This time he practiced his deep relaxation technique two hours before-
> hand, practiced his speech before the mirror one hour beforehand, and accepted the
> modest tension build-up during the hour before the talk as natural. Immediately

> *before his turn arrived, he did a deep breathing exercise, relaxed his muscles, took his time, and presented a flawless speech with composure. Afterwards, he gave himself several internal pats on the back for doing so well—and for mastering his fear of speaking.*

Joe's challenge was to control his stress response in such a way that his speech would be effective the second time around. In short, he needed to learn to control his stress response so his behavior could be up to potential.

In this situation and others like it, emotions, thoughts, and behavior are interwoven in an intricate, complex web. The parts can be separated only for purposes of discussion and analysis. In reality, they occur together.

Yet, which do we focus on in the immediate stress situation like Joe's class presentation? A key assumption in this book is that while emotions, thinking, body, and behavior are interwoven and inseparable, there are key targets.

Controlling interpretation of the stressor

Controlling the physical stress response

Controlling the behavior or coping response

This leaves out emotions. This does not mean that emotions are unimportant or to be denied. To the contrary, I believe them to be a valuable, central part of human experience, during stress and all other parts of life. But emotions occur and change largely in response to what we think, do, and experience in our bodies. While we will give attention to feelings in this chapter, we assume they can best be controlled or altered by regulating what we think and do and by regulating our bodies.

This view is consistent with Lazarus (1975, 553) who emphasizes the role of mental and behavioral coping in determining emotions. "You will note that this analysis reverses the usual wisdom that coping always follows emotion (or is caused by it) and suggests that coping can precede and even influence its form and intensity."

Parrino expresses a similar view within his holistic "human response system" framework (Parrino, 1979).

> In the human response system model, emotions do not precipitate problems. Rather problems or maladaptive responses lead to emotional upset and disturbance. Human responses such as disordered thinking habits can precipitate anger in frustrating situations. A nervous system that is easily aroused by threatening life events can produce a state of chronic anxiety and tension. Behavioral habits such as procrastination can induce deep states of depression. In summary, habits of living are seen as the instigators of emotional reactions.

Of course, through a loop-back effect, emotions in turn affect physical arousal, thinking, and behavior. But in terms of a stress control strategy, it is best in stressful situations to approach emotions indirectly through one of these other channels, rather than directly. In fact, this probably is the only way.

This chapter focuses on methods for eliciting the relaxation response. These methods are divided into two categories, on-the-spot tension reducers and deep relaxation methods.

ON-THE-SPOT TENSION REDUCERS   ▼

BREATHING TECHNIQUES

Below are a number of simple breathing techniques for controlling or reducing the physical stress response in the immediate stressful situation. Each counters the arousal associated with either a mini or maxi fight-or-flight response with a brief release of the relaxation response. Contraction and relaxation are intrinsic parts of the breathing cycle as you inhale and exhale. These exercises simply build upon this fact.

Each of the following is presented as an exercise that you are invited to experience as you read, as well as in later stressful situations.

EXERCISE 9-1. SIX-SECOND QUIETING RESPONSE

This simple technique is amazingly effective. Do it many times each day, beginning with at least once per hour. Use it routinely, whether or not you face challenge. Then do it especially when needing an on-the-spot tension reliever.

1. Draw a long, deep breath.
2. Hold for two or three seconds.
3. Exhale long, slowly, and completely.
4. As you exhale, let your jaw and shoulders drop. Feel relaxation flow into your arms and hands.

This can be done with eyes open or closed, with others or alone. Few people will ever detect you doing this exercise.

EXERCISE 9-2. THREE-BREATH RELEASE

Here is another technique that you can practice on-the-spot, during or before meetings, tests, performances, confrontations. It is very simple and very effective. Try it at least once each day or week.

1. If possible, let your eyes fall closed. (This is not essential.)
2. Draw a comfortably deep breath, preferably into the deeper end of your lungs (this is diaphragmatic breathing). As you let go, allow your whole body to loosen and go slack at once. Feel your entire musculature relax and soften. As you let go, recall how your body feels at the end of a good, deep relaxation session, and let your body sink toward that feeling of slackness and heaviness—all in one long, comfortable exhale. (Don't worry if you are standing or sitting, you will not fall over. If you are standing and want to let your eyes close, you can keep your balance by placing your hand on something solid next to you.)

3.   Draw a comfortably deep second breath. As you inhale, randomly choose a particular muscle (or pair) in the head, neck, or shoulder area. Usually you will find yourself focusing on a muscle that you suspect to be tense—the brow, the jaws, the shoulder-lifting muscles. As you exhale, focus all your awareness on that muscle, and imagine you feel it dissolving, draining of tension even more completely than it might have during exhale number one.

4.   Draw a comfortably deep third breath. As you release it, focus inside your forearms and hands, and imagine them feeling heavier, warmer and calmer, as if you just completed a full deep relaxation session.

5.   Open your eyes and continue about your business. No judgment, no analysis. Just let it go at that. You do not have to "perform" this technique—just do it, with your awareness clear and inward for the moment, but without effort. With practice, its value will become more and more obvious.

Source: Gelb (1980, 153)

EXERCISE 9-3. FOCUS ATTENTION ON BREATHING

This simple technique can help your mind and body in tense situations. It is very simple. Without trying to change anything, simply allow your mind to be fully aware for several moments of your breathing. Dwell on the rise and fall of your chest, the cooler air coming in, the warmer air passing out. Be aware of whether your breaths are shallow or deep, quick or slow, comfortable or uncomfortable. Dwell on the passage of air in and out of your right nostril for a few breaths, then your left. Simply allow this attentiveness to settle you, to quiet distracting or racing thoughts. It is important to accept what you observe, simply be with it. Do not concern yourself with trying to change it.

EXERCISE 9-4. BREATHING SLOWLY FOR CALMING EFFECT

Another technique, very effective for many people before a difficult speech, performance, interview, physical performance, or athletic performance, is to deliberately breathe calmly and slowly, thinking of this slow breathing as soothing and calming your entire body. Leaving your breath out longer than normal can be especially helpful.

EXERCISE 9-5. DIAPHRAGMATIC BREATHING

You are invited to experience the following diaphramatic breathing exercise, written by relaxation expert Jonathan Smith (1985, 114).

First sit comfortably with your feet on the floor. Place a clock or watch with a second hand in front of you. When the second hand reaches 12, hold your ribcage and collarbone as still as possible and breathe in through your stomach as slowly as you can. Imagine you are filling your stomach with air. See how long you can draw out the inhalation and exhalation. How slowly did you breathe? Now place your hands over your stomach and hold your stomach as still as you can. Try not to let it move at all. Breathe by moving only your ribcage. See how slow you can make this breath.

EXERCISE 9-6. BREATHING AWAY TENSION

1.   Sit or lie in a comfortable position with hands open and legs uncrossed.
2.   Be aware of the weight of your entire body on the floor, bed, couch, or chair. Your muscles need not help support your body at all.
3.   Softly close your eyes.
4.   Focus attention on your nostrils and "see" the air entering each side. Follow its path down into your lungs, "watch" it swirling around, and "observe" it moving back up and out.
5.   As it leaves, tell yourself it is carrying away tension, pain, and disease if present.
6.   Continue for 1–5 minutes.

Remember, the better your physical fitness, the better your ability to extract and process large amounts of oxygen during exercises such as these throughout the day will be.

MUSCLE RELAXATION TECHNIQUES

The techniques described below are brief, on-the-spot tension reducers, intended to be used throughout the day, especially during or between challenging situations.

Exercise While Standing

EXERCISE 9-7. STRETCHING

Notice how a cat often enjoys a full-body stretch and yawn after eating or before settling down. Try it, especially before a challenging event. Reach upward as high as possible with both hands. Then spread your feet and reach up and over your head with one straight arm while sliding the other down your opposite leg. Put both arms behind you, hands clasped. Pull down and back strenuously, opening up your chest and shoulders. Then yawn if you feel like it, with both arms falling easily to your sides.

EXERCISE 9-8. MUSCLE SLAPPING

Gently slap the muscles all over your body. This can help relax them, as well as provide stimulation and mild toning.

EXERCISE 9-9. TRUNK ROTATION

Large trunk rotations provide an excellent warm-up and relaxation method. Extend both arms straight out to the side. Slowly and gently rotate from the waist, first right, then left. Repeat several times with your hands resting on your hips. Be gentle, avoiding quick or strenuous movements. Never push beyond a point of mild tightness.

EXERCISE 9-10. JOGGING IN PLACE

With your arms gently hanging at your side, slowly run in place for one to three minutes. Your feet need hardly leave the ground. You can release muscle tension, while mildly oxygenating your brain and the rest of your body.

Exercise Your Arms

EXERCISE 9-11. FLOPPY DOLL

Stand with feet set apart to provide good stability. Allow your arms to dangle at your side. Then rotate your upper trunk back and forth with your arms and hands swinging gently and effortlessly along. Allow your entire upper body to relax as you slowly rotate back and forth. Repeat several times with a brief breather in between.

EXERCISE 9-12. SWIMMER'S SHAKE-OUT

You will see competitive swimmers do this exercise during the few moments before the starting gun. Allow both arms to hang very loosely at your side. Beginning with your hands, rotate each arm from fingertips to shoulder. At the same time, let them swing gently from front to back. This will be relaxing only if you let your arms hang loosely, rather than raise them outward to the side. Notice how this relaxes your shoulders as well as your arms.

EXERCISE 9-13. ISOMETRIC ARM RELIEVER

Pull or push for a few seconds with each hand against a desk, a doorway, or another immovable object. Relax for a few seconds. Repeat several times. Notice the release of muscle tension during each rest interval.

Exercise While Sitting

EXERCISE 9-14. TENSE AND RELAX NECK AND SHOULDERS

The most common location of muscle tension for most people is back of the neck and shoulders. One easy way of releasing this tension is to tighten the neck and shoulders, hold for five or ten seconds, then completely release. Repeat a number of times. Be aware of more relaxation in this area than before.

EXERCISE 9-15. CIRCLING SHOULDERS

Be aware during the day when your shoulders are tight. Consciously release this tension while gently rotating them first in one direction, then in the other. You can do this quite inconspicuously. A gentle massage by a friend is a great follow-up. Remember that you look more confident and at ease with loose rather than tight shoulders.

EXERCISE 9-16. LEG LOOSENER

Many women make it a habit to hold their legs tightly together, even when alone. Similarly, men often keep their legs quite tight, especially when pushed for time or in an intense situation. This commonly is reflected in foot jiggling or knee bobbing. Deliberately allow your leg muscles to let go. Let your thighs fall apart a little. Keep your ankles relaxed.

EXERCISE 9-17. FACE LOOSENER

Your facial muscles are closely tied to your emotional state. Tension or relaxation in your face are important forms of non-verbal communication. Especially telltale is forehead muscle contraction, which for many people is a chronic condition. You may find it quite useful, therefore, to do the following.

Check whether your teeth are clenched. If so, let them release so your jaw is more relaxed. Next check out your forehead. If you detect muscle tension there, lift your eyebrows gently and release lines of tension or fatigue. Turn a furrowed, frowning brow into a smooth, relaxed forehead. Coordinate each step with a relaxing breathing away of tension.

EXERCISE 9-18. NECK PRESS

A simple method of reducing neck tension is to press the head back against a wall or bookcase for a few seconds, then release, much like you did above with your arms. Or try pressing your forehead into your hand, release, repeat several times. This is a brief form of progressive relaxation.

EXERCISE 9-19. HEAD ROLL

Gently rotate your head from side to side and from front to back in a full circular motion. Repeat in the opposite direction. Continue a number of times. It is very important to do this exercise slowly and gently in order to avoid muscle strain.

EXERCISE 9-20. SELF-MASSAGE

Use your finger tips or your cupped hands to massage your facial muscles. This can also be done to your neck, shoulders, arms, or hands. You will find this to be surprisingly restful and tension-reducing.

EXERCISE 9-21. SITTING STRETCH

Extend your one leg forward and upward from a sitting position and hold for a few seconds. Then release and let it fall. Repeat with the other leg. This can also be done with shoulders and arms. For example, reach your hands behind your chair, clasp, then stretch backward. You will find your shoulders, arms and chest relaxing, ready to return to a lower tension level than before.

EXERCISE 9-22. BRISK FIVE-MINUTE WALK

The next time you have already accumulated physical tension or are about to enter a potentially distressful situation, take a brisk five-minute walk. This can release muscle tension, allow greater oxygenation in your brain and body, allow for mental diversion or positive affirmations. It can be amazingly effective.

MENTAL TECHNIQUES

EXERCISE 9-23. THOUGHT STOPPING

This is a simple technique for stopping unpleasant, disabling, or other negative thoughts that threaten to interfere with full concentration or peace of mind. Simply "hear" the word "stop" shouted inside your mind. This can help bring your thinking process to a halt, even briefly. Then immediately substitute a more positive, productive, useful line of thought. This technique can prove especially useful in situations that create personal fear or tightness.

EXERCISE 9-24. MENTAL DIVERSION

This technique, an extension of thought stopping, merely involves substituting more positive thoughts for thoughts that are unnecessarily preoccupying or anxiety-provoking. Here is one man's experience.

I discovered some time ago that, if I allowed myself to, I would spend the hour or two before conducting a large management seminar in worrying about whether I would do a good job. I'd go over my notes, check and recheck my materials, and keep asking myself whether I'd overlooked anything. After discovering the technique of mental diversion, I changed that pattern. Thereafter, I would prepare thoroughly for the seminar (or a meeting with executives, or an important presentation, or any other challenging task), get everything in order well in advance, and put it aside. I would then deliberately indulge in other mental activities that would bring me positive feelings, with the complete assurance that everything was taken care of. Driving to the location where I am to conduct a seminar. I frequently sing songs in the car—one of my favorite activities. This keeps my mind too busy to worry about the task ahead. I usually arrive at the location wishing I had more time to sing a half dozen other songs that have come to mind. (Albrecht, 1979, 204).

EXERCISE 9-25. POSITIVE AFFIRMATIONS

As a sure confidence-builder, repeat affirmative statements over and over just before or even during a difficult situation. These can help alter your perception of threatening situations, relax your body, and drain away emotional anxiety. For example, tell yourself the following.

I am prepared.
I am in control of this situation.
I have no reason to be afraid.
I like myself.
I will do this very well.

EXERCISE 9-26. DESENSITIZATION

Sometimes a serious aversion develops toward a specific activity, such as giving a speech, meeting a new person of the opposite sex, travelling by air, taking a test, interviewing for a job, or speaking freely in a meeting. Desensitization is a systematic technique, developed several years ago by Wolpe (1958), by which the person overcomes the fear or phobia by associating low physiological arousal with the anxiety-producing situation through deep relaxation and visualization. Sometimes an intermediate step of practicing the activity alone or with a friend also is used. Here is one way to use desensitization. If possible try it the first time under guidance of someone trained in this technique.

1.   Choose a challenging event, one that precipitates disordered thinking, fear, anxiety.

2.   Elicit the relaxation response by one of the muscular relaxation techniques described in this chapter. It is desirable to relax during imagery, but you can proceed with the following steps even if you are not completely relaxed.

3.   Imagine the anxiety-provoking situation as vividly as possible. Continue to imagine the situation until you feel that you are deeply involved in it. It helps to imagine it vividly enough to get mildly emotionally aroused by what you are imagining.

4.   Alternate between imagining the scene and relaxing until you get more and more comfortable with the imagined event.

5.   Plan a time to confront yourself with the situation and do it. If you aren't as comfortable in the situation as you would like to be, repeat the steps outlined above and try it once again.

DEEP RELAXATION   ▼

In Chapter 3 we noted that just as the body possesses the natural ability to arouse, to prepare for action, it has a built-in ability to relax. Through the parasympathetic nervous system and quieting of the endocrine system, the ability is a natural tendency, on its own, to restore homeostasis through quieting of the fight-or-flight response. Unfortunately, our fast-paced lifestyle often keeps the stress response activated so permanently that the body and mind stay aroused at an excessively high level for days, weeks, or even years, without release or recovery. The result is wear and tear, breakdown, and stress illnesses such as those reviewed in Chapter 4.

Research during the past decade on biofeedback and meditation has shown conclusively that the mind is able to deliberately produce the relaxation response, not just back down to the level of beginning homeostasis, but below that to a psychological and physical state of *deep* quiet or deep relaxation. Research also has shown that when this condition of deep relaxation is produced once or twice every day for 15 or 20 minutes, substantial benefits follow for stress control and health enhancement. (Benson, 1975) We now will describe in detail what deep relaxation is, how it can be created, and practical issues in beginning to practice deep relaxation.

HYPOMETABOLIC AND HYPERMETABOLIC APPROACHES TO STRESS CONTROL

Aerobic exercise and deep relaxation are opposite approaches to controlling stress and tension. Running, swimming, and other aerobic activities temporarily elevate metabolism—indeed the entire physical system—in order to meet the demands for more energy output voluntarily placed on it by the person exercising.

Deep relaxation, on the other hand, temporarily quiets metabolism and all the physical processes associated with it. With both activities, the mind and body both return to a level below the starting point in terms of subjectively felt tension and even objectively measurable body activity. With aerobic exercise, it takes longer for the body to reach that post-exercise level of deeper quiet, perhaps even several hours after an intense workout as the body cools down.

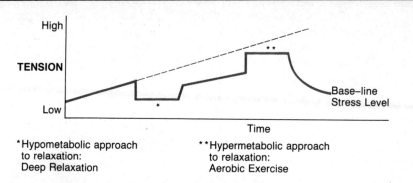

As shown in Figure 9-1, a common pattern is for baseline stress level to begin low in the morning, then to rise as the day progresses, finally falling off with two martinis, T.V., or sleep in the evening. Another even more destructive pattern is for baseline stress level to begin at an elevated point as soon as the person awakens, then to stay up all day, never returning even at night.

As shown by the solid line, aerobic exercise and deep relaxation are complementary approaches to keeping baseline stress level down so it seldom leaves the person's zone of positive stress. Note that in both cases, the post-session level of stress is lower than beforehand. It makes eminent good sense, then, to practice both nearly every day, preferably with several hours separating the two.

Remember, they both are preparation for activity and stress, as well as recovery from tension already accumulated. Therefore, they are best done every day whether you subjectively feel you need them or not. Their effect is cumulative over weeks, months, and years in keeping tension under control.

METHODS OF DEEP RELAXATION

Meditation

Meditation is a practice of sitting or reclining comfortably and quietly with eyes closed for 10 to 20 minutes once or twice a day and using a mental focus to quiet the mind, thereby quieting the body. (Carrington, 1984).

Jonathan Smith, an expert on relaxation exercises, has noted that:

> Meditative exercises have been around for thousands of years. They appear in just about every world culture. Some have deep ties with religion, while others are completely secular. All have one thing in common: the calm directing of attention toward a simple stimulus. (Smith, 1985, 183)

Meditation often is confused with contemplation. They are not the same. Contemplation refers to thinking about something— contemplating the meaning of an event yesterday, considering a theological idea, dwelling on a poem and its application to your life. Contemplation sometimes is done with eyes closed, as is meditation.

Meditation, however, does not involve thinking. Rather, it is indifferent **mental focus on a stimulus.** Indifferent means the focus is carried on "with complete indifference, expecting nothing, desiring nothing" (Smith, 1985, 183). Examples of a stimulus are a silent sound or mantra—"Ieem," "ohm," "hmmm," "maroom," "varoom," or "aroom." Others might be a short prayer or sacred word, a line of music, or your breathing. A light or spot on the wall sometimes are used.

HOW TO MEDITATE

As you begin to meditate, you will note a tendency for your mind to wander. This is quite all right. In fact, it is part of the meditation process. It is important not **to concentrate** on the stimulus—concentration is something different altogether. Meditation means to allow your mind to wander, as it surely will. Gently return to the focus as you become aware your mind is wandering.

Smith describes the process in this way.

> Thus, meditation is not so much a focusing exercise as a returning exercise, a way of coming home. In fact, all you need to know in the way of instruction for meditation is this:
>
> CALMLY ATTEND TO A SIMPLE STIMULUS
>
> AFTER EACH DISTRACTION CALMLY RETURN
> YOUR ATTENTION.
>
> By patiently doing this, again and again and again, the mind is very gradually conditioned to attend for longer and longer periods of time. It is important to emphasize this return of attention should be patient, easy, and gentle—not forced or strained. The goal is not to keep your mind vigilantly glued on the focal task, as if you were playing baseball or a video game. Instead, as calmly and restfully as possible, ease your attention back to the task. Let your mind wander. Every time your mind drifts from the task, you have another opportunity to calmly return your attention. It is only through such opportunities to return that you gradually condition your mind to attend to the focus. It is through distraction and diversion that the experience of meditation deepens and embraces more and more of the world (Smith, 1983, 184).

Another meditation expert, Patricia Carrington, (1978, 25), describes the focus aspect of meditation in this way.

> When meditating, never force thoughts out of your mind. All kinds of thoughts may drift through your mind while you are meditating. Treat these thoughts just as you would treat clouds drifting across the sky. You don't push the clouds away—but you don't hold onto them either. You just watch them come and go. It's the same with thoughts during meditation, you just watch them, and then when it feels comfortable to do so, go back.

BENEFITS OF MEDITATION

Since 1970, thousands of careful studies have been conducted on various forms of deep relaxation, especially Transcendental Meditation and the Benson Meditation Method (sometimes called the Relaxation Response). They show a number of specific benefits, including the following (Benson, 1975; Ferguson and Gowan, 1975; Frew, 1977; Aron and Aron, 1986; Smith, 1986).

Increased measured intelligence

Increased recall, both long-term and short-term

Better "mental health" (decreased anxiety, depression, aggression, and irritability, and increased self-esteem and emotional stability)

Greater perceived self-actualization or realization of potential

Better academic performance in high school and college

Improved job performance

Improved job satisfaction

Improved athletic performance

Better mind-body coordination

Increased perceptual awareness

Normalization of blood pressure

Relief from insomnia

Normalization of weight

Reduced drug abuse

Glasser (1976, 32) who maintains that meditation is a positive addiction similar to running, comments about the subjective benefits from Transcendental Meditation:

> Subjectively, almost everyone remarks that he or she feels "less tense, less worried." Most mention that they had previously experienced some kind of tension, some degree of strain. Students even speak of the "anxiety I felt about school and my future" but "now," said one man, "I feel a certain easiness, everything is smoother." "The main benefit of meditation for me," said another, "is the almost total reduction of serious worry." That means worry in the sense of non-productive, nervous disruption. I can still be deeply concerned about important matters.

> One man stated that "for the first time since I can remember, I can relax, without drugs or drink." A girl wrote, "Before I began the Transcendental Meditation program, I used drugs, methedrine and narcotics. The effects of the drugs were that I was incredibly tense. Physically, my shoulders were up so high that one could barely see my neck." She said that, immediately after receiving instruction in the TM technique, "my shoulders had dropped, all the tension in my face was gone so that my whole facial structure had changed, and most important to me, I was completely at ease. My tension didn't come back."

Advocates of TM maintain that the positive effects of meditation result not only from physiological processes, but also from coming into greater harmony with one's inner nature. Later in this chapter, this is referred to as "centering" or tuning into one's "inner light." Whatever the term, there is growing evidence that meditation and other forms of deep relaxation foster realization of higher potentials—and help to reduce stress.

MEDITATION EXERCISES

Below are several simple meditation exercises. Find which one works for you. The important thing is consistency and regularity. Meditate once or twice each day for 10 to 20 minutes each session.

EXERCISE 9-27. THE BENSON METHOD OF MEDITATION

Dr. Herbert Benson of the Harvard Medical School has shown that the following method of meditation can produce the same physiological changes associated with Transcendental Meditation. (Benson, 1975, 114).

Sit quietly in a comfortable position.

Close your eyes.

Deeply relax all your muscles, beginning at your feet and progressing up to your face. Keep them relaxed.

Breathe through your nose. Become aware of your breathing. As you breathe out, say the word, "ONE": IN . . . OUT, "ONE": IN . . . and so on. Breathe easily and naturally. Continue for 10 to 20 minutes. You may open your eyes to check the time, but do not use an alarm. When you finish, sit quietly for several minutes, at first with your eyes closed and later with your eyes open. Do not stand up for a few minutes.

Do not worry about whether you are successful in achieving a deep level of relaxation. Maintain a passive attitude and permit relaxation to occur at its own pace. When distracting thoughts occur, try to ignore them by not dwelling upon them and return to repeating "ONE." Practice the technique once or twice daily, but not within two hours after any meal, since the digestive processes seem to interfere with the elicitation of the Relaxation Response.

SOURCE: Benson (1975, 114).

EXERCISE 9-28. BREATHING COUNTDOWN

1. Close eyes in sitting or supine position.
2. Take one deep breath, hunching shoulders and holding breath for six seconds.
3. Breath out slowly and completely.
4. Resume normal breathing.
5. On first out-breath, silently say "10." On the next out-breath, silently say "9." On the next out-breath, silently say "8," etc., down to "1."
6. When you reach "1," you can repeat "1" over and over, count back to "10" or let your mind wander.
7. Continue for 10–20 minutes.
8. Slowly open your eyes, resume normal activities.

EXERCISE 9-29. I AM RELAXED

1. Sit or recline quietly and comfortably.

2. Begin by drawing a long deep breath, hold, exhale long and completely. As you exhale, allow your jaw and shoulders to drop.

3. With each in-breath, silently say, "I am." With each out-breath, silently say, "Relaxed."

4. As you become aware of your mind wandering, gently return to the focus: I AM RELAXED.

5. Continue for 10-20 minutes.

Biofeedback

A good deal of research has been conducted in recent years on biofeedback—the use of various detectors to give feedback to the user about her or his physiological arousal at a given moment, thereby aiding the individual in learning to lower arousal (Green & Shellenberger, 1991).

The point of biofeedback training is to discover how relaxation feels and then to learn to induce the feedback indicator downward through conscious focus of the mind (Green & Green, 1977). This usually is done with a therapist, stress consultant, or technician in a comfortable chair in an office or other clinical setting, although sometimes simple devices are used by the individual at home or work. The individual then learns to elicit the same state of relaxation in the absence of the detective device. Biofeedback can be used to create on-the-spot arousal, as well as deep relaxation (Brown 1977).

BIOFEEDBACK TECHNIQUES

A variety of biofeedback techniques have been developed to make visible otherwise invisible internal processes (Budzynski & Stoyva, 1984). **Electromyographic feedback (EMG)** detects muscle contraction through electrodes affixed to the skin surrounding a specific muscle in order to detect small electrical discharges that accompany muscle contraction. Like other types of biofeedback, the feedback may be in the form of a sound, a dial, or a graph. Occasionally, more exotic feedback is used: music, lights, even an electric train. The greater the muscle contraction, the higher the tone, light, dial, or graph. As the individual relaxes, muscle tension drops, and so does the feedback. This information is used by the person to induce still more quieting. EMG biofeedback is often used to help the individual learn how to relax a tight forehead, neck, lower back—or the body generally.

As early as 1928 (Rice, 1987) Hans Berger discovered that the very small electrical discharges from the brain can be amplified and recorded. Thus, the **electroencephalograph** (EEG) was developed. This sensing device is attached to specific locations on the head and attuned to detect alpha, beta, theta or delta waves. Alpha waves are associated with the deep quiet of meditation or falling off to sleep. EEG biofeedback is sometimes used for general relaxation training, but more often to assist the individual in reducing or preventing headaches or for improving attentiveness or concentration.

Another form of biofeedback measures **skin temperature.** Usually some type of finger thermometer is used. As tension mounts, skin temperature in the hands and feet falls. This is the result of constriction of capillaries, a process that shunts blood back into main muscles to be available during the stress response. Remember, your body cannot distinguish between physical threats and other stressors, so it assumes you are in physical danger, whatever the stressful situation. On the other hand, elicitation of the relaxation response brings more blood into the hands and feet, raising their skin temperature.

Even beginners usually are able to raise skin temperature several degrees when skin temperature monitoring is combined with other relaxation techniques. More advanced practitioners sometimes are able even to control temperature to the extent of raising temperature in one ear lobe, while lowering it in the other.

Skin temperature biofeedback sometimes is used to reduce migraine headaches, as well as to treat Raynaud's disease, a problem of constricted blood vessels in the hand, producing extreme cold and pain. This type of biofeedback also is used for general relaxation training.

The **galvanic skin response (GSR)** measures the skin's resistance to electrical conductance across its surface. The greater the relaxation, the greater the resistance—for reasons not entirely understood by experts. The most likely explanation is that with increased tension there is increased sweating. This rise in moisture in turn conducts electricity more quickly. Whatever the physiological process involved, the GSR can be useful for general relaxation—as well as for demonstrations to groups, for which I use the device in my classes and workshops.

Cardiovascular activity measures comprise another type of biofeedback. Whether measuring heart rate, arrhythmias, or blood pressure, this practice can be useful, especially with people who have cardiovascular problems. Of course, monitoring heart rate is a simple practice anyone can constructively use to monitor in a gross way one's physiological arousal.

QUESTIONS ABOUT BIOFEEDBACK

Two key questions are debated by relaxation experts about biofeedback. First, does biofeedback yield benefits beyond those of other relaxation techniques such as meditation, autogenic relaxation, or progressive muscle relaxation? Probably not. Biofeedback may enhance learning or enable it to occur more quickly, but there probably is nothing unique about biofeedback-aided elicitation of the relaxation response, with one notable exception. Biofeedback may be useful for relaxing specific muscles or specific processes such as blood vessels in the hands or forehead.

Second, can relaxation training in the biofeedback clinic be readily transferred to the individual's ongoing life? Again, perhaps and probably with no greater effectiveness than with other relaxation methods.

In sum, biofeedback has been demonstrated to be a useful aid in assisting individuals to learn how to relax—generally and in specific body locations. It is best seen as an adjunct to other relaxation methods, rather than as an independent method standing alone. For some, it may provide the type of feedback and structure that aids learning. For others, learning other techniques of deep relaxation and on-the-spot tension reduction can be accomplished just as well without biofeedback.

Autogenic Relaxation

This technique was first introduced by the German psychiatrist Johannes Schultz in 1932 and continues to have high popularity in Europe. (Schultz & Luthe, 1959). Like meditation, autogenic ("self-produced") relaxation depends on a relaxed body state (sitting with or without back support, or reclining) and a passive, accepting attitude. While this technique takes on several variations, it usually is practiced by focusing self-suggestions of warmth and heaviness in specific muscle groups throughout the body. Done to completion, one needs to devote 30–60 minutes to the technique. Yet limited positive results can be experienced in as few as five minutes.

Norris and Fahrion (1984) have summarized a number of conditions for which autogenics have been employed, including anxiety, phobic disorders, and hysteria. They have also presented research findings showing positive results. Many other studies have produced similar positive results for clients suffering from everything from tension headaches to hypertension, smoking addiction, epilepsy, sexual dysfunction, and alcoholism.

While healthy skepticism is warranted in evaluating this technique, like the others described here, there does appear to be convincing evidence that autogenics can sometimes work to elicit the relaxation response with positive results for health and coping (Rice, 1987). Try Exercise 9-30 for yourself.

EXERCISE 9-30. AUTOGENIC RELAXATION

1. Recline or sit in a comfortable position in a quiet place.

2. Begin with the Six-Second Quieting Response. Close your eyes if you wish.

3. Repeat each stage three to six times in a 30-60 second period. The self-suggestions are to be done silently. After you have finished each location, open your eyes so you will be fresh as you move on the next step (Rice, 1987, 284).

Stage 1. "My right (left) arm is heavy."
"My right (left) leg is heavy."
"Both my arms are heavy."
"Both my legs are heavy."
"My arms and legs are heavy,"

Stage 2. "My right (left) arm is warm."
"My right (left) leg is warm."
"Both my arms are warm."
"Both my legs are warm."
"My arms and legs are warm."

Stage 3. "My heartbeat is regular and calm."

Stage 4. "My breathing is calm and relaxed.'
"It breathes me."

Stage 5. "My upper abdomen is warm."

Stage 6. "My forehead is cool."

Like the other techniques described here, you might find it beneficial to begin with small steps. Be patient. Find the relaxed position and the length of each session that best fits you.

Progressive Muscle Relaxation (PMR)

First written about by Edmund Jacobson in 1929, progressive muscle relaxation has come to be widely practiced and studied with consistent positive results (Jacobson, 1929). Very simply, PMR calls for alternately tensing and relaxing specific muscles throughout the body. In the more technical language of Chapter 3, it alternates between eliciting the sympathetic and parasympathetic nervous systems—the emergency and calming branches. The technique can be practiced for periods ranging from one to 20 or 30 minutes. Some people find this to be a useful tool for falling asleep. Exercise 9-31 describes an abbreviated version for you to try. Other sources provide more detailed instructions.

EXERCISE 9-31. PROGRESSIVE MUSCLE RELAXATION (PMR)

1.   Find a quiet place where you can recline or sit comfortably.
2.   Begin with the Six-Second Quieting Response.
3.   Squeeze each of the following, hold for 10 seconds, then release and draw a deep breath. Move on to the next location.

>   Right fist
>   Right forearm
>   Right upper arm
>   Left fist
>   Left forearm
>   Left upper arm
>   Shoulders and neck
>   Head and face

If you wish to continue, move to your feet and legs, then to your abdomen.

4.   As you proceed, be aware of the contrast between tension and calm. Be aware of the pleasant sensation of relaxation. Most of all, be aware of your power to produce deep quiet.

Hypnosis and Self-Hypnosis

Hypnosis is a very old and effective method of producing deep relaxation (Green & Shellenberger, 1991). Hypnosis is a condition of very deep mental and physical quiet, induced by the hypnotic suggestion of a trained person who uses key words and images to elicit the desired internal change. He or she then gives post-hypnotic suggestions, which, acting through the subconscious, can be very powerful in reducing fears, phobias, smoking, overeating, anxiety, and other problems. When deep relaxation is suggested, the physiological changes associated with the relaxation response can be induced. Hypnosis should only be attempted under the guidance of a trained and experienced hypnosis practitioner.

As Morse and Furst (1979, 245) have noted, different degrees of depth occur during hypnosis.

> Some individuals can only achieve a light trance. In a light trance, a person often feels relaxed, both mentally and physically, but he is completely aware of his surroundings. In a medium trance, an individual is often able to take a mental "trip" and achieve an even deeper state of relaxation. A deep trance is called the somnambulist stage. In this stage, a person can generally realize the more distinctive phenomena of hypnosis, which include the following:
>
> 1. Hand levitation; a hand or an arm rises, apparently of its own free will.
> 2. Eyelid catalepsy—an inability to open the eyes.
> 3. Limb rigidity; an arm or a leg locks in a straightened position.
> 4. Automatic writing; a hand appears to write of its own free will.
> 5. Automatic movement; a hand or a leg moves continuously.
> 6. Dream induction; vivid dreams occur easily.
> 7. Dissociation—an ability to feel either as if one is in two places at the same time or that one can separate the mental from the physical state.
> 8. Hallucination—to be able to see, smell, hear, or feel objects that are not present (known as positive hallucination) or not to see, smell, hear or feel objects that are present (known as negative hallucination).
> 9. Age regression and progression; the former is the ability to go back in time, while the latter is the belief that one can go ahead into the future.
> 10. Amnesia—to be able to forget that which has occurred during the hypnotic state.
> 11. Posthypnotic suggestibility—to act out, at a later time, a suggestion given by the hypnotist.
> 12. Analgesia—the ability not to perceive pain (perhaps, more appropriately, an example of a negative hallucination).

Experts estimate that about 70 percent of people can enter a medium hypnotic trace, while 20 percent seem capable of entering a deep trance.

Hypnosis can be useful in several ways in managing stress. For instance, it can help remove internal barriers and resistances, such as unfinished emotional trauma from the past. Second, it can help build "immunity" against harmful effects of specific future stressful events. Third, through suggestion it can help the individual achieve deep relaxation at a later time.

Self-hypnosis most commonly is used to induce deep relaxation, rather than for medical or dental reasons. Usually self-hypnosis is learned from a trained hypnotist, although it can be self-taught. The point is to induce deep quiet through self-suggestion, much like meditation, autogenic relaxation, progressive muscle relaxation, or visualization, which we will explore next.

Visualization

Visualization, also called mental imagery, guided daydreaming, or "movies of the mind," is another technique that reduces rational mental activity and induces deep quiet. (Samuels, M., and Samuels, N., 1975; Brye, 1978; Green and Shellenberger, 1991) This is a method of imagining yourself in some very pleasant place, usually a natural setting, where you take yourself or someone guides you, live or by audiotape, taking you into a deep, pleasant quiet.

This technique usually is used to induce deep relaxation, although it also can be used as a form of mental rehearsal, as briefly described in Exercise 9-32 and presented in more detail in Chapter 14.

You are invited to try Exercises 9–32 to 9-35 to experience various types of visualization.

EXERCISE 9-32. MENTAL REHEARSAL

Five or ten minutes before entering a difficult situation, use any of the relaxation techniques described elsewhere in this chapter to take your mind and body to a more relaxed state. Then visualize yourself moving through the situation with confidence and competence. Repeat several times before entering the actual situation. This is discussed in more detail in Chapter 14.

EXERCISE 9-33. A PRIVATE PLACE.

You are invited to try the following visualization exercise, reprinted here from the *Wellness Workbook*.
A PRIVATE PLACE: An exercise in Creative Imagination.
This exercise serves a number of useful purposes. Doing it will take you into a state of relaxation. The images you form will stay with you for a long time and provide you with an imaginary place to retreat to for refreshment and healing. Then too, it will exercise your imagination, and excite you as you realize how resourceful you can be. Finally, it may suggest some possibilities for changing your real environment.

Find a quiet, relaxing place, and give yourself thirty uninterrupted minutes to do this exercise. It is helpful to have a friend read it to you so you can close your eyes and give your imagination free rein. You could also tape record it and play it back to yourself. Now, in your mind, journey to your bedroom. See it as vividly as possible. Look it over, wall by wall, remembering what is there. Notice that a new door has appeared on one wall. The door has a door knob. Approach it and put your hand on the knob, notice its texture and temperature. When you open the door, you are going to find yourself in a new room, an addition to your house, a room that you have never seen before. The room will be empty, except that it will have several windows. Go inside now and survey your space.

First, decide upon the light in the room. Where are windows placed? Determine what views you would like to have out of each. (One woman looked out upon the ocean from one, a redwood forest from another, and a snow-covered mountain from a third.)

Now cover the floors if you wish. Next attend to the walls—color, paintings, murals, shelves? Now furnish it for yourself—include a special chair or pillow or couch on which you can rest and dream. Want a work space?—an art studio, a dance floor, a writing desk? Make it happen immediately. If you like music, listen for it. Or add a piano, organ, flute, and music stand. Many people who have done this report that they added elements of the outdoors into their environment—an indoor waterfall, a floor-to-ceiling bird cage, a tree in the middle of the room.

Be as courageous and as outrageous as you can be. Remember there are no limits. Now sit back and enjoy your place. Tell yourself that you can go to it to solve your problems, to relax in the midst of a hassled day, to prepare yourself for sleep. The uses are as many and as varied as your needs. Have fun with it.

Now you may wish to draw or paint what you have created in your mind. Share it with a friend. Build an addition. It's up to you.

SOURCE: Ryan & Travis (1981, 143).

EXERCISE 9-34. THE BEACH

1.   You are invited to become comfortable in a reclining or sitting position, preferably in a quiet place.

2.   Begin by completing the Six-Second Quieting Response.

3.   Visualize the following, allowing your mind to roam free in its own way. If you find it useful, you might dictate the following instructions onto an audiotape, then play it back as you go. Feel free to modify as you wish.

Imagine you are on vacation. No cares, no worries. You feel completely free from your usual daily pressures and hassles. You are walking along the water's edge on a quiet, barely inhabited, warm ocean beach. You are in your bathing suit, either alone or with someone close to you, whichever you prefer. As you stroll, you feel the coolness of the damp sand under your feet. You hear the gentle rolling of the waves. Under one arm is a rolled-up towel. You turn away from the water onto soft, white, warm sand. You pick a spot where you can be alone and still. You put down your still-rolled towel as a pillow. You lie down on the soft, pleasantly warm sand. You feel the warmth of the sand on your back, the backs of your legs, the backs of your arms. You note the deep blue of the late morning sky. It is completely clear, except for one wispy cloud near the horizon over the water. You feel the gentle warmth of the sun on your skin, the pleasant warmth of the sand beneath. You feel utterly relaxed and still. For the next several minutes, continue to experience this place, allowing your mind to wander as it wishes. Enjoy this very pleasant sensation of stillness, warmth and quiet....

And now, imagine getting up, gathering up your towel, walking back to the water's edge. Again, you experience the cool, damp sand underfoot. You continue on along the beach, feeling alert, refreshed, peaceful, and renewed. You give yourself credit for this positive experience.

Bring your attention back to the present. Draw a deep breath. Resume your normal activities.

EXERCISE 9-35. COMBINING DEEP RELAXATION METHODS

You are invited to try this brief technique which combines meditation (repeated mental focus), autogenic relaxation (warmth and heaviness in hands), and visualization (imagining your hands in warm water or in the warm sun). This text was written by the relaxation expert Jonathan Smith (Smith, 1985, 1).

> Let both of your hands fall to your sides. Let them become as relaxed as possible. Give yourself a while to settle into a position that feels very comfortable. Let your breathing be calm and even. Now, focus your attention on your hands. Simply repeat to yourself the phrase, "My hands are warm and heavy." Let those words go over and over like an echo. There is nothing for you to try to do. Do not try to force your hands to feel warm and heavy. Simply let the words go over and over in your mind, like the words of a simple song or nursery rhyme. You might want to imagine your hands in warm water, or in the warm sun.

To purchase a 25-minute audiotape, with music and oral instructions much like these, write for information to:

Walt Schafer, Ph.D.
Enloe Hospital Stress and Health Center
West Fifth Avenue and Esplanade
Chico, CA. 95926

There are many other ways of producing deep relaxation. What you have read here is a sampling of some of the main methods. A number of written sources are available for other methods. See for example, Smith (1985, 1986), Hanson (1986), Schwartz (1982), Carrington (1978), LeShan (1974), Charlesworth and Nathan (1982), and Davis, Eshelman, and McKay (1982).

MAKING DEEP RELAXATION PART OF YOUR LIFE

The greatest challenge in practicing deep relaxation is not learning the techniques. With practice, they come rather easily. The greater challenge is building the practice into your daily life with regularity and consistency.

Since there seems to be a cumulative effect of deep relaxation, much like aerobic exercise training, it is important that for maximum effect you do it over a period of many months, even years—10 to 20 minutes once or twice a day.

As noted above, daily deep relaxation combined with daily aerobic exercise is a very powerful combination. Try it.

Exercise 9-36 is intended to help you get started.

EXERCISE 9-36. PLANNING TO BEGIN DEEP RELAXATION

1. What type of deep relaxation exercise are you most attracted to?
2. When will you start?

3. What steps will you take to learn a deep relaxation technique (through reading, an audiotape, a videotape, a class or workshop, individual instruction, for example)?

4. When and where will you practice deep relaxation each day?

5. What difficulties do you expect to encounter?

6. How will you overcome each of these difficulties? For example, what will you do six months from now when you become so busy you "just don't have time" to practice deep relaxation every day?

We now have covered perhaps the three most powerful clusters of tools for managing stress for maximum wellness: self-talk skills, health buffers, and relaxation methods. In combination, they hold promise, not just for minimizing distress, but for turning stress into a positive force for maximizing your potential and reaching peak performance. They are important ingredients of the whole-person, lifestyle approach to stress management which is the theme of this book.

There are still other ingredients. In the next chapter, we will discuss managing time and change—key stress management and wellness skills in a fast-paced, rapidly changing world.

REFERENCES　　▼

Albrecht, K. (1979). *Stress and The Manager*. Englewood Cliffs, N.J.: Prentice-Hall, Inc.

Aron, E., & Aron, A. (1986). *The Maharishi Effect*. Walpole, N.H.: Stillpoint Publishing.

Benson, H. (1975). *The Relaxation Response*. New York: Morrow.

Brown, B. (1977). *New Mind, New Body*. New York: Harper and Row.

Brye, A. (1978). *Visualization: Directing The Movies of Your Mind*. New York: Barnes and Noble.

Budzinski, T.H., & Stoyva, J.M. (1984). Biofeedback methods in the treatment of anxiety and stress. In Woolfolk, R.L., & Lehrer, P.M. (Eds.), *Principles and Practice of Stress Management*. New York: Guilford Press, 188-219.

Carrington, P. (1978). *Freedom In Meditation*. New York: Anchor.

Carrington, P. (1984). Modern forms of meditation. In Woolfolk, R.L., & Lehrer, P.M. (Eds.), *Principles and Practice of Stress Management*. New York: Guilford Press, 108-141.

Charlesworth, E.A., & Nathan, R.G. (1982). *Stress Management: A Comprehensive Guide To Wellness*. New York: Ballantine.

Davis, M., Eshelman, E.R., & McKay, M. (1982). *The Relaxation and Stress Reduction Workbook*, 2nd. Ed. Oakland, Ca.: New Harbinger Publications.

Ferguson, P.C., & Gowan, J.C. (1975). Psychological findings on Transcendental Meditation. *Scientific Research on the Transcendental Meditation Program*. Switzerland: MERU.

Frew, D.R. (1977). *Management of Stress: Using TM At Work*. Chicago: Nelson.

Gelb, H. (1980). *Killing Pain Without Prescription*. New York: Harper and Row.

Glasser, W. (1976). *Positive Addiction*. New York: Harper.

Green, E., & Green, A. (1977). *Beyond Biofeedback*. New York: W.W. Norton.

Green, J., & Shellenberger, R. (1991). *The Dynamics of Health and Wellness: A Biopsychosocial Approach.* Fort Worth: Holt, Rinehart and Winston.

Hanson, P.G. (1986). *The Joy of Stress: How To Make Stress Work For You.* Kansas City: Andrews and McMeel.

Jacobson, E. (1929). *Progressive Relaxation.* Chicago: University of Chicago Press.

Lazarus, R.S. (1975). A cognitive-oriented psychologist looks at biofeedback. *American Psychologist,* 30, 553-561.

LeShan, L. (1974). *How to Meditate.* New York: Bantam.

Nicklaus, J. (1976). *Golf My Way.* New York: Simon.

Norris, P.A., & Fahrion, S.L. (1984). Autogenic biofeedback in psychophysiological therapy and stress management. In Woolfolk, R.L., & Lehrer, P.M. (Eds.). *Principles and Practice of Stress Management.* New York: Guilford Press, 220-254.

Parrino, J.J. (1979). *From Panic To Power: The Positive Use of Stress.* New York: John Wiley.

Rice, P.L. (1987). *Stress and Health: Principles and Practice for Coping and Wellness.* Monterey, CA.: Brooks/Cole.

Samuels, M. & Samels, N. (1975). *Seeing with The Mind's Eye; The History, Techniques and Uses of Visualization.* New York: Random House.

Smith, J.C. (1985). *Relaxation Dynamics: Nine World Approaches To Self-Relaxation.* Champaign, Il.: Research Press.

Smith, J.C. (1986). *Meditation: A Sensible Guide To A Timeless Discipline.* Champaign, Il.: Research Press.

Schultz, J., & Luthe, W. (1959). *Autogenic Training.* New York: Grune & Stratton.

Schwartz, J. (1982). *Letting Go of Stress.* New York: Pinnacle Books.

Wolpe, J. (1958). *Psychotherapy by Reciprocal Inhibition.* Stanford, CA.: Stanford University Press.

Coping With
a Busy World:
Managing Time, Pace,
and Change

Chapter 10

CHAPTER 10

I. INTRODUCTION: THE CHALLENGE OF TIME

II. TIME, CHANGE, AND STRESS
A. Different Concepts of Time
B. Accelerating Change: The Context of Personal Stress
   1. Factors in Social Change
   2. Social Change and Personal Stress

III. STRESSORS RELATED TO TIME, PACE, AND CHANGE
A. Overchoice
B. Overload in Pace of Daily Life
   1. Variations in Pace of Life
   2. How Overload Leads to Stress
   3. Personal Roots of Overload
      a. Irrational Beliefs about Time
      b. Type A Behavior
      c. The Type E Woman
      d. Work Addiction
C. Transitions
D. Clustering of Life Events
   1. Clustering and Stress: Research Evidence
   2. Minimizing Distress From Clustered Change

IV. DAILY HASSLES
A. Measuring Hassles and Uplifts
B. Daily Hassles, Clustering of Life Events and Stress

IV. MANAGING STRESS FROM TIME, PACE, AND CHANGE
A. General Guidelines
B. Learning to Manage Time

INTRODUCTION: THE CHALLENGE OF TIME   ▼

"I don't have time."

"I need 25 hours in a day."

"There's just not enough time."

"I am so disorganized."

"I'm the world's worst procrastinator."

These familiar lines reflect a common concern we all share: how to cope with time.

Time is a universal feature of human experience. Wherever and whenever we live, we must deal with time:

filling time

making time

organizing time

using time

saving time

passing time

and more.

For some people, time is a friend—it brings challenge, pleasure, satisfaction. For others, time is an enemy, bringing anxiety, boredom, or confusion. For some, there is too little time, for others too much.

TIME, CHANGE AND STRESS   ▼

DIFFERENT CONCEPTS OF TIME

Our notions of time are culturally influenced. In the U.S. Virgin Islands, where two of my sisters lived for many years, time is approached quite differently than "on the mainland." If you arrive at a dinner party within an hour or so of the appointed time, that's quite acceptable. For many on the island of St. Croix, the concepts of punctuality and hurry are entirely foreign. Similarly, in rural Kenya, where I recently visited my daughter, a Peace Corps volunteer, the main mode of transportation is walking. Patience and endurance, rather than quickness and efficiency, are virtues. In this country, by contrast, we are brought up to value punctuality, hurry, efficiency.

Variation in the cultural context of time is illustrated by a study reported by Levine and Wolff (1985), of time tolerance among college students in Brazil and the United States. When asked what they would consider "late" arrival for a lunch appointment with a friend, Brazilian students averaged over 33 minutes. Americans averaged 19 minutes. Brazilian students allowed an average of 54 minutes before they would consider someone "early" for such an appointment, while American students would allow an average of 24 minutes.

International differences are also illustrated by national rankings in the accuracy of public clocks, walking speed and post office speed in selling stamps, as shown in Table 8-1. Levine and Wolff note that even within the United States, standards of time and punctuality vary from place to place according to the rhythm and rules of different regions and cities. "Seemingly simple words like 'now,' snapped out by an impatient New Yorker, and 'later,' said by a relaxed Californian, suggest a world of difference" (Levine and Wolff, 1985, 32).

	TABLE 10-1. PACE OF LIFE IN SIX COUNTRIES.		

	Accuracy of Bank Clocks	Walking Speed	Post Office Speed
Japan	1	1	1
United States	2	2	2
England	4	2	3
Italy	5	4	6
Taiwan	3	5	4
Indonesia	6	6	5

Numbers (1 = top value) indicate the comparative rank of each country for each indicator of pace.
SOURCE: Levine and Wolff (1985)

Two important implications flow from awareness of these cultural influences in our ideas about time. First, there are no absolute rights and wrongs about punctuality, productivity, pace or anything else about time. These standards are culturally influenced. This fact, of course, is difficult for many Americans, especially those with rigid expectations of self and others about punctuality, efficiency, and pace, to accept. Second, as modern communication increasingly puts people in contact across national and regional boundaries, it is important to be aware of cultural differences in time. This can avoid a misunderstanding of others' intentions and behavior.

Within a given cultural context, how we organize, fill and pace our time influences stress and how we deal with it. Wise management of time, taking account of social context and personal preferences, is a vitally important ingredient in effective stress management.

Our experiences with time—especially pacing and change—are not only influenced by where we happen to live but when. A dominant fact of life these days is that we live in an era of rapid social change.

ACCELERATING CHANGE: THE CONTEXT OF PERSONAL STRESS

Social Change: changes in the social world surrounding the individual.

Note at the outset that *social* change refers to the world outside the person. *Personal* change refers to change in the individual's life, such as moving, changing jobs, getting older, becoming more assertive.

Perhaps the best description of the accelerating pace of social change is found in Alvin Toffler's *Future Shock* (1971). Toffler offers considerable evidence that things are moving faster than they did in the past, certainly faster than in our parents' or grandparents' time.

Factors in Social Change

One reason for the increase in the pace of social change is rapid *population growth* around the world. The world's population is expected to double in about 35 years at its present growth rate. In many countries, population will double in only 25 years. Already we number about 5.4 billion people. An increase, of course, will mean more mouths to feed, more bodies to clothe, more houses to build, more goods and services to be produced, more crowding.

A second reason for the faster rate of change *is technology*—the increasing use of sophisticated mechanical and electronic devices to solve problems and produce goods. Our reliance on science, combined with the need for more goods and services and the need to keep ahead of competition, leads manufacturers to constantly produce new goods and devices. What used to take weeks, months, or even years now can be accomplished in seconds. Yet technology exists not only in factories and computer centers. It has rippled outward to affect entire communities. One look at a modern kitchen, compared with one in your grandparents' time, should be enough to convince you of the broad impact of technology.

As Toffler points out, if we think of technology as the great engine of change, then knowledge is the fuel on which that engine runs. The fantastic speed-up in the generation of *new knowledge* is the third factor responsible for the faster rate of social change. The computer is partly responsible for this increase in knowledge, especially in the sciences. The number of new scientific books and articles is staggering—and still growing. A chemistry professor comments that he could pass few college examinations these days because so much has been discovered in recent years. Another professor notes that more than half of all knowledge has been developed in his own brief lifetime.

C. P. Snow, the novelist and scientist, has remarked that "until this century, social change was so slow that it would go unnoticed in one person's lifetime. That is no longer so. The rate of change has increased so much that our imaginations cannot keep up" (Toffler, 1971, 22). Signs of this speed-up are all around us— faster transportation, consumer fads, whole new skylines in big cities and the disappearance of old ones, new shopping centers, people moving from one place to another, a higher divorce rate.

Social Change and Personal Stress

Accelerating social change since the turn of the century has brought with it four major trends that bear on personal stress.

From rural living to urban living

From stationary to mobile

From self-sufficient to consuming

From physically active to sedentary

As these social changes have occurred—and continue—a speed-up in *personal* change also takes place. One way of understanding how social change affects the person is to think of daily life as consisting of situations, each of which is made up of five simple elements.

Things

Places

Persons

Organizations

Ideas

Each of these elements is more temporary than before, speeding up the "flow of situations" (Toffler, 1971, 33). *Things* are more and more transient. If you are like most people, you buy things, then discard them more quickly than your parents did. Consequently, you make and break emotional ties with things more often than people did 25 to 50 years ago. Each time you do, you must adjust.

Advertising is a prime reason for this faster turnover of things. We think we need new products partly because we are told that we do. Another reason is we move more often and cannot take all our possessions with us. Still another is we think we need to "keep up with the Joneses." If your friends or neighbors have a snowmobile, a new car, a swimming pool, or new skis, you may believe you need them too. So you adopt a "throw-away mentality." You come to expect more temporary connections with such things as clothing, cars, houses, toys, art, and furniture.

With *places,* too, we make and break ties more often. Think about place of residence, for example. Many Europeans are the ninth, tenth, or fifteenth generation in their communities. Many visit their nearby churchyard cemetery every Sunday to pay respects to their ancestors—and to reinforce their linkages with the past. In contrast, one of every four Americans—about 55 million—moves each year. Place loses much of its emotional meaning as we come and go.

Our changing relationship with place also is affected on a daily basis. In times past, home and work were close together. Shop and farm were next to living quarters. But with the development of the large factory and the large store, people went away from home to work. Now the daily commute to work may take up to an hour or two each way. One college professor travelled every Wednesday from Northern California to Salt Lake City to complete his graduate studies—returning in time for his full load of teaching duties the next day. A minister travelled from Phoenix to Chicago for studies every Tuesday, then returned to Phoenix for pastoral duties on weekends. Place is more fleeting than ever before.

People also are less permanent in your life than they were for your parents and grandparents. Because you move more often (and if you don't, your neighbors do), you must make and break relationships more often. In the college dormitory, for example, very close friendships develop during a school year. For many students, these relationships are the most meaningful of their lives. Yet the year ends and the entire dorm social system for that year disappears. Some friendships remain steadfast, but most disappear. Each time you make and break ties, an adjustment must be made. Stress—and sometimes distress—results. And many people wonder why they should get involved, since they, their neighbors, or their friends probably will be leaving soon.

The *organizations* in which you work, play, worship, and study also flow through your experience more rapidly. This occurs in two ways. One is that organizations appear and disappear more often. The other is that organizations change more quickly. Whereas organizations once tended to be rigid bureaucracies, resistant to change, many now are much more fluid. More and more workers—and students—must adjust more often and more quickly to shifting organizational environments. As a result, many people sink roots less deeply into their organizations and groups, just as they hesitate to get too attached to their neighborhoods and friends.

Finally, *ideas* and *information* come and go more quickly, requiring increasingly rapid turnover of images in your mind. The English language is changing constantly, as illustrated by the change in ethnic terms from "Negro" to "Black" to "African-American," and by the rapid appearance and disappearance of such words as "teach-in," "sit-in," "hassle," "psychedelic," "fast-back," "wash-and-wear." Toffler points out that if William Shakespeare were alive today, he would be virtually illiterate because so many English words are new. Faster change also occurs in intellectual fads, best-selling books, and trends in art and music. Referring to the rapid pace at which we must change our conception of reality and our mental images of the world, Toffler raises the question: "How fast and how continuously can the individual revise his inner images before he smashes up against these limits?" (Toffler, 1971, 180). No one knows for sure. But we may be approaching those limits.

In his more recent book, *The Third Wave*, Toffler (1980,2) points out that confusion and ambiguity are other realities we face in this era of rapid change.

> A powerful tide is surging across much of the world today, creating a new, often bizarre, environment in which to work, play, marry, raise children, or retire. In this bewildering context, businessmen swim against highly erratic economic currents; politicians see their ratings bob wildly up and down; universities, hospitals, and other institutions battle desperately against inflation. Value systems splinter and crash, while the lifeboats of family, church, and state are hurled madly about.

In this rapidly changing and confusing world, more and faster adjustments are needed. More stress sets in. One way of looking at this is to think of the individual as a channel through which a multitude of experiences flow—as diagrammed in Figure 10-1.

In the 1990s you must process more experiences than did people in the 1920s, 1940s, or even the 1970s. In short, you must face a greater number, variety, and intensity of stressors than people did in earlier times. While you can and do adjust to this faster tempo, there is a greater chance of distress. Not only do individuals risk illness, intellectual and emotional distress, or behavioral difficulties, our entire society may be showing symptoms of too rapid change (Toffler, 1970, 2, 9).

> The malaise, mass neurosis, irrationality, and free-floating violence already apparent in contemporary life are merely a foretaste of what my be ahead unless we come to understand and treat this illness...unless man quickly learns to control the rate of change in his personal affairs as well as society at large, we are doomed to massive adaptational breakdown.

FIGURE 10-1. FASTER FLOW OF EXPERIENCE

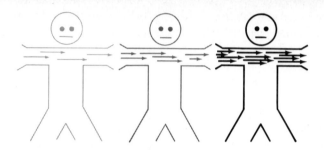

One way of illustrating how faster social change causes stress and distress is shown in Figure 10-2.

A recent study by Levine and others (1989) reported that pace of life can be studied not only at the individual level, but at a community and regional level as well. They reported that when pace of life is measured by aggregate averages of walking speed, talking speed, work speed, and concern with clock time, strong correlations are found between a U.S. city's or region's pace of life and mortality from coronary heart disease. This may partly result from unhealthy habits (for example, more smoking) in faster-paced areas. Whatever the reason, pace of life can affect stress and health.

FIGURE 10-2. SOCIAL CHANGE AND STRESS

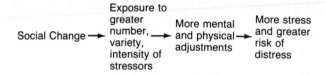

Social Change → Exposure to greater number, variety, intensity of stressors → More mental and physical adjustments → More stress and greater risk of distress

BOX 10-1. DEPRESSION AND SOCIAL CHANGE

Martin Seligman (1988) recently pointed out an astounding fact: the rate of depression has risen roughly tenfold over the last two generations. He went on to raise the pressing question, "Why have we become more depressed?"

Seligman notes that in less developed countries, depression is almost nonexistent. When depression does occur in China, which is only occasionally, its symptoms tend to be physical rather than psychological. While manic-depression, which tends to have physiological origins, was found to be almost the same (1–2 percent) among residents of Baltimore and the Amish, the rate of unipolar depression (depression without mania) among the Amish is about one-fifth to one-tenth that of Baltimore residents.

These findings suggest there must be something about our society, our way of life, not just about individual depressives, that explains the rise in depression in this country.

Seligman suggests two main causes. First, we have moved toward individual explanations for events, especially bad events. For a variety of cultural and economic reasons, this has become the "age of the individual." We expect individual happiness, ease, and comfort. If an individual falters, we see it as his problem—a lack of effort, character, or personal gumption.

Second, we have become loosened from older attachments to the larger society. Viet Nam, Watergate, assassinations, political scandal have combined to cause questioning the value of relying on larger institutions. This has happened at the very time extended family, neighborhood and church are fading as significant attachments for the individual.

The result of these two trends is predictable, according to Seligman: When the person goes through troubling or unsettled times, what can she or he rely on for support? Mostly self. And self is, at best, a precarious anchorage upon which to lean. Widespread depression results as the individual, in relative isolation from external supports, blames self and does his or her best to draw upon inner resources, often to find little there.

Seligman (1988, 55) contends that to slow the rising tide of depression, we need to reach a better balance between individual and collectivity, between self and society.

> There is a final possibility, a more hopeful one: We can retain our belief in the importance of the individual but scale down our preoccupation with comfort and discomfort and make a renewed commitment to the common good. A balance between individualism, with its perilous freedoms, and commitment to the common good should lower depression and make life more meaningful. In this age of choice, this choice, surely, is ours.

In Chapter 15, we return to issues of transcending our own problems by focusing more on the common good.

STRESSORS RELATED TO TIME, PACE, AND CHANGE ▼

Within the context of accelerating change, a number of change-related and time-related stressors confront us in everyday life. We will examine four: overchoice, chronic overload, transitions, and clustering of life events. Along the way, you will be given the opportunity to explore a number of options for dealing with these stressors.

At the outset, you are invited to complete Execise 10-1, the Time Stress Questionnaire. This will help you discover both the extent to which time problems are stressors for you and which ones stand out as especially significant.

EXERCISE 10-1. TIME STRESS QUESTIONNAIRE

Below are several time-related difficulties people sometimes experience. Please indicate how often each is a difficulty for you, using numbers as follows:

___0___ Seldom or never a difficulty for me
___5___ Sometimes a difficulty for me
__10__ Frequently a difficulty for me

_____ My time is controlled by factors beyond my control

_____ Interruptions

_____ Chronic overload—more to do than time available

_____ Occasional overload

_____ Chronic underload—too little to do in time available

_____ Occasional underload

_____ Alternating periods of overload and underload

_____ Disorganization of my time

_____ Procrastination

_____ Separating home and work

_____ Transition from work to home

_____ Finding time for regular exercise

_____ Finding time for daily periods of relaxation

_____ Finding time for friendships

_____ Finding time for family

_____ Finding time for vacations

_____ Easily bored

_____ Saying "yes" when I later wish I had said "no"

_____ Feeling overwhelmed by large tasks over an extended period of time

_____ Avoiding important tasks by frittering away time on less important ones

_____ Feel compelled to assume responsibilities in groups

_____ Unable to delegate because distrust quality of others' performance

_____ Unable to delegate because no one to delegate to

_____ My perfectionism creates delays

_____ I tend to leave tasks unfinished

_____ I have difficulty living with unfinished tasks

_____ Too many projects going at one time

_____ Get into time binds by trying to please others too often

_____ I tend to hurry even when it's not necessary

_____ Lose concentration while thinking about other things I have to do

_____ Not enough alone time

_____ Feel compelled to be punctual

_____ Pressure related to deadlines

1. How do you measure up to the following standard?
   0–49   Low difficulty with time-related stressors
   50–99   Moderate difficulty with time-related stressors
   100 or more   High difficulty with time-related stressors
2. How satisfied are you with your time-related difficulties?
   Quite satisfied
   Somewhat satisfied
   Not very satisfied
3. Now go back and underline the five most significant time-related stressors for you.
4. By yourself or with the aid of someone else, determine concrete steps you can take to remedy each of these key time-related stressors. Write them on a separate sheet of paper, in your stress diary, or in notebook.
5. When will you begin each of these steps?

OVERCHOICE

As Toffler (1971, 264) points out, an important by-product of rapid change is a vast increase in options:

> Ironically, the people of the future may suffer not from an absence of choice, but from a paralyzing surfeit of it. They may turn out to be victims of that peculiarly super-industrial dilemma; choice.

Many social critics have attacked the creeping standardization of modern life, believing we are all being pressured toward fewer choices—toward acting, thinking, and feeling the same. Their protest is symbolized by the computer card, which they see as a tool for making everyone alike. But they probably are wrong. The real problem seems to be too much choice, too many options. Many Americans feel overwhelmed by the choices they must make: what to do, how to live, what to believe, what to buy, where to move, how to look, what to wear. Overchoice adds to stress and distress, since every option is a stressor.

One aspect of overchoice is the tremendous increase in the variety of consumer goods. Some people feel uncomfortable in the supermarket; they are numbed by so many options on the shelves. Toffler points out that two economic factors account for this trend toward diversification of goods (Toffler, 1971, 266).

. . . first, consumers have more money to lavish on their specialized wants; second, and even more important, as technology becomes more sophisticated, the cost of introducing declines.

This is the point that our social critics—most of whom are technologically naive—fail to understand: it is only primitive technology that imposes standardization. Automation, in contrast, frees the path to endless, blinding, mind-numbing diversity.

Automobiles are a good example: The number of options can be staggering. In Toffler's words (1971, 268–269):

Thus the beautiful and spectacular Mustang is promoted by Ford as the "one you design yourself," because as critic Reyner Banham explains, "there isn't a dung-regular Mustang anymore, just a stockpile of options to meld in combinations of 3 (bodies) × 4 (engines) × 3 (transmissions) × 4 (basic sets of high performance engine modifications)—1 (rock-bottom six cylinder car to which these modifications don't apply) × 2 (Shelby Grand Roaring and Racing setups applying to only one body shell and not all engines/transmission combinations)." This does not even take into account the possible variations in color, upholstery and optional equipment.

The same kind of diversification—and overchoice—has taken place in movies, magazines, television sets, soaps, houses, clothing, arts, and illegal drugs (Toffler, 1971, 269).

The material goods of the future will be many things, but they will not be standardized. We are, in fact, racing toward "overchoice"—the point at which the advantages of diversity and individualization are cancelled by the complexity of the buyer's decision-making process.

Another aspect of overchoice is the increase in *lifestyle* options. Should you live in the country or in the city? If in the country, should you live in the mountains, on the coast, in the forest, in the desert? What size city? What type of house—ranch-style, modular, suburban cardboard, corner duplex? And with whom should you spend your time—with drug users, hot-rodders, Jesus converts, Zen Buddhists? With vegetarians, meditators, executives, scientists, gays, athletes? To consider all possible options—or even a few of them—is to be bombarded by choices. The mind boggles. Subcultures are everywhere. Which to join? None? Try a few, one at a time? Which ones? Why?

Meanwhile what happens to you? Are you still there? Or are you simply whatever you are *doing*, whichever group you are with, wherever you live this year, this month, this week? This is the third aspect of overchoice: more frequent *identity crises*, especially among young people. Identity crisis refers to uncertainty—and sometimes intense anxiety—over these questions: Who am I? What kind of a person am I? Do I want to be? Can I not be? Can I be? In a stable, slow-moving society such questions do not arise. A person's position in life, beliefs, and identity are given. There is little choice. In our society, at least for many of us, there is too much (Toffler, 1971, 269).

> The level of personality disorder, neurosis, and just plain psychological distress in our society suggests that it is already difficult for many individuals to create a sensible, integrated, and reasonably stable personal style. Yet there is every evidence that the thrust toward social diversity, paralleling that of the level of goods and culture is just beginning. We face a tempting and terrifying extension of freedom.

In the face of overchoice, you must be centered and self-directed in order to retain your sainty, dignity, and self-control. Otherwise you risk being overwhelmed by too many options.

OVERLOAD IN DAILY PACE OF LIFE

Consider this: experts estimate that the average American is exposed to 65,000 more stimuli *per day* than our ancestors a mere 100 years ago (Ferguson, 1980). This means we live a much faster daily pace of life.

Pace of life: the number, variety and intensity of stressors, per day, week, or year.

Variations in Pace of Life
It is likely that the average American can be described by the faster pace depicted. We process more situations; we cram more into an hour, a day, a week. If you live at a faster pace, you probably experience the following.

A greater number of stressors

A greater variety of stressors

A higher proportion of new, unfamiliar stressors

A greater number of intense stressors

Faster movement from one stressor to the next, with frequent overlap

More demands for adaptation or adjustment

A greater amount or intensity of stress

Higher chances of distress because of the greater amount and intensity of stress

Faster and slower paces of life theoretically are measurable, assuming separate actions could be recorded, counted, and weighted in terms of the stressfulness to the person. In that sense, pace of life is quantifiable in the abstract. Practically, of course, this is virtually impossible. However, it is worth noting that analytically, a faster pace of life may or may not breed distress. It depends entirely upon the upper limit of the individual's zone of positive stress. "Racehorses" thrive on a pace that would overwhelm a "turtle." Often, however, Type A persons and others delude themselves into believing that they are racehorses by nature. At the onset of physical breakdown, such as heart attack, persistent dizziness, or chronic trembling, they begin for the first time to realize they have overestimated their tolerance for a fast pace. An important point of this book is that effective health buffers probably can increase our tolerance of fast pace, thereby increasing the amount of potential pro-ductivity and the number of other experiences that we can experience with less hazard to health and emotional life.

How Overload Leads to Stress

Associated with any activity are two necessary time periods—lead-time and afterburn. Consider, for example, a student facing an examination in history, an especially important one because she needs a "B" to qualify for a scholarship to college. *Lead-time* is the period of emotional and intellectual preparation she needs the day before and on the morning of the examination. *Afterburn* is the time needed after the exam to think about how she did, feel it, talk to her friends, set it to rest. If she has neither enough time to prepare nor enough time afterward to "come down"—to relieve the pressures of the exam—she will feel slightly off-balance, a bit tense. No single instance is terribly significant. But ignoring the need for adequate lead-in and afterburn time thousands of times during a lifetime can create an enormous build-up of many small tensions and stresses.

A fast pace of life, especially for someone who needs quite a bit of lead-in and afterburn time, can be a significant source of tension, stress, and distress. Various ailments—colds, asthma, chest pains, high blood pressure, and sore back—often result if too many activities are crammed into too short a span of time.

Research on role overload on the job further supports the notion that a fast daily pace may be hazardous to health. Work overload may be of two types: quantitative and qualitative.

> When employees perceive that they have too much work to do, too many different things to do, or insufficient time to complete assigned work, a condition of *quantitative* overload exists. *Qualitative* overload, on the other hand, occurs when employees feel they lack the ability to complete their jobs or that performance standards are too high regardless of how much time they have. An engineer asked to design a containment system for a new nuclear power plant within three months may feel that, given the other projects he/she is already responsible for, three months is insufficient time. This is quantitative overload. The same assignment given to a non-engineer may cause qualitative overload, since the individual may lack the necessary skills to complete the project (Ivancevich and Matteson, 1980, 113).

Among the adverse effects of job overload are elevated cholesterol, increased incidence of heart attacks and hypertension, lowered confidence, decreased work motivation, increased absenteeism, sharply reduced numbers of suggestions contri-buted, and increased drinking behavior. Clearly, too fast a pace of life on or off the job, especially when it results in overload, is dangerous when it becomes a chronic condition.

Later in the chapter, you will read abut a number of specific strategies and techniques for managing time in ways that will minimize chronic overload. Meanwhile, it is useful to examine several personal roots of overload: irrational beliefs about time, Type A behavior, Type E behavior, and work addiction.

BOX 10-1. AMERICANS' STRUGGLE WITH TIME

Americans who struggle with time are not alone. A recent Gallup poll demonstrates just how pervasive constant time pressure is in American life (Gallup Poll, 1990). Here are key findings from a recent nationwide survey.

* Nearly eight of 10 Americans report that time moves too fast for them.

* More than half (54 percent) feel under pressure to "get everything done that you need to."

* The lower the age, the greater the struggle with time. For example, 68 percent of those 50 and older say they have enough time, compared with 44 percent of those younger than 50. Baby boomers with a college education struggle the most: only 33 percent say they have enough time.

* The majority of Americans (54 percent) would prefer to work a four-day, 10-hour week, with only 37 percent preferring the conventional five-day, eight-hour day.

* Responses clearly suggest work has a negative impact on people's experiences with time. Monday is by far the least favorite day of the week. Friday, Saturday, and Sunday are most preferred. Least favorite hours of the day are 6:00 AM and 7:00 AM.

* When given several choices, Americans say they wish they had more time for personal exercise and recreation (47 percent), hobbies (47 percent), reading (45 percent), family (41 percent), and thinking or meditating (30 percent).

Widespread struggle with time led *Time Magazine* recently to publish a story on "How America Has Run Out of Time" (Gibbs, 1989, 58).

There was once a time when time was money. Both could be wasted or both well spent, but in the end gold was the richer prize. As with almost any commodity, however, value depends on scarcity. And these are the days of the time famine. Time that once seemed free and elastic has grown tight and elusive, and so our measure of its worth is dramatically changed. In Florida a man bills his opthalmologist $90 for keeping him waiting an hour. In California, a woman hires somebody to do her shopping for her—out of a catalog. Twenty bucks pays someone to pick up the dry cleaning, $250 to cater dinner for four, $1,500 will buy a fax machine for the car. "Time," concludes pollster Louis Harris, who has charted America's loss of it, "may have become the most precious commodity in the land."

This sense of acceleration is not just a vague and spotted impression. According to a Harris survey, the amount of leisure time enjoyed by the Average American has shrunk 37 percent since 1973. Over the same period, the average workweek, including commuting, has jumped from under 41 hours to nearly 47 hours.

✓

EXERCISE 10-2. OPTIONS FOR REDUCING CHRONIC OVERLOAD

A number of specific techniques for managing time to reduce chronic overload are presented at the end of this chapter. Below are eight broad options for reducing chronic overload. Which one or ones seem most promising for you (other than the first)? What concrete steps will you take to carry them out?

1. Continue present pace—stay distressed.
2. Continue present pace but learn to live with it.
   a. Self-talk
   b. Relaxation methods
   c. Health buffers
3. Cut back on present activity level
4. Say "no" to new opportunities if needed
5. Be more efficient
   a. Delegate
   b. Organize time better
   c. Waste less time
6. Stop hurrying when not needed
7. Periodically step back, contemplate, re-establish priorities, and reorganize time
8. Leave the role or the environment

Personal Roots of Overload

IRRATIONAL BELIEFS ABOUT TIME

Chronic time urgency is not just a result of external pressure. It is also a product of inner forces—beliefs, drives, wants, needs. A key step for reducing time urgency is to examine your beliefs or assumptions about time—and where needed, to alter those that are irrational or unreasonable. Below are 11 common irrational beliefs about time. Others are presented in the section on the Type E Woman. After reading these 11, you are invited to complete Exercise 10-3.

1. I must always be productive.

2. What matters most in life is getting ahead, being productive, or winning competitive struggles.

3. I cannot delegate because no one can meet my standards.

4. I will be able to enjoy myself only after catching up with all I have to do.

5. I must always get the most possible done in the least possible time.

6. I must usually hurry to get everything done.

7. If I spend time relaxing, resting, or exercising, I will certainly fall behind in more important things.

8. I cannot help but be upset or anxious when a task is incomplete.

9. I have no control over constant overload in my life.

10. There is no way I can be happy if I'm overloaded. I can't stand it.

11. I must be all things to all people.

EXERCISE 10-3. EXAMINING IRRATIONAL BELIEFS ABOUT TIME

1. Using the following categories, assess how much each of the 11 irrational beliefs applies to you.

Applies QUITE A BIT to me
Applies SOMEWHAT to me
Applies VERY LITTLE to me

2. Rewrite those you noted as applying somewhat, quite a lot, or a great deal to you.

3. How would your life be different if you were to genuinely accept and act upon these alternative beliefs?

4. What step will you take first to act on one of these beliefs?

TYPE A BEHAVIOR

You read a detailed discussion of Type A behavior in Chapter 5. It is worth noting here that Type A behavior, widely regarded as a major risk factor for coronary artery disease, is a common personality source of chronic overload. Friedman, one of the originators of the concept, defines Type A behavior as follows (Friedman & Ulmer, 1984, 31):

> Type A behavior is above all a continuous struggle, an unremitting attempt to accomplish or achieve more and more things or participate in more and more events in less and less time, frequently in the face of opposition—real or imagined—from other persons. The Type A personality is dominated by covert insecurity or hyperaggressiveness, or both.

Type A behavior almost invariably breeds a faster pace of life because such a person is driven to accomplish as much as possible in the shortest possible time and is chronically impatient with "wasted" time, as well as with others' slower pace. Many work organizations actively promote Type A behavior, especially if the management at the top is Type A and if the organization is rapidly growing. Some families also promote it, as shown in a number of recent studies of how Type A behavior and a fast-paced pattern are taught to children in certain types of families. Thus, Elkind (1981) speaks of the "hurried child."

Friedman and Rosenman point out that American culture places high value on a fast pace (Friedman and Rosenman, 1974). Speed, numbers, accomplishments, competitive success, incessant upward climbing—all are held up as elements of the American ideal of the "good life" and the "successful" man or woman. Urban living, with its crowding, commuting, and rush, reinforces this pattern, especially among the middle and upper classes.

Type A behavior is more common in men than women. The Type E pattern seems to be more characteristic of women.

THE TYPE E WOMAN

Harriet Braiker, a clinical psychologist, believes the Type A pattern does not accurately capture the distress-producing experiences of most contemporary women. In response, she has developed the concept, Type E (Braiker, 1986, 5).

Success for achievement-oriented women today is defined as achievement in both realms: career and personal. But the success formula is a calculus that often yields enormous frustration and exhaustion. There seems to be only one way for women to play the game and win: be Everything to Everybody. Many working women adapt to the enigmatic problems of trying to "have it all" by pushing themselves to do "it" all themselves, and to excel in all their roles, often at tremendous cost to their physical and emotional health.

Bombarded with daily life stress, working women are swelling the epidemiological ranks of ulcer cases, drug and alcohol abuse, depression, sexual dysfunction, and a score of stress-induced physical ailments, including backache, headache, allergies, and recurrent viral infections and flu.

They suffer in legion numbers in various degrees from what stress specialist Barbara B. Brown calls "states of unwellness"— those in-between states in which one is not sick enough to have a real diagnosis, but where stress incubates and serious stress illnesses, such as heart attacks, strokes, and ulcers, insidiously breed.

Of course, many women seem able to accomplish truly dazzling feats. In spite of heavy workloads, they manage a host of other commitments to family, personal relationships, community and other organizations—for a while. But behind the dazzle, behind the multifaceted competence and ostensible strength, you can almost hear the stress bombs ticking away.

Too often, the high-achieving woman is the proverbial candle burning at both ends. What's worse, she has unwittingly baited a trap with her own competence: she is the victim of her own success. Paradoxically, the more she demonstrates that she can do, the more others demand of her. She, indeed, proves that she can do it all, and her admiring fans—at home and at work—scream for more. Her driving achievement needs force her to stretch her resources even thinner until she gets caught in a self-perpetuating *dis*-stress cycle.

At some point, her complicated life may begin to backfire, and everything that she has worked so hard to attain and maintain may appear threatened. The stress takes its toll on her physical health— in short, on her life. Recognition of her own limitations may further threaten her self-esteem and heighten feelings of inadequacy. She may fight back by trying to do even more, but it won't work; it can't work.

It is not difficult to see how chronic overload emerges from the Type E pattern (Wellington-Jones, 1989). Braiker points out that the Type E pattern is both sociological and psychological in origins. The complex roles of working women result in excessive, incompatible demands—this is the external or sociological source. But partly in response to these demands, many women develop a series of what Braiker calls "erroneous expectations." It is this internal, psychological source that is the immediate source of the Type E pattern.

According to Braiker, there are 10 common erroneous expectations or beliefs. These form the cognitive basis of the stressful behavior and feelings of Type E women (Braiker, 1986, 151).

1. I have to do things perfectly.

2. I should be able to accomplish more in a day.

3. I should be able to do everything without feeling stressed or tired.

4. I have to please others by doing what they ask me to do.

5. I have to prove myself to everyone.

6. "Having it all" should make me happy.

7. I can't be happy until "I have it all."

8. I can't relax until I finish what I have to do.

9. If I can make people need me because of everything I do for them, they'll value me.

10. I should be everything to everybody.

Braiker provides two Type E scales. One measures Type E behaviors, the other Type E beliefs. A recent study by Faulkner demonstrates a strong relationship between both scales and distress symptoms (Faulkner, 1987).

EXERCISE 10-4. ASSESSING AND REWRITING TYPE E BELIEFS

1.   How much does the Type E beliefs characterize your own thinking? For each belief, rank yourself, using the following categories:

Applies QUITE A BIT to me
Applies SOMEWHAT to me
Applies VERY LITTLE to me

2.   Rewrite those that apply somewhat, quite a bit, or a great deal so they become more reasonable, moderate and helpful. You might want to review Chapter 7 to refresh your memory on the criteria of "reasonable" beliefs.

3. What concrete differences would occur in your life if you were to apply these alternative, reasonable beliefs?

4. What specific decisions and actions can you take to begin to implement these new beliefs?

Braiker also proposes several exercises for reducing Type E beliefs and behavior, along with a 21-day plan for carrying them out (Braiker, 1986, Chapter 10).

1. Redefine role requirements

2. Prioritize your activities in rank-order

3. Create and rehearse "No" scripts

4. Develop a pleasurable activities schedule

5. Brainstorm and problem-solve with friends to find practical, personal solutions

6. Use guided imagery and deep relaxation for desensitization

7. Practice stress inoculation with role-playing and script rehearsal

8. Use constructive self-talk

9. Take mental mini-vacations

10. Correct faulty time allocations with time-management analysis

WORK ADDICTION

A third source of chronic overload is addiction to work or "workaholism." This "disorder" can have many origins. Common to all of them is equating self-worth to performance. The pursuit of approval and self-esteem can become a compulsive, endless self-generating quest (Machlowitz, 1980; Kiechel, 1989).

Commonly, work addiction is an adaptation to being an adult child of an alcoholic parent. Rather than becoming addicted to alcohol or some other chemical, the person finds a socially acceptable way to express her or his addictive tendency.

Bryan Robinson, author of an insightful book on the subject, summarizes this view as follows (Robinson, 1989, 26):

> Work abuse is a serious compulsive disorder. It is as ravaging and insidious as alcoholism or eating disorders. How many times have you been told, "Keep up the good work"? And then there's, "Boy, is he dedicated!" or "What a go-getter!" We all hear these accolades from time to time on the job. Work addicts take them to heart. Work is the drug of choice for many adult children from chemically and dysfunctional homes because excessive work medicates emotional pain by making them feel better. It can repress rage, hurt, fear, guilt, sadness and just about any emotion. Work abusers get hooked because work anesthetizes them from dealing with unpleasant feelings that they have stored in their bodies since childhood. Work addicts suffer some of the same symptoms as alcoholics. They have similar denial systems, reality distortion and need to control. Careers zoom, and marriages and friendships falter because of compulsiveness, self-absorption, overindulgence, mood swings, and highs

and lows. Work addicts get high from work, go on binges and get hangovers as they ultimately start to come down. The downward swing is accompanied by withdrawal, irritability, anxiety and depression. Work abusers can never be fully happy, self-content, and peaceful until they face their neglected inner feelings without the medication of work.

Robinson rightly notes that work addiction needs to be distinguished from healthy commitment to work. The difference is largely one of balance (Robinson, 1989, 33).

Work addiction is a general approach to life that consumes the abuser's time, energy and thoughts. The major difference between abuse (or addictive) work and healthy (or constructive) work is the degree to which excessive work interferes with physical health, personal happiness, or intimate and social relationships. Healthy workers give the amount of time and thought to their work that is proportionate to other activities in their lives. They enjoy their work, are productive, and generally are effective in what they do. They balance their lives with social and leisure activities, hobbies, and personal and family time. Work abusers cannot control their compulsive work habits and even use different words that reflect their true feelings about "the great divide": work responsibilities and family obligations.

Generally, constructive workers are thinking about and enjoying the now. They're not thinking about work during off times. But addicted workers think about work all the time, and it takes precedence over and interferes with all other areas of life.

EXERCISE 10-5. THE WORK ADDICTION RISK TEST (WART)

You are invited to complete this scale developed by Robinson to help you find out the extent to which you may be work addicted.

Read each of the 25 statements below and decide how much each one pertains to you. Using the rating scale of 1 (*never true*); 2 (*seldom true*); 3 (*often true*); and 4 (*always true*), put the number that best fits you in the blank beside each statement.

_____ **1.** I prefer to do most things myself rather than ask for help.

_____ **2.** I get very impatient when I have to wait for someone else or when something takes too long, such as long, slow-moving lines.

_____ **3.** I seem to be in a hurry and racing against the clock.

_____ **4.** I get irritated when I am interrupted while I am in the middle of something.

_____ **5.** I stay busy and keep many "irons in the fire."

_____ **6.** I find myself doing two or three things at one time, such as eating lunch and writing a memo, while talking on the telephone.

_____ **7.** I overly commit myself by biting off more than I can chew.

_____ **8.** I feel guilty when I am not working on something.

_____ **9.** It is important that I see the concrete results of what I do.

_____ **10.** I am more interested in the final result of my work than in the process.

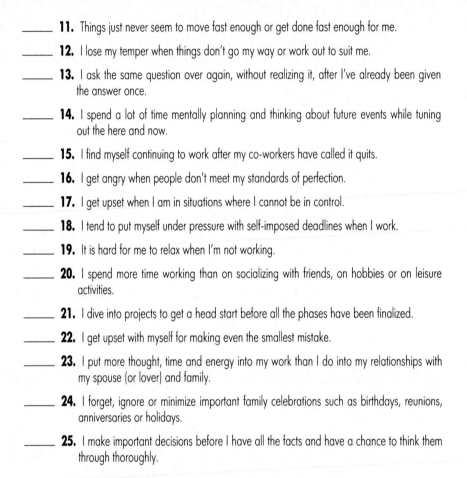

_____ **11.** Things just never seem to move fast enough or get done fast enough for me.

_____ **12.** I lose my temper when things don't go my way or work out to suit me.

_____ **13.** I ask the same question over again, without realizing it, after I've already been given the answer once.

_____ **14.** I spend a lot of time mentally planning and thinking about future events while tuning out the here and now.

_____ **15.** I find myself continuing to work after my co-workers have called it quits.

_____ **16.** I get angry when people don't meet my standards of perfection.

_____ **17.** I get upset when I am in situations where I cannot be in control.

_____ **18.** I tend to put myself under pressure with self-imposed deadlines when I work.

_____ **19.** It is hard for me to relax when I'm not working.

_____ **20.** I spend more time working than on socializing with friends, on hobbies or on leisure activities.

_____ **21.** I dive into projects to get a head start before all the phases have been finalized.

_____ **22.** I get upset with myself for making even the smallest mistake.

_____ **23.** I put more thought, time and energy into my work than I do into my relationships with my spouse (or lover) and family.

_____ **24.** I forget, ignore or minimize important family celebrations such as birthdays, reunions, anniversaries or holidays.

_____ **25.** I make important decisions before I have all the facts and have a chance to think them through thoroughly.

Once you have responded to all 25 statements, add up the numbers in the blanks for your total score. The higher your score, the more addicted you are to work. The lower your score, the less work addicted you are. The following key will help you interpret your score.

A score from 25 to 54 = You are not work addicted.
A score from 55 to 69 = You are mildly work addicted.
A score from 70 to 100 = You are highly work addicted.

SOURCE: Robinson (1989, 35).

Robinson proposes steps that can be taken to break out of the damaging trap of work addiction (Robinson, 1989, 144). In addition to steps that can be taken for employees in the workplace, he suggests the following steps for personal recovery. Several are based on the same principles as Alcoholics Anonymous.

▾ Slow down your pace

▾ Learn to relax

▾ Work on moderation

▾ Improve family climate

▾ Strengthen family ties

▾ Celebrate life's rituals

▾ Get back in the social swing

▾ Live in the now

▾ Build social networks outside of work

▾ Develop social pastimes

▾ Pamper yourself

▾ Eat properly, rest and exercise

▾ Validate yourself

▾ Mourn the loss of your childhood

▾ Seek spiritual healing

▾ Attend a 12-Step program

▾ Apply the 12 Steps of AA

We have discussed chronic overload, a key time-related stressor. We also have surveyed four common sources of chronic overload, together with several approaches to reducing overload. Next we will examine other time-related stressors.

TRANSITIONS

"Who are you?" said the Caterpillar...

"I—I hardly know, Sir, just at present," Alice replied rather shyly, "at least I know who I was when I got up this morning, but I think I must have been changed several times since then."

Alice's Adventures in Wonderland (Carrol, 1960)

Another stressor related to change and time is transition. In a fast-paced society, you no doubt experience less permanence than your parents or grandparents did. You make and break ties to the world around you more often. You more frequently change how you live and what you do. Each change requires a transition. Each transition requires an adjustment. Stress always results, distress sometimes follows. In her excellent book *Overwhelmed: Coping With Life's Ups and Downs*, Nancy Schlossberg presents a summary of types of transitions (1989, 28).

Types of Transitions: A Summary

Elected: some are social milestones; others are individual choices

- ▼ Graduating from school
- ▼ Moving away from home
- ▼ Changing jobs
- ▼ Having a baby
- ▼ Retiring
- ▼ Moving
- ▼ Divorcing
- ▼ Becoming a grandparent

Surprises: When the unexpected happens

- ▼ Car accident
- ▼ Winning the lottery
- ▼ Death of a child
- ▼ Plant closing
- ▼ Getting a raise

Nonevents: When the expected doesn't happen

- ▼ Infertility
- ▼ The promotion that doesn't occur
- ▼ The book that is never published
- ▼ The fatal illness that disappears
- ▼ The child who never leaves home

Life On Hold: The transition waiting to happen

- ▼ The long engagement
- ▼ Waiting to die
- ▼ Hoping to become pregnant
- ▼ Waiting for Mr. or Ms. Right

Sleeper Transitions: You don't know when they started

- ▼ Becoming fat or thin
- ▼ Falling in love
- ▼ Becoming bored at work

Double Whammies: It never rains but it pours

- ▼ Retiring and losing a spouse
- ▼ Marrying, becoming a stepparent, and being promoted to first supervisory job
- ▼ Having a baby, developing a serious illness, getting a new job
- ▼ Caring for ill children and parents at the same time

And many others

Schlossberg points out that a particular transition can affect the individual in a number of ways, some positive, some negative.

▼ It can change your roles—you have a baby, and suddenly you've become a parent; you change jobs, and you take on a whole new set of responsiblities.

▼ It can change your relationships—being a parent puts you in touch with new people, as does a new job. Both experiences may also transform your existing relationships.

▼ It can change your routines—a new baby alters living and sleeping habits; a new job may require a shift in schedule and in commuting patterns.

▼ It can also affect your assumptions about yourself and the world—a new father discovers he's more protective and responsible than he thought he would be; a person in a new secretarial position may discover personal strengths and weaknesses that went unrecognized in the old clerk-typist job.

Three types of transitions stand out as especially significant for many people.

Geographic mobility—moving from one community or neighborhood to another—is a type of transition experienced by millions of Americans each year. When a family moves, each member must pass through a host of transitions—from familiar to unfamiliar places, from one set of friends to another, from one school or work setting to another, from old routines to new ones. Research has shown that the stresses of moving are especially painful for children between the ages of two and four and for teenagers, for whom the trauma of leaving their home towns and their friends may be extreme. Research also has shown that a variety of illnesses, including coronary heart disease, occur more frequently among uprooted adults.

Role transition also can create substantial stress. Promotions, demotions, marriage, divorce, remarriage, becoming a parent, a job transfer, or becoming a high-school or college student cause stress and sometimes distress. A distress reaction is especially likely under certain conditions: if the transition is from a high to a low-stimulation environment (or vice versa); if the transition is involuntary; or if several role transitions occur simultaneously. When a person's new role requires behavior that falls outside his or her comfort zone, the chances of distress will be heightened.

A *lifestyle change* also can be highly stressful, yet thousands of Americans undergo changes in lifestyle each year. Part of the problem with such transitions is the in-between space—the void, the search, the uncertainty, the absence of anchorage.

Severe stress symptoms are common during such transitions. Yet they do not always show up in the short run. A 19-year-old youth once described his experiences of the previous four years as follows: In the ninth grade, he was into athletics. Finding that world unsatisfying, he took up with a motorcycle gang in the tenth grade. The following summer, he became involved with heavy drug use. A year later—his senior year—he was "rescued" from that lifestyle by the "Jesus people." In a discussion group that included a 75-year-old woman who had lived on the same ranch for 50 years, he later commented: "It took me a whole month to get over that one." There were few immediate signs of stress or distress in this case, yet one wonders about the outcome over the long run.

A serious loss is a wrenching transition. Death of a family member is almost always traumatic. So is loss of a home through fire, separation and divorce, termination of a professional career, involuntary retirement, theft of a valued personal possession, disappearance of a family pet, loss of an arm. In each case, one must "say goodbye" and adjust to life without the loss object or person. Whatever the loss, people pass through remarkably similar steps of mourning. As described by Horowitz, these steps are shown in Figure 10-3.

Horowitz points out that individual differences affect the order of entry into phases, how much time is spent in each phase, and the signs of stress or distress that occur in each phase. But in general, people tend to follow this pattern. Let us focus, for example, on the loss of a spouse.

Outcry is an almost automatic emotional response that may take varied forms— weeping, screaming, panic, or fainting. For example, a woman told that her husband has just died in an accident may cry out in anguish, "No, no, It can't be true!"

Denial refers to a numbing avoidance of the reality of the loss. For example, relatives of the widow just described might come to help out and provide comfort. Since they are less deeply affected by the loss, they may already have entered the intrusive phase. For example, they are likely to think of the deceased constantly, to cry, and to express intense sadness. The widow in contrast, may be numb, busy with planning and "entertaining," giving the appearance of strength. But she only appears to be "doing very well."

Intrusion, which follows denial and/or outcry, is a preoccupation with the lost spouse through dreams, recurrent reminders of past events, even visual images of the deceased. This phase my not begin until after the relatives have left. Weeks or months later, "she might begin to oscillate between periods of denial and numbing episodes in which she experiences waves of searching grief, ideas about the emptiness of her life, and even an hallucinatory sense of the 'presence' of her lost husband" (Horowitz, 1976, 52).

Working through is gradually coming to terms with the reality of the loss and adjusting to life without the spouse. In most cases involving the death of a family member, this requires six months to one year of emotional adjustment, decisions and planning, and changing of daily routines.

Completion is reached when the person is able to get on with a new stage of life without denial or serious intrusion of the loss.

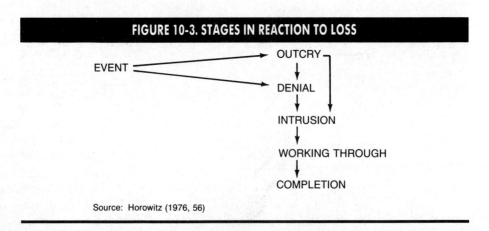

FIGURE 10-3. STAGES IN REACTION TO LOSS

EVENT → OUTCRY → DENIAL → INTRUSION → WORKING THROUGH → COMPLETION

Source: Horowitz (1976, 56)

People always have had to cope with the expected and the unexpected. Even for our ancient ancestors, the uncertainties of climate, food supplies, and relations with neighboring tribes made life a continuing process of adaptation. In contemporary times, change is inherent in the life cycle itself. One writer refers to these predictable life cycle events as "marker events." Marker events begin early. The five-year-old entering kindergarten experiences a dramatic confrontation with the unfamiliar— new faces, new routines, new expectations, new challenges. To some extent, this is repeated every time a student enters the next level of school. The move from high school to college can be especially stressful because of the need for greater self-reliance, increased financial concerns, keener competition, and new social demands. Marriage is another stressful "passage," pleasurable as it may be. Having children, especially if several are closely spaced, creates stress on each parent and on the marriage. So does the child-rearing process and, later on, the departure of children from the home. Retirement is a difficult and sometimes lethal adjustment. Death of a spouse is the last major change for many people.

Throughout the life cycle, a number of intense personal adjustments must be made, regardless of the pace of social change. But rapid social change and a faster pace of life bring a number of additional life changes. These are relatively new in human history, at least on such a mass scale. Among the most important of these are divorce, remarriage, and geographic mobility.

Schlossberg contends four potential resources—four S's—are vital for managing change:

▼ Your overall **Situation**

▼ Your **Self**

▼ Your **Supports**

▼ Your **Strategies** for coping

Exercise 10-6 provides an opportunity to analyze the nature and impact of a specific transition in relation to one of these resources, **supports,** drawing on the work of Schlossberg. She provides similar exercises for the other three resources as well.

EXERCISE 10-6. YOUR SUPPORT REVIEW

Are you getting what you need for this transition in terms of:

Affect?	Yes	No
Affirmation?	Yes	No
Aid?	Yes	No
Do you have a range of types of support—spouse or partner, other close family or friends, co-workers/colleagues/neighbors, organizations, strangers?	Yes	No
Have you checked the institutions that are available to you?	Yes	No

Has your "convoy of social support"—from intimate to institution—been interrupted by this transition?	Yes	No

Do you regard your **support** for this transition as:

A high resource?	Yes	No
A low resource?	Yes	No
A mixed bag?	Yes	No
Okay?	Yes	No

SOURCE: Schlossberg (1989, 62)

EXERCISE 10-7. COPING STRATEGIES FOR TRANSITIONS

Below are a number of coping strategies for transitions. Which do you now use? Which will you use in the future?

COPING STRATEGIES	NOW USE	WILL USE
*Taking action to change or modify the transition		
Negotiating	_____	_____
Taking optimistic action	_____	_____
Seeking advice	_____	_____
Asserting yourself	_____	
Brainstorming a new plan	_____	_____
Taking legal action (if needed)	_____	_____
*Changing the meaning of the transition		
Applying knowledge of the transition process	_____	_____
Rehearsing	_____	_____
Developing rituals	_____	_____
Making positive comparisons	_____	_____
Rearranging priorities	_____	_____
Relabeling or reframing	_____	_____
Selectively ignoring	_____	_____
Using denial	_____	_____
Using humor	_____	_____
Having faith	_____	_____
*Managing reactions to stress		
Playing	_____	_____
Using relaxation skills	_____	_____
Expressing emotions	_____	_____
Doing physical activity	_____	_____
Participating in counseling, therapy, or support groups	_____	_____

Reading   _____   _____

*Doing nothing   _____   _____

*Other strategies

_____   _____   _____

_____   _____   _____

_____   _____   _____

SOURCE: Schlossberg (1989, 89, based on work from Pearlin and Schooler, 1978).

CLUSTERING OF LIFE EVENTS

We noted in Chapter 2 that an important line of theory and research in recent years has focused on the impact of too much personal change in too short a time—the clustering of life events.

In the preceding section, we focused on stressful single life transitions. Emphasis here is on the high risk to health, life satisfaction, and productivity of the accumulation of too many life changes in too short a time.

When referred to the Enloe Hospital Stress and Health Center by her physician, Carolyn, 55 years old, suffered from diarrhea, insommia, hemorrhoids, hypertension, and swings between severe anxiety and depression. The symptoms had appeared within a few short months quite unexpectedly to Carolyn, who had been emotionally stable and free of illness throughout most of her adult life. An interview and paper-pencil test revealed a clustering of the following events in her life during the preceding nine months.

She retired after 32 years of elementary school teaching.
Her husband sold his hardware business and retired.
They decided to move to a retirement community in another part of the state.
They sold their home.
They left their neighborhood, church, and extended family.
They bought a new home.
They adapted to a new climate.
They developed a new friendship group and entered a new church.
They readjusted their marriage to both being at home.
They adjusted to a 50 percent reduction in income.
She deliberately lost 50 pounds, which seemed a good idea at this transition time.
She and her new doctor decided it was time to stop hormone treatments prescribed earlier for menopause.
Their only daughter filed for divorce.
Their 15-year-old cat died.

> Clearly, this woman faced an enormous number of virtually simultaneous adjustments in mind, body, and behavior. She was overwhelmed. Her body and spirit began to break. She felt near a "nervous breakdown."
>
> Fortunately, greater awareness of why she was experiencing these difficulties, together with proper temporary medications, daily deep relaxation, and daily brisk walking, brought her out of this intense period of worry and frustration. Our program, combined with medical treatment, restored her health and emotions to a normal level after a few brief months.

Carolyn is but one illustration of a common pattern among highly stressed patients referred to the Center by physicians: too much change in too short a time. Her experience is consistent with a growing number of studies showing that the greater the clustering of life events, the greater the chances of becoming ill.

Clustering and Stress: Research Evidence

One study, for example, examined the illness rates of 2,500 sailors at sea for six months (RAHE, 1968). Just before embarking, the sailors were given a long checklist of life changes to determine how many they had experienced the previous year. These ranged from apparently insignificant changes in daily habits to dramatic, wrenching changes.

> The questionnaire went on to probe such issues as the number of times he moved to a new home. Had he been in trouble with the law over traffic violations or other minor infractions? Had he spent a lot of time away from his wife as the result of job-related travel or marital difficulties? Had he changed jobs? Won awards or promotions? Had his living conditions changed as a consequence of home remodeling or the deterioration of his neighborhood? Had his wife started or stopped working? Had he taken out a loan or mortgage? How many times had he taken a vacation? Was there any major change in his relations with his parents as the result of death, divorce, marriage, etc.? (Toffler, 1971, 331).

The questionnaire did not ask whether the sailor thought the change was pleasant or unpleasant, good or bad, but simply whether or not it had happened. Results showed that "life-change scores" for the previous year were correlated with illness rates while at sea. The greater the number of life changes, the greater the chances that illness would occur. Furthermore, the more significant or serious the changes, the more serious the illness was likely to be.

This study is illustrative of hundreds during the past two decades, consistently showing that the greater the clustering of life events, the greater the harmful impact on health, emotions, and quality of life. These studies have been conducted across all age groups and in such diverse countries as the United States, England, Wales, El Salvador, Malaysia, Japan, France, Belgium, Denmark, Sweden, Norway, and Peru (Rice, 1987, 157). A fascinating recent study in Beirut found that the greater the number of violence-related events an individual had encountered, the greater the incidence of cardiac problems.

Like adults their own age and older, college students are likely to be negatively affected mentally and physically by a clustering of life changes. One recent study found that students with high life-change scores experienced greater number and severity of illnesses during the following semester (Marx, Garrity and Bowers, 1975).

College athletes are not immune from these effects, as first reported in a study of the impact of life changes on football injuries among University of Washington football players. As shown in Table 10-2, I found a similar pattern among football and soccer players at California State University, Chico: the more numerous the life changes during the year preceding the season, the greater the number and severity of injuries (Schafer and McKenna, 1981). We found a similar pattern in the study of 572 adult runners: the higher the life change score, the greater the number of injuries, the more days missed running, the more often the runners sought medical attention for an injury, and the more often they got sick for reasons other than running injuries (Schafer and McKenna, 1985).

Many studies now have documented the contribution of individual life changes to physical and psychological distress (Dohrenwend and Dohrenwend, 1974; Dohrenwend and Dohrenwend, 1981; Dohrenwend, 1986). While technical and scientific questions still remain about some of these studies, the overall pattern of findings is clear: the greater the number, clustering, and intensity of life changes, the greater the chances of illness, injury, or psychological problems. Two scientists have summarized these findings as follows (Rabkin and Struening, 1976, 1014):

> In both retrospective and prospective investigations, modest but statistically significant relationships have been found between mounting life change and the occurrence or onset of sudden cardiac death, myocardial infarctions, accidents, athletic injuries, tuberculosis, leukemia, multiple sclerosis, diabetes, and the entire gamut of minor medical complaints. High scores on checklists of life events have also been repeatedly associated with psychiatric symptoms and disorders, and such scores have been found to differ between psychiatric and other samples.

Exercise 10-8 presents the original Holmes-Raye Social Readjustment Rating Scale for the population at large. You are invited to complete this scale to determine the clustering of events in your life.

TABLE 10-2. DISTRESS SYMPTOM SCORE BY LIFE CHANGE SCORE

DISTRESS SYMPTOM SCORE

Life Change Score	High	Medium	Low	Total	(N)
High	53%	42%	6%	101%	(36)
Medium	32%	27%	41%	100%	(34)
Low	14%	31%	55%	100%	(29)

P = <.001 N = 99

EXERCISE 10-8. SOCIAL READJUSTMENT RATING SCALE

This scale is useful for determining the clustering of life events in your own life. To use the scale, record the values (Life Change Units) corresponding to the events you have experienced **during the past year.** These values indicate the average stressfulness of each event on a scale of 0–100. Thus, if you experienced one personal injury or illness, record 53. If two injuries or illnesses record 53 twice.

LIFE EVENT	MEAN VALUE
1. Death of spouse	100
2. Divorce	73
3. Marital separation from mate	65
4. Detention in jail or other institution	63
5. Death of a close family member	63
6. Major personal injury or illness	53
7. Marriage	50
8. Being fired at work	47
9. Marital reconcilliation with mate	45
10. Retirement from work	45
11. Major change in health or behavior of a family member	44
12. Pregnancy	40
13. Sexual difficulties	39
14. Gaining new family members (through birth, adoption, oldster moving in, etc.)	39
15. Major business readjustment (merger, reorganization, bankruptcy, etc.)	39
16. Major change in financial state (a lot worse or a lot better off than usual)	38
17. Death of a close friend	37
18. Changing to a different line of work	36
19. Major change in the number of arguments with spouse (more or fewer arguments than usual, about child-rearing personal habits, etc.)	35
20. Taking out a mortgage or loan for a major purchase (home,business, etc.)	31
21. Foreclosure on a mortgage or loan	30
22. Major change in responsibilities at work (promotion, demotion, lateral transfer)	29
23. Son or daughter leaving home (for marriage, to attend college, etc.)	29
24. Trouble with in-laws	29
25. Outstanding personal achievement	28
26. Wife beginning or ceasing work outside the home	26
27. Beginning or ceasing formal schooling	26
28. Major change in lining conditions (building a new home, remodeling, deterioration of home/neighborhood)	25
29. Revision of personal habits (dress, manners, associations, etc.)	24
30. Trouble with boss	23
31. Major change in working hours or conditions	20
32. Change in residence	20
33. Changing to a new school	20
34. Major change in usual type and/or amount of recreation	19
35. Major change in church activities (a lot more or fewer than usual)	19

36. Major change in social activities (clubs, dancing, movies, visiting, etc.)	18
37. Taking out a mortgage or loan for a lesser purchase (for a car, TV, freezer, etc.)	17
38. Major change in sleeping habits (a lot more or less sleep, or a change in part of day when sleep occurs)	16
39. Major change in number of family get-togethers (more or fewer than usual)	15
40. Major change in eating habits (a lot more or less food intake, or very different meal hours or surroundings)	13
41. Vacation	13
42. Christmas	12
43. Minor violation of the law (traffic tickets, jaywalking, disturbing the space, etc.)	11

Source: Holmes and Rahe (1967, 213).

Minimizing Distress from Clustered Change

Mental and physical illness is not inevitable, by any means, during or after clustering of life changes. But the chances do increase. The question becomes, what can I do to protect myself, to minimize chances of distress from clustered change?

Consider the following advice from Holmes and Holmes in a booklet published by Blue Cross, a health insurance company with a great deal at stake in minimizing illness (Holmes and Holmes, 1974, 75).

It all sounds pretty grim. But there may be ways in which you can soften the blow. Change is not entirely random. You have a large amount of personal control over whether and when to marry, go to college, move or have a family. You may have little control over whether to get divorced, change jobs, take out a loan or retire. But you may have a pretty good idea of when these events might take place.

So the future is not a complete blank. You can predict it to a certain degree. And to this degree, you can order your life by managing the change that is a vital part of living. You can weigh the benefits of change against its costs, pace the timing of the inevitable changes and regulate the occurrence of voluntary change to try to keep your yearly life-change score out of the danger zone.

If you are considering your third job change in two years, you might stay for a while and consider a more long-lasting alternative. Or if divorce is imminent, you might avoid the temptation to plan to remarry right away and give yourself time to sort out the implications of all the changes that divorce brings with it. If you are approaching 65, a gradual rather than sudden transition from full-time work and responsibility could help reduce the feeling of uselessness that often accompanies retirement.

Here are six useful strategies for dealing with clustering of life events.

1.   Insofar as possible, minimize the clustering of life events.

2.   Anticipate the likely additive effects of stress of a life change you are considering—before deciding.

3. Maintain effective health buffers to be prepared for unavoidable clustering of life changes.

4. Manage your self-talk during periods of clustered change in order to keep events in perspective.

5. Cope constructively rather than destructively with any distress that does result from clustering of life changes.

6. When experiencing change, control those parts of your life that are controllable.

EXERCISE 10-9. APPLYING STRATEGIES FOR HANDLING CLUSTERING OF LIFE EVENTS

Read carefully the above six strategies for handling change.

1. Looking back over recent periods of clustering of life events, which of these strategies have you used? Be specific.
2. Which strategies might you strengthen as you deal with future clustering of life events?
3. What specific step(s) will you take to apply one or more of these strategies?

DAILY HASSLES   ▼

You may recall that Lazarus (Lazarus & Folkman, 1984) views stress as a transactional, interpretive, coping process. Distress is the result of an individual's appraisal of an event or situation as personally important and exceeding her resources for effectively coping with it. It is not surprising, then, that Lazarus and his colleagues at the Berkeley Stress and Coping Project would focus on small events as potentially stressful for some individuals. Thus, they decided to study micro-events—daily hassles—as the person moves through time (DeLongis et al., 1982; Lazarus & Folkman, 1984). At the same time, they studied the effects of daily uplifts.

Measuring Hassles and Uplifts
A sample of 100 middle-aged people were asked to check how often 117 different hassles and 135 daily uplifts had occurred during the past month and how severe or pleasant the hassle or uplift was. Thus, two scales resulted: a Hassle Scale and an Uplift Scale. Table 10-3 lists the frequency with which leading items were checked.

Daily Hassles, Clustering of Life Events and Stress
Others previously had suggested that these familiar, seemingly minor daily events often are taken for granted because they seem so innocuous compared with major life events, yet can have harmful effects on the individual. Still earlier, Cason (1930) measured what he called "common annoyances."

TABLE 10-3. TEN MOST FREQUENT HASSLES AND UPLIFTS

ITEM	PERCENTAGE OF TIMES CHECKED
Hassles	
1. Concerns about weight	52.4%
2. Health of a family member	48.1%
3. Rising prices of common goods	43.7%
4. Home maintenance	42.8%
5. Too many things to do	38.6%
6. Misplacing or losing things	38.1%
7. Yard work or outside home maintenance	38.1%
8. Property, investment, or taxes	37.6%
9. Crime	37.1%
10. Physical appearance	35.9%
Uplifts	
1. Relating well with your spouse or lover	76.3%
2. Relating well with friends	74.4%
3. Completing a task	73.3%
4. Feeling healthy	72.7%
5. Getting enough sleep	69.7%
6. Eating out	68.4%
7. Meeting your responsibilities	68.1%
8. Visiting, phoning, or writing someone	67.7%
9. Spending time with family	66.7%
10. Home (inside) pleasing to you	65.5%

SOURCE: (Kanner, et al., 1981, 61).

Lazarus and Folkman (1984) point out that life events and daily hassles tend to supplement each other in the sense that a major change, such as divorce or job change, sets in motion a whole series of minor adjustments. A man who just left his wife and family, for example, may need for the first time to confront paying bills, taking care of his laundry, fixing his lunch, cleaning his new apartment, and shopping for groceries (Oppenheimer, 1987). Thus, one might expect a positive correlation between clustering of life events and daily hassle scores.

Yet Lazarus and Folkman (1984) note that only a modest association has been found between these two measures. This means that, while clustering of life events partly explains the occurrence of daily hassles, hassles most often occur independently of major life events.

Which experience, clustering of life events or daily hassles, are most likely to produce distress? In summarizing several years of research, Lazarus and Folkman (1984, 311) note:

> Our research findings have shown, in a regression-based comparison of life events and daily hassles, that hassles are far superior to life events in predicting psychological and somatic symptoms. Hassles accounted for almost all the outcome variance attributable to life events, whereas life events had little or no impact on health outcomes independent of daily hassles.

In other words, it seems to be the accumulation of small rather than large negative events that wears the individual down mentally and physically. Interestingly, uplift scores added little predictive power for distress beyond that of hassles scores alone, although respondents tended to check uplifts more often than hassles. Wolf, and others, (1989), also found that hassles correlated more strongly with mood over a nine-year period than did life events. Burks and Martin (1985) reported a similar result, using their own measure of "everyday problems."

These findings point again to the role of interpretation or, in Lazarus' terms, appraisal, in understanding and predicting individual distress. Whether something is a hassle depends entirely upon the person's self-talk about that event. If, for example, a person tends to awfulize, negativize, or catastrophize, he or she is much more likely to see daily events as hassles.

Yet in an increasingly fast-paced, changing world marked by overchoice, overload, transitions, and clustering of life events, chances increase that events indeed will be experienced as hassles by many.

Thus far in this chapter you have read about the cultural context of time, about rapid social change as the context of personal stress, and about five stressors related to change, pacing, and time: overchoice, chronic daily overload, transitions, clustering of life events, and daily hassles. You also read about some of the personal roots of these stressors and about a number of strategies and techniques for handling them effectively.

We now will focus on a number of other specific time management approaches and tips.

MANAGING STRESS FROM TIME, PACE, AND CHANGE ▼

GENERAL GUIDELINES

Habit is a double-edged sword. On one hand, it makes life easier by adding predictability and routine. On the other hand, habit can stunt growth, prevent exploration, lead to blind inertia.

Habit exerts tremendous force in all of our lives. So much, in fact, that it can be called a basic drive. The force behind habit is the *repetition compulsion*. Like everyone else, you possess a strong drive to be and to do what is familiar. Habit is comfortable and secure. Risk and change create tension. Habit requires little effort. Changing can require that you exert yourself as never before.

Becoming aware of the force of habit in your own life can be very important in helping you to manage stress because, like most people, you may need to work hard to overcome destructive habits. As pointed out earlier, some stressors—death of a loved one, fire, injury—cannot be changed. These you must learn to accept, with as little harmful effect as possible. But most stressors in your daily life can be controlled—some easily, others with great effort.

Learning to tailor to your own needs the number, variety, and intensity of stressors to which you expose yourself is most important. This requires attention both to pace of life and to major life changes. There are a number of specific ways you can improve your ability to manage your stressors. All of these are based on what you have already learned in previous chapters.

1. Become more aware of the nature of stressors in your daily life. Understanding and anticipating stressors can strengthen you in advance, help to reduce their harmful impact, and assist you in controlling them. For example, knowing in advance that starting a new job probably will upset your sleep patterns, energy level, personal relationships, and appetite can help you to handle this potentially difficult transition.

2. Take personal responsibility for your pace of life and for major life changes. You are partly a product of your social environment, and your roles and responsibilities shape your behavior to a large extent. But you need not—in fact, you must not—be entirely passive. You can act upon your world as well. Ultimately *you* are responsible for how fast or how slow you live or how many changes you bring upon yourself in a year's time. Blaming society, your teacher, your boss, your parents, or your spouse is passing the buck. They may play a part in creating the stressors you must face. But over the long haul, you must control your own stressors.

3. Know your comfort zone. People vary in the range of stimulation that is comfortable, healthy and productive of growth. You need to discover how much stimulation is right for you. Too much activity for too long can lead to distress from overload. Too little can lead to boredom and stunted growth. Becoming more sensitive to internal cues that tell you your limits in both directions is an important step toward the wide management of your pace of life.

4. Find a good fit between your own needs—your comfort zone—and the demands of your environment. If you need to live relatively slowly, don't become a corporation executive. If you thrive on a relatively rapid pace, find friends, an intimate partner, and a job that will allow and support such a lifestyle. A bad fit can lead to continuing tension both within you and between you and others. A good fit can minimize stress-related problems.

5. Know how rapidly and how much your comfort zone can change. Your comfort zone is not set for all time. You can change stimulation activity levels according to circumstances and personal choice. Flexibility is essential. Become sensitive to how rapidly and how much you can change your comfort zone.

6. Anticipate the probable stressful effects of major life changes. Many people consider only financial benefits or prestige in changing jobs. Others consider only emotional factors in beginning or ending a romantic involvement. Few of us think about the likely effects of a major life change on stress levels. Is the timing right? Are the likely stress effects too great to justify the change—at least for now? Are too many major changes occurring simultaneously? Are the long-run gains from a major change likely to offset the temporary stress effects? For example, how large an adjustment is needed in a prospective geographic move? How long is it likely to take? Are the potential benefits great enough to justify this amount of stress?

7. Avoid clustering too many major life changes. If you have experienced a death in the family, a change of residence, the end of an intense romance, and a major illness within the past few months, this may not be a good time to change jobs. Correct spacing of major life changes is vital to intelligent management of stress. To the extent that you can control your major life changes, you should keep them in line with your comfort zone.

8. Manage daily life—micro-engineer your time—so you have optimal lead time, afterburn time, and time for unfinished business. Again, what is "optimal" depends on the person. You may be able to move quickly from one intense activity to another or to carry, with few adverse effects, a host of unexpressed feelings and incomplete tasks. Your "correct" lead-time, afterburn time, and number of pieces of unfinished business may differ drastically from those of a friend whose time needs are different. Control your time, insofar as possible, to fit your own needs and style.

9. Establish clear priorities and values so you can select opportunities and challenges wisely in a world of overchoice. The Quakers refer to this as being "centered." Others call it "being clear" or "having your head on straight." Whatever words you prefer, know what is important and unimportant, desirable and undesirable for you. If you don't, you run the risk of being overwhelmed by options and of having decisions made for you by others. Clear values can provide guidelines for specific decisions.

10. Select activities and challenges that are meaningful to you and avoid meaningless ones whenever possible. Dr. Selye (1974) maintains that we possess two types of adaptive energy: superficial and deep. Superficial adaptive energy is not depletable. In fact, it can be increased through good health and fitness. Deep adaptive energy is like an inherited fortune, held in reserve for times of intense stress. Selye suggests that our deep adaptive energies may be limited and finite, like oil reserves in the earth. In times of distress, we use up small amounts of this reserve. "Chemical scars" remain. As the reserve is depleted, we wear down. This is aging. Total depletion brings death.

Wise management of pace of life means using deep adaptive energies sparingly and for the right purposes. As Selye states (1974, 40) "we can squander our adaptability recklessly, 'burning the candle at both ends,' or we can learn to make this valuable resource last long, by using it wisely and sparingly, only for things that are worthwhile and cause least distress." Proper pacing is vital in daily life, just as in running a marathon. So is choosing activities and goals that are meaningful—worth using up some of our deep adaptive energy.

Many people hate their work; others hate their social life. Alienation, boredom, and symptoms of distress too often follow. Sometimes, of course, you must do things that have little meaning or make little sense to you. But when you can exercise choice, spend your time on challenges and activities that are meaningful to you. Develop sensitivity to your talents, deep interests, and personal preferences. Become good at things you enjoy. Enjoy those things you do best. Being "centered" helps. Some people refer to this as following your own destiny.

11. Take enough risks so you are challenged but not so many you are overwhelmed. Abraham Maslow, the humanistic psychologist, wrote that we all face a tug and pull between the drive for safety and the drive for growth through risks. Taking risks in work, in school, in your relationships, or in sports is essential for growth. Always staying safe—out of fear of failure, rejection, or the unknown—causes stagnation.

Taking too much risk can be foolish, leading to distress or disaster. Intelligent, properly aimed risk-taking is essential for fulfilling your potentials. Knowing when to take risks and when not to, when to be content and when to push into new frontiers, knowing your best *pace* of growth—these are vital ingredients of stress management and making stress work for you.

LEARNING TO MANAGE TIME: TIPS AND EXERCISES

Below are a series of exercises for improving your time management skills. Pick those that fit your needs. Guidelines and exercises specifically for college students are provided in Chapter 12.

EXERCISE 10-10. SINS OF TIME MISMANAGEMENT

Rice (1987, 327) has identified seven deadly sins of "time mismanagement":

1. Confusion: Where am I going?
2. Indecision: What should I do?
3. Diffusion: Mental and physical overload.
4. Procrastination: That will keep for another day.
5. Avoidance: Escape to fantasyland.
6. Interruptions: Getting started is the hard part
7. Perfectionism: I was raised a perfectionist.

With which of these "sins" can you identify? How do they affect your performance, relationships, and satisfaction?

EXERCISE 10-11. AVOIDING PROCRASTINATION

Procrastination means that one part of you puts off doing what another part of you knows you need to do. For some, procrastination takes the form of difficulty in starting a task, for others difficulty in finishing something.

Whichever is true for you, remember that procrastination is a combination of thinking and action. Changes in both may be needed. Below are several guidelines. Pick the ones that you believe would be most useful for you.

1. Be aware of procrastinating self-talk. Substitute new self-talk.
2. Prioritize. Selectively procrastinate.
3. Break large tasks into smaller ones.
4. Set intermediate deadlines.
5. Block off escape routes—diversions and excuses.
6. Remember, momentum will carry through the task, once you begin.
7. Start.
8. Chip away at small tasks.
9. Consider each step toward your goal as a small accomplishment.
10. Stop perfectionism.
11. Set aside blocks of time to catch up.
12. Finish tasks before starting others whenever possible.

EXERCISE 10-12. THE PROCRASTINATOR'S CODE.

In their helpful book, *Procrastination: Why You Do It, What To Do About It,* Burka and Yuen (1983, 16) set forth the "procrastinator's code."

I must be perfect.
Everything I do should go easily and without effort.
It's safer to do nothing than to take a risk and fail.
I should have no limitations.
If it's not done right, it's not worth doing at all.
I must avoid being challenged.
If I succeed, someone will get hurt.
If I do well this time, I must always do well.
Following someone else's rules means I'm giving in and I'm not in control.
I can't afford to let go of anything or anyone.
If I expose my real self, people won't like me.
There is a right answer, and I'll wait until I find it.

1. Using the criteria for rational and irrational beliefs in Chapter 7, would you regard these as rational or irrational?
2. Identify those that apply to you.
3. Rewrite each of those you identified.
4. What other self-talk do you use to procrastinate—for example, "This is too hard (too unpleasant, too big a job). I'm too tired (busy, unprepared, overwhelmed)."

EXERCISE 10-13. CONTROLLING YOUR TIME

Webber (1972), a time-management specialist, points out that our time can be divided into two categories: discretionary (under your own control) and non-discretionary (controlled by others). One important step in controlling the stressors in our work and non-work lives is to put as much time under your own control as possible. Once this is done, Webber suggests, you can protect your discretionary time by the following means.

Insulation: Screening and sorting incoming information and tasks one time each day for processing outgoing information

Isolation: Finding a place to work without interruption

Delegation: Especially those activities over which you need not exercise direct control and which others are competent to perform

Simplification: Grouping similar tasks into time-blocks whenever possible

Concentration: Working from prioritized lists and doing one thing at a time.

EXERCISE 10-14. RISK FACTORS FOR BOREDOM

When you have experienced periods of extended boredom, which is in many ways the opposite of Type A behavior, which of the following "risk factors" was present?

	Very True	Quite True	Not Very True
Not enough challenge	_____	_____	_____
Too much isolation	_____	_____	_____
Too much routine	_____	_____	_____
Meaninglessness	_____	_____	_____

1. What steps can you take, based on personal responsibility, for minimizing such experiences in the future?

2. Remember that experiences are never boring of themselves—they become boring only when they are interpreted that way. What self-talk might you use to turn boredom into a positive experience?

EXERCISE 10-15. SETTING PRIORITIES

MY PRIORITIES FOR THE WEEK OF: _____

PRIORITY A—MUST DO

_____

_____

_____

_____

_____

_____

PRIORITY B—SHOULD DO

_____

_____

_____

_____

_____

_____

PRIORITY C—NICE TO DO

_____

_____

_____

_____

_____

_____

_____

EXERCISE 10-16. USING LISTS

To-do lists can be very helpful. Try the following.

1. Use different categories for your list. For example,

    Calls
    Shopping
    To Read
    Office tasks
    Household tasks

2. Lists can be daily or they can cover several days.

3. Avoid creating unrealistically long lists or setting unrealistic deadlines.
4. Do the best you can. Give yourself credit for chipping away at your list.

EXERCISE 10-17. MISCELLANEOUS TIME MANAGEMENT TIPS

Here are a number of specific time management tips. Check those you might benefit from using. Underline the two you plan to begin first. Then start.

If you are usually too busy, leave details to someone else whenever possible—the income tax return, fixing your car, office details.

Move through your day slowly enough to experience beauty in your environment—on your way to school or work, for example.

Learn to live with unfinished tasks—only a corpse is completely finished.

Leave enough time between activities so that you minimize overlap.

Schedule only as many tasks each day as you can reasonably finish without pressure.

Leave time in your schedule for the unexpected.

Leave early enough so that you need not rush to get where you are going, even if this means rising 20 minutes earlier in the morning.

Say "no" to new opportunities or responsibilities if they would overload or rush your day.

Take steps to "center"—listen to your inner voice of wisdom.

Find a work environment that is not chronically high-pressured or harried. Avoid Type A organizations. Find another job if necessary.

Learn to slow your pace of talking, walking, eating.

Find time each day to relax, meditate, exercise.

Avoid doing more than one thing at a time.

Tell yourself at least once each day that failure seldom results from doing a job too slowly or too well. But failure often is caused by mistakes of judgment or from too much hurrying.

Ask yourself at least once each week: Apart from eternal distress and hurry, what is really important to me?

Measure success by quality, rather than a quantity.

"Screen out" whenever possible—even if this risks disapproval or missing something you may have thought important.

Surround yourself with symbols of tranquility—soft music, plants, pleasant colors, and lighting.

Use your noon hour for deep relaxation, exercise, or something else that will slow you down, lift your spirits, and restore energy.

Find time and space to be alone each day other than at your desk or in your car.

Associate with Type B's or Type C's whenever possible.

Practice effective listening. Avoid interrupting out of impatience.

Catch your free-floating hostility in progress. Stop it. Take deliberate actions of graciousness and patience.

Ask whether something in fact must be done this hour or this day. Would catastrophe ensue if you could not squeeze it in?

Use waiting in line to observe people around you and to practice deep breathing techniques while you are waiting.

Whenever you find yourself jiggling your knees or tapping your fingers, immediately practice the six-second quieting response.

Use realistic to-do lists to free your mind from preoccupation with all you have to do and to organize tasks. Prioritize items. Avoid self-downing if you don't finish the list.

Stop blaming others for falling short of your day-to-day accomplishment goals. Accept responsibility for trying to do too much in too short a time or for being poorly organized.

Whenever you catch yourself racing through a yellow light, immediately turn right and go around the block.

You have read about time, pace and change—important contexts of personal stress. We have explored some of the societal and personal roots of time-related distress. You have been given a number of guidelines and exercises for effectively managing time and change.

In the next chapter, we will focus on social support, an important resource for building resistance against distress from time, change and other sources.

REFERENCES ▼

Braiker, H.B. (1986). *The Type E Woman.* New York: Dodd, Mead and Company.

Burka, J.B., & Yuen, L.M. (1983). *Procrastination: Why You Do It, What To Do About It.* Reading, MA.: Addison-Wesley.

Burks, N., & Martin, B. (1985). Everyday problems and life change events. *Journal of Human Stress,* 11, 27-35.

Carroll, L. (1960). *Alice's Adventures in Wonderland.* New York: Signet Books.

Cason, H. (1930). Common annoyances: A psychological study of every-day aversions and irritations. *Psychological Monographs,* 40, (Whole No. 182).

Delongis, A., Coyne, J.C., Dakof, G., Folkman, S., & Lazarus, R.S. (1982). Relationship of daily hassles, uplifts, and major life events to health status. *Health Psychology,* I, 119-136.

Dohrenwend, B.S., & Dohrenwend, B.P., (Eds.). (1974). *Stressful Life Events: Their Nature and Effects.* New York: John Wiley and Sons.

Dohrewend, B.S., & Dohrenwend, B.P. (Eds.). (1981). *Stressful Life Events and Their Contexts.* New York: Prodist.

Dohrenwend, B.P. (1986). Note on a program of research on alternative social psychological models of relationships between life stress and psychopathology. In Appley, M.H., & Trumbull, R. (Eds.), *The Dynamics of Stress: Physiological, Psychological, and Social Perspectives.* New York: Plenum Press, 283-294.

Faulkner, G. (1987). *Type E and Distress Among Working Women.* Unpublished Masters Thesis, California State University, Chico.

Ferguson, M. (1980). *The Aquarian Conspiracy.* Los Angeles: Tarcher.

Friedman, M., & Rosenman, R.H. (1974). *Type A Behavior and Your Heart.* New York: Fawcett.

Friedman, M., & Ulmer, D. (1984). *Treating Type A Behavior and Your Heart.* New York: Alfred A. Knopf.

Gallup Poll. (1990). People feel time is running out. *San Francisco Chronicle,* November 5, 1990, B3.

Gibbs, N. (1989). How America has run out of time. *Time Magazine,* April 24, 58-67.

Holmes, T.H., & Rahe, R.H. (1967). The social readjustment rating scale. *Journal of Psychosomatic Research,* 11, 213.

Holmes, T.H., & Holmes, T.S. (1974). How stress can make us ill. *Stress.* Chicago: Blue Cross.

Horowitz, M.J. (1976). *Stress Response Syndromes.* New York: Jason Aronson, Inc.

Ivancevich, J.M., & Matteson, M.T. (1980). *Stress and Work.* Glenview, Il.: Scott, Foresman and Company.

Kanner, A.D., Coyne, J.S., Schaefer, C., & Lazarus, R.S. (1981). Comparison of two modes of stress measurement: Daily hassles and uplifts versus major life events. *Journal of Behavioral Medicine,* 4, 1-39.

Kiechel, W. (1989). The workaholic generation. *Fortune,* April 10, 50-62.

Lazarus, R.S., & Folkman, S. (1984). *Stress, Appraisal, and Coping.* New York: Springer Publishing Company.

Levine, R., & Wolff, E. (1985). Social time: The heartbeat of culture. *Psychology Today,* 19 , 29-35.

Levine, R.V., Lynch, K., Miyake, & Lucia, M. (1989). The type A city: Coronary heart disease and the pace of life. *Journal of Behavioral Medicine,* 12, 509-524.

Marx, M., Garrity, T., & Bowers, F. (1975). The influence of recent life experiences on the health of college freshmen. *Journal of Psychosomatic Research,* 19, 87-98.

Machlowitz, M. (1980). *Workaholics: Living With Them, Working With Them.* New York: New American Library.

Oppenheimer, K. (1987). The impact of daily stressors on women's adjustment to marital separation. *The Journal of Family Practice,* 24, 507-511.

Pearlin, L.I., & Schooler, C. (1978). *Journal of Health and Social Behavior,* 19, 2-21.

Rabkin, J.G., & Struening, E.L. (1976). Life events, stress and illness. *Science,* 194, 1013-1020.

Rahe, R.H. (1968). Life-change measurement as a precipitor of illness. *Proceedings of the Royal Society of Medicine,* 61, 1124-1126.

Rice, P.L. (1987). *Stress and Health: Principles and Practice for Coping and Wellness.* Monterey, CA.: Brooks/Cole.

Robinson, R.E. (1989). *Work Addiction: Hidden Legacies of Adult Children.* Deerfield Beach, Fl.: Health Communications, Inc.

Schafer, W.E., & KcKenna, J. F. (1981). Life change, stress and injury: A study of male college athletes. Unpublished paper.

Schafer, W.E., & KcKenna, J.F. (1985). Life changes, stress, injuries, and illness among adult runners. *Stress Medicine,* I, 237-244.

Schlossberg, N.K. (1989). *Overwhelmed: Coping With Life's Ups and Downs.* Lexington, MA.: Lexington Books.

Seligman, M.E.P. (1988). Boomer blues. *Psychology Today*, 21, 50-55.

Selye, H. (1974). *Stress Without Distress*. Philadelphia: Lippincott.

Sheehy, G. (1976). *Passages: Predictable Crises of Adult Life*. New York: E.P. Dutton.

Toffler, A. (1971). *Future Shock*. New York: Bantam.

Toffler, A. (1980). *The Third Wave*. New York: Bantam.

Webber, R.A. (1972). *Time Management*. New York: Van Nostrand.

Wellingham-Jones, P. (1989). *Successful Women: Their Health & Handwriting*. Tehama, CA.: PWJ Publishing.

Wolf, T.M., Elston, R.C., & Kissling. (1989). Relationship of hassles, uplifts, and life events to psychological well-being of freshmen medical students. *Behavioral Medicine*, 15, 37-45.

SOCIAL SUPPORT: GIVING AND RECEIVING

Chapter

11

CHAPTER 11

I. SOCIAL TIES: A STRESS RESISTANCE RESOURCE
A. Dimensions of Social Support
B. Gains and Costs of Social Support

II. TWO RELATIONSHIPS OF SOCIAL SUPPORT TO WELL-BEING
A. Direct Effects
B. Buffering Effects

III. THE CHALLENGE OF BUILDING AND USING SOCIAL SUPPORT
A. Satir's Model of Communication
B. Communication Guidelines for Direct, Honest Communication
C. Self-Disclosure
D. Active Listening
E. Giving and Getting Negative Feedback
F. Assertiveness
G. Communication Style and Stress

SOCIAL TIES: A STRESS RESISTANCE RESOURCE   ▼

Margaret had been married for 28 years to a prominent attorney. They were parents of two grown sons. Although their marriage was far from perfect, she was nearly devastated when he announced one day he was leaving to marry another woman. For several days, Margaret hardly slept or ate. During ensuing months, she went through a host of changes in her living situation and daily routines. Yet, she survived these tough early days. In fact, she went on after several months of pain and mourning to new levels of strength.

Fortunately, Margaret had several close friends and a broad social network for support through this period. They listened as she expressed her loss. They helped with details of the adjustment. They cared. In looking back a year later, she marveled at the support she had received from her friends. She felt immensely grateful for the part they played in her survival—indeed her growth—through this transition.

This story illustrates the vital role social support often plays as a stress resistance resource. In the previous chapter, you read that clustering of life events increases risk of illness. You also read that not everyone gets sick during periods of transition and change. Both theory and research point to the protective influence of social support when people go through stressful events.

In Chapter 2, we noted that Durkheim, an early sociologist, found that the more integrated individuals are in social systems, the less vulnerable they are to suicide. This finding fit his more general theory that social connection plays a supportive and protective role in individuals' lives (Durkheim, 1951).

You also read that Antonovksy (1979, 1987) contends that generalized resistance resources (GRRs) help provide protection through assisting the person in the belief that events are fairly predictable and will turn out reasonably well. That is, social support promotes a sense of coherence. He identifies social connectedness as an important GRR and cites several studies to support his view.

Similarly, Lazarus and Folkman (1984) suggest in their transactional, process-oriented, coping approach to stress that social support can play a vital role as a resource in dealing with difficult life events. They state, "The social environment is not just a major source of stress; it also provides vital resources which the individual can and must draw upon to survive and flourish" (Lazarus and Folkman, 1984, 243).

The importance of social support as a stress resistance resource is reflected in the entire issue of a major academic journal recently devoted to "predicting, activating, and facilitating social support" (Hobfoll, 1990).

DIMENSIONS OF SOCIAL SUPPORT

Before going on, it is important to be clear about our terms. Social network refers to the "specific set of linkages among a defined set of persons or a given person" (Mitchell, 1969). The larger the social network, the greater the number of ties. Being socially connected is the opposite of being isolated. A social network can be characterized not only by its scope, but by its composition (for example, coworkers, friends, relatives, neighbors) and quality (close or distant, friendly or unfriendly, supportive or indifferent). Stated differently, social ties can vary in two ways: number of ties and intensity or closeness of ties.

Social support refers to relationships that bring positive benefits to the individual. Perceived social support means social ties the person perceives or experiences as yielding positive gains. Thus, not all social networks—or persons within those networks—bring social support. Sometimes quite the opposite occurs, as we all know (Pagel, Erdly & Becker, 1987).

Different types of social support can be identified. Dean and Lin (1977) identify two main types: expressive (emotional support) and instrumental (task-related support). Weiss (1974) speaks of six functions of social support, all essential for well-being: attachment, social integration, opportunity for nurturance, reassurance of one's worth, a sense of reliable alliance, and obtaining guidance. House (1981, 39) defines social support as: ". . . an interpersonal transaction involving one or more of the following:

1. Emotional concern (liking, love, empathy)

2. Instrumental aid (goods or services)

3. Information (about the environment)

4. Appraisal (information relative to self-evaluation)."

Greenberg (1980, 142) points out that social support often flows through social support groups. Support groups exist in so many kinds and forms and affiliations that it is sometimes confusing to identify what the basic ingredients are. Some of the necessary factors seem to be the following.

1. The same people attend.

2. The group meets regularly, once a week or more.

3. The group has met for an extended period of time—until closeness develops.

4. There is an opportunity for informality, spontaneity, and incidental contacts.

Greenberg (1980, 144) also maintains that the most important way true social support takes place in groups like those above is not through the central activity of the group, but through informal, incidental contacts, such as the following.

Driving to and from meetings with someone

Having dinner together before or after the meeting

Having a group potluck meal

Meeting in someone's house

Talking during coffee breaks, in the social get-together after the "formal" meeting

Chats, separate social get-togethers, and the like

Solving problems and making decisions together

Pairing up outside the group with another group member

Going on a trip together, to a convention, or to a retreat setting

Which of these types of contacts do you engage in? Might you in the future?

Gains and Costs of Social Support

Like other areas of social, psychological and medical research, not all studies confirm the direct and buffering relationship of social support to mental and physical well-being. And like other topics of research and theory, the nature of the linkages is quite complex. In fact, as Lazarus and Folkman point out, social ties are not always positive and beneficial. Indeed, "When we think about the value of social networks, therefore, we must bear in mind that social relationships create problems which comprise a significant share, probably the lion's share, of the sources of stress in life.

TABLE 11-1. POSITIVE AND NEGATIVE EFFECTS OF SOCIAL SUPPORT

	Positive Effects	**Negative Effects**
PREVENTION	Reduce uncertainty and worry Set good example Share problems Calm model Distract	Create uncertainty and worry Set bad example Create new problems Calm model Distract Germs
COPING	Label beneficial Provide sympathy Give helpful information	Label negative Subject to irritation and resentment Give misleading information
RECOVERY	Maintain regimen Contrast with health (incentive) Create desire to stop being a nuisance	Discourage regimen Contrast with health (depressed) Create power/dependence need

SOURCE: Suls (1982, 264).

The balance between costs and benefits probably differs among persons, social roles, and stressful encounters" (Lazarus and Folkman, 1984, 248). Table 11-1 lists some of the potential positive and negative effects of social support. The actual balance of gains and cost depends, of course, on the combination of the external reality and the person's perceptions and utilization of those external resources.

The point remains: social support can be an important "stress resistance resource," contributing to mental and physical well-being (Ornstein, R., and Sobel, D. 1985; 1989).

TWO RELATIONSHIPS OF SOCIAL SUPPORT TO WELL-BEING   ▼

Direct Effects

It is important to note that social support can have two different types of relationships to mental and physical well-being. First, it can have a direct effect. That is, the greater the social support, the more positive the mental and/or physical health. This type of relationship has been widely studied and widely supported. In a review of these studies, the sociologist James House cites one of the classic studies (House 1981, 39).

Berkman and Syme . . . analyzed data gathered between 1965 and 1974 on 2229 men and 2496 women, aged 30 to 69 in 1965 and randomly sampled from the population of Alameda, California. They assessed whether the presence or absence of four kinds of social ties in 1965—marriage, contacts with friends, church memberships, and informal and formal group associations—affected the likelihood of the person dying over the next nine years. People low or lacking in each type of social tie were 30 percent to 300 percent more likely to die than those who had each type of relationship. Generally, these trends held for both sexes and at all age levels, although marriage had the strongest protective effect for men, while contact with friends was most protective for women. . . . The more intimate ties of marriage and friendships were stronger predictors than were ties of church and group membership.

The Alameda County study just cited measured only the number of ties. Other studies point to the importance of quality of support for health (Pines, 1980, 43).

Recently 10,000 married men who were 40 years of age or older were followed for five years in Israel. The researchers, Jack H. Medallie and Yuri Goldbourt, wanted to find out how many new cases of angina pectoris developed. They assessed each man's medical risk factors for heart disease and then asked, among other items, this question: Does your wife show you her love?

The answer turned out to have enormous predictive power. Among high-risk men—men who showed elevated blood cholesterol, electrocardiographic abnormalities, and high risk of anxiety—fewer of those who had loving supportive wives developed angina pectoris than did those whose wives were colder (52 per 1000 versus 93 per 1000).

These and other studies strongly suggest that the more the individual is tied into positive, supportive relationships, the more positive one's mental and physical well-being. For reviews of this literature, see, for example, Berkman and Syme (1979); Thoits (1982); Turner (1981); Cohen (1988); House, Landis and Umberson (1988); Dunkel-Schetter and Skokan (1990); Hobfoll, et al., 1990; and Sarason, Pierce, and Sarason (1990).

Buffering Effects

The second type of relationship between social support and well-being is the buffering relationship. Here, social support softens the impact of potentially stressful events. Stated differently, it serves as a buffer between difficult life experiences and health outcomes. As Lazarus and Folkman state, "It can help to prevent stress by making harmful or threatening experiences seem less consequential, or provide valuable resources when stress does occur" (1984, 246). This is illustrated, of course, in Margaret's experience: given the marital separation, she benefitted from friends' support.

An example of a study on the buffering role of social support is that of Lin, Woelfel, and Light (1985). Not surprisingly, they found that depression increased as the importance and undesirability of a major life event also increased in their sample. However, they found that the amount of depression diminished as social support increased, especially from people with whom the subject had strong ties. Curiously, social support did not help in the case of marital breakup (as it did in Margaret's case). The authors speculate that ". . . marital disengagement may have a substantial disruptive impact on a person's social environment so as to render it, although apparently only temporarily, incapable of providing the necessary support. Such disruption may be due to the transition from old support resources to new ones" (Lin, Woelfel, and Light, 1985, 260).

The key conclusion of this study, however, was that social support from close friends provided a buffer against depression, given a major and undesirable life event, except for marital separation.

Marriage, even with its ups and downs, repeatedly has been shown to play an especially powerful protective role. For example, Pearlin and Johnson (1977) found that when stressful life events were relatively infrequent or minor, marrieds and unmarrieds had similar levels of depression. But when social and economic circumstances became more trying, marrieds experienced substantially less depression than unmarrieds. "The combination most productive of psychological distress is to be simultaneously single, poor, isolated, and exposed to burdensome parental obligations." They conclude (Pearlin and Johnson, 1977, 714):

> What we have learned suggests that marriage can function as a protective barrier against the distressful consequences of external threats. Marriage does not prevent economic and social problems from invading life but it can apparently help people fend off the psychological assaults that such problems otherwise create. Even in an era when marriage is an increasingly fragile arrangement, this protective function may contribute to its viability, at least in the absence of alternative relations providing similar functions.

Lazarus and Folkman (1984) correctly point out that when social support is viewed as a resource available in the social environment, we need to focus on cultivating and using it. Most of all, this means communicating effectively. In this chapter, therefore, we focus on the communication process as a vital part of stress coping. You will note that attention is given to both giving and receiving.

At the outset, you are invited to complete a personal assessment of current social support in your own life in Exercises 11-1, 11-2, and 11-3.

BOX 11-1. SOCIAL SUPPORT AND SELF-TALK

An undergraduate student in my Human Stress class wrote the following, used here with her permission.

> This past week has been a bit of a stressful and depressing week for me. On Monday, I found out about a problem I have that is somewhat personal. I was depressed and gloomy all day. I went from class to class, not really paying attention to the instructors and not talking to anyone else in class. I moped around all day basically feeling sorry for myself.
>
> Once I got home, I did not say much to my roommates, ate dinner and then went to my room. I could not concentrate on anything and felt very worn out. Around 6:30 I laid down and didn't awake until 8:30. I still felt empty inside, lonely and depressed. The nap obviously didn't cure my gloominess.
>
> Well, I then ventured out of my room and began talking to one of my roommates. I hadn't told anyone of my problem yet and wasn't sure if I wanted to or not. Well, sooner than I thought, I was babbling the whole story to my roommate. She sat and listened and was very sincere through the whole conversation.

Towards the end, she looked at me and said, "Really, Judy (not real name), it's no big deal. I've had the same problem before and it's really nothing to worry about. It could be worse, you know."

When she said that, the comment we use in class all the time—"Is this truly worth getting upset about?"—hit me, and I realized I was blowing this whole ordeal out of proportion. I suddenly felt a huge burden lifted off my back, and I knew this was something minor that I will get over. In time it shall pass, just like most other problems.

I learned basically that confiding in others helps a great deal with many of our problems. Often these problems are ones that others can hopefully help you with or make you understand that it's not so bad. I also realized that the sayings you give us do have a tremendous amount of relevance to our everyday lives.

EXERCISE 11-1. REVIEW OF SOCIAL SUPPORT NETWORK

You are invited to answer the following, either in writing or in discussion.
Daily Social Support

1. The person(s) I count on for day-to-day support includes:
2. Agree or disagree? For the most part, my current social support network is quite sufficient for meeting my day-to- day needs. Explain.
3. I wish the following were different in terms of my day-to-day social support network:
4. Steps I will take to make this happen include:

Social Support During Stressful Times

1. When I am going through a difficult period, those I call on for support include:
2. Agree or disagree? For the most part, my current social support network is quite adequate during periods of high stress. Explain.
3. I wish the following were different in terms of my social support network during my periods of personal difficulty:
4. Steps I will take to make this happen include:

EXERCISE 11-2. GIVING SUPPORT TO OTHERS

Daily Social Support

1. Those to whom I give support on a daily basis include:
2. Agree or disagree? I am quite satisfied with the amount and quality of support I give to others on a daily basis. Explain.
3. I wish the following were different in terms of my giving of support to others on a daily basis:
4. Steps I will take to make this happen include:

Social Support During Stressful Times

1. Those to whom I give support during their stressful times include:

2. Agree or disagree? I am quite satisfied with the amount and quality of support I give to others during their stressful periods. Explain.

3. I wish the following were different in terms of my giving of support to others during their stressful times:

4. Steps I will take to make this happen include:

EXERCISE 11-3. ASSESSING YOUR SOCIAL SUPPORT GROUPS

List groups to which you belong under the appropriate column.

	Do Not Belong	Belong, Not an Important Social Support for Me	Belong, an Important Source of Support for Me
An informal group of co-workers	———	———	———
A formal co-worker group, for example, a weekly luncheon group, a monthly management organization, an executive club, and the like	———	———	———
A sports or hobby group, for example, a singing group, a square dance club, a racquetball club, and the like	———	———	———
One's own large, kinship family (there are still some around)	———	———	———
An activity group, for example, a weekly discussion, book reading, play reading, and the like	———	———	———
Service group (Kiwanis, Rotary, and so on, and especially small informal satellite shoot-offs from these large groups)	———	———	———
Extended families (artificial, intentional families developed in churches, community organizations, and so on)	———	———	———

Racial, ethnic, and nationality
groups (associations, clubs, and so
on)
Vocational groups (organized and
formal)
Church and other community
groups
Strictly social groups; for example,
singles' clubs, men's groups,
women's consciousness raising
groups, and the like

SOURCE: Greenberg (1980, 143).

BOX 11-2. PETS AS SOCIAL SUPPORTS

It has long been known by owners of cats, dogs, horses, and other domesticated animals, that pets can be a meaningful personal anchorage. Recently, researchers have begun to study whether pets might also enhance health—and perhaps even extend life. Their findings are indeed noteworthy. Consider the following:

A British psychologist found a significant increase in health and morale among research subjects who received a parakeet (Ferguson, 1984).

When children between the ages of nine and 16 were asked to read aloud, blood pressures invariably went up. However, when a dog was present in the room, blood pressures did not rise as much (Lynch, 1985).

A group of college students had their blood pressure monitored while interacting with a dog tactually, verbally, and visually (Vormbrock and Grossberg, 1988). Subjects' blood pressures were lowest during dog petting, higher while talking to the dog, and highest while talking to the experimenter.

When a group of adults communicated in a laboratory with the human experimenter, blood pressures went up. When communicating with their pets, however, blood pressures remained the same or actually decreased (Lynch, 1985).

Among 92 heart patients discharged from the University of Maryland's coronary-care unit, six percent of pet owners died during the next year, compared with a death rate of 28 percent of non-pet owners—a four and one-half times higher risk to non-pet owners (Friedman, 1980).

Clearly, pets serve as a meaningful personal anchorage and apparently can not only aid in improving the quality of life but even length of life.
Consider the following questions:

> **1.**   What are the implications of the above research findings for you?
>
> **2.**   What are the implications for your present or future childrearing?
>
> **3.**   Do you know of older adults without pets who might benefit from one's presence?

THE CHALLENGE OF BUILDING AND USING SOCIAL SUPPORT   ▼

Lazarus and Folkman note that, "The basic assumption underlying the current interest in social support is that, other things being equal, people will have better morale and health, and function better, if they receive or believe they will receive social support when it is needed" (1984, 250). As Caplan states, "significant others help an individual mobilize his psychological resources and master his emotional burdens; they share his tasks, and they provide him with extra supplies of money, materials, tools, skills and cognitive guidance to improve his handling of the situation" (Caplan, 1974, 6). Thus, building social networks and drawing on social support becomes an important part of the process of coping. In cultivating networks and supports, of course, one must be mindful of giving as well as receiving. And as one learns early in life, giving is the key to receiving. The more you provide support, the more you have available for yourself when needed.

Lazarus and Folkman correctly point out that when social support is viewed as a resource available in the social environment, we need to focus on cultivating and using it. Most of all, this means communicating effectively. In this chapter, therefore, we focus on the communication process as a vital part of stress coping. You will note that attention is given to both giving and receiving.

Entire books have been written, of course, on communication skills for minimizing stress for self and others. Here we can touch only on a few key facets of the communication process. We begin with Virginia Satir's ideas about communication and wellbeing.

SATIR'S MODEL OF COMMUNICATION

According to psychologist and family therapist Virginia Satir, communication ". . . is the giving and receiving of meaning between any two people" (Satir, 1976, pages unnumbered). Key questions about the communication process are these:

What meaning is made? How is it given?

How is it received?

What happens to each person as a result and what happens to the relationship?

The main point to communication, for Satir, is to enhance self-esteem of self and others. Effective communication also needs to promote the Five Freedoms (Satir, 1976):

The freedom to see and hear what is here instead of what should be, was, or will be.

The freedom to say what one feels and thinks instead of what one should.

The freedom to feel what one feels instead of what one ought.

The freedom to ask for what one wants instead of always waiting for permission.

The freedom to take risks in one's own behalf instead of choosing to be only "secure" and not rocking the boat.

According to Satir (1976) a key to good communication is **congruence** within yourself.

The power in congruence comes through the connectedness of your words matching your feelings, your body and facial expressions matching your words, and your actions fitting all. You come from a state of strength because all of your parts have flow with other parts. You are not blocking anything off.

You can easily be believed. Your energy goes to developing trust. You do not cause suspicion. You can be easily understood because you are clear. Other persons feel given to.

You feel open can therefore feel excitement instead of fear.

You can live the Five Freedoms.

You know that you can choose, that you have many choices you can make.

Satir contends that true communication can be attained by:

Inviting someone to make contact with you. The message is, "I want to communicate with you. Are you available?"

Arranging yourself physically so as to make contact. This means making eye contact and using affable body language.

Being prepared to take risks in conveying authentic thoughts and feelings.

Making your statement begin with "I." For example, state, "I am upset," rather than "You upset me."

Asking questions for elaboration or clarification. Questions can be intimidating or stimulating; put-downs or affirmations of interest.

Thinking of interpersonal difficulties as opportunities rather than as threats.

Satir points out that "Communication is to relationship what breathing is to maintaining life . . ." (Satir, 1976). She further notes four ways of communicating often used by people with low self-esteem— "those who have not yet learned to live their Five Freedoms." These communication styles can negatively affect physical health. Moreover, "they box in relationships so they become destructive, dead, distant, and frustrating." They limit a person's potential for personal growth and for developing cooperative, satisfying relationships. They promote fear and dependence.

These four styles are (Satir, 1988):

Placating: talking in an ingratiating way; never disagreeing, no matter what; constantly apologizing.

Blaming: fault-finding; dictating; acting superior; putting fault on others.

Computing: being very correct, very reasonable with no semblance of feeling; acting calm, cool, and collected.

Distracting: doing or saying whatever is irrelevant to what others are doing or saying; not responding to the point.

Satir points out that these styles of responding do more than interfere with open and honest communication. They also reinforce the person's feeling of low self-esteem.

COMMUNICATION GUIDELINES FOR DIRECT, HONEST COMMUNICATION

Below are a number of guidelines for direct, honest communication. They can be useful for making all your face-to-face relationships rich and supportive for you and others. They are adapted from Egan's book, *You and Me* (1977), and from Rossiter's *The Human Potential* (1984).

1.   **Own your feelings and thoughts.** Practice speaking in the first person rather than generally. For example, say "I would like to see a movie tonight," instead of "I hear there are some good movies in town."

2.   **Address the other person directly.** Look at the person for whom your remarks are intended and speak to him or her directly. If you are communicating in a group setting, communicate directly to the person you intend to receive your remarks, rather than abstractly to the group as a whole.

3.   **Make statements rather than ask questions** if you have a point to make. Instead of asking, "Thai menus are usually pretty good, aren't they?", say, "I really would like a Thai dinner tonight. Let's go."

4.   **Don't sandbag your negative feelings.** This probably is the most common source of relationship-induced distress. When feelings of frustration, resentment, or hurt accumulate, they block energy, cloud one's thinking, and turn into bound physical energy—that is, tension. This is probably the greatest single

source of stress-related illness. Unexpressed negative feelings also increase chances of blow-ups. In expressing these feelings, be sure to use "I" messages rather than "You" messages. "I feel hurt by what you said," rather than "You make me so mad when you act like that."

5.   When giving feedback, describe the effects of the other's actions rather than be accusatory. This way, you communicate your awareness of your own experience and avoid putting the other person on the defensive. Say, "When you talk to me that way, it makes me feel discounted and not appreciated," rather than "You said that just to put me down."

6.   Be generous in giving positive feedback to others. It is easy to move through our days with many unexpressed positive feelings and thoughts. Expressing a few more of these can make a real difference in the quality of others' lives— and in how people respond to you. Give a lot, you will get a lot.

7.   Practice active listening. Genuine listening is one of the most meaningful gifts you can give to others. It feels wonderful to be with someone who expresses interest and caring about you by attending to what you are saying, asking followup questions, and giving honest feedback. The returns to you will far outweigh the effort. Someone said there are two kinds of listeners: those who genuinely listen and those who wait their turn to speak. Try being a good listener. See the section below on Active Listening.

8.   Speak only for yourself and not for others. Husbands and wives, for example, often fall gradually into the habit of speaking for each other. If someone addresses a question to your spouse (or friend or lover), don't interrupt and answer yourself instead. Respect your partner by allowing him or her to respond. Speak directly and honestly for yourself—and give others the opportunity to do the same.

EXERCISE 11-4. ASSESSING AND APPLYING COMMUNICATION GUIDELINES

1.   For each of the eight communication guidelines, assess how often you currently practice each one, using the following:

    I do this MOST OF THE TIME
    I do this SOMETIMES
    I do this SELDOM

2.   The guidelines I would most like to apply more in my life are:
3.   The specific actions I will take to apply these include:

Part of congruence, Satir writes, is honest disclosure of inner thoughts and feelings, the topic to which we now turn.

SELF-DISCLOSURE

> *Bill R. has trouble making friends. His acquaintances all like him, but no one knows what he is really like.*
>
> *Dorothy W. also has no close friends. Unlike Bill, however, she is not reluctant to let others know what she is feeling or what her problems are. In fact, she reveals personal things to almost everyone. People regard her as somewhat strange.*
>
> *Terry is contemplating a divorce from her husband Ken. She now realizes that she has never really known him. For five years, she has lived with him, cooked and cleaned for him, and slept with him. In all that time, they have talked only about day-to-day concerns: what was for dinner, their week-end plans, and so forth. What is he really like? What were his hopes, dreams, and fears? She really doesn't know. (Derlaga and Chaikin, 1975, 1).*

Self-disclosure, the process of revealing authentic, personal thoughts and feelings to others, is to allow oneself to be seen, known, understood. Self-disclosure entails risk. Normally it is worth risk taking. Yet discretion is needed, as illustrated by Dorothy's experience above.

Self-disclosure helps build the type of relationships that can be vital, not only for ongoing emotional health, but especially in times of difficulty. Self-disclosure can promote helpful, supportive relationships. When used inappropriately, it can increase, rather than reduce, distress. (Tavris notes (1974, 71):

> Self-disclosure occurs through the content of words (revealing or protective), the tone and quality of words spoken (harsh or warm), non-verbal behavior (eye contact, distance from listener, gestures, and facial expressions), and actions taken (reflecting deep love, vulnerability, or animosity, for example). Self-disclosure can take place in breadth (sharing a great deal of information about yourself, but nothing in much detail) or in depth (sharing intimate, deeply personal emotions).

One book on self-disclosure refers to "the lonely society" to describe the fact that with urbanization, mobility, and the fast pace of life in most modern societies, self-disclosure becomes more difficult, indeed even risky (Derlaga and Chaikin, 1975). Familiarity does not necessarily mean closeness. This is reflected in experiences with "familiar strangers," as described by the social psychologist, Stanley Milgram.

> For years, I have taken a commuter train to work. I noticed that there were people at my station whom I have seen for many years but never spoken to, people I came to think of as familiar strangers. I found a peculiar tension in this situation, when people treat each other as properties of the environment, rather than as individuals to deal with. It happens frequently. Yet there remains a poignancy and discomfort, particularly when there are only two of you at the station; you and someone you have seen daily but never met. A barrier has developed that is not readily broken.

The "familiar stranger" phenomenon, indeed the absence of self-disclosure in general, is partly the result of a necessary decision to "screen out" most people we meet. We simply cannot give time and energy to be open in a personal way with the dozens or hundreds of people we meet each day. We would be overwhelmed.

Nor is full openness even in everyone's best interest all the time. "Plungers," who too quickly and too completely reveal themselves, often are scorned and avoided. So, too, are those who perpetually engage in "ego-speak"—the boosting of one's ego by speaking only about what we want to talk about. . . . According to Derlago and Chalkin (1975), "Ego-speak is mental masturbation."

Solitude can be golden at times. Insulating yourself from the opportunity to participate in self-disclosure sometimes is healthy and productive. According to Tillich, the theologian, solitude "is the experience of being alone, but not lonely." Henry David Thoreau (1946) once said, "I never found a companion that was so companionable as solitude."

Full self-disclosure is inadvisable in certain circumstances.

▼ When you clearly would be rebuked or hurt

▼ When revealing a thought, feeling, or intention would result in harmful reactions toward you

▼ When the situation clearly calls for completion of a task rather than sharing of feelings

▼ When the other person clearly is disinterested

▼ When a feeling or thought is best reserved for intimate partners

You probably can identify other situations in which concealment to some degree is appropriate.

On the other hand, a number of benefits often flow from self-disclosure.

▼ Expressing inner thoughts and feelings promotes self-awareness and self-understanding. By putting thoughts and feelings into words, they become clear to the sender.

▼ Communication becomes more complete. Intentions, background information, and associated emotions are better known.

▼ Emotional pressure is avoided or reduced, reducing chance of stress build-up.

▼ Expressing emotions promotes physical health. Unexpressed emotions block energy, get stuck in muscles and joints, help cause high blood pressure and other illnesses, perhaps even shorten the span of life.

▼ Expressing authentic feelings and thoughts puts the other person at ease, reducing his or her tension.

▼ The possibility of later depth, warmth, and honesty in a relationship increases.

▼ You open yourself to caring, verbal and action responses.

▼ You increase the chances of creative problem-solving, both by you and with others.

▼ You promote expansion of your feelings, ideas, abilities.

In his lifelong study of self-actualizing persons, Abraham Maslow found that every individual he studied was fully open and disclosing to at least one or two other persons. Maslow concluded that the inability to be honest and revealing to at least a few others blocks growth and prevents fulfillment of potential. He recommends "when in doubt, be honest rather than not" (Maslow, 1971, 45).

A consistent research finding is that "self-disclosure begets self-disclosure" (Derlaga & Chaikin, 1975, 38). Openness by A tends to elicit openness by B. On the other hand, a distant communication brings the same thing back. Thus, an important step to bring down unnecessary barriers both for you and for those you interact with is to be open whenever appropriate and possible. You thereby promote your own well-being and that of others around you—and you help build a social climate of support, forthrightness, mutual honesty, and authenticity.

EXERCISE 11-5. ASSESSING SELF-DISCLOSURE

_____ **1.** I seldom share my true feelings with anyone.

_____ **2.** Those with whom I work (or go to school) know little about what I'm thinking most of the time.

_____ **3.** I usually feel better after expressing myself to someone I'm close to.

_____ **4.** I wish I could get closer to others.

_____ **5.** I wish I could open up more to others.

_____ **6.** I would like to be more open to others and their feelings.

_____ **7.** Being open with others usually ends up hurting me.

_____ **8.** Others see me as quite honest and open.

_____ **9.** My physical tension usually mounts when I hold in my feelings for very long.

_____ **10.** My sleep is often disturbed by unexpressed bad feelings.

What can you learn from your answers?

EXERCISE 11-6. RISKING SELF-DISCLOSURE

During the next two days, take the following risks:

Express inner feelings to someone new.
Invite the same from someone new.

1. What happened?
2. What did you and the other person feel?

3.   What steps can you take to be more self-disclosing in the future? Through what specific actions of listening or speaking?

ACTIVE LISTENING

Listening effectively is a basic ingredient in any effort to cope constructively with others. Any exchange between two or more people contains four basic elements.

▼ Sender

▼ Message

▼ Feelings

▼ Receiver

Active listening is a simple skill that is too seldom practiced. When used correctly, it can do wonders to assure that these four elements are in harmony. Clear and crisp exchanges of information and positive feelings between sender and receiver then are possible. Task accomplishment also benefits.

Let us assume the following message at 4:00 P.M. one day:

11-year-old boy to mother: "I'm sick of school."

At this point, mother can respond in any number of ways.

Mother to boy:

"You are tired from staying up too late watching T.V. last night." (Psychologizing)

"Are you saying you don't believe learning is good for you?" (Questioning)

"No you're not." (Denying)

"Oh, you are always complaining." (Discounting)

"I can tell. I know school is a drag." (Sympathizing)

"You know I have to send you to school every day. The law says so." (Defending)

"You have no business feeling that way. You are only a sixth grader and will have to stay in school at least six more years." (Judging)

"You must get to bed earlier, get your homework done on time and take a better attitude towards school. Then you will like it. No more of this." (Ordering)

"Sounds like you're sick of school." (Parroting)

"Let me tell you about one time I was sick of school when I was nine years old, blah, blah, blah." (Flipping to own story)

These are common, but defective responses. The boy is likely to feel no better. In fact, he probably will go away feeling unheard, put-down, intimidated, judged, belittled, attacked, and/or misunderstood.

Alternative responses, each an example of active listening, might be:

Mother to boy:

"You seem pretty discouraged about school today."

"You sound pretty tired today."

"You sound really pooped."

"You appear really down on school."

Any of these responses is likely to set in motion a fruitful exchange for the following reasons.

▼ The initial sender, the son, feels he is being truly heard.

▼ He will feel he is worthwhile because he is heard.

▼ The receiver, mother, checks out the accuracy of what she thinks she has heard. She invites him to say more, lowering his stress level by letting off steam and further reinforcing his sense of worth.

▼ She withholds her feelings, at least until she is clear what he is saying.

▼ He is given the chance to search for solutions himself, thereby promoting his own responsibility for his actions.

▼ Warmth and understanding are promoted between mother and son.

▼ The basic format for active listening is simple:

▼ You sound _____ about _____.

The words cannot be mechanical or stilted, of course, but must flow naturally within the context of the person's own vocabulary and communication style.

The active listener is non-critical and non-controlling, at least in the early stages of the exchange. Sometimes it is appropriate, of course, to respond with an order, command or judgment—but usually only after the sender has been fully heard. In most common daily interchanges at work and home, active listening is entirely appropriate and beneficial. Chances are reduced that sender or receiver will unnecessarily build up tension or resentment.

In short, active listening includes the following.

Showing attentiveness

Clarifying content of sender's spoken message

Verifying non-verbal messages

Inviting more information and expression of feelings

Providing a genuine personal response

Promoting joint problem-solving or problem-solving by the sender alone

Active listening is useful because it promotes the following.

Accuracy of communication

Warmth and acceptance between sender and receiver

Self-worth of the sender

Elaboration of content

Full expression of feelings

Equality

Openness

Faith in sender's ability to solve problems

The most important features of active listening can be summarized in three simple do's and three simple don'ts:

Do's

Do be and appear attentive.

Do ask follow-up questions.

Do rephrase what you have heard.

Don'ts

Don't interrupt

Don't give immediate judgments or solutions.

Don't divert the conversation to yourself.

Active listening, then, is a vitally important skill for minimizing distress for both self and others.

BOX 11-3. LISTENING TIPS

Today's Supervisor notes that 80 percent of the typical workday is spent communicating with others. Of that time, nearly half is spent listening. Yet the typical person remembers only a quarter to half of what was heard. Viewed this way, poor listening is very expensive because of lost information and damaged relationships.

Today's Supervisor has identified some of the most common and harmful habits associated with poor listening.

FAKING: Putting on a good show of listening by nodding and giving verbal cues, but not listening at all.

INTERRUPTING: Breaking in while the other is talking.

DOMINATING: Waiting your turn to talk, gathering your thoughts together, then cutting others short.

CORRECTING: Lying in wait for factual errors, then immediately correcting these errors in the other's remarks.

CRITICIZING: Rather than listening, passing judgment on the other person while he or she is talking—her voice, mannerisms, appearance, point of view, attitude.

On the positive side, *Today's Supervisor* suggests several simple methods for better listening:

▼ STOP TALKING

▼ FOCUS YOUR ATTENTION AND ACTIONS

▼ NOTICE HOW THINGS ARE SAID

▼ NOTICE WHAT ISN'T SAID

▼ STOP FOR "CLARITY CHECKS"

SOURCE: *Today's Supervisor* (1989, 12)

EXERCISE 11-7. ACTIVE LISTENING: WRITING OR DISCUSSION EXERCISE

Provide an active listening alternative to each of the following responses. You may work on them orally or write them down.

Sender: "I don't have time for this nonsense."
Listener: "You sure as –ell do. Do it." (Ordering)
Active Listener:

Sender: "Why doesn't anyone ever take me seriously around here?"
Listener: "Poor John, no one ever listens to you." (Discounting)
Active Listener:

Sender: "I'll show those bums."
Listener: "You have no business talking like that." (Judging)
Active Listener:

Sender: "Nothing ever works around here."
Listener: "Oh, come on, you are just tired and hot tonight." (Psychologizing)
Active Listener:

Sender: "The administration of this place has no understanding of our problems."
Listener: "What business do you have talking like that?" (Judging)
Active Listener:

Sender: "I'm going to jump off the bridge, for sure."
Listener: "Poor John—feeling sorry for yourself again." (Discounting)
Active Listener:

Sender: "This workload is overwhelming."
Listener: "I know you've been putting in long hours." (Supporting)
Active Listener:

Sender: "I'm so angry, I could scream."
Listener: "What do you mean? I did the best I could." (Defending)
Active Listener:

Sender: "I'm convinced I'm going to keep everything to myself from now on. You can't trust anyone around here."
Listener: "You sound like you can't trust anyone around here." (Parroting)
Active Listener:

EXERCISE 11-8. ROLE-PLAYING ACTIVE LISTENING

With a cooperative partner, role-play several exchanges using active listening. Extend the number of communications beyond one or two until you get the full feeling of active listening throughout the conversation.

EXERCISE 11-9. ACTIVE LISTENING IN REAL LIFE

Deliberately try active listening in at least two situations today. Observe the consequences for you and your communication partner. What words best describe what happened? What was the result?

GIVING AND GETTING NEGATIVE FEEDBACK

Among the most volatile interchanges between one person and another is giving and receiving negative feedback. If bungled, stress created by the original unhappiness is multiplied many times. Thus, an ensuing stress build-up mounts for both.

Assume you are under a time deadline at work. The deadline is tomorrow at noon, when you and your work team must turn in a report to management. Also assume that at 3:00 P.M. a member of the team has just produced a rather deficient segment that clearly needs more work and will require you as a team leader to stay up late tonight and revise it. You are quite angry and disappointed. This is not the first time he has come up short. Your patience is wearing thin. How can you best give negative feedback? You want to accomplish several things through this feedback: Make known your own disappointment and frustration and let him know specifically what is deficient; let him know what the consequences may be for him, the team, and you; and indicate that in the future his performance must improve in specific ways (Steinmetz, 1980, 81).

Here is an approach for the above situation developed by Steinmetz (1980) both for you as boss in giving the negative feedback and for your subordinate in receiving it.

1. Describe the situation and the deficiencies in specific and objective terms. Limit your remarks to the present, excluding, for now, the past. Give only what is directly useful and avoid overloading the recipient with unnecessary details or irrelevant points. Avoid sarcasm. Remain objective in order to minimize chances of defensiveness by the recipient. For example, "You had time available to work on this. We badly need it. It does not include these specific bits of information, which are vital to the overall report. Further, it is not written clearly."

2. Express your own feelings, using "I feel" messages. Share these feelings, rather than denying them. Avoid put-downs, attacks, or accusations. For example, "I feel disappointed and frustrated."

3. Give the recipient a chance to respond here. If he or she agrees, you need not proceed further. An interchange with active listening both ways can be very productive.

4. Specify changes you want in specific terms. Be objective and firm. For example, "I will want such and such data by 6:00 this evening though it may require staying overtime. Then I want to meet you at 8:00 A.M. to go over what I have rewritten tonight."

5. Avoid being demanding, authoritarian, or patronizing. Simply be firm. "In the future, I would like you to ask if you are unclear about what is needed and to do a complete, thorough job."

6. Share your perception of the possible or likely outcome of the changes you request. Use positive terms, avoiding "you had better do it, or else" remarks. A threat of punishment muddies the waters. For example, "If you do, we all can be proud of our work, have better feelings as a team, and help out management."

A four-step format also applies in receiving negative feedback. Your goal is to focus objectively on the message being sent in order to remedy the situation through effective individual or joint problem-solving.

1. Describe the situation as you perceive it in objective and specific language.

2. Express your perception of the other person's feelings.

3. State in your own words the changes you think he or she wants.

4. State your perception of the likely consequences of the changes objectively, candidly, and specifically.

These formats must be adapted, of course, to specific people and situations. They can be effective for minimizing further negative feelings and for getting the job done well. The more these techniques are practiced and used, the easier and more natural they become.

EXERCISE 11-10. GIVING NEGATIVE FEEDBACK

Think of a situation in which you gave (or wish you had given) negative feedback. Using the above format, write what you might have said in your stress diary.

EXERCISE 11-11. RECEIVING NEGATIVE FEEDBACK

Now think of a situation in which you were given negative feedback. How might you have responded differently using this format? Write your answers.

BOX 11-4. DO'S AND DON'TS OF GIVING AND TAKING CRITICISM

GIVING IT

DO'S	DON'TS
1. Know the facts	1. Attack the person.
2. Pinpoint specific behavior.	2. Criticize past behavior without linking to desired future behavior
3. Criticize in order to change future attitude or behavior.	3. Overgeneralize
4. Be sure criticism is understood.	4. Dump your own frustration or anger through criticism.
5. Show empathy—how would you take it?	5. Criticize without having facts.
6. Think before speaking—organize facts and approach.	6. Criticize and run.

7. Criticize only if change is possible.

8. Use good timing—other's mood, your mood, context.

9. Maintain calm in your body.

7. Criticize, then punish through silence.

8. Publicly humiliate.

9. Heap on too much at one time.

TAKING IT

DO'S	DON'TS
1. Take criticism as opportunity rather than threat.	1. Overgeneralize by taking criticism as negative reflection on your total performance or your character.
2. Be thick-skinned.	
3. Listen attentively.	2. Allow defensiveness to prevent accurate listening.
4. Understand fully.	3. Believe you must always defend yourself.
5. Ask for more information.	
6. Watch for repeated patterns.	4. Be thin-skinned.
7. Look for grain of truth.	5. Automatically discount criticism
8. Acknowledge grain of truth.	6. Attack back.
9. Assess the source.	
10. Relax—use a Six-Second Quieting Response.	
11. Repeat back what you are hearing.	

EXERCISE 11-12. ROLE-PLAYING NEGATIVE FEEDBACK

With a cooperative partner, role-play the above steps, alternating between giving and receiving negative feedback.

EXERCISE 11-13. REAL LIFE PRACTICE IN NEGATIVE FEEDBACK

Try the four steps described above for giving and receiving negative feedback in a real-life situation. Then answer the following.

1. Did the exchange accomplish what you had hoped?
2. What were the consequences for you? For your partner? For accomplishment of tasks? For others in the environment? Distinguish between immediate and longer-term effects.

3.   What might you do or say differently next time?

4.   What did you learn about yourself by using this format?

ASSERTIVENESS

Our framework of stress and stress management assumes that a stressor is perceived and appraised by the individual. Throughout this chapter, we have focused on constructive options for coping with people-stressors, active listening, appropriate self-disclosure, dealing with angry feelings, giving and receiving negative feedback. Another useful approach to coping effectively (that is, responding so you get what you want but not at others' expense) is assertiveness.

TABLE 11-2. PASSIVE–ASSERTIVE–AGGRESSIVE TYPES

PASSIVE	ASSERTIVE	AGGRESSIVE
This person is:	This person is:	This person is:
Shy	Usually more extroverted	Somewhat hostile
Withdrawing		
Reluctant to assert rights and privileges	Aware of rights and privileges and uses them constructively	A vehement defender of own rights yet often violates or usurps the rights of others
		Unmindful of where own rights end and the violation of where other's begin
Socially inhibited	Socially productive	Socially destructive

SOURCE: Girdano and Everly (1979, 148).

EXERCISE 11-14. ASSERTIVENESS SELF-ASSESSMENT

Read the above table carefully. Underline the items that describe you. Do you tend toward passivity, assertiveness, or aggressiveness? How does your behavior vary, if at all, at home, work, school, and social events?

Generally, assertiveness is desirable behavior for reducing tension in situations where there is potential build-up of resentment or anger, or when strength must be used to get what you want or to prevent someone else from imposing upon you unnecessarily. Yet we must retain choice and option. Aggressiveness is seldom called for, except perhaps in situations of physical attack or danger. Passive behavior sometimes is appropriate. Certainly, *temporary,* timely passivity represents simple good judgment in certain circumstances. Being quiet sometimes is best. Assertive behavior must be exercised with discretion and perceptiveness.

What are the specific characteristics of assertiveness? Steinmetz (1980) suggests the following.

1.   Eye contact: Steady, eye-to-eye contact while speaking. Not staring or glaring, but firm and unyielding.

2. Hand gestures: Use strong gestures to emphasize important points. Loses effectiveness if overdone.
3. Posture: Standing or sitting tall and straight, rather than slouching, slumping, or hiding.
4. Voice firmness: Maintaining a steady, firm volume, tone, and pace throughout, without imposing too much volume. Avoid yelling as well as weak trail-offs through drop of volume or "you-knows."
5. "I" statements: Just as with expressing disappointment, assertiveness calls for such openers as, "I feel," "I want," "I need," "I would appreciate." "I request." By contrast, the passive opener is "Don't you think that," while a common agressive opener is "You should." "I" statements imply responsibility for what you are feeling and requesting.
6. Short sentences: These are clearly understood and imply firmness. Avoid long, rambling sentences that lose the listener and the potential impact of your message.
7. Pauses for feedback; Strategic breaks can both underscore what has just been said and provide an opportunity for clarifying a response.

EXERCISE 11-15. POSITIVE SELF-TALK FOR ASSERTIVENESS

Try some of the following self-talk statements before, during, and after encounters requiring assertiveness. Be an experiment-of-one. Find which ones work for you (Butler, 1981).

Preparing for self-assertion
No negative statements. I'm just going to express my feelings.
My purpose here is not to be liked and approved of by everyone.
It isn't awful to make a mistake.
I'll express my feelings. If I'm honest and direct, then I've been assertive.
I'm not going to apologize for where I am now.
Stop catastrophizing. I'm doing them a favor by letting them know what I feel.

Handling an assertive encounter
I'll go at my own rate. I can back up if I'm feeling overwhelmed.
I have a perfect right to express my feelings.
Everyone doesn't have to agree with me for me to be OK.
It's OK to feel nervous. That's part of entering new territory.
There is no perfect way of saying this.
I can not think of something to say if I just express my feelings.
If my mind goes blank, it's OK to say, "My mind has just gone blank."

Giving yourself credit
I'm really glad that I was honest.
I'm really pleased. That was hard for me to say.
I'm still feeling a little shaky, but I did it. I deserve a lot of credit.
I was terrific.
Hey, the roof didn't fall in. I'm getting better every time.
They didn't respond as I would have liked, but that's not important. The important thing is that I asserted myself.

EXERCISE 11-16. SELF-MONITORING ASSERTIVENESS DURING NEXT 24 HOURS

Watch yourself for the next 24 hours. Enter in your stress diary what you observe about the fit between your overall pattern of behavior and the three described here. Also observe the degree to which you display each of the seven assertiveness behaviors just described.

EXERCISE 11-17. OBSERVING OTHERS' ASSERTIVENESS

Repeat Exercise 11-15 with someone you know well. What do you see?

EXERCISE 11-18. RECALL QUIZ

1. In your own words, what is assertiveness? Passivity? Aggressiveness?
2. What are the seven behaviors associated with assertiveness?

EXERCISE 11-19. ROLE-PLAYING ASSERTIVENESS

Try role-playing more assertive behavior with a cooperative, safe partner. Create hypothetical, recalled, or anticipated situations. Switch parts.

EXERCISE 11-20. ASSERTIVENESS IN REAL LIFE

Now try to be more assertive in a real-life situation where it is timely and appropriate.

1. What did you feel?
2. How successful were you in doing what you wanted to do?
3. In getting what you wanted?
4. What were the consequences for self? Others?
5. What would you do differently next time a similar opportunity arises?

COMMUNICATION STYLE AND STRESS

In Chapter 1 we noted that many people are distress provokers, sometimes intentionally and with full awareness, other times quite unintentionally. In this chapter, we have reviewed a number of means whereby you can keep your stress at a reasonable level without causing undue distress for others and while getting what you want.

Viewing your communication as a whole, do you give a preponderance of positive strokes (communication messages that add to others' self-worth or reduce tension) or negative strokes (acts that add to stress and lessen self-worth, comfort, and emotional well-being)? Of course, the communication process is never clearly one way or the other, but rather a mixture of the two. Most of us are somewhat in the middle. Yet the following principles generally are valid.

Positive strokes prevent and reduce distress for others, and, through a loop-back effect, for self.

Negative strokes cause or add to distress for others, and, through the same loop-back effect, for self.

Karl Albrecht, in *Stress and the Manager* (1979, 265), has presented a list of positive and negative behaviors. We will re-label them "distress-provoking" and "stress-reducing."

Distress-Provoking (punishing) actions include:

Monopolizing the conversation

Interrupting

Showing obvious disinterest

Keeping a sour facial expression

Withholding customary social cues such as greetings, nods, "uh-huh," and the like

Throwing verbal barbs at others

Using nonverbal put-downs

Insulting or otherwise verbally abusing others

Speaking dogmatically; not respecting others' opinions

Complaining or whining excessively

Criticizing excessively; fault finding

Demanding one's own way; refusing to negotiate or compromise.

Ridiculing others

Patronizing or talking down to others

Making others feel guilty

Soliciting approval from others excessively

Losing one's temper frequently and easily

Playing "games" with people; manipulating or competing in subtle ways

Throwing "gotcha's" at others; embarrassing or belittling others

Telling lies; evading honest questions; refusing to level with others

Overusing "should" language; pushing others with words

Displaying frustration frequently

Making aggressive demands on others

Diverting conversation capriciously; breaking others' train of thought

Disagreeing routinely

Restating others' ideas for them

Asking loaded or accusing questions

Overusing "why" questions

Breaking confidences; failing to keep important promises

Flattering others insincerely

Joking at inappropriate times

Bragging; showing off; talking only about self

Stress-Reducing (rewarding) behaviors include:

Giving others a chance to express views or share information

Listening attentively; hearing other person out

Sharing oneself with others; smiling; greeting others

Giving positive nonverbal messages of acceptance and respect for others

Praising and complimenting others sincerely

Expressing respect for values and opinions of others

Giving suggestions constructively

Compromising; negotiating; helping others succeed

Talking positively and constructively

Affirming feelings and needs of others

Treating others as equals whenever possible

Stating one's needs and desires honestly

Delaying automatic reactions; not flying off the handle easily

Leveling with others; sharing information and opinions openly and honestly

Confronting others constructively on difficult issues

Staying on the conversational topic until others have been heard

Stating agreement with others when possible

Questioning others openly and honestly; asking straightforward, non-loaded questions

Keeping the confidences of others

Giving one's word sparingly and keeping it

Joking constructively and in good humor

Expressing genuine interest in the other person

EXERCISE 11-21. MONITORING YOUR COMMUNICATION STYLE

1. Check those items that apply to you most of the time.
2. Ask someone close to you to check which items apply to you most of the time.
3. Which communication actions would you like to decrease in the future? Increase?
4. Ask someone close to you which ones he or she would like you to increase or decrease.
5. If he or she is willing, tell that person what you would like him or her to increase or decrease for the sake of your stress level.

In the next chapter, we will focus on social support, an important resource for building resistance against distress from time, change, and other sources.

In the next chapter, you will read about coping styles— dealing effectively with stressful events and with temporary distress.

REFERENCES ▼

Albrecht, K. (1979). *Stress and The Manager.* Englewood Cliffs, NJ: Prentice-Hall, Inc.

Antonovsky, A. (1979). *Health, Stress and Coping.* San Francisco: Jossey-Bass Publishers.

Antonovsky, A. (1987). *Unravelling The Mystery of Health: How People Manage Stress and Stay Well.* San Francisco: Jossey-Bass Publishers.

Berkman, L., & Syme, S.L. (1979). Social networks, host resistance, and mortality: A nine-year follow-up study of Alameda County residents. *American Journal of Epidemiology,* 109, 186–204.

Butler, P.E. (1981). *Self-Assertion For Women*. San Francisco: Harper and Row.

Caplan, G. (1974). *Support Systems and Community Mental Health*. New York: Behavioral Publications.

Cohen, S., & Wills, T.A. (1985). Stress, social support, and the buffering hypothesis. *Psychological Bulletin*, 98, 340–355.

Dean, A., & Lin, N. (1977). The stress-buffering role of social support. *Journal of Nervous and Mental Disease*, 169, 403–417.

Derlaga V.J., & Chaikin, A.C. (1975) *Sharing Intimacy*. Englewood Cliffs, NJ: Prentice-Hall, Inc.

Dunkel-Schetter, C., & Skokan, L.A. (1990). Determinants of social support provision in personal relationships. *Journal of Social and Personal Relationships*, 7, 437–450.

Durkheim, E. (1951, 1897). *Suicide*. Glencoe, Il.: Free Press.

Egan, G. (1977). *You and Me: The Skills of Communicating and Relating to Others*. Monterey: Brooks/Cole.

Ferguson, T. (1984). Pets. *Medical Self-Care*, No. 27, 29–32.

Friedman, E. (1980). Animal companions and one-year survival of patients after discharge from a coronary care unit. *Public Health Reports*, 95.4, 307–312.

Greenberg, H.M. (1980). *Coping With Job Stress*. Englewood Cliffs, NJ: Prentice-Hall, Inc.

Hobfoll, S.E. (Ed.). (1990). *Predicting, Activating and Facilitating Social Support*. Special Issue of *Journal of Social and Personal Relationships*.

Hobfoll, S.E., Freedy, J., Lane, C., & Geller, P. (1990). Conservation of social resources: Social support resource theory. *Journal of Social and Personal Relationships*, 7, 465–478.

House, J.S. (1981). *Work Stress and Social Support*. Reading, MA: Addison-Wesley.

House, J.S., Landis, K.R., & Umberson, D. (1988). Social relationships and health. *Science*, 241, 540–544.

Lazarus, R.S., & Folkman, S. (1984). *Stress, Appraisal and Coping*. New York: Springer Publishing Company.

Lin, N., Woelfel, M.W., & Light, S.C. (1985). The buffering effect of social support subsequent to an important life event. *Journal of Health and Social Behavior*, 26, 247–263.

Lynch, J.J. (1985). *The Language of the Heart*. New York: Basic Books.

Maslow, A. (1971). *The Farther Reachers of Human Nature*. New York: Viking.

Mitchell, J.S. (Ed.). (1969). *Social Networks in Urban Situations*. Manchester, England: Manchester University Press.

Ornstein, R., & Sobel, D. (1985). The healing brain. *Psychology Today*, 21, 48–52.

Ornstein, R., & Sobel, D. (1989). *Healthy Pleasures*. Reading, MA: Addison-Wesley Publishing Company.

Pagel, M.D., Erdly, W.W., & Becker, J. (1987). Social networks: We get by with (and in spite of) a little help from our friends. *Journal of Personality and Social Psychology*, 53, 793–804.

Pearlin, L.I., & Lieberman, M.A. (1977). Marital status, life- strains and depression. *American Sociological Review*, 42, 704–715.

Pines, M. (1980). Psychological hardiness: The role of challenge in health. *Psychology Today*, 14, 43–45.

Rossiter, C. (1984). *The Human Potential.* Alexandria, VA: Human Potential.

Sarason, I.G., Pierce, G.R., & Sarason B.R. (1990). Social support and interactional processes: A triadic conceptualization. *Journal of Social and Personal Relationships*, 7, 495-506.

Satir, V. (1976). *Making Contact.* Berkeley: Celestial Arts.

Satir, V. (1988). *The New Peoplemaking.* Mountain View, CA.: Science and Behavior Books, Inc.

Steinmetz, J. (1980). *Managing Stress Before It Manages You.* Palo Alto: Bull.

Suls., J. (1982), Social support, interpersonal relations, and health: Benefits and liabilities. In Sanders, G., & Suls, J. Eds.), *Social Psychology of Health and Illness.* Hillsdale, NJ: Erlbaum.

Tavris, C. (1974). The frozen world of the familiar stranger: A conversation with Stanley Milgram. *Psychology Today*, 8, 71–74.

Thoits, P.A. (1982). Conceptual, methodological, and theoretical problems in studying social support as a buffer against life stress. *Journal of Health and Social Behavior*, 23, 145–159.

Thoreau, H.D. (1946). *Walden.* New York: Random House.

Today's Supervisor. (1989). Listening Better, March, 12.

Turner, R.J. (1981). Social support as a contingency in psychological well-being. *Journal of Health and Social Behavior*, 22, 357–367.

Vormbrock, J.K., & Grossberg, J.M. (1988). Cardiovascular effects of human-pet dog interactions. *Journal of Behavioral Medicine*, 11, 509–518.

Weiss, R.S. (1974). The provisions of social relationships. In Z. Rubin (Ed.), *Doing Unto Others.* Englewood Cliffs, NY.: Prentice-Hall, Inc.

PART

THREE

Special Applications

Passing the Test
of College Stress

Chapter 12

CHAPTER 12

I. INTRODUCTION: WORSENESS VS. WELLNESS
A. Allison: A Model of Worseness
B. Jennifer: A Story of Wellness
C. Challenge and Opportunity During the College Years

II. COLLEGE IN THE 1990S: THE SOCIAL CONTEXT

III. COPING WITH STRESSORS OF THE COLLEGE YEARS
A. Clustering of Life Changes
B. Separation from Parents
C. Reintegration: Developing New Relationships
D. Love and Sex
E. Daily Hassles
F. Financial Uncertainty
G. Grade Pressures
H. Role Difficulties
  1. Role Overload
  2. Role Conflict
  3. Role Strain
  4. Role Ambiguity
I. Substance Abuse

IV. LIFE SCRIPTS, IDENTITY FORMATION, AND CAREER CHOICE

V. COPING AND SUCCESS IN COLLEGE

INTRODUCTION: WORSENESS VS. WELLNESS ▼

ALLISON: A MODEL OF WORSENESS

Allison came to CSU, Chico as a freshman from a Bay Area high school, where she had averaged B+ grades and had been active in a number of school activities.

Slightly insecure, she immediately put out her antennae to detect what was expected around her. She was eager to please and fit in.

During the first two weeks, Allison slept about four hours a night, less on weekends. She spent lots of time sharing stories with new friends.

She went to class most of the time, but missed several Thursday and Friday classes during those early weeks. She didn't study much, sure she could catch up. It had been no problem in high school.

Allison had been physically active as a high school field hockey and soccer player. But now she just couldn't seem to find the time to exercise here.

She missed a lot of dorm meals, especially breakfast, and she readily admitted to being hooked on junk food, especially late at night.

Allison met some very attractive young men and was sexually active—sometimes rather foolishly. She loved "partying," although she felt pretty wiped out afterwards.

By the fourth week of school, she was beginning to feel lonely and slightly depressed. None of her new relationships was very meaningful or supportive. Allison missed her family, but seldom called.

She awoke one morning at the end of the fifth week with a sore throat, which turned into a lingering bad cold. She missed classes for about a week. Allison virtually panicked at her first mid-term exam and performed poorly.

She continued to feel lousy—out of control, lonely, overwhelmed, TATT (Tired All The Time), short of money (which she had failed to ration), behind in school, and losing confidence by the day. Allison ended that first semester with a C+, 3 Cs, and a D and was put on academic probation.

Allison's story is the story of worseness.

JENNIFER: A STORY OF WELLNESS

Jennifer came to CSU, Chico, from a background much like Allison—fairly well-to-do family, a record of modest academic success, vague goals of wanting to "work with people"—and, of course, to meet and marry a handsome and wealthy young man.

She, too, came to college with a certain degree of insecurity, yet she got off to a rather different start. She made two or three very good friends who were available when needed for support and fun. They also loved to exercise together, alternating running and aerobics for a total of four or five days a week.

She talked by phone each week with her parents and younger brothers. Jennifer soon became active in CAVE (Community Action Volunteers in Education), a campus-based community volunteer program.

She went to bed by a reasonable hour during the week, averaging more than seven hours of sleep per night. She ate consistently well and kept healthy snacks on hand in her room.

Jennifer studied about two hours each weekday and another two hours or so each evening, more when needed. She was able to stay focused on her homework from the start and missed only one class during the first five weeks, because of a time conflict with her academic adviser.

At mid-term time, Jennifer felt prepared and confident. She got good grades right away, which bolstered her confidence and reinforced her habit of carefully managing

> *her time. She didn't get sick all semester and ended up with an A, 3 Bs, and a B−. She was delighted and optimistic.*
>
>   *Jennifer's story is a story of wellness.*

EXERCISE 12-1. A SECOND LOOK AT ALLISON AND JENNIFER

1. Make a list of all the attitudes and actions by Allison that represent worseness. (For a review of worseness and wellness, see Chapter 1.)

2. Make a list of all the attitudes and actions by Jennifer that represent wellness.

3. If you are a college student, which attitudes and actions of these two students most closely resemble your own? Be specific.

CHALLENGE AND OPPORTUNITY DURING THE COLLEGE YEARS

The stories of Allison and Jennifer are repeated every year on every college campus in America. The college years bring to mind the Chinese character with a dual meaning: crisis and opportunity. Whether the new student is an 18-year-old, fresh out of high school, or a 38-year-old working-class single mother returning to school as a step toward a better life, the college journey puts him or her to personal tests that most likely are beyond anything experienced before. This can be approached as an opportunity or a threat, a chance to practice wellness or worseness.

How you respond will determine how much is gained from the college experience. Practice of a wellness lifestyle, including turning challenges into positive stress, can facilitate your academic learning and personal development (Whitman, Spendlove and Clark, 1984, 1986). But more, how you cope during these years can shape habits that last a lifetime, vitally influencing your well-being for years to come.

In a host of ways, the college years present a wonderful opportunity to apply many of the ideas and skills you have read about in this book.

COLLEGE IN THE 1990s: THE SOCIAL CONTEXT   ▼

To possess the **sociological imagination** is to see individual experience within a broader social context. This certainly applies to the college experience during the 1990s.

Most students entering college in 1992 were born in about 1974. As Hoffman (1989, 4) has noted, the early life experiences of this cohort took place during the late 1970s and the 1980s—"a period of economic stagnation, falling expectations, and rising social dislocations."

During these years, unemployment fluctuated, we experienced record-high inflation, we were still reeling from the disillusionment of Viet Nam and Watergate. The stock market experienced a mini-crash, we became a debtor nation, our space program endured a traumatic tragedy.

We were frightened by Chernobyl, international terrorism became widespread, AIDS created fear. Crime and drugs became everyday realities. Our national debt soared to previously unthinkable levels. The condition of the natural environment continued to deteriorate with little evidence of social or political will to reverse the destruction.

The profit motive and self-aggrandizement took extreme forms in the rhetoric of our government leaders and in the unethical conduct of many in business. We witnessed a corresponding decline in concern with the common good.

Our rate of divorce reached a new high, with fully half of all new marriages expected to end in dissolution. A record high number of new students thus entered college having grown up in a climate of separation, divorce, single-parenting, remarriage, and reconstituted families. An increasing number of students, in fact, themselves had been involved in family dissolution, often returning to college as a next step after a separation, divorce, or remarriage. Most often, at least on my campus, these are women in their late twenties to early forties.

This period saw progress in ethnic and women's rights, yet sharp divisions emerged over abortion and freedom of choice. On many campuses, ugly incidents of racism and sexism were reported. Prejudices remained.

Economic pressures in families, combined with declining federal support, meant that financing college became a major stressor. Consequently, many students could expect to work while going to school. For millions, the four-year college experience turned into five—at the very time when, perhaps, for the first time in our history, students had reason to question whether they would be better off than their parents.

To be sure, this is not a pretty picture. Yet, it is real. Hoffman (1989, 7) recently summarized implications of this context for college students in the 1990s as follows:

> . . . the contemporary generation of students is growing up in an era which has not provided for them a sense of future possibilities, which has indeed called into serious question the legitimacy of traditionally valued institutions. Their life choices are made in an economic context which provides severe constraints on their ability to establish independent households, not to mention, for those who would so desire, forming committed relationships and their own families. Their expectations, encouraged by the affluence of many of their families of origin, are high; they are anxious about their ability to realize their expectations. The culture says of them (and they of themselves) that they are self- interested, disinclined to develop a meaningful set of principles or values beyond the self. They are a relatively small generation; their social and political influence, therefore, is not strongly felt. They, and we, are confused about how to think about their place in adult society.

Given this context, it should not be terribly surprising that this generation of college students is perceived by faculty as ill-informed and uninvolved in national and international affairs (Curtis, 1989; Henry, 1989).

The social and cultural context described above also has produced a new generation, according to one observer, that . . . "acts as if the world owes them, as if they have a right to win, as if they need whatever they want and deserve whatever they need" (Associated Press, 1990b).

Yet, there are signs that many college students are moving beyond self-preoccupation and political alienation to a new era of social concern and political activism. For example, enrollment in social science and social work undergraduate majors is up, perhaps reflecting a turn from the Me-First perspective of the Reagan years to the beginnings of a greater concern with the common good (Kleiman, 1990). This positive trend is reflected in a recent report about college students traveling to Florida in order to use spring break to build homes for the homeless through Habitat for Humanity, rather than to party in the sun (Associated Press, 1990a).

The college years are never easy, then, yet they become even more difficult— and potentially distressful—within the context we have described, because of added uncertainty and ambiguity.

COPING WITH STRESSORS OF THE COLLEGE YEARS ▼

As Lazarus and Folkman (1984) have noted, the individual continually appraises stressors through time, sees some as more threatening than others, copes in ways that seem appropriate at the moment according to available personal and social resources, and moves along to the next stressors in the process. Often, of course, these stressors confront the person in combination, even at the same time.

A recent study identified a number of serious concerns in the lives of college students, based on their reports of what was happening to them in the past week (Roscoe, 1987). These concerns ranged from academic pressures to illness and injuries, dating-related problems, sex/pregnancy concerns, and death in the family. In the following discussion, we will identify a number of key stressors for college students along with suggestions for coping with each stressor.

CLUSTERING OF LIFE CHANGES

Most students face enormous clustering of life changes. The number of simultaneous transitions can seem awesome, illustrated by the following.

▼ Leaving home (parents, siblings, one's room, family routines), perhaps for the first time

▼ Leaving familiar friends and community surroundings

▼ Entering a dorm or apartment living arrangement—very different from home

▼ Developing new friends and acquaintances

▼ Becoming familiar with new ethnic and social class groups

▼ Becoming accustomed to new class organization and teaching styles that are different from high school

▼ Confronting the need to manage one's time

▼ Facing greater academic competition than in high school

▼ Dealing with less feedback about performance

▼ Entering new clubs and other campus organizations

▼ Assuming greater responsibility for personal finances

▼ Making and breaking intimate relationships

▼ For older students, balancing new demands on time and family resources

Most students make these multiple, clustered transitions smoothly, with no ill effects. Large-scale studies of more or less normal college students suggest that four of five (around 80 percent) will experience some degree of anxiety or turmoil but will proceed along a relatively normal path of personal development, despite this clustering of change (Katz, 1968; Giddan and Price, 1985; Giddan, 1987). Yet among college students, just as others, the higher the life change scores, the greater the risk of illness and other difficulties.

Powell (1987) classifies student adjustment to this clustering of life changes into four categories, which vary according to success of coping style:

▼ The Green Zone: Normal Adaptation

▼ The Yellow Zone: Temporary Adjustment Reactions

▼ The Orange Zone: Neurotic Symptoms

▼ The Red Zone: Severe Maladjustments

Table 12-1 shows that, among a sample of college athletes, the higher the life change score, the higher the distress symptom score. The difference in the percentage of high distress symptom scores was large: 53 percent among those with high life change scores, compared with only 14 percent among those with low life change scores. The chances of a low distress symptom score were nine times greater if athletes had lower than high life change scores (54 percent vs 6 percent).

This clustering of life changes is inherent in the very process of entering college, especially if one has left home for a campus elsewhere. Yet, distress from these multiple stressors varies a great deal among students, depending upon a number of factors:

TABLE 12-1. DISTRESS SYMPTOM SCORE BY LIFE CHANGE SCORE

LIFE CHANGE SCORE	DISTRESS SYMPTOM SCORE				
	HIGH	MEDIUM	LOW	TOTAL	(N)
High	53%	42%	6%	101%	(36)
Medium	32%	27%	41%	100%	(34)
Low	14%	31%	55%	100%	(29)

P = <.001 N = 99
SOURCE: Schafer and McKenna (1981).

▼ Self-talk habits (for example, interpreting these stressors as a challenge, rather than a threat; believing the demands can be mastered; displaying hardiness)

▼ Social supports from family and friends (for example, isolation or exchanging support and caring when needed; drawing upon campus resources when needed)

▼ Health buffers (for example, exercise, nutrition and sleep habits)

▼ Coping style when pressed (for example, denial, alcohol abuse, procrastination vs. careful time allocation, continuation of regular exercise, talking about the pressure with a supportive friend)

▼ Relaxation practices (for example, daily deep relaxation, conscious use of deep breathing, and mental rehearsal)

See Chapter 10 for a discussion of steps for coping with clustering of life events. These apply during the college years as well as at other times.

EXERCISE 12-2. SELF-APPRAISAL OF COPING WITH CLUSTERED LIFE CHANGES

1.   List the life changes you have experienced during the past year.
2.   Which have been pleasant, which unpleasant?
3.   What have you done (thoughts or actions) to minimize their harmful effects on your mind, body, performance, and relationships?
4.   What have you not done that you might in the future? Be specific.

SEPARATION FROM PARENTS

Concerning younger students, one of the most central factors among these clustered changes is separating from parents. As a student, you may be unaware that your challenge of breaking away happens at the very time your parents are going through difficult changes of their own. As Philip (1988, 18) states:

> Parents of college age students are generally facing what has come to be called, perhaps somewhat dramatically, the mid-life crisis. Among other things, this may involve anxiety and depression at getting older, a sense that they no longer will be quite as central to their children's lives as they had been (perhaps not an unmixed blessing), a foreboding about their own future as they see the aging of their own parents and, as husband and wife, perhaps having to become reinvolved as a couple no longer having children at home to act as buffers between them.

Separation from parents occurs in the context of a number of developmental tasks facing the young person. Included are these, according to Long and Long (1970, 6):

1. The development of competence

2. The management of emotions

3. The management of interpersonal relationships

4. The development of purpose

5. The development of integrity

6. The development of identity

7. The development of autonomy

In the course of curricular and extracurricular pursuits, the college student gradually progresses toward resolution of each of these issues—never reaching closure, of course, since each is a life-long challenge.

Part of the challenge of autonomy is separation from parental control. This has not always faced young people, of course, but in the context of our society's emphasis on separate nuclear families, the decline of the extended family, and our Western tradition that once a person reaches 18 or 21, parental control should cease (or at least dramatically diminish), separation from parents becomes a central task for the young adult. The flip side of this process is individuation—becoming one's own person in terms of emotions, direction in life, and decision-making.

Philips (1987, 20) notes:

> Entering college marks the end of childhood/adolescence and the beginning of adulthood. Important aspects of this transition for freshmen include (1) leaving the family for membership in the college community; (2) new responsibilities for decision-making and caring for their own physical needs if they are living away from home; (3) mourning the losses involved in leaving home, such losses including parents, friends, and various forms of support networks.

For some college youth, this transitional process goes smoothly with little disruption or tension. For others, the process is not so clean. Students sometimes are beset by loneliness, others by rebelliousness, still others by depression. One recent study found 15 categories of problems in relations between college students and their parents (Anderson and Younger, 1987). These difficulties centered on lack of emotional contact, too much control, and perceived manipulation by parents. Yet another study (Bogat, et al., 1985) found parents to be the most important source of generalized social support among college students.

Using constructive coping steps is vital to turning this process of separation into one of growth and maturation, rather than one of staying stuck and dependent—or turning to alcohol, drugs, disorganization, and disarray. A key to constructive transition is maintaining contact with home through telephone calls, letters, and visits—at the same time that new, supportive friendships are developed at college.

REINTEGRATION: DEVELOPING NEW RELATIONSHIPS

The process of developing new friendships, thereby reintegrating into a new social network, is an important step in the developmental process for all students. This new network can become an important source of support and well-being. One study showed, for example, that perceived social support can make a difference in problem-solving (Lakey and Heller, 1989). Another showed that the greater the social support, the more favorable the immune response (Jemmett and Magloire, 1989). It can also be a source of considerable worry and tension.

In an excellent book on coping in college, *Do We **Have** To Know This For The Exam?*, Virshup (1987, 24) suggests the following to new students about reintegrating into a new social support network:

> Eventually the feeling of homesickness will pass, and you will begin to establish new friends, new caring relationships. Some people seem to need a lot of friends, others need just one or two good friends with whom they can share their deepest thoughts and feelings. Whichever style fits you better is right for you. But everyone needs friends to help cope with life. Otherwise, college can be very lonely.

Developing new friendships does not always just happen. You have to make it happen. A first step is to make yourself available to others. Being with others is necessary. Greeting people gives the impression you are open to talking. You have many opportunities to meet people—in your place of residence, in classes, in study groups, in the halls, in the snack bar.

Joining an interest group is another way. Special interest groups may be based on sports, computers, music, arts, language, politics—the list is endless. One of the best ways to meet people in a more than superficial way is to find study partners. This shared activity develops into lasting and meaningful friendships.

Appropriate self-disclosure also helps. The term "appropriate" is important to remember. The antithesis of appropriate is the "plunger," the person who too quickly and too openly shares personal experiences.

One also needs to avoid "ego-speak," which is the tendency to always steer the conversation to what you want to talk about. Empathy and effective listening are absent in the student who practices ego-speak.

So, appropriate openness and honesty are important. As we noted in Chapter 11, self-disclosure begets self-disclosure. Virshup's advice to students is worth noting (Virshup, 1987, 24).

> . . . trying to make too good an impression is obvious and puts people off. Giving people a little bit of what they expect makes them like you. Trying too hard to be what you are not makes you a phony, and that reputation is the kiss of death. There is a fine line which you mustn't cross. It is best to err on the side of authenticity, so that who you are is what you are offering, no more nor less. You must, therefore, learn candor, authenticity, and open self-disclosure; nothing less will do. You must be reasonably honest from the first encounter.

Another key guideline is to be authentic. It is very easy during the early college years to try to put on an image that you think others will like but that turns out to be quite unreal. Others will see through this facade very soon. Being the real you is the best way. Chances are you will be valued and accepted—not by everyone, but by some who will become your friends and support persons.

Some of the guidelines and communication methods proposed in Chapter 11 can be very useful in building new social connections in college as the bonds with parents gradually are weakened.

LOVE AND SEX

Developing intimate relationships is another development task that becomes an important source of satisfaction and growth for the college student and, at the same time, a common source of worry, anxiety, guilt, and frustration.

We live in a culture that tells us to expect much from love and sex. We admire those who attain satisfaction in these realms. In fact, we probably share a basic psychological need for intimacy. Our physiological drive for sexual expression takes us in the same direction.

As a consequence of these social, psychological, and physiological influences, almost all students are drawn into erotic feelings during the college years. Making and breaking intimate relationships are significant potential sources of stress.

A high percentage of students enter college already sexually experienced (Associated Press, 1990c). Many already have had a variety of sexual partners. As earlier, sex during the college years can be an authentic expression of caring and commitment or a casual, passing encounter. Uncertainty of meaning and intention of sexual attraction and sexual activities becomes a source of anxiety and worry, especially for females.

As Virshup (1987) notes, college is a time when the individual often struggles to reach a proper personal balance between casual sex and sex based on commitment. For some, sex is disassociated from intimacy and caring. For others, intimacy and love begin with casual sex. For still others, sex only seems right as an expression of intimacy, following a period of courtship. Finding the personal balance that fits one's background, wants, needs, and ethics is a continuing issue during the college years.

The breakup of intimate relationships is a major source of upset for many students. Many times, students over-react, upsetting their emotional life, their study habits, academic performance, and other relationships. It is important to keep the making and breaking of relationships in perspective and to avoid magnifying, awfulizing, catastrophizing—and the destructive behavior such as heavy drinking, use of drugs, procrastination, social withdrawal, that often accompany such negative self-talk.

Concern with pregnancy has always been a focus of concern for young adults, of course, and it continues. Added to that in recent years has been concern about AIDS and other sexually transmitted diseases. Normal anxieties associated with sexuality among college students thus have heightened.

Another sexual issue for many students relates to sexual orientation. Experts estimate that probably about 10 percent of college students are gay in orientation, although more than that among college men probably have had some homosexual contact (Virshup, 1987). Many struggle with the hidden identity of bi-sexuality. The college years often serve as the time when decisions about sexual orientation are made, or at least grappled with. Counseling sometimes is appropriate for students dealing with this issue.

Sexual harassment concerns most female college students at one time or another, sometimes from faculty, other times from male students. Date rape probably is more common than most realize. Clear communication about intentions and limits is most important to prevent misunderstanding, exploitation and sexual violence.

DAILY HASSLES

In Chapter 10, you read about Lazarus' study on the harmful effects of daily hassles (Lazarus, 1981). These micro-stressors are the ". . . irritating, frustrating, distressing demands that, to some degree, characterize everyday transactions with the environment" (Kanner, et al., 1981, 3). The more filled people's lives are with these negative daily annoyances, the more the emotional difficulties.

As we previously noted, the presence or absence of daily hassles is not a matter of adverse circumstances alone. Such events only become "hassles" if they are seen that way. What is a neutral occurrence for one person becomes a hassle for the next if it is seen as a threat, imposition, or burden.

Following publication of Lazarus' study, my students and I developed the Daily Hassle Index, a measure designed for college students. After my own students listed the ten most frequent sources of irritation in their daily lives, they asked four of their friends to do the same. These were then codified into the 49 most common daily hassles. The resulting scale is presented in Box 12-1.

This scale can be used in two ways. First, comparison of individual total scores yields a measure of irritability. Second, comparison among items tells us something about the "hassle ranking" of events and circumstances among respondents.

The 10 most irritating daily hassles among a sample of 185 of CSU, Chico students were these:

▼ Too little money

▼ Too little time

▼ Constant pressure of studying

▼ Writing term papers

▼ Taking tests

▼ Future plans

▼ Boring instructors

▼ Getting up in the morning

▼ Weight

▼ Parking problems around campus

BOX 12-1. DAILY HASSLE INDEX FOR COLLEGE STUDENTS

Below is a list of daily hassles that commonly irritate college students. Please indicate how often each one is an irritation to you. Use numbers as follows:

__0__ Almost never an irritation to me
__5__ Sometimes an irritation to me
__10__ Frequently an irritation to me

_____ Parking problems around campus

_____ Careless bike riders

_____ Library too noisy

_____ Roommate too noisy

_____ Preparing meals

_____ Too little time

_____ Too little money

_____ Deciding what to wear

_____ Laundry

_____ Materials unavailable in library

_____ Getting up in the morning

_____ My weight

_____ Not enough time to exercise

_____ Noisy neighbors

_____ Conflicts with roommate

_____ Instructor not available

_____ Boring instructor

_____ Constant pressures of studying

_____ Instructor diffcult to understand

_____ Not enough close friends

_____ Not enough time to talk with friends

_____ Too few dates

_____ Room temperatures

_____ How I look

_____ Too little intimacy

_____ Other students are unfriendly

_____ Getting to class on time

_____ Car problems

_____ Quality of meals

_____ Future plans

_____ Relationships at work

_____ Tensions in love relationship

_____ Conflict with family

_____ Crowds

_____ Other drivers

_____ Missing my family

_____ No mail

_____ Being lonely

_____ Being unorganized

_____ Others' opinions of me

_____ Roommate's messiness

_____ Problems with own or roommate's pet

_____ Too little sleep

_____ Shopping

_____ Taking tests

_____ Writing term papers

_____ Household chores

_____ Fixing hair in morning

_____ Physical safety after dark

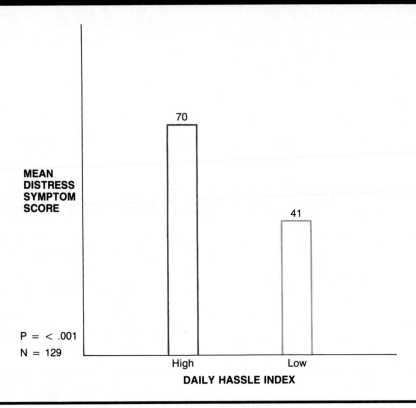

FIGURE 12-1. DISTRESS SYMPTOM SCORE BY DAILY HASSLE INDEX SCORE

Does high irritability contribute to elevated distress symptoms and to other signs of a less satisfying quality of life, as we might expect?

Figure 12-1 reveals that, among another sample of 129 CSU, Chico undergraduate students, those who scored in the highest quartile on the Daily Hassle Index averaged 70 on the Distress Symptom Scale, while those scoring in the lowest quartile averaged only 41 on the Distress Symptom Scale, a statistically significant difference.

EXERCISE 12-3. ASSESSING YOUR DAILY HASSLE INDEX SCORE

1. What is your Daily Hassle Index score?
2. Is it higher than you would like?
3. To what degree is your score a result of objective life circumstances?
Your attitudes and interpretations?
4. What specific realistic or postive self-talk statements can you use to avoid turning the experiences in the Daily Hassle Index into negative hassles?

Additional analysis revealed other correlates of high Daily Hassle Index Scores:

▼ Lower levels of internal control

▼ More depression

▼ More emotional tension

▼ Lower life satisfaction

▼ Less vitality and energy

▼ Lower self-esteem

▼ Less fun and playfulness.

EXERCISE 12-4. SPECULATING ABOUT CAUSE AND EFFECT OF DAILY HASSLE SCORES

Each of the factors we have shown to be statistically associated with daily hassle scores might be either cause or effect—or both at the same time. For example, high irritability can contribute to high distress symptoms—and/or vice versa.

1. For each of the variables listed as correlating with daily hassle scores, speculate about the direction of cause and effect.

2. In each case, create a reason why you think the causal arrow would run in this direction.

3. In these speculations and supporting arguments, how might one or more of the theories described in Chapter 2 be useful?

A recent study by Johnnie-Len Call (1990), a student at Coastal Carolina College, found a significant correlation in a sample of 95 undergraduate students between external locus of control (based on scores on the Rotter Internal-External Control Scale) and Daily Hassle Index scores. This finding is consistent with previous findings that persons with external locus of control are more vulnerable to distress because of their greater attribution of events to luck, chance, or fate—rather than to their own ability to cope (Johnson and Sarason, 1978; Sandler and Lakey, 1982; Zika and Chamberlain, 1987; Caldwell, Pearson and Chin, 1987).

Call also found a significantly higher daily hassle score for females than males, as shown in Figure 12-2. This finding is consistent with results each time I have administered these scales to CSU, Chico students.

EXERCISE 12-5. WHY DO FEMALES SCORE HIGHER ON THE DAILY HASSLE INDEX?

Table 12-3 describes a significantly higher average daily hassle scores among females than males. In your opinion, what factors associated with female/male socialization patterns, roles, and/or thought processes might account for this difference?

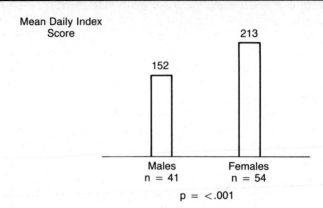

FIGURE 12-2. DAILY HASSLE INDEX SCORES BY GENDER

Mean Daily Index Score

152   213

Males
n = 41

Females
n = 54

p = <.001

Sources: Call (1990).

The key point about daily hassles, of course, is that there is nothing inherently irritating about any of the events or experiences listed in the Daily Hassle Index. Rather, interpretation of these events determines how stressful or irritating they become. As Marcus Aurelius said, "Our life is what our thoughts make of it" (Bedford, 1980). Chapter 7 described a number of techniques for managing your interpretations and perspectives in such a way that you can minimize irritation and upset, especially over daily micro-stressors.

Several of the daily hassles are not so minor for many students and represent significant stressors in their own right. One of these is financial uncertainty.

FINANCIAL UNCERTAINTY

We noted earlier in the chapter that increasing numbers of students face financial strain, partly as the result of reductions in federal support for students in the form of grants and loans.

College students' financial strain is quite different from low-income members of the community in that the "plight" of students usually is temporary. For many non-college families, low income brings not only limited money for basic needs, but limited job opportunities, poor community services, substandard schools, inadequate health care, poor housing. Children in poor families often grow up amidst insecurity, despair, anger, crime—and high stress. Poverty happens among ethnic minorities more often than among whites.

Whether white or black, rural or urban, young or old, most poor people face an array of stressors. Predictably, rates of stress-related illness, psychological disturbance, violence, and crime are higher among low-income people than others. For example, African-American men have very high rates of hypertension in the United States, although their difference with whites disappears when economic status is the same.

In a report to the Congressional Joint Economic Committee, Harvey Brenner (1979) identified seven indicators of social stress as statistically related to unemployment in the United States: homicide, suicide, deaths from cardiovascular disease and kidney disease, deaths from cirrhosis of the liver, total deaths, number of people sent to jail, and admissions to mental hospitals.

This study suggests that the stressors of economic uncertainty affect not only those who are poverty-stricken or members of an ethnic minority. They may affect anyone faced with the threat of not being able to make ends meet. This is especially true of those on fixed incomes, such as the disabled and the elderly.

For many college students, this pressure may be temporary but nevertheless real. This takes its toll in several ways. Included are anxiety and distraction, associated with wondering about one's ability to pay the next set of bills, including registration fees, tuition, and books. Another is the need to hold one or more jobs while going to school. Students have always worked, of course, but more and more students work longer hours at more jobs in order to make ends meet. This can cause time pressure, erode sleep, and decrease time devoted to exercise, healthy play, and friendship. Academic performance and health often suffer.

This problem is especially prominent among older students returning to school, most often single mothers. Financial uncertainty combines with overload and role conflict to generate special challenges for this group.

In the face of financial uncertainty, careful budgeting (with assistance if needed), maintaining good health buffers, social supports, self-talk habits, and coping styles become especially critical.

GRADE PRESSURES

The reality is that grades are important—for athletic eligibility, scholarships, job applications, and more. Grades are the center of a host of complex challenges, motivations, rewards—and problems.

In many ways, our grading system serves as a reflection of the larger society. It is based on the belief that competition is intrinsically good, that rewards should be in scarce supply, that accomplishment should be attained only after an open contest and considerable hard work, that people's futures—indeed their worth—should be ranked according to their achievement, and that self-image should reflect one's accomplishment.

Without debating here the merits of the American grading system, it is worth noting that this system motivates many students toward higher levels of learning and achievement than they otherwise might achieve. Yet, the same system risks a great many difficulties for some students.

It is not the system, of course, that gets individuals into problems of distress, it is their interpretations and reactions to it. As Virshup (1987, 16) points out,

> There are many ways in college to feel good or bad about yourself. There are many ways you can decide whether or not you are a good and worthwhile person. You may believe you are only as good as your latest grade. Then that you must spend your life studying harder and doing better, and generally proving yourself through your performance. You may develop "test anxiety," freeze in tests, fail to measure up to your own standards, and generally feel inadequate.

BOX 12-2. CAUSES AND PREVENTION OF TEST ANXIETY

CAUSES	PREVENTION
1. Inadequate preparation	**1.** Pacing and planning
2. Negative self talk	**2.** Using realistic and positive self-talk
3. Negative mental images	**3.** Using mental rehearsal
4. Physical tension	**4.** Practicing daily deep relaxation and using Six-Second Quieting Response
5. Inadequate exercise, nutrition, sleep	**5.** Maintaining a wellness lifestyle, especially during exam weeks

---

A key step in handling the challenge of grades is to make a dual commitment to yourself: to do your very best and to separate your self-esteem from your grades.

A central cause of grade-related distress is test anxiety. We noted in previous chapters that positive stress can be very helpful in motivating you to peak performance. Yet, too much stress can interfere with your preparation, concentration, and performance. This is test anxiety. The key is to attain optimal arousal, optimal anxiety, and optimal tension.

Over the years, my observations of students lead me to believe that five key factors contribute to test anxiety. Box 12-2 is a list of these five, together with steps for preventing each one. This formulation is consistent with studies (Crouse, Doffenbacher, and Frost, 1985; Lent, Lopez, and Romano, 1983) showing that test anxiety can indeed be reduced.

EXERCISE 12-6. UNDERSTANDING AND PREVENTING YOUR OWN TEST ANXIETY

1. To what extent do you suffer from test anxiety—that is, anxiety that interferes with your performance?
2. When you do, what part does each of the causes listed in Box 12-2 play?
3. What specific steps might you take to prevent test anxiety in the future?
4. When will you start?

Other common difficulties with grades are **fear of failure** and **fear of success.** Fear of failure is common to most of us. To fall short of our own or others' expectations in school, job, athletics, or any other activity as to risk both external and internal costs: threat to academic or career prospects, disapproval, rejection, humiliation, guilt, chagrin, a blow to self-esteem. Fear of failure, then, is perfectly natural and can help motivate you to prepare and perform well.

Sometimes, however, fear of failure becomes so extreme that it creates unnecessary emotional and physical distress.

Ellen is a college sophomore who carries an intense fear of failing from early childhood when her parents humiliated her several times in front of friends for having gotten C's on tests. This lingering memory continues to create intense anxiety every time she faces a test. Ellen is intensely afraid she will "fail" again, thereby "ensuring" rejection by others. While she is almost always well prepared, she often underperforms because her fear creates "static" in her thinking process during exams. Moreover, she deliberately avoids challenging situations whenever possible because of this fear of failure. For Ellen, a normal desire to perform well and to avoid a poor showing has turned into an irrational, nearly debilitating fear of failure, which creates much unhappiness and threatens to stunt her continued academic and occupational progress.

Less common is fear of success. To succeed is to convey the message to others that you are capable, bright, and dependable. The natural result is that others will expect you to succeed again in the future. This is a frightening prospect for persons so lacking in self-confidence and so fearful of rejection that they don't want anyone to expect anything of them, now or tomorrow. The solution is to avoid succeeding.

Since such persons also fear failure because of the rejection that would result, they cannot risk total failure in school, job, athletic, or community situations either. Two alternatives present themselves: Either avoid performance situations altogether or be sure to perform in a mediocre fashion, neither clearly succeeding nor failing. Hovering continually somewhere between these two extremes is not very rewarding, to be sure, but it allows an individual to remain safe from the rejection inherent in either failing now or falling short of others. Those who fear success, then, usually destine themselves to a lifetime of banality, neither realizing performance potential nor enjoying the rewards of accomplishment.

Figure 12-3 shows the growing gap through time between actual performance and perception of others' expectations. The consequence is ever-mounting anxiety, despite or because of rising performance. The solution for some persons, though usually not a conscious choice, is to fail dramatically, as in not answering any of the test questions at all, being totally unprepared for an important job meeting, going to work drunk, or oversleeping for a conference with the boss. Figure 12-3 shows that such failure quickly brings others' expectations down to a low level again. Anxiety thereby is reduced again to a tolerable level, while low self-esteem is reconfirmed. For others, the answer is to hover between success and failure, never really trying.

FIGURE 12-3. PERFORMANCE AND PERCEIVED EXPECTATIONS

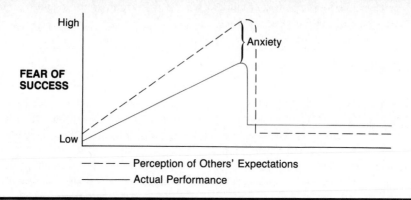

– – – – Perception of Others' Expectations
———— Actual Performance

ROLE DIFFICULTIES

A number of key challenges during the college years relate to role difficulties. A role is a cluster of expectations associated with a given social position. For example,

TABLE 12-2. NUMBER OF HOURS STUDENTS SPEND EACH WEEK ON SELECTED ACTIVITIES (BY PERCENT RESPONDING)

ACTIVITY	HOURS PER WEEK						
	NONE	1–2	3–4	5–6	7–8	9–10	11 OR MORE
Talking informally to other students	3	19	16	13	9	9	31
Watching television	13	22	18	14	11	8	14
Leisure reading	23	35	17	11	6	4	4
Talking to faculty members	26	56	11	4	1	1	1
Studying in the library	27	24	14	9	5	6	15
Attending campus cultural events	46	36	11	4	1	1	1
Participating in organized student activities (other than athletics)	50	26	10	6	3	2	3
Participating in intramural sports	70	16	8	3	1	1	1
Participating in intercollegiate athletics	93	1	*	*	1	1	4

* = less than 1 percent
SOURCE: The Carnegie Foundation for the Advancement of Teaching, National Survey of Undergraduates, 1984.

the position of college student brings with it a host of expectations from role partners: instructors, classmates, friends, librarians, study partners, roommates, and others. We will examine several role difficulties during the college years: role overload, role conflict, role strain, and role ambiguity. In each case, becoming aware of the stressor can be a first step to effective coping.

Role Overload

You may recall that two of the top three daily hassles reported above were "Too little time" and "Constant pressure of studying." In short, chronic overload is almost endemic to the college years. This probably is more true today than ever, as more and more students work part-time and more are returning to school between ages 25 and 40 (especially single mothers).

Table 12-2 presents a picture of how a large sample of students spend their time. For many students, this adds up to too much to do in too few hours. The result can be a feeling of chronic hurry, hassle, and struggle with time.

EXERCISE 12-7. HOW ORGANIZED ARE YOU?

To assess how organized you are, please complete the following scale. Score one point for every question you answer "yes."

1. Are you almost always late to meetings and appointments?
2. Do you find yourself always making apologies for being disorganized?
3. Do you plan only a day at a time—never weeks or months in advance?
4. Do you find that you "don't have time" for those essential activities that help you take care of yourself—exercise, relaxation, preparing and eating good food, music and arts, quality time with family and friends?
5. At the end of a day do you often feel that you've been dealing with trivia and haven't done the more important things?
6. Do you feel you'd like to be more organized, but your life is such a mess you wouldn't know where to begin?
7. Is your refrigerator badly in need of cleaning?
8. Do you often forget or misplace your keys, glasses, handbag, briefcase appointment book, and the like?
9. Do you find yourself constantly running out of essential supplies at home or at work?
10. Have you forgotten a scheduled appointment within the past month?

If you score:

0–1
Congratulations! You have things pretty well under control

2–4
Somewhat disorganized.

5–7

Fairly disorganized. Following guidelines in this article should be helpful.

8–10

Highly disorganized. Life is probably pretty difficult. The guidelines in this book could change your life.

SOURCE: *Medical Self-Care,* 16 (Spring, 1982), 26.

EXERCISE 12-8. IDENTIFYING TIME CONSUMERS

Walter and Seibert (1990, 35) present a list of time wasters with the following introduction. "Wasting time is one of the most enjoyable pastimes known to college students. You should be able to do whatever you wish with your time. But, if you feel that you are losing control of your time and not accomplishing what you want, you might review the following list of time consumers."

COMMON TIME CONSUMERS

Talking with friends
Talking on the telephone and telephone interruptions
Daydreaming
Watching television
Sleeping
Listening to music
Drop-in visitors
Reading (other than school material)
Playing sports or games/hobbies
Cleaning rooms/apartments/doing laundry/groceries/cleaning desk
"Goofing around" or "partying"
Eating/snacking
Spending too much time in the dining hall
Procrastination/worrying

Which of these do you find yourself doing most? What will you do, specifically, to spend your time more constructively?

EXERCISE 12-9. TIPS FOR EFFECTIVE SCHEDULING

Walter and Seibert offer several useful suggestions for scheduling by the college student:

As we've said before, one of your greatest aids will be to use and follow a time schedule. Obtain a month-by-month calendar with spaces that you can fill in with important dates and obligations—when examinations will take place and when papers and projects are due. Next, fill in all the times that you plan to go to concerts, shows, family gatherings, meetings; plan for trips or other events; and so on.

After developing a picture of your major commitments for the months ahead, you are now ready to make up a weekly schedule of your classes, study hours, and other obligations. A weekly schedule gives you a clear picture of what you are doing with your time; it helps you spot an extra hour or two during the day that you can use for studying or other responsibilities. This way you can plan more free evenings to do what you want.

Follow these steps for effective scheduling:

1.   Establish a well-defined and reasonable schedule, one that you can live with.
2.   Budget time to prepare for each class and all examinations.
3.   Budget time to take care of all of your other personal responsibilities.
4.   Study course notes as soon as possible after each class period, rather than waiting until the last few days before the exam.
5.   Give difficult subjects preferred times with the fewest possible interruptions and disturbances.
6.   Reserve time for leisure activities, and make sure that you do not study during these periods!
7.   Stick to your schedule and reward yourself for having achieved your study goals in the allotted time.

There are no simple answers to avoiding chronic overload, but a number of potentially helpful guidelines sometimes can help.

1.   Be cautious about saying yes to new time obligations. Give yourself an hour or a day before saying yes. Be aware of your reasons for saying yes. Do they include a desire to please or a wish to avoid disapproval, rather than intrinsic value or interest in the activity? Question your motives.

2.   Carefully organize your time and set up semester, weekly and daily schedules. See Exercise 12-7 for an assessment of how organized you are. See Exercise 12-9 for tips from Walter and Siebert (1990) about effective scheduling by the college student.

3.   Avoid procrastination, drawing on the suggestions in Chapter 10. The key, according to Walter and Seibert, is to listen to your self-talk. They point out that two voices vie for dominance in most college students' minds: the "Take Action Now Voices" and the "Do It Later Voices." Here is what they usually say (Walter and Seibert, 1990, 37):

Take Action Now Voices	Do It Later Voices
Let's get it over with.	I don't feel like it now.
It's already late.	There's still time.
You know it, just do it.	I'll do it later.

They'll be pleased with what I've done.	This other thing is more important.
It's a challenge.	I'll be better prepared later.
It'll be fun when I get into it.	It may solve itself if I wait.
Once I get started it'll go quickly.	If I wait, someone else may do it.
If I don't do it now, I'll have to do it later.	I need more information.

EXERCISE 12-10. LISTENING TO YOUR INNER VOICES ABOUT PROCRASTINATION

1. Which of the inner voices about procrastination typically dominates in your own mind?
2. Which specific statements do you most often "hear?"
3. During the next week, listen carefully to your self-talk about procrastination. Use the P and Q or Instant Replay methods to change from negative to constructive self-talk about getting things done.

Role Conflict

College students face two types of role conflict. One is incompatible expectations associated with two or more different roles. Examples include student-employee, student-mother, student-daughter, student-friend. Role demands often bump into one another, as in the case of Kim.

Kim is a college junior who occupies several roles: student, roommate, lover, daughter, employee. Usually others' expectations do not seriously conflict, but sometimes she does feel in a bind. On a recent Thursday, for example, her history professor and classmates expected her to present an oral report on the life of Calvin Coolidge at their 12:00 class, her roommates wanted her to help clean the apartment all morning, her boyfriend wanted to have lunch with her, she felt pressured to answer her mother's letter of last week, and her boss called at 7:30 AM to ask her to substitute for a sick employee.

The second type of conflict is incompatible expectations from different role-partners within a single role. For example, a student's five professors each put a claim on the time and energy of the person. Two may expect her to be fully prepared for mid-term exams on the same day that another expects her to present a top-notch oral presentation, and the last one expects her to turn in a well-written term paper.

The result of role conflict can be confusion, anxiety, tension, underperformance, irritability, even illness. Studies in occupational stress indicate that the greater the role conflict on the job, the lower the job satisfaction, the greater the anxiety, the higher the blood pressure, the greater the incidence of heart attacks, the higher the cholesterol, the greater the obesity, the higher the heart rate, the greater the occurrence of abnormal EKG's, the greater the absenteeism, and the greater the worker turnover (Matteson and Ivancevich, 1987). Some of the same effects are likely to occur among students when these pressures are accompanied with ineffective coping.

Potentially harmful effects of role conflict in college can be minimized by recognizing when role conflict occurs and that it can have adverse effects. Other preventive steps include proper time management practices, careful planning and pacing, effective health buffers, and constructive self-talk.

EXERCISE 12-11. EXAMINING YOUR ROLE CONFLICTS

1. Identify several of your own between-role conflicts. What are the roles? Who are the role partners? What are their conflicting expectations? Be precise.
2. Do the same with within-role conflicts.
3. How do you think you are affected by these role conflicts?
4. How do you cope with these role conflicts—effectively and ineffectively.

Role Strain

Still another type of role difficulty is role strain—when personal desires conflict with other's expectations. Many instances can be identified in the lives of college students:

▼ A student wants to attend an unusually appealing Tuesday night concert, while his instructor expects him to attend his Tuesday night class.

▼ A student would rather watch the World Series game than attend a biology lab session.

▼ A student wants to take his girlfriend to a movie. His fraternity brothers expect him to attend an emergency meeting.

▼ A student wants to write about the Kennedy policy toward Cuba in the early sixties. His instructor wants the paper to be limited to Central America.

Balancing personal wants and desires with others' expectations is a lifelong challenge, of course, with no single, simple formula. Awareness helps. So does having clear goals and priorities. So does having good sense as to when to compromise or accommodate. Balancing self-interest, on one hand, and social responsibility and concern for others, is the long-run guideline to follow.

Role Ambiguity

Roles sometimes lack clarity in what is expected. That is, the guideposts by which a person finds direction may be ambiguous. Young people today face role ambiguity in a host of ways.

> Probably no society makes the transition from childhood to adulthood more difficult than we do in America. We have developed very few patterns that dramatize the "coming of age" of the adolescent. We have provided him with few guideposts by which to find directions. At adolescence, we expect the boy or girl to stop being a child, yet we do not expect him to be [an adult]. Any definitions he has of his changing age positions are quite inconsistent. He may drive an automobile at sixteen, leave school at eighteen, be subject to the draft at nineteen, and vote at twenty-one. He is told he is no longer a child, but he is treated like a dependent, supported by his parents, and mistrusted for the tragedies that befall some adolescents—auto accidents, juvenile delinquency, pre-marital pregnancies, and drug addiction. In a word, there are many situations in which he scarcely knows whether he is expected to act like an adult or a child (Vander Zanden, 1975).

Role ambiguity arises from several sources, all of which can affect college students. One is rapid social and cultural change. Relationships between younger college students and their parents undergo continual redefinition, with both experiencing uncertainty as to how to make decisions, communicate, and reach a mutually agreeable accommodation in terms of autonomy and control.

A second source of role ambiguity is passage from one life cycle stage to another. Transition from childhood into adolescence and from adolescence into adulthood are classic examples. This source relates to virtually every younger college student, especially combined with the rapid change noted above.

Third, role ambiguity can result from incomplete, fuzzy, or otherwise inadequate communications from role partners. This can happen to the college student, for example, when a faculty member is not clear as to what is expected, when roommates do not develop clear understanding about noise, visitors, cooking, shopping, or housecleaning.

Whatever the cause, role ambiguity can heighten distress and increase stress-related illness, emotional disturbance, and troubled behavior. Research in the workplace has identified a wide range of negative effects of job-related role ambiguity: more job dissatisfaction, more job-related tension, lower self-confidence, higher blood pressure, lower self-esteem, greater depression, greater anxiety, and greater resentment toward the employer (Matteson and Ivancevich, 1987). College students who cope ineffectively with role ambiguity risk some of the same effects.

Effective coping with role ambiguity can occur by means of clear internal goals and priorities, assertiveness in clarifying unclear role expectations from others, constructive self-talk rather than awfulizing or negativizing, and maintaining effective health buffers.

SUBSTANCE ABUSE

A freshman enrolling in nearly any college or university enters a subculture where alcohol and drugs are readily available and where considerable social pressure prevails to become at least a casual user. States the director of a college counseling center, "The greatest instigator of alcohol and drug use in college is a friend. Roommates get roommates to try drugs, older students influence freshmen to drink and use drugs" (Walter and Siebert, 1990, 143).

Alcohol is used more frequently than any other drug, in large part, of course, because it is legal after age 18 or 21 and because its use is widely accepted and promoted in our society. About eight of 10 college students report drinking within the past month and about five percent drink daily—more on some campuses than others. Over half of all males and one in three females report frequent bouts of heavy weekend drinking. About one in five use marijuana at least once a month and about seven percent report using crack or cocaine at least that often (Walter and Siebert, 1990).

Students drink and use drugs for two main reasons. The first is to gain social acceptance. The National Institute on Drug Abuse found, in a nationwide study of use of alcohol and other drugs by high school and college students, that the reason most often given for using any substance was "to have a good time with my friends" (Walter and Siebert, 1990, 143).

The second reason is to feel better. In this respect, Virshup (1987, 169) states this:

> I raised three teenagers who were exposed to the drug scene, yet survived and thrived. I like to think that advice I gave them was of some help. I suggested: don't use *anything* in order to feel *better* when you are feeling *bad*.

Walter and Siebert (1990, 143) present several signs of addiction and substance abuse:

Use the substance more and more frequently;

Develop a toleration for it, need a bigger dose to experience the effects, the effect lasts a shorter time;

Feel "off" when not using it, feel shaky, anxious, edgy, physical discomfort without it;

Have little awareness of how much used; believe usage is normal and under control;

Friends notice personality changes, goes from happy, "up," social, and self-confident to unhappy, grumpy, withdrawn, depressed, fearful, and paranoid;

Friends, family, and acquaintances express concern, encourage less use or stopping;

Person says more than once, I could stop if I wanted to, I just don't want to;

Rationalizes use, blames other people, events, situation for use;

Becomes unmotivated, performance at work or in school deteriorates, less done of poorer quality;

Has auto accidents, increase in traffic tickets (alcohol);

Cannot remember the next day what happened the night before (alcohol);

Warnings from officials, notices of delinquent payments;

Tries to borrow money, makes excuses for not repaying loans, sells belongings, may steal money or items to sell;

Promises to improve when confronted, asks for another chance, asks to be trusted.

Evidence mounts that problem drinkers differ biochemically from social drinkers. Care must be taken especially by students with a family history of alcoholism.

Alcohol advertisements add to the problem by helping reinforce the beliefs, now translated into widely shared social norms, that by drinking you will be transformed into someone better than you are—and that you "deserve a drink."

Alcohol ads tell us that alcohol will make us sexier, more creative, more powerful, more creative and will help us to buffer the punches of a cruel world. They tell us we have a right to drink—we worked for it; we deserve it.

We deserve to Partyyyy! After a long week of dealing with professional egos (at school or work), irate customers, demanding mates, George Bush with his finger on the trigger, a hole in the ozone, we deserve a cold one, or two—and we don't need to feel guilty about it. We can handle it. We know when to stop. We know what our limits are. And if we want to start the weekend early on Thursday or Wednesday, that's okay too. We're Americans, we have rights, so pour us up another one! (Virshup, 1987, 168)

Clearly, advertising and social norms create a climate in which alcohol becomes a convenient means of dulling anxiety and depression. Students must be aware that alcohol and drug abuse can be harmful to their educational process—as well as to their health. Certainly, they are destructive approaches to "feel better" in times of pressure.

LIFE SCRIPTS, IDENTITY FORMATION, AND CAREER CHOICE ▼

During the college years, every student continues to deal with the questions that have been the central focus of his/her life from childhood: Who am I? Whom will I become?

Eric Berne (1964, 1972, 1976) the founder of transactional analysis, contended that nearly everyone emerges from adolescence with a *life script*—a blueprint for thinking, feeling, and living. As an actor follows a stage script, people spend their lives blindly living out their own life script. Included in the script are directions related to matters such as the following.

How to be masculine or feminine

How to get love and attention

How to feel about oneself

How to feel about others

How to cope with stress

How to spend time

Whether and how to succeed or fail

Your life script emerges during childhood and adolescence out of early messages from parents and other adults and early decisions you make. Early messages—given through example, reward and punishment, and direct instruction—include attribution (you are, you aren't) and injunctions (you should, you shouldn't, you must, you must not). Because you have the power of choice, you are not merely a passive receiver of these messages. Choice is possible, including acceptance, rejection, or modification of early messages. Many people raised in destructive homes are exposed to "losing" or violent messages, yet they turn out well because they choose their own life plan.

Life scripts are inherently limited because they stifle authenticity and spontaneity. By definition, they are harmful. But they are damaging in another way as well—they often lead to distress. Life scripts can cause distress in several ways.

1. By directly calling for a life of unhappiness, failure, pity, half-effort, depression, boredom, illness, or loneliness. These are *banal life scripts.*

2. By directly calling for tragedy—suicide, a life in prison, premature death through alcoholism, accident, or heart attack. These are *tragic life scripts.*

3. By indirectly calling for either a banal or a tragic life through inept or harmful coping responses—violence toward others, drugs, schizophrenia, impulsive spending, or compulsive overeating.

Life scripts reflect in part the norms and values of the surrounding culture and subculture. Yet each script is unique in many ways. Scripts maintain their lifelong hold over a person through the *repetition compulsion*—the drive to be and do what is familiar. This drive probably is stronger than the "pleasure principle." Doing and feeling what is familiar often takes priority even over enjoying life—not out of choice, but out of habit. A tragic illustration of the power of the repetition compulsion is the fact that as many as 90 percent of parents who abuse their children are repeating their own histories of abuse by their parents—a pattern currently scarring the lives of as many as 2.2 million children between the ages of three and 17 in the United States.

Not everyone has a life script. A small minority of people are raised by parents to be *self*-directed, to make up their *own* minds about what to believe and how to live—rather than to be controlled by a script from childhood. Yet most people are bound by their script, spending their lives blindly following it or struggling somehow to break free. Many adults succeed—attaining a genuine authenticity, autonomy, and self-direction. Through awareness, effort, and support from others, life scripts can be left behind or at least rewritten in major ways. Full development of potential depends on script-free living.

A central challenge during the college years, then, is to become fully aware of one's life script as it has been shaped by culture, subculture, family, and self. Simultaneously, one must sort and select, retaining those elements we want and discarding those early decisions that no longer fit the self and the future one wants.

Part of this process is choosing a career that fully is one's own, reflecting one's deepest interests and social values. Often, of course, students concern themselves more with expediency, material gain, and short-run opportunity in their choice of career than with more important issues of values, ethics, personality-career fit, and lifestyle options. Attentiveness to these broader concerns is important from the time students arrive at college, through choice of major, until their final job interview and job choice.

COPING AND SUCCESS IN COLLEGE ▼

Throughout the book, we have noted that coping with difficult events and circumstances is most usefully understood as an ongoing, transactional, fluctuating process of appraisal and response as the individual deals with the multitude of stressors in his or her life. In this chapter, we have briefly described a number of common potential distressors in the lives of college students. We have suggested that the key approaches to managing stress set forth in previous chapters apply here as in other stages of life. Included are:

▼ Awareness of the nature and effects of stress—positive, neutral, and negative

▼ Management of self-talk

▼ Practicing effective techniques for eliciting the relaxation response

▼ Maintaining effective health buffers (exercise, nutrition, and sleep)

▼ Managing time and change

▼ Participating in strong, stable, supportive social support networks

▼ Employing effective coping techniques in dealing with specific stressors

A recent study by DeGrauw and Norcross (1989) provides useful information about what a sample of 469 students experienced as their most distressing episode of the last three years, what they did to cope, and which coping methods were most effective.

Students were asked in a questionnaire to focus on their worst period of psychological distress during the past three years. They then were asked whether there was a particular event associated with this period of distress. Nearly eight of 10 reported affirmatively. Table 12-3 presents the types of precipitating events reported by the students. It is apparent most have to do with stressors discussed previously in this chapter. Others, such as family death or illness relate to life back home.

Next, respondents in the study were asked what specific steps they took to cope with their distress. Table 12-4 shows the most and least often used types of coping processes.

In summarizing these results, DeGrauw and Norcross (1989, 67) state, "In other words, college students tended to lean on others, restructure their thinking

TABLE 12-3. PRECIPITATING EVENT OF DISTRESS EPISODE

EVENTS	PERCENT OF STUDENTS REPORTING
Relationship Conflicts	38
School Related	20
Family Death	12
Moving/Relocation	4
Death of Friend	3
Family Illness	2
Personal Illness	2
Occupational Difficulty	0
Other	18
	99

SOURCE: DeGrauw and Norcross (1989, 64)

TABLE 12-4. MOST AND LEAST USED COPING PROCESSES

MOST OFTEN USED

Helping Relationship

Wishful Thinking

Logical Analysis

Active Cognitive Coping

Seeking Social Support

LEAST OFTEN USED

Environmental Evaluation

Stimulus Control

Social Liberation

Catharsis

Medication

SOURCE: DeGrauw and Norcross (1989, 66)

and wish for a better outcome. They tended not to restructure their environments, use prescription drugs, or emotionally release their feelings."

Female students were found more often to use helping relationships, catharsis, information seeking, and social support, while males were more likely to keep to themselves and to avoid other people.

Finally, the authors studied success in coping—what worked and what did not work in dealing with the distressing episodes. They summarized their results as follows:

> The methods positively correlated with success in the present study of distressed students and previous investigations of non- students were active—problem solving, behavioral, positive focus—and interpersonal—helping relationship—in nature. Methods negatively associated with success were largely passive—wishful thinking, blame self—and avoidant—keep to self, avoidance. The recommendations for student self-changers would thus be to maximize supportive relationships, maintain an optimistic attitude, employ action strategies, avoid self-recriminations, and resist the temptation to withdraw into themselves.

EXERCISE 12-12. LOOKING BACK AT DISTRESSING EPISODES IN YOUR COLLEGE LIFE—AND HOW YOU COPED.

1.   Identify the 3-5 most distressing episodes during your past year or two in school.
2.   For each episode, what was the precipitating distressor(s)?
3.   For each episode, what coping steps or processes did you use? With what outcomes?
4.   Looking back, what coping methods, if any, might you have used that would have been more effective?

In another recent study, Schafer and King (1990) found no association between frequency of great stress and four measures of religiousness: religious affiliation (Catholic, Protestant, Jew); frequency of attendance at religious services; importance of religion; and Christian rebirth (born-again vs. non-born-again). It would appear from these findings that, although religious faith and practice certainly have been widely used coping methods, they had no visible effect in protecting the 194 students in our random sample from experiencing high stress.

Hicks, Grant, and Chancellor (1986) recently found that the greater the Type A behavior, the greater the self-reported stress, and that among both Type A's and Type B's, the longer the average amount of sleep, the less the stress.

Walter and Siebert (1990, 30) note that the difference between successful students and unsuccessful ones is that ". . . successful students persist. They keep going. The less successful students give up too easily. They quit when they become frustrated, don't do well at first, or do less well than others."

Walter and Siebert also state that the students who persist through times of difficulty do several things differently:

▼ They practice mental rehearsal of desired accomplishments.

▼ They handle the challenge and uncertainty of college by developing a healthy balance between self-reliance and acceptance of guidance.

▼ They develop self-confidence and a positive self-image through a healthy balance of self-praise and self-criticism.

▼ They accept nervousness, fear, and not always doing well at first as natural.

Walter and Siebert (1990, 29) consider healthy self-esteem, self-confidence and a positive self-image as most important of all. They point out that these provide an inner stability that yields several benefits. It lets you:

Accept praise, recognition, success, and friendship as legitimate;

Examine and learn from mistakes and failures;

Not be pressured into undesirable actions or situations out of fear of being disliked;

Resist and not be manipulated by insincere flattery;

Reject undeserved criticism;

Admit mistakes and apologize to others for them;

Handle new, unexpected developments knowing you can count on yourself; and

Value yourself as a unique, special human being.

Researchers recently asked nearly 2,400 graduating seniors from nine colleges what factors contributed most to their success in college. Their responses are summarized in Table 12-5. Social contacts, with both fellow students and faculty/staff are high on the list. So is organizing time well and getting involved in campus activities outside the classroom.

In the next chapter, you will learn more about characteristics and habits of people who thrive under pressure.

TABLE 12-5. PERCENTAGE OF STUDENTS WHO SAID THE FACTOR CONTRIBUTED TO A SUCCESSFUL AND SATISFYING COLLEGE CAREER

FACTOR	PERCENTAGE
Personal contacts with students	89
Personal contacts with faculty and staff	78
Time I have spent on special interests and activities out of class	73
Ability to organize tasks and use my time effectively	72
Work experience during college or in the summer	63
Social life on campus	62
Sense of direction; knowing why I am in college and what career I would like to work toward	56
Availability of financial resources	52

SOURCE: Walter and Siebert (1990, 5); adapted from Willingham, 1985)

EXERCISE 12-13. APPLYING THIS CHAPTER

After carefully re-reading this chapter, you are invited to complete the following sentence:

In order to better manage my stress and enhance my own wellness during the remainder of this academic year, I will (based on what I have learned in this chapter):

In Chapter 13, we will examine managing stress and preventing burnout in the workplace.

REFERENCES ▼

Anderson, W., & Younger, C. (1987). Parents as a source of stress for college students. *College Student Journal*, 21, 317-323.

Associated Press. (1990a). Some college students using spring break to build up, not party down. *Chico Enterprise-Record*, March 16, 2C.

Associated Press. (1990b). Study criticizes ethics of younger generation. *San Francisco Chronicle*, October 11, A12.

Associated Press. (1990c). Teen sexual activity increases. *Chico Enterprise-Record*, November 8, 4A.

Bedford, S. (1980). *Stress and Tiger Juice*. Chico, CA.: Scott Publications.

Berne, E. (1964). *Games People Play*. New York: Grove.

Berne, E. (1972). *What Do You Say After You Say Hello?* New York: Grove.

Berne, E. (1976). *Beyond Games and Scripts*. New York: Grove.

Bogat, S.A., Caldwell, R.A., Rogosch, F.A., & Kriegler, J.A. (1985). Differentiating specialists and generalists within college students' social support networks. *Journal of Youth and Adolescence*, 14, 23-35.

Brenner, H. (1979). Mortality and the national economy. *Lancet*, 2, 568-573.

Caldwell, R.S., Person, J.L., & Chin, R.J. (1987). Stress-moderating effects: Social support in the context of gender and locus of control. *Journal of Personality and Social Psychology*, 13, 5-17.

Call, J.L., (1990). The relationship between daily hassles, gender, and locus of control in college students, (Unpublished manuscript, University of South Carolina, Coastal Carolina College).

Crouse, R.H., Doffenbacker, J.L., & Frost, G.A. (1985). Desensitization for students with different sources and experiences of test anxiety. *Journal of College Student Personnel*, 28, 315-318.

Curtis, D. (1989). Professors say their students are shallow. *San Francisco Chronicle*. November 7, 1.

DeGrauw, W.P., & Norcross, J.C. (1989). Students coping with psychological distress: What they do and what works. *Journal of College Student Psychotherapy*, 4, 55-76.

Giddan, N.S., & Price, M.K. (1985). *Journey of Youth: Psychological Development During College*. Schenectady: Character Research Press.

Giddan, N.S. (1987). Coping and identity development in college students. *Journal of College Student Psychotherapy*, 2, 33-58.

Henry, T. (1989). Survey reveals young Americans turned off by politics. *Chico Enterprise-Record*, November 22, 3C.

Hicks, R.A., Grant, F. & Chancellor, C. (1986). Type A-B status, habitual sleep duration, and perceived level of daily life stress of college students. *Perceptual and Motor Skills*, 63, 793-794.

Hoffman, F.L. (1989). Development issues, college students and the 1990s, *Journal of College Student Psychotherapy*, 4, 3-12.

Jemmett, J.B. & Magloire, K. (1989). Academic stress, social support, and secretory immoglobulin A. *Journal of Pesonality and Social Psychology*, 55, 803-810.

Johnson, J.H., & Sarason, I.G., Life stress, depression and anxiety: Internal-external control as a moderator variable. *Journal of Psychosomatic Research*, 22, 205-208.

Kanner, A.D., Coyne, J.C., Schaefer, C., & Lazarus, R.S. (1981). Comparison of two modes of stress measurement: Daily hassles and uplifts versus major life events. *Journal of Behavioral Medicine*, 4, 2-39.

Katz, J. (Ed.) (1968). *No Time for Youth*. San Francisco: Jossey-Bass.

Kleiman, C. (1990). Students abandon big bucks for social sciences. *San Francisco Examiner*, September 30, 44.

Lakey, B., & Heller, K. (1989). Social support from a friend, perceived social support, and social problem-solving. *American Journal of Community Psychology*, 16, 811-824.

Lazarus, R.S. (1981). Little hassles can be hazardous to your health. *Psychology Today*, 15, 58-62.

Lazarus, R.S., & Folkman, S. (1984). *Stress, Appraisal, and Coping*. New York: Springer.

Lent, R.W., Lopez, F.G., & Romano, J.L. (1983). A program for reducing test anxiety with academically underprepared students. *Journal of College Student Personnel*, 24, 265-266.

Long, N.J., & Long, J. (1970). *Conflict and Comfort in College*. Belmont, CA.: Wadsworth.

Matteson, M.T., & Ivancevich, J.M. (1987). *Controlling Work Stress*. San Francisco: Jossey-Bass.

Philips, A.F. (1987). Parents, sons and daughters: Growth and Transition during the college years. *Journal of College Student Psychotherapy*, 2, 17-32.

Powell, D.H. (1987). Is my college student normal? *Journal of College Student Psychotherapy*, 2, 149-186.

Roscoe, B. (1987). Concerns of college students: A report of self-disclosures. *College Student Journal*, 21, 158-161.

Sandler, I.N., & Lakey, B. (1982). Locus of control as a stress moderator: The role of control perceptions and social support. *American Journal of Community Psychology*, 10, 65-80.

Schafer, W., & McKenna, J.F. (1981). Life change, stress and injury: A study of male college athletes. Unpublished paper.

Schafer, W.E., & King, M. (1990). Religiousness and stress among college students: A survey report. *Journal of College Student Development*, 31, 336-341.

Vander Zanden, J.W. (1975). *Sociology: A Systematic Approach*. 3rd Ed. New York: Ronald.

Virshup, B. (1987). *Do We Have to Know This for the Exam?* New York: W.W. Norton.

Walter, T., & Siebert, A. (1990). *Student Success.* Fort Worth: Holt, Rinehart and Winston.

Whitman, N.A., Spendlove, D.C., & Clark, C.H. *Student Stress: Effects and Solutions.* Washington, C.D.: ASHE-ERIC Higher Education Research Report No. 2.

Whitman, N.A., Spendlove, D.C., & Clark, C.H. (1986). *Increasing Students' Learning.* Washington, D.C.: ASHE-ERIC Higher Education Research Report No. 4.

Willingham, W.W. (1985.) *Success In College: The Role of Personal Qualities and Academic Ability.* New York: College Entrance Examination Board.

Zika, S., & Chamberlain, K. (1987). Relation of hassles and personality to subjective well-being. *Journal of Personality and Social Psychology, 53,* 155-162.

Managing Job Stress and
Preventing Burnout

Chapter 13

CHAPTER 13

I. INTRODUCTION
   A. Costs of Job Stress
   B. The Need for Optimal Job Stress

II. HIGH-RISK STRESSORS IN THE WORKPLACE
   A. Organizational Stressors
      1. Centralization and Lack of Participation
      2. Shift Work
      3. Inadequate Social Support
      4. Organizational Climate
   B. Role-Related Stressors
      1. Role Conflict
      2. Role Ambiguity
      3. Role Overload
      4. Role Underload
      5. High Role Expectations—Low Control
      6. Difficult Relationships
      7. Career Insecurity and Inopportunity
      8. Sexual Harassment
      9. Other Common Role-Related Stressors

III. JOB BURNOUT
   A. What Is Burnout?
   B. Burnout Stages
      1. Involvement
      2. Stagnation
      3. Detachment
      4. Juncture
      5. Intervention
   C. Organizational Factors Contributing to Burnout
   D. Preventing Burnout
      1. Managers and Supervisors
      2. Individuals

INTRODUCTION

Joan is conscientious and competent. She may be a book-keeper, a mathematical analyst, or an executive secretary. She is well recognized by her fellow employees and her supervisor. She often feels tugged from many different directions; she feels splintered—at times, even overwhelmed. She doesn't find it easy to say "no"; she takes on a great deal but always manages to accomplish it successfully. At times, however, the cost seems high. She doesn't have time to enjoy herself; she says it's difficult to relax; she would like to find ways to unwind a little. She feels tension headaches after a tough day that often ruin her evenings. Joan wants to learn new ways to cope with her job stress.

Joe may be an engineer, a production worker, a sales manager, or the boss of a small retail establishment. He is proud of his Mediterranean heritage; he believes in letting his feelings out. "I don't have stress; I give it to others," he says. He sure does. If criticized by the boss or a customer, he is angry and complains all day. He dumps it on his fellow workers or subordinates. He ridicules his wife and puts down the kids. He seems to enjoy being angry. But lately the feedback from his co-workers, wife, and children is beginning to get to him. He wants to learn ways to control his emotions, to be less excitable, to feel less guilty. He, too, is experiencing stress. He would like to be angry less often. Joe's ready for a change (Greenberg, 1980).

Joan and Joe are typical of a growing number of American workers whose quality of life and health are damaged by job stress—and who recognize it and want to do something about it. In this chapter, we apply many of the facts, concepts, and guidelines already presented in previous chapters to the specific problem of job stress. Approaches available both to the organization and to the individual are presented.

COSTS OF JOB STRESS

A recent article in *The Wall Street Journal* headlined, "Fear and Stress in the Office Take Toll" (O'Boyle, 1990, B1) states:

> Human resource managers, as well as doctors, psychologists and pollsters agree that workplace stress is way up. Layoffs—and the pervasive fear of dismissal—are jangling nerves. Even survivors aren't secure; many must work longer hours amid more belt tightening. Moreover, workplace stress is often compounded by troubles at home: tighter personal finances, for instance, or marital tensions.

"Stress is here. You can feel it rise right up off the page in the newspapers we read," says Clinton G. Weiman, corporate medical director for Citicorp in Manhattan. "People feel the crunch, and eventually it gets reflected in the health care system."

In Chapter 1, we noted that stress is very costly for our society. Job stress by itself has been estimated to cost billions of dollars to employers, primarily through the following areas:

Underproductivity (quality and quantity)

Absenteeism

Health insurance payouts

Worker turnover

Workers' compensation claims

Theft and sabotage

Matteson and Ivancevich (1987) estimate that, in combination, these costs amount to over $2,773 per worker per year for a medium-sized manufacturing concern—adding up to more than the company's annual profits. These figures say nothing, of course, about the decreased quality of everyday work life suffered from excessive negative stress. We will see that such negative stress is caused partly by employers through the job climate they provide and partly by employees in how they maladaptively cope with the pressures of work.

Drugs and alcohol have become a serious and costly problem in the American workplace. In a cover story on "Drugs on the Job," for example, *Time* magazine stated: "Illegal drugs have become so pervasive in the U.S. workplace that they are used in almost every industry, the daily companions of blue- and white-collar workers alike. Their presence on the job is sapping the energy, honesty and reliability of the American labor force even as competition from foreign companies is growing ever tougher" (Castro, 1986, 54).

Factors accounting for increased drug use on the job extend beyond the workplace itself, of course, into the society at large. Thus, the National Institute on Drug Abuse estimates that nearly two-thirds of the people now entering the work force have used illegal drugs. Yet job stress clearly is a contributing factor to the drug problem—and to a host of others—at work.

Another cost of widespread job distress in this country is burnout—a process of progressive mental and physical exhaustion. Burnout is thought to be especially prevalent in human service work, where in recent years professionals and their staffs have been faced with diminishing financial resources and lowered public esteem at the very time when work load has increased (Patrick, 1981; Cherniss, 1980; Maslach and Jackson, 1982).

According to Patrick (1981), the symptoms of burnout include the following.

Diminished sense of humor

Skipping rest and food breaks

Increased overtime and no vacation

Increased physical complaints

Social withdrawal

Changed job performance

Self-medication with alcohol, tranquilizers, and other mood-altering drugs

Emotional changes

Burnout results in higher rates of worker turnover, decreased effectiveness, increased absenteeism, lowered morale, and other harmful effects. No one knows for certain how widespread this problem is, but it is significant enough to draw the attention of many experts in human resource management and organizational psychology.

THE NEED FOR OPTIMAL JOB STRESS

Recall that the goal of managing job stress, just as any other type of stress, is not to avoid it (an impossibility) but to harness it so that it becomes a positive force toward alertness, energy, and productivity. The goal, then, is to create optimal job stress—neither too much nor too little arousal. Most of the time, we want to stay within our zone of positive stress, while periodically pushing our limits in order to learn gradually to take on new responsibilities and challenges with minimal negative stress. How best to accomplish this is an ongoing issue facing both the organization and the individual.

Forbes (1979) has identified the following as indicators of optimum stress among employees.

High energy

Mental alertness

High motivation

Calmness under pressure

Thorough analysis of problems

Improved memory and recall

Sharp perception

Optimistic outlook

Forbes suggests that managers use these indicators to assess stress levels at any given time among those supervised. According to Forbes, indicators of either underload or overload include the following.

Boredom

Apathy

High accident rate

Frequent grievances

Absenteeism

Negative outlook toward employer

Widespread fatigue

Insomnia

Change in appetite

Increased use of tobacco, drugs, or alcohol

Errors

Indecisiveness

Short-range attitude

While these indicators are difficult to measure, they can be observed by the sensitive, perceptive manager. When apparent to the degree that individual and organizational effectiveness are impaired, constructive steps are needed to deal with employee stress—and the conditions in which those employees work.

HIGH-RISK STRESSORS IN THE WORKPLACE   ▼

What factors in the work setting seem to increase chances that people who work there will suffer inordinate job-related distress? In their book, *Managing Job Stress*, Brief, Schuler, and Van Sell (1980) have identified a host of such factors, some

TABLE 13-1. SOURCES OF JOB STRESS

ORGANIZATIONAL CHARACTERISTICS AND PROCESSES

Organizational Policies
Inequitable or inadequate performance evaluations
Pay inequities
Ambiguous or arbitrary policies
Rotating work shifts
Frequent relocation
Idealistic job descriptions before hiring

Organizational Structure
Centralization; low participation in decision-making
Low opportunity for advancement or growth
Size
Excessive formalization
Excessive specialization and division of labor
Interdependence of organizational units

Organizational Processes
Poor communication
Poor or inadequate feedback on performance
Ambiguous or conflicting goals
Ineffective delegation
Training programs

JOB DEMANDS AND ROLE CHARACTERISTICS

Working Conditions
Crowding
Lack of privacy; poor spatial arrangements
Noise
Excessive heat or cold
Lights: inadequate, glaring, or flickering
Presence of toxic chemicals
Safety hazards
Air pollution, including radiation

Interpersonal Relationships
Inconsiderate or inequitable supervisors
Lack of recognition or acceptance
Lack of trust
Competition
Difficulty in delegating responsibilities
Conflict within and between groups

Job Demands
Repetitive work
Time pressures and deadlines
Low skill requirements
Responsibility for people
Underemployment; overemployment

Role Characteristics
Role conflict
Role ambiguity
Role underload/overload
Role-status incongruency

SOURCE: Brief, Schuler, and Van Sell (1980, 66–67)

---

related to the organization as a whole and others related to the more immediate job roles played by the individual workers (see Table 13-1).

EXERCISE 13-1. JOB STRESSOR QUESTIONNAIRE

Below is a questionnaire that has proven useful for identifying a variety of potential distressors at work. It can be used for self-awareness by individuals, for identification of common problems experienced by a work group or total organization, or for comparison of subunits within a workplace. This instrument has been used in individual stress counseling, in consultations with employers, and in research studies. It is intended to be used here for increasing your personal awareness of job stressors in your work environment.

The list below contains possible sources of stress on the job. For each item please indicate the frequency with which this condition is a source of stress for you. Place a number next to each item as follows:

4 *Always* a source of stress
3 *Frequently* a source of stress

2 *Sometimes* a source of stress
1 *Rarely* a source of stress
0 *Never* a source of stress

_____ Not sure what is expected of me

_____ Isolated from others during work

_____ Work is meaningless to me

_____ Pay is too low

_____ Bad fit between my personality and demands of the job

_____ Unchallenging

_____ Too little time to do all that's expected of me

_____ Lack of influence over my job conditions

_____ Little positive feedback from my superiors

_____ Different people expect different things from me

_____ Long hours

_____ Rotating shifts

_____ Graveyard shift

_____ Swing shift

_____ Bad lighting

_____ Little feedback about whether or not I am doing a good job

_____ Too much noise

_____ Too many people around me, too little privacy

_____ Too many interruptions

_____ Too little freedom to do the work my own way

_____ My abilities are not fully used

_____ Too much routine

_____ Personality conflicts among my co-workers

_____ Workload sometimes too heavy, other times too light

_____ Little opportunity for advancement

_____ Sexual harassment

_____ Irritable customers or clients

_____ Need to act contrary to personal ethics

_____ Lack of appreciation from public

_____ Other

As noted at the beginning this questionnaire is intended to help you identify specific stressors at work. You may also find it helpful to use the following categories in assessing the overall potential of your job for creating distress:

50 or higher   High potential for job distress

20 to 49   Moderate potential for job distress

19 or lower   Low potential for job distress

Space does not allow detailed descriptions of all potential distressors in the workplace. Thus, we will focus here on a number of factors that have been studied by stress researchers. These are divided into two categories: organizational stressors and role-related stressors.

ORGANIZATIONAL STRESSORS

1.   **Centralization and Lack of Participation.** Work organizations vary in the degree to which decision-making is centralized in one or a few positions at the top or spread throughout the system. Centralization may be efficient when an organization is small and circumstances are stable. However, as the work setting grows in size and as circumstances require a rapid response, centralization becomes

inefficient. Moreover, this pattern of control has the effect of excluding middle- and lower-level employees from participating in decisions that affect their work. The result can be decreased morale and increased stress-related symptoms. For example, in a study of over 1,400 American workers, lack of participation in decision-making was the most consistent and notable predictor of negative job stress and health problems (Brief, Schuler and Van Sell, 1980). Similar findings have been reported in a study of Canadian workers (Zalesnick, de Vries, and Howard, 1977).

Clearly, the organization and its employees benefit from a decentralized pattern of decision-making, with a concomitant sense of influence over the work process and work conditions by employees.

2. Shift Work. Perhaps one of five American workers works on an evening, night, or rotating shift, rather than during the daytime (Brief, Schuler, and Van Sell, 1980). This pattern has developed mainly in industries where continuous production is a requirement—for example, in utilities, steel, petroleum, and food processing. Sometimes, human service areas also demand such schedules—in law enforcement, fire fighting, and hospitals, for example.

While organizational demands may provide ample reason for shift work, individual workers often experience substantial strain because of it. In a social world where most people live according to a daytime work schedule, adaptation is often difficult. Sleep patterns are different, social contacts are affected, noise and quiet needs are reversed, and more. Family life, friendships, health, and emotions often suffer. Wilkinson (1971, 35) has suggested an evolutionary reason.

. . . the human adult is an animal whose body is tuned by evolution and training to go about its business during the hours of daylight and sleep during those of darkness. Ask it to work at night and sleep during the day and it does both rather badly.

Brief, Schuler, and Van Sell (1980, 74) have summarized the stress symptoms found to be associated with shift work in the list shown in Table 13-2.

One aspect of shift work is difficulty with the circadian rhythm, which concerns 24-hour cyclical fluctuations in such body functions as temperature, metabolism, heart rate, sleep cycle, adrenal hormone production, and mental alertness. There is little question that shift work interferes with these normal rhythms (Toufexis, 1990). The more frequent the shift change (for example, every seven days, as in some companies), the more severe the interference.

Organizations, then, need to minimize shift work to the extent possible. When it is required by the nature of the tasks to be performed, it seems best to allow workers to stay on a given shift for perhaps three or four months at a time. Individuals who must work on a non-daytime or rotating shifts need to do all possible to maximize stability, good health habits, and good health buffers, as described in Chapter 8. Avoiding awfulizing, negativizing, and catastrophizing can help avoid making matters worse.

3. Inadequate Social Support. In Chapter 11, you read that social isolation is a risk factor for boredom, distress symptoms, and illness. Chapter 11 referred

TABLE 13-2. STRESS SYMPTOMS ASSOCIATED WITH SHIFT WORK

PHYSIOLOGICAL SYMPTOMS

Inability to obtain enough sleep
Fatigue
Disturbances in appetite, digestion, and elimination
Upper gastrointestinal disorders
Respiratory problems

DISTURBANCES IN FAMILY AND INTERPERSONAL RELATIONSHIPS

Parenting role difficulties
Higher divorce rate
Higher incidence of sexual problems
Unfavorable family reactions
Increase in solitary leisure activities
Lower participation in social, religious, and civic organizations
Fewer contacts with friends

WORK PRODUCTIVITY

More mistakes
More accidents
Lower productivity

PSYCHOLOGICAL REACTIONS

Impaired mental health
Fewer needs fulfilled at work
Lower commitment to the organization

SOURCE: Brief, Schuler and Van Sell (1980, 74)

to social support as an important buffer, helping to build resistance against distress. Social support in the workplace is just as vital to wellness as it is in the family and the community.

Perhaps the most useful research on this topic is by sociologist James House. In his book, *Work Stress and Social Support* (1981) he points out that social support at work can exert two positive impacts on the person. First, the greater the social support from supervisors and co-workers, the less the stress and the better health becomes. This he calls the "direct effect" of social support. A study of 1809 workers in the rubber industry provides evidence that supervisor support and co-worker support were positively associated with job satisfaction and were inversely associated with such health problems as itch and rash, ulcers, angina pectoris, cough, and neurosis (House, 1981).

Second, social support can have an "indirect or buffering effect," whereby it can soften the harmful effects of other stress-producing conditions, such as autocratic leadership style, shift work, or excessive routine on the job. House reports several studies showing that social support does in fact exert this buffering effect as well. For example, those workers with a high workload, with role conflicts, and with underutilization of abilities all had fewer health complaints when social support at work was high than when it was low.

For supervisors and managers, a continuing challenge is to develop means of promoting work group cohesion and supportiveness, as well as to provide it directly themselves. The individual worker needs to avail herself/himself of support that may be available, as well as to give of herself/himself in ways that will contribute in a positive way to a supportive environment for co-workers.

EXERCISE 13-2. WORK SOCIAL SUPPORT SCALE

Here is a useful measure for assessing social support at work. A slightly modified version of one used by House and associates, this scale yields four scores: a supervisor support score, a co-worker support score, a support score for others outside work, and an overall, total social support score. For illustrative research using the original scale, see House (1981, 71).

	Very much	Somewhat	A little	Not at all
		(put one check by each item)		

How much does each of these people go out of his/her way to do things to make your *work life* easier for you?

Your immediate superior	_____	_____	_____	_____
Other people at work	_____	_____	_____	_____
People outside work	_____	_____	_____	_____

How much can each of these people be relied upon when things get tough at work?

Your immediate superior	_____	_____	_____	_____
Other people at work	_____	_____	_____	_____
People outside work	_____	_____	_____	_____

How often are the following people willing to listen to your personal problems?

Your immediate superior	_____	_____	_____	_____
Other people at work	_____	_____	_____	_____
People outside work	_____	_____	_____	_____

How easy is it to talk with each of the following people?

Your immediate superior	_____	_____	_____	_____
Other people at work	_____	_____	_____	_____
People outside work	_____	_____	_____	_____

4.   Organizational Climate. Just as individuals have personalities, work settings have a "climate" or a "feel" about them (Matteson and Ivancevich, 1987). Each is distinctive in its tone and in the effect it leaves among those it serves—customers, students, patients, clients—as well as those who work there. Organizational climate, which admittedly is difficult to measure, is the result of several factors.

Centralization—decentralization

Amount of worker involvement in decision-making

Degree of trust among fellow employees and from supervisors to employees

Overall worker commitment to organizational goals

Pace of work (slow, optimal, fast)

Group attitudes toward those served

Cohesion within work groups

Health practices among employees

Overall stress level in the organization

Predictability of events

Pace of change in the organization

Quality of the physical environment

The more positive the organizational climate in a holistic sense, the more favorable its likely impact on workers' stress and health will be. Attending to these not-so-apparent variables is an important challenge facing the successful manager.

ROLE-RELATED STRESSORS

The stressors (potential distressors) discussed below have to do not with the larger organizational climate of work, but with the immediate work roles within which the person performs. A role is a cluster of expectations associated with a given social position (for example, father, student, employee, citizen, neighbor, friend). Researchers have identified a number of role-related conditions that can and often do contribute to worker distress and illness. Knowing about these can be an important step toward minimizing their harmful effects.

Role Conflict
Role conflict refers to incongruent expectations associated with social roles. It comes in two forms. One is within-role conflicts, in which role partners associated with a single position send incompatible expectations. For example, a school superintendent is expected by teachers to raise salaries, but taxpayers expect him to keep taxes down. Another example is a waitress expected by management to serve more tables but is expected by customers at a specific table to give prompt and courteous service.

The second form of role conflict is incompatible expectations associated with two or more roles. A common illustration is mother-employee. Here there often is a direct conflict in what others expect. Meeting the expectations associated with one role results in falling short of the expectations sent by partners of the second role.

Periodic role conflicts of these types are, of course, unavoidable in all jobs. But when they are a chronic condition of work, stress and health can suffer. Early researchers on this, for example, found that the greater the presence of role conflicts, the less the job satisfaction, especially when conflicting messages are received from persons in authority (Kahn, et al, 1964). Other studies have linked role conflicts with heart disease, high blood pressure, elevated cholesterol, and obesity (Cassel, 1974; Warr and Parry, 1982). Ivancevich and Matteson (1980, 111) have summarized these studies by stating:

> Thus, as a stressor, role conflict undermines job satisfaction (with all the negative outcomes so frequently found to be associated with that) and is associated with physiological changes that have both personal and organizational costs. Other difficulties, such as decreased quality of decisions made and reduction of creativity, are very likely to result from the tension and anxiety associated with conflict.

While role conflicts sometimes cannot be avoided in jobs with multiple role partners, managers need to be sensitive to creating conditions with as few conflicts as possible. Individual workers need to feel confident about bringing supervisors' attention to avoidable role conflicts; they should be reasonable and clear when giving directions or expectations to their role partners, as well. And, as with other role difficulties, the more a person practices the stress management methods described in this book, the less role conflict is likely to have harmful effects on morale, productivity, and health.

Role Ambiguity

Rose, a new secretary at a weight control clinic, is quite confused about what her job priorities should be. This confusion is partly the result of the newness of the clinic itself and partly the result of an unclear definition of her duties by her supervisor. Understandably, Rose is more anxious and uncertain than she expected to be in this new job. Her sleep has been affected, and she is more irritable at home than before she took the job.

Rose is suffering the effects of role ambiguity—lack of clarity about the work role. Lack of certainty about role priorities, about the balance of duties, and about how to do specific tasks are unavoidable, of course, when one is new to a job, when the job itself is new or redefined, or when the organizational policies or procedures are in a state of flux. However, when role ambiguity is a long-term condition of work, a number of adverse consequences are likely, according to research studies (Matteson and Ivancevich, 1987).

Job dissatisfaction

Job-related tension

Lower self-confidence

Elevated blood pressure

Depression

Anxiety

Less work motivation

Feelings of resentment

No organization can be structured to avoid role ambiguity entirely. Nor can individual workers ever hope to avoid it completely, whether they are self-employed or work for others, lower level workers, or professionals. However, managers need to do all possible to define work responsibilities clearly, to keep policies and procedures updated, and to maintain clear communication channels. The individual needs to be assertive in seeking clarification when needed.

Role Overload

We are all familiar with periods of time when there simply is more to do than time available. When this is a temporary condition, we seem to be able to adapt fairly easily. However, when the condition becomes chronic, the result can be burnout and breakdown. As Ivancevich and Matteson have stated (1980, 113):

> An electrical system that is unable to handle all of the electricity introduced to it is overloaded. In most instances a fuse blows or a circuit breaker is tripped, stopping the input and preventing damage to the system. When an individual is unable to handle all the work input, that person may become overloaded. Unfortunately, unlike the electrical system, people do not have an automatic safety device, and the overload condition can lead to physical, mental, and job performance problems.

Overload can take two forms: quantitative (too much to do in time available) and qualitative (impossibly demanding expectations by supervisors). Either type, when chronic, can lead to stress and health difficulties. Overload among tax accountants around April 15, for example, has been found to lead to elevated cholesterol in the blood (Friedman, Rosenman and Carroll, 1958). Other negative outcomes reported by researchers include increased risk of heart attacks, low job satisfaction, escapist drinking behavior, high absenteeism, low confidence, high accident rates on the job, and high cigaret consumption (French and Caplan, 1973).

Occasional overload is probably unavoidable. Overload as a chronic condition can be avoided through wise role definitions, proper assessment of manpower resources needed to carry out a given workload, and establishing a good fit between individual capabilities and needs of the job. Learning to cope effectively with temporary overload and to be assertive enough, individually or collectively to minimize chronic overload when working for others can be useful steps for minimizing distress from role overload. Finally, role overload often is self-created. We need to be sensitive to our limits of time and energy in order to avoid chronic overload when we can.

Role Underload

This occurs when the occupant experiences too little to do or insufficient variety on the job. This is especially true of repetitious jobs, such as assembly-line work (Brief, Schuler & Van Sell, 1980). Like role overload, underload can occur from time to time in most jobs. We usually adapt to these conditions with little difficulty. When understimulation is an ongoing experience, demoralization, anxiety, depression, and physical symptoms of distress become common. One study found that executives at the high and low end of a stress scale had more medical problems, suggesting a curvilinear association between stimulation and health (McLean, 1979). This study ". . . seems to demonstrate that those who are bored or understimulated and those who feel highly pressured represent the two ends of a continuum, each with a significantly elevated number of symptoms" (McLean, 1979).

Role underload more often results from too little variety in work tasks (qualitative underload) than from too little to do (quantitative underload). The challenge facing managers, then, is to structure work so it has sufficient variability over the long run. The individual employee needs to seek out a job with sufficient variety and quantity for her/his needs, to structure the job's pace and variety for one's tastes insofar as possible, and to tolerate temporary underload—perhaps even welcome it.

High Role Expectations—Low Control

Among the most risky conditions of all for worker distress is a role that has heavy responsibilities and high expectations combined with little opportunity to control how the job is carried out or the conditions of work (Cooper and Payne, 1978). A good example is the position of secretary, say, in a lawyer's office. She (Have you ever seen a male legal secretary?) is likely to be besieged with time deadlines, heavy time demands from her boss, unhappy clients over the phone, and the need for precision in filling out forms and in typing documents. Yet she is likely to have little to say about the physical conditions of work, about interruptions, about the workload, or about the format of reports and forms she must complete.

Another example is the hospital technician whose work must be very carefully executed because a life and certainly the patient's comfort may depend upon it. Expectations of superiors, the public, and the patients are high. Yet technicians in the X-ray department, the surgery room, the cardiology laboratory, or the respiratory department are likely to have little to say about their pace of work, about the demeanor of physicians, or about the layout of the hospital facility in which they work. The result for occupants of such positions often is a high incidence of distress symptoms.

Managers can minimize such symptoms by giving employees as much opportunity as possible to determine the manner and pace with which tasks are carried out. Decentralized decision-making with maximum involvement by work groups can help, as we saw earlier. As with other role stressors, the individual is challenged here with being assertive in requesting as much leeway as possible in controlling conditions of work. Maintaining good mental and physical coping habits is vital for handling effectively the distress that sometimes does occur from these conditions.

Difficult Relationships

Difficult role partners may be supervisors, co-workers, or those served by the role occupant: patients, students, customers, or clients, for example. The potential for distress is especially likely among those at boundary-spanning points in the organization. That is, where members of the organization deal with others outside the organization. Illustrations include teachers, customer service representatives, nurses, ministers, and lawyers (Bramson, 1981).

The degree to which distress in fact occurs depends on the skill of the role occupant in handling difficult role partners, especially those who are angry. Here are several suggestions for handling an angry person at work.

1. Be attentive. Use effective listening, as described in Chapter 11.

2. Avoid allowing your self-esteem to be threatened. Be thick-skinned, using positive self-talk.

3. Allow the angry person time to vent.

4. See her/his anger as a problem to be solved, rather than as something to be angry back at.

5. Use the "grain of truth" approach. Try to acknowledge even a small degree of truth in what the person is saying.

6. Show empathy. This itself often will defuse the other's anger.

7. If needed, be assertive. There comes a point where it is OK to tell the angry person that enough is enough—to stop dumping on you. This can be done assertively, without hostility or aggressiveness, as described in Chapter 11.

Even the most tactful and patient individuals have their off-days, of course. Effective managers ensure that their employees are adequately trained in listening skills, in handling angry persons, and in problem-solving for difficult persons served by the organization. The effective employee makes certain that she/he continues to update and refine these vital job skills.

Career Insecurity and Inopportunity

This role-related stressor has to do with those features of a person's career development affecting her/his perceptions of present and future options. These features may become sources of concern, anxiety, frustration, or loss of motivation (Ivancevich and Matteson, 1980).

One of these factors is job insecurity. Another is lack of opportunity for job advancement. Erikson and his associates found that job satisfaction was greatest among individuals whose promotion matched or exceeded their hopes (Erickson, Pugh, and Gunderson, 1972). As advancement rates fell behind expectations, job satisfaction decreased. Blau found a number of stress-related consequences including reductions in work output, high accident rates, alcoholism and/or drug abuse, worsening interpersonal relations on the job, and increased resentment and resistance to supervision (Blau, 1978).

Such career problems may be inherent in certain job settings and job categories. Further, they may be partly caused by nonwork factors in the private lives of employees, such as a midlife crisis, faltering career commitment, or self-doubt.

Yet it is incumbent on the sensitive manager to be alert to evidence of such conditions. For the individual worker, this is an example of using personal distress signals as a sign of disharmony between inside ideals and outside reality—which can lead either to further distress or to constructive steps to alter or advance one's career direction.

Sexual Harassment

From 70 to 90 percent of employed women report that they have been subjected to sexual harassment—"unwanted, repeated and coercive sexual advances" (Farley, 1978). According to Brief, Schuler, and Van Sell (1980, 193), "Sexual harassment can take the form of innuendoes, lewd comments, sexual gestures and touching, demands for dates, and outright demands for sexual involvement. Often, promises of career advancement in return for sexual favors, or threats of harm if demands are rejected, are implicitly or explicitly made." A study of sexually harassed women found that three of four were negatively affected emotionally or physically (Safran, 1976).

The most insidious manifestation of this problem may be sexual advances from a higher status male who gives explicit or implicit promise of advancement or other favoritism in return for sexual favors. Women usually find this situation intimidating, demeaning, and exploitative.

Such behavior violates the integrity, freedom and rights of women on the job. The U.S. Equal Opportunity Commission has made clear through its regulations that sexual harassment by supervisors is a violation of civil rights. Increasingly, employers are issuing explicit guidelines and rules prohibiting such conduct and specifying procedures to be followed when it does occur.

Employers and supervisors need to be aware of this subtle yet pervasive problem. Educational campaigns are needed for employees and employers, males and females, young and old. Employers must do all possible to stop it. Women need to practice on-the-spot assertiveness and to know grievance procedures to follow when such harassment does occur.

Brief, Schuler, and Van Sell (1990, 194) suggest a number of options for women who are sexually harassed on the job.

1. Be aware that the come-on is not a response to you or a comment on your competence, but reflects stereotypes attached to women as a group.

2. Make it clear you dislike the sexual attention and want it stopped. If needed, repeat in front of others.

3. Share your experiences and concerns with other women at work so you don't feel you are alone and so you can receive support.

4. Keep a written record with details of what happens.

5. Complain to your supervisor in writing. Go one step higher if needed.

6. If your complaints are not dealt with effectively within the organization, you can file an official complaint with your local or state Human Rights Commission, Fair Employment Practices Agency, or the Federal Equal Employment Opportunity Commission. Expect long delays.

7. If you decide to quit, apply for unemployment benefits. Be clear exactly why you quit.

8.   Be especially good to yourself while you cope with the stresses of this threat to your career.

Other Common Role-Related Stressors

Those stressors listed thus far are hardly exhaustive. Other common ones, which in fact may be primary in given situations, include:

Lack of appreciation by supervisors

Low public image

Low wages

Conflict of work with childbearing

Underutilization of abilities

Irritating habits of co-workers

Having to act contrary to personal ethics

We next examine job burnout, a common result of stress overload, combined with inability to cope effectively.

JOB BURNOUT ▼

WHAT IS BURNOUT?

According to Matteson and Ivancevich (1987, 241), "Burnout is a psychological process, brought about by unrelieved work stress, that results in emotional exhaustion, depersonalization, and feelings of decreased accomplishment."

Job burnout is a progressive state of mental and physical exhaustion. It is marked by physical depletion and chronic fatigue, feelings of hopelessness and helplessness, a deteriorating self-image, and growing negative feelings toward work and other people (Matteson and Ivancevich, 1987). As Jackson (984) notes, the first sign of burnout usually is emotional fatigue. Since this is an unpleasant emotional state, psychological distancing from other people predictably follows. A decreasing sense of personal effectiveness and accomplishment also is common.

BURNOUT STAGES

Matteson and Ivancevich (1987, 242) maintain that burnout consists of up to five stages.

1.   INVOLVEMENT

This is the stage of enthusiasm, commitment, and exhilaration. If the person's expectations can be sustained, burnout may never occur. However, if job reality falls short of expectations, burnout chances increase.

2. STAGNATION

Hardly detectable at the beginning, stagnation creeps into one's work experience in such a way that satisfaction diminishes, and fatigue begins to occur. Involvement and excitement at work level off, and the individual begins to turn elsewhere for satisfaction—family, leisure, hobbies, social contacts.

3. DETACHMENT

Many people become aware at this point that something is missing from their work experience and that they are becoming chronically tired emotionally and physically. They find themselves simply "putting in time." They begin to avoid challenges and opportunities and grow increasingly negative about work.

4. JUNCTURE

This is the stage that can devastate the individual, her/his career and even the family. Self-doubts prevail, self-esteem is at a very low level, extreme cynicism exists toward clients or patients, absenteeism mounts, relationships become troubled. At the extreme, the person may even fail to function on the job, quit, or contemplate suicide.

5. INTERVENTION

At this stage, the individual or the organization intervenes in such a way that the person retrieves morale, health and productivity. The intervention may take the form of changing assignments within the workplace, beginning an exercise program, entering counseling, or simply a personal choice to change one's attitude or perspective.

Intervention may not work, however, if the organizational environment continues to be flawed.

ORGANIZATIONAL FACTORS CONTRIBUTING TO BURNOUT

Pfifferling and Eckel (1982, 264) have identified a number of work conditions carrying a high risk of employee burnout. According to the authors, presence of three or more of these conditions qualifies an organization as burnout-prone.

Continuously high stress levels

A norm of constantly giving to others

Discouragement of hierarchical staff interaction

Expectations of extra effort with minimal rewards

No reinforcement for suggestions on improving morale

Repetitive work activities

Minimal additional resources available for extra-effort tasks

Lack of encouragement for professional self-care

Discouragement of mutual participation in decision-making

Evangelistic leadership styles

Policy changes unrelated to problem priority

Policy changes too frequent to be evaluated

Rigid role typing for workers

A belief that playfulness is unprofessional

Pervasive "isms" (ageism, sexism, nepotism, and so on)

Emphasis on past successes

Constant shifting of ground rules for policy

Minimal emphasis on positive feedback

Minimal emphasis on comfort of environment

PREVENTING BURNOUT

Managers and Supervisors

Shapiro (1982) maintains that burnout is not the result of either the person or the organization alone, but of the interaction between the two. He contends that supervisors can follow several constructive practices to minimize burnout potential.

Leadership that provides support, structure, and information

Communication that is timely, appropriate, and accurate

An environment that is planned, efficient, and orderly

Workers who participate meaningfully in decision making

Support and nurturing from supervisory staff

Encouragement of employee creativity and innovation

Peer friendship and support networks

Especially important to minimizing burnout potential is anticipatory socialization of new employees (preparation for potential burnout traps and how to avoid them). Kramer (1974) reports a program of anticipatory socialization that significantly reduces the reality shock for new nurses, thereby lessening chances of burnout.

Effective managers and supervisors not only push for maximum short-run productivity. They know that healthy and satisfied workers are also vital for the long-term benefit of all concerned—managers, workers, and clients. They know that optimal job stress needs to be sought.

Here are several ways managers and supervisors can move toward achieving this ideal.

1.   They can make the organization a sufficiently appealing place to work so that satisfaction is high and turnover is low.

2. They can assure that role expectations are as clear and congruent as possible in order to minimize role conflicts and role ambiguity.

3. They can manage the work process so that it is appropriately varied and is chronically neither overloaded nor underloaded.

4. They can strike a good balance between continuity and change in the organization. While self-renewing change is vital for keeping up with shifting conditions outside the organization, such change must not occur at a pace so fast that it produces widespread distress among employees.

5. Managers and supervisors can provide continuing support and encouragement to their employees. They can ensure that each employee feels needed and appreciated. Similarly, they can encourage the formation of cohesive, supportive work groups among co-workers.

6. To the degree possible, every person can be given maximum flexibility to work at the pace and manner that will ensure maximum long-term health, satisfaction, and self-expression—as well as short-term productivity.

7. They can provide meaningful opportunities for ongoing involvement by all employees in decisions affecting them.

8. They can be attentive to stress levels within the organization—and to work conditions that might contribute to unnecessary distress.

9. They can provide supportive stress management services for employees in distress. Such services, ranging from fitness programs to counseling services, can be provided within the organization, or referral networks can be established.

10. Managers and supervisors can provide opportunities for all workers—themselves included—to learn more about stress and distress, especially related to work.

EXERCISE 13-3. ASSESSMENT OF YOUR WORKPLACE

1. To what extent do you think each of these conditions is met in your place of work?

2. If you are a manager or supervisor, to what extent are you doing each of these things? What changes might you make to better meet these ideals?

3. As an employee, what might you do to bring these ideals to the attention of your supervisors or managers—assertively and not aggressively?

Individuals

Individuals can prevent burnout by following many of the guidelines and methods presented in previous chapters of this book. Perhaps most important of all is realistic self-talk, personal pacing, and good health buffers.

When confronted with distressors, chronic or acute, there are a number of options open to you. These have all been presented in more detail in previous chapters. The initials <u>AAAABBCC</u> will help you remember them. These have been expanded from the work of Tubesing and Tubesing (1983).

Awfulize about the stressor

Alter the stressor—through individual or group action

Avoid or withdraw from the stressor

Accept the stressor, by

> Breathing away tension (Six-Second Quieting Response)
>
> Building health buffers
>
>> Regular exercise
>>
>> Adequate sleep
>>
>> Good nutrition
>
> Changing your interpretation of the stressor
>
> Communicating differently with the stressor

EXERCISE 13-4. APPLYING THE AAAABBCC OPTIONS

1.   Identify three work-related stressors that have led to tension or upset for you recently.
2.   Which of the AAAABBCC options might you have used to minimize your distress in each instance?
3.   Which might you use in similar situations in the future?

In this chapter, you have read about some of the high costs of job stress and about the need for optimal job stress for peak performance and good health. You also read about high risk stressors related to the organization and the work role. The nature and roots of burnout also were explored. Finally, you read about options for the organization and the individual to prevent and remedy job stress, especially burnout.

Many people, of course, work under very demanding conditions and pressures, yet stay well. Many even thrive under these conditions. What can we learn about their habits, attitudes and qualities? The next chapter focuses on theories and research related to thriving under pressure, especially at work.

REFERENCES

▼

Blau, B. (1978) Understanding mid-career stress. *Management Review, 67,* 57-62.
Bramson, R.M. (1981). *Coping with Difficult People.* Garden City, NJ: Anchor/Double-day.

Brief, A.P., Schuler, R.S., & Van Sell, M. (1980). *Managing Job Stress*. Boston: Little, Brown & Company.

Cassel, J. (1974). Psychosocial processes and stress: Theoretical formulation. *International Journal of Health Services*, 4, 471- 484.

Castro, J. (1986). Battling the enemy within. *Time Magazine*, March 17, 1986, 54-61.

Cherniss, C. (1980). *Staff Burnout: Job Stress in the Human Services*. Beverly Hills: Sage.

Cooper, C.L. & Payne, R. (Eds.) (1978). *Stress at Work*. New York: John Wiley & Sons.

Erickson, J., Pugh, W.M., & Gunderson, E.K., Status Incongruency as a predictor of job satisfaction and life stress. *Journal of Applied Psychology*, 56, 523-525.

Farley, L. (1978). *Sexual Shakedown: The Sexual Harassment of Women On The Job*. New York: McGraw.

Forbes, R. (1979). *Corporate Stress*. Garden City, NJ: Doubleday.

French, J.R.P., & Caplan, R.D. (1973). Organizational stress and individual stress. In Morrow, A.J. (Ed.). *The Failure of Success*. New York: AMACOM, 30-36.

Friedman, M. R., Rosenman, R.H., & Carroll, V. (1958). Changes in serum cholesterol and blood-clotting time in men subjected to cyclic variation in occupational stress. *Circulation*, 17, 852- 861.

Greenberg, H.M. (1980). *Coping with Job Stress*. Englewood Cliffs: Prentice-Hall, Inc.

House, J.S. (1981). *Work Stress and Social Support*. Reading: Addison-Wesley.

Ivancevich J.M., & Matteson, M.T. (1980). *Stress and Work: A Managerial Perspective*. Glenview: Scott.

Kahn, R.L., Wolfe, D.M., Quinn, R.P., Snoek, J.D., & Rosenthal, R.A. (1964). *Organizational Stress*. New York: John Wiley and Sons.

Kramer, M. (1974). *Reality Shock: Why Nurses Leave Nursing*. St. Louis: Mosby Press.

Maslach, C. & Jackson, S. (1982) Burnout in health professions: A social psychological analysis. In B. Sanders and J. Suls (Eds.) *Social Psychology of Health and Illness*. Hillsdale, NJ: Lawrence Erlbaum.

Matteson, M.T., & Ivancevich, J.M. (1987). *Controlling Work Stress*. San Francisco: Jossey-Bass.

McLean, A. A. (1979). *Work Stress*. Reading: Addison-Wesley.

O'Boyle, T.F. (1990). Fear and stress in the office take toll. *Wall Street Journal*, November 6, B1.

Patrick, P.K., (1981) *Health Care Worker Burnout: What It Is, What To Do About It*. Chicago: Blue Cross/Inquiry.

Pfifferling, J.H., & Eckel, F.M. (1982). Beyond burnout: Obstacles and prospects. In Paine, W.S. (Ed.), *Job Stress and Burnout*. Beverly Hills, CA: Sage.

Safran, C. (1976). What men do to women on the job: A shocking look at sexual harassment. *Redbook*, 149, 217-224.

Shapiro, C.H. (1982). Creative supervision: An underutilized antidote. In Paine, W.S. (Ed.). *Job Stress and Burnout*. Beverly Hills, CA: Sage.

Toufexis, A. (1990). Drowsy America. *Time Magazine*, December 17, 78-85.

Tubesing D., & Tubesing, N. (1983). *Structured Exercises in Stress Management: Vol. I.* Duluth: Whole Person Associates.

Warr P., & Parry, G. (1982) Paid employment and women's psychological well-being. *Psychological Bulletin,* 91, 498-516.

Wilkinson, R. (1971). Hours of work and the twenty-four hour cycle of rest and activity. *Psychology of Work.* Ed., Warr, P. Middlesex: Penguin.

Zalesnick, A., F.R. deVries, & Howard, J. Stress Reactions in organizations: Syndromes, causes, and consequences. *Behavioral Sciences,* 22, 151-162.

Thriving Under Pressure

Chapter 14

CHAPTER 14

I. INTRODUCTION

II. FOUR THEORIES OF THRIVING UNDER PRESSURE
   A. The Self-Actualized Personality
   B. Hardiness
   C. The Survivor Personality
       1. Biphasic Traits
       2. Serendipity
       3. Synergy
       4. Self-actualization
       5. Creativity
       6. Intuition
       7. Humor
       8. Competence Under Pressure
   D. Type C Behavior

III. THRIVING UNDER PUBLIC PRESSURE

IV. TIPS FOR THRIVING UNDER PRESSURE
   A. Chronic Pressure
       1. Methods from Previous Chapters
       2. 10 C's for Thriving Under Pressure
   B. Short-Term Episodes of Pressure
       1. Mental Rehearsal
       2. Positive Self-talk for Peak Performance
   C. Building Confidence

INTRODUCTION ▼

> Pressure's the name of the game today. Not just the pressure to get ahead, but the stress of trying to make it in a world where every time you look up, the rules of the game have changed. There's good reason we feel pressured. The world around us is becoming more competitive and less predictable with each passing day. In the past forty years the human race has entered the atomic age, the space age, and the computer age (Kriegel and Kriegel, 1984, xiii).

In a rapidly changing, fast-paced, competitive world, thriving under pressure is vital for health, enjoyment, and success. Sometimes pressure is a specific event (a final exam or speech), other times an ongoing circumstance (senior year in college or adapting to single parenthood after a divorce). Here are other examples.

▼ The high school student striving for a respectable grade point average.

▼ The university sophomore (a music major) taking a chemistry final.

▼ The college athlete performing at a young age before thousands or even millions.

▼ The young professional seeking upward mobility in her corporation.

▼ The NBA star stepping to the free throw line with the score tied in the final 20 seconds of the seventh game of the championship series.

▼ The single working mother with a family to care for at the same time that her job exerts high demands.

▼ The business executive with hundreds of employees and stockholders depending upon her decision-making abilities.

▼ The surgeon making vital decisions and moves under the operating room spotlight and with a life depending on him.

▼ The public official whose every move is watched by the public and the press while he makes decisions affecting thousands of people and millions of dollars.

Thriving under pressure, then, is a challenge in many circumstances and at any age. *Stress Management for Wellness* means more than relaxing or escaping in order to avoid pressure. It means being all you can be. It means reaching higher and higher levels of well-being, performance, and fulfillment. In short, it means not only surviving but thriving, even under the most difficult circumstances.

In discussing "how to learn lessons from life experiences," Walter and Siebert (1990) cite the old saying that, "Good mariners are not created by calm seas." They note that during times of severe adversity, some people survive remarkably well.

> During the Depression in the 1930s, some people went against the tide and refused to be swept away by mass despair. Even though thousands were destitute, some people found ways to be happy and to enjoy being alive. Using their imaginations and inner resources, they maintained a positive direction for themselves and their families during hard times (Walter and Siebert, 1990, 162).

Guidelines and skills from previous chapters—combined with new information presented here—can aid you in reaching peak performance and staying well under pressure.

FOUR THEORIES OF THRIVING UNDER PRESSURE   ▼

We can learn a great deal by examining four theories of high-functioning persons. Each of these is based on research by psychologists interested in discovering the qualities of outstanding individuals who stand apart from the rest.

THE SELF-ACTUALIZED PERSON

A classic study of high-level mental health was carried out by Abraham Maslow. Conducted rather informally over a long period of years, Maslow's investigations began while he was still a young Ph.D. in New York City. He noted with curiosity two older professors who seemed to be different from others, to be truly outstanding human beings. After watching them for some time, he came to discover they shared certain distinguishable qualities. He then decided to broaden his observations to include others around him—friends, students, present and past public figures (Goble, 1970).

After a time, Maslow put into writing his discoveries (Maslow, 1954; 1959; 1962; 1965; 1966; 1971). Self-actualization is the state of highest possible functioning, usually reached only in later years and only by a small percentage of people. He loosely described self-actualization as "the full use and exploitation of talent, capacities, potentialities, personalities, etc. Such people seem to be fulfilling themselves and doing the best that they are capable of doing" (Maslow, 1954). He later used the term "fully human."

Maslow included a number of qualities in his description of the self-actualized person (Goble, 1970, Chapter 3). It is useful to understand thriving under pressure in the context of this cluster of high-level qualities of model human beings.

▼ The ability to see reality as it is, rather than as they wish it to be.

▼ Perception and understanding undistorted by desires, anxieties, fears, hopes, false optimism, or pessimism ("desireless awareness").

▼ The ability to see people for what they are and to see through the fake and the phoney.

▼ The ability to be decisive in decision-making.

▼ A clear sense of what is right and just.

▼ A sense of humility, combined with willingness to listen to others and to learn.

▼ Dedication to some work, mission, or value larger than themselves.

▼ The ability and commitment to work very hard, yet experiencing a blurring of work and play.

▼ High creativity, along with spontaneity, willingness to make mistakes, openness, and flexibility.

▼ Uninhibited and hence expressive, natural and simple.

▼ Ability to ignore criticism, ridicule, and cultural constraints, with resulting "psychological freedom."

▼ More concerned with the task or outcome than with building image or ego— "self-transcendent."

▼ Relative absence of inner conflict. "He is not at war with himself; his personality is integrated" (Goble, 1970, 29).

▼ Pleasure at seeing pleasure in others.

▼ Confidence and self-respect; absence of severe self-condemnation.

▼ Sense of control over events and his reactions to events.

▼ Ability to thrive alone or with others.

▼ Tolerance of others' shortcomings.

▼ Ability to develop long-lasting, stable, supportive intimate relationships and friendships.

▼ Ability to maintain composure under pressure.

This last quality—composure under pressure—emerges naturally from a context of confidence.

These healthy individuals are not often threatened by the external situation as they have great confidence in their ability to handle whatever confronts them. They are almost uniformly unthreatened by the unknown and the mysterious. In fact, they are usually attracted to the unknown (Goble, 1970, 35).

We must keep in mind again Maslow's observation that this cluster of "fully human" qualities is attained only by a relatively few individuals. Certainly, they represent high ideals. Yet it is important not to discount or criticize yourself because you are "not there yet." Remember Maslow's contention that those few who are so fortunate usually reach this level only after age 60.

HARDINESS

In previous chapters, you read about the studies by Maddi and Kobasa (1984) in which they searched for characteristics of people who stayed healthy even during the clustering of multiple life changes. They identified a pattern they termed "hardiness"—a personality style showing a liking of challenge, a strong sense of commitment, and a strong sense of control.

Hardiness has not yet been studied as a quality facilitating peak performance under pressure, but it has been shown to help the person maintain good health in the face of challenging life circumstances and transitions, which is one form of thriving under pressure.

Hardiness is a perspective, a set of beliefs and attitudes that aids the individual in enduring and remaining optimistic during difficult times. Such a person is able to turn adversity into challenge, to sustain a strong commitment to herself and the task at hand, and to have a strong sense of control over events. As we noted previously, the opposites of challenge, commitment and control are threat, alienation, and helplessness—hardly the qualities that contribute to thriving under pressure.

THE SURVIVOR PERSONALITY

Psychologist Al Siebert for years has been fascinated by why some people survive a major setback such as a serious illness or injury, while others do not (Walker,

1988; Siebert, 1983; Walter and Siebert, 1990). He observes that some individuals rise to the occasion and are better for the experience, while others wither, weaken, or become embittered by adversity.

Siebert points to several examples. During the Nazi era, millions experienced horrible torture in concentration camps. Some victims were able to protect themselves by retreating to a reserve of inner strength. If they survived the gas chambers, many of these individuals emerged stronger, not weaker, and went on to live long, healthy, and productive lives.

Some Viet Nam veterans have never recovered from the trauma of the war; others have been able to put the memories to rest and get on with their lives.

Physicians marvel at the fact that two patients of similar age, socioeconomic status, and disease state can respond quite differently to treatment. One recovers and resumes a normal life, the other withers and dies.

In the same way, students respond quite differently to the heavy pressures of college. Why do some thrive and others become overwhelmed, discouraged, ill, and dispirited?

After studying hundreds of "survivors," Seibert discovered several patterns.

Biphasic Traits

Siebert observed that survivors display counterbalanced, seemingly paradoxical traits. They are playful and serious, trusting and cautious, intuitive and logical, impulsive and stable, gentle and strong, easygoing and strongwilled, childlike and mature. These qualities might seem at first glance to make for unpredictability, even schizoid tendencies. But Seibert believes they serve an important positive function: allowing the individual to respond with versatility under a wide range of demanding circumstances.

Serendipity

Survivors have a knack for responding with insight and wisdom under the pressure of an accident or other misfortune. They don't waste time moaning and groaning, but instead look ahead to how best to survive or solve the problem. Instead of asking, "Why did this terrible event happen to me?", they look ahead and ask, "Now that this has happened to me, what am I going to do about it? How can I turn this around?"

They are able to respond to events that would be highly distressing for others, turning them into a possible challenge, from negative stress into positive stress. Their ability to find seemingly fortuitous answers and solutions works for them in remaining level-headed and centered during adversity.

Synergy

Survivors need and produce synergy—having things go well for themselves and others. Their inner "life force" seems to take them in directions that work out, even under enormous pressure and hardship. They care so deeply about the wellbeing of others that they are unusually flexible and adaptive, with little ego investment in a given solution and willingness to learn and listen. They leave whatever world they pass through better than they found it. Siebert notes that survivors are "foul-weather friends."

Self-Actualization
Survivors enjoy taking reasonable risks. They challenge themselves and welcome the unknown. Like those studied by Maslow, these people are curious and self-motivating. They become better and smarter as they grow older. Able to adapt easily to change, they have no fear of looking foolish. They focus more on discovery than safety, security, or looking good.

Creativity
Survivors are less judgmental than others. They are not as quick to label something as good or bad, right or wrong. They accept others' fallibilities. Most of all, they are inventive in finding solutions to problems and adversities. This results from not being limited by fear of ridicule. They think spontaneously as the need arises. Their solutions are often a surprise to others.

Intuition
Survivors can sense subtle, even subliminal cues and clues. They are unusually sensitive to feelings and nuances and consider them valuable sources of information. Siebert believes this extraordinary sensitivity and perceptiveness sometimes even borders on extrasensory perception (ESP). He states, "My guess is that people who are fully functioning as humans achieve harmony with some unknown energies in the universe" (Walker, 1988, 15).

Humor
The trait most often found in survivors, according to Siebert, is humor. The survivor personality is able to laugh at what has happened and to find something amusing even in the midst of difficult events. Siebert noted that even hardened Korean War combat veterans, with whom he served in the 1950s, were able to respond to their own mistakes with humor. Rather than feel threatened or deeply disappointed, they were able to take difficulty with good humor and light-heartedness.

Competence Under Pressure
According to Siebert (1983, 21), trying circumstances are transformed into positive challenges because the person:

- ▼ can sit back and let things run themselves

- ▼ expends much less energy than people who are struggling

- ▼ has chunks of optional time for being curious about the early signs of new developments

- ▼ can spot early indications of potential trouble and take action to prevent it

- ▼ can work on future happenings so that when they occur things fall into place easily

▼ can put high quality time and energy into emergency developments without having other basic matters interrupted

▼ responds to an emergency or crisis with an attitudinal reflex of both expecting and needing things to work out well

Finally, Siebert (1983, 21) notes that:

> The really competent, synergistic people in every sphere of human activity are those individuals who have gone beyond their teachers. They have learned what no one can teach them. Competence results from self-motivated, self-managed learning. People who follow instructions on how to function successfully are never as skillful as people who are self-motivated learners.

TYPE C BEHAVIOR

A fourth theory of thriving under pressure, whether such pressure be difficult ongoing circumstances, such as the Great Depression, or a specific event, such as an athletic contest or a job interview, is Type C behavior. The Type C pattern draws some of the best attributes from the Type A and Type B patterns and adds new elements to form a cluster of ingredients for meeting challenge head-on with success and vitality. Originators of this concept, Robert and Marilyn Kriegel (1990, xvi), note:

> Type C behavior is a performance model for us all. Everyone . . . can perform as a Type C. Whether you're directing a multi-billion-dollar corporation or managing a small office, selling or speaking, running a machine or running for election, marketing or manufacturing, teaching or training, researching or reporting, out looking for a first job or wanting to change careers—WHATEVER YOU DO, YOU CAN DO IT AS A TYPE C.

The Type C model is based on the Type C experience—where everything seems to flow naturally at a very high level of performance. States Congresswoman Barbara Boxer, "It's like being on a roll. I feel confident and enthusiastic and everything seems to work. I am able to accomplish a great deal with a minimum of effort. My energy keeps building and gets transferred to whomever I am working with" (Kriegel & Kriegel, 1990, 1).

An award-winning reporter describes his Type C episodes this way: "Sometimes when I'm rushing to meet a deadline, I become so involved in what I am doing that I am unaware of anything going on around me. I get calm and everything becomes easy. It's unbelievable. I've done my best work at these times" (Kriegel and Kriegel, 1990, 2).

Type C episodes are marked by several qualities, experienced by most people at one time or another (Kriegel and Kriegel, 1984, 2).

Transcendent. You go beyond your usual level to new heights of personal performance.

Effortless. Your performance flows easily, without special effort or struggle.

Positive. You are optimistic and confident, thoroughly enjoying what you are doing.

Spontaneous. There is a natural unity of thought and action. Choices come easily.

Focused. Your concentration is complete. You are fully engaged with the process. You are totally involved and fully connected.

Vital. You feel unusually alive and energetic. You feel total joy in what you are doing and accomplishing.

The "C" in this model stands for three C's in the Type C pattern: **challenge, confidence** and **control.** These are the characteristics most often reported by people asked to describe their Type C experiences.

Based on countless workshops and consultations, as well as interviews with over 400 business executives, the Type C concept closely resembles the three C's of hardiness. Curiously, however, Kriegel and Kriegel never cite the work of Maddi and Kobasa, even though scientific publications on hardiness had appeared several years before. Despite this flaw, the Type C model does merit attention as a tool for better understanding how to thrive under pressure.

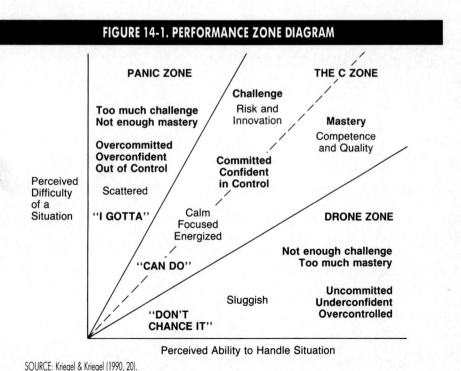

FIGURE 14-1. PERFORMANCE ZONE DIAGRAM

SOURCE: Kriegel & Kriegel (1990, 20).

According to Kriegel and Kriegel, everyone possesses Type C potential. However, this potential often remains blocked by bad habits, unexamined fears, and, simply, lack of recognition of its existence and potential. This potential can be unleashed with proper attitude training and skill development.

Mastery of the skill required for a task is one important prerequisite to the Type C experience. Before you can feel the exhilaration of mountaineering, kayaking, basketball, public speaking, writing, or decision-making, you must master the required skills.

Yet mastery must alternate with challenge. You must occasionally leave your comfort zone to take on new and more demanding challenges. In reflecting on the balance between mastery and challenge, a young and very successful corporate president states, "I love challenging myself. There's a certain tension when you are on your edge that is exquisite. I feel drawn to the front lines. However, before I put myself out there, I always try to know as much as possible about what I am doing" (Kriegel & Kriegel, 1990, 9).

Kriegel and Kriegel's chart describing the balance between mastery and challenge and the place of the "C Zone" between the "Panic Zone" and the "Drone Zone" is presented in Figure 14-1.

Kriegel and Kriegel identify several blockages to Type C experiences and the Type C pattern: negative beliefs about one's abilities, negative self-talk, the vicious cycles referred to in Chapter 5, negative mental pictures, low self-esteem, unwillingness to take risks, and overestimating one's abilities relative to the challenge. Several of the steps proposed later in this chapter can assist you in overcoming these barriers.

THRIVING UNDER PUBLIC PRESSURE   ▼

A colleague of mine, Barbara Gard, served for 12 years as a city councilperson in a northern California community. During that time, she was struck by the many local elected officials she met at statewide meetings who seemed to love their political service, despite its time demands and frequent public criticism. We decided to look into the matter further by conducting an informal survey of local elected officials at several conferences she attended (Schafer and Gard, 1986).

When asked, "Do you enjoy your job as an elected official?", 90 percent of the 85 subjects responded "very much," and the other 10 percent said "somewhat." None responded "not very" or "not at all." It would appear, then, that the vast majority thrive on the pressures of this elected position.

We were also interested in how these people cope with the stress they do experience. A number of options were given, and they could write in their own responses as well. The most commonly used methods were these:

Exercise

Taking vacations

Watching television

Reading

Participating in sports

Watching movies

Written comments included (Schafer and Gard, 1986, 8):

"I believe in taking the job seriously but not personally."

"Through the years I've learned that all you can do is your best. As long as I have done my best, I don't worry."

"Interpersonal conflict with fellow council members—I love it."

"I rarely feel stress about anything."

"Keeping a balance in job council position and family is a never-ending struggle. With a large family still at home, I feel the diversity of my roles helps eliminate stress."

This modest study suggests that respondents in our small sample of elected local officials genuinely enjoyed their public service, and that they experienced relatively little distress despite the presence of a host of potential irritants. Moreover, they seemed to cope quite effectively with the little stress they did develop. They thrive under pressure.

LOW-STRESS CITY MANAGERS

After reading about the above study of city council members, several city managers—those persons hired by city councils to manage city government—requested "equal time." They asserted that, although city council members might score low on measures of their own stress, they often are stress-givers—to city managers. They wondered how city managers might compare with city council members, as well as with other professions.

Our curiosity whetted, we decided to conduct a mailed survey of city managers in California to investigate how stress is experienced by members of this very challenging profession. Two hundred nineteen of the 404 city managers responded (Schafer and Gard, 1988a and 1988b). Comparison of our sample with a previous study suggested we had tapped a representative sample of California city managers. The average age was 46 years, 71 percent had graduate degrees, and 96 percent were male. The average time as a city manager was 10 years, the average time in present position was six years.

One of our objectives was to identify the stressors causing these city managers the most distress during the past year. Table 14-1 shows the 15 top-scoring stressors. It is clear that city managers found themselves the objects of frequent role conflict and role overload, pressures to perform, lack of support, inadequate resources, weighty decisions, and more.

To our surprise, their average distress symptom score (see Chapter 4 to understand this measure) was only 18—very low compared with most other occupations we had studied. Clearly, most city managers seemed to sustain very well the rigors of a very challenging job.

TABLE 14-1. RANKING OF STRESSORS REPORTED BY MANAGERS DURING PAST YEAR

1. Having to tolerate council members who spend too much time on trivial matters and too little time on larger policy matters

2. Chronic overload

3. Pressures from individual council members

4. Too little funding to provide needed level and quality of services

5. Constant interruptions in work

6. Having to discipline or fire employees

7. Too few staff

8. Staff not sufficiently competent or responsive

9. Weight of responsibility for entire city government

10. (Tie) Lack of support from council
    Conflict between politics and professional management

11. Dealing with uninformed, unintelligent, or incompetent council members

12. Work intrudes into personal or family life (for example, after-hours calls, meetings)

13. Labor relations

14. Dealing with unethical or illegal requests from council members

SOURCE: Schafer and Gard (1988a, 15)

We went one step further. Among these high-functioning officials, who seemed especially to thrive? What were the characteristics, attitudes, and habits of those who scored especially low in distress symptoms?

To investigate these questions, we divided the sample into two groups: those who scored in the highest 75 percent on the Distress Symptom Scale and those who scored in the lowest 25 percent. We then compared key differences between the two groups.

Here are some of the key findings (Schafer and Gard, 1988b).

Low-stress city managers scored lower in Type A behavior, measured with the Framingham Type A Scale.

Low-stress city managers scored higher in hardiness, measured with a 12-item hardiness scale (Kobasa, 1984).

Low-stress city managers reported better health and higher energy levels. Of course, good health can be seen as both cause and effect in relation to job stress. Stress drains energy and contributes to illness. Viewed differently, good health helps buffer against distress. Since our survey was cross-sectional (a single point in time), we cannot distinguish between cart and horse. For clues as to why low-stress city managers scored higher in health and energy, it is useful to note differences in their patterns of exercise.

Low-stress city managers were more likely to engage in some form of aerobic exercise, they exercised longer per session, and they exercised more times per

week. Nearly nine of 10 in the total sample reported regularly engaging in some form of exercise. Three of four participated in some form of aerobic fitness activity.

Low-stress city managers were set apart, not by their more frequent use of constructive coping methods, but by their less frequent use of negative ones. Specifically, low-stress city managers were less likely to do the following to help them cope with temporary distress, based on responses to a checklist of more and less constructive coping methods:

▼ Drink more wine, beer or liquor than usual

▼ Just suffer through and endure the problem as best you can

▼ Become more careful and conscientious than usual—like checking and re-checking your work

▼ Allow yourself to become more irritable

▼ Treat or indulge yourself—like buying something you wanted

▼ Avoid other people, get away by yourself

▼ Work harder than usual—either at home or at your job

▼ Sleep more than usual

▼ Get in the car and drive

Caution is needed in drawing conclusions from these findings about the effectiveness of specific coping methods. Yet it does appear that low-stress city managers were less inclined toward escapism, withdrawal, and irritability, as well as toward less compulsiveness in work. No statistically significant differences appeared among constructive coping methods.

Low-stress city managers reported higher job satisfaction, more inclination to choose the same career again, and higher overall happiness scores.

The city manager profession is among the most challenging—and potentially stressful—of any in this country. Yet as a group this sample of city managers scored low in distress symptoms and high in job satisfaction. We have noted a number of attitudes and behavior patterns of those who scored especially low in distress symptoms. These are people who seem to thrive under pressure.

Having examined several theories and our own two studies of high-functioning individuals, let us next examine several approaches and methods available to you to increase your own abilities to thrive under pressure. Many of these methods emerge from the theories we have reviewed.

TIPS FOR THRIVING UNDER PRESSURE   ▼

We noted at the beginning of this chapter that thriving under pressure means thriving under difficult chronic conditions and thriving under short-term episodes of pressure.

CHRONIC PRESSURE

Consistent application of the techniques discussed in the later section for dealing with episodic pressures also help cope effectively with long-term chronic pressure. So can application of the stress management methods presented in the earlier chapters of this book, including the following:

Methods from Previous Chapters

▼ Use realistic and positive self-talk. Maintain a perspective of hardiness and a sense of coherence.

▼ Maintain effective health buffers—regular exercise, good nutrition, and consistently adequate sleep.

▼ Use consistent and effective deep relaxation methods and on-the-spot tension reducers.

▼ Manage time with intelligent pacing, balance, and organization.

▼ Maintain strong, supportive relationships.

▼ Cope constructively with difficult events and with temporary distress.

10 C's for Thriving Under Pressure

Thriving during periods of chronic stress can be enhanced by practicing the 10 C's for thriving under pressure (Schafer and Gard, 1986). These steps and their relationship to one another are shown in Figure 14-2. You will note that they combine the components of hardiness, Type C behavior, health buffers, coping, and more.

Conditioning refers especially to regular exercise, but also includes good nutritional and sleep habits.

Caring refers to participating in supportive, caring relationships with family, friends, and co-workers. It includes both giving and receiving.

When these two ingredients are present, then the four key C's of this expanded version of hardiness (incorporating one from Type C behavior) become more likely.

Challenge is the ability to interpret difficulty and change as a positive challenge or opportunity.

FIGURE 14-2. THE 10 C'S FOR THRIVING UNDER PRESSURE

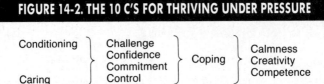

Conditioning ⎱
            ⎰ Challenge ⎱   ⎱ Calmness
              Confidence ⎰ Coping   ⎰ Creativity
              Commitment   Competence
Caring   Control

Confidence is belief in your ability to master whatever difficulties and challenges come along.

Commitment is positive involvement in your activities and strong belief in your ideals—giving it your best shot.

Control is belief in your ability to influence events and your reactions to events.

Given the presence of these four core ingredients of a "thriving perspective," another C becomes more likely.

Coping is your ability to respond constructively to challenging events and to your own temporary distress.

When one copes constructively, three other C's follow.

Calmness is your ability to maintain a moderate level of physical and emotional arousal in the face of difficulty.

Creativity refers to the ability to generate innovative and situationally specific solutions to difficulties and dilemmas.

Competence is your ability to handle the demands of a job or task effectively.

While no research has been conducted on these 10 C's for thriving under pressure, it is likely that their presence, especially in combination, will lead to thriving under the pressure of long-term stressors.

Thriving under long-term, chronic pressure also becomes easier to the degree that you move along the continuum of maturation toward the level Maslow called "self-actualization," as you read above. This does not happen overnight through the application of any specific technique, of course, but is the result of long-term personal growth and development. To the degree that such growth occurs, change and adversity come to be seen as one more challenge in the flow of experience— difficult but hardly overwhelming. The same holds for the gradual emergence of the Type C pattern in your own life.

SHORT-TERM EPISODES OF PRESSURE

Mental Rehearsal

Your mind is capable of creating two types of images: those that enter your brain through the senses and those that you create through your power of imagination (Bry, 1978). Evidence from sports psychology and other fields of performance has confirmed that mental rehearsal, one form of imagination, can be highly effective in enhancing performance under pressure. Kreigel and Kriegel (1984) refer to this as "previewing" the challenging activity.

Whether the situation is athletics, music, theater, public speaking, a crucial examination, or conducting a meeting, peak performance depends upon two main factors. First is technical preparedness through intense and repeated practice. Second is proper use of mental imagery or visualization before the event.

Several well-known athletes have used mental rehearsal quite deliberately and systematically, though they may never call it that (Sperling, 1981; Lynch, 1982).

Jean-Claude Killy, the multiple Olympic Gold Medalist, reported that preparation for one of his races was completely mental for several weeks beforehand. He skied the slope again and again in his mind. That is all he could do since he was recovering from an injury at the time. It turned out to be one of his best-ever performances.

Jack Nicklaus maintains that 50 percent of a good golf shot is proper mental imagery beforehand. He runs a color mental movie through his mind before each shot. In his book *Golf My Way*, he states, "First I 'see' the ball where I want it to finish, nice and white and sitting up high on the bright green grass. Then the scene quickly changes, and I 'see' the ball going there, its path, trajectory, and shape, even its behavior on landing. Then there is a sort of fade out, and the next scene shows me making the kind of motion that will turn the previous images into reality" (Nicklaus, 1976).

Jack Fosbury, former high jump world record holder, Olympic Gold Medalist, and inventor of the Fosbury Flop method of jumping, used the same technique of mental movies before each jump. "I would do a sequence of events. I would think of the last jumps, in practice or competition, and I would try to think what I was doing wrong, where I would come close to the bar. Then I would visualize what it felt like to do it right. I would remember back to my last good jump and try to emulate that. I would go over that in my mind a couple of times until I was sure, until I have the feeling in my head exactly what I was going to do for a good jump. Then I moved to another thought— all positive thinking—I was going to make the jump. When I had convinced myself, I would go. I made my body sensitive to my mind" (1980 Olympic Trials, *Daily Program*).

Kubistant (1986) has noted that the effectiveness of mental rehearsal is based on two physiological facts. First, the basal parts of the brain and the central nervous system cannot distinguish between actual experience and imagination—between something that is actually happening and something that is being vividly visualized (Jacobsen, 1932; Shaw, 1940; Maltz, 1969; Bry, 1978). Second, mentally practicing an activity causes all those nerves that in actuality fire the muscles to be fired at a lower, yet significant magnitude during the imaginary activity.

EXERCISE 14-1. A MENTAL REHEARSAL METHOD

Here is a technique for practicing mental rehearsal and for applying it in specific demanding situations. Included are two stages.

STAGE 1. MENTAL REHEARSAL

Complete these steps many, many times during the weeks, days, and hours leading up to the event in question. You can do this during deep relaxation; while walking, exercising, or driving; or just as you are falling to sleep.

1. Develop a clear mental picture of a demanding forthcoming event. Create as much imaginary detail as possible—place, persons, events.

2. Create a clear, detailed image of how you want to handle this situation. Experience yourself as calm, confident and effective.

3. While imagining this positive, successful response to the situation, use a **cue—form your thumb and forefinger into a circle.** Whenever creating the mental rehearsal, use this cue, so that, in your mind, the cue comes to be linked to the image.

STAGE 2. APPLICATION
1.   Enter the situation.
2.   As you do, use the cue. This will bring to your mind your oft-rehearsed positive response, and the positive feelings associated with it.
3.   In turn, chances will be enhanced that this desired response—and desired outcome—will occur.

Practicing a physical activity, then, results in your brain and body actually believing it is happening. Since your brain, body, and behavior tend to go in familiar directions, your mental rehearsal then increases chances of success. Of course, mentally rehearsing failure also heightens chances of actual failure.

In short, positive mental rehearsal can become self-fulfilling, whatever the pressure.

Positive Self-Talk for Peak Performance
In Chapter 7, you read about the potential of self-talk for creating misery and burnout, on one hand, and hardiness and stress-resistance, on the other hand. Positive or realistic self-talk is a key ingredient in thriving under pressure, both long-term and short-term.

In his helpful book on performing your best, Kubistant (1986, 164) has identified several types of negative self-talk that can interfere with peak performance in athletics and academics. First are distractive self-statements, to which mediocre performers seem to be most vulnerable:

▼ Look at that good looking man (woman) up there in the second row.

▼ That baby's crying is really starting to get on my nerves.

▼ I wish I had more time to complete this.

▼ My teammates are always goofing around.

▼ I remember back when I was in a similar situation to this.

▼ That sequence wasn't supposed to be in there.

▼ Those lights are too bright.

Another type of negative self-talk is to focus on how teammates or competitors are doing.

▼ What does she have that I don't?

▼ How is my practice partner doing over there on the adjacent court?

▼ Wow, Joan is already done with the examination.

▼ How can he do better if we prepared in the exact same way?

▼ Everybody except me seems to be breezing through this section.

▼ My potential next opponent over there looks really sharp.

▼ The rest of the class seems to be much brighter than I.

Third is focus on poor self-image.

▼ I am terrible at this.

▼ This is just awful.

▼ I'll never amount to anything.

▼ After I fail, I won't be able to face anybody.

▼ I was a fool to think that I could ever do this.

▼ If only I were smarter, then I could learn this movement.

▼ This poor performance will prove to everybody that I am totally incompetent.

Kubistant (1986, 165) notes that, "Like an unchecked infection, these types of negative self-statements fester and spread throughout the entire individual. These put-downs serve no other purpose than to reinforce pessimistic attitudes, low self-concepts, and, eventually, resignation."

In Chapter 7, you read about two techniques for turning negative self-talk around into realistic or positive self-talk: the P & Q Method (pause and question) and the Three C's of Instant Replay (catch negative self-talk, challenge it, change it). Kubistant (1986, 172) suggests a number of "basic affirmations" that can be helpful for thriving under pressure:

▼ Everyday in every way I am better and better.

▼ I like myself.

▼ I am the captain of my ship; I am the master of my fate.

▼ I trust my abilities.

▼ I am relaxed.

▼ I forgive my errors.

▼ Sure I can.

▼ Can do.

▼ I enjoy what I do.

▼ I am on my side.

▼ I always do the best job I can.

▼ I am proud of my efforts.

▼ I can do anything I choose to do.

You will note that these affirmations meet the criteria set forth in Chapter 7 for effective new self-talk. Each statement is:

▼ Personal

▼ Positive

▼ Present-tense

▼ Practical

▼ Brief

Kubistant (1986, 173) also suggests that you develop your self-talk statements that will remind you of the specific skills and attributes you need for peak performance. For example:

I am a good _____

I am an efficient _____

I am a creative _____

I am a relaxed _____

I am a courageous _____

I am a strong _____

I am a purposeful _____

I am a graceful _____

I am a _____

I am a _____

EXERCISE 14-2. SELF-TALK AND CHALLENGE

1. Think of a difficult task or event you will face in the near future (or have faced in the recent past).
2. List negative self-talk statements (beliefs and/or situational interpretations) for turning this event into a negative threat.
3. Then list positive self-talk statments for turning this event into a positive challenge or opportunity.
4. Which list most closely resembles your actual self-talk tendencies?
5. During coming days and weeks, be aware of your self-talk when facing changes or difficulties.

Thriving under the pressure of a performance situation can be enhanced by combining positive mental rehearsal with positive self-talk, deep relaxation, pacing, concentration, and other skills (Sperling, 1981; Lynch, 1982; Rotella, 1984; Abraham, 1985). In a workshop for competitive roller skaters (figure, dance, and speed), I presented an integrated plan for preparing for competition. It met with remarkable success with several competitors. This sequence, presented in Exercise 14-3, can be adapted to almost any type of challenging performance situation.

EXERCISE 14-3. HARNESSING THE MIND TOWARD PEAK ATHLETIC PERFORMANCE

1. Know why you are training and competing; be sure it's for the right reasons.
2. Don't be an extreme perfectionist. Set realistic, personal goals.
3. Don't gunnysack your feelings. "Unfinished business" can interfere with concentration and block energy.
4. Be totally prepared through thorough practice.
5. Avoid these traps: fear of failure and fear of success.
6. Learn to use visualization—"positive mental movies."
7. During the day of competition, be unhurried, uncluttered, soothed, focused.
8. Perform well for you, not for your impression on friends, teammates, coaches, parents.
9. Stop negative thoughts and feelings. Substitute positive feelings and images through "positive mental movies" and key confidence-building words.
10. Be aware of body and emotional signals of your own best "activation level."
11. Let yourself do it, rather than make yourself do it. Concentrate; don't bear down. Be totally absorbed.
12. Don't be distracted, discouraged, or stopped by an error in performance.
13. Use the following steps in preparing for competition.
    a. The night before competition, do deep relaxation, with a positive mental movie of your performance.
    b. Two to five hours before the event, repeat deep relaxation.
    c. On the site, use deep breathing and key relaxing words to control physical tension. Then create a brief, positive, relaxed mental movie of your performance.
    d. Now let your mind become totally absorbed in your performance. Create "a cocoon of concentration"—not bearing down but becoming "one" with your movement and your partner, if present.
    e. Let your body take off and do its job.
14. After finishing, stroke yourself for what you *did* do well.
15. Remember the keys: practice, positive mental movies, and concentration.

BUILDING CONFIDENCE

Your ability to thrive under pressure can increase through time as you become more experienced, mature, and self-actualized. Building confidence is part of this process.

Confidence refers to trust in one's abilities to master a difficulty or task (Kriegel and Kriegel, 1984). The opposite of confidence is self-doubt. Confidence is more likely, of course, among individuals who were given lots of positive early messages from their parents about their self-worth and abilities. Yet confidence can be strength-

BOX 14-1. RIVER LESSONS

During a summer raft trip through the Grand Canyon with my wife and daughters, I watched with fascination as five accompanying kayakers and a canoeist maneuvered through the eddies and rapids of the glorious Colorado. On one occasion, my wife and I spent an adrenaline-charged morning in a stable, forgiving inflatable tandem kayak, successfully traversing several modest-sized rapids, our life jackets firmly secured. A first-time experience, we were both exhilarated.

A few weeks later, we decided to take the plunge (so to speak) by enrolling in a hard-shell kayaking class. We progressed through learning basic strokes, "wet exiting," and rolling. At the end of that first week, we took our first white-water river trip down a rather tame section of a northern California river—under close supervision of our instructor.

Throughout, I experienced a child-like thrill from entering new territory and mastering new skills.

I was reminded again that one does not grow by always taking the easy way. Challenge is vital. Staying within my comfort zone is safe, to be sure. But sometimes pushing my limits takes me to new levels of competence, satisfaction, and enjoyment.

But I soon discovered that knowing my limits is equally vital. I could quickly see the foolhardiness of venturing into waters that are unknown or beyond my capabilities.

Kayaking in one sense is a solo activity. I am tucked alone in my shell with one paddle. Yet when done properly, kayaking is highly social. I would never go down a river alone or out of reach of a nearby partner, readily available if needed—an illustration of the essential balance between individuality and interdependence.

Another lesson is composure under pressure—riding the smooth but ominous flow of the V just before the first wave of the rapid; looking down into the next drop and into the large wave just ahead; hanging upside down while getting set up to roll back up—or to do a quick "wet exit."

For fun, my wife and I also decided to buy an inflatable tandem kayak. I now understand what a good friend and white-water mentor means when he tells us that tandem canoes and kayaks are known as "divorce boats" by veterans of the river. By the end of the day, fortunately, my wife and I did get our signals straight. We are still married.

Lots of learning on a river.

ened later on, whatever one's previous experiences. Figure 14-3 describes the process of building confidence. There are three key points in this process:

Challenge → Mastery → Confidence

The confidence-building process includes other steps, both internal and interactive.

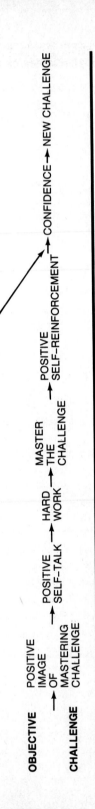

FIGURE 14-3. BUILDING CONFIDENCE

OTHERS'
POSITIVE
REINFORCEMENT

OBJECTIVE   POSITIVE
IMAGE
OF   → POSITIVE   → HARD   → MASTER   → POSITIVE   → CONFIDENCE → NEW CHALLENGE
MASTERING   SELF-TALK   WORK   THE   SELF-REINFORCEMENT
CHALLENGE   CHALLENGE   CHALLENGE

EXERCISE 14-4. IMPROVING STEPS FOR BUILDING CONFIDENCE

1. Where are your strengths and weaknesses in the confidence- building process shown in Figure 14-3?

2. Which steps will you strengthen during coming weeks?

3. What specific steps will you take?

In this chapter, you have read about a number of approaches and techniques for thriving under pressure of two types: chronic pressure from difficult life circumstances or demands and short-term demanding episodes. Applying many of these methods can enhance your chances of surviving adversity—even thriving under the pressure.

Learning to thrive under pressure can benefit not only your own effectiveness and well-being. It can also enable you to transcend your own problems by contributing to the well-being of others around you, the focus of Chapter 15.

REFERENCES ▼

Abraham, H. (1985). Three steps to peak performance, *Skiing*, 38, 217-220.

Bry, A. (1978). *Visualization: Directing The Movies of Your Mind*. New York: Barnes & Noble Books.

Sex rarely impairs athletic performance, (1989). *Family Practice News*, Dec. 15-31.

Goble, F. G. (1970). *The Third Force: The Psychology of Abraham Maslow*. New York: Pocket Books.

Kobasa, S.C. (1984). How much stress can you handle? *American Health*, 2.

Kriegel, R., & Kriegel, M.H. (1984). *The C Zone: Peak Performance Under Pressure*. Garden City, NY: Anchor Press.

Kubistant, T. (1986). *Performing Your Best*. Champaign, Ill.: Life Enhancement Publications.

Lynch, J. (1982). Positive thinking techniques for improving performance, *Runner's World*, 4, 22.

Maslow, A. H. (1954). *Motivation and Personality*. New York: Harper & Row.

Maslow, A.H. (1959). *New Knowledge in Human Values*. New York: Harper & Row.

Maslow, A.H. (1962). *Toward A Psychology of Being*. New York: Van Nostrand.

Maslow, A.H. (1965). *Eupsychian Management*. Homewood, Ill.: Irwin-Dorsey.

Maslow, A.H. (1966). *The Psychology of Science*. New York: Harper & Row.

Maslow, A.H. (1971). *Toward The Farther Reaches of Human Nature*. New York: Viking.

Maddi, S., & Kobasa, S.C. (1984). *The Hardy Executive*. Homewood, Ill.: Dow Jones-Irwin.

Nicklaus, J. (1976). *Golf My Way*. New York: Simon.

Olympic Trials. (1980). *Daily Program*.

Rotella, R.J. (1984). "The psychology of performance under stress," *FBI Law Enforcement Bulletin*, 1-11.

Schafer, W., & Gard, B. (1986). How elected officials handle the stress and pressure of public office . . . and thrive! *Western City, 62,* 7-10.

Schafer, W. & Gard, B. (1988). Stress and California's city managers, *Western City, 64,* 13-15.

Schafer, W. & Gard, B. (1988). Stress: How low-stress city managers differ from the rest, *Western City,* 64:7, 15-17.

Siebert, A. (1983). The Survivor Personality, *Association for Humanistic Psychology Newsletter,* 19-22.

Sperling, D. (1981). The myth of the natural athlete, *Success Magazine,* 28, 31.

Walker, M. (1988). The survivor syndrome, *The Courier Journal Magazine,* 14-15.

Walter, T. & Siebert, A. (1990). *Student Success,* 5th Ed. Fort Worth: Holt, Rinehart & Winston.

Balancing Self-Care and Social Responsibility

Chapter 15

CHAPTER 15

INTRODUCTION   ▼

> The center of human nature is rooted in ten thousand ordinary acts of kindness that define our days.
> —Stephen Jay Gould (1990, 33)

The theme of this chapter is that living a wellness lifestyle includes balancing self-concern with concern for others. Truly effective stress management includes modifying conditions in the social environment, not just adapting to them. True self-fulfillment embraces contributing to the well-being of others as well as taking care of yourself.

CONSTRUCTIVE MALADJUSTMENT   ▼

The term "adjustment" sometimes is used in discussions of mental and physical health. Well-adjusted persons, it is said, are those who adapt effectively to the world around them. As a result, they experience minimal frustration and tension.

"Adjustment," like stress management, can be taken too far. If, by adjusting, the individual passively accepts conditions in the world around her that are destructive, unjust, cruel, or unfair, she has done a disservice to herself and her world.

Constructive maladjustment is being appropriately discontented about conditions in the surrounding social, political, or natural environment that in the judgment of the person are wrong and need to be changed—and being motivated to change those conditions.

Here are several examples.

▼ Candy Lightner lost her 13-year-old daughter to a drunk driver. She did not passively accept the loss. She did not simply focus on adjusting to her grief and to the new reality of living without her precious daughter. Instead, she decided to do everything in her power to lobby for tougher drunk driving laws. She founded Mothers Against Drunk Drivers—MADD (Babbie, 1985).

▼ Curtis Sliwa, a young MacDonald's manager, decided to do something constructive about urban violence. Rather than stopping with the usual individualistic (and necessary) steps of taking care for his own safety, he persuaded 12 friends to join him in riding subways together in New York City to head off crime. The group expanded to become the Guardian Angels, promising to break up muggings, rapes, and other acts of violence. It was not long before several thousand Guardian Angels were active in many American cities (Babbie 1985).

▼ Monique Grodski was a nine-year-old in 1979 living in suburban New York when by chance she watched a TV documentary on the plight of Cambodian refugees. She was moved by these people's strong spirit. "I found it amazing that they were still singing and had the hope and strength to go on. After I saw that, I actually cried. I really had to do something about it" (Babbie, 1985, 113). She was especially disturbed by the plight of the children. Monique made a personal decision to do something to enable the children to have a greater say in this and other world problems. She was instrumental in forming the Children's Peace Committee, which went on to circulate petitions, raise funds for several causes, and speak to community groups.

You may recall from Chapter 2 the idea that **personal problems** and **public issues** often are closely linked (Mills, 1956). Individual unhappiness, depression, anxiety, even ill health are tied to public spending priorities, unemployment, community crime rates, the work climate, war and peace, social density, the rate of community growth, and more. These influences of society on self are one reflection that "no man is an island entire and of itself," as we noted in Chapter 2.

What is needed, then, is **"the sociological imagination"**—the ability to understand that personal experience is influenced by larger social forces (Mills, 1956). Mills correctly maintained that we need not only to pursue our personal solutions to personal problems. We need also to do what we can to modify positively those surrounding conditions that help cause the problems. This may take the form, for example, of getting involved in the political process, contributing to a favorite candidate's campaign, writing or calling an office-holder, getting involved in a local committee or commission, participating in a task force to work on a problem in the workplace.

In short, truly effective and holistic stress management for wellness includes constructive maladjustment, based on the sociological imagination, and the ability to link personal problems with public issues.

At a more personal level, we need to balance self-care with care for those in our immediate environment.

EXERCISE 15-1. LINKING PERSONAL PROBLEMS AND PUBLIC ISSUES

1.   Make a list of personal stress-related symptoms of several people in your immediate environment, yourself included.
2.   Next to each one, list two or three social or public factors that you think might be causally linked to that personal problem.
3.   Next, write or discuss what might be done through public or governmental action to reduce this negative social force.

ALTRUISTIC EGOISM AND EGOISTIC ALTRUISM ▼

SELYE'S ALTRUISTIC EGOISM

After several decades of physiological research on the nature of the stress response, Hans Selye was frequently asked about the implications of his studies for how to live a healthy and worthwhile life.

At first, he was quite uncomfortable in this realm of prescriptive philosophy. After all, his life's work had been devoted entirely to the realm of objective science. After further thought, however, he found it was possible after all to remain true to scientific principles, on one hand, and to provide a fundamental guideline for "the good life," on the other.

This guideline is captured in the term, **altruistic egoism—"to earn thy neighbor's love"** (Selye, 1974, 5). While expressing appropriate caution about telling others how to live or passing judgment on others' lifestyle, Selye did believe it was possible to draw on basic biological laws to arrive at two conclusions. On one hand, humans historically have been and continue to be self-interested. That is, each living creature possesses a fundamental life force that impels it to take care of itself in ways that ensure its growth, well-being, and survival.

Yet, on the other hand, the human species has survived only through cooperation and commitment to the welfare of the whole. Thus, it is biologically natural that humans balance concern with self with consideration for others.

As a guideline for individual motivation and behavior, altruistic egoism incorporates that necessary balance. That is, the individual ought to work hard, even sometimes to the edge of personal stress, in order to contribute to the common good, thereby earning others' affection and esteem. Both the person and the society stand to gain.

The person benefits through assuring ". . . his own homeostasis and happiness by accumulating the treasure of other people's benevolence towards him." Altruistic egoism, the ". . . hoarding of the goodwill, respect, esteem, support, and love of our neighbor, is the most efficient way to give vent to our pent-up energy and to create enjoyable, beautiful, or useful things" (Selye, 1976, 452).

The society gains through the contributions of its individual members to the well-being of the whole. If enough individuals merge self-satisfaction with social gain in this way, small groups, organizations, communities, and the whole society surely benefit.

As with all good ideas, altruistic egoism has its traps. For example, the individual can focus excessively on whether others in fact appreciate her altruistic actions as much as she deserves. Moreover, she can give so much to the common good that her own spiritual, mental, or physical health goes downhill. This leads to burnout, discussed in Chapter 13.

My own consideration of values dealing with self, society, and stress has led me to a variant of Selye's altruistic egoism. I call it egoistic altruism. It is an alternative guideline for merging self-interest and concern for others.

EGOISTIC ALTRUISM

> Joan Fernandez finds great personal satisfaction through her work as a nurse. She goes home nearly every afternoon with a sense of genuine pride in the knowledge she has made a real difference in patients' lives.
>
> Fred Rogowskie works as an accountant with a firm that specializes in service to nonprofit and other community service organizations. His career provides him deep meaning and purpose, since he knows that recipients of these organizations ultimately benefit from the financial guidance he provides these organizations.
>
> Jack Burt's work as a line supervisor in an auto manufacturing plant may seem mundane to some. But to him it offers a special opportunity to make a difference, since he does everything he can to make the work process humane and healthy for his supervisees.

Each example illustrates **egoistic altruism—self-fulfillment through contributing to others' well-being.** Contributing to others' well-being can occur in many ways, and does not depend upon a career of social or public service.

▼ A college student can facilitate the study habits and fitness routine of his roommate through encouragement and cooperation with household chores.

▼ Mothers and fathers can contribute to the well-being of their children in a host of small ways.

▼ Neighbors can enhance the well-being of each other through sharing when needed and by being considerate of noise and air pollution.

▼ Co-workers can contribute to the well-being of each other by providing support and encouragement.

▼ An attorney can make the world a better place by providing sound advice and counsel to clients in time of need.

▼ A full-time mother and homemaker decides she can make a difference by getting involved in the neighborhood school's PTA as a way of working with others to improve street safety for children walking to and from school.

▼ Parents in a crime-ridden public housing project can enhance their own self-fulfillment by joining with others in the project to work with police to reduce drug sales in local playgrounds.

BOX 15-1. REFLECTIONS ON ALTRUISM

Altruism is a spontaneous and natural expression of our fundamental relatedness, not a form of deviance. Psychologist Alfie Kohn noted, "Helping may be as dramatic as agreeing to donate a kidney or as mundane as letting another shopper ahead of you in line. . . . Caring about others is as much a part of human nature as caring about ourselves."

Altruism does not necessarily involve self-denial or sacrifice. In acting on behalf of others, both ordinary volunteers and those whose lives are devoted to service report feeling joy and fulfillment. Such joy is a natural consequence of caring.

Being tender-hearted does not mean being soft-hearted. Those we have recognized as creative altruists work in the most challenging situations. Those they serve—youth at risk, addicts and drug abusers, juvenile delinquents, the mentally ill, the homeless—are unimpressed by do-gooders and bleeding-heart liberals. But their lives are transformed by the pragmatic intelligence and unconditional support they encounter in creative altruists.

While much altruistic behavior is indeed directed at the relief of immediate suffering, creative altruism involves innovative efforts to address the fundamental causes of deeply rooted social inequities. In the words of psychologist Howard Gruber, "Creative altruism, when it goes the limit, strives to eliminate the cause of suffering, to change the world, to change the fate of the Earth."

SOURCE: Hurley (1990, 33)

As with Selye's concept of altruistic egoism, the notion of egoistic altruism merges self-interest with contributing to the common good. Both self and others benefit. Like Selye's altruistic egoism, egoistic altruism takes the person outside himself/herself. This is **self-transcendence** (Kohn, 1990).

A key difference beyond my concept and Selye's is that egoistic altruism brings fulfillment through self-satisfaction, through the knowledge that one has been true to her/his value of enhancing others, whether or not others express their appreciation or indebtedness. In this sense, egoistic altruism promotes self-reliance. The individual thus values, but does not depend upon others' feedback, acknowledgement, or praise.

As Ray has noted (1989, 12), ". . . altruism affirms the ultimate value of the existence, or being, of other persons." He notes that this may be why people acting altruistically are truly perplexed when bystanders ask them why they helped others, the implication being, 'what was in it for you?' Altruists respond, 'It just seemed to be the right thing to do,' or 'It was the human thing to do.' Satisfaction and a sense of personal gratification does not depend on others' praise. It rests on doing the deed."

David Sobel, a physician and author (Ornstein and Sobel, 1989), says this about egoism and altruism:

> One thing that really helps is volunteer work, helping those less fortunate than yourself. Volunteer work is an old-time folksy approach to stress management. Put another way, there are a lot of selfish reasons to be altruistic. In addition to the good that comes from the volunteering itself, assisting people in dire straits helps the helpers keep their own problems in perspective. It also boosts self-esteem (Castleman, 1990, 39).

EXERCISE 15-2. UNDERSTANDING AND APPLYING ALTRUISTIC EGOISM AND EGOISTIC ALTRUISM

1. Define altruistic egoism and egoistic altruism and give one or two illustrations of each.
2. Which concept appeals more to you as a guideline in your own life? Why?
3. Which do you think would be more advantageous to the whole society if widely practiced? Why?

HELPING AND WELLNESS ▼

Helping is healthy. This is the conclusion from a report on several surveys of volunteers throughout the country (Andrews, 1990). For example, a national study of more than 1800 members of more than 20 volunteer organizations showed that 57 percent of respondents reported increased self-esteem during or after helping others. Fifty-four percent said they experienced a "feeling of warmth." Nearly one in three reported increased energy and one in five noted a "high" feeling—perhaps the result of increased endorphins from the helping experience.

Approximately 95 percent of respondents from several combined samples of

BOX 15-2. THE CARTER ETHIC

Jimmy Carter and Rosalynn Carter live out their lives in headlines. During his presidency, Jimmy Carter informed the nation that ecological conservation, human rights and conflict resolution based on mutual understanding were immediate global issues. He established a comprehensive energy policy based on the National Energy Act of 1978 and plowed windfall profits from decontrolled domestic oil prices into conservation. Tax incentives were enacted for the use of solar and other alternative energies. He said he would never lie to us. Then, in a resounding defeat over the hostage crisis, Carter lost the election for what would have been his second term to Ronald Reagan. The Carters returned to their farm in Plains to find the business in ruins, themselves nearly bankrupt, their hopes and plans shattered.

Much has happened to the Carter family since. Above all, they have not only survived, but prevailed. A recent *Washingtonian* article lists Jimmy Carter (with former Surgeon General C. Everett Koop and George Bush) as one of the capital's three most-admired men.

Christopher Matthews, the *San Francisco Examiner's* Washington bureau chief and former Carter speechwriter, attributes this comeback in public esteem to changing values in the nation. He goes on to say, "The stands he took as president, together with the things he did afterward, have finally paid off."

The September 1989 issue of *The Economist* says, "His opinions of what is right and necessary for the world have not changed much since he was president, and in that sense he can be said to be using the Center (The Carter Presidential Library and Center) to pursue the unfinished business of the Carter administration, so abruptly interrupted by his electoral defeat in 1980. Conflicts, denials of human rights, hunger, disease, military competition, unproductive agriculture, economic error: Mr. Carter . . . takes off to Panama, Beijing, Khartoum, or Addis Ababa, meanwhile convening conferences on the Middle East, on Latin American debt, on the weaknesses of government in Africa and on the means of combating avoidable disease. The level of quality at these conferences has been high. Good people turn up for Mr. Carter."

The Carter ethic is not only gaining popularity in the United States, but elsewhere around the world as well. Casimir Yost, president of the World Affairs Council of Northern California, noted "The invitation [to be a neutral observer and mediator for the Dominican Republic's recent presidential election] illustrates his very considerable popularity and prestige in Latin America as the man who concluded the Panama Canal treaties and pressed for human rights and democracy. Indeed, as Carter toured voting sites around Santo Domingo last week, voters waiting in lines spontaneously broke into cheers."

"Carter is like the patient investor who sits on the same portfolio for years and suddenly finds himself rich," adds Christopher Matthews. The Carters, no longer constrained by the demands of the "please everybody" political arena, have continued to follow their hearts.

SOURCE: Miller (1990, 32)

volunteers reported feeling good while helping. Eight of ten said these good feelings kept recurring long afterwards, whenever the helping experience was recalled.

The researchers asked respondents about their health—whether it was perceived to be excellent, good, fair, or poor. They found that those volunteers in excellent health were significantly more likely to report four or more positive effects of helping. Those whose helping was direct reported better health than those who helped indirectly, that is, not face-to-face. The more frequent the helping, the better the health—and the fewer the visits to a doctor.

Helping others through a group was found to relate more strongly to health outcomes than helping through individual effort. Finally, helping strangers was more positively associated with health than helping family or friends.

Many of the respondents reported feeling greater calmness during and after helping. One woman reported that doing something nice for someone actually snapped her out of bouts of depression. Another reported she treated her stress-related headaches by shopping for clothing for needy children.

Herbert Benson, noted expert on the relaxation response, states, "For millennia, people have been describing techniques on how to forget oneself, to experience decreased metabolic rates and blood pressure, heart rate and other health benefits. Altruism works this way, just as do yoga, spirituality and meditation" (Luks, 1988, 42).

These studies did not prove, of course, that helping causes good mental and physical health. The causal influence could be reversed. That is, healthier people might simply help more often than unhealthy people, accounting for the positive associations found in these surveys.

Yet Andrews (1990, 32) correctly concludes that the results ". . . provide strong support for the hypothesis that there is a relationship between helping others and a number of health-related factors." He continues:

> In summary, the results of this study suggest that volunteer activity, particularly when performed frequently and directed toward strangers, can be added to the growing list of life-style and social network factors associated with physical and mental well-being. More research is required to establish a causal relationship between helping and health and to determine whether the perception of superior health reflects the individual's actual medical condition. However, the findings reported here are consistent with the view that volunteer activity produces real benefits for the provider as well as for the recipient.

What is needed, of course, to demonstrate fully that helping actually causes better health, is a longitudinal study in which the mental and physical health of a large group of nonvolunteers is measured initially and then later comparisons are made between those who go on to volunteer and those who don't. Meanwhile, it is reasonable to suggest that helping others through volunteer activities may be one way to practice egoistic altruism—to heighten one's own self-fulfillment and well-being through contributing to the well-being of others.

Luks (1988, 42) points out:

> Taking time to help, then, may be a basic step to protect health. Stress assaults us: Seventy percent of Americans say there is a lot or some stress in their lives, and 40 percent believe stress has made

them sick. Yet only 25 percent volunteer regularly. Those who don't say they are too busy and don't want to neglect important responsibilities. The health benefits they're passing up may turn out to be only part of their loss. At this early stage of altruism research, all those selfless people seem to have found ways into a wonderful glow.

A continuing challenge is to find your own optimal balance between giving to community groups and other organizations, on one hand, and meeting personal and family needs, on the other. Like other good things, giving to others can turn sour if your own health suffers or if your children, lover, or spouse are seriously neglected. For brief periods, of course, intense commitment to a cause or activity is fully warranted. Over the long haul, the key is balance.

HEROISM AND SOCIAL RESPONSIBILITY   ▼

THE NEW HEROES

In his inspiring and informative little book, *You Can Make a Difference*, sociologist Earl Babbie contends that "You and I are the heroes who will save America and the world" (1985, 18).

In the past, the term "hero" typically was applied to a select few—those who stood apart from the rest by performing extraordinary feats. Examples of this classic view of heroism were Beowolf, Robin Hood, Joan of Arc, David. Contemporary fictional heroes of this type persist in comics and films: Batman, Superman, the Marvels, Sky King, John Wayne characters, Rocky.

What sets heroes apart? Babbie maintains that the essential core of heroism remains the same, namely, **social responsibility—willingness to assume personal responsibility for public problems** (Babbie, 1985, 26). Assuming social responsibility is to devote one's energies to improving something in the social environment—in the absence of personal gain from doing so. In other words, a person who assumes responsibility for a wrong or deficiency in a small group, organization, community, or society does so because she believes to do so is the right thing to do, not because she stands to gain in any direct way. Babbie (1985, 27) notes that social responsibility ". . . is assumed, not assigned, undertaken rather than imposed." It is a matter of declaration, rather than duty with a total absence of guilt, burden, or blame.

BARRIERS TO ASSUMING SOCIAL RESPONSIBILITY

Social Barriers
Assuming social responsibility is not easy. The sheer size of organizations in which problems develop—and must be solved—often intimidate potential ordinary heroes like you and me. At the same time, specialization structures responsibility. We readily assume that someone must have been assigned a given task. Thus, it becomes very easy to walk by a piece of litter on the sidewalk, passing by this small opportunity for assuming social responsibility by telling oneself that the city government hires people to pick up litter. It's most certainly not my job—or my responsibility.

It is only a small step next to convince oneself that it's not my responsibility to pick up the phone and call for help when a neighbor is being robbed, beaten, or even murdered, as was Kitty Genovese a few years ago in New York—while 38 of her neighbors silently watched. None wanted to get involved.

Another less obvious social influence to avoiding responsibility is the high rate of cynicism, apathy and alienation in America (Babbie, 1985; Oreskes, 1990). When surrounded by apathy and cynicism, when in fact this attitude seems the normal way to be, it becomes easy to remain detached, concerned only with self-gain.

Finally, Charles Simpkinson (1990), in a fascinating and useful article on "compassionate living," observes that empathy is an essential ingredient in altruism, and that self-love is needed for empathy. "Since it is impossible to truly love others

---

BOX 15-3. VACLEV HAVEL: TO HIS WIFE, OLGA HAVEL, FROM PRISON

We must constantly, here, now,
at once and everywhere,
withstand the temptation
to be utilitarian
and we must weigh what is true
against what is a lie,
what is genuine against what is false,
what is moral against what is immoral,
what is life-giving against what is
deadening.

We must never forget
that the first little lie
told in the interest of truth,
the first little injustice
told in the name of justice,
the first tiny immorality
defended by the morality of things,
the first careless lapse
in this constant vigilance
means the certain beginning of the end.

Hope is a dimension of the spirit.
It is not outside us but within us.
When you lose it you must seek it again
Within yourself
and with people around you
Not in objects
Or even in events.

SOURCE: Havel (1990, 36)

unless one loves oneself, our strong cultural bias against any overt form of self-love is one of he biggest blocks against empathy and, therefore, altruism" (Simpkinson, 1990). "Healthy narcissism," on the other hand, is healthy not only for self but for our ability to love others.

Personal Barriers

According to Babbie (1985, Chapter 9), several self-talk barriers are commonly used to prevent assumption of social responsibility for public problems.

▼ I'll seem "goody-goody."

▼ I'll seem holier than thou.

▼ My motives will be suspect.

▼ It's not my responsibility.

▼ I don't know what to do.

▼ I may make things worse.

▼ I may look stupid.

▼ Nothing I could do would make a difference.

True heroes do not let such self-talk (excuses) stand in their way. They hold values that impel them to see a need and respond, regardless of what others might think.

EXERCISE 15-3. ASSESSING YOUR SELF-TALK ABOUT SOCIAL RESPONSIBILITY

1.   Do you sometimes find yourself using any of the above self-talk statements? If so, which ones? In what kinds of situations?

2.   How might each of these self-talk statements be rewritten to promote rather than impede social responsibility?

3.   What differences would occur in the world if more people used these alternative self-talk statements?

OPPORTUNITIES ARE EVERYWHERE

Several years ago while teaching at the University of Hawaii, Earl Babbie gave his undergraduate students in a social problems class an unusual assignment: to find a social problem and fix it. Credit would not be given for finding out who was to blame for the problem, only for solving it. Nor would credit be given for "bitching about how bad things are" (Babbie, 1985, 145). They could only solve a problem others, as well as themselves, were concerned about. And they had to do more

BOX 15-4. LESSONS FROM THE HOLOCAUST

For the past 20 years, Samuel Oliner has been a sociology professor at Humboldt State University. When I met him recently during a visit to that campus, I had no idea what he had been through in his "other life." I later learned his astounding story.

Before dawn on August 14, 1942 German trucks coldly rolled into the walled-in Jewish ghetto of Bobowa, Poland, where he lived as a 12-year-old boy. Nazi soldiers leaped out of the trucks, yelling, "All Jews outside." The horrified people were brutally beaten, then herded into trucks and driven off into the darkness. Their corpses later were found in a pit in a nearby forest. They had been machine-gunned down. Included were Samuel's (then known as Shmulek) parents, grandparents, brother, sister, other relatives, and thousands of others.

Only Samuel survived, hiding on the rooftop of his house, so terrified he wasn't sure if he was dead or alive.

He managed to climb down the next day. As a blond, blue-eyed boy who looked like a Christian Pole, he hiked to a nearby village where he begged, then was taken in by a benevolent Christian woman. He left the area, fearing he would be recognized.

Later freed by Russian troops, the 15-year-old orphan was sent to England by a refugee committee. He was educated, eventually migrated to the United States, served in the armed forces in Korea, then went on to raise three children and over a period of 20 years to obtain his doctorate in sociology.

In 1978, he began teaching a course, "On Causes and Consequences of the Holocaust." An unexpected result was unleashing of a flood of painful memories: his teenage sister weeping the night she was raped by Gestapo officers; his grandfather pushed against a hot stove by a Nazi officer, then knocked to the floor; the screaming throughout the ghetto the night his family and others were rounded up and taken away. Oliner was forced to confront his past and attempt to come to terms with it.

Another result was even more unexpected—emergence of a burning desire to learn more about those who, like his rescuer, Balwina Piecuch, put themselves at great risk to rescue Jews. Oliner began reading about ordinary people from all over Nazi-occupied Europe who performed these acts of courage. As a social scientist, he wanted to know more about what had created the altruistic nature in these 20th century heroes.

He and his staff gathered 600 detailed stories of rescue from aging rescuers in Poland, France, Italy, the Netherlands, Denmark, Norway, and Germany itself. They also interviewed 200 people from the same areas and of similar ages and backgrounds who had done nothing to save the Jews.

They then analyzed differences between the two groups. Their findings cast light on the origins of compassionate behavior.

Rescuers were not especially adventurous, self-confident, or religious.

They were more empathic, more caring, and displayed a greater sense of responsibility for others.

Rescuers had developed their compassionate natures in part through having lived among people unlike themselves in terms of faith and background. They had learned to tolerate—even defend—diversity.

Early family experiences set rescuers apart from bystanders. Rescuers' parents were more likely to use reason in disciplining their children, thereby instilling values as well as compassion. Bystanders were more likely to have been beaten and abused by their parents.

Rescuers were more likely to have been raised by parents who themselves were models of caring and kindness.

This research helped heal Oliner. States Rabbi Harold Schulweis, a close friend, "He found the spark of decency in human beings." Oliner now is a man of 60 who has made peace with his past and maintains optimism and hope about his future. He says, "The notion that we are each other's keeper is gaining. Maybe we've reached a point where another Holocaust is unimaginable." After pausing, he adds, "It's because of the people who cared that I'm here. There are such people in the world—and we can teach our children to be like them."

SOURCE: Oliner (1986); Oliner and Oliner (1988); Hunt (1990a; 1990b)

than make a mere dent on the problem or give it the good ole' college try. They had to solve it. Thus, tackling the nuclear arms race, world hunger, or racism in America was discouraged.

During the rest of the summer, Babbie was amazed—and rewarded beyond his expectations. All the social problems that were recognized, tackled, and solved were close to home. They included these:

▼ Potholes in a neighborhood street. A student and 20 neighbors who watched him get started worked together to fill them.

▼ A student who was acutely aware of widespread loneliness in her dorm organized a dorm cookout.

▼ Picking up litter.

▼ Cleaning up broken glass on a nearby street that had been left after a vehicle accident.

▼ Moving an errant sprinkler that had been spraying a sidewalk and one lane of auto traffic.

▼ Tying up and supporting a small tree that had been blocking a sidewalk due to roots loosened by a recent rainstorm.

▼ Trimming a bush on public property that had blocked vision on a dangerous corner.

▼ Removing a fallen branch that was a danger to drivers.

▼ Helping push a stalled car out of traffic.

▼ Taking a purse left on a bus seat up to the driver.

▼ Asking a nearby gas station attendant to help in spraying with insecticide an overflowing trash can at a bus stop that had become infested with bees, endangering awaiting bus passengers.

▼ Cleaning up a mess in a dormitory bathroom.

▼ Purchasing note pads and pencils for each pay telephone on the dormitory floor—along with a note requesting that they not be taken.

While these social problems may seem trivial—and they may be in the larger scheme of things—they do illustrate a valuable point: opportunities are everywhere for everybody to make a difference.

Opportunities exist at every level:

▼ Among friends

▼ In families

▼ In apartments and dormitories

▼ In classrooms

▼ In the immediate workplace

▼ In the organizations in which we work

▼ In our neighborhoods

▼ In community organizations

▼ In our communities

▼ In our regions

▼ In our states

▼ In our nation

▼ In our world, on our planet

EXERCISE 15-4. SOLVING A SOCIAL PROBLEM IN YOUR IMMEDIATE ENVIRONMENT

Pick a social problem to solve, using Babbie's criteria described above. After you have taken steps to solve the problem, write or discuss the following questions.

1. Identify and describe the social problem.
2. Describe what you did.
3. Describe the reactions of others who saw you doing it.
4. Describe your own reactions to the experience.

SOURCE: Babbie (1985, 149)

BOX 15-5. WELLNESS AND ENVIRONMENTALISM

We usually think of wellness as an individual thing—healthy personal habits for enhancing quality and length of life. Environmentalism typically is seen as a social movement focusing on the earth and its precious resources.

A legacy of Earth Day 1990 is recognition that wellness and environmentalism overlap. Wellness is the process of promoting environmental as well as personal health. You read in Chapter 1 that environmental wellness habits are included in a whole-person wellness lifestyle.

Personal wellness cannot flourish in a polluted natural environment or on a globe headed toward depletion of nonrenewable resources.

In short, a wellness lifestyle at once benefits self and environment.

For example, the U.S. Department of Energy reminds us that the average family can save $70 to $100 per year through energy-conscious driving and good car maintenance—while saving energy and contributing to clean air.

Below are several specific tips for practicing conservation on the roads, as suggested by the Department of Energy.

Use public transportation, try biking, or walk if you can.

Share your ride.

Eliminate unnecessary trips.

Vacation at home or nearby this year.

Travel by train or bus instead of by car.

Rediscover the pleasures of walking and biking during your vacation.

Observe speed limits.

When driving, accelerate smoothly and moderately, drive at a steady pace, and minimize braking.

Wellness means caring about the earth as well as your own mind-body. Energy-saving habits on the road are one practical way to unite wellness and environmentalism in your own life. Think about it.

Egoistic altruism—self-fulfillment through enhancing the well-being of others—has one other virtue: it leads to self-transcendence. It takes us outside ourselves and our own problems. Focusing on how we can contribute to the well-being of others is one of the best ways to prevent and cope with our own distress.

We will next examine some of the social approaches that are needed to minimize unnecessary distress. Working together, individuals can make a difference in improving the social conditions out of which widespread distress arises.

MODIFYING THE SOCIAL CONTEXT OF STRESS   ▼

In Chapter 2, you read about an area of stress theory emphasizing that you do not experience stress and distress alone. You are vitally affected by the same social and historical forces that affect others. Stress and distress are *patterned*. Many adults, for instance, experience heart attacks partly in response to the pressures of an accelerating, fast-paced society. Many youth become alienated and delinquent in part because of poor schools, limited job opportunities, and adult crime in their neighborhood.

If distress is to be minimized throughout American society, not only must individuals manage their own stress wisely, but social approaches to stress management must also be followed. Working on these efforts constitute some of the ways individuals can transcend their own stress-related problems to contribute to a better world.

THE FAMILY

The family can help children learn about stress, live so that stress plays a positive role in their lives, and establish good stress-control habits for adulthood. If families can become more effective in teaching children to handle stress effectively, many instances of painful distress later in life may be avoided. Better stress management must begin in the early years of life—and the family is where the first, and sometimes the strongest, habits form.

1. *Parents need to understand stress and promote awareness of stress in their children.* Effective parenting depends on awareness of the nature, causes, and effects of stress and methods for its control—in parent and child. If children and young people learn more about stress, they also will be able to apply this understanding later as adults. Most people who are now parents need to learn more. Most of the ideas discussed in this book can be fully understood by 10 or 12 year olds if explained and applied in the normal course of family living.

2. *It is important for parents to provide unconditional love that in turn will contribute to positive self-esteem.* Many of the steps suggested in earlier chapters for managing stress wisely are based on self-control and conscious choice, which themselves depend on self-esteem. Self-esteem develops naturally when children are loved, not for what they do, but for who they are.

3. *Security and stability within the family are vital.* No matter what else changes, no matter what the personal stresses, the child must sense that parents are there and that they care. Children also need a good deal of routine and predict-

ability in their daily lives. Maintaining this climate is difficult enough in a rapidly moving society in which family members often are involved in many activities outside the home. It becomes more difficult when families are troubled and go through divorce. The single parent often faces an even greater challenge.

4. *It is important to teach children to take responsibilities for their actions.* In this way, they are more likely to grow into adulthood already able to choose wisely and used to taking control of events. They are less likely to grow up habitually helpless or overly dependent on others.

5. *Parents need to promote early value clarification and choice—what is important, unimportant, desirable, and undesirable, valuable and not valuable.* Children and young people need to know what they believe in—through their own thoughtful choices—as early as possible. This does not require a "hands-off" approach by parents. Controls and limits are important. But where the child's welfare and the welfare of others are not at stake, promotion of the child's independent awareness and moral choice will help develop internal guidelines for action. In this way, the child will become self-directed and less like a paper boat on the stormy seas of change, option, and pressures.

6. *Parents can set an example by adopting a pace of life that is within their comfort zone.* Children learn more from what they see than from what they hear. Parents who are perpetually either bored or overloaded are likely to raise children in the same mold.

7. *Parents need to set examples of good health and fitness and constructive coping responses to distress.* The most important means by which parents can aid children in developing good stress buffers and constructive coping responses is to practice sound habits themselves. It is vital for young people—before they marry and have children—to become aware of stress and to develop sound habits of stress management.

8. *To enhance family security, every family ought to be assured a guaranteed annual income—through paid work in private or public sectors or through family assistance grants; and discrimination in housing, education, and employment must be reduced.* Millions of children, youth, and parents encounter unnecessary distress because of poverty or discrimination and the family problems they cause. A nation genuinely committed to "life, liberty, and pursuit of happiness" among all its citizens must do everything it can, publicly and privately, to reduce discrimination and to promote economic security of families as a foundation for stress reduction.

THE SCHOOL

The school is the second major influence on children and youth. And the school, like the family, can minimize pressures toward distress and teach students how to deal with stress.

1.   *Schools need to provide more "affective" learning—that is, learning about emotions, relationships, and stress.* These topics in turn should be related to larger social influences. For example, students need to understand that many "mental health" problems are really stress-related and that they are caused partly by rapid social change. Affective education can best be carried out through experiential learning. Students learn more easily if they can apply ideas to daily life or if actual life situations are simulated in the classroom through role-playing. This type of learning should begin in the elementary years.

2.   *The learning process must be designed to require high standards and offer enjoyment for more students.* Much of the distress experienced by young people is caused by oppressive, irrelevant, excessively standardized schooling. Research has shown that this is especially true for students who are not headed for college. Schools must recognize individual differences, provide varied options along the way, be accompanied by reasonable rules and enforcement, offer many opportunities for involvement, and be enjoyable. Education must foster a positive sense of self-worth, as well as respect for others, among all who attend school. At the same time, schools should teach basic skills of thinking and communicating so that students will not experience unnecessary distress later in life because of poor preparation.

3.   *Schools can reduce youthful distress by responding to deviant students in more positive ways.* Too often the feelings of anger, despair, and hopelessness among marginal and troublesome students are exaggerated by the way in which the school responds to deviants. Too often the school emphasizes humiliation and exclusion rather than genuine concern and individualized handling of deviant cases. Often, substantial stress is created, setting in motion a vicious progression: rebellion, alienation, withdrawal, despair, dropping out, unemployment, and crime.

4.   *Schools need to enhance students' self-worth by offering varied opportunities for success.* Handling stress wisely, as we have seen, depends partly on a sense of control over events, which in turn is based upon self-confidence. Self-confidence can be fostered by providing every student with meaningful experiences he or she can master. Positive reinforcement from others builds self-esteem. This is one of the most important benefits of a wide-ranging extracurricular activity program, as well as community-related internships or field experiences.

5.   *Learning ought to emphasize preparation for living in the world of today—and tomorrow.* Schools too often prepare youth for yesterday's world. And, as Toffler notes, "It is no longer sufficient for Johnny to understand the past. It is not even enough for him to understand the present, for the here-and-now environment will soon vanish." In this chapter, "Education in the Future Tense," Toffler (1971) provides many concrete examples of how schooling can be more future-oriented. Included are steps for emphasizing basic skills, for updating rapidly changing information, for relating to others in a fast-paced world, and for making wise decisions in a world filled with overchoice. Also needed are entirely new, creative alternative schools.

THE WORKPLACE

Substantial distress often arises in the work setting—from oppressive supervision, higher worker turnover, meaningless routines, social isolation, and chronic overload. A humane work setting affords opportunities for creative expression and self-development and it contributes to the physical and mental health of people who work there. A number of ways in which work organizations can minimize unnecessary distress and maximize self-development and good health are discussed in Chapter 13.

THE COMMUNITY

Even the best family or school can do little to reduce stress if the youth who passes through them enters a community filled with strain, limited opportunity, and limited support for its residents. In a number of ways, the community can play a constructive part in minimizing distress, even in a fast-moving world.

1. *Communities must preserve the neighborhood, promote stability, and foster a sense of unity among residents.* Social anchorage is vital. So are mutual support and a lasting attachment to place and neighbors. These elements of good community life are constantly threatened by geographic mobility and perpetual change. Programs and activities to support a genuine sense of community are most important.

2. *The community needs to provide programs for stress-ridden residents.* A good community is one that cares and shows that it does, both by promoting person-to-person interactions and by meeting the special stress-related needs that cannot be met by individuals or their families. The latter includes, for example, family and individual counseling services, aid for senior citizens, youth crisis centers, child abuse programs, emergency housing services, and "reintegration aid" to those leaving mental hospitals and prisons.

3. *The community needs to provide varied opportunities for youth to become involved in constructive and meaningful roles.* For the past several decades, young people have spent most of their time in school. Relatively few part-time or summer job opportunities exist, and they are becoming fewer. Years ago, young people worked in the family fields, market, or shop. They had a sense of competency, belonging, and usefulness. Now, most youth—especially those in the inner city—are uninvolved in meaningful activities and roles because most of these have disappeared. Fortunately, many communities now are recognizing this need and are creating work and school-related opportunities for young people, as well as opportunities for involvement in decision-making.

4. *Each community ought to carefully examine its rate of growth and, if it is too fast, slow it down.* Americans seem to be addicted to the idea that progress equals growth—growth in numbers of people, space, profit, and standard of living. There are two severe problems with this conception. We are rapidly

running out of energy. And fast community growth inevitably means perpetual change. Rapid change means high stress for large numbers of people. Small alternative communities can play a useful role in illustrating stability, simplicity, neighborliness, and low energy use.

5. *Each community needs to find ways of integrating its senior citizens into the mainstream of productive, socially useful living.* America's way of handling the elderly is tragic: out of sight, out of mind—but not really. The suffering of the elderly is great—in nursing homes, cheap hotels, isolated apartments, even next door. For many retirees, there is too little to do, too few who care, too little money, little reason to hope. The fundamental reason for this sad circumstance is that we isolate the elderly and exclude them from full participation. We must find ways of reducing their distress—by bringing them back into the workplace, strengthening their family ties, seeking them out in our neighborhoods, and drawing upon their talents and wisdom in educating the young.

GOVERNMENT ACTION

Stress management must be the responsibility primarily of individuals, families, groups, and the local community. It should be a private concern. But there are several important roles to be performed by government at federal, state, and local levels:

1. Federal, state, and local governments must provide some financial support for stress-prevention community services.

2. Federal, state, and local governments need to examine the stress-creating potentials of new policies and programs.

3. Federal and state governments should support research into the causes, consequences, and control of stress, as well as dissemination of knowledge gained by such research.

4. Federal and state governments need to monitor stresses and distresses throughout the population through various "social indicators."

5. Federal, state, and local governments need to ensure equal opportunity for all citizens to maximize their potentials and to reach their highest possible levels of achievement and reward.

6. Governments at all levels owe it to their citizens to provide security from crime and from genuine threats from other governments.

7. The Federal government needs to take constructive steps to reduce the likelihood of war and especially nuclear holocaust.

The greatest stressor of all is the threat of nuclear catastrophe. Increasingly, citizens of all ages, including small children, find the quality of their lives dampened by the real possibility of extinction through nuclear war. During a speech in 1957, President Dwight D. Eisenhower recognized this reality.

War in our time has become an anachronism. Whatever the case in the past, war in the future can serve no useful purpose. A war which becomes general, as any limited action might, could only result in the virtual destruction of mankind.

President Eisenhower also spoke of the vested interest of the "military-industrial complex" in building more and more armaments. There now is widespread belief that doing so has heightened rather than lessened the likelihood of all-out nuclear war. Each new technological advance in weapons results not in reduced risk of war, but in further escalation by the other side.

Moreover, diversion of vast resources to military weaponry has diverted money, manpower, and other resources here and abroad away from progress toward improved length and quality of human life for millions through food, agricultural means to produce food, health care, education, housing, care of the elderly and the young, and much more.

Whatever one's political position on these issues, there can be little doubt, if we care about reducing the ultimate source of human distress, that governments and the people they govern need to search for new ways of relating to one another on this ever-smaller globe. As Albert Einstein stated in 1946, "the unleashed power of the atom has changed everything save our modes of thinking and we thus drift toward unparalleled catastrophe (Beyond War, 1986, i)."

Because of vested political, industrial, and military interests in continuing the arms race by those in positions of power, as described by President Eisenhower, it seems likely that a more peaceful future rests on large numbers of citizens here and abroad agreeing and acting upon two simple ideas.

ALL WAR IS NOW OBSOLETE

General Douglas MacArthur recognized this in 1961 when he stated:

> The very triumph of scientific annihilation (the atom bomb) has destroyed the possibility of war's being a medium for the practical settlement of international differences . . . Global war has become a Frankenstein to destroy both sides. No longer is it a weapon of adventure—the shortcut to international power. If you lose, you are annihilated. If you win, you stand only to lose. No longer does it possess even the chance of the winner of a duel. It contains now only the germs of double suicide.

Also in 1961, President John F. Kennedy spoke of the ultimate stressor:

> Unconditional war can no longer lead to unconditional victory. It can no longer serve to settle disputes. It can no longer be of concern to great powers alone. For a nuclear disaster, spread by winds and waters and fear, could well engulf the great and the small, the rich and the poor, the committed and the uncommitted alike. Mankind must put an end to war or war will put an end to mankind.

Many believe that all war is now obsolete because even limited, small scale wars carry the real risk of escalating to nuclear conflict. Therefore, new solutions to disputes between nations must be sought.

WE ARE ONE

When astronauts and cosmonauts view the globe from space, they see one, unified whole with no frames and no boundaries. Humans share one important thing in common: the desire to survive. They share one common space—the earth—on which to survive.

Apollo IX astronaut Russell Schweikert said this upon his return:

> When you go around it in an hour and a half, you begin to recognize that your identity is with that whole thing. And that makes a change.
>
> You look down there, and you can't imagine how many borders and boundaries you cross, again and again and again, and you don't even see them. There you are—hundreds of people killing each other over some imaginary line that you're not even aware of, that you can't see. From where you see it, the thing is a whole, and it's so beautiful. You wish you could take one person in each hand and say, "Look at it from this perspective. What's important?"
>
> You realize that on that small spot, that little blue and white thing, is everything that means anything to you. All of history and music and poetry and art and birth and love; tears, joy, games. All of it on that little spot out there that you can cover with your thumb.

In past centuries, we identified with smaller units in order to survive: the family, the clan, the tribe, the nation. Now, we need to shift our identification to the level of the globe in order to survive, because it is only in this way that all people together can ensure that our common interest of survival is protected.

To be sure, there always will be differences between peoples and nations on this globe. But we must come to agree upon a common set of rules to govern our relations between nations and a set of procedures for settling differences. Only then can we truly act as one and dramatically reduce the risk of war—as we must if we, our children, and our grandchildren are to survive.

Most of all, then, we as humans need to think differently about war and peace. When millions of people here and broad come to accept these two ideas— "all war is obsolete" and "we are one"—political leaders will then follow. Alternative solutions to war will be found.

There are many social approaches to stress management. Only a few have been mentioned here. Social approaches must be aimed at reducing the structural social forces that produce distress. All the same, individuals must attempt to reduce their personal stress levels. Attempts by government or social groups to reduce some of the causes of large-scale stress and distress should complement the individual approaches discussed in earlier chapters.

REFERENCES ▼

Andrews, H.F. (1990). Helping and health. *Advances: The Journal For Mind-Body Health,* 7, 25-34.

Babbie, E. (1985). *You Can Make A Difference.* Anaheim Hills: Opening Books.

Babcock, D.E., & Keepers, T.D. (1976). *Raising Kids Okay.* New York, Avon.

Beyond War. (1985). *Beyond War: Selected Resources.* Palo Alto: Beyond War Foundation.

Beyond War. (1986). *Beyond War: A New Way of Thinking.* Palo Alto: Beyond War Foundation.

Castleman, M. (1990). How the stress experts deal with theirs. *Medical Self-Care,* 56, 35-40.

Coleman, J.S. (1973). *Youth: Transition To Adulthood.* Chicago: University of Chicago Press.

Elkind, D. (1981). *The Hurried Child: Growing Up Too Fast Too Soon.* Reading: Addison-Wesley.

Gordon, T. (1970). *Parent Effectiveness Training.* New York: McKay.

Havel, V. (1990). To his wife, Olga, from prison. *Noetic Sciences Review,* No. 14, 36.

Helmstetter, S. (1989). *Predictive Parenting.* New York: William Morrow and Company.

Hunt. M. (1990a). Can goodness be taught? *Parade Magazine,* May 6, 28-29.

Hunt, M. (1990b). *The Compassionate Beast: What Science Is Discovering About The Humane Side of Humankind.* New York: William Morrow and Company.

Hurley, T.J. (1990). Reflections. *Noetic Sciences Review,* No. 16, 33.

Kohn, A. (1990). *The Brighter Side of Human Nature: Altruism and Empathy in Everyday Life.* New York: Basic Books.

Leonard, G. (1968). *Education and Ecstasy.* New York: Dell.

Luks, A. (1988). Helper's high. *Psychology Today,* 22, 39-42.

Miller, J. (1990). Hello, this is Jimmy Carter. *Noetic Sciences Review,* No. 16, 32.

Mills. S.W. (1956). *The Power Elite.* New York: Oxford University Press.

Oliner, S. (196). *Restless Memories: Recollections of the Holocaust Years.* Berkeley: Judahl Magnes Press.

Oliner, S., & Oliner, P. (1988). *The Altruistic Personality: Rescuers of Jews in Nazi Europe.* New York: Free Press.

Oreskes, M. (1990). "Astonishing" U.S. voter apathy. *San Francisco Chronicle.* May 7, A10.

Packard, V. (1974). *A Nation of Strangers.* New York: Pocket Books.

Polk, K. & Schafer, W.E. (1972). *Schools and Delinquency.* Englewood Cliffs: Prentice-Hall.

Ray, P.H. (1989). Altruism as value-centered action. *Noetic Sciences Review,* No. 12, 10-14.

Schafer, W.E. & Olexa, C. (1971). *Tracking and Opportunity.* San Francisco: Chandler Publishing Company.

Selye, H. (1974). *Stress Without Distress.* Philadelphia: Lippincott.

Selye, H. (1976). *The Stress of Life,* Rev. Ed. New York: McGraw- Hill Book Company.

Silberman, C. E. (1970). *Crisis In The Classroom.* New York: Vintage, 1970.

Simkinson, C.H. (1990). Compassionate living: Can we integrate healthy narcissism and social responsibility? *Common Boundary,* 8, 7-9.

Steiner, C. (1974). *Scripts People Live.* New York: Grove.

Toffler, A. (1971). *Future Shock.* New York: Bantam.

Epilogue

EPILOGUE

I. THE BEST OF TIMES AND THE WORST OF TIMES

II. MANAGING STRESS IN A CHALLENGING WORLD

III. STRESS MANAGEMENT FOR WHAT?

IV. A FOUR-PART GUIDING PHILOSOPHY

THE BEST OF TIMES AND THE WORST OF TIMES   ▼

We live in the best of times and the worst of times. Through technology, we are able to leave behind most of the struggles of daily existence which in the past burdened humankind. We are gifted with options. We are not bound by space, by the vagaries of climate, or by the rampages of pestilence. There are no apparent limits to what we can discover and do.

Yet technology has brought unintended traps—too much change in too short a time, an ever-faster pace of daily life, a never-ending quest for material goods, loss of anchorages, uprootedness, transience, isolation, neglect of our bodies. Most of all, technology has brought something entirely new to human history: humankind's ability to destroy civilization, indeed life itself on this planet, if not through planetary pollution then by nuclear catastrophe.

What have changed more slowly are our ideas about how to adapt our way of life to technology. Sociologists refer to this as **cultural lag.** One result has been the rise of new types of distress—the distresses and diseases of "civilization." Relationships are strained, families break up more quickly and more often. Chronic fatigue has become an epidemic in American life.

Yet there is reason for optimism, certainly at the personal level and, perhaps, collectively. The medical and behavioral sciences have made great strides in providing guidelines on how we can face the inevitable, incessant stressors of daily life, yet survive—even thrive.

George Sheehan (1978), the cardiologist who runs and writes, has stated that we live in a society where the body is a second-class citizen. He correctly maintains that first of all, we need to be "good animals." What is needed is to treat your body as a first-class citizen, providing the basis for emotional and spiritual health, satisfying relationships, and a productive life.

MANAGING STRESS IN A CHALLENGING WORLD   ▼

This book has set forth a framework for understanding stress and its effects, positive and harmful. Within this framework, we have examined a wide variety of specific techniques for monitoring and managing stress. These stress management methods have been presented within several categories:

▼ Monitoring early warning signs of distress (Chapter 4).

▼ Practicing constructive coping responses in dealing with challenging stressors and with your own temporary distress (Chapter 6).

▼ Managing your perspectives and interpretations of stressful events (Chapter 7).

▼ Maintaining good health buffers—exercise, nutrition and sleep (Chapter 8).

▼ Using effective relaxation methods, including on-the-spot tension reducers and deep relaxation methods (Chapter 9).

▼ Applying effective steps for pacing and balancing time, for making transitions, and for dealing with change (Chapter 10).

▼ Utilizing effective communication skills to relate effectively with others around you and participate in caring networks of social support (Chapter 11).

▼ Properly balancing self-care with social responsibility in order to help modify the social context of personal stress when needed and to contribute to the well-being of others (Chapter 15).

BOX E-1. QUALITY LIVING

To live content with small means,
to seek elegance rather than luxury,
and refinement rather than fashion;
to be worthy, not respectable,
and wealthy not rich;
to listen to stars and birds, babes and sages
with open heart;
to study hard;
to think quietly, act frankly, talk gently,
await occasions, hurry never;
in a word, to let the spiritual,
unbidden and unconscious,
grow up through the common—
this is my symphony.

—William Henry Channing

SOURCE: Channing (1989, 48)

In Chapter 1 we identified several assumptions that need to guide your quest for effective stress management approaches that will work for you over the long run:

▼ Personal responsibility

▼ Holism

▼ Gradualism

▼ Balance

▼ Rhythm

▼ Awareness

▼ Action

▼ Experiment-of-one

▼ Lifelong process

Perhaps most important of all personal qualities for implementing suggestions in this book is a strong sense of internal control. As noted previously, the opposite of internal control is helplessness—the sense that one's life is controlled entirely by external forces, by one's inner drives or needs, by fate, or simply by inertia.

The best path to confidence for turning adversity into challenges is the belief that you can make things happen, that you control your own destiny.

In his excellent book, *Control Theory*, William Glasser (1984, 2) puts it succinctly.

> If I believe that the motivation for all I do, good or bad, comes from within me, not from the outside world, then, when I am miserable, I cannot claim that my misery is caused by uncaring parents, a boorish spouse, an ungrateful child, or a miserable job. If I were a machine, this claim might be valid. I could be programmed to "feel good" only if those I "needed" treated me well. But I am not a machine, and although I strongly desire good treatment from everyone in my life, if I don't get what I want, it is my choice whether or not to be miserable.

Glasser is correct in noting that it is totally warranted sometimes to be discontented with present circumstances. We referred to this in Chapter 5 as positive anger or indignation. It is our dissatisfaction that motivates us to improve reality within or around us. Dissatisfaction with aspects of work, with community growth patterns, or national medical care policies will motivate you to take constructive, corrective action as an employee or citizen. Dissatisfaction does not always feel good. Yet it is vital to improving our existence.

You read about hardiness as a cluster of attitudes and beliefs—including internal control—that can help you survive, even thrive under the pressure of change and adversity. Hardiness will enable you to become involved in making the world a better place, as well as to enjoy it more and stay healthy. Using hardiness to leave this planet in better shape for your children means attending to the social context of stress, as well as to your personal existence.

You have read that there is an upside to stress as well as a downside. Managed effectively, stress can be turned into a positive force to help you reach your highest possible level of well-being and performance.

STRESS MANAGEMENT FOR WHAT? ▼

You read in Chapter 1 that the primary goal of stress management is **wellness— living at one's highest possible level as a whole person.** We noted that wellness, or optimal wellbeing, includes:

- ▼ Absence of illness

- ▼ Low illness risk

- ▼ Maximum energy for daily living

- ▼ Enjoyment of daily life

- ▼ Continuous development of one's abilities

- ▼ Commitment to the common good.

Stated differently, wellness takes you beyond normal health to a higher plane. The effect of wellness is to maximize your potentials while enjoying the process and maintaining optimal health along the way.

You read that wellness is attained through positive habits in the following areas:

Environmental
Intellectual
Emotional
Spiritual
Physical
Social
Time

A FOUR-PART GUIDING PHILOSOPHY ▼

As discussed in Chapter 15, a continuing challenge is not only to maximize personal wellness but to balance self-care with social responsibility. In closing, I want to share my own four-part philosophy that provides the guidance and coherence I need to balance self-care with my desire to make a difference. I invite you to consider this for yourself.

1. Continually have visions and dreams, some of which have social significance—that will benefit others.

2. Work hard, at least partly with others, to bring these dreams and visions to reality.

3. Balance that hard work with play, care of body and spirit, intimacy, and friendship.

4. Enjoy the process.

I wish you well.

REFERENCES   ▼

Channing, W.H. (1989). Unnamed poem. *Noetic Sciences Review*, No. 13, 48.
Glasser, W. (1984). *Control Theory*. New York: Harper.
Sheehan, G. (1978). *Running and Being*. New York: Simon & Schuster.

Glossary

ACTH (adreno-corticotropic hormone) A stress hormone produced by the pituitary gland. Triggers the adrenal cortex during the stress response.

Active Listening An active process of being attentive, taking in information and feelings accurately and completely, and rephrasing what you have heard to check its accuracy.

Adaptive Reactions to Distress Reactions that reduce rather than increase one's distress in the long run.

Adrenal Cortex The outer part of the adrenal gland which, in response to ACTH, produces corticoids.

Adrenaline (Also known as epinephrine) A stress hormone produced by the adrenal medulla. Prepares the body for direct, immediate, physical action.

Adrenal Medulla The inner part of the adrenal gland which, in response to the sympathetic nervous system, produces adrenaline (epinephrine) and noradrenaline (norepinephrine).

Aerobic Exercise Physical movement involving sustained elevation of heart rate. To be effective in producing the aerobic training effect, a person must elevate heart rate to 70% to 85% of maximum heart rate for at least 20 or 30 minutes per session at least three times per week. Illustrated by brisk walking, running, swimming, and bicycling.

Aerobic Training Effect The body's adaptation to repeated aerobic exercise. Includes improved abilities to take in oxygen (respiration), transport oxygen to the muscles (circulation), and burn oxygen (metabolism).

Affective Learning Learning about emotions, relationships, and stress.

Afterburn Time The time needed after an event to complete it behaviorally and emotionally before moving on to the next activity.

Aggressive A style of relating that includes being hostile, insensitive, angry, or abusive.

Altruistic Egoism Hans Selye's term for doing things others will appreciate and for which they will return their love. Earning others' love.

Anger Negative anger is a feeling, expressed or unexpressed, of hostility, aggressiveness, or a desire to hurt. Wanting to punish the source of frustration. Positive anger is motivation to change or correct the source of frustration. Both are based on wanting something, not getting it, and being frustrated.

Anticipatory Stress Arousal created by thinking about a forthcoming event or challenge. May be helpful or harmful.

Anxiety Mental and physical arousal in anticipation of a negative future experience. Usually includes fear and tension. May be chronic or acute.

Apathy Lack of emotion, concern, or interest.

Arrhythmia A disturbance in the electrical rhythm of the heart.

Assertive Communicating in a manner that does not intentionally offend or hurt others, yet includes strong statements or actions by the individual to express what he/she wants.

Autogenic Relaxation A relaxation technique based on repeated thoughts of warmth and heaviness in specific parts of the body.

Autonomic Nervous System The peripheral nervous system of the body which sends electrical messages of arousal (sympathetic nervous system) or quieting (parasympathetic nervous system) to muscles, glands, and organs.

Awfulizing Turning a difficult situation into something awful, terrible, or intolerable.

Balance A guideline for managing stress involving effectively balancing such things as rest and activity, risk and safety, change and stability, thought and action.

Banal Life Script A blueprint for living calling for a life of unhappiness, failure, pity, half-effort, depression, boredom, illness, or loneliness.

Behavioral Distress Symptoms Symptoms of distress reflected in one's actions. Illustrations include irritability, withdrawing, attacking someone, or difficulty sitting still.

Being Right Believing that it is intolerable to be seen as wrong and that one's beliefs or opinions are always right. A negative style of self-talk.

Belief An enduring assumption.

Benson Method of Relaxation A type of meditation involving sitting comfortably in a quiet place, relaxing muscles, and then repeating "one" for 10 to 20 minutes once or twice per day.

Big Circle An active relaxation technique involving large trunk rotations from the waist.

Biofeedback Use of any device to detect internal physiological processes. Learning to relax by controlling this feedback.

Blaming Attributing responsibility for events, especially negative ones, to someone else, even when such responsibility rightfully belongs to self.

Boredom Being uninterested, unmotivated, and listless. Ennui.

Bound Energy Physical tension from unexpressed or unresolved arousal.

Breathing Away Tension A relaxation technique in which you imagine tension, upset, or pain leaving your body with each exhalation.

Burnout A condition of mental and physical exhaustion resulting from overstimulation, meaninglessness, or hopelessness.

Cancer A life-threatening disease in which cells in one part of the body reproduce uncontrollably.

Career Inopportunity Lack of opportunity for job advancement.

Career Insecurity Lack of assurance of continuation of one's job.

Catastrophizing Expecting the worst almost certainly will happen. Worrying about perceived impending catastrophe.

Catecholamines Hormones produced by the adrenal medulla, including adrenaline and noradrenaline (epinephrine and norepinephrine).

Centering Listening to your inner voice of wisdom. Being centered is knowing what you need, want, or believe.

Cerebral Cortex The outer layer of the brain where most thinking occurs.

Challenge Objective challenge refers to a difficult situation or event. Subjective challenge (a component of hardiness) refers to seeing a change or difficulty as a positive opportunity rather than as a threat.

Cholesterol A waxy-type lipid used in construction of cell walls and certain hormones. Excessive amounts in the bloodstream contribute to coronary heart disease.

Chronic Stressors Stressors that are ubiquitous or recurrent.

Circling Shoulders Rotating the shoulders in a circular fashion to reduce muscle tension.

Clustering of Life Events Occurrence of many unusual life experiences within a relatively few days, weeks, or months.

Cognitive Distress Symptoms Disturbed thinking associated with the chronic or acute excitation of the stress response. Illustrated by difficulty in concentrating, forgetfulness, mental block, and disorganized reasoning.

Commitment Being positively motivated toward and involved in your daily life (for example, school, work, or community groups). A component of hardiness. Opposite is alienation.

Computing Being very correct, very reasonable with no semblance of feeling; acting calm, cool, and collected.

Concentration In relation to time management, refers to working from prioritized lists and doing one thing at a time. In relation to listening, refers to focusing attention on what speaker is saying. In relation to peak performance, refers to focusing attention and energy on accomplishing a task or goal.

Confidence Belief in one's ability to master a task or difficulty. A component of hardiness. Opposite is self-doubt.

Conscious Interpretation Pathway Conscious appraisal of the nature and degree of threat from stressors.

Constructive Maladjustment Being appropriately discontented about conditions in the surrounding social, political, or natural environment that in the judgment of the person are wrong and need to be changed—and being motivated to change those conditions.

Content of Stress The larger physical and social environment within which stressors and personal stress occur.

Control Fallacy The belief that happiness depends on cajoling or coercing others to do what you think they should.

Coping Constantly changing cognitive and behavioral efforts to manage specific external and/or internal demands that are appraised as taxing or exceeding the resources of the person.

Coronary Artery Disease Partial or complete blockage of one or more coronary arteries with plaque.

Corticoids Stress-related hormones preparing the body for direct, immediate, physical action. Produced by the adrenal cortex.

Cultural Lag When one element in society lags behind in adjusting to change in another element.

Current Stress Arousal occurring during an event. May be helpful or harmful.

Daily Hassles Minor, recurrent, daily events that are experienced as minor distressors.

Deep Adaptive Energy The body's deep chemical and energy reserves that can be depleted by major or recurrent experiences of distress.

Deep Relaxation Mental and physical relaxation in which metabolism goes below baseline during a relaxation exercise.

Defensiveness Responding to negative feedback or criticism with efforts to protect your image or opinion.

Deliberate Reactions to Distress Reactions to your distress that are not scripted by parents but are based on awareness and choice.

Denial Not recognizing or accepting your distress symptoms or life situation. Also a stage in the grieving process following death of a loved one or in anticipation of one's own death.

Depressants Drugs such as tranquilizers, alcohol, and barbiturates used to relieve tension. May be prescribed or illegal.

Depression A multi-faceted experience of lowered energy and motivation, flattened affect, loss of sleep and appetite, and other symptoms.

Desensitization A technique for overcoming phobias and fears. Involves progressive exposure to a distressor (such as flying) through such steps as imagery, role playing, and brief practice.

Destructive Coping Response A response to stressors that contributes to distress for self or others.

Discounting Not taking seriously what another person says and putting the speaker down.

Disputation A technique for challenging unreasonable beliefs or negative self-talk.

Distortants Drugs such as LSD and mescaline, which distort perception of reality.

Distracting Doing or saying whatever is irrelevant to what others are doing or saying; not responding to the point.

Distress Too much or too little arousal resulting in harm to mind or body.

Distressor Any demand on mind or body resulting in too much or too little arousal.

Ego-Speak Talking about oneself excessively and inappropriately.

Egoistic Altruism Self-realization through giving to others.

Emotional Distress Symptoms Symptoms of distress reflected in emotions or feelings. Illustrated by depression, hopelessness, anxiety, fear, and joylessness.

Endocrine System The network of glands that secrete hormones directly into the bloodstream.

Epinephrine See *Adrenaline*.

Episodic Stressor A stressor that occurs irregularly or only once.

Escapism A destructive reaction to distress in which you escape the situation or deny your feelings of disharmony by immersing into television, books, fantasy, drugs, or flight. Not same as temporary, constructive withdrawal.

Eustress Helpful arousal. Same as positive stress.

Experiment-of-One Discovering through trial and error which stress management techniques work best for you.

External Perfectionism Holding impossibly demanding expectations of others.

Face Loosener A passive method of deliberately concentrating on allowing facial muscles to loosen.

Fallacy of Fairness The belief that it is impossible to achieve any degree of personal happiness because of perceived unfairness in the world.

Familiar Stranger Someone you regularly see but do not know, such as a student in the same college classroom.

Fear A feeling of fright, apprehension, or dread based on a perceived threat or danger.

Fear of Failure Apprehension about failing based on the belief that to fail is to risk unacceptable rejection by others or severe damage to self-esteem.

Fear of Success Apprehension about achieving based on the belief that to succeed will result in escalation of others' future expectations beyond one's ability to perform.

Fight-or-Flight Response A multi-faceted, genetically programmed response of the body preparing the person for immediate action in response to a perceived threat.

Floppy Doll An active relaxation method in which the person stands and rotates the upper trunk with arms dangling and swinging at the side.

Flow of Situations The pace at which events pass through a person's experience.

Food Scripting A blueprint for relating to food, usually developed in childhood through early messages and early decisions about food. A subtype of life script.

Foresight Perceiving and sometimes stopping an action or thought before it occurs, as in foreseeing and catching one's anger response when his/her public image is threatened.

Frustration A feeling of disappointment or irritation at being thwarted from one's goals or wants.

Game Interpersonal exchanges, usually with underlying or implicit messages, which people use to make themselves or others feel bad.

General Adaptation Syndrome Hans Selye's theoretical model of the body's response to sustained stress, which includes a sequence of three stages: alarm, resistance, and exhaustion.

Generalized Resistance Resources Any characteristic of the person, the group, or the environment that can facilitate effective tension management.

Geographic Mobility Moving place of residence from one locality to another.

Gradualism Incorporating new stress management techniques into your life gradually and one or two at a time rather than precipitously or in larger clusters.

Hardiness Personal strength. As used by Maddi and Kobasa, includes challenge, commitment, and control. The 10 C's also include confidence, conditioning, caring, coping, calmness, creativity, and competence.

Head Roll Gently rotating your head from side to side and from front to back in a full circular motion. Repeating several times in opposite directions.

Health Buffers Health habits that help build resistance against distress.

High Blood Pressure A higher than normal (repeated readings higher than 140/90) amount of pressure against the inner walls of arteries and capillaries. Also known as hypertension.

High Density Lipoprotein Protein substances in the blood that act as scavengers by picking up excess cholesterol from artery walls and transporting it back to the liver where it is converted into bile acid and discharged through the stool.

High-level Wellness A goal of stress management that includes good health (absence of illness and maximum energy and vitality), life satisfaction, productivity, and self-development.

Hindsight Becoming aware of or understanding an event or experience after it has occurred.

Holism The assumption that since the human is a multi-dimensional being, a number of complementary approaches to managing stress are needed involving mind, body, and behavior.

Homeostasis An equilibrium state of the body in which neuromuscular and chemical conditions are relatively constant.

Hydrotherapy Relaxation through immersion in warm water as in a shower, hot tub, or flotation tank.

Hypermetabolic Stress Control Active relaxation methods, such as aerobic exercise, in which metabolism is temporarily elevated.

Hypertension See *High Blood Pressure.*

Hypnosis A condition of very deep relaxation, induced by self or another person, in which the person is especially open to suggestion.

Hypometabolic Stress Control Passive relaxation methods, such as meditation or autogenic relaxation, in which metabolism temporarily drops below normal.

Hypothalamus Portion of the lower brain which, in response to perceived threat, sends a chemical message to the nearby pituitary gland to prepare for fight-or-flight.

"I" Messages An assertive communication in which the person begins the statement with "I" rather than "you."

Inappropriate Response to Stressors Coping responses in which the person reacts to stimuli in inappropriate ways. Illustrated by rebellion, rescuing, or drinking.

Insomnia Difficulty sleeping. May refer to disturbed sleep onset or to interrupted sleep.

Instant Replay A method of correcting distorted or negative thinking involving three steps: catch negative or distorted self-talk, challenge it, change it.

Insulation A time management method involving screening and sorting incoming information and tasks one time each day for processing outgoing information.

Intellectual Distress Disturbed thinking, such as difficulty organizing thoughts, forgetfulness, and mental block, associated with the stress response.

Internal Control A sense of being able to influence events and one's reactions to events. Opposite is helplessness.

Internal Perfectionism Impossibly demanding expectations of self.

Interpretation of Stressor Thoughts, automatic or deliberate, about the nature and degree of threat from a stressor.

Intersender Role Conflict Incompatible expectations sent from two or more role partners.

Intrasender Role Conflict Incompatible role expectations sent from a single role partner.

Isolation When used in the context of time management, refers to finding a place to work without interruption. When used in the context of social relationships more broadly, refers to being alone or without social support.

Isometric Arm Reliever Briefly pushing or pulling each arm against an immovable object, then relaxing.

Jogging In Place A method of relieving tension through brief elevation of muscular and cardiovascular activity.

Judging In relation to active listening, refers to passing judgment on the speaker's statement rather than remaining neutral.

Judging Total Human Worth Evaluating total worth of self or others on the basis of traits or behavior.

Lead time Time needed to prepare for an event.

Leg Loosener A passive method of deliberately concentrating on allowing leg muscles to loosen.

Life Script A blueprint for living, usually developed during childhood as a result of early messages from significant others and early decisions by self.

Limbic System The midlayer of the brain in which emotions are created.

Low Density Lipoprotein Protein substances in the bloodstream that transport cholesterol from the liver to be deposited along the inner walls of the arteries and elsewhere in the body.

Macro-Stressor A stressor experienced as major in nature, resulting in an intense stress response. May be a positive or negative stressor.

Magnifying Making more of an event than it actually is. Also known as making mountains out of molehills.

Maladaptive Reactions to Distress Reactions to personal distress that increase distress for self or others in long-run if not immediately.

Marker Event A significant, predictable event in the life cycle, such as graduating from high school, marrying, or starting one's first full time job.

Martyrdom Seeking out misery, usually because of the repetition compulsion. Common among distress seekers.

Massage A relaxation technique in which one person uses touch to loosen muscle, joint, or connective tissue tightness in another person.

Meaninglessness Lack of direction or sense of significance in one's life. A risk factor for boredom.

Meditation A relaxation technique in which the person focuses on a mantra, sound, word, or phrase (that is, a repeated mental focus) to quiet the mind, thereby quieting the body.

Mental Diversion Switching one's thoughts to another subject in order to avoid fear, anger, or another unwanted emotion. Also known as thought switching.

Mental Rehearsal Using imagery and self-talk to rehearse a forthcoming experience.

Micro-stressor A stressor experienced as minor in nature, resulting in a low intensity stress response. May be positive or negative.

Midsight Recognizing or understanding an experience while it is occurring, rather than before or afterwards.

Migraine Headache A recurrent, painful condition in the head associated with alternating constriction and dilation of cerebral blood vessels. Often accompanied by nausea and visual disturbance.

Minimizing Diminishing the value or importance of something to less than it actually is.

Missing the Mark An inappropriate coping response in which the person responds to or does what was not asked or vice versa.

Muscle Slapping A method of reducing one's muscle tension by gently slapping muscles throughout the body.

Musturbation Albert Ellis' term referring to the distorted belief that events must turn out precisely as the person wants—otherwise they will inevitably be very upsetting. Putting unreasonable "musts" on the world.

Myocardial Infarction Death of heart tissue resulting from insufficient supply of oxygen. Also known as heart attack.

Neck Press Briefly reducing neck tension by pressing the head forward or backward against an immovable object such as a wall or bookcase, then relaxing.

Negativizing Filtering out positive aspects of a situation while focusing only on negatives.

Neustress Neutral arousal. Stress that is neither helpful nor harmful.

Noradrenaline A stress hormone produced by the adrenal medulla. Also known as norepinephrine.

Optimal Arousal That level of arousal resulting in maximum productivity, satisfaction, and good health. Also known as positive stress.

Optimal Health Absence of illness, low illness risk, and maximum energy for daily living. May not be the same as "normal" health.

Organizational Stressors Conditions in an organization with a potential to result in distress among those who work there.

Overchoice The existence of so many options that the person feels overwhelmed.

Overgeneralizing Generalizing from a single event or piece of information to all such events or facts.

Overstimulation Experiencing stimuli so numerous or intense that one feels overwhelmed.

Parasympathetic Nervous System Part of the autonomic nervous system, which regulates the relaxation response of the body.

Parroting An ineffective response while listening in which you repeat back the exact words you just heard.

Passivity A style of interacting in which the person does not express genuine wants, needs, or opinions and allows himself/herself to be controlled by others.

Peak Performance Attaining a very high level of excellence relative to one's abilities.

Perfectionism Impossibly demanding expectations of self and/or others.

Personal Change Changes within the person's life, such as moving, changing jobs, becoming more assertive, and starting to exercise.

Personalizing A style of distorted thinking in which the person believes others' actions or feelings are entirely caused by self.

Personal Responsibility Believing that events and one's reactions to events to a large degree are the result of personal choice. Accepting the possibility of self-determination.

Physical Distress Symptoms Distress symptoms reflected in the body. Illustrated by neck pain, fatigue, stomach upset, and headache.

Pituitary Gland Endocrine gland located at base of brain below the hypothalamus. Considered the master gland. Secretes ACTH and TTH during the stress response.

Placating Talking in an ingratiating way; never disagreeing, no matter what; constantly apologizing.

Plunger Someone who too quickly and too completely reveals himself or herself in social situations.

Polarized Thinking The tendency to think in terms of black–white, good–bad, perfection–failure. No middle ground.

Positive Affirmations Positive self-talk statements intended to elevate self-esteem or confidence.

Positive Mental Image A positive picture in the mind of a forthcoming event or challenge.

Positive Stress Arousal that contributes to health, satisfaction, or productivity.

Procrastination Putting off starting or completing tasks perceived as being unpleasant.

Prodrome The first stage of a migraine headache in which cerebral blood vessels constrict, resulting in such symptoms as dizziness, flushness, visual static, or a generalized sense of uneasiness.

Progressive Relaxation An active relaxation technique in which specific muscles are tensed, then relaxed.

Psychologizing An ineffective listening response in which the listener inappropriately or inaccurately attributes thoughts or feelings to the speaker.

Psychosomatic Illness An illness in which the mind plays a significant etiological role.

Qualitative Overload Feeling overwhelmed by the difficulty of one or more tasks.

Quantitative Overload Feeling overwhelmed by a large number of tasks or stimuli.

Race Horse Someone who thrives on the fast pace of life.

Rackets Patterns of thinking in which the person keeps himself/herself miserable—for example, anxious, afraid, or angry. Often practiced by distress-seekers.

Reactions to Distress Mental and/or behavioral ways of handling acute or chronic distress. May be deliberate or scripted, adaptive or maladaptive.

Reasonable Belief An enduring assumption that is factual, moderate, and helpful.

Relaxation Response Quieting of mind and body.

Repetition Compulsion The drive to repeat that which is familiar. The force of habit.

Residual stress Mental and/or physical arousal that remains after an experience. May be positive or negative.

Reticular Activating System Complex network of nerve fibers through which nerve messages are sent among layers of the brain.

Rheumatoid Arthritis A chronic disease of unknown origin in which joints become inflamed, swollen, and painful, May be aggravated by stress.

Rhythm In relation to assumptions about stress management, refers to recognition that stress and distress come and go in rhythms and stages. In relation to the heart and heart disease, refers to repeated electrical stimulation of the heart muscle resulting in heart beats.

Risk-taking Engaging in actions that are new, dangerous, or have potential for failure. Moderate amounts needed for personal growth.

Role Ambiguity Unclear expectations associated with a social position, such as student, employee, or mother.

Role Conflict Incompatible expectations associated with a social position, such as student, employee, or mother.

Role Overload Expectations associated with a social position call for more activity than time allows, as experienced by the role occupant.

Role Strain Conflict between personal desires and others' expectations.

Role Transition Movement of an individual from one social position to another. Illustrated by graduation, marriage, divorce, becoming a parent, a job transfer.

Role Underload Expectations associated with a social position that call for too little activity, resulting in boredom, understimulation, or lethargy.

Sadness The dreary, dark feeling associated with a real, imagined, or anticipated loss.

Scripted Reactions to Distress Reactions to distress that are embedded in one's life script as a result of early messages and early decisions about how to handle distress.

Self-actualization State of highest possible human functioning, usually reached only in later years. Being fully human. Includes the full use and exploitation of talent, capacities, potentialities, personalities, etc.

Self-disclosure Communicating one's authentic feelings or thoughts. Allowing oneself to be known, seen, understood.

Self-hypnosis A method of producing deep relaxation in which one silently repeats self-suggestive statements, thereby quieting the mind and quieting the body.

Self-massage Using your fingertips or palms to massage the face or other areas that might be tense.

Self-monitoring Becoming aware of one's thoughts, feelings, and action patterns.

Self-talk Internal dialogue; conversation with self; includes interpretations of events.

Self-transcendence Devoting energy to goals beyond yourself.

Sense of Coherence A pervasive, enduring though dynamic feeling of confidence that one's internal and external environments are predictable and that there is a high probability that things will work out as well as can reasonably be expected.

Sensory Deprivation The experience of being deprived of most or all external stimuli. When prolonged, can result in extreme distress.

Sexual Harassment Unwanted, repeated, and coercive sexual advances.

Shoulding Constant imposition of "shoulds" and "should haves" on self, others, or both.

Simplification When used in context of time management, refers to grouping of similar tasks into time blocks.

Six-second Quieting Response A simple relaxation technique with four steps: draw a deep breath, hold briefly, exhale completely, let jaw and shoulders drop.

Slow Motion Suicide Destructive habits such as smoking, overeating, excessive drinking, and drug-taking.

Social Approaches to Managing Stress Group efforts to reduce social forces that create distress and to assist people in distress.

Social Change Change in the environment surrounding the person.

Social Network The specific set of linkages among a defined set of persons or a given person.

Social Responsibility Willingness to assume personal responsibility for public problems.

Social Support An interpersonal transaction involving sharing of one or more of the following: liking, love, empathy, information, goods, or services.

Sociological Imagination The ability to understand that personal experience is influenced by larger social forces.

Solitude Being alone, secluded, or isolated. Usually means the person experiences aloneness positively.

Stimulants Drugs, such as caffeine and amphetamines, that arouse mind and body.

Stress Arousal of mind and body in response to demands made upon them.

Stressor Any demand on mind or body.

Stretching An active method for relaxing muscle tension, done standing, or sitting.

Superficial Adaptive Energy Energy for coping with life that can be replaced through rest, exercise, good nutrition, and other good health habits.

Swimmer's Shake An active relaxation method in which you allow your arms to hang loosely

at your sides, then shake each one from fingers to shoulder in a rotary motion.

Swimmer's Shake-out Rotating and dangling each arm at the side, much like a competitive swimmer before the race start.

Sympathetic Nervous System That part of the peripheral nervous system which regulates the stress rsponse of the body.

Sympathizing To show understanding, pity, or compassion. An effective interactional style, except in active listening, when remaining neutral may be more effective.

Sympathomimetic Agent A substance such as caffeine, which stimulates the sympathetic nervous system.

Tense and Relax Neck and Shoulders An active method, drawn from progressive relaxation, for reducing muscle tension in the neck and shoulders.

Thought Stopping Using an internal command to stop an unwanted stream of thinking.

Three-breath Release A method of relaxing mind and body in which, during each of three long and deep exhalations, specific muscles are relaxed.

Thyroid Gland Endocrine gland, located in the neck, which secretes thyroid hormones such as thyroxine.

Thyrotropic Hormone (TTH) A hormone secreted into the bloodstream by the pituitary gland during the stress response to activate the thyroid gland.

Thyroxine A hormone produced by the thyroid gland during the stress response. Speeds up metabolism and increases sensitivity of tissues of the body to adrenalin.

Time Demands Pressures, obligations, and tasks requiring your time.

Time Supply The amount of time you have available to complete a given set of tasks.

Trackdown A method of tracking down the meaning of specific distress symptoms.

Tragic Life Script A life script calling for tragedy, such as suicide, imprisonment, alcoholism, or heart attack.

Turtle A person who thrives on a relatively slow pace of life. Easily overloaded.

Type A Behavior A pattern of thinking, feeling, and acting marked by intense drive, perfectionism, time urgency, and easily aroused hostility and anger.

Type B Behavior A pattern of thinking, feeling, and acting marked by the relative absence of Type A qualities.

Type C Behavior A pattern of thinking, feeling, and acting in which the person thrives and reaches peak performance under pressure. The Type C perspective includes challenge, confidence, and control.

Type E Woman The woman who believes she must be everything to everybody and feels overwhelmed in the process of carrying out this belief.

Ulcer An open sore on the lining of the stomach or just inside the small intestine.

Unconditional Love Unyielding love based on a person's existence rather than on his/her actions.

Unconscious Interpretation Pathway Activation of the stress response without conscious appraisal or interpretation. Illustrated by the body's automatic response to low grade sound or lighting.

Under-reactions Reactions to stressors that are less than called for by the situation.

Understimulation Stimuli that are too few or not intense enough for the person. Can result in underload distress symptoms.

Unfinished Business Incomplete tasks or unexpressed feelings.

Unreasonable Belief A belief that is not based on fact, is extreme, or is harmful.

Value Clarification A learning process in which the person clarifies his/her beliefs about what is important/unimportant, valuable/not valuable, desirable/undesirable.

Vicious Cycle A negative cycle of thinking, feeling, acting, and others' responses, beginning with an unreasonable belief.

Visualization The process of deliberately creating positive mental pictures for the purpose of mental rehearsal or relaxation.

Vital Cycle A positive cycle of thinking, feeling, acting, and others' responses, beginning with a reasonable belief.

Wellness The state of living at one's highest possible level as a whole person. Maximizing one's potentials while enjoying the process and maintaining optimal health along the way.

Work Addiction Compulsive involvement in work, usually stemming from the obsessive pursuit of approval and from equating self-esteem with performance. Commonly an adaptation to being an adult child of an alcoholic parent.

Yoga A discipline of relaxation and spiritual growth involving prescribed body postures and movements while carrying on specific breathing and mental exercises.

Zone of Overload Distress On a hypothetical continuum of arousal, this is the zone above a person's upper limit of tolerance in which overload distress symptoms appear.

Zone of Positive Stress The tolerance range of stress in which a person is healthy, productive, and satisfied.

Zone of Underload Distress On a hypothetical continuum of arousal, this is the zone below a person's lower limit of tolerance where underload distress symptoms appear.

Name Index

Subject Index

CREDITS